PRINCIPLES AND PRACTICE OF PLANT CONSERVATION

IUCN
The World Conservation Union

Founded in 1961, WWF (World Wide Fund for Nature) is the largest international, private nature conservation organization in the world. Based in Switzerland, WWF has national affiliates and associate organizations on five continents. WWF works to conserve the natural environment and ecological processes essential to life on Earth.

WWF aims to create awareness of threats to the natural environment, to generate and attract on a worldwide basis the strongest moral and financial support for safeguarding the living world, and to convert such support into action based on scientific priorities. Since 1961, WWF has channeled over U.S. $130 million into more than 5000 projects in some 130 countries, which have saved animals and plants from extinction and helped to conserve natural areas all over the world. It has served as a catalyst for conservation action, and has brought its influence to bear on critical conservation needs by working with and influencing governments, private organizations, scientists, industry, and the general public.

Founded in 1948, IUCN—The World Conservation Union brings together states, government agencies, and a diverse range of private organization in a unique world partnership: some 680 members in all, spread across 111 countries.

As a union, IUCN exists to serve its members—to represent their views on the world stage and to provide them with the concepts, strategies, and technical support they need to achieve their goals. Through its six commissions, IUCN draws together over 5000 expert volunteers in project teams and action groups. A central secretariat coordinates the IUCN program and leads initiatives on the conservation and sustainable use of the world's biological diversity and the management of habitats and natural resources, as well as providing a range of services. IUCN has helped many countries prepare national conservation strategies, and demonstrates the application of its knowledge through the field projects it supervises. Operations are increasingly decentralized and are carried forward by an expanding network of regional and national offices, located principally in developing countries.

Above all, IUCN seeks to work with its members to achieve development that is sustainable and that provides a lasting improvement in the quality of life for people all over the world.

PRINCIPLES AND PRACTICE OF PLANT CONSERVATION

David R. Given

TIMBER PRESS
Portland, Oregon

Reprinted 1996

ISBN 0-88192-249-8

Printed in Hong Kong

Timber Press, Inc.
The Haseltine Building
133 S.W. Second Ave., Suite 450
Portland, Oregon 97204-3527, U.S.A.

Library of Congress Cataloging-in-Publication Data

Given, David R.
    Principles and practice of plant conservation / David R. Given.
        p.   cm.
    Includes bibliographical references and index.
    ISBN 0-88192-249-8
    1. Plant conservation.   2. Biological diversity conservation.
    I. Title.
    QK86.AIG54   1994
    333.95'316--dc20   93-5240
                                                            CIP

Contents

Foreword   vii

Acknowledgments   viii

1   Reasons for Conserving Plant Diversity   1
    Conservation and Development   2
    Developing a Rationale for Conservation   3

2   How Plants Become Threatened or Extinct   13
    The Process of Extinction   15
    Characteristics of Declining Populations   17
    The Influence of Humanity   20
    Future Losses and Gains   35

3   Documentation and Databases for Plant Conservation   37
    Types of Data   38
    Types of Databases   44
    Collecting and Describing Data   46
    Data Processing   56
    Access to Databases   59

4   Plant Population Management   61
    Biological and Ecological Considerations   62
    Maintaining Population Characteristics   63
    Viable Population Planning and Risk Analysis   68
    Maintaining Essential Habitat   72
    Field Study Techniques   73
    Population Management in the "Real" World   83

5   Plant Conservation in Protected Natural Areas   85
    Considerations in Designating Protected Areas   87
    Protected Area Categories   96
    Managing Protected Areas   100

6   Off-site Plant Conservation   115
    The Role of Botanic Gardens in Conservation   117
    Gene Banks and Germ Plasm Conservation   130
    Experimental Gardens   133
    Other Off-site Conservation Areas   135

Research and Liaison Between Sites 136
Constraints to Off-site Conservation 142

7 Plant Conservation in Modified Landscapes 145
Types of Modified Landscapes 146
Habitat Restoration 156
Translocation and Reestablishment 161

8 Awareness and Education 165
Environmental Awareness Programs 166
Environmental Education Programs 168
The Education Function of Protected Areas 171
The Contribution of Professionals 180
Environmental Education Resources 181
The Media 183
Social Ethics 184

9 Conservation Legislation, by Cyrille de Klemm 189
The Basis for Legislation 189
Species-centered Legislation 191
Collection Controls 193
Trade Controls 196
Habitat Protection 197
Dynamic Conservation 199
Ecosystem-centered Legislation 200
Future Directions 203

10 Economics and Plant Conservation 205
Valuing Resources 206
The Costs of Development 211
The Costs of Conservation 213
International Trade and Foreign Aid 214
Allocating Resources for Conservation 225
Economic and Environmental Stability 226

11 Putting It Together: Integrated Conservation 229
Conservation—A Crisis Discipline 229
Cross-sectoral Conservation—Integrated Approaches 230
International Organizations 232
Multinational and Development Agencies 234
Volunteers 236
Research Priorities for Conservation 238
The Funding Crisis 240
The Information Crisis 241
Focal Points 241
The Last Frontier 242
People and Plants 245

Conversion Formulas 249

Bibliography 251

Index 281

Foreword

It is paradoxical that, despite the key role of plants in the environment and our dependence on plant life for our very existence, the conservation movement has not given plants attention that is commensurate with their importance. In an attempt to redress the balance of effort between plant and animal conservation, IUCN and WWF established in 1984 a joint Plant Conservation Programme, the aim of which was to "assert the fundamental importance of plants in all conservation activities."

One of the main themes of the joint Plant Conservation Programme was "building the capacity to conserve." This included a project, "Plant Conservation: Principles and Practice," aimed at providing practicing conservationists with a handbook that explained the concepts and principles underlying successful plant conservation. The IUCN–WWF Plant Advisory Group, which oversaw the program, under the chairmanship of Dr. Peter H. Raven and, later, Professor Arturo Gómez Pompa, recommended that Dr. David Given be contracted to prepare the handbook. This was made possible by the cooperation of New Zealand's Department of Scientific and Industrial Research, for whom Dr. Given was then working.

An outline for the book prepared by Dr. Given was debated by the Plant Advisory Group in 1986. Many members of that group contributed substantially to the book's preparation by reviewing manuscripts or providing literature and case studies for inclusion. The preparation of the text, which went through various drafts, involved Dr. Given in a great deal of research and travel for fact finding and consultation.

The completed draft was edited by Martin Walters, who also prepared it for publication. Professor Vernon Heywood (IUCN) undertook a scientific edit of the final draft.

Both IUCN and WWF would like to express their gratitude to Dr. Given for the enormous effort and painstaking labor that he has invested in the preparation of this book over a period of six years. The result is the first detailed overview ever to be published of this vitally important subject. We feel it will be a landmark publication and will greatly advance the cause of conserving plant diversity. It is fitting to publish this book following the United Nations Conference on Environment and Development (UNCED) because it will provide a clear statement of the principles and practice of plant conservation and be a valuable contribution to the debates arising from the Earth Summit.

Vernon H. Heywood
Former Chief Scientist, Plant Conservation
IUCN—The World Conservation Union

Acknowledgments

This book originated in recommendations by the IUCN Plant Advisory Group in 1987 and I am grateful for the vision and support of the Group under the able chairmanship and inspiration of Peter Raven and Arturo Gómez Pompa. Other members of the Group were Peter Ashton, L. Ake Assi, Enrique Forero, Ole Hamann, He San-an, Kuswata Kartawinata, T. N. Khoshoo, E. van der Maarel, Nanuza Menezes, Ghillean Prance, P. Quezel, Voara Randrianasolo, Richard E. Schultes, A. Takhtajan, and Wang Xianpu. The parallel support of staff of WWF International and IUCN was instrumental in developing the manuscript and seeing it through to publication, particularly the support of Eva Hansen (who supervised initial writing of the book) and successive chairs and permanent staff members of the IUCN Species Survival Commission.

Space does not allow me to thank individually the many people who assisted with this project by providing information, answering questions, expediting my travel, and facilitating visits to institutions and field sites. I trust that all those who gave of their time will accept this acknowledgement of their individual efforts: your cooperation and interest has been instrumental in the writing of this book, which is a compilation of the concepts, experiments, techniques, and aspirations of many people working in many different aspects of conservation, within numerous countries. It has been a privilege to share experiences and wisdom, and to come to know so many as good friends.

My special thanks go to colleagues who have had a particular influence on my twenty-five-year pilgrimage into the conservation of plants. Special mention must be made of Robert Boden, Susan Cochrane, Don Falk, Al Gentry, Roger Good, Tony Hall, Warwick Harris, Vernon Heywood, John Leigh, Gren Lucas, Jeff McNeely, Colin Meurk, David Norton, Graeme Patterson, Bruce Pavlik, Peter Raven, Simon Stuart, Hugh Synge, Cathy Wilson, Dennis Woodland, and Keith Woolliams.

The former Department of Scientific and Industrial Research in New Zealand generously allowed me to undertake the writing of this book as WWF International contract 3329. Martin Walters patiently edited the initial text. I am grateful also to the staff of Timber Press for their assistance throughout this project. Finally, I owe a considerable debt to Karina and to Bronwyn, Andrew, and Craig for their forebearance during many nights of word-processing and weeks of absence from home.

CHAPTER 1

Reasons for Conserving Plant Diversity

We share the earth with at least 5 million—perhaps as many as 30 million—species of organisms. About 235,000 of these species are flowering plants and about 325,000 are nonflowering plants such as lichens, mosses, and seaweeds. All are important parts of the web of life, contributing to the fragile green mantle clothing our planet. This mantle is essential to life, and we depend on plants for our survival. All people, no matter where they live, depend on plants for food, clothing, shelter, and fuel. Even when we use things obtained from animals, plants are used indirectly, because all animals ultimately depend on plants for their energy. It follows that the earth's ecosystems are also dependent on plants.

Consequently, the well-being of the world of plants and the maintenance of biodiversity—a wide range of animals and plants, communities, ecosystems, biological processes, and interactions—is of vital importance. Throughout history, people have equated the vitality of the natural world—its plants, animals, water, soil, air, and landscapes—with the health of human populations.

It makes sense to ask, How can people feel affinity with, and be part of, nature yet be able to use it? As people and nations try to find a balance between a range of attitudes toward the natural world, tensions are inevitable. World conservation strategies and national conservation strategies are attempts to resolve such tensions. Basic to these strategies are the concepts of sustainability and the interdependence of conservation and development (IUCN/UNEP/WWF 1990). Actions that are necessary include limiting human impact on the biosphere, maintaining biological wealth, using nonrenewable resources at a rate that does not exceed creation of renewable substitutes, equitably distributing costs and benefits, promoting technologies that increase benefits from a given stock of resources, using economic policy to help maintain natural wealth, anticipatory and cross-sectoral approaches to decision making, and promoting cultural values that help achieve sustainability.

The biodiversity program of the Commonwealth Science Secretariat stresses the importance of "life support species"—those that are crucial to human well-being. Such approaches involve complex issues, and mistrust and misinterpretation can easily occur as people look at resources and needs from different viewpoints and with differing priorities. What some see as priorities may be far from the priorities perceived by others. Developed and developing countries, and both developers and conservationists, must listen and be aware of the needs and values that various viewpoints express.

Conservationism is sometimes construed as "a position aiming to keep the environment as untouched as possible," whereas there are arguments for "explicit inclusion of the environmental dimension within development planning" (Weil 1986). In the first World Conservation Strategy, conservation is defined as,

> The management of human use of the biosphere so that it may yield the greatest sustainable benefit to present generations, while maintaining its potential to meet the needs and aspirations of future generations. Thus, conservation is positive, embracing preservation, maintenance, sustainable utilization, restoration, and enhancement of the natural environment (IUCN 1980: 1).

In the broadest sense, conservation incorporates elements of both preservationism and of sustainable use, restoration, and enhancement. One of the greatest difficulties for conservation is to recognize intrinsic values of species and their right to life, while not giving conservation an air of both unreality and remoteness from human concerns (Prescott-Allen 1984).

It is extremely important that experiences of nature be positive. Positive experiences of a transforming nature lead to changes of view and values in people's lives. Too much of science, and particularly conservation, environmentalism, and preservationism, is pervaded with doom and gloom. Bad news is depressing, and as advertisers and politicians know, "voters don't elect prophets of doom" (Soulé 1988: 469).

Conservation and Development

Twentieth-century discussions of the use of nature often take place against a backdrop of uncontrolled exploitation or consumption. Consumption is the use of a resource so that it will not, in the foreseeable future, be available again. Conventional mining for some minerals such as coal and petroleum is an obvious example of consumption. Consumption of living species sometimes involves single species, such as the hunting of elephants for ivory, but it also involves destruction of habitats, such as felling of forests and draining of wetlands (Figure 1.1). This can decimate plants and wildlife and destroy indigenous cultures. Consumptive or exploitative regimes have tended to be associated with highly technological cultures, in contrast to long-established traditional cultures, which tend to be less exploitative.

Nineteenth-century colonial invasion by European countries, coupled with erroneous assumptions regarding the inexhaustible nature of resources, resulted in depletion that has continued to the present day.

Figure 1.1. In many parts of the world, plants are increasingly threatened with extinction as ecosystems are disrupted by human activities. Clearing in primary rain forest, Tai Region, Ivory Coast. (Courtesy of WWF–U.K.)

Often, land was cleared of natural vegetation and soils were exhausted, leaving eroded slopes and dust bowls. Indigenous peoples were sometimes enslaved, massacred, and displaced (Gunn and Edmonds 1986). Many nineteenth-century accounts of exploration tell as much about the firearms, hunting expeditions, and trophy shooting of the explorers as they do of the native land, people, and geography.

Attitudes toward development that are based on conservation are a move to redress the balance. Concepts such as *optimal harvest* and *maximum sustainable yield* are increasingly incorporated in planning for development.

The reasons for advocating species protection are varied. They range from the belief that all plants and animals have a right to exist, to the belief that future generations of people have a right to expect adequate resources (Taylor 1986; Norton 1987; Engel and Engel 1990).

Strict preservationism is not the same as conservation. Conservation may advocate preservation of species and ecosystems but may also advocate use of them, providing this is not wasteful. The preservationist is concerned with preventing destruction of species, ecosystems, and wilderness, even when they may be regarded by many others as legitimate resources. Broadly, preservationists appeal to intrinsic values of nature, while conservationists may appeal to other values as well (e.g., the use of plants by humankind).

To adopt a strictly preservationist stance would probably result in worldwide starvation through nonuse of resources. To hold to uncontrolled consumption and exploitation risks leading to the same endpoint through exhaustion of resources. A challenge for conservation is to seek a middle stance, sometimes promoting preservation, but at other times supporting controlled exploitation.

Developing a Rationale for Conservation

It is worth noting that the governments of the world have already made an important, but little-noticed, commitment to nature conservation through The World Charter for Nature, adopted by the General Assembly of the United Nations in 1982 (McNeely et al. 1990). The charter recognizes that humanity is part of nature, that every form of life is unique and warrants respect, and that lasting benefits from nature depend upon the maintenance of essential ecological processes. Drawing on the charter and the World Conservation Strategy (IUCN 1980), IUCN's Working Group on Ethics and Conservation has produced an ethical foundation for conservation (see IUCN/UNEP/WWF 1990). The implications of this are elaborated in Engel and Engel (1990).

It is not surprising that arguments seeking to demonstrate economic use or utility (even if currently unproven) are the most pervasive in Western developed countries. In these countries, there tends to be a generally exploitative relationship with nature. Technology is given extreme prominence, and economic analyses (especially in the form of cost-benefit analyses) are important planning tools. As might be expected, older traditional societies in developing nations tend to have a stronger orientation toward moral arguments for conservation.

The question of the extent to which economic arguments are needed, as against esthetic and moral arguments, is vigorously debated. Especially where balances of payments are paramount considerations, "the economic climate now and for some time is likely to give men every incentive to be gimlet-eyed and stony-hearted" (Allen 1974: 529). Nevertheless, there are strong efforts to develop persuasive and soundly based arguments for conservation that do not depend on conventional economics. Several types of argument are used to promote conservation of plants.

- The economic value of plants as resources for humanity, both now and in the future.
- The role of plants in maintaining a stable environment. This largely involves the regulation and stability of environmental processes.
- The scientific value of plants, and the opportunity to study and determine ecological processes.
- Maintaining future options.
- Cultural values and symbolic use.
- The role of plants in inspiring people and in transforming their values.
- Worth, including the right of species to exist and their inherent moral value.

Each of these arguments can be presented in a variety of ways and incorporates a range of related arguments. Collectively, they provide a framework on which plant conservation can build. There is also some debate regarding the strict validity of arguments such as "scientific value."

Economic contribution of plants

Since the dawn of history, people have drawn heavily on certain plants to satisfy the needs of daily life—food, shelter, clothing, fuel, and medicines, as well as recreational and cultural needs. Selection of particular plants has led to the development of major crops, such as rice, barley, maize, wheat, and potato, and has also led to utilization of many thousands of plants for medicinal use. Sources of fuel are fundamentally of plant origin, whether directly as wood or charcoal, or indirectly as coal, petroleum, or animal dung.

In highly technological countries, it is a worthwhile exercise to think about the economic benefits people derive from plants from the time they wake to the end of the day when they retire to sleep (Myers 1985a, 1985b). Each day, most people enjoy a long list of goods that derive from plants. This will include obvious items such as food, but it will include many less obvious things. Even in developed Western countries such as the United States, there is one chance in four that a prescribed medicine will owe its origin to starting materials from flowering plants. Approximately 119 pure chemical substances extracted from such plants are used in medicine throughout the world; 80 percent of the people in developing countries rely on traditional medicine for primary health care and 85 percent of traditional medicine involves the use of plant extracts (Farnsworth 1988).

Natural rubber, latexes, gums, resins, waxes, dyes, and essential oils from plants are key components of innumerable products from paper, varnish, and plastics to deodorant, lipstick, and clothes. We have long ceased to use the plants just from our own geographic regions, but make use of plant materials originally found in many parts of the world. In this sense the contribution of plants to humanity is global.

It is a tragedy that direct use of wild plants makes its greatest contribution to human survival and well-being in poor, rural economies where there may be greatest depletion of biodiversity. The rate of loss is alarming but is not surprising; such areas are under intense pressures. This comes from developed countries who want to trade for their resources and indigenous people who need to use the plants to survive. Where population pressure is intense or economics dictate, use of plants may not be particularly selective.

Just one resource—fuelwood—can be considered. In the Himalayan foothills, sites supporting forests where rhododendron, oaks, and conifers flourished until the middle of the twentieth century are now eroded, bare hillsides. In Mali, the scarcity of fuel-wood rose by 15 percent every year between 1973 and 1980, and around some African towns, deforestation extends for distances in excess of 100 kilometers (Myers 1985b).

The plant kingdom has the potential to contribute far more than it does to the material welfare of people. Already, it contributes more overall than the animal kingdom, although the latter is larger in terms of number of species. The list of potentially useful plants requiring investigation is almost endless, especially as we cannot predict what may be of interest in the future. Today, there is considerable interest in so-called fuel trees. Yet during the last century, it is unlikely that anyone would have thought there would be interest in plants providing combustible hydrocarbons for fuel.

The potential contribution of the plant kingdom can be appreciated by considering chemicals derived from plants. Thousands of plants containing useful chemical substances are known. Some are used as traditional medicines, but many are almost unknown outside the regions where they are gathered and used. Then there are the chemical pesticides derived from plants. To cope with predation, plants have developed a host of chemical compounds that provide biological defenses. Species of the tropics and of regions with climatic extremes seem particularly rich in these. Only a very small percentage of these compounds have been investigated for their direct value to humanity.

Food plants provide a second example of the usefulness of plants. At least 75,000 plants are edible. Plants are basic to the food requirements of all people, yet the main food resources of the world depend on little more than a handful of species. During the course of history, about 3000 plants have been used for food, though far fewer have been commercially cultivated. There is potential for many other plants to become food crops. Despite the considerable efforts already underway in this area, thousands more species are likely to have desirable characteristics for breeding into existing crop plants (Myers 1985b).

Conservation of a wide variety of plant species can be justified on the grounds that they are of direct economic importance to humans. What we currently use is a fraction of the potential, and only about one percent of the earth's plants have been thoroughly screened for use. It is a beginning, and there is room for sustainable use of many hundreds, if not thousands, of other plants. It seems very likely that new plant materials of the future would more than pay for the costs of preserving species and developing sustainable harvesting or cultivation (Myers 1979).

Maintenance of environmental stability

Much is currently being made of the need to conserve a wide range of species and natural biological systems—the world's biodiversity. One of the major arguments for conservation proceeds from the assumption that diversity is good. Thus it is reasonable to ask if there are good arguments in favor of diversity.

Ecosystems are complex, with many interactions and feedback loops (Figure 1.2). General study of complex systems indicates that they are subject to instability and breakdown when they lack adequate protection against the risk of a systems component failure, and because of a lack of homeostatic mechanisms. The following are specific causes for systems failure (Watt et al. 1977):

The all-the-eggs-in-one-basket phenomenon—lack of diversity. Where a system has limited diversity, it becomes vulnerable to a systems component failure. If a country depends on only one product for its income, and serious problems occur such as lower world prices or depletion, then the entire country may face economic disaster. Increased diversity promotes system stability because an increase in the number of items that can independently support a system decreases the probability that all will fail simultaneously. This applies not only to social systems but also to natural communities and ecosystems.

Increased complexity of the system. This is sometimes confused with diversity, but the two are different. Complexity refers not only to size but also to a high degree of interconnection among components of the system. A disturbance or shock applied from the outside to one component travels along interconnected pathways and eventually affects a large number of components. Consequently, the total system becomes more vulnerable and fragile as it becomes more complex. The only devices that protect a system from this type of instability are homeostatic negative feedback mechanisms with short response times. Natural ecosystems have evolved to include species that promote these homeostatic responses and thus buffer the effects of external shocks, even in highly diverse systems.

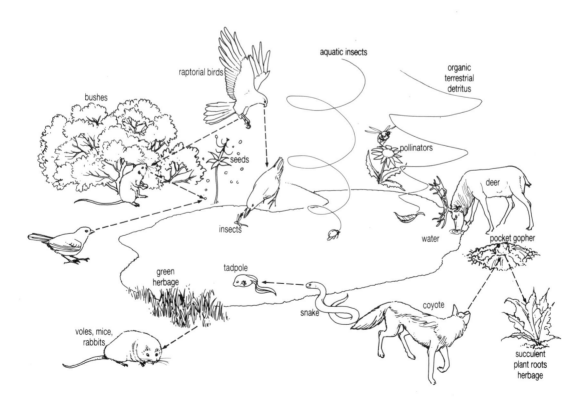

Figure 1.2. Interactions between a vernal pool and its terrestrial surroundings. (Redrawn by permission from Zedler 1987)

Increase in catastrophic shocks. Instability can be caused by sets of factors that can, to varying degrees, operate independently of the size of the system. These are the numerous shocks that affect systems, such as drought, flooding, depletion of resources, significant climate alteration, pollution, and extreme population increase. Some of these factors are beyond human control, but many are caused or exacerbated by human destruction or lack of long-term planning. Thus humanity can contribute to stability maintenance by designing and implementing homeostatic control mechanisms, and by maintaining a range of species that buffer against catastrophe.

One of the difficulties in managing natural biological communities that have been modified is that there is often little indication of which species are critical to long-term functioning and buffering. Identification of critical species, linkages, and pathways is important. Loss of just one species in a complex ecosystem, such as tropical moist forest, may lead to major disruption of linkages within the local community and an eventual cascade of other species losses.

In the absence of definitive information, it is not surprising that many experts are suggesting caution in reducing plant diversity. Collection and interpretation of essential data are needed. This demands sufficient funds for research into fundamental ecosystem functioning (Myers 1979). The logical course is to adopt an approach in which we avoid extinction unless the social (and biological) costs of doing so are unacceptably large.

The loss of a single species from a community may not necessarily cause great change, although loss of a key species could. The loss of many (perhaps at least 10–20 percent), however, is likely to be critical. There is no clear-cut answer to the question, "When do losses become critical?" At some point losses will affect local communities, and at a higher level they will affect global stability. Particular value needs to be placed on *indicator species* that signal when there is something wrong with the health of an ecosystem, and on those species that are key biological links or on which many other species depend.

An extension of these arguments concerns the use of communities or ecosystems as models for the reconstruction of similar but destroyed or depleted habitats. The original is preserved as a "blueprint" and as a source of living components (Bunnell and Williams 1980). It is often assumed that human-dominated systems have not functioned as well as natural systems, so most land managers approximate natural environ-ments in managed systems by using information derived from real systems. Examples include rehabilitation of strip-mined areas, forest replanting, and reconstruction of wetlands. Actual cases of totally rebuilt ecosystems are still rare.

In many parts of the world, alteration and depletion of plant cover is so great that it is not just the effect on key species that is important: the loss of whole communities of plants and animals is likely (Figure 1.3). All organisms require appropriate habitats to survive. A concern of many ecologists is that habitat destruction and modification are creating new habitats that are increasingly unsuitable for many of the species existing today. Greater human appropriation of the earth's total energy budget; increases in water, soil, and atmospheric contaminants such as fluorocarbons; and changes in the constituents of the atmosphere, especially carbon dioxide, are just some of the changes occurring.

CASE STUDY: HUMAN IMPACTS ON GLOBAL NET PRIMARY PRODUCTION

Net primary production (NPP) is the energy that green plants bind into organic molecules in the process of photosynthesis, minus the energy those plants use for their own life processes. Globally, this amounts to about 225 billion metric tons of organic matter annually, nearly 60 percent of it on land.

Humanity is now using directly (e.g., by eating, feeding to livestock, using lumber and firewood) more than 3 percent of global NPP, and about 4 percent of that on land. This is a minimum estimate of human impact on terrestrial systems. Yet humans can be thought of as co-opting NPP not only by direct use but also by indirect use. Thus if we chalk up to the human account not only the NPP directly consumed, but also such other categories as the amount of biomass consumed in fires used to clear land, the parts of crop plants not consumed, the NPP of pastureland (converted from natural habitat) not consumed by livestock, and so on, the human share of terrestrial NPP climbs to a staggering 30 percent. And if we add to that the NPP foregone when people convert more productive natural systems to less productive ones (such as forest to farm or pasture, grassland to desert, marsh to parking lot), the total potential NPP on land is reduced by 13 percent, and the human share of the unreduced potential NPP reaches almost 40 percent.

There is no way the co-option by one species of almost two-fifths of the earth's annual terrestrial food production could be considered reasonable, in the sense of maintaining the stability of life on this planet. Most demographers project that the human race will double its population

Figure 1.3. Fragmentation and fixation of landscapes with elimination of natural vegetation are increasingly familiar scenes worldwide. Top: Montane grassland and scrub cleared for farming in central North Island, New Zealand, leaving only marginal strips of indigenous vegetation. Bottom: Lower reaches of the Manawatu River, North Island, showing almost total conversion of landscape to farms, roads, and houses. (D. R. Given)

within the twenty-first century or so. This implies a belief that our species can safely commandeer upwards of 80 percent of terrestrial NPP, a preposterous notion to ecologists who already see the deadly impacts of today's level of human activities.

Source: Ehrlich 1988.

Scientific value of plants

The array of species found on earth can be compared with the books of a library: once removed, they cannot be readily replaced. More than this, a particular journal rapidly loses value when individual volumes or issues are lost. The analogy for conservation is that series of species, the communities they make up, and entire land masses of life contain information that becomes rapidly degraded as components become extinct. The many unknown and unnamed species are part of this treasure-trove of important information. If such species are lost before they are investigated, then the human race will have lost forever these "volumes" of knowledge.

The value of biological diversity to science, and ultimately to humanity as a whole, is a function of many things. These include the data individual species provide for research and the lessons they provide for students. Biodiversity allows measurement of environmental quality through fluctuations in population size, behavioral change, physiological change, or the concentration of human-generated pollutants in tissues (Bunnell and Williams 1980). It is very easy to undervalue such contributions from plant diversity because so often our primary concern is whether a plant can be eaten, burned, cut for timber, or used for stabilizing hillside soils and riverbanks. We need to appreciate that individual plants as well as the communities they form may be many things to different people. Many disciplines benefit from attributes peculiar to particular species. Cell biologists benefit from the odd life cycle of the slime molds, paleobotanists from the longevity of bristlecone pines, and evolutionists from the occurrence of localized relicts and isolated centers of species richness.

Unfortunately, it seems that it is often the species in trouble—those with some biological quirk that makes them vulnerable to change and habitat change—that are the ones which can tell us much about the peculiarities of the world in which we live. Such species can greatly help us understand the processes of extinction itself, perhaps one of the most pressing research areas in biology. There is great need to conserve not only those plants that are widespread and robust, but also those that are local and vulnerable, and thereby learn how to manage less vulnerable species before they too become threatened.

Maintenance of future options

Uncertainty about the future is often implied in arguments for conservation. Total destruction is an irreversible process. Even the best of contemporary technology cannot re-create species if there is nothing of that species left. Re-creation of habitats and biomes from remnants may be theoretically possible in some instances, but tends to be beyond available resources except on a very small scale. Therefore, it can be argued that there are obligations to minimize destruction and fragmentation out of regard for the future. The future includes not only future options for humanity—the availability of resources and choices for future generations of people—but also future options for continued evolution.

There is considerable emotional and philosophical appeal for a sustainable use approach to resource management. Survival concerns not just the present generation but also succeeding ones. For humanity, most ethical and religious systems place high value on ensuring the survival of one's children's children. There is nothing new or unnatural in maintaining reasonable options for the future.

Sometimes the objection is raised that consideration for future generations does not generate an absolute rate of use for nonrenewable (or only slowly renewed) resources (Hunt 1986). Fortunately, most plant resources are renewable at rates that can be estimated. Demand for a product and rate of use can be fitted to the rate at which the resource is renewed. The important point is that sustainable rates of use for harvest of species and use of habitat should be determined and use should be matched accordingly.

One argument against a conservationist, sustained yield approach states that, as natural resources become scarce, progress in technology results in the development of substitutes. Certainly it is true that as natural products have provided the models for synthetic products, need for natural products often declines. Yet rarely does the use of natural products decline totally. For example, there is still a considerable demand for natural rubber despite the extensive use of synthetic rubber. Another consideration is that synthetics themselves require raw products that are often nonrenewable. Hence, in the long term, it can be argued that there are disadvantages in relying largely or entirely on the substitution of synthetics for natural products. There would seem to be a strong case for mixed synthetic–natural product industries, the major use of technology being to develop better and more economical use of all resources so that waste is minimized.

Esthetic appeal of plants

Many people—perhaps most—react positively to plants that are visually appealing. Through the ages, poets, writers, and artists from many cultures have testified to the effect of plant beauty on the human mind and emotions. Other species may appeal because they are bizarre or have the reputation of being "odd." An example is provided by carnivorous plants, which have a considerable horticultural following. A number of plant groups have wide appeal in many countries, which has sometimes led to their depletion, examples being the commercially exploited tropical orchids, carnivorous plants, cacti, and bromeliads.

The esthetic argument has two limitations, one general and one applying to plant conservation. First, esthetic value (for example, of works of art) depends on the object's potential to produce enjoyment and pleasure in onlookers. Therefore, absolute esthetic value is very dependent on current taste and fashion. Further, esthetic value may differ according to a person's situation. Guy Mountfort summarized this well when he accepted the 1978 World Wildlife Fund Gold Medal: "An old Bedouin in the Jordan desert once said to me, 'When I am hungry, a date palm gives me food. When my belly is full, behold the tree is beautiful'" (Leigh et al. 1984). Esthetic value will differ from one society to another: what one group of people find esthetically satisfying will not always appeal to others.

A second limitation to the esthetic argument is that many plants that particularly deserve protection are unlikely to have esthetic appeal. They may be commonplace or even ugly. Nevertheless, the esthetics argument can be useful: there are a number of "flagship" plants that can be used as symbols for conservation. Outstanding examples among the animals include the tiger and panda; among plants one can point to orchids such as the Cooktown orchid of Australia, the bizarre parasitic *Rafflesia* of tropical southeast Asia, giant redwood trees in California, and some endemic species of oceanic islands. The conservation of such flagship plants leads to the conservation of associated plants by heightening awareness of the problems faced by other, less appealing species and the need to conserve these as well.

A variation on the esthetic argument is the appeal to rarity. This argument places value on rarity itself—an expression of unavailability or limitation of the opportunity to possess a particular plant. In developed countries, rare species attract a lot of attention just because they are rare (Heywood 1988b). Sometimes people place an additional value on a species because they regard it as surviving but struggling against the "titanic forces of destruction."

Morals and values

The simplest form of moral argument for conservation is expressed as, "It is immoral to take life and exterminate species." This is a value judgment, generally based on some personal credo or religious belief. In the past it has mostly been addressed at animals. Moral arguments are often associated with other arguments or value judgments. Even where persons expressing a moral case for conservation do not claim to hold particular religious beliefs, their moral position on animals and plants will often reflect a particular religious heritage. Because of their connection between spiritual belief, heritage, and morality, moral arguments concerning conservation ought not to be ignored or minimized.

Perceptions and standards of society change through time. The relative merit given to various objects such as plant species also changes. Even our understanding of what is "natural" can change from one generation to another. A pioneer farmer's perception of what is natural may include large tracts of undisturbed forest and impenetrable wetlands. The farmer's grandchild, on the other hand, may consider only tracts of grassland, hedgerows, and woodland remnants natural. As with the esthetic argument, some habitats or species may receive greater attention than others, although the latter may be just as deserving of attention.

Almost unconsciously, most people value certain species more than others, and some groups of organisms more than other groups. Thus, ardent conservationists may give generously to a campaign to save tropical forest or may visit a nature reserve to see orchids, but without any further thought may go home and drain the swampland beside their houses. Nevertheless, the moral argument "that species are, therefore they ought to be" is a sufficient motivation for some people. Intuitive, culturally related feelings do not require rigorous philosophical proof for their general acceptance. That they are felt and valued is sufficient for most people.

Restricting oneself to scientific statements does not free one from value judgments. Science has its own set of values. References to "the importance" of scientific knowledge ultimately depend on some nonscientific source of value. Science serves human values. This includes the discovery of penicillin from the *Penicillium* fungus, and the discovery of chemicals in Mexican yam suitable for manufacture of birth control drugs. Science can provide its own motivation, and knowledge need not be pursued for the sake of technological advances. Advancing our understanding of the beauty and functioning of natural systems can be a valued human goal.

In the broadest sense, three kinds of values can be distinguished: demand, intrinsic, and transformative (Norton 1987). *Demand value* occurs when an object such as a species provides satisfaction for some felt preference. Commonly, demand value is seen in terms of economics, but there are actually a range of demand values including, use values, which include gathering plants for food and fuel as well as esthetic enjoyment and use of plants for research; option values, which recognize that plants have value for use even if they are not being used at the present time; quasi-option values, which are option values enhanced by the expectation that growth in knowledge will find as yet unknown uses; and existence values, which are defined independently of actual use.

Intrinsic value recognizes the value in existing—that something can have value because it is, not because it is particularly useful to humanity. In contrast to demand and transformative value, this is not an "instrument" value (that is, it cannot be quantified in terms of use of the object being valued). Arguments for intrinsic value are complicated by questions of the place of anthropocentrism and whether intrinsic values can be separated from human valuations (even whether objects apart from humans can have intrinsic worth).

Transformative value exists where the object provides occasion for examining or altering a felt presence rather than simply satisfying it. It involves a transformation of, or change in, a person's previous set of felt preferences.

Demand values may seem the most persuasive, but for many people, they are not the whole answer. For scientists, the use of demand values can be particularly irksome. It is a simple fact that the functions and interactions of ecosystems are not understood well enough to allow accurate monetary values to be computed for even the best known species or ecosystems.

Plants do not fare well in discussions of intrinsic values. Most discussions of rights involve higher animals, and plants are tacked on as an afterthought. For instance, some arguments for rights in nature are based on consciousness or the capacity for subjective experience. But plants are not generally considered to be conscious—at least as we understand it. Sometimes it is suggested that the presence of life is enough—that duties are owed to all living things as a matter of principle. This premise has been adopted by drafts of the successor to the World Conservation Strategy, which notes, "People are part of nature. They should respect nature at all times, for nature is life. . . . Every life form warrants respect and preservation independently of its worth to people" (IUCN/UNEP/WWF 1990).

Many environmentalists are moralists to the extent they believe the human world view requires change and is capable of change. They believe the values of society ought to be in harmony with nature, and draw on three substantive premises for support. The first premise is that the human species has evolved, along with other species, within a complex and interrelated system. In countless ways *Homo sapiens* remains dependent on a functioning natural environment, and both present and potential needs are determined by the interaction of genetic systems with this environment. The second premise states that the universe is extraordinarily complex. Disturbance at one point has effects elsewhere in it, sending a rippling cascade through the system. The third premise is that the ecological world view embodying the first two points justifies a humble approach to values and objectives. We are in no position to grossly manipulate the system when all we have is knowledge based on a single relationship.

It could be objected that humans (and other species) have withstood the loss of many species, perhaps thousands, without any obvious negative result. Europe probably bears little resemblance now to its prehistoric appearance, and much of this change must be ascribed to human influences. The continent is a "mosaic of edge effects," yet more than 500 million people live there, most in considerably greater comfort than many people in other parts of the world. Against this, we can ask why it is that places such as the Galapagos Islands, the Antarctic seas, and the arctic tundra (none of which is the most salubrious of environments) attract a steady stream of visitors who are prepared to pay dearly for the experience of going to these places. One could ask why people value botanic gardens and woods or grow flowers and shrubs in their gardens.

Natural biological systems can withstand some changes but not others. Changes that mimic natural processes, such as taking older and weaker organisms to fulfil human needs, or controlling an outbreak of a pest species by encouraging its natural enemies, work within the established patterns of the system of nature. These changes set off compensating mechanisms, often already in place; information flows through the system, allowing other organisms to react. On the other hand, abrupt changes with no parallels in normal biological or climatological processes scramble the feedback messages and leave the system in disarray (Norton 1987).

Opportunities need to be created to allow people to experience transformative values. It is not enough to preserve areas of wilderness merely for those few hardy trekkers and alpinists who have the physical capacity to get to them. Rather, experiences of nature need to be made available close to where all people live. James Lovelock (1988: 489) points out the problem for the rapidly expanding urban dwellers of this world:

> Because we are city dwellers we are obsessed with human problems.... We are so alienated from the world of nature that few of us can name the wild flowers and insects of our locality or notice the rapidity of their extinction.

It is curious that no fully coherent, holistic philosophy of conservation has developed, at least in Western society (Norton 1987). The discord of many communities may well have its roots in failure to understand the holistic nature of our world, the interdependence of its parts, and the futility of isolation. Biologically, the human race is set a little apart from the rest of life, and in particular, plants. This opens up particular responsibilities for other species and demands a position of stewardship—a partnership forged between people and nature (e.g., Salim 1981; Boyd 1984; Engel 1990).

Humanity cannot exercise wise stewardship in the absence of justice and equity. As long as people are struggling for survival—whether it be for the essentials of life, such as food and water, or for cultural survival—they will put such matters ahead of conservation considerations. A woman whose family is starving or needs a fire to cook food will be justifiably interested in immediate use of a food or fuel plant rather than leaving it in the ground to conserve soil or genetic diversity. The tragedy is that her situation is rarely self-inflicted or caused by nature. It is likely to result from the greed and selfishness of others who may be far distant.

Human communities involve unique and distinct kinds of relationships that bind their members, but to enter into these relationships demands that we know who belongs to the community as the basic unit of life on earth. This has been recognized in various forms such as the foundational value of reverence for life

(Skolimowski 1990) and the concept of the noosphere to describe a world dominated by human influence and reasoning (Laptev 1990).

Within the mixed community, many elements affect one another. The elements exist for each other but also for one another and for the whole. The community is interdependent, and it follows that choices are not between the environment and people, or between preservation and jobs, but between different kinds of mixed communities of people, plants, and animals. It also follows that individuals in the community are not totally free to act as individuals, independently of all others about them.

There will, in all likelihood, never be a perfect community or solution, but there is the opportunity to redirect and restructure. Sustainable community development can be a reality and may be the only viable reality in the longer term. Nonetheless, the effectiveness of sustainable development is largely dependent on developing ethics of sustainable development (Engel 1990). These ethics must incorporate evaluation of existing moral values, understanding of peoples' motivation, clarification of the moral implications of choices, conflict resolution, and definition of a new social paradigm.

Meanwhile, concerned scientists predict that as many as one quarter of all species could be lost by the early twenty-first century. It would be a tragedy for biodiversity and the human race if an acceptable sustainable society arrived too late to negate this.

Case Study: The Assisi Initiative

In autumn 1986, a unique alliance was forged between conservation and five of the world's major religions, at Assisi in central Italy. The event marked the twenty-fifth anniversary of World Wildlife Fund and included a pilgrimage, conference, cultural festival, retreat, and interfaith ceremony in the Basilica of St. Francis.

A major part of the initiative was the issuing of declarations by the five religions involved. Other religious groups have followed since by issuing their own statements on conservation or by announcing their intention to do so. The conference and retreat provided opportunity for religious philosophers to help inject moral perspectives into conservation's somewhat ill-defined ethical foundations.

Five brief extracts from the Assisi declarations are followed by a subsequent statement on nature by the Baha'i faith:

> **Buddhist.** Buddhism is a religion of love, understanding and compassion and committed towards the ideal of non-violence. As such it also attaches great importance

towards wildlife and the protection of the environment on which every being in this world depends for survival.

Christian. Man's dominion cannot be understood as license to abuse, spoil, squander or destroy what God has made to manifest his glory. That dominion cannot be anything else than a stewardship in symbiosis with all creatures.

Hindu. Hinduism believes in the all-encompassing sovereignity of the divine, manifesting itself in a graded scale of evolution. The human race, though top of the evolutionary pyramid at present, is not seen as something apart from the earth ... man did not spring fully formed to dominate the lesser life forms, but rather evolved out of these forms itself, and is therefore integrally linked to the whole of creation.

Islamic. For the Muslim, mankind's role on earth is that of a khalifa, vice-regent or trustee of God. We are God's stewards and agents on earth. We are not masters of this earth; it does not belong to us to do with it what we wish. . . . Unity, trusteeship and accountability, that is ta-wheed, khalifa and akhrah, the three central concepts of Islam, are also the pillars of the environmental ethics of Islam.

Jewish. In the Kabbalistic teaching, as Adam named all of God's creatures, he helped define their essence. Adam swore to live in harmony with those whom he had named. Thus, at the very beginning of time, man accepted responsibility, before God, for all of creation.

Baha'i. Nature in its essence is the embodiment of My Name, the Maker, the Creator. Its manifestations are diversified by varying causes, and in this diversity there are signs for men of discernment. Nature is God's Will and is its expression in and through the contingent world. It is a dispensation of Providence ordained by the Ordainer, the All-Wise.

Source: WWF 1986.

CHAPTER 2

How Plants Become Threatened or Extinct

The 1980s saw the appearance of numerous books with graphic titles such as *Extinction is Forever, Where Have All the Flowers Gone, Vanishing Heritage,* and *Plant Extinction: A Global Crisis.* These titles reflect concern that the world is losing plant species at a faster rate than ever before in geologic history (Figure 2.1). Trees that were at one time important components of forests and provided food and fuel to tribespeople are disappearing. Shrubs and herbs that had evolved over millions of years are reduced by habitat

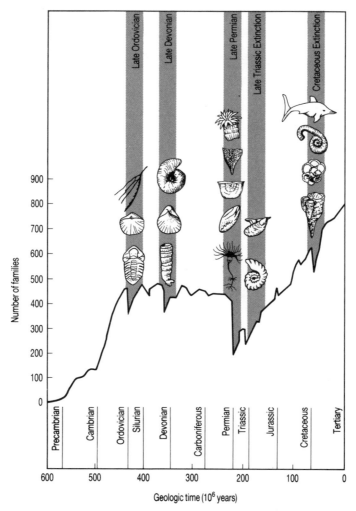

Figure 2.1. Geologic extinctions. A summary of mass extinctions showing the principal groups of animals affected by each event. (Redrawn by permission from Jablonski 1986)

13

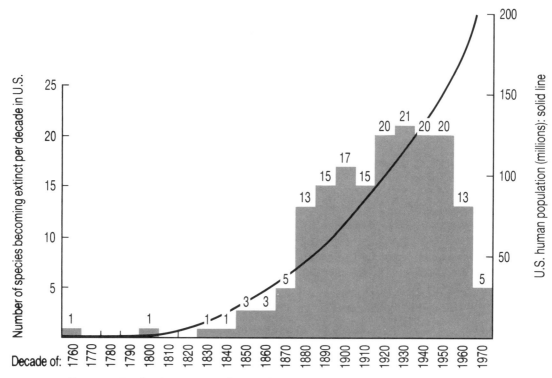

Figure 2.2. Historic extinction rates in the United States. Extinctions of U.S. flora and fauna (exclusive of Hawaii) by decade since 1760 (histogram), compared with growth of the U.S. population (solid line) during the same period. (Redrawn by permission from Bunnell and Williams 1980)

conversion to a few individuals in a few days. Aggressively invading plants and animals are driving out native species. The plantscapes of many regions are altering dramatically as more and more land is required for agriculture, housing, roads, industry, and energy sources. Extinction rates for flora and fauna in the United States since 1760 are graphically illustrated in Figure 2.2.

Increasingly, humanity is implicated in this depletion and loss. Even such large-scale effects as climate change are influenced by people, through such phenomena as the "greenhouse effect." What humanity has done is to magnify natural threats many times over, as well as to introduce new threats.

The diverse mechanisms involved in most extinctions fall into five general categories (Diamond 1986; Fitter 1986): overkill, habitat destruction, impact of introduced animals and weeds, pollution, and secondary losses.

The following represent specific major threats to plants (based on Falk 1987): organized land conversion, including agriculture, housing, roads, industrial development; dam construction and inundation; soil compaction or disturbance; erosion; mining disturbance from coal, oil (including shale), sand and gravel

quarrying; wetland draining and filling, and changes in water-table; herbicide spraying; trampling and over-grazing by range animals and feral animals; slash-and-burn (shifting) cultivation; fire and fire suppression; competition from introduced exotic plants; recreation—off-road vehicles, skiing, trampling, camping; diseases (e.g., fungal blight) and insect predators; natural and induced vegetation succession; commercial, and sometimes scientific, collecting; vandalism; and disappearance of symbionts, pollinators, dispersers.

CASE STUDY: THE LOSS OF *ASTIRIA ROSEA* FROM MAURITIUS

Astiria is a monotypic genus, related to *Dombeya*, in the family Sterculiaceae. In the nineteenth century, this beautiful small tree was collected in a few localities in the humid forest of high altitudes of Mauritius. Since 1860, no botanists have seen it again although a lot of time has been spent searching for it.

Astiria was introduced into cultivation and grown in the Sir Seewoosagur Ramgoolan Botanic Garden of Mauritius and in Syon Park near Kew, England, where it flowered in 1833. Since this epoch, classic works like the *Dictionary of*

Horticulture of the Royal Horticultural Society give information on how to care for and propagate this plant. Unfortunately, it is probably also extinct in cultivation! There is very little hope that it will be rediscovered in cultivation, although it is not impossible that a specimen or two survive in an old forgotten Victorian greenhouse. The loss of this species is a major one for science, to be compared with that of the dodo. It is also a great loss for horticulture for the plant's bunches of pink flowers and large velvety leaves were very attractive. It may be that *Astiria* still survives in a remote corner of the mountains of Mauritius. Some parts of the region still have not been fully explored botanically. The recent discovery of two new palms, *Hyophorbe vaughanii* and *Tectiphiala ferox* (new genus), on the island suggests that unexpected treasures are still to be found. If *Astiria* survives, it is probably only as a very few specimens; these forests are invaded increasingly by exotics. In the Mascarenes, *Astiria* is the only genus considered to be extinct although two others survive as single specimens in the wild: *Ruizia* (in Reunion) and *Ramosmania* (in Rodrigues). Both have now been rescued and are conserved in botanic gardens.

Source: Lesouef 1988.

The Process of Extinction

Extinction of a species involves reduction in its numbers until it ceases to exist. It is the antithesis of persistence. Extinction generally occurs when an environmental change or challenge exceeds the adaptive capacity of individuals, and there is no safe place to which they can retreat. Extinction is dynamic in nature, involving ongoing processes of disturbance. Only recently has extinction been studied from a systems perspective and, even now, little is understood about what it really involves.

Two classes of events lead to extinction. *Deterministic* events are those involving unalterable change, such as deforestation or climate shift. A deterministic extinction occurs when something essential is removed or when something else that is lethal is added. Small oceanic islands provide good examples of deterministic extinction: essential bird or insect pollinators may disappear and, along with them, the plants that depend on them; feral animals such as goats may invade and eat all the plants.

The other kind of events are *stochastic* or chance events. These occur as a result of normal, random changes or environmental disturbance. Usually, this does not destroy a population—at least not immediately. But once numbers or density, or both, are decreased, there is greater risk from the same or other random events. The smaller and more dispersed a population, or the smaller the intervals between disturbances, the greater the risk of stochastic extinction. Stochastic extinctions can involve a number of events, each of which is unlikely to cause extinction on its own but which additively wreak havoc.

In nature, deterministic and stochastic events interact (Gilpin and Soulé 1986; Schaffer 1987). Many extinctions are the result of a deterministic event that brings the population down to a size where stochastic (or chance) events are influential. Environmental variability is a very significant component, and high environmental variability may present the greatest barrier to persistence. It is even likely to swamp other stochastic factors such as demographic and genetic uncertainty.

It is sometimes assumed, especially by lay people, that the longer a species has survived, the more successful it will be in overcoming forces leading to extinction. This is not true. The chances of events happening that will lead to extinction—especially stochastic events such as storms and landslides—are quite independent of the previous history of the species (Koopowitz and Kaye 1983). Perhaps the most obvious examples of deterministic extinction today are provided by habitat conversion, especially in the tropics. Deterministic forces are particularly devastating in regions with high densities of species with very restricted geographic ranges. The total extinction of a species as opposed to the extinction of one component population is most likely when the species is a local endemic, the species is already near extinction, or there is widespread habitat destruction.

Stochastic forces are somewhat different. Three kinds of stochasticity can be recognized (Gilpin and Soulé 1986). The first, demographic stochasticity, is the chance variation in individual births and deaths. In a small population extinction can occur randomly because of low birth rates or high death rates. This means that a population is not secure from extinction while it remains small, especially if it is outbreeding. A second type of stochasticity known as genetic stochasticity includes inbreeding depression, chance effects of lethal genes, and the loss of genetic diversity and heterosis. Debilitating diseases caused by recessive genes increase greatly in frequency as population size decreases. The third type of stochasticity is environmental. It includes environmental shocks received by all members of a population. In a more spread-out population, there is likely to be more habitat variation that buffers against change. No environment is static, and consequently all populations run the risk of suffering from environment stochasticity.

Deterministic events (e.g., storms, fires, and destruction of vegetation by feral animals) are readily observed. Stochastic events, however, may be unnoticed until it is too late. Effects such as decreasing reproductive rates and reduced fitness are not readily observed unless appropriate measurements and monitoring are carried out. Such monitoring includes observations on reproductive strategies, the spacing of individual plants, seed and other propagule production, and reproductive success.

CASE STUDY: A MODEL OF EXTINCTION VORTICES

Environmental change can set up positive feedback loops of biological and environmental interaction that have further negative impact on the population. These are termed *extinction vortices*. Four vortices are distinguished in the Gilpin and Soulé model. These are the R, D, F, and A vortices:

The R vortex. Chance lowering of population size (N) and increases in population growth rate [Var (r)] make the population vulnerable to further disturbances, in turn reducing N further and increasing Var (r). An example would be alteration in sex-ratios in an obligately outcrossing species, with increased variation in birth and death rates because of decreased fertilization.

The D vortex. A lowering of N and an increase in Var (r) can alter the spatial distribution of a population and can increase the patchiness of its distribution. Rates of local extinction vary because the probability of extinction varies inversely with the population size at each patch. Fragmentation can have negative consequences for the genetic effective population size (N_e).

The F vortex. A decrease in N_e can lead to the start of two genetically based vortices, resulting from increased genetic drift and loss of genetic variation. Inbreeding depression and loss of heterozygosity can lead to decreased efficiency, growth rate, reproduction, and disease resistance. In turn, r and N_e are reduced.

The A vortex. Any reduction in N_e also reduces the efficacy of stabilizing and directional selection. This, in turn, accelerates the rate of lack of fit between population phenotype (PP) and the environment (E). This reduces r and N still further.

Source: Gilpin and Soulé 1986.

Minimum critical area and viable population size

Population vulnerability analysis (PVA), a recent development in the study of population viability and extinction, is based on three constantly changing and interacting fields: population phenotype, the environment, and population structure and fitness. The components of these three fields are as follows (Gilpin and Soulé 1986):

1. Population phenotype
   A. Morphology
      (1) Variation of sizes, shapes, and patterns
      (2) Geographic and temporal variation
   B. Physiology
      (1) Metabolism
      (2) Metabolic efficiency
      (3) Reproduction
      (4) Disease resistance
   C. Interspecific interactions
   D. Distribution
      (1) Dispersal
      (2) Genetic migration
      (3) Habitat selection
2. Environment
   A. Habitat quantity
   B. Habitat quality
      (1) Abundance (density) of resources
      (2) Abundance of interacting organisms
      (3) Patterns of disturbance—duration, frequency, severity, spatial scale
3. Population structure and fitness
   A. Dynamics of spatial distribution
   B. Patch distribution—metapopulation structure and fragmentation
   C. Age structure
   D. Size structure
   E. Sex ratio
   F. Saturation density
   G. Growth rate
   H. Variance of growth rate
      (1) Individual
      (2) Within patches
      (3) Between patches

From data relating to the interactions of these fields, models are being developed to show which of several extinction pathways is most likely.

In recent years there has been considerable emphasis on minimum viable population (MVP) concepts and the search for a "magic number" for a general, universal minimum population size. Much data for this and PVA comes from studies of animals (especially mammals and birds). As a generalization, animal demography is relatively clear-cut; numbers of breeding animals, fecundity, mortality, and so forth, can be readily calculated for many species. It is more complex to calculate such numbers for many plants. The precise number of breeding individuals may not be a useful concept, especially among long-lived perennials, where there is a substantial seed bank, or for species with both sexual and vegetative reproduction. Often there is no standard "size" in adults as there usually is in animals. Even if one decides to count individuals, is the fundamental unit a stem, clump, tiller, or a discrete "patch"? For those plants capable of forming clones, does one count ramets or genets? In a vegetatively reproducing population, it may be very difficult to determine the number of genets. A further complication is that long-lived perennials may be genetic mosaics in which there are mutation-induced variants within the one plant.

The idea of a minimum viable population implies there is a minimum threshold that will ensure that a population will persist in a viable state for a given interval of time. Early investigations of the problem em-phasized demographic approaches, based chiefly on birth and death analyses; these found that there were critical limits below which extinction was likely. Recent approaches have tended to concentrate on genetic aspects of the problem. These findings also conclude that there are critical factors of population size and structure. In very small populations, inbreeding and loss of selectable variation can facilitate extinction.

The probability of extinction cannot be pegged to population size alone. Each particular situation will depend on various interacting factors such as life history, temporal and spatial distribution of individuals, and genetic variation.

Priority candidates for population viability analysis and estimates of minimum viable population size include species whose activities create critical habitat for several other species; mutualist species whose behaviors enhance the fitness (e.g., reproduction and dispersal) of other species; predatory or parasitic species that regulate the populations of other species, and whose absence would ultimately lead to a decrease in species diversity; species that have spiritual, esthetic, recreational, or economic value to humans; and critically rare or endangered species (Soulé 1987).

Characteristics of Declining Populations

Early investigators of extinction theory hoped that models incorporating stochastic factors would reveal threshold values below which populations will quickly succumb to extinction. It is unlikely that such universal thresholds exist. It now seems reasonable to state that the probability of extinction increases gradually as effective population size decreases. For each particular case, a series of acceptable levels of risk have to be identified. Specific strategies to protect species have to be based on a case-by-case approach (Jensen 1987). Each particular situation will depend on many interacting factors such as life history, distribution of individuals through space and time, periodic fluctuations in habitat conditions, predator relationships, and inherent genetic variation.

Such interrelated events can be modeled mathematically, although mathematical models tend to simplify, not taking into account all the possibilities in nature. Nevertheless, such models can yield interesting conclusions, which then can be applied more widely than the confines of the model itself. Current attitudes tend to treat the various factors affecting population and species survival as separate; a synthesis that combines a wide range of factors is needed (Goodman 1987).

Given the expense of maintaining protected areas over long periods of time, the "persistence time and extinction rate" problem has practical implications for conservation management. In some instances, extremely large populations (requiring large areas of habitat) may be required to ensure the viability of a species. In contrast, some plants seem to be able to persist for long periods, perhaps hundreds of years, in quite small numbers, again demonstrating that there is no set of universally applicable magic numbers (Gilpin and Soulé 1986).

As reduction in size of available habitat occurs and mere remnants are left, several related effects may become apparent. A species may migrate into a site even though the species was not present when the fragment of habitat was formed. Species are also increasingly occupying marginal and suboptimal habitats. Although populations must be able to maintain themselves through cycles of change, lack of habitat may prohibit the build-up of numbers of individuals from periodic lows. There may be significant genetic changes in populations isolated for even a small number of generations. It may be hard to predict beforehand just how these effects will show and how they will interact, especially as it is not yet clear if extinction-prone populations tend to show universal trends.

Certainly the factors just enumerated have greater effect as populations become smaller. A countering force does occur in some species, especially these that have previously undergone a reduction in population size to very low levels (genetic bottleneck). This is the elimination of lethal genes—the purging of those individuals that are less able to survive in small populations. Conservative genetic architecture has been suggested as a protective mechanism in such instances. The result is that those individuals that continue to survive in small populations are simply those that are most capable of doing so.

Loss of genetic variability as a result of diminishing population size is likely to reduce a population's ability to respond adaptively to changing environmental conditions. The smaller the population, the more vulnerable it becomes to loss of genetic diversity in successive generations (Figure 2.3). The fact that plants are sessile has two profound consequences. First, there can be significant genetic variation over a few meters. Second, whereas many animals can move to new sites when conditions become unfavorable, plants essentially cannot do this. As a counter to this, they often have a greater variety of reproductive options and genetic structures than do animals. These factors complicate management and make it hard to predict genetic consequences of reduction in population size, although they do potentially lead to a wide range of management options.

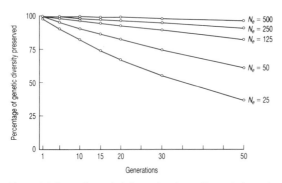

Figure 2.3. Loss of genetic information in small populations. As the effective size (N_e) of a small population decreases, the genetic diversity also declines rapidly over the generations. (Redrawn by permission from Foose 1986)

The importance of distribution of individual breeding units or subpopulations within a larger population system—the *metapopulation* structure—is only now being appreciated. It is not just the total size of a population that figures into vulnerability analysis; geometric character of distribution and the patterns of gene flow within the population are important as well. All populations, to a greater or lesser extent, exhibit *patchiness* (contagion)—varying densities within the whole area occupied.

Two considerations follow. On the one hand, because sedentary organisms such as plants are not free to wander away looking for breeding partners, proximity to nearest neighbors can be crucial to reproduction. If nearest neighbor distance is greater than the foraging distance of a pollinating insect, local extinction is very likely. This has led to the concept of minimum viable density (MVD). Although hundreds of individuals of a species may exist within a protected area, density of the population may be below the MVD threshold. A second consideration is that subdivision of a population into discrete patches increases the chance of inbreeding within patches. Excessive patchiness can lead to frequent local extinction and recolonization, greatly complicating the calculation of what is, in effect, a greatly lowered effective size of the whole population.

Although there is danger in seeking universal levels for MVDs, in general terms, an effective population size of about 500 may be a practicable and reasonably satisfactory first approximation. This should lead to reasonable persistence times for most species, as a minimum necessary to continue evolution and to sustain long-term adaptability for change. Most populations of this size will maintain nearly as much variation in quantitative characters as an indefinitely large population. In the case of a variable or widespread species, each endangered and distinct ecotype should be conserved at a minimum of 500 individuals (Frankel and Soulé 1981; Roche and Dourojeanni 1984; Lande and Barrowclough 1987).

Genetic diversity itself has two components. The first is *allelic richness,* which is defined as the number of alleles in a population sample—a measure of variability within a population. Trees with widespread natural distributions tend to have high allelic richness values compared with other plant groups. The second component is the distribution of genetic diversity across the geographic range of a species—*allelic evenness.* The pattern of genetic diversity for a particular species has great significance for management. If there are considerable genetic differences between populations (allelic unevenness), then numerous reserves may have to be set aside. On the other hand, few larger reserves may be more appropriate where there is genetic evenness. The nature and distribution of genetic variation also becomes extremely important when natural populations are being sampled for gene bank collections, botanic gardens, or for supply of stock material to be used in restoration projects.

It is a general assumption in conservation biology that long-term persistence is enhanced by high genetic variability and that low levels of variability should be avoided. Very small populations (the extreme being single plants) are particularly at risk, as are populations growing at the limits of geographic or altitudinal range. In such instances, breeding programs to maximize variation by controlled crossing between particular sets of individuals may have to be considered. Nonetheless, some examples of extremely low genetic variability among narrow-range endemics have been recorded. *Moraea loubseri* occurs as one population of a few plants in the Cape Region of South Africa; existing cultivated plants appear to be unusually uniform with respect to flower color markings (Hall 1984). *Pinus torreyi,* of California, is known from two small populations and electrophoretic studies have revealed no significant intrapopulation variation (Ledig 1986).

Lack of genetic diversity and inbreeding may not necessarily of themselves lead to extinction. Following an extreme population crash and the resulting inbreeding depression, if a population does survive it will have lost most recessive lethal alleles. This loss may shield the population against some degree of inbreeding, at least in the immediate generations because there will be a lack of lethal genes in the genetic system. This may provide an explanation for the observation that some crops (e.g., garden vegetables grown in small numbers for personal use by home and village gardeners) may persist for many generations as selfed lines.

The fact that in the course of fluctuations in population size, some species have survived "bottlenecks" (extreme reduction in population size) does not prove that smaller numbers are justified (Figure 2.4). The question may well be, How long do you want the population to survive? If it is only for a few generations, then small populations may be satisfactory. We cannot argue from "some bottlenecks do not lead to immediate extinctions" to "bottlenecks do not lead to extinctions" (Soulé 1987). The only bottleneck examples that can be observed are those that have survived: perhaps the rare survivors. When examples of species that have recovered from bottlenecks are examined, genetic diversity generally is found to be very low, which makes the population or species vulnerable to future extinction events.

In the very long term (extending over hundreds of years), survival and persistence depend on *adaptability*—the ability of a population to change its genetic composition in response to long-term changes in the environment. This in turn depends on a broader array

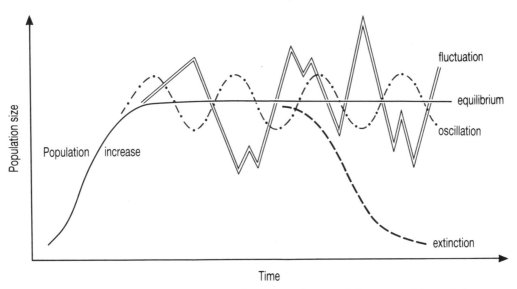

Figure 2.4. Fluctuations in abundance and rarity through time. Few, if any, populations are so stable as to be in constant equilibrium (solid line); most oscillate seasonally or annually (dashes and dots) or irregularly fluctuate (double line) reflecting changes in various limiting factors. Where mortality exceeds reproductive success, extinction (dashed line) is inevitable. (Reproduced by permission from King 1987)

of genetic resources than are required for short-term survival, hence the need for reasonably large effective population sizes. For example, at an average size of 50 individuals, roughly 64 percent of a population's neutral (or currently unselected) genetic variation will be lost through genetic drift within 100 generations. Since evolutionary change depends on the presence of heritable variation, this represents a serious loss of adaptive potential.

Four final matters must be stressed. First, in most instances, size estimates assume the absence of management except to reduce such factors as poaching. Second, some viable populations will be so large that it will be impossible to contain this many individuals in reserves and parks of modest size. The most recent modeling studies are indicating that some populations must be so large that the only solution will be to establish the species in new sites with a range of suitable environments. Third, one of the oldest ecological principles is Liebig's Law of the Minimum—the limiting factor for viability is the factor that is in shortest supply. The limiting factors in the long run for most biological systems will be keystone species. Therefore, there is need to estimate approximate minimum viable population sizes for those species whose health and well being may well determine the viability of other species and the whole ecosystem in the long term.

Finally, effective population size is not the same as total population size. Just counting the total number of individuals of a species is not sufficient. Effective population size may be reduced by presence of non-breeding individuals, skewed sex ratios, some degree of inbreeding, random variation in progeny survivorship, the loss of genetic variability that may have occurred during previous periods of low population size (the "bottleneck" effect), and patterns of pollination (population structure). Some populations simply may be far too small even when they appear healthy and viable. Such species may be well on the way to extinction unless there is rapid intervention.

The Influence of Humanity

It has been suggested that because extinctions are "natural" they ought to be allowed to occur without human intervention, but the present extinction crisis has been precipitated by our own species. Within a few years, depletion of habitat has increasingly threatened thousands of plants with extinction. Many more species have highly reduced reservoirs of genetic variation. Fragmentation is resulting in a mosaic of small habitat remnants unsuited to the survival of many species. Natural extinction climbed to a rate of about 1 species every 10 years between 1600 and 1950, and is much higher (and increasing) at the present time (Bunnell and Williams 1980). By the end of the twentieth century, extinction rates may rise as high as 40–400 times the background rate. Perhaps a reasonable guess is that species extinction in many groups will become about 100 times the average level for the last 50 million years (Ehrlich 1986).

What are the primary causes of human-induced extinction? Hunting, habitat disruption, and introduction of predators or competitors are common factors. Oceanic islands seem particularly vulnerable. Even remote oceanic islands of the world are just as prone to settlement as continents. In the wake of settlement, island ecosystems are quickly affected by habitat loss, predation by grazing mammals, and weed competition. On many islands, the amount of habitat affected by each person has grown at a faster rate than the human population itself. The situation on islands demonstrates that a host of secondary factors may operate synchronously and reinforce each other. Different factors affect plants at different times of the year or at different stages of their life cycle. Assessment of the contribution of such threats cannot be made at the office desk, but must be made on-site, through monitoring and experimentation (Messick 1987).

In summary, about 25,000 flowering plants are threatened today with extinction. Many more are genetically depleted. Prime causes of human-induced depletion are over-exploitation, habitat loss and fragmentation, and loss of resilience through local extinction of key species (Figure 2.5). Most examples of plant depletion through harvesting involve plants for the medicinal, timber, or horticultural trade.

Habitat or ecosystem destruction shows little sign of abating in intensity. High technology allows clearing of extensive areas of land, and slash-and-burn disturbance cycles are becoming shorter in many regions. Such activities are reaching farther into formerly pristine habitats supporting highly diverse and complex biological communities. Rapid human population increase, and greater demands by technological societies for resources are two driving forces behind this trend.

CASE STUDY: EXTINCTION OF *FRANKLINIA* IN NORTH AMERICA

The most famous North American endangered plant is probably *Franklinia altamaha,* a tree named after Benjamin Franklin. The history of the tree is well documented. It was first noticed on 1 October 1765, by John Bartram and his son William along the banks of the Altamaha River in Georgia. William returned to the site a number of years later and collected some of the plants.

In 1790, Moses Marshall, a nurseryman, went to the same spot and also collected material. He was probably the last person to see a *Franklinia* in the wild.

The plant is closely related to the camellia, and has shiny leaves and large white blossoms. When mature, *Franklinia* grows to about 9 meters tall and makes a handsome garden plant. During late summer and early fall, *Franklinia* bears large flowers with five rounded white petals and a central boss of golden stamens. Sometimes the 7-centimeter-wide flowers are borne just as the foliage turns scarlet at fall.

These trees have been popular in cultivation for more than 200 years. What happened to them in the wild? There is really no clear explanation. The species was rare when first discovered, with just a small patch growing on that site in Georgia. The trees must have been already on the verge of extinction, and so the small collections made by the Bartrams and Marshall merely hastened the species' natural end.

A number of attempts have been made to relocate *Franklinia* trees in the wild. Although there have been a few claims of success, all attempts ended in failure. This is one of the lucky species to be successfully cultivated prior to its demise in the wild.

Source: Koopowitz and Kaye 1983.

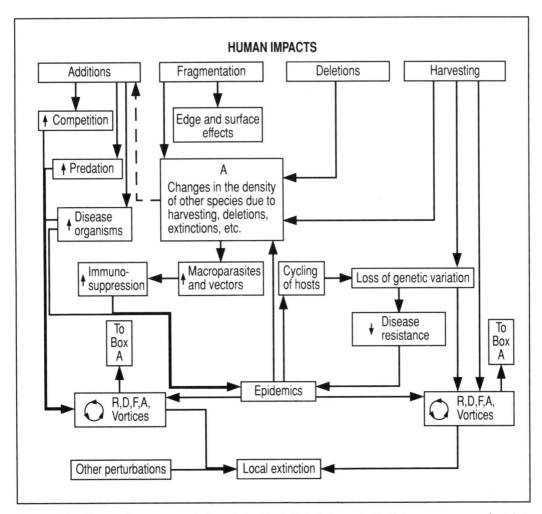

Figure 2.5. Flow diagram of some cause-and-effect relationships in biological communities that are consequences of certain human impacts. The dashed arrow from box A to "Additions" indicates that an increase in the density of a species may behave ecologically like a species addition. (Reproduced by permission from Gilpin and Soulé 1986)

Extinction typically is discussed in the context of species, but it is also important to recognize what is happening in particular populations. Monitoring activities and the recording of events that may lead to extinction should be focused on populations. Within a target species, especially one scattered over a large geographic area or a range of habitats, some populations may be increasing, some may be static, and others may be declining.

Community level interactions may be critical to species extinctions but do not necessarily result in loss of a population. Loss of a pollinator, or competition between a natural pollinator and exotic flower visitors that are ineffectual pollinators, can cause all populations of a species to become depleted through reproductive failure. If the pollinator or species of plant is a keystone member of the community, its loss can in turn lead to the loss of other species throughout their distribution range; this is the classic *extinction-* or *trophic-cascade* (Jensen 1987).

Loss of habitat

Loss of habitat is a fundamental threat for living organisms. All organisms have particular habitat requirements; they have evolved to survive and reproduce in a specific niche. If the niche is reduced in size or even eliminated, species occupying it will be unlikely to persist. They will be squeezed out of the community. Every human activity has an effect on habitats and niches—what can be termed *essential habitat.* Human influence on natural ecosystems cannot be avoided. People must be fed, clothed, and sheltered. But attending to the necessities of life is one thing; excessive and thoughtless damage through exploitation is another. Too often habitat loss is greater than necessary, as shown by historic changes in land use and distribution of natural habitat (Figure 2.6). This comes from lack of forethought and often arises out of maladjusted development and squandering of natural resources (Prescott-Allen 1984).

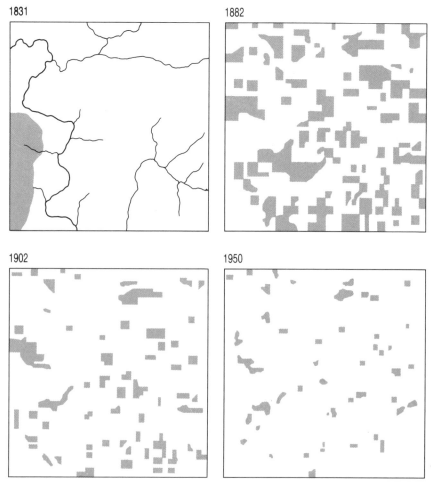

Figure 2.6. Progressive loss of habitat. Changes in wooded area of Cadiz Township, Wisconsin, during the period of European settlement. (Reproduced by permission from Curtis 1956)

Most important are habitats that support major processes, especially those habitats that may be "biosphere regulators" or that govern global processes (Prance 1981; Myers 1984b). Examples include moist tropical forests, large freshwater wetlands, coastal wetlands, and tidal meadows (Prescott-Allen 1984). Yet these are the very habitats that are frequently under threat, either because they are in regions with high population densities or because they appear to be useless or marginal habitats that, to the lay person, serve no obvious purpose. Industrial and nonindustrial plantations in the tropics are estimated to increase by about 1.1 million hectares each year. For the 76 countries subject to a 1981–85 FAO/UNEP study, there was replacement by about 1 hectare of plantation, on average, for every 10 hectares of closed or open tree formation cleared (Roche and Dourojeanni 1984).

Worldwide, forests receive much publicity, but the same cannot be said for some other species-rich habitats. The high diversity levels of open habitats such as grassland, savanna, and tundra are often overlooked (Prescott-Allen 1984). Transformation of open habitats is permitted because people consider such areas to be wasteland, or forget that plants of open sites may have highly specific requirements. Coastal habitats are particularly vulnerable; many of the component plants do not grow readily elsewhere. Coastal regions often are heavily populated and are in demand for development of recreational and industrial facilities. It is all too easy to quarry sand or flatten and reshape sand dunes to develop housing, industrial parks, and recreational sites. Sand dune vegetation in many countries is only a remnant of its former extent, and often, little has been done to protect the plants found growing naturally in such habitats (Marangio and Morgan 1987). Other threats tend to follow an initial degradation of habitat. An influx of weeds is often associated with opening up of habitat. In turn, these may crowd out native plants, prevent seedling germination, or compete for scarce commodities such as water.

Desertification

Desertification currently affects much of arid Africa (chiefly the Sahel), especially in regions with 200–800 millimeters of annual rainfall. Other large areas affected are in the eastern Mediterranean and southwest Asia, the western coast of South America from northern Peru to northern Chile (Keel 1987), and Australia. In 24 countries in these areas, land that is not already desert is at high risk of becoming desert. A further 23 countries have land that is at moderate risk.

Desertification has important consequences for threatened plants and vegetation. The dry lands that may be subject to desertification generally are not highly productive, but they often contain unusual assemblages of species that have evolved to cope with climatic and edaphic (soil) extremes. A significant number of plants of arid regions are of economic interest, and some have developed unusual chemical features that probably constitute a response to the harshness of their environment. An example is the jojoba shrub (*Simmondsia chinensis*) of the southwestern United States and northern Mexico. Jojoba is the only producer of liquid wax in the plant kingdom; the product now has numerous industrial applications including substitution for sperm whale oil (Myers 1984a). In addition, the value of grasslands as carbon sinks increasingly is recognized.

The lands in greatest danger of desertification are in semidesert zones where climate and vegetation allow some grazing and cropping, but where water is a limiting factor. Most of the regions subject to desertification are continental and lie between 10 and 40 degrees latitude in the Northern Hemisphere and between 10 and 30 degrees latitude in the Southern Hemisphere. Semiarid ecosystems may fluctuate between grassland and shrubland thicket within a few decades, depending on climate, grazing, and burning regimes. Such cyclical changes may do little harm when usage is not intense. With increasing intensity of use, however, succession may cease to be cyclical and linear decline takes place.

The process of desertification often results from the following specific activities (Le Houérou and Gillet 1986):

Cultivation of unsuitable terrain and soils. These are excessively arid, too sandy, too stony, too shallow, too saline, or too steep to sustain crops. In African arid zones, agricultural crops are expanding over rangelands at about the same rate as population growth. One effect of this is that lands less suitable for production are being brought into use, but lower and lower yields demand that yet more land be developed.

Cultivation methods that enhance wind erosion. This includes disc plowing, clear fallowing, and use of short-cycle annual crops without wind breaks.

Excessive removal of woody plants for fuel. In some areas, the only fuels available are cow dung and wood. Currently, wood consumption for fuel in the African arid zone is about 16.5 million metric tons per year. Destructive wood-cutting extends in concentric circles of 50- to 100-kilometer radius around large towns of the zone. In the Sudan, 548 million *Acacia* shrubs are pulled up and burned annually to supply energy for cooking.

Faulty irrigation practices. Large areas are sterilized by use of excess water or water that is too saline.

Inappropriate water and livestock management policies. Deep bores for water often result in concentration of animals in the immediate vicinity.

Careless mineral resource surveys (e.g., excessive use of heavy vehicles).

Unregulated tourism development.

Overstocking, overgrazing, and poor range management. This can result in reduction of perennial plant cover to less than 10 percent of original cover.

Of these activities, crop expansion, overstocking and firewood collection are the most harmful: these initiate about 80 percent of desertification in the African arid zone and a similar scenario probably prevails in most other desert regions (Le Houérou and Gillet 1986).

Typically, desertification occurs in two main stages. First, the herb layer is lost. Too little importance is sometimes attached to this. In savanna communities this stage may falsely appear beneficial in that increased growth of trees and shrubs occurs and a severely degrading grassland appears to be a flourishing woodland. But following this, there is a loss of trees and shrubs with severe and increasing losses of other plants and soil. Once desertification is under way, wooded perennial grassland may change to annual grassland and then to bare soil, which is vulnerable to erosion. Up to this point, reversal is possible if intensity of exploitation is reduced. Once soil loss takes place, however, reversal becomes impossible within reasonable limits of time and expense, although slow recovery is possible. A further and more drastic threshold is reached with erosion of the subsoil.

Loss of wetlands and aquatic habitats

Wetlands and aquatic habitats take many forms—marshes, swamps, mires, floodplains, rivers and lakes, shores of artificial lakes, and estuaries (Maltby 1986). Many animals and plants have evolved to cope with the peculiarities of a water-dominated environment. Wetlands occur in all climates and on all continents; most are geologically young and ecologically fragile. Many are ephemeral or physically unstable, and often change dramatically with time and season. Wetlands are created, change, or vanish as vegetation changes, sediments are deposited, or land sinks or rises.

The value of wetlands is often underestimated. Many thousands of plant species are restricted to them and are locked into complex relationships. The fluctuating water levels of wetlands often correlate with high numbers of plant species, many of them generally uncommon (Keddy 1985). Most water-dominated systems are highly productive, and complex food chains therein actually sustain species living far beyond the immediate wetland boundaries. It is ironic that many people regard wetlands as unproductive wastelands, not realizing these systems moderate flooding and drought, and act as sinks, trapping nutrients and maintaining high water quality. Wetlands ecologically couple land and water. In addition, wetlands are often focal points for recreation.

Direct threats to wetlands include drainage, dredging, and stream channel modification; waste disposal; construction of dikes and other structures for flood control; and mining of peat and soil. Indirect threats include sediment diversion by dams, hydrological alteration, and subsidence caused by extraction of groundwater. Few large-scale *polder* (wetland reclamation) projects now completed have been subjected to serious environmental and ecological study (Sioli 1986).

Although new wetlands are being created in some parts of the world, it is difficult and costly to duplicate precisely the conditions found in natural wetlands. Most natural wetlands are adapted to periodic fluctuations in water level; such fluctuations can be extremely difficult to replicate, especially when other users such as waterfowl hunters and farmers demand management to different water levels. Artificial wetlands do fulfill a valuable function but rarely do they adequately replicate all the functions of natural wetlands.

Loss of moist tropical forest

Humanity's current degree of interference with vegetation throughout the world is seen at its most acute in the case of tropical rain forest. Ironically, many of the best moist tropical forests are in countries that can least afford expensive conservation measures, and where pressure to utilize forested lands to grow crops and generate income is greatest. Perhaps the biggest single factor in tropical deforestation is clearance for agriculture. Nevertheless, many pressures to utilize tropical forests, especially moist lowland forests, come from wealthier countries, which look to these forests to supply pulp and hardwood lumber (Whitmore 1980; Jacobs 1988).

Description of species new to science cannot keep pace with current rates of destruction of tropical vegetation—chiefly forests. During the nineteenth and twentieth centuries, about 1.4 million animal and plant species have been formally described and named, and at least 5 million (but perhaps as many as 30 million) remain to be cataloged (Wilson 1988).

While about one million temperate organisms have been named, it is probable that less than one in five tropical species is known to science, although the general situation for flowering plants is much better than for many other taxonomic groups.

Despite the abundance of both popular and scientific articles on tropical forest deforestation, it is surprisingly difficult to determine precise rates of change. Still less is known about the full effect of deforestation on forest genetic resources.

An offshoot of FAO forest inventories in the late 1970s concluded that the overall figure for depletion of closed forests in the tropics was less alarming than the generally quoted figure of 50,000 hectares of clearance per day (Lanley and Clement 1979). Lanley and Clement, however, defined vegetation as closed forest when the trees were 5 meters high and the crown cover was 40 percent or above. This meant the finest rain forests of western Malaysia still just qualified as closed forest when, after logging, they were virtually beyond repair (Jacobs 1988). A second report concluded that worldwide destruction of tropical moist forest was occurring at a rate of 240,000 square kilometers per year, or 65,750 hectares each day (Myers 1980). This figure is in the same order of magnitude as an estimate given by the director of FAO in 1978, and a 1982 figure calculated by Norman Myers (quoted in Jacobs 1988): deforestation in the sense of virtual elimination amounting to 115,000 square kilometers per year, with deforestation in the sense of gross disruption of ecosystems amounting to a further 85,000 square kilometers annually.

The most recent estimates of destruction rates of moist tropical forest conclude that global rates of loss are high and still increasing (Sayer and Whitmore 1991; Blockhuis et al. 1992), although for some regions and countries deforestation rates have started to decrease since the late 1980s. Sayer and Whitmore (1991) point out that some alarmist predictions are probably overstated, although rates are greater than some earlier estimates (e.g., by FAO) suggested. They also point out that it is misleading to extrapolate towards a zero base.

Within the tropical forest biome, the greatest threats are to moist tropical forests, especially gathering of fuelwood, cattle ranching, and small-scale cultivation. Commercial logging is becoming of lesser concern with development of sustainable forestry policies, although significant illegal logging continues in some regions. Forest zone ranches in Brazil were estimated to cover over 100,000 square kilometers in the 1980s, although removal of clearance subsidies has resulted in a rapid decrease in area. In Central America, the number of cattle and the amount of pastureland increased two and a half times between 1950 and 1981 (Koopowitz and Kaye 1983; Myers 1984a, 1984b). China has lost much of its forest. Detailed study of the rare and threatened plants of the Yunnan tropics has not been completed; however, study of this region shows that in an area of about 19,000 square kilometers, there are about 4000 vascular plant species, of which 345 have been proposed as rare (Xu Zaifu 1987). Among these, 53 species require urgent protection within China. More than 10 percent of the regional flora may be rare and threatened, because roughly one-half of the tropical forests of Yunnan have disappeared through deforestation since the 1950s.

The greatest threats to moist tropical forests include spread of small-scale agriculture, spread of commercial farms (whether plantations or ranches), commercial forestry, and collection of poles and firewood.

Machinery allows extractive forestry at a rate undreamed of in the past, and the forests are no longer inexhaustible (Whitmore 1980; Prance 1986; Jacobs 1988). If just one type of moist tropical forest is considered—the Atlantic forest of southern Brazil and northeastern Argentina—a mere one percent of the Brazilian element remains, while 40 percent of the tropical forest in Argentina has been completely altered. Even in Argentina, however, the rate of forest removal has rapidly increased in the 1980s with the advent of high technology logging procedures (Johnson 1989). Despite what is said about the many values of forests, they are still exploited principally for their hardwoods. Making tree replanting a requirement for permits to exploit private forestland can actually hasten rain forest removal by encouraging replacement with fast-growing exotic conifers, unless the replacement species are specified.

In Colombia, Ecuador, and Peru, major loss of the genetic diversity of *Theobroma cacao* has occurred. In Southeast Asia, the lowland tropical rainforest habitats of wild relatives of mango (*Mangifera*), durian (*Durio*), rambutan (*Nephelium*), and other local fruits have been reduced as a result of logging and clearing for agriculture. The habitat of *Coffea arabica,* the most valuable of the coffees in southwestern Ethiopia, is threatened but unprotected. Other examples of endangered genetic resources are some south Gippsland populations of *Eucalyptus globulus* in Australia, and the Agaun population of *Araucaria hunsteinii* in Milne Bay Province of Papua New Guinea (Roche and Dourojeanni 1984).

Although most emphasis is on moist tropical forests, other tropical forest types are exploited as well. In Mesoamerica today, one of the most threatened of the once widespread habitat types is dry forest. Only 0.08 percent of the original 550,000 square kilometers of dry forest is preserved, and less than 2 percent of this exists as relatively undisturbed natural lands. Habitat restoration will have to be an essential part of conserving the remnants. The conservation of dry forest is essential to the long-term persistence of other vegetation types including moist forest. Many insects and some birds spend the dry season in rain forests but spend the rainy season in dry forests (Janzen 1986a).

Industrialization of developing countries results in other major threats to tropical forests. In Brazil, the Grande Carajas Programme threatens to consume large areas of tropical forest in the eastern Amazon through the extraction of raw material for charcoal to be used in smelting pig iron (Fearnside 1989). This project illustrates a host of subproblems: the difference between assumed "zones of influence" and the real areas affected, the overall impact of many small operations (which may be as great as a single scheme), impacts on third parties who may not be considered in environmental impact studies, and problems in enforcing noncompliance conditions attached to multinational finance.

In terms of total area affected, it has been suggested that there has been already a loss of 37 percent of moist tropical forest, but this may be an overestimate; the figure may be nearer 27 percent (Simberloff 1986). Unless there is a full commitment to sustainable logging and major cessation of land clearance, a projected decrease in area of 12–25 in the last two decades of the twentieth century is possible. National parks and other reserves in tropical America total about 96,700 square kilometers of forest (Simberloff 1986). Estimates for protected area coverage of tropical moist forest in 16 countries of Asia and the Pacific indicate that just over 27 percent of remaining forest areas are in existing or proposed protected areas (extrapolated from Collins et al. 1991). Total area likely to be protected in the near future is still not large, and even established parks may become threatened as adjacent areas are eliminated.

CASE STUDY: CRITICALLY ENDANGERED AND EXTINCT PLANTS OF SRI LANKA

Out of the 26 plant genera endemic to Sri Lanka, 12 have endangered species. Nine of these genera are monotypic, and one has two species, both of which are endangered. About 190 of the 850 endemic species are very rare and may be considered endangered. In addition to the above, many species with wider distributions are becoming more and more scarce. This leads to 300–350 endangered species for

Sri Lanka in these major families:

Orchidaceae. Of 159 species in 68 genera, 31 are rare and 18 are endemic. About five species have not been collected in the twentieth century.

Apostasiaceae. Only one species occurs in Sri Lanka, but it is very rare.

Amaranthaceae. *Cyathula ceylonica* is endemic but has not been collected for over 100 years. Its only close relative occurs in Africa.

Connaraceae. *Ellipanthus unifoliatus* has not been seen since 1888.

Leguminosae. *Sophora zeylanica* is endemic but has not been seen in the wild since 1925.

Clusiaceae. *Mesua stylosa* is endemic and has not been collected for over 100 years.

Myrtaceae. *Eugenia* is represented by 12 species; 4 endemic species are now very rare.

Apocynaceae. One endemic species is disappearing rapidly; another is also endemic but has not been seen for over 100 years.

Asclepiadaceae. One endemic *Ceropegia* has not been collected for over 100 years, and six other species in this family also have not been collected in the twentieth century.

Asteraceae. Six species have not been collected in the twentieth century; three of them are endemic to Sri Lanka.

Source: Abeywickrama 1983.

CASE STUDY: DEGRADATION AND LOSS OF VEGETATION IN NEPAL

Sixty-one percent of Nepal's 14 million people live in the hills and mountains, and about 93 percent of the population is engaged solely in agriculture. In the mountains, the average landowner holds only one-tenth of a hectare. The forest, agriculture, and livestock form such a compact and complex relationship that one is always dependent on the other and all are intimately related to the fragile hill ecosystem. The growing human and livestock populations are exploiting forests at an accelerated rate. The area of cultivated land in the mid-hills correlates fairly well with the number of cattle kept. Higher elevations offer minimal opportunities for agriculture, so higher pasturelands are utilized for limited livestock only.

Green and dry fodder crops are used as cattle feed for three months of the year, and for the rest of the year farmers lop down twigs, branches, and leaves of the forest trees. Such trees, large and small, are being continually hacked and hewn and most of them stand without leaves or twigs.

The scrubby landscape of the Nepalese mid-hills has experienced a sharp recession of forest cover over the last few decades. Even smaller stands that could have regenerated have not been spared. The increasing demands for fodder in the hills and exploitation of forest flora has already pushed back the foliage line to the mountain tops, which are hardly accessible. It has become increasingly difficult for the hill farmers to maintain their livestock, and they have been forced to reduce the size of herds.

Fuelwood is the primary source of energy in Nepal. The gross timber requirement in the country is 70 cubic meters per household. Most of the poor people near towns earn additional income through the sale of firewood or manufacture of charcoal. All these activities, as well as some manufacture of paper, have contributed to the accelerated destruction of hill vegetation.

Source: Khadka 1983.

Harvesting and overexploitation

For many plants, traditional harvesting has not involved the total death of individuals (the exception would be annual crop plants in cultivation). On the other hand, harvesting of animals often does result in death. This scenario is changing with increasing destructive harvesting of plants, for instance, of tropical hardwood trees for lumber.

Most current examples of overexploitation involve gathering of plants for pharmaceutical chemicals, for wood for the lumber industry, or for horticultural use (Figure 2.7). Sometimes these activities can have devastating results. The 23 species of so-called mahoganies are one group of trees that have suffered espe-

cially severely from the demands of the timber trade. Unfortunately, no mahogany plantations have proved viable. On St. Helena Island in the South Atlantic Ocean, the endemic ebony, *Trochetia melanoxylon*, was felled to provide fuel for burning the lime for fortifications erected during the Napoleonic Wars. Today, this is a very rare species (Cronk 1986).

An increasingly important type of plant exploitation involves the taking of species with horticultural potential. It is only in recent years that the full extent of the horticultural trade has been realized. Orchids, cycads, palms, some rock garden plants such as cyclamen, lilies, carnivorous plants, and succulents and cacti are also particularly vulnerable to this form of exploitation (Koopowitz and Kaye 1983). The extent of the horticultural trade is indicated by the number of cacti legally imported into the United States. In 1977–78, this was a staggering 6,850,000 plants from more than 50 countries. Although some of the species involved sell for very high prices, there is considerable waste.

Inclusion of populations of highly desirable species in protected areas is not sufficient to ensure their survival (Bennett et al. 1987). Illegally collected cacti sell in the United States for $5 to $500 each. Private citizens are known to collect cacti for their own use, and some cactus and succulent clubs and guidebooks have been known to publish explicit directions for finding rare and endangered species. Offenders are not always easily located, and courts frequently regard plant thefts as minor. Fines, when they are imposed, sometimes do not greatly exceed the cost of commercially obtained plants.

Figure 2.7. Destruction of oak - rhododendron forest in the Himalayan foothills, through overgrazing and firewood gathering. Mussooree, India. (D. R. Given)

Although harvesting may not totally eradicate a population, it may reduce genetic variability by selectively depleting races with particularly desirable features. Examples of this are coming to light among plants harvested for pharmaceutical use (Rao et al. 1983). Increasing volumes of wild material have to be harvested to give the same yield of the end product. Genetic erosion is a natural consequence of this and has been observed in densely populated regions such as parts of Indonesia (Sastrapradja 1983). Genetic variability parallels environmental variation and can be used to improve productivity of species grown in plantations and gardens. Relatively few species have been intensively studied for regional variation, especially in chemical characters.

CASE STUDY: LOSS OF HIGH-YIELDING GENOTYPES OF MEDICINAL PLANTS THROUGH HARVESTING

Dioscorea deltoidea is a very important plant of the Himalayas whose tubers have been found to contain high concentrations of diosgenin, a corticosteroid used in production of sex hormones. Earlier collections of the species made in Kuku and Simla Hills (western Himalaya) by several workers indicated that the genetic material contained up to 6 percent or more of diosgenin. Fifty-eight additional collections made from these hills were analyzed for several characters including diosgenin content. Surprisingly, none of the accessions yielded higher than one percent diosgenin. The high diosgenin yielding genotypes seem to have been lost from these habitats through the activities of herb collectors. Certain areas in Kashmir and Himachal Pradesh, which used to have genotypes high in diosgenin content, have been completely denuded. The exploitation of this species has been promoted by the uncontrolled granting of contracts: in certain cases, states have given long leases to multinational companies with the result that the species is almost extinct in some areas.

Rauvolfia serpentina, another Himalayan plant, is a valuable source of reserpine and other hypotensive alkaloids used extensively to control hypertension and as a tranquilizers in certain mental disorders. The plant has been collected indiscriminately for the last 20 years. There is very little supply of *R. serpentina* left, and many of the high-yielding gene pools have been lost.

Source: Gupta and Sethi 1983.

Alien plants and feral animals

Invasions by alien plants and animals are nothing new. They have occurred throughout geologic history under the influence of tectonic processes and climatic changes, and as new species have evolved they have migrated and established in regions far from their place of origin (Di Castri 1989). In terms of conservation, however, human-induced invasions are most significant. From the early times of agriculture about 10,000 years ago, there has been an accelerating spread of plants—both deliberate and accidental—as part of civilization's baggage. In some oceanic islands such as New Zealand and the Hawaiian archipelago, the ratio of native to introduced plants may approach one. Three crises of human history have had a particular impact with respect to invasions: neolithic increase in human-induced disturbance, expansion of European trade, and the present acceleration of change in land use and development of areas of formerly intact vegetation.

Alien plants can be regarded as belonging to one of three categories (McClintock 1987). The first category includes introductions persisting only locally within urban areas, where they derive benefits from cultivation such as out-of-season watering. Not all of these introductions are properly naturalized, nor do they all have an impact on the native vegetation. The second category includes introductions that occupy disturbed habitats such as wastelands, edges of roads, fire sites, and earthfill sites. In many such places, indigenous plants were displaced by the original disturbance and may be prevented from recolonizing such sites, or the disturbed areas may act as nuclei for colonization of undisturbed sites. The third category includes introductions that have moved further afield, invading areas of native habitat where they displace native plants. These introductions are generally highly aggressive weeds, sometimes with wide distributions throughout the world.

Some types of habitats are more prone to invasion than others, a concept that has become a recurring theme in ecological literature (Ashton and Mitchell 1989). Open habitats including grasslands, sand dunes, and many wetlands tend to be particularly vulnerable to opportunist weeds (Ranwell 1981). These readily spread once disturbance has been initiated by events such as fire. Woody, tall-growing alien species are a particularly severe problem in many nonwoody habitats because some have the capacity to form dominant communities and shade out other species. Other particularly successful weeds are those that can change the direction of ecological succession. In a habitat where native plants rely on instability, stabilizing species such as sand-dune binders can eliminate suitable sites very rapidly. One of the ironies of invasions is illustrated by temperate grasslands: some are extremely susceptible to invasions while others have produced many of the most aggressive plant invaders (Mack 1989).

Invading plants can exert a profound influence on resident species (Figure 2.8). Open habitats such as coastal sand dunes, river beds, cliffs, and talus slopes are particularly vulnerable to invasion by aggressive plants, which can rapidly cover large areas. Plants such as lantana, marram grass, gorse, European broom, and Kikuyu grass are able to choke out pre-existing native species and form a new vegetation in only a few years. By modifying the soil and changing the environment near the ground, they can change the direction of succession. The explanation for why some communities are far more vulnerable to invasion is a frequent objective of ecological studies. Invasive success is the result of interactions between the invading species and the target habitat, but it can be profoundly modified by timing in relation to chance events (Crawley 1989). Post-invasion successional changes may be just as important as conditions during early phases of invasion (Ashton and Mitchell 1989).

Figure 2.8. Weeds, such as Cape daisy (*Cryptostemma calendulacea*) at Alexandria, Victoria, Australia, can sometimes cover many hundreds of hectares. (D. R. Given)

Feral animals, especially mammals, are quite another issue but no less important. Many continental regions have a long geologic history of animal browsing and grazing; plant species are adapted to coexist with such animals. Plants of oceanic islands, on the other hand, have evolved in the absence of grazing and browsing mammals, or their place has been taken by birds such as the flightless rattite moas of New Zealand. Many temperate and tropical oceanic islands have suffered severely from introductions of animals such as goats, pigs, rabbits, and cattle. An additional factor is that many feral mammals are generalists who eat a wide range of plants. As more palatable species become scarce, they switch to alternative food sources; sometimes they change their food preferences even when a range of palatable species is present (J. Flux, pers. com.).

On both continents and islands, feral pigs are a common problem. Their feeding methods can root up many hectares of land, in a short time drying out and exposing soil to erosion and preventing regeneration. In North America, heavy infestations of feral pigs can reduce herbaceous ground cover by up to 98 percent, with actual species reductions being over 50 percent (De Benedetti 1987). Reductions in leaf litter can exceed 30 percent and soil chemistry is significantly altered. Feral pigs are believed to spread fungal diseases, causing loss of native trees in Hawaii. At Pinnacles National Monument in California, feral pigs cause soil disturbance, consume native species such as valley oak (*Quercus lobata*), compete with and pass disease to wildlife (some of which may be important dispersers of seed), and cause structural damage in forests.

Feral animals affect plants directly and indirectly. Direct effects include eating of foliage, roots, and bark; mechanical damage to low branches; rubbing on lower parts of trunks; and predation on flowers and seed. Sometimes adult plants may appear to be quite healthy but a population is doomed because all seed or seedlings are destroyed by animals. Indirect effects are mainly to the habitat. One of the most common is intense grazing pressure, which removes or weakens ground cover and disturbs top soil, leading to erosion. Such opening up of vegetation and changes in soil favors ephemeral weeds that may secondarily inhibit reestablishment of indigenous species.

Invading weeds and animals can do more than change habitats and compete with indigenous plants directly. Sometimes their most significant effects may be indirect, especially in contributing to trophic cascades. The Argentine ant provides two examples of this. The first is the possible future extinction of fynbos plant species as a result of displacement of native ants formerly responsible for the dispersal of seed (Bond and Slingsby 1984). The second is the same ant's potential role in elimination of endemic Hawaiian plants. The Hawaiian biota lacks endemic ants and those that are introduced have had a devastating effect on the indigenous insect fauna, some of which are major pollinators of indigenous plants. The Haleakala silversword (*Argyroxiphium macrocephalum*) and some of its near relatives are self-incompatible, reproduce only by seed, and would decline rapidly if pollination failed (Macdonald et al. 1989).

CASE STUDY: INVASIVE PLANT SPECIES ON THE
GALAPAGOS ISLANDS

The known number of exotic plants in the Galapagos
Islands rapidly increased from 77 species in 1971 to 260 species in 1987. This presumably resulted from the growing
human population and the introduction of plants for ornamental and cultivation purposes. The exotics are found
chiefly on the four inhabited islands: Santa Cruz (198 species), Floreana (91 species), San Cristobel (111 species), and
Isabela, Sierra Negra (68 species). Several species have naturalized and established in national park areas. Although
the majority of species have not yet altered the ecological
equilibrium significantly, some species have invaded large
areas to form monocultural stands or, at best, very altered
vegetation types. These latter species and their current distribution are listed below.

Invasion by exotic plant species is still occurring, and
large areas with unique vegetation, such as the evergreen
Scalesia forests and *Miconia* shrublands, could face extinction if the current invasion is allowed to continue. Very few
resources have been available to initiate effective control of
exotic plants. A few small-scale experiments have been carried out with herbicides to control *Psidium*. Far greater input of money is needed, and the cultivation of "noxious"
species should be made illegal. A coordinated effort involving national park authorities and research interests is
needed.

Representative species	Introduction date	Island distribution (hectares)			
		SC[1]	F	I	C
Psidium guajava	1910	100	8000	20,000	12,000
Eugenia jambos	?	1	1	5	50
Lantana camara	1940	1	2000	--	1
Cinchona succirubra	1941	4000	--	--	--
Furcraea hexapetala	?	10	1	10	10
Kalanchoe pinnata	?	+	50	10	10
Rubus sp.	1983	1	--	--	100
Pennisetum purpureum	?	5000	150	?	?

[1] SC = Santa Cruz, F = Floreana, I = Isabela, C = San Cristobel

Source: Lawesson 1987.

It is important to know which invasive organisms
will cause disruption, and which will merely slip into
an existing community with no significant displacement of other species. An ideal (from the point of
view of the plant) invasive plant is frequently described as a "plastic" perennial that germinates under
a wide range of physical conditions, grows quickly,
flowers early, is self-compatible, produces many seeds
that disperse widely, reproduces vegetatively, and is a
good competitor (Baker 1965). Such a list of characteristics can serve as a checklist of potential warning
signs (Noble 1989). The success of invasions (and
conversely, resilience to invasion), however, is influenced by many factors. Niches must be available and
the invader must be able to compete successfully for
resources against species already present. The invading species must be able to reproduce and establish a
new generation with greater numbers of individuals.
Reproductive strategies are an important consideration in the success of invading species. There are obvious limitations on dioecious species, which require
the establishment of more than one plant or
propagule if they are to survive (unless they can produce occasional monoecious plants). Obligate vegetative propagators are also at risk of not establishing and
spreading because of limited dispersal. Annual plants
tend to invade over long distances less often than perennials.

Communities that have widely spaced species,
where there are available niches for invaders to slip in,
will tend to be less resistant to invasion. Other communities are surprisingly resistant to invasion, at least
in the absence of substantial disturbance. Because of
this resilience, many invading species may be temporary occupiers of ground rather than permanent additions to the community (Pimm 1986).

One of the vexing questions about invasion is
whether islands are more vulnerable to introductions
than continental regions. There are numerous examples of island ecosystems being invaded by large numbers of introduced plants and animals (e.g., Loope
and Mueller-Dombois 1989). Certainly, many islands
have experienced proportionally more species introductions in recent historic times than most mainland
areas. It can be argued that oceanic islands are only
now experiencing what many continental regions
went through many thousands of years ago. The high
percentage of island extinctions in recent times reflects a truly greater number of species introductions
than on continents. One can also argue that the dis-
harmony of island floras makes them more vulnerable
and that invasive species exploit "niche vacancies." A
high degree of disruption is likely to occur when a

previously absent factor such as a grazing herbivore is introduced into an ecosystem. With a greater number of introductions, there is a greater chance of a particular introduced species having a devastating effect (Pimm 1986).

Particularly in the tropics, the effects of invasions must be carefully considered in species and ecosystem management. Increasing numbers of vegetation remnants and protected areas are surrounded by highly modified agricultural and urban land, or by second-growth vegetation. Such areas become more vulnerable to invasion by opportunistic species, particularly where buffer zones are absent. Sometimes the protected area appears to experience an increase in diversity and, possibly, overall plant density; but often these increases are at the expense of regeneration of species originally found in primary vegetation (Hubbell and Foster 1986).

Invading species are not all bad. They contribute to the study of conservation biology in that they are contemporary examples of the processes of immigration and persistence (or extinction), which have been occurring for many millions of years. They provide experimental situations in which to test the tenets of island biogeographic theory, and they are, in a sense, field experiments on the success or failure of invasions and of theoretical predictions of extinction. Lessons from these "experiments" contribute to the planning of deliberate reintroductions of species that are threatened in their natural area of occurrence. Invasions may seem undesirable, but they have been a real part of nature since the first organisms evolved.

CASE STUDY: EFFECTS OF ANIMAL AND PLANT INTRODUCTIONS

A review of 10 papers covering over 850 animal and plant introductions reveal three common features. First, less than 10 percent of introductions caused definite species extinctions (71 extinctions). The highest number of these were recorded for birds, which are very vulnerable to predation, especially poor fliers or ground-nesting birds of oceanic islands. Overall, introductions may tend to increase numbers of species (i.e., gains are greater than losses). Second, of 55 documented extinctions, over 90 percent were on islands. Third, predation was the principle cause of extinction. Habitat change accounted for 11 of 71 extinctions; and direct competition from the introduced species was a distant third factor, accounting for three extinctions.

Source: Pimm 1986.

Pollution

Whereas smoke and human wastes have been pollutants of air and water for many centuries, the twentieth century has seen the advent of novel pollutants such as heavy metals, radioactive isotopes, and long-lived injurious chemicals such as chlorinated hydrocarbons, detergents, and plastics. Some are particularly damaging to plant life. Heavy metals can readily poison plants, particularly where soils are highly acid. Organic herbicides discharged into waterways affect sensitive species, even though they may be highly diluted. Surprisingly, such commonplace chemicals as detergents discharged in sewer lines can adversely affect coastal plants by removing the cuticle wax that prevents intake of salt.

Much publicity has been given to "acid rain" (or acid deposition), which results chiefly from the burning of fossil fuels and the production of a range of gases, of which the most important are probably sulfur dioxide and nitrogen oxides. These gases are soluble in water; thus they make rain acidic and are absorbed into the water cycle. The pollutant gases may themselves be absorbed by natural surfaces, forming more acid. Acid rain and acidification is nothing new (Gorham 1989); acidified ecosystems have been studied scientifically for about two centuries, but such study has accelerated in the twentieth century. Full realization of the seriousness of human-induced acidification has led to a concentrated effort to fully investigate the effects of acid pollutants on natural ecosystems.

For many years, huge and increasing amounts of pollutants have been poured into the atmosphere of regions such as North America and Europe, so that rainfall in some areas may be up to 100 times more acid than normal. This acid precipitation can have disastrous effects on both habitats and species. Especially affected are waters of lakes and streams, and the soil of coniferous forests.

The effects of acid deposition are many and varied, ranging from corrosion of metal pipes and building stone to acidification of water, death of fish and birds, and dieback of forest trees and mosses. Damage to trees caused by smoke, dust, and sulphur dioxide has been recognized for over 100 years, but it is mainly since the early 1970s that the widespread nature of acid rain has been fully appreciated. In the late 1960s, over 500,000 hectares were affected in the Ruhr region of Europe. Surveys of coniferous forests of Europe suggest that more than half of the total forest area of the former West Germany may be damaged. Up to 87 percent of silver fir (*Abies alba*), 59 percent of Scots pine (*Pinus sylvestris*), and 51 percent of Norway spruce (*Picea abies*) may be affected (see Table 2.1). There are predictions that in some areas, all spruces and firs may be dead by the end of this century unless swift action is taken.

Table 2.1. Comparative damage from acid rain for four tree species in Europe, as determined from representative surveys.

Species	Survey	Damage class (%)[1]			
		0	1	2	3+4
Scots pine	U.K. 1984	48	29	17	--
	Germany 1983	57	32	10	1
Norway spruce	U.K. 1984	71	26	2	0.5
	Germany 1983	59	30	10	0.9
Sitka spruce	U.K. 1984	65	28	6	0.5
Silver fir	Germany 1983	24	27	42	7

[1] Damage classes: 0 = healthy; 1 = slight damage;
  2 = medium damage; 3+4 = severe damage and dead.

Sources: Ling and Ashmore 1987, Table 14 adapted; data from Rose and Neville 1985, cited in Ling and Ashmore 1987.

Not only trees, but also smaller plants such as mosses and lichens are affected by acid deposition (Woodin 1988). The centers of many cities are sometimes referred to as "lichen deserts" because of the small number of lichens able to grow there. Lichens are, in fact, good indicators of pollution levels. *Sphagnum* moss, which grows in abundance on moors and bogs, especially of temperate and mountain regions, is also generally sensitive to pollution. In the United Kingdom, smoke pollution killed many areas of *Sphagnum* during the industrial revolution. Smoke pollution has now been reduced but in its place acid deposition is preventing the moss from growing back. A range of herbaceous plants, especially those of moorland, are affected and the growth of some crop plants is reduced by acid deposition.

The precise effect of acid rain on both individual species and ecosystems is hard to assess. One of the problems is that by the time macroeffects are evident, much irreversible damage is likely to have been done. Indeed, one of the points of controversy is whether dieback in areas suspected to be affected by acid rain is attributable just to acid rain or to a range of causes, of which acid rain is only one. Although many scientists now believe that atmospheric pollution is in-

volved, in combination with other biotic and abiotic stress factors, an incontrovertible cause-effect relationship has yet to be proved (Ling and Ashmore 1987). Among the causes suggested for dieback are extreme climate events, planting of trees of unsuitable provenance, soil deficiencies, viruses and fungi, changes in ozone concentration, increased ammonium concentrations, and stress resulting from the additive effects of a host of factors.

Lack of certainty regarding the precise mechanisms and primary and secondary causes of dieback ascribed to acid rain makes it difficult to mitigate effects. Where acidity is a problem, emission reduction is an obvious step and the only realistic long-term solution. Liming of lakes that have become acidic can help, but usually has to be continued even beyond the period of acid deposition and can be very costly in remote regions. Liming changes other chemical parameters as well. Critically affected plants can be shifted to regions of similar climate and soils that are less affected, but this, too, is only a temporary expedient (Woodin 1988).

What is the global pollution situation, for instance, with acid rain? What is emerging is a picture of highly acidified regions covering much of Europe and the eastern parts of North America. These are well documented and it is expected that major increases will not be experienced, although levels are already high and some ecosystems will experience further severe deterioration (Galloway 1989). Less publicized is the emergence of an acidified region in southern China, fueled by large emissions of sulfurous gases from coal burning in urban parts of Guishow and Sechuan provinces.

In most tropical countries, emissions are low but increasing. Several studies, for instance, in Venezuela and Nigeria, have indicated that particular regions with naturally acidic soils may be highly sensitive to acidification (Rodhe 1989). Overall, given the reality of population growth and potential for industrial expansion in the tropics, future emissions of gases such as sulfur dioxide and nitrogen oxides could greatly exceed current emissions (Galloway 1989). It may be that creating reserves for tropical ecosystems will be insufficient to conserve the wealth of tropical biodiversity; social issues such as urban development, industrialization, and fuel use will require just as much attention.

Water-borne effluents from industry and agriculture are highly varied and may affect aquatic communities in many ways. Chlorine, chromates, cyanides, heavy metals, phenols, and aromatic solvents are toxic, even in low concentrations. Mixtures of poisons are often more toxic than their individual constituents, through enhancement of the physiological action or formation of new ultratoxic compounds such as cyanogen chloride, which is produced in mixtures of chlorine and thiocyanates (Kaul 1983).

Many tropical wetlands are under particular threat from pollution. While the waters of temperate wetlands cool during the winter, those of the tropics remain at elevated temperatures so that tropical rivers and lakes frequently support perennial mats of floating plants. These mats can grow to gigantic sizes, as with the floating matupa islands in Amazonian lakes. In tropical lakes, initial disturbance is usually through pollution from sewage and runoff from fertilized fields. Both of these lead to eutrophication (increase in nutrients), production of toxic gases such as hydrogen sulphide, and loss of water oxygen. With expansion of human population needs and industrialization, some rivers have literally become sewers themselves, and in rural areas rivers may become polluted with byproducts of agricultural industries.

In the long term, perhaps the greatest fears are held for global pollutants that threaten to affect the basis of life on earth or that may cause long-term climatic changes. Increase in carbon dioxide, methane, and other gases is indisputable, but its full contribution to climatic warming through the "greenhouse effect" is not yet fully known. Similarly, the effect of fluorocarbons on the fragile ozone layer of the upper atmosphere is a matter of intense interest and is leading to international agreements on reductions in emissions of such chemicals. Thinning of the ozone layer will increase markedly the amount of ultraviolet radiation reaching the earth's surface, with resultant increases in mutation rates and carcinomas.

Climate change

The most catastrophic effects on plant diversity worldwide could be those that result from climatic changes induced by our mismanagement of the earth. One of the major driving forces in climate is the greenhouse effect, which allows short-wave solar radiation to pass through the atmosphere, but which partially absorbs long-wave radiation emitted by the earth's warm surface. A number of trace gases in the atmosphere—chiefly carbon dioxide, methane, and nitrogen oxides—are responsible for this absorption. Since, on average, the outgoing long-wave radiation balances the incoming solar radiation, both the atmosphere and the surface of the earth will be warmer than they would be without the greenhouse gases. The natural greenhouse effect is influenced also by dust, especially that resulting from volcanic eruptions.

Natural fluctuations in greenhouse gases have occurred in the geologic past and are associated with periods of climate change. Since preindustrial times, concentrations of these gases have been increasing slowly because of human activities, but the rate of increase has markedly accelerated since 1800: atmospheric carbon dioxide is estimated to be increasing by 0.5 percent each year, aerosols by about 4 percent, and methane by 0.9 percent (Intergovernmental Panel on Climate Change 1990). In the absence of any steps to reduce emissions, this could raise average global temperatures by 1.5–4.5°C, which is about the total temperature change experienced during past glacial and interglacial periods. Such changes are likely to lead to rising sea levels; changing rainfall patterns, with some regions becoming drier and others wetter; some increased seasonality of climate; and melting glaciers and polar ice caps.

A second long-term climatic effect that has resulted from human interference is reduction in levels of ozone in the upper atmosphere. This has led to ozone holes, especially prominent over Antarctica during summer months. Fluorocarbons such as chlorofluoromethane, a gas used as a refrigerant and propellant, have been implicated as major contributors to this effect. Consequences of this are extremely grave as it is the ozone layer that shields the biosphere from mutagenic ultraviolet radiation from the sun. Both the ozone problem and the greenhouse effect have sparked a rash of studies and conferences and the drafting of international conventions.

How serious is the problem? What are the likely effects on plant diversity? What steps can be taken to mitigate the effects? These and many consequent questions need to be addressed, yet they cannot be answered because of uncertainties and conflicting scenarios. Three features of the greenhouse effect receive general agreement (Cohn 1989). First, it seems likely that individual species will respond differently. Some species will not be able to adapt or migrate fast enough; some may become extinct; and others may be drastically reduced in range. It is possible some rare species that are poor competitors but reasonably stress-tolerant may do better than at present. Second, new plant and animal communities are likely to be formed. These will include mixtures of indigenous and naturalized species. Weed invasion may become one of the most significant phenomena for several decades. Similar formation of new communities occurred during fluctuations in climate associated with glaciation in the Pleistocene epoch. Third, the effects of warming will be greatest on plants that are directly influenced by rainfall and temperature, plants that are sensitive to small changes in these areas but which cannot readily migrate.

Global warming may be affecting animal and plant populations already. For some plants, migration rates may need to increase to something like 20 to 25 times the rate of migration at the end of Pleistocene glaciation. Although there is dispute over the details, the rate of anticipated climate change could be several orders of magnitude faster than climatic changes in the geologic past. Major impacts are likely to result, not so much from average changes but from extreme events such as drought and rain storms (e.g., Peters 1988; Bruce 1990).

Uncertainty exists regarding the possible demise of whole plant associations. It has been suggested that arctic tundra could be extirpated as global temperatures increase, especially as permafrost is lost from the top 2 to 3 meters of existing tundra. Much may depend on the ability of species to migrate altitudinally. A vertical ascent of around 500 meters could compensate for a 3°C rise in average temperature, but because available land area decreases with increasing altitude, species with large habitat area requirements may become extinct. In any case, associations of species will be squeezed into decreasing areas as they ascend.

In tropical habitats, the most catastrophic effects may result from changes in rainfall pattern rather than temperature changes. Decreases in wet season rains, or increases during dry seasons, will disrupt finely tuned breeding systems that depend on regular patterns of resource and nutrient availability. Another important effect concerns the spread of tropical and warm temperate weeds, which will be able to spread into regions formerly unsuitable for colonization.

Around 20 percent of the excess carbon in the atmosphere originates from fires in Amazonia. To achieve a 50 percent reduction in present levels of carbon dioxide in the atmosphere would require complete cessation of rainforest destruction as well as planting of 2 million square kilometers of forest (Dobson et al. 1989). Industrial pollution adds a significant contribution to atmospheric carbon dioxide as well, and major criticisms are being directed toward industrialized countries for their continued promotion of models of environments with "unlimited resilience" (G. Woodwell, qtd. in Dobson et al. 1989). Reduction in emissions of pollutants is an obvious step that must be accompanied by replacement of at least some of the forest that has been lost. Underlying these themes is a need for a change to a philosophy of renewable resource use. In forestry, for instance, cutting cycles will probably have to be increased.

It is easy for sensationalism to creep into discus-

sions of possible climate change. Worst-case scenarios can be picked up by prophets of gloom and projected as the only picture of the future. Such scenarios have to be considered among others, recognizing the inherent uncertainty of the future effects of climate change. This is particularly the case with respect to rises in sea level, which may, in fact, vary considerably in different parts of the world. It is difficult to quantify future warming and changes in rainfall even if cause-effect relationships can be indisputably established. Present analyses of data are insufficient. Nevertheless, there is genuine cause for concern regarding the implications of climate change.

Perhaps the greatest problems will be political (Gleick 1989). Some of the worst impacts will fall on developing countries least able to prevent or adapt to changes. This scenario, together with the long history of political frictions and disputes worsened by environmental stresses, suggests that global climatic changes have the potential to exacerbate international tensions. Increasing importance is being made of international cooperation and conservation treaties, but these can only be effective in a climate of cooperation. Changes in the earth's atmosphere bring the risk of more than just changes to the physical climate, but also deterioration in the political and social climate of this planet.

Human population increase

Like a classic epidemic, worldwide growth of the human species is accelerating. Even the medium-growth studies of the Global 2000 report published in 1980 (Barney 1980) forecast an increase to about 6.35 billion people by the end of the twentieth century. Despite marked declines in birth rates per family in some countries, it will take until into the twenty-second century to achieve zero population growth—as much as 130 years from now. In the meantime, barring unforeseen catastrophe, the world human population could climb to two and a half or three times its present level.

Most population growth will occur in underdeveloped countries rather than industrialized ones. In the year 2000, the less developed regions will have about 80 percent of the world's people. Some of the countries that will experience greatest increases, and that may be last to stabilize population levels, are also those with the most to lose biologically. Madagascar has 10,000 endemic plants and is expected to increase its 9.5 million people to 45 million early in the twenty-second century. Colombia, with its rich rain forests and tens of thousands of plant species, now has 27 million people, but may reach 60 million within 90 years. The Philippines support more tree species on a single mountain than are found in the whole United States; that country now totals 48 million people, but is projected to reach 125 million before population stability is achieved.

Population increases of such magnitude put a strain on the natural environment and biodiversity. For one, they result in direct competition for the same land, water, and air that plants require—often the plants that both directly and indirectly support the country's economic base. Degradation and loss of habitat occurs as people migrate or are resettled into formerly undisturbed areas. Irresistible social and political pressures force development of more land for food and fuel, and for harvesting of wild plants such as hardwood trees. Where there are balance of payment and monetary inflation problems, land is likely to be required for growing cash crops. This puts additional pressure on both existing agricultural land, which is being used to supply food and fuel to indigenous people, and on wildlands.

An examination of the conservation status of the flora of the Cape region of South Africa—one of the richest areas in the world for plant diversity—revealed a 61 percent reduction in the area once occupied by indigenous plants (Hall 1978). About 20 percent of the component plant species may be in danger of extinction. Human populations in the region are growing by 60,000 people each month. Clearly, reduction in population growth, along with education and a better economic status, are necessary.

Responsibility for the consequences of human population growth lies in part with those who are living "on site" (e.g., the peasant farmers of the tropical forests and grasslands). Those who live in more distant developed countries, however, are also responsible for what is happening. Many of these problems stem from disproportionate distribution of global resources. To come to grips with human population increase—with famine, lack of resources, and use of natural resources that cannot be sustained—demands a global solution. The solution must include equitable allocation of resources, especially by developed countries that have for many decades used a disproportionate share of natural resources. Just one person from a developed and industrialized country in Europe or North America consumes at least 10–15 times as much vegetable food as a person in Uganda or Bangladesh. In the tropical forest debate, it is valid to ask, Whose hand is really on the chain saw at work in tropical forests? and to question international pricing systems for natural commodities (Myers 1984a; Jacobs 1988).

Ultimately, there are few winners and many losers in the human population race. Some of the immediate losers are the species that are displaced, extirpated, or genetically impoverished. In the long term, the human species also loses opportunities to utilize natural resources such as forest trees and desert shrubs that may have a host of as yet unknown uses. This is the serendipity argument for maximizing biological diversity. Furthermore, decrease in environmental quality negatively feeds back into the system and creates further stresses. Finally, there is a loss of local distinctiveness as the world assumes a greater uniformity in its plant cover. The unique regional peculiarities of plants and vegetation are a major part of the fabric that forms the rich and varied tapestry of human society today.

Future Losses and Gains

The earth is entering a period when, for the first time, a major extinction event will have been precipitated by a single species—*Homo sapiens*. Between half a million and 2 million species—15–20 percent of all species on earth—could be extinguished by the year 2000, mainly because of loss of wild habitat, but also in part because of pollution. This will be an extinction rate possibly surpassing the mass-extinctions of former geologic periods (Jablonski 1986; Kaufman 1986; Simberloff 1986). Loss of tropical forest will account for half or more of these extinctions, but current trends are also causing great disruption of aquatic ecosystems, temperate rain forests, grasslands, and other major ecosystems and habitats.

The twentieth century may well see the end of significant evolution of large plants and terrestrial vertebrates, at least in the tropics. There simply may not be large enough areas left for some important evolutionary processes to occur. This will impinge on social and political systems. Wild strains of crop relatives are rapidly disappearing and threaten to limit future options for crop improvement and especially disease and pest resistance. The increasing practice of monoculture of a few crop strains makes crops more vulnerable to disease epidemics or plagues of pests. This is occurring at the same time the genetic resources to resist such disasters are being lost.

Rain forests—and not only those of the tropics— remain one of the greatest areas of concern. No matter which figures one accepts or which assumptions one makes, there is no room for complacency about the world's major reservoirs of biodiversity. Even the lowest of current estimated rates imply disastrous losses of populations and species in the near future. Half the forests will be destroyed in a hundred years; they could be largely gone in two centuries. This is not a problem that can be left to future generations. It would be highly imprudent to operate on the conservative assumption that the rate of destruction can be held to that which is current (Ehrlich 1986). As rich nations seek to maintain their position in a world of dwindling resources, the pressures they put on the rest of the world seem certain to increase.

In the long term, catastrophic impacts on human life may result not only from loss of genetic resources but also from changes in environmental quality and climate. Large-scale destruction of forests could dramatically alter the hydrological regimes and climate of regions such as Amazonia. In turn, this will induce cycles of depletion, even in areas set aside for nature preservation (Myers 1984a; Janzen 1986b).

Part of the problem lies in decision makers and major consumers being geographically distant from trouble spots. Another problem of attitude is that for any particular activity or incident, it might be fairly easy to shrug off the effects. Can just a little more do any real damage to other species? If things get really bad, can we not stop polluting for a while and life will return? Maybe we would be better off in a world dominated by people and their cattle, sheep, goats, and pigs? These and other questions taken in isolation, as they always are, continually lead reasonable people to make decisions that contribute to the human assault on the ecological systems of earth.

The essential message is that global effects are the sum of local effects. It is not improved protected area systems, legislation, or changed systems of resource use that will conserve biodiversity so much as changed attitudes of ordinary citizens. At its most fundamental level, biological diversity is threatened because people are out of balance with their environment (McNeely et al. 1990).

CHAPTER 3

Documentation and Databases for Plant Conservation

Information about threatened species and habitats is a need of the times. Landowners want to know which rare plants grow on their land. Protected area managers want to know which plants should be preserved before others and how best to manage them. Plant growers want to know which garden plants are rare. Crop breeders want to know which local endemics have desirable characteristics for incorporation into new crops. Ethnobotanists seek information on the traditional uses of disappearing plants. Without good information, action is based on hearsay and unproven assumptions. In their description of the database established for the flora of Israel, Shmida and Ritman (1985) list the kinds of requests that might be made of a floristic database with an ecological orientation:

- How many chamaephyte species with red flowers, spiny leaves, and fleshy fruit flower in May in the Judean hills in Israel?

- List the endemic and rare species that grow in a natural area planned for development.

- How many species (or genera or families) are common to both Israel and California?

- What is the taxonomic diversity (e.g., species/genus ratio) of Mount Carmel in Israel? Or, compare the taxonomic diversity of the Lamiaceae (Labiatae) with that of the Brassicaceae (Cruciferae).

- List the plants in the Jerusalem region that flower in April.

- Compare the annual/perennial ratio of Asteraceae (Compositae) in the Mediterranean region of Israel with that of the desert region.

- How many plants with the specific name *cretica* and author name Boissier grow in Israel?

The primary goal of threatened plant documentation is to ensure that the information needed to

reduce dramatically the decline in plant diversity, plant resources, and plant habitats is readily available. Such documentation often takes the form of databases that monitor changes in plant diversity, plant resources, and their habitats; that hold data on the survival of plant taxa and vegetation types as part of an overview of the decline of plant diversity; that promote and achieve strategies for effective conservation of target plants, habitats, and geographic areas; and that provide and interpret information for individuals and agencies involved in conservation, encouraging the use of these data and making them widely available (Synge and Heywood 1987, modified).

For many people the term database conjures up a picture of massive computer facilities, high technology, and escalating expenditure on data retrieval; but any body of information is a database. A single herbarium specimen is a database of information about a plant at a specific site. A drawer of file cards with addresses, notes on flowering times, or bibliographic references is, similarly, a database. Databases do not have to be complex or sophisticated; their structure and the form in which information is stored need only be sufficiently complex to allow them to perform the tasks for which they were set up.

A database should provide the information essential to determining priorities for areas as well as species—the basic "elements of diversity." These elements reflect biodiversity from biomes down to single gene variants. It may not be possible to save every plant species or key site, and not every species or site can be acted on at the same time. The primary elements of diversity are therefore those groups of plants and those areas given highest priority for action. These include known threatened species, extinction-prone species, plants useful to humanity (economically useful plants and those plants used traditionally by indigenous people), and areas and vegetation types of known or suspected high diversity (Synge and Heywood 1987).

Databases for conservation place a lot of emphasis on endemism. The term endemic is applied to any taxonomic group confined in distribution to a particular region. Without qualification, the term is meaningless. Every species is confined to some area, small or large. Generally, endemic is used for countries, islands, and climatic areas, including vegetation units such as neo-tropics, tropical forest, and arctic tundra. One convenient way to limit the use of the term is to apply it only to taxonomic units whose geographic

extent is smaller than average for their kind.

Frequently the assembling of data on the elements of biodiversity—whether in terms of major ecosystems, rare species, or genetic resources—is hampered by a shortage of technical and scientific personnel, a lack of economic resources to purchase or rent technological devices such as computer equipment, a lack of ready access to literature, and a shortage of professional taxonomists. Inaccurate or uncertain data is the result. Even when these resources are available, efforts frequently are hampered by the large number of species to be dealt with, gaps in geographic patterns of collection, and the urgency of the task.

Types of Data

Many plant conservation databases concentrate on threatened species (including subspecies, varieties, etc.). These are plants that are not expected to be able to persist; included are those plants known only from restricted geographic areas or small populations. Various systems for defining and categorizing threat have evolved. The concept of threat and its subcategories works best for narrow endemics known from one or very few adjacent sites because the threat to a site then equates with the threat to a whole species. The concept works least well for large tropical floras where many species are known imperfectly.

As lists grow, categorizing species to create subsets becomes increasingly important. A list of 400 species may be little help to a protected area manager with very limited resources unless it can be broken down to show priorities, usually by categorizing species. Probably the most widely used general categories are those adopted in the IUCN *Red Data Books*. These categories do not differentiate between geographic range, threat, population size, and habitat specificity. They have have led to the independent development of multiple systems designed to separate components of threat, such as the Californian R-E-V-D code (based on the four components of rarity, endangerment, vigor, and distribution; York 1987), and the alpha-numeric code used for national lists in Australia (Briggs and Leigh 1989).

known or likely places.

Endangered (E): taxa in danger of extinction and whose survival is unlikely if the causal factors continue operating. Included are taxa whose numbers have been reduced to a critical level or whose habitats have been so drastically reduced that they are deemed to be in immediate danger of extinction.

Vulnerable (V): taxa believed likely to move into the Endangered category in the near future if the causal factors continue operating. Included are taxa for which most or all the populations are decreasing because of overexploitation, extensive destruction of habitat, or other environmental disturbance; taxa with populations that have been seriously depleted and whose ultimate security is not yet assured; and taxa with populations that are still abundant but are under threat from serious adverse factors throughout their range.

Rare (R): taxa with small world populations that are not at present Endangered or Vulnerable, but that are at risk. These taxa are usually localized within restricted geographical areas or habitats or are thinly scattered over a more extensive range.

Indeterminate (I): taxa known to be Extinct, Endangered, Vulnerable, or Rare but where there is not enough information to say which of the four categories is appropriate.

UNKNOWN CATEGORIES

Status Unknown (?): no information.

Candidate (C): taxa whose status is being assessed and which are suspected but not yet definitely known to belong to any of the above categories.

Insufficiently known (K): taxa suspected but not definitely known to belong to any of the above categories, following assessment, because of the lack of information.

NOT THREATENED CATEGORY

Safe (nt): neither rare nor threatened.

CASE STUDY: IUCN CONSERVATION CATEGORIES OF THE
RED DATA BOOKS

THREATENED CATEGORIES

Extinct (Ex): taxa that are no longer known to exist in the wild after repeated searches of their type localities and other

Note: Some combinations of these categories are permitted. Within the threatened categories, for example, the following combinations signify that a plant definitely belongs to one of the two named categories:

Extinct/Endangered	Ex/E
Endangered/Vulnerable	E/V
Endangered/Rare	E/R
Vulnerable/Rare	V/R

Combinations between the threatened and not threatened categories, however, do not signify that a plant could be anywhere on the scale encompassed by the two categories; if that was the case, the category Unknown should be used. Instead, combintaions between threatened and not threatened categories signify that a plant is on the borderline between the two categories or that the plant is in one category in part of its range and in the other elsewhere:

Vulnerable/not threatened	V/nt
Rare/not threatened	R/nt

Source: IUCN Species Survival Commission.

Categories must be applied to entities in relation to a predefined area, which can be as large or small as one likes. Consequently, a plant may be placed in different categories of threat depending on the area considered. A plant that is extinct in one place can be endangered in one country and rare in another, but might be only rare or even not under threat at the worldwide level. The categories themselves give some indication of priority, but this usually has to be balanced with other information (for instance, land availability for protection and cost) when priorities for action are set. As databases are built up, they feed back not only into themselves but also into other databases. This feedback is important, as is the capacity to change categories or to add or remove species. Such changes demand rapid assessment and updating capabilities, which in turn depend on a close liaison among various databases.

Undescribed taxa should not be omitted from consideration simply because they do not have formal scientific names. If they can be readily recognized and are known to qualify on the basis of risk, they can be included in a database, preferably under informal names (e.g., *Bellis* "white spot," *Olearia* "Glenhope form," etc.). It helps to append a brief diagnosis or specimen reference to such an informal name (Shevock and Taylor 1987). For large undescribed elements, alternative approaches are being developed: for example, the concept of extinction-prone species, or the "hot spot" approach, which identifies major centers of diversity. Such hot spots are well shown in maps of threatened species of Australia, where southwestern Australia and the eastern seaboard emerge as centers of regional diversity (Figure 3.1).

Even where floras may not be well known in total,

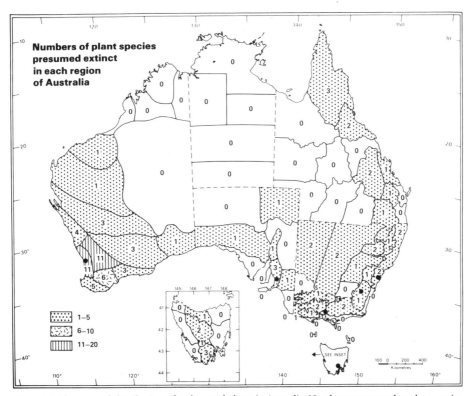

Figure 3.1. The unequal distribution of endangered plants in Australia. Numbers correspond to plant species presumed extinct in each biogeographic region. (Reproduced by permission from Leigh and Briggs 1992)

it is usually possible to identify assemblages of species, such as plants confined to geographically very restricted habitats that have been reasonably well documented (e.g., plants of the lomas of coastal Peru); plants that may be widespread but have been heavily overexploited virtually everywhere they occur (e.g., American mahoganies, west African medicinal plants, minor forest products in Southeast Asia); plants that are threatened by similar factors throughout their range (e.g., species of wetlands, or those palatable to widespread predators); and plants from genera or families that have been studied to a considerable extent (e.g., ferns, orchids, legumes, and, in particular, economic plants and their relatives).

Categories of threat and setting priorities

Even lists of only a few hundred species can be little more than a compilation of meaningless names unless there is some attempt to subdivide that list. There are several reasons to move beyond a mere list of plants, places, or habitats for the purposes of conservation, including to inform the public about which species are most threatened; to draft and eventually implement laws, regulations, and treaties on threatened species; to set priorities for funding and action to preserve species; and to break up large lists into groups that can be readily perceived by those using them (Holt 1987 in part; Mace and Lande 1991).

One of the most important objectives of a listing and categorization process is to suggest priorities for action. How best to categorize is an issue that is hotly debated and is still far from settled. In part, this is because the process is, in a sense, a matter of judgment. Causes of rarity are often complex and obvious factors may only tell part of the story. Several factors will usually be interacting at any one time: biology, habitat, evolutionary history, chance dispersal, disturbance frequency, predation, and harvesting are only some of the more obvious. Changes in the environment and interactions with other organisms combine with qualities inherent in the species or population to create rarity or vulnerability to extinction (Messick 1987). Concepts such as *threat, rarity,* and *endangerment* attempt to combine different facets that collectively are expected to provide a measure of the risks faced by a species or habitat.

CASE STUDY: FACTORS USED TO DETERMINE DEGREE OF RARITY FOR A GIVEN PLANT SPECIES

1. Age of taxon
   A. Old and senescent
   B. Young, incipient
   C. Intermediate age
2. Genotype of taxon
   A. Depauperate/depleted
   B. Genotype comparable to closely related common species
   C. Product of hybrid speciation
3. Evolutionary history
   A. Effects of past climatic changes or stasis
   B. Mode of origin of species
4. Taxonomic position
   A. Meaningful taxonomic level (Is rarity an artifact?)
   B. Systematic relationships (e.g., generic, specific, subspecific)
5. Ecology
   A. Habitat
   B. Effects of present climate
   C. Effects of edaphic conditions
   D. Effects of predators/pathogens—density changes
   E. Competitive ability
6. Population biology
   A. Life history information
   B. Status of populations (e.g., declining, stable, increasing)
   C. Factors influencing mortality and recruitment
7. Reproductive biology
   A. Average number/range flowers/fruits, seed-set
   B. Pollination biology
   C. Seed dispersal methods and/or agents, distance
   D. Seed germination and establishment
8. Land use history
   A. Habitat alteration (e.g., fire history—suppression; introduction of exotic herbivores and plants)
   B. Pollinators, or exotic plant competitors; effects of current land management policies)
9. Recent human uses
   A. Horticultural trade
   B. Aboriginal uses
   C. Role in ancient or modern medicine and/or industry

Source: Fiedler 1986.

Many simple scoring systems are geographic-based (area occupied and number of populations), but these parameters do not necessarily correlate with an element of diversity's expected persistence time. Rarity in terms of distribution and abundance also is not always an indication of impending extinction. Relatively widespread species may be in far greater risk of extirpation than some narrow endemics known only from single populations (Fuller 1987). Figure 3.2 shows the relationship between several of these parameters.

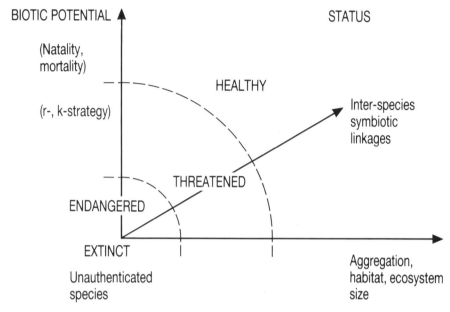

Figure 3.2. Relationship between categories of threat, geographic range and habitat, and population size. (Reproduced by permission from Furtado 1987)

Traditionally, many people have opted for simple categories such as threatened, at risk, and endangered, although there is little agreement on just what terms should be used and how many are appropriate. From 151 lists of threatened species, *Red Data Books,* and *Red Lists,* 57 categories were identified, these falling within eight general classes (Munton 1987). Perhaps one of the reasons for this confusion is that a comprehensive knowledge of the biology, evolutionary and recent history, and population structure and dynamics would be required before an extremely precise assessment of threat could be made. Such data are rarely available in full, so scientists and conservationists are forced to make estimates of threat on an intuitive basis (Reveal 1981; Fiedler 1986). This creates problems for those administering conservation laws, who want categories to be as unambiguous as possible (Bean 1987).

Ideally, threatened species that are candidates for conservation should be assessed very broadly for a range of factors (Whitson and Massey 1981). The greater the number of factors considered, the more effective the database is for management. As just noted, frequently, little is known about species at risk, and for many species, resources and time do not allow in-depth study before decisions about priority have to be made. Thus one arrives at the importance of monitoring, which can signal problems as they are about to arise. A simple type of early warning system presents a series of fields for which binary factors can be readily scored.

CASE STUDY: A METHOD FOR ASSIGNING CONSERVATION PRIORITIES TO THREATENED SPECIES

Field	Higher Priority	Lower Priority
Geographic	Small range	Wide range
	Endemic to region	Not endemic to region
Taxonomy[1]	High level taxon	Low level taxon
	Small genus/family	Large genus/family
	Probably relict	Not relict
Habitat	Under threat	Not under threat
	Fragile	Resistant
	Specificity narrow	Wide habitat range
	Successional	Climax
Life form	Annual or short-lived perennial	Long-lived perennial
Populations	Small	Large
	Few	Many
Biology[2]	Rarely flowering	Often flowering
	Specific pollinator	Nonspecific pollinator
	Dioecious	Monoecious
	Obligate outcrossing	Selfing readily
	Seed short lived	Seed long lived
	Poor class structure	Good class structure
	Poor vegetative reproduction	Good vegetative reproduction
Miscella-neous	Harvested	Not harvested
	Region of high endemism	Region of low endemism

[1] High level taxa = family, genus; low level taxa = subspecies, variety.

[2] Poor class structure = disproportionate representation of one age class; good class structure = spread of population through age classes.

Source: Given 1984.

In a simple early warning system it should be possible to rapidly assess the fields, in some instances from standard floras supplemented by field surveys (Given 1984). Such a system needs to recognize that three biological components of rarity are related to present occurrence: a within-habitat component, a between-habitat component, and a geographic component.

Traditionally, the last of these components has been the most emphasized, although research indicates that the others are very important as well. One of the reasons for this emphasis is the "sample" or "scale" problem. The majority of areas sampled tend to be small, but the smaller the sampling universe, the greater the number of so-called rare species. This occurs because some species will be absent simply by chance in small sample areas or because the species concerned are only present at a particular successional stage (Soulé 1986). Therefore, a geographical component of rarity is unavoidable.

Populations are dynamic: vulnerability, area of occurrence, and population size change through time. Time itself should be considered in assessments of rarity: both short-term and evolutionary causes of rarity may lead to similar effects, but for vastly different reasons. There is an urgent need to build a synthetic approach into the way rarity and threat is assessed and species are categorized (Fiedler 1986).

An advance on the single-term system is to separate and rate different aspects of rarity. A first step is to separate distribution (itself made up of geographic, habitat or ecosystem, and population size components) from threat. Widespread species can be under greater threat than narrow endemics. As an example, a plant known only from an inaccessible and remote canyon may be under less threat than a species known from numerous sites over some thousands of square kilometers, because the latter is at risk from epidemic disease. Further categorization can be made on the basis of present management (whether protected in a reserve), biological factors (such as poor reproductive potential), and ratings for various types of "value."

Multiple rating systems can be extended in various ways. The simplest is to score for a wide range of factors and to sum these to produce a single overall rating. This is the approach used for the *Red Data Book* of the British Isles and for the Threatened Plants Register of New Zealand. In both instances, emphasis is on geographic factors and human threats. Such a system can be a useful supplement to others, such as the IUCN system, as it has the potential to highlight some of the particular aspects of threat and risk to a species. Use of this approach in an expanded form might go some way toward providing a more meaningful assessment of rarity. The approach can be extended further by aggregating scores or profiles of individual threatened species at particular sites to arrive at an overall site rating. Protected area proposals can then be prioritized by ranking according to the sum of the conservation indices for all threatened species they contain (Given and Williams 1984). The summing approach has been criticized on several grounds, notably that to score various factors and add them is like taking chalk, cheese, and tree leaves and adding them together to provide an overall figure that is not mathematically meaningful. Weighting of scores is identified as a further problem. Geographic distribution and protection in a reserve both may be scored from 0 (i.e., widely distributed or well protected) to 3 (i.e., single site or not reserved). But who is to say that these should be equivalent in their scaling, or whether the scale for distribution should be from 0 to 50? What this means is that additive scores have an arbitrary element; the final score is an artifact and as such its use to generate a strictly linear list of conservation priorities is probably unwise.

One way out of this problem is to group factors that are being scored into four major sets, which can then be collectively analyzed:

1. Rarity. Includes factors such as geographic area, population size or density, endemism.
2. Vulnerability. Includes those factors that not only threaten (e.g., harvesting, habitat sensitivity), but also biological factors such as longevity, obligate pollinators, and reproductive success.
3. Benefits. Includes factors such as known and potential demand values, support value for other species, and spiritual or traditional values.
4. Costs. What other options are given up by saving a species (or population), including opportunity to use resources to conserve other plants?

Where many individual factors are unrelated, it is better to look at score profiles rather than cumulative scores. By using agglomerative sorting techniques (e.g., clustering analysis), species or sites that have a similar score profile are grouped together rather than arranged in a linear sequence from low to high. Clustering analysis can be used to generate a dendrogram expressing the taxonomy of the threat list (A. Hall, pers. com.) or to generate groups with similar management characteristics (Given and Norton 1993). Each species is regarded as being somewhere within a multidimensional space based on many parameters. To group species one must be able to predict which regions of that space are more desirable than others.

Portrayal of rarity in this manner helps one appreciate that extinction is not a simple linear progression from common to rare to very rare to extinct (Holt 1987). It also highlights the importance of time-frame. This little used approach deserves further development. Figure 3.3 illustrates the three basic ways of analyzing threat scores—a linear scale, clustering analysis, and multidimensional analysis.

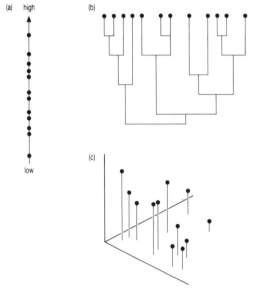

Figure 3.3. Three ways of analyzing data using threat scores: (a) linear scale; (b) clustering analysis in two dimensions; (c) three-dimensional analysis (e.g., principal components analysis).

Many of the currently accepted categories of threat, rarity, and endangerment tend to ignore species that are not quite at the level where they qualify for critical threatened lists. These include species that are quite widespread but whose habitat is potentially threatened, species that are still locally common but where peripheral or small populations are declining, and widespread species with generally low densities wherever they occur. Many such species may be future candidates for rare and threatened plant lists. Such plants are conveniently classed as "local" (a term used in New Zealand) or "sensitive," although the use of the latter term in the United States is a little different (Smith 1987).

It is naive to suggest that all threatened species, once identified, can be allocated maximum resources required to ensure their survival and well-being. In extreme instances, it may not even be possible to protect all species, and resources may have to be used for those plants with the best chance of long-term survival, or the survival of which will maximize the survival of other plants, animals, and ecosystems. Such

priorities, distasteful though they may be, are a necessity in some situations; in fact, setting priorities may become one of the most important issues in conservation management if biodiversity decreases to critical levels.

In many parts of the world, whole floras are in danger, yet not enough is known about the species to document each individually. Plant groups such as mosses, liverworts, and lichens are particularly poorly documented in many regions. Biodiversity is at such a high level in some regions that it is not possible to assess in a short time which particular species are under threat, which may become threatened, and which are secure. Some may have to be abandoned to be certain of saving others. Lack of specialist botanists and resources for conservation, combined with low density of target species in natural communities, highly scattered distribution, and inaccessibility of key sites, make the problems particularly acute in some parts of the tropics.

Setting aside large geographic areas to include a wide range of ecosystems for preservation will provide some short-term solutions, even though this may have to be done on the basis of unproven presuppositions about diversity and patterns of endemism. This will not cover all threatened species, however; some will slip through the safety net. Thus has arisen the concept of an *extinction-prone species:* a species whose individual threat status is unclear but which belongs to an endangered vegetation type.

Lists of extinction-prone species can be compared with plant inventories for protected areas to ascertain which species are protected already. Satellite imagery can be used for some regions to indicate the extent of critical habitat and the magnitude and patterns of threat. But for many critical regions, only estimates can be made for biodiversity. For instance, by 1982, 3426 species had been recorded for the endangered Chocó vegetation of northern Colombia, but it is predicted that there may be up to 9000 species, of which 25 percent are endemic. Identification of extinction-prone species demands interrogation of vegetation survey databases to find key sites and allow quantitative estimates of particular types of vegetation.

The concept of extinction-prone species is of most use in the moist tropics where there is high regional diversity, but it is also useful for threatened but little-studied vegetation types, such as halophytic communities of central Asia. It also may be very useful for azonal habitats such as wetlands, vernal ponds, and geothermal sites, which are often highly vulnerable because of small size and a tendency to be overlooked in regional habitat inventories.

Types of Databases

It is convenient to divide conservation databases into two groups—universal and specialist. Universal databases are those that are comprehensive in scope, often dealing with plants worldwide and relying either on massive storage and processing capacity or on a network of linked databases. Specialist databases are narrower in scope and may include only a very restricted range of data fields. There are pitfalls in both kinds of data sets. Universal databases are difficult to maintain because of the volume of data coming in from many different (often distant) sources. Specialist databases may be difficult to integrate with related databases when the need arises. The relative merits of universal and specialist databases continue to be debated, although they are complementary and both are needed.

Both global and specialist databases have their advantages and disadvantages. Smaller databases are likely to lack an overall perspective and output from them may be incompatible with other databases. There is no doubt, however, that they are easier to maintain and update, and can be run on less sophisticated equipment and with fewer trained personnel. Achieving the objectives of universal databases may require sophisticated data-processing skills, a large operating staff, and computing equipment capable of rapidly processing data. Nonetheless, the task of setting up even quite large databases is becoming easier through the increasing availability of "user friendly" software, greater availability and lower cost of microcomputers (PCs) with considerable computing power, and more efficient networking systems both locally and globally. Several years ago microcomputer systems were very limited in memory and speed. The advent of hard-disk technology and chip evolution has changed that, and there is every reason to believe that technology will rapidly change the picture in the next few years. A sophisticated system can now be maintained with relatively little training in computer technology, apart from routine typing skills and some knowledge of efficient data management.

Universal databases serve five basic functions (Synge and Heywood 1987):

1. Answering inquiries that require comparisons of regions or countries, or global analyses or comparisons.
2. Acting as clearinghouses for requests, passing them on to more specialist databases; requests can be preempted to some extent by books and papers outlining where data may be found.
3. Providing initial basic data for other conservation databases, to avoid needless repetition of information entry.
4. Filling gaps in the global coverage of regional, national, or more specialist databases; inevitably there will be some countries where national databases cannot be created or will not be effective.
5. Providing a test-bed for systems and standards under development for other databases.

Operators of universal databases should see them as public assets with a wide range of potential clients. Even where cost recovery is necessary because of administration policies, fees should not be so high as to discourage genuine users. This means keeping search costs to a minimum and providing just the information required; clients do not want to be hampered by a lot of redundant information they do not need. Thus it is useful to design a database on two levels. On the first level, a database should be designed to provide core information. For example, in a database of threatened species, provide the names of target species in a specified area, perhaps with a summary of threats, status, habitat, most recent record, and so forth. On the second level, a database should be designed to provide, as required, detailed records for individual sites and populations.

One characteristic of a well-designed database and supporting program is that it should readily answer frequently asked questions from clients. It should also be able to handle (not necessarily as fast) many other incidental questions. This facilitates creation of an intellectual meeting point and encourages others to become interested in plant conservation and contribute information.

The ability of universal databases to promote and assist specialist databases can be overlooked. Where there are a large number of smaller or more specialist systems, universal databases can provide information on what is held in the specialist ones, and can facilitate information interchange by formulating acceptable data transfer formats. As in work with individuals and local interest groups, good public relations are essential; managers of specialist databases must see that cooperation with universal systems is worthwhile.

The range of possible databases relevant to conservation is almost unlimited. Some common examples include the following:

- Regional databases on protected areas and their management, tenure, and main vegetation or floristic components.

- Taxonomic databases (for a particular plant group, e.g., orchids, ferns, legumes, palms; or for a growth form, e.g., trees).
- Herbarium collection and botanic garden databases indicating what is held in current collections.
- Ecological databases (e.g., plants of wetlands, deserts, or other ecosystem types).
- Economic databases (e.g., economic plants of a particular region, oil sources, wild relatives of agricultural crops).

In a specialist database there is generally less necessity to establish complex retrieval procedures, especially if the database is set up for a very particular type of output. Maintaining the integrity of records and updating is easier—the database manager is closer to the primary sources of records. Advances in computer technology and increasing availability of user-friendly programs mean that small- to medium-scale databases can be set up at quite moderate cost. These do not require access to large mainframe computers but can be designed around personal desk-top computer technology.

It is tempting, when setting up a specialist database, to include elements of data "in case they may be useful." Managers of such a database may want to make it more "significant" to attract funding. Increasing the scope of a specialist database without considerable forethought can be a fatal mistake. The system becomes choked with information that is rarely used, some of which can be obtained by other means. Hall (1974: 24) described the problem of too much data in an inaccessible form in relation to herbaria:

> Vast stores of data may be close at hand, but for want of efficient curating may be almost unusable. One must dig for long hours for data that may be widely important. From a DATA BANK, the museum has become a DATA CRYPT! The problem of access to literature has strengthened the defenses of this data crypt, in spite of valiant efforts to avert a crisis situation.

Regional or local databases profit from organizational links and close association. A series of data centers were set up in Latin America in the late 1980s and early 1990s at the initiation of The Nature Conservancy, Arlington, Virginia (USA). The design of these data centers is based on that used in "natural heritage programs" for individual states in the United States. The Latin American centers are now organized into an association, of which Conservation International forms the secretariat. The function of the secretariat is to organize, stimulate, and help fund the network of data centers and to extend the system throughout Latin America and the Caribbean (Synge and Heywood 1987).

It is easy to see ways in which specialist and universal databases depend on each other. Ideally, there should be a worldwide network of compatible specialist databases covering a wide range of types of information and geographic areas. When assessments of losses in biodiversity are needed, lists of relevant threatened species can be prepared from these databases for subsequent comparison with similar lists for neighboring countries or other taxonomic groups and vegetation types. International universal databases would assign global categories for each taxon and pass this back to the local database, so species threatened on a world scale can be given priority for national action. In reality, this is not likely to happen, at least not in the short term. Small and large databases are independently developed in many countries and institutions. Autonomous databases exist for economic plants, crops, forestry interests, legal matters, and land inventory. There is an urgent need for policymakers to recognize the efficiencies that would result from close interplay between these various types of data systems. They can and should depend on each other.

CASE STUDY: THREATENED PLANTS DATABASE OF THE WORLD CONSERVATION MONITORING CENTRE

The World Conservation Monitoring Centre (WCMC) provides a unique service on the status of threatened plants on a global scale. Data has been gathered on tropical timber species, plants of ethnobotanical or pharmaceutical value, and plants present in protected areas. Plant information comes from a variety of sources and in a variety of formats, including published and unpublished material, lists, and correspondence with several thousand contacts worldwide.

Computerized data on 80,000 taxa are currently managed on the plants database (BG-BASE) at WCMC and are extensively referenced. Increasingly datasets arrive in computerized form using agreed transfer formats. These data are then incorporated electronically.

Information from the plants database, together with information from other units at WCMC, is regularly provided to users, either on paper or electronically. WCMC's connection to Internet greatly facilitates data transfer in the future. The *WCMC Biodiversity Map Library* (a Geographic Information System running under *ArcInfo*) provides the capability to map plant distribution and extensive data on habitats, protected areas, and centers of species diversity.

A wide user community is served. The data are shared with contributers, and data and analyses are provided for a wide range of government and nongovernment users, the press, and the general public.

Source: World Conservation Monitoring Centre 1993.

As an independent, private, national land conservation organization emphasizing the protection of natural diversity, particularly within the United States, The Nature Conservancy needs well-organized, readily accessible scientific information on the plant and animal species and natural community (vegetation) types (called the elements of natural diversity) of North America north of Mexico.

Site-specific data on the actual occurrences on the landscape of populations or stands of these elements is generally developed state-by-state through state Natural Heritage Inventory Programs. Overall status summaries of each species are developed at The Nature Conservancy's national office in Arlington, Virginia, drawing upon the status data of the various state heritage programs (not including detailed locality data).

The Nature Conservancy's national databases are implemented as several distinct but interrelated files on an in-house minicomputer. Collected are data on plant and animal species and their global (rangewide), national, and state statuses; on priority sites for conservation; and on existing and desired protection. Conservation ownership and related topics are primarily used internally within The Nature Conservancy. A national file on pertinent bibliographic references and other sources of information is also developed.

The species files are organized hierarchically, with a single record for each species, subspecies, plant variety, or other taxonomic entity, and a state-tracking record for each state in which the entity occurs. These files currently contain species-level records for all vascular plants and vertebrate animals native or naturalized in North America north of Mexico. Associated files handle synonymy. Less complete data on nationally rare invertebrates and nonvascular plants are also included. State status information is currently most complete for the states in which an entity is rare or protected, but status data are also now being added for states in which the plant in question is abundant or secure. For certain species of high conservation interest—primarily national rarities and aggressive invasive exotics—more detailed documentation in loosely organized text form is also maintained.

Sources: The Nature Conservancy, unpublished; L. Morse, pers. com.

Collecting and Describing Data

In the early stages of developing a plant conservation database, it is important to collect data from primary sources, for instance, from the actual sites where plants grow. Increasingly, agencies with legal responsibilities are requiring field documentation—a policy that may be time-consuming, but which is quite proper (Nelson 1986). Only by checking what is actually happening where plants grow or are used can there be reasonable certainty about the presence, health, and persistence of individuals, populations, and vegetation types.

The simplest type of data is information on the location of target species and number of plants at each location; this is usually supplemented with a general description of habitat, threats, and management needs. Even at this level, information should be site-specific and field-checked. Where possible, surveys should gather specific data on the ecology, predation, mortality, and reproduction of the population. For critically threatened species in very small populations, the spatial relationships of plants can be mapped and representative plants numbered and marked. General notes should be taken on the condition, size classes, and reproduction of individual plants, and on physical and biological characteristics of the site. Photographs of the whole site, the habitat, and selected individuals should be standard procedure. Taken together, these steps yield insight into the ecology and population dynamics of a species (Schwegman 1986).

Data elements

Descriptors are required regardless of the size and purpose of a database. The most essential descriptor is a consistent naming unit, usually a species, area name, or vegetation type. This name is usually cross-referenced to a geographic or administrative unit. Within a particular database, similar elements of data will be required and the actual number of descriptors usually need not be large. Some of the useful types of descriptors to consider are (Ray 1984; Synge and Heywood 1987) the name of a plant taxon (species, subspecies, etc.); the eco-geography, or precise distribution and community type where the plant occurs; physical factors (i.e., data of ecological importance that determine the distribution of species); biotic factors (e.g., distributions of vegetation types and habitat, productivity, reproduction, mortality, etc.); economic and social factors (i.e., the human activities that affect species and environments); legal and administrative factors (e.g., agencies responsible for regulation, management, and legislation); and conservation status and trends with recommendations for action.

The IUCN's Plant Existence Categorization Scheme (PECS) is designed to provide an internationally agreed upon set of descriptors to record the status of a plant, whether native or introduced. It provides a way of categorizing the relationship between individual plants and individual areas.

CASE STUDY: THE IUCN PLANT EXISTENCE
CATEGORIZATION SCHEME (PECS)

1. Occurrence
   A. Certain (C)
   B. Doubtful (?)
   C. Predicted (R)
   D. Recorded in error (E)
   E. No information (-)
2. Endemism
   A. Endemic (E)
   B. Doubtfully endemic (D)
   C. Not endemic (N)
   D. No information (-)
3. Origin
   A. Native (N)
      (1) Restocked (S)
      (2) Reestablished (E)
      (3) Bulked (B)
      (4) Not as above
      (5) No information (-)
   B. Introduced (I)
      (1) Naturalized (N)
         (a) Invasive (V)
         (b) Noninvasive (I)
         (c) No information (-)
      (2) Casual (C)
      (3) No information (-)

Source: Synge and Heywood 1987.

Point locality information is essential for population-specific management. Data should ensure that a particular plant population can be relocated where it occurs. Point locality information, especially when transferred to maps, can seem expensive, but in the long run it can be more expensive to try to relocate a critically endangered plant in a poorly defined locality. Detailed mapping clearly is justified for highly threatened species, for genetically important populations, and for plants of economic importance. Occur-

rences of invasive exotics or the distribution of predators may also merit detailed site-specific mapping, particularly when these are in or near established natural areas. This is where use of computerized GIS technology can pay dividends (e.g., Myatt 1987).

Habitats and ecosystems are important descriptors, but there is often a lack of consensus on the best way to describe vegetation. Generally, much local terminology is used, and experts disagree on the use of floristic versus physical parameters as the basis of habitat classification. Nevertheless, consistent classification of vegetation and landscape units, at least within a particular database, is vital.

The purpose of a conservation database should be to assess change over time as well as to give an up-to-date view at any time. Threats to species can be divided into many different kinds: some are natural and others are human-caused, some affect individual plants and others affect whole communities. Threats can be classified according to severity, or degree, and imminence (whether immediate or just a possibility in the future). Each aspect of threat has a differing impact on persistence time. Threat, like so many other parameters of a conservation database, is difficult to quantify. Degree of threat, particularly, is a subjective concept simply because until a threat has been in operation for some time, we are unlikely to know precisely how it will affect a target plant.

Of the more specialized databases for plant diversity, those dealing with living plant materials, especially botanic garden holdings and genetic resources, are probably the most commonly encountered. These require additional descriptors, which should include the following:

- Accession data (institution plus internal reference number, and reference to those of donors).
- Identification and verification qualifiers (certainty of identity of the plant).
- Sex of the plant material.
- Source (e.g., donor, provenance).
- Sampling data, including the form in which propagating material or propagules were obtained and sampling techniques used.
- Propagation history (e.g., whether propagated vegetatively or from seed) and regeneration history.
- Methods of storage (whether as seed, tubers, tissue, DNA, whole plants).
- Distribution of plants or propagules and subsequent use of this material, including records of breeding trials, incorporation of genetic cultures into breeding lines, and so forth.

Efficient databases are critical to the smooth running of international and national networks, such as the currently forming international one for botanic gardens, the regional networks coordinated by the Center for Plant Conservation in the United States, and the system of national plant collections in the United Kingdom. Germ plasm collections are recorded in databases through user networks involving the International Board for Plant Genetic Resources (IBPGR) and the United Nations Food and Agriculture Organization (FAO). Sometimes network databases need be no more than "indexes to other databases," rather than monolithic storage houses of information.

Coordinating data input

Selection of the building blocks is not the end of the matter. It is still necessary to construct the database by relating the various elements with each other. It is vital that data structures match the real world. It costs far more to correct a mistake in database design after the database has been constructed than before it is completed. For example, it is critical to have a naming system for plants that is consistent, and for which a compromise between simple and complex nomenclature has been achieved. It is also vital to consider the sorts of questions the database will be expected to answer and to ensure that it is capable of doing this. For instance, there is little point defining records in terms of administrative areas only if the majority of requests require point locality or vegetational data.

In the case of the Threatened Plants Unit of IUCN, the database was built around the relationships between the following sets of entities (Synge and Heywood 1987): plant taxa (species, genus, etc.), areas where taxa occur, plant communities, botanical institutions, and books and papers.

A typical organizational structure of a plant conservation database is given in Figure 3.4. Such a structure is necessary to systematize data from a variety of sources that will be used for several purposes.

Bibliographic files are important and serve three major functions. First, they store references generally relevant to plant conservation, perhaps to be published eventually as a bibliography. Second, they store references that function as additional data sources. Third, they validate information on the database. At the initial stages, literature records can be handled by screening library accessions and bibliographies and then recording references on index cards. Bibliographies expand rapidly, however, and once several thousand references are included, it is logical to put the system on computer and to access electronically based bibliographic data systems. As an example, between 1974 and 1979, incoming books at the library of the

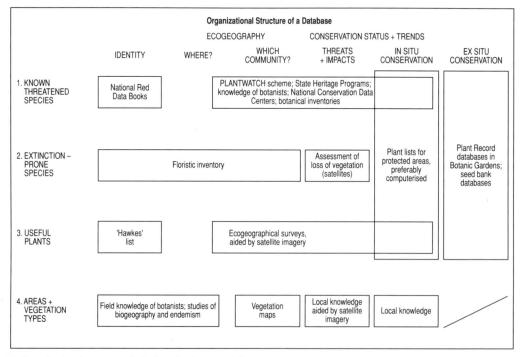

Figure 3.4. Organizational structure of a database for threatened plants. Rows refer to groups of plants of similar conservation status or need; columns refer to classes of information required. (Reproduced by permission from Synge and Heywood 1987)

Royal Botanic Gardens, Kew, were screened for conservation references. From 1979 to 1985, references were added in the course of preparing the *Kew Record*, an annual taxonomic bibliography. Citations were stored in a computer data file. During 1986, a volunteer worker increased the file from 3000 to 8000 references, utilizing additional resources such as commercial databases and recently published bibliographies. By April 1987, the data file had about 10,000 references (Synge and Heywood 1987). Sometimes, extensive cross-referencing must be developed, using such categories as general subject, plant family, plant name, protected area, and area of occurrence.

Data sources do not have to be limited to published references but can include letters, questionnaires, and unpublished reports. As with other types of databases, it is vital to decide the scope of a bibliographic system and to relate it to clients' needs. How far, for example, can other bibliographic databases supply needs? Would an abstracting service be worth the very large investment required? Are there clients who would pay for the service? These questions must be answered before expensive database development is undertaken (Synge and Heywood 1987).

Case Study: Criteria for References in the Joint IUCN–Kew Plant Conservation Bibliography

Rare and threatened plants and their conservation. Include papers that outline the status of a species that is threatened nationally or locally, but which may be common on a world scale.

Erosion of genetic resources. Conservation of genetic resources, in situ or ex situ, especially accounts of the conservation of individual crops.

Conservation of other plants. Includes widespread species and threats to plants.

Threats to plant life. Include papers on introduced species describing threats and their effects on native plant species and vegetation.

Extent and loss of habitats and vegetation. Emphasis should be on including general and substantial papers, but omit papers of local scope.

Techniques for plant conservation.

Protected Areas. Especially plant lists for them and accounts of their vegetation; but not urban parks, or research results in protected areas, unless directly relevant to conservation. Papers on plant sites under threat or proposed for protection are included if they cover these aspects.

Substantial papers on conservation organizations.

Role and work of botanical institutions. Especially botanic gardens doing plant conservation work (but not lists of, or papers on their plant holdings).

Ex situ plant collections held for conservation purposes.

Conservation thinking and policy. Especially background papers on conservation in a country or region; reviews of the legal basis for conservation (but not citations of the laws themselves).

Bibliographies on the above topics. If the title does not specify the relevance to one or more of the above topics, this should be explained in the notes.

Source: Synge and Heywood 1987.

The collaboration of scientific and management agencies is essential in designing and setting up databases. Universities, natural history museums, management authorities, and botanical gardens all have a role to play. Actively growing herbaria and research organizations may have more up-to-date information than government agencies. Given the large number of universities in the tropics, particularly in Latin America, their role in documenting tropical plants must not be underestimated (Roche and Dourojeanni 1984). Especially for genetic resources, there are many public and private international agencies that are both useful data sources and potential clients. These include FAO, UNEP, UNESCO (especially through its Man and the Biosphere Program [MAB]), IBPGR, and IUCN (especially through its commissions). At the regional level, agencies such as the Organization of American States (OAS) and the Tropical Agronomic Center for Research and Instruction (CATIE) in Costa Rica have a vital part to play in assembling and using data for plant conservation (Roche and Dourojeanni 1984).

It is easy to be carried away with enthusiasm about professional organizations and to forget that amateur naturalists, special interest societies, and ad hoc groups of people in a particular district often have the intimate knowledge that larger national organizations lack. These groups need to feel that they are contributing usefully to conservation. Some of the best supporters of databases are farmers, hikers, and retirees who are interested in just a few square kilometers around their homes. Local natural history groups can be encouraged to record and document the plants of their area and to provide information on ecology and distribution, threats to persistence, and strategies to preserve threatened plants. Good public relations are essential. People must know that their observations are not just disappearing into a "black box," never to be seen again; they deserve regular information on the database and visible appreciation of their role.

Joining the various components of a database into a series of workable relationships does not mean that all parts of a database have to be implemented initially. Some parts may not be fully designed or implemented until several years have elapsed. It is advantageous to be flexible about altering the database so that additional fields can be added and existing ones merged without loss of data or overall structure. Most databases, especially large ones, will have to be altered at some point. Even as people start to retrieve information, unanticipated inquiries sometimes suggest new types of data or new ways of using information. Most databases incorporate ideas from existing ones, yet each—regardless of scope and degree of specialization—will have its own peculiarities and requirements.

CASE STUDY: DEVELOPMENT OF NATIONAL AND
INTERNATIONAL DATA COLLECTIONS ON
TROPICAL WOODY RESOURCES

Stage 1: Collection of basic information
1. Preparation of national lists of woody genetic resources.
2. Compilation of information on the distribution of each species on the list.
3. Compilation of information on the exploitation or present use of each species on the list.
Stage 2: Allotment of priorities
1. Representation of each listed species within each country's protected areas.
2. Grading of the listed species in terms of present or potential social and economic importance.
3. Indication as to whether each listed species is endangered or not.
Stage 3: Detailed information on prime target species
1. Progressive compilation of information on intraspecific variation of the most important species.
2. Progressive compilation of biological information, especially plant phenology, of every listed species.
Stage 4: Monitoring

A national list of woody species with value as genetic resource species (Stage 1) could be based on lists of flora and fauna species being exploited and traded; lists of native woody species being planted; lists of species of ethnobotanical interest; lists of wild plant relatives of cultivated crops; and review of information from forest inventories.

Additional information could be gleaned from lists of native plant species that exist in herbaria and botanical gardens, and a literature review on national and international taxonomy of the country's flora.

Source: Roche and Dourojeanni 1984.

Transfer formats

Transfer of information from one place to another has always been hampered by lack of agreement on how information is to be processed and stored. In conservation work, there is a growing need to transfer data from one locality to another and to compare data from a variety of sources to obtain regional and global perspectives on issues such as trade in rare species, depletion rates, and effectiveness of conservation strategies. Few databases have been set up for exactly the same purpose, and each uses different information sources, elements of data, and storage and retrieval systems.

A *transfer format* is a set of standards for exchanging (generally computerized) data on a given topic (Botanic Gardens Conservation Secretariat 1987). It consists of a set of definitions for the fields within each record. The format does not necessarily define the limits of information or fields, both of which may go far beyond what is needed for a transfer format. Rather, the standards define what is minimally acceptable and specify a core format that will facilitate transfer of information from one database to another. The use of the transfer format does not limit use of a computer because its definition is independent of the storage method and machinery. It simply declares how the data elements are stored on the medium used for the data transfer. Obviously, the organizations exchanging data need to agree on the physical medium and on the recording format whereby the file is written on the medium. The overriding consideration is to produce a format that will not unduly confine the local user but will facilitate transfer of information while being as clear, simple, and unambiguous as possible.

Transfer formats can help during the planning of new, especially smaller databases and record systems. The format definitions of fields include useful data for the systems analyst and computer programmer. They outline the structure of each field, showing how long it should be and what logical tests can be applied to it to ensure accuracy of the data. For example, the International Transfer Format (ITF) for botanic gardens has a module on plant names (Fields 6–15) incorporating taxonomic and nomenclatural facets designed by leading specialists; as a result the module is the minimum needed to cover virtually all types of wild and cultivated plant names. Those not wanting to write complex computer programs for their own databases, or lacking access to computer software, can simply use such a transfer format as the internal record structure for a single flat file on their computer.

Additional fields can be added on the end and removed when one is writing files for transfer. In more complex solutions, commonly repeating items like generic names can be held in look-up files, with their associated families, using invisible numeric codes in the main accession file. In this case conversion of data to and from the transfer format is a little more complex.

International transfer formats are important globally for linking previously unrelated databases. As an example, many managers of protected areas are anxious to develop their inventories into databases that can contribute to management of resources in their area, and that can answer requests for information from outside. To encourage consistency, the UNESCO Man and the Biosphere (MAB) program has developed a project that will permit electronic comparisons to be made easily between conservation databases (listing, for example, the names of species prone to extinction) and protected area databases (Synge and Heywood 1987). It will also allow comparisons between protected areas in different states and continents, and development of management packages that can be applied to many different reserves and national parks.

Remote sensing and geographic information systems

Remote sensing has been used since the simplest devices allowed people to gather data from a distance (Oldman 1985). Remote sensing was transformed through the development of aerial photography. Space research over the last three decades has seen a further technological revolution in the use of images from satellite surveys. Remote sensing of activities taking place over a few square meters from many thousands of kilometers away is a fact of life.

A region may first be sensed remotely through the "eye" of a camera, perhaps mounted on a satellite. Such remote images show the region with its mountains, valleys, rivers, and forests. Extent and speed of events such as deforestation can be monitored by regular observation. But these images are not self-explanatory: they yield blind maps, which must be interpreted. Remote sensing at this level needs to be combined with ground checks by more conventional surveys. It is part of a continuum from on-the-ground surveys to aerial photographs to satellite imagery. With very precise satellite images or aerial photographs, more detailed information becomes available. Different vegetation types, plant heights, patterns of disturbance, and various forms of land use can be detected. Further remote sensing over a period of time can show and interpret changing gaps, mosaics, and patches of different ages, and different growth patterns.

One of the most obvious uses for remote sensing is the rapid documentation of major environmental trends over large areas, such as changes in the extent of the world's forests and deserts. The Global Resources Information Database (GRID) is designed to provide such information as part of the Global Environment Monitoring System (GEMS) (Gwynne 1985). GRID is a geographical data management system on a global scale. It uses data gathered in all the other GEMS databases and combines them with conventional base maps and remotely sensed images from satellite survey programs, aerial surveys, and (where possible) corroborative ground data. The existing GEMS database offers very comprehensive coverage of environmental factors. The whole system, utilizing various forms of remote sensing and a range of databases, can, for instance, help protected area managers take biological, geologic, demographic, and development factors into account in planning.

There is potential for remote sensing to be used in many types of data gathering and interpretation. This includes locating of rare habitats or mapping of the extent of critical habitat on large areas not amenable to conventional survey. Remote sensing does have limitations. It works best, for instance, in areas of low relief and, thus, is ideally suited for use in plateau and lowland regions of the tropics; it is less appropriate in rugged, mountainous regions. For satellite technology, on-the-ground receiving stations are necessary and, up until now, these have been chiefly in developed countries, although many of the needs for remote sensing are in developing regions. Satellite data gathering also requires access to interpretive expertise so that costs of using it can rapidly mount even with a relatively simple program for a restricted geographic area.

Satellite technology, perhaps surprisingly, can contribute to conservation documentation through the accurate fixing of positions on the earth's surface. Working out precise location can be a great problem in some areas such as dense tropical forest, regions with few obvious topographical features, or countries poorly served by accurate maps. The equipment needed for such position fixing is not yet fully portable, but the required miniaturization should be available in the very near future. Automatic recording of point location on a portable computerized data-logger could eliminate errors that occur routinely in vegetation surveys, critical population surveys, and transcription of location information from field notes.

A recent innovation made possible by computers is the development of geographic information system (GIS) technology in which data on many different factors such as climate, vegetation, land-ownership, and so forth are combined to provide a summary for a particular site or information for a particular species or other defined item in the GIS database (e.g., Myatt 1987; Beardsley and Stoms 1993). A GIS database of management area boundaries and protection-level categories is far more useful than a simple tabular database, a dot map of managed areas with attribute information linked to the points, or a traditional paper map (Beardsley and Stoms 1993). A GIS system visually and statistically summarizes land and biodiversity characteristics, permits sensitive analysis of management effectiveness, and identifies gaps in protected area and habitat systems (gap analysis). Such a system stores data from these fields and links them together by one or more common denominators (Curran 1985). The usual linking items are geographic location (generally defined according to a standard map grid system or latitude and longitude) and altitude. Thus, each item of information can be expressed in terms of an infinite number of points in three-dimensional space. The principles of a GIS are described in Figure 3.5.

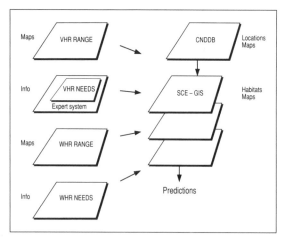

Figure 3.5. The principles of a GIS with linked databases, as applied to habitat predictions in southern California; CNDDB = California Natural Diversity Data Base; SCE–GIS = Southern California Edison Geographic Information System; VHR = Vegetation Habitat Relationship Database; WHR = Wildlife Habitat Relationship Database. (Reproduced by permission from Myatt 1987)

Each of the different types of information can be visualized as a shell or layer of information. A simple type of GIS uses transparent overlays for an equivalent geographic region, each overlay showing a different parameter such as rainfall, geology, soil type, popula-

tion density, or vegetation type. The physical limitations of such a system only allow incorporation of a very small number of parameters. In contrast, sophisticated computer-based GIS systems are capable of incorporating many tens or even hundreds of shells, and results are plotted as three-dimensional models.

GIS technology obviously demands considerable coordination and cooperation. It also requires the staff and commitment to constantly up-date information. It is not necessary to start with an enormous database; one can start only with topography, geographic features, generalized vegetation, distribution of rare species, and landownership, adding, as each become available, such parameters as soil types, climate, and protected areas. As a greater number of information sets are involved, and retrieval and analysis become more powerful, greatly sophisticated analyses are possible. GIS systems offer, perhaps for the first time, the possibility of integrated management, hazard prediction, and scenario modeling over entire regions.

CASE STUDY: USE OF SATELLITE IMAGERY TO MONITOR THE VEGETATION OF TUNISIAN GRAZING LANDS

Rangeland monitoring using satellite imagery has been employed to map and monitor large areas, especially since the formation of the Global Inventory Monitoring and Modeling Studies (GIMMS) group in 1982. Over the first few years of the project, research included land-coverage mapping and monitoring of the phenology of global vegetation.

The Tunisian project used red and near infrared channels of the advanced very high resolution radiometer (AVHRR) of satellite NOAA-9. This was supplemented by ecological information obtained by conventional ground survey techniques. Fifteen, five-channel scenes of AVHRR coverage were obtained. One of these was selected on the basis of near-nadir viewing and low percentage cloud cover for each month of 1985 plus March 1986. Particular images were selected to correspond to those periods when ground surveys were undertaken.

Atmospherically corrected normalized difference vegetation index (NDVI) data were used because they exemplify the differential reflectance properties of green vegetation in the visible red and near infrared spectral regions. These can be correlated with green leaf biomass, percentage vegetation cover, and absorbed photosynthetically active radiation. High values show dense green vegetation, and low values show senescence or absence of plants.

The north-south aridity line shows well in the results. Interesting anomalies show up as well, probably reflecting favorable local conditions resulting from fluctuations in groundwater during the growing season, or large areas of exposed soil with seasonally high water content or a veneer of reflective salt crystals. A strong correlation was shown between NDVI and percentage vegetation cover. Generally, strong correlations were found between NDVI and dry aboveground green biomass as well as percentage vegetation cover. Close correspondence was found between monthly rainfall and NDVI. The time lag between a fall in NVDI (declining green biomass) and decreasing rainfall was found to be greater than for increasing NVDI (vegetation growth responding to increases in rainfall).

Generally, the project showed that AVHRR–NDVI data can be used for monitoring the dynamics of vegetation at both regional and local scales. Monthly fluctuations in NDVI for four selected sites showed that seasonal changes can be followed and interpreted in conjunction with ground survey checks. Such data has considerable potential for estimating length of growing seasons.

Source: Kennedy 1989.

Documentation of plants directly useful to people

Usefulness is a somewhat subjective term; it is not always easy to decide what is a significantly useful plant, as all plants have or can acquire a use of some sort. Any tree species growing in arid-zone Africa may be used for fuelwood, but that does not mean that every species should be given high priority for conservation. Other plants may assume usefulness only when preferred species are absent; they may even be very poor substitutes. There is a big difference between a regular food plant and one that is edible simply because it is not poisonous! Serendipity creates another problem: the total range of uses that may arise in the future.

It is helpful to give conservation priority to plants that are regularly used by humans (whether cultivated outside botanic gardens and genetic collections, or systematically gathered from the wild) or plants that are relatives of species included under the above criterion. A range of categories emerge when plants useful to people are classified (Hawkes 1987a):

- Major food and fruit tree crops and their close wild relatives.
- Minor food and tree crops and their close wild relatives.
- Forage plants for animal feed, silage, and so forth.
- Agricultural and ruderal weeds and wild plants gathered for food.
- Trees, bushes, and other plants used for firewood, housing, boat-building, bridges, and so forth.
- Medicinal and drug plants, stimulants, spices, aro-

matics, flavorings, food colorings, and so on.
- Plants used for chemical and/or industrial purposes (e.g., oils, fats, resins, rubber, insecticides, vermicides, fish poisons).
- Fiber plants used for textiles, ropes, twine, and nets.
- Plants used for basketry, furnishing, food containers, and so forth (e.g., bamboo, rattan, gourds).
- Plants used for textile dyestuffs and body ornamentation.
- Plants used as ornamentals for home and sport.
- Plants used for ritual and magic.

There are inherent problems to assessing the value of wild or weedy species related to plants of known economic value. Most will accrue a very low rating on their own, their value being related to their affinity with harvested species. One must know how closely related a species is to a harvested one. Some are close enough to exchange genes easily; for others, gene transfer is not possible or requires radical techniques. For still other plants, degree of genetic closeness simply is not known. One solution is to give these related wild species percentage scores related to their assumed closeness to cultigens (cultivated relatives) (Hawkes 1987a):

- Primary gene pool (the same biological species)—80 percent.
- Secondary gene pool (gene transfer difficult but possible)—60 percent.
- Tertiary gene pool (gene transfer at present very difficult) or genetic relationship unknown—40 percent.

Data about germ plasm accessions are nearly as valuable as the plant material itself. Inadequate evaluation is a serious problem and lessens the value of many otherwise useful samples of seed and other plant material. An important concept is that of passport data. These include field notes on the sample, perhaps only as simple as the local name of the sample (which might be what a farmer calls it), date of collection, and a brief site description. Other useful information includes obvious morphological characteristics, abundance or population size, and associated crops and wild plants (Plucknett et al. 1987). Once the material is received by a collection center, further notes can be made on the plant material and a detailed description drawn up using standardized descriptors designed for the particular plant group or crop type. The descriptors allow rapid data entry and ease of comparison with other samples.

Full evaluation of samples in germ plasm banks often lags behind the rate of collection of new samples. This is primarily the result of lack of trained staff, and to breeders being busy developing new varieties. It was estimated in the mid-1980s, for example, that less than half the maize collection maintained by Centro Internacional de Mejoramiento de Maiz y Trigo (CIMMYT) in Mexico had been evaluated (Plucknett et al. 1987).

The IBPGR plays a major role in documentation of "useful plants" by developing standardized descriptors on a crop-by-crop basis, by printing gene bank catalogues and directories of germ plasm collections, and by assisting with the computerization of gene bank holdings. Repositories of plant material are being encouraged to use standard *passport data* to systematize holdings, and to sort out redundant samples and "junk"—data with inadequate documentation and of very limited use for this aspect of conservation.

CASE STUDY: RANKING PLANTS OF ECONOMIC VALUE

Plants are used to different extents by different tribes, communities, and nations, and the uses to which they are put vary greatly. Therefore, it seems logical to use several different criteria to measure a plant's importance. Six distinct scoring criteria are suggested:

Utilization based on area. Eventually, it may be possible to consider this criterion completely objectively, based on the exact area where the species is cultivated or gathered.

Utilization based on time. A crop species eaten every day but harvested only once a year would attract a very high score. A tree species cut down and used to construct a house or bridge, on the other hand, would be given a low score since it would not actually be consumed every day and might be replaced no more than every 5 to 10 years, or even longer.

Importance to community and tribe. This criterion attempts to assess how those people who actually use the plant species regard it in terms of its importance to their lives, customs, religious beliefs, and so forth.

Use in commerce and barter. This criterion is fairly self-explanatory. The final score may need to be an average value if, for instance, a plant species in one area is never sold or exchanged, while in another it is sold or exchanged quite frequently.

Actual or potential use for development as a world commodity. For a crop or plant product that is already developed on a world scale, or even partly so in certain areas, a score near 100 would be appropriate. Score may vary according to the knowledge of the scorer and also if further information is forthcoming or if the potential for development is found to be increasing or decreasing.

Range of uses. Certain plants possess a range of uses, while others possess only one or a few.

Using these six scoring criteria, the following priority list for economic plants is suggested (revised scoring, 2 June 1987):

Extent of utilization based on area

A. Pantemperate, pantropical; generally common — 100
B. Same as (A) but moderately common in most countries — 75
C. The same, but rare in most countries — 50
D. Restricted to one country or region but common — 30
E. As (D) but localized — 20
F. As (D) but very restricted — 10

Extent of utilization, based on time gathered or harvested

A. All the time; article of daily use — 100
B. From time to time throughout the year — 75
C. Seasonally gathered/harvested — 50
D. Occasionally gathered/harvested — 30
E. Rarely gathered/harvested — 20
F. Hardly ever gathered/harvested — 10
G. Never gathered/harvested — 0

Importance to community and tribe

A. Important for tribe or national community — 100
B. Fairly important (some do without it) — 50
C. Low level of importance (could get on well without it) — 25
D. Very low importance (also if use is dying out) — 10

Use in commerce and barter

A. Widely sold internationally — 100
B. Sold to some extent internationally — 80
C. Widely sold nationally; rarely internationally — 60
D. Sold or exchanged in certain areas — 40
E. Occasionally sold or exchanged — 20
F. Never sold or exchanged — 0

Actual or potential use for development as a world commodity

A. Already developed — 100
B. Of great potential value and undergoing development — 80
C. Of apparent great potential but no development yet — 60
D. Possible potential value — 30
E. Little potential — 10
F. Potential zero or unknown — 0

Range of uses

A. Multiple (10 or more) — 100
B. Many (5–9) — 75
C. Few (2–4) — 50
D. One (1) — 30

Source: Hawkes 1987a, adapted.

Whereas the known uses of a plant can be assessed objectively, its use in the future is a matter for speculation. Some plants jump from relative obscurity to prominence, as did jojoba (*Simmondsia chinensis*). Potentially useful plants fall into two clear categories: relatives of useful plants, and useful plants that have the potential to be more useful in the future (including underexploited plants). Some plants have experienced spectacular rises as crops. Soybean, for example, has risen from being a very minor localized crop to one of the main exports of the United States, in 20 years or so. Others, such as winged bean (*Psophocarpus*), are minor crops at the moment but they are increasingly more widely grown. Some plants, like sorghum, are slowly declining in importance.

What is needed are concepts similar to the way economists discount future values. There are already ways of assessing utility, so for a potentially useful plant, we can work out its ranking today and its most likely rating in, say, ten years. The final ranking we give to the plant logically should be the rank for its present use plus a discounted value of its likely rise in ranking in future. The percentage by which we discount the likely rise should depend on both the time delay for this rise to happen and the likelihood of its occurrence. Because these assessments are subjective, and because the rises will be heavily discounted, say by as much as 10 times, it is probably best not to try to develop a complicated mathematical model to calculate the discount rate and then apply it, but rather to use a table such as the one in Table 3.1.

Table 3.1. A mathematical model for discounting future usefulness of plants.

Plant's potential rise in ranking	100–200	200–300	300–400
High—likely in 10 years or less	70	80	100
Medium—likely in 20 years or so	60	70	80
Low—likely to be as much as 50 years	30	60	70

Documentation of areas of high diversity

Which areas around the world are highest priority for plant conservation? How are they brought to the attention of governments, aid agencies, and conservation organizations? Detailed information on individual species may be lacking but botanists often have a feeling for those areas that are rich in diversity—the so-called hot spots of diversity. Several international projects are currently underway to identify concentrations of biodiversity, for instance, the Centers of Plant Diversity Project (IUCN Plant Conservation Office 1990), and the WCMC tropical forest atlas. The concept of high diversity areas includes two types of *site units*, each having rather different emphases. The first type of site unit includes geographically defined units that are botanically rich areas and often the location of narrow endemics or relicts, for example, Mt. Mulanje (Malawi), Mt. Nimba (Liberia), or Kinabalu Park (Borneo). The second type of site unit includes vegetation types that are exceptionally rich in diversity or endemism, but which are under extreme threat. In this second type of site unit it is often only practical or possible to conserve part of the target area (e.g., the lowland rain forests of Cameroon, the Atlantic forests of Brazil, shrublands of southwest Australia, and the limestone flora of Peninsular Malaysia).

Quantity and quality of information varies markedly. Detailed knowledge may be nonexistent, yet preliminary studies may indicate that an area is of outstanding importance. Analysis of presumed extinctions is likely to indicate regions with high levels of both local endemism and threat (Figure 3.1), In some cases, botanically rich areas are remote and therefore inadequately explored (e.g., the Sierra de Periga in Venezuela). Collections and data may be highly selective in coverage of plant groups.

For small areas such as oceanic islands, information may be quite sketchy. The island of Rapa in the southeastern Pacific Ocean has a remarkable flora with a high level of endemism, but data on conservation status of the endemic flora are scanty (Synge and Heywood 1987). Fieldwork to determine major uses of local plants, and the ecology, biogeography, and floristics of key areas should be undertaken. If this can be supplemented by floristic studies of the key sites, so much the better.

Although species richness is the primary criterion defining a hot-spot, other characteristics should also be considered, especially for more detailed site selection at a local level, such as within a vegetation type. Included in these criteria are the following four questions (Synge and Heywood 1987):

1. Is the site threatened or under imminent threat of large-scale devastation?

2. Does the site include a diverse range of habitat types?

3. Does the site contain a significant proportion of species adapted to special edaphic conditions (e.g., obligate limestone and ultramafic plants)?

4. Does the site contain an important gene pool of plants of value to people, or plants that are potentially useful?

The more plant species in a community, the greater the spatial heterogeneity, both for other plants and for dependent animals, because new habitats are created. This has led to the concepts of alpha-diversity and beta-diversity. The former is diversity within habitats, and the latter is diversity between habitats or the number of habitats within a particular community.

Case Study: The Centers of Plant Diversity Concept to Document Areas and Vegetation Types of High Diversity

A new approach to the problem of conserving the maximum amount of plant diversity is to prepare a directory of some of the world's most important plant sites and vegetation types. Approximately 250 sites and regions have been selected worldwide for consideration. A *site* can be a botanically rich area that can be defined geographically (e.g., Mt. Kinabalu in Borneo); a geographically defined region with high species diversity or endemism (e.g., the Atlas Mountains in Africa, or the Cordilleras Baeticas in Spain); or a vegetation type of exceptionally high diversity (e.g., the Amazon rain forests and Atlantic forests of Brazil).

The main objectives of this approach are (1) to identify which areas around the world, if conserved, would safeguard the greatest number of plant species; (2) to document the many benefits, economic and scientific, that conservation of those areas would bring, and to outline the potential value of each for sustainable development; and (3) to develop a strategy for the effective conservation of centers of plant diversity worldwide.

For some parts of the world, site selection is easy, especially when there is only one major remaining area of natural habitat in the region. In many areas it is not possible to pinpoint specific sites. In these instances regional accounts are planned. These emphasize the need for a representative coverage of the region. In some instances areas are still poorly known botanically, while in others designation of protected status is no guarantee of safety from threats.

Standardized data sheets have been prepared for some regions and sites. For each site, information is arranged under the following headings: geography; vegetation; flora; useful plants; and other values, threats, and conservation. In addition, information on the site, including statistics on the flora, is summarized at the beginning of each account.

Source: IUCN Plant Conservation Office 1990.

Data Processing

People sometimes assume that in some mysterious way electronic data processing methods are necessarily superior in every respect to manual methods of assembling, sorting, and maintaining information. It is easy to forget that large quantities of information— databases of considerable size—have been maintained for hundreds of years without the benefits of computer technology. Historic information sources such as the Doomsday Book of William I after his conquest of Britain, and Josephus's histories of the Jews were achieved without any of the modern technology that is often taken for granted. Similarly, many traditional societies have perfected oral transfer of information over many generations. Even in recent decades, the first edition of the *Atlas of the British Flora* was accomplished using 40-column cards and mechanical/manual sorting techniques. Many small but useful databases are maintained on standard file cards. Hard copy records are still the basis of many rare species locality systems.

Electronic data processing becomes necessary when data must be manipulated, the amount of data is very large, the data are accessed from a wide variety of sources, and the data will be used for a variety of purposes. Nevertheless, there are some things that computers will not do, and "biologists have been quite unrealistic in their predictions of what the computer can do for them in the realms of computerized data banking" (Shetler 1974). Electronic data processing is really made for the fastidious organizer and not for the unorganized who would delight in discovering a machine to clean up the mess in scientists' and managers' files. The most commonly encountered data processing problems are listed.

Data. Raw data for the processing system may have serious imperfections such as unclear handwriting; missing or inferred information; and obscure, out-of-date, or vague place names. The raw data usually have to be interpreted, rearranged, and supplemented with standard codes, indices, or abbreviations. Typically, changes have to be made so that the data meets standards for efficient processing.

Editing, proofreading, and correcting. Some computer-based editing of the input is usually possible, or checking is carried out by reading computer-printed proofs of the input. Misspelled words or incorrect abbreviations will give a glaringly wrong result that should be noted during proofreading. When errors have been found, a simple mechanism for entering corrections into the data bank is most important.

Data bank files. Once input has been completed, the information is stored in one or more files, which can be linked by indexing into groups and super-groups, giving a hierarchy. The structure of hierarchies may be highly significant for retrieval, so it is important to know that a program being considered for data banking can manage hierarchies in an effective way.

Retrieval. For small data banks, retrieval may be done very simply for some queries, using bound printouts on which the requested information is sequenced and printed in various ways by the computer. Such an approach may be efficient enough in many working environments. In other instances, retrieval may be better carried out interactively under program control.

People are easily put off to the idea of using computers for database management because they "lack computer skills and are too old to learn." At one time it was true that use of a computer demanded familiarity with complex operating languages. Although the complexity of programs involved in electronic data processing is increasing, many programs have been made user-friendly through the use of menu systems, clear instructions, and plain language prompts.

Nevertheless, it is always worth checking if a manual system can do a job satisfactorily before becoming committed to electronic data processing. Among the questions to be asked are the following:

- Is the database always going to be small, and are the questions simple enough to be adequately answered manually?

- Are there other potential uses for the data that would be enhanced by use of a computer?

- Is computer hardware and software already available on-site?

- What are the present and future requirements for hardware, software, and staff?

- Is there a readily available labor market that could provide people to do the job manually?

- Will the database provide information for other databases? If so, can data transfer be facilitated by computer technology?

Quality control and updating

A database is only as good as the information it contains. There is considerable truth in the adage, "garbage in, garbage out." If information is tentative, out-of-date, inaccurate, or unsubstantiated, the database will reflect this. Information from conservation databases is needed increasingly as evidence in land-use planning hearings and legal proceedings. Such uses demand strict attention to accuracy. Problems and inadequacies can arise many places in a database; errors commonly occur in latitude and longitude, map references, and locality names.

One of the keys to efficient database management is to ensure that data are reliable. From the moment data are collected they start to "decay." In the case of plant populations and vegetation, some sites may be relatively unchanging over a number of years, but at others change can be rapid. This is a particular problem with rare plants or vulnerable vegetation types. What was found at a site last year may be under threat this year and extinct next year. There may be natural fluctuations in population size, habitat degradation, ongoing and new threats, and changes in landownership—all should be recorded. All information should be checked periodically. Particularly critical information needs to be tagged, not only with source, but also the date of acquisition. Periodicity of checking will depend on the "half-life" of the information—that is, the time it takes for the information to have only half the value or reliability it had when first gathered. Some information has a particularly short half-life (for example, abundance of an aquatic plant in a rapidly drying marsh), whereas other information can have a very long half-life (location of a national park).

To update records, it is necessary to evolve a system for regular checking of sites. Sites requiring most frequent checking are obviously ones that are most fragile, most prone to the effects of development, or that have concentrations of threatened species. It is also useful to adopt a systematic approach to data gathering when sites are being checked, for instance, by using a standard checklist. The condition of a site, description, numbers of rare plants, and other similar details can be compared directly with the results of former visits. Information evaluation is an important aspect of this and must be an integral part of any model (Whitson and Massey 1981). Such evaluation must involve experts on the biology and habitat of target species, and not just land managers. It should be the basis for revision of the threat status or score of individual species, and for setting priorities for protection.

Data are rarely complete in every respect, especially if a large number of fields of information are involved. A lot of time is likely to go into increasing information accuracy and content of a database. Often information can be cross-checked against an evaluation checklist, such as the following:

1. What data and map show: single source, compiled, new?
2. Justification
   A. Value: of subject matter, of itself, and for analyses
   B. Choice: of data mapped—why presented as it is
3. Completeness and quality of data
   A. Mapped data: result of comprehensive analysis, partial
   B. Scale: adequate for element, too generalized
   C. Confidence: poor–excellent, obvious data needs
   D. Problems encountered: data availability, form
4. Need for additional study
   A. As a part of this analysis
      (1) Specific sites and/or problems
      (2) Specific data gaps
   B. As a consequence of this project
      (1) Specific sites and/or problems
      (2) Specific data gaps
5. Relationships to other categories
   A. For analysis and/or synthesis
      (1) Possible conflict and/or compatibility
      (2) Cumulative and/or synergetic effects
   B. Seasonal needs or problems
   C. Other
6. References

Source: Ray 1984.

Inadequacies in documentation

Documentation systems will be inadequate when recording and database systems are poorly designed, and when the wrong questions are asked of a database. Inquirers may be unsure of the relevance of some fields or may not appreciate the limitations of data. Some errors and inadequacies may be the result of mistakes made at the data collection stage. For example:

Essential information is not entered on data sheets at the field site. To leave data entry until days, or even hours, later is to invite errors; memories are fallible.

Data forms are inadequate, perhaps even ambiguous. Forms should be designed to be filled in from top to bottom, each item in logical sequence.

Data is transcribed from draft field notes or temporary forms onto permanent forms or report sheets. Because of the potential to introduce errors, transcription should be minimized and every transfer of information must be carefully cross-checked.

Codes are used excessively. Where possible, numerical codes should be avoided in favor of full data entry or alpha-numeric codes that have meaning to the user (e.g., FOR for forest and NATPR for national park).

Most of the time, information systems fail because organizational behavior problems brought on by people were ignored and too much emphasis was put on solving the technical problems. If steps are not taken to understand and deal with human factors, systems will continue to fail. In computer-based systems, problems can arise in such diverse operations as transcribing and encoding data, keying the data into computerized form, modifying and editing the data, and programming and debugging. Data processing staffs rarely see the whole design of data use; they tend to follow a set of simple rules and do not have the background for understanding what the data relationships are or how the information will be used in decision-making processes.

Quality control is of the utmost importance. When errors are found, data may have to be extensively searched at the point of origin to correct the errors. Modern computer software increasingly can incorporate machine-based checks on such errors as spelling, format, and locality data. These checks should be built into the systems as much as is practicable. As the data system grows larger, lack of quality control can cause an incremental reduction of new data acquisition, bringing about data management bottlenecks, rendering the existing data worthless, or even bringing the entire data management operation to a halt (Moyseenko 1981, in part). It is tempting to include some fields in a database system in case they may be useful in the future. Fields should be evaluated using a subset of the database, and redundant fields should be eliminated. In the case of a herbarium database set up by the National Herbarium, Pretoria, South Africa, data were rarely entered for several fields. Examples included soil type (4 percent), plants woody or herbaceous (1 percent), actual or potential use (2 percent), slope of site (4 percent), and biotic effects (2 percent) (Morris and Manders 1981).

Original records should be retained so that serious errors can be checked back to their source and unusual records validated. If data are combined or simplified, for example, where precise point localities are converted into larger grid squares for mapping, the original data must be retained as a check. Use of a computer does not remove the need to store original field records, notebooks, data sheets, and herbarium specimens. Whenever data are queried, one needs to be able to access the original source of information. This is critically important in conservation databases.

Problems can also arise when manual systems are converted to electronic data retrieval, or when manual and computerized systems are merged. The ever-popular assertion that computer speed and storage capacity can overcome all obstacles in data management is misleading. Larger and faster computers simply provide faster and bigger mistakes. Information systems may fail because they have incorporated too much unstructured data, so that the output consists of massive amounts of disorganized and undigestible data.

Most conservation databases do not require high-speed turnaround, which can be relatively expensive. In the past, batch processing often was preferred for handling large amounts of data, chiefly because it was cheaper. More efficient technology increasingly has made it possible to consider interactive processing and data retrieval on even quite modest computer systems. Interactive systems can give the illusion that data is controlled more effectively (Moyseenko 1981). On the other hand, more complex systems and techniques are involved. A valuable axiom of computer science states that the cost and difficulty of operating a system increases exponentially with the size and complexity of the programs. The larger and more complex the system, the greater the opportunity for it to fail in larger and more complex ways.

A database must be continuously maintained; information integrity can be lost if this is not done. User evaluation, feedback, and continuous program operation must be integral parts of the overall database management system. Clearly, a revolution is taking place in information gathering and dissemination. Information transfer is a rapidly growing industry. Plant conservation—with its local and global needs for accurate data and the constantly changing nature of the resource—must take every opportunity to utilize the best of new information technology.

Access to Databases

Databases are largely wasted unless the information is available for use. Managers of databases deny access to information for a variety of reasons. For one, they do not want to see information on sensitive sites or species misused. A database may have been developed for in house use only. Appropriate retrieval packages may not be developed yet. Users themselves may be quite unreasonable when making requests, asking for complex information at a moment's notice without being prepared to pay for it.

Care does have to be taken when releasing sensitive information. Some data should not be freely available but should be released on a "one-off" basis, only to those who want to use it for legitimate reasons (e.g., to establish a nature reserve or in a land-use inquiry). Confidentiality is perhaps the greatest problem in endangered species data systems. Nevertheless, data needs to get to those who can use it effectively to protect and manage biodiversity. For every case where there has been misuse of information, other instances can be quoted where local extinction occurred because landowners and local government authorities were ignorant and did not appreciate the importance of a site. This is no reason to broadcast far and wide where sensitive sites and plants are located. Published records in particular must be disclosed with discretion. Locality details can be manipulated so that, for instance, they are publicly referred to only in terms of a 10-kilometer grid. Ironically, sometimes when data are withheld, they can be obtained from herbarium sheets in a herbarium freely accessible to the public.

There is considerable argument for establishing a formal or informal information network or clearinghouse for database inquiries (Morse et al. 1981). Two vital aspect of information transfer are communication between ongoing projects, and information transfer from researchers to land managers. It is easy to get duplication between managers of projects, or noncomparable data that are of little use when regional syntheses are attempted or data are compared from year to year. It is surprising how many times the same information is requested by the same agency (sometimes even by people in the same office). Often protected area managers are not aware of the current work of academic or contract researchers, or of work conducted by government agencies.

There are many ways of presenting data to clients, but the actual format of data presentation is probably not as important as its clarity. The user should not be required to undertake complex interpretation of the information. Retrieval packages tend to be ignored in the rush to accumulate data but must be considered at an early stage of database development, particularly if graphic presentations are envisaged. Conversion of in-house databases for wider use can involve considerable time and expense, but if the potential clients really want the information, then they should bear some of the costs of this conversion. Since the early 1970s, the *Red Data Book* format has become internationally recognized as one means of summarizing data on target species for a wide range of interest groups. It is not the only possible format and must be backed up by much more detailed and accessible data. Many inquiries are likely to be management oriented, and although *Red Data Books* are useful for overall assessment and case histories, they are not sufficiently detailed to be of use in precise site management.

In most countries where successive compilations of threatened species have been made, many changes are necessary in lists, even over the short term. Clients do not want out-of-date data. The problem can only be overcome by reliable local observers who can look for species that are critically rare or of uncertain status (Perring and Farrell 1983). Observations made by these people can be used to plan surveys to collect precise and up-to-date information not only on the location of the species, but on the size and exact boundary of each population, on the biology of the species at the site, and on the conservation status of the area.

Every record should be backed up by some form of hard copy. Often this is standardized sheets or cards. Computer records must be adequately backed up on disk or tape stored away from the major working records. Observations on different dates or by different people should be treated as separate records. These records can become the basis of a computerized data bank. Records carry basic information about the date of the sighting, location and habitat, as well as any notes made by an observer. Subsidiary notes should not be discarded even when there is no immediate use for them. In surveys of the threatened plants of Britain, a population form, separate from the geographic site form, was designed for biological information, although biological notes were included on the site record if an observer did not complete a population form (Perring and Farrell 1983). If, however, a population form was completed, this was noted on the site record card, but the extra details on the form were not transferred to it. Both sets of forms have been major sources of information for the preparation of a "Table of Threat Numbers" and the systematic account of the present status of each taxon that forms the core of the *Red Data Book*.

Another widely recognized system is that of Element Stewardship Abstracts, developed by The Nature Conservancy (TNC) in the United States. These provide TNC stewardship staff and other land managers with current management-related information on those species and communities that are most important to protect, or most important to control. TNC

provides abstracts to users free of charge, encouraging them to contribute their own information. This sharing of information benefits all land managers and ensures the availability of up-to-date information on management techniques. Information contributors and major users receive updated editions of stewardship abstracts.

CASE STUDY: GUIDELINES FOR REPORTING SURVEY RESULTS

A rare plant survey report should include the following:

1. *A description of the project.* This should include maps of development that will cause disturbance, and a discussion of construction and operational aspects of any proposed projects or disturbance.
2. *A detailed description of the study methods.* Early in the report, the methods employed in collecting background information and conducting the fieldwork should be discussed; this should include an overview of the research design and its rationale.
   A. *Background information*—the kinds of information considered necessary, methods used to obtain data, and sources actually used.
   B. *Fieldwork*—all methods employed in the field to search for rare plants, in sufficient detail for the reader to understand the methods and why they were used; includes methods used to define the boundaries of populations, methods to identify the plants and the characteristics of the population. Also report areas that were examined and gave negative results.
3. *A discussion of the survey results.* Describe the dates surveys were conducted, what was found (include detailed maps and descriptions), and the characteristics of the populations and their habitat. Standardized data forms should be attached if used as part of the study. A list of all species identified should be attached.
4. *References used in preparing the survey report.* References cited, persons contacted, herbaria visited, and the location of voucher specimens should be included.

If space is a problem, major points should be briefly summarized. The summary within the environmental report should include a statement that a floristic survey was conducted (if this is the case), the dates of fieldwork, the methods employed, and the results of the survey. Environmental reports must also include a discussion of potential impacts and mitigation measures. The full report should be cited and its location given to enable reviewers to examine the report. It should be made available to appropriate institutions.

Source: Nelson 1986.

CHAPTER 4

Plant Population Management

Many aspects of plant population biology must be considered during the development of conservation or preservation strategies. Effective conservation or preservation requires that many factors be taken into account (Given 1984; Fiedler and Ahouse 1992). These include breeding systems, life-cycle patterns, dispersal modes, and in John Harper's (1977) words, "all of those other peculiarities that distinguish the biology of individual species." The ultimate test of conservation biology theory is its application to actual management situations—the so-called real world. Until recently, much plant population management has been relatively benign, involving as little interference as possible. Active management, when utilized, has often been intuitive rather than based on well-grounded theory and case histories. In a surprising number of instances, this has worked—a testimony to the resilience of many plants and their habitats. But in other instances, the approach has been insufficient: numbers have continued to decline.

A necessary relationship exists between management of ecosystems, species, and populations. Species management comes down to management of particular populations at specific sites. Nevertheless, even when the primary concern is the conservation of a particular population and site, there will be broader considerations. Species conservation cannot be considered independent of habitats and ecosystems. The use of land adjacent to the target site is also relevant to conservation of particular populations. Management of populations includes several distinct components: selecting a precise target for management, determining the characteristics of the target, selecting measurable goals of management, and developing techniques to achieve these and contingency plans. Social issues are important. A particular site or species may be of interest to several different groups, each of which has different goals; some of these goals may be incompatible with the conservation of plants (P. Keddy, pers.

com.). There are likely to be budgetary and staff requirements (and constraints). Present and future threats and social constraints need to be considered.

Sometimes effective management simply consists of initial survey, followed by protection of the site from unwanted human interference, and periodic visits to check the state of habitat and number of plants. If manipulation is necessary, the management choices multiply and selection of an appropriate technique becomes more difficult. This is where the advice of professional biologists becomes essential.

It is appropriate to ask: Why be concerned with population management? Should not management be at the ecosystem level? Population management needs to be considered separately for the following reasons:

- Ecosystem management depends on maintenance of key species. If these are in trouble and declining, the whole ecosystem eventually suffers.

- Particular species may be threatened or in decline because of factors that are independent of the ecosystem as a whole. Examples include harvesting, predation, and the consequences of small population size.

- Some species may require specific habitat manipulation independent of that applied to the whole system where they occur.

- It cannot be assumed that because a species is in an area now it will still be there in 50 or 100 years time. Strategies need to be set in a time frame where expected persistence time into the future is considered.

- People generally find it easier to understand conservation of biodiversity at the species level than at other levels (e.g., ecosystem and gene). Species conservation and preservation is best done at the level of populations.

The ultimate test of management success is

whether it promotes persistence of biodiversity into the future. Given adequate habitat protection and assistance with reproduction, many rare and endangered plants can recover their numbers and vitality. It is the role of conservation biology to shift the odds in their favor (Csuti 1984).

Biological and Ecological Considerations

Although there may be some generalized trends among threatened plants, such as frequent lack of competitive ability, niche selection, and specialized biotic relationships, such species are not necessarily characterized by any single set of life history features. They have as wide a range of reproductive strategies, histories of evolution, disturbance responses, and relationships with the environment as other species. Each species has its own unique blend of characteristics, genetic diversity, and lifestyles. Management of the diversity of plants around us will only be as good as the information available, but often there is distressingly little known about target species. As a result, much management proceeds in an information vacuum. Not enough is known about the way even simple ecosystems function and respond to disturbance. For few species do we know details of reproduction, dispersal, and establishment. The problems are well demonstrated by lack of agreement on what factors lead to high local levels of species richness (Ashton 1992). Although a general theory might be derived, species richness certainly is not mediated by a single factor. High predictability (low year-to-year variation) may play a part by providing conditions for narrow niche differentiation to develop. On the other hand, frequent perturbation can also lead to species richness (Grubb 1977; Keddy 1985) especially on low nutrient soils (e.g., Hopper 1977).

What is the minimum information one should try to have? At the very least one must know what are the target species and where they are found, and have some measure of how well they are persisting. An assessment should provide information on the following (Hopkins and Saunders 1987; Messick 1987):

Taxonomy: often confused, inadequately described, or based on poor sampling; with uncertain affinities, and poorly distinguished from closely related species.

Life history: often poorly known but required for understanding the interaction of species and environment. Critical requirements should be identified, including soil and nutrient needs.

Reproductive biology: type of breeding system and essential pollinators and dispersers; it is necessary to know what other plants and animals interact with target species and, hence, must be preserved at the same site.

Seeds: presence and persistence of a seed bank or dormant stages.

Vegetative reproduction: the extent of this.

Population size and density: if there are few breeding plants, the population becomes vulnerable to random events that can cause further decline. Density and population size are closely linked to reproductive strategies of species.

Population number and variation: number and size of other populations of the species, and relative magnitude of within- and between-population variation.

Disturbance and stress: need for and adaptation to natural disturbances and stress.

History: original distribution and history, and reasons for rarity.

Other strategies: associated strategies that may be available, such as conservation in a botanic garden, habitat restoration, or transfer of plants to a new site.

Uses: actual and potential use—economic, traditional, or other—and need for chemical screening or other tests. This may influence the number of populations needing protection as well as priorities for protection.

Collecting detailed information can be time-consuming and expensive. To gather the information, do research, and actively manage a population requires even more time and effort. Unlimited resources are rarely available, so it is necessary to decide at the outset which species should be subjected to detailed analysis and which should be given only minimal attention. The choice is not always easy, and one is often influenced by personal preferences for certain organisms.

In setting priorities, important target species are those whose persistence interrelates with that of other species. An evolutionary change in one population may impose selection pressures on coexisting populations and induce change in them. Such mutually adaptive changes in populations are called coevolution. This produces both mutualistic relationships (those where the two populations benefit) and antagonistic responses. Coevolution is frequent in plants, where it often involves the plant and its animal dispersers and pollinators. Assumptions regarding the species which others shelter must be made cautiously. Incorrectly assuming that other species are receiving protection as a result of the protection of another umbrella species can result in inadvertent loss. One of the perhaps unexpected results of identifying target species is that they are not necessarily the most prominent or the rarest species in the community. There are three important categories of target species:

1. *Indicator species* known to be particularly sensitive to pollutants, human activity, ecological instability, or other disturbance.

2. *Umbrella species* whose existence often requires an unusually large area, and which provide protection for other species within the area, or species that rely upon a scarce resource also critical for the survival of many other species; very small areas with remnants of vegetation may lack umbrella species—they may have been lost from the system.

3. *Keystone species* that play a central role in the ecology of the resident community.

Major criteria for choosing the target species of a plant conservation program include the following (Baker and Schonewald-Cox, 1986, modified):

Type	Criteria
Indicator	Sensitivity to pollutants Sensitivity to human activity Sensitivity to ecological instability
Umbrella	Requires large area Requires scarce resource
Keystone	Essential to ecological integrity of community Essential to survival of other species
Charismatic	Socially significant Culturally significant Unusually attractive Anthropomorphic
Recreational	Popular for picking or growing Popular for observation
Economic	Provides material that can be sold or harvested for personal use Related to agricultural species
Threatened	May be extirpated

The concept of *modules of species* is useful. Modules are groups of strongly interacting species within a community. A conservation program should aim to identify and conserve intact modules and, as resources allow, attempt to reconstruct fragmented or lost modules. The module approach demands sufficient knowledge of the ecosystem to appreciate the interactions between species.

Maintaining Population Characteristics

Maintenance of population characteristics should be a fundamental objective of plant management programs. This is not only so that populations continue to function as they have throughout their evolutionary history. The higher level units of biodiversity (vegetation types, ecosystems, and biomes) also must maintain those characteristics that allow them to function. Population biology has relatively recently entered into plant ecology, providing a focus for the links that tie ecology to genetics, evolutionary theory, management, and conservation (Harper 1984). This focus is an important one.

A critically important point is that in highly localized species the spread of age classes within individual populations may not be even. Many plants occur in approximately even-aged stands, where most of the individuals fall within an age range of not much more than 10 percent of the normally attainable age—even-aged cohorts that may indicate cyclical events such as periodic mast seeding or catastrophe.

Populations cannot be regarded as static (Figure 4.1). Study of vegetation dynamics in relation to population characteristics shows that the floristic composition of most vegetation types changes from year to year. Furthermore, reactions of populations and vegetation to changes in environmental conditions may last for decades, and during a sequence of change, some species disappear while others become established or behave as ephemerals (van der Maarel 1984). The biology of the species concerned—the popula-

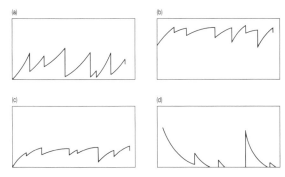

Figure 4.1. Idealized diagrams of plant population dynamics showing the types of changes that can occur through time: (a) dynamics dominated by phases of population growth after recurrent disasters or episodes of colonization; (b) dynamics within a habitable site dominated by limitations on environment carrying capacity —carrying capacity is high and species are abundant; (c) as for B but carrying capacity low and species rare; (d) dynamics within a habitable site dominated by population decay after more or less sudden episodes of colonization or recruitment from the seed bank in the soil. (Reproduced by permission from Harper 1981)

tion characteristics—will largely determine the precise nature of such changes.

Conservation is largely concerned with questions of persistence and extinction and the replacement of one individual by another. Perhaps the best known framework for considering life cycles is that which recognizes two contrasting types of life history: those of organisms adapted for dispersal, colonization, and rapid population growth (r-strategists), and those adapted for persistence and reproduction in stable populations (k-strategists). A very useful way of considering rare species, in particular, is their ability to withstand competition, disturbance, and stress (Grime 1977, 1979). These factors can be arranged as a triangular matrix, allowing particular species to be plotted so as to show their susceptibility and strengths in each of these areas.

Another critically important point is that in highly localized species the spread of age classes within individual populations may not be even. Many plants occur in approximately even-aged stands, where most of the individuals fall within age range of not much more than 10 percent of the normally attainable age—even-aged cohorts that may indicate cyclical events such as periodic mast seeding or catastrophe.

Maintaining effective population size

Effective population size is an important element of population management. A positive correlation often exists between population size and genetic fitness, al-

though this must not be assumed in every instance. As a population is reduced in size it becomes more prone to a range of both deterministic and stochastic effects, which can lead to extinction. Finally, small populations are vulnerable to extinction through catastrophe.

Every effort should be made to build populations up to an acceptable size. Past estimates of what this might be have ranged from a minimum of 50 interbreeding individuals to 500 or even more. It is now generally accepted that there is no magic number below which populations are necessarily doomed and above which they are safe. Rather, as size decreases the risks of extinction become greater and persistence times become shorter. Similarly, management becomes more intensive, manipulative, and costly. In most instances, and in the absence of more precise data, an effective population size of 500 for a target species is probably a good figure to aim for. Certainly, once numbers drop below 50–100 there should be concern and urgent planning for intervention. Trends may change and even reverse. Some species show fluctuations suggesting that their populations spend much time recovering from the last disaster. Examples include weedy species of cultivated land—classic r-strategists (Harper 1981).

A species may be uncommon simply because its habitat is only suitable for occupation for short periods of time. The plant may even rely on continual migration from one suitable site to another. Such survival may depend on seeds reaching suitable sites elsewhere before the parent plant is extirpated (Harper 1981).

Concern for minimum population sizes (regardless of the reasons) translates to a goal of setting aside protected areas of large size (Roche and Dourojeanni 1984). Assuming that a minimum viable size for a sexually mature population of outbreeding trees should be 200 individuals, Ashton (1976) calculated that reserves in species-rich Borneo should be at least 2000 hectares. The presence of biological and ecological links between species (both plant and animal) strongly influences the presence and survival of particular species in a community; thus the area required by the target species should not be the only consideration.

Distribution patterns and population sizes change, sometimes radically, over time. Older plant groups, such as southern podocarps (Podocarpaceae), some fern allies, southern beech (*Nothofagus*), and "living fossils," such as dawn redwood (*Metasequoia*), now occupy very different areas from those they occupied in the past.

Assessing genetic variability

The extent and pattern of genetic variability in natural populations are critical to conservation, especially where species are highly endangered. These can indicate the evolutionary history and origins of species, the interrelationships between populations, and the abilities of populations to withstand present and future perturbation of the environment. Knowledge of natural patterns of variability is necessary if reintroductions and translocations are to simulate natural processes. Three questions must be asked:

1. What is the amount of genetic variation through the whole range?

2. What is the distribution of that variation within and among populations?

3. What is the effectiveness of gene dispersal throughout a population and between populations through pollination and dispersal?

Until recently, assessment of genetic variability generally has been through measurements of gross features such as length, number, form, and color of various parts of the plant. There are many hundreds of such features that can be measured, and chemical, ecological, and physiological characters can be used as well. Several difficulties are encountered in assessing genetic variability. First, it may be difficult to decide which are the most important characters, or which few should be measured. Second, it may be difficult to separate inherited features from those that reflect habitat differences. A third difficulty is that the small number of characters looked at are often biased toward those that can be measured easily; these may not be important characters in terms of relationships. Finally, examination of macro-characters may not readily allow objective estimates of how different species are.

It is very difficult to distinguish genetic from environmental effects. Techniques have been developed to allow these effects to be separated, perhaps one of the simplest still being to grow plants in uniform environment plots using randomized planting patterns for several growing seasons (Ashton 1987). Careful measurement and analysis of macrocharacters and their variation should be a first step in assessing genetic variation, and it may give all the answers necessary. Sophisticated electrophoretic techniques (e.g., analysis of flavenoids, isozymes, proteins, and mitochondrial DNA), however, provide more precise methods for direct evaluation of the genetic variation of a population (e.g., Moran and Hopper 1987).

Many *loci* (positions of the gene on a chromosome) that synthesize proteins, especially enzymes, are *polymorphic*, or have more than one alternate state. The association between this polymorphism and population variation is strong enough to use protein variability as a first-order approximation of overall population variation. Soluble proteins that differ in electrical charge can be separated by dyes that produce colored substances on the gel. Enzymes with different mobilities appear as more than one band on a gel stained for a specific enzyme–substrate reaction. Such different molecular forms of enzymes that catalyze the same reaction are called isozymes. If these occur at the same locus in different allelic states, they are called allozymes.

Allozyme features can be read directly from gels, and in most cases they have a one-to-one correspondence with genotypes. The allozyme technique gives biologists their first straightforward means of visualizing gene products. Allozyme frequencies allow estimation of the amount of heterozygosity or variability present in a population.

The plant breeding system is an important determinant of genetic structure. Plants that primarily reproduce through self-fertilization may have little genetic variability within populations. Those that predominantly outcross may have as much as 90 percent of their variation within populations. Plants that reproduce primarily by asexual means tend to have more variability between populations than within. In extreme environments survival may best be served by every plant closely fitting the environment and minimizing within-population variation.

CASE STUDY: GENETIC STRATEGIES FOR SURVIVAL UNDER CONDITIONS OF HIGH STRESS IN *DEDECKERA*

Dedeckera eurekensis is a rare, relictual species confined to a few small populations in the mountains fringing the northwestern Mojave Desert of California. The habitat occupied by *Dedeckera* can be described as extremely arid.

The species has enormous genetic variability (heterozygosity), greater than that which might be expected for a desert species, although by no means extreme for woody perennials in general. This high variability should increase the chances of survival for individual plants, although it is also likely to increase mortality at ovule through seedling stages of the life cycle. In the case of *Dedeckera*, heterozygosity appears to be inversely correlated with reproductive success. The plant has an exceptionally low seed-to-ovule (S/O) ratio. This is countered to some extent by prolific flowering, suggesting that sufficient seeds are produced to permit establishment of rare seedlings under favorable circumstances.

One scenario is that *Dedeckera* evolved in a less extreme habitat and is now adopting a strategy that allows it to survive under conditions to which it is not ideally suited.

Sources: Weins et al. 1988; Gee 1989.

Breeding systems and dispersal problems

Some aspects of plant breeding and dispersal systems tend to make the conservation of plants simpler than that of many animals. Plants do not wander and do not have complex social interactions. Many plants can be propagated by vegetative means, they do not usually require daily care, and the majority are bisexual, which means that genetic integrity frequently can be maintained with fewer individuals. On the other hand, because there are so many types of breeding systems, when a plant population is failing the range of factors that have to be investigated can be very wide (Bawa and Webb 1984).

If male and female flowers are on different plants (plants are dioecious), sexual reproduction may be restricted when population numbers become very low and one or the other sex is reduced to only one or two plants. In the extreme instance, of complete loss of one sex, further reproduction must be vegetative unless plants of the missing sex can migrate into the area. This can be a particular problem in regions where dioecism is high, for example on some island groups such as New Zealand, where 12–13 percent of the species are dioecious (Godley 1979).

An associated problem is imbalance in sex ratios, such as excesses of males over females. This reduces the effective size of a population. Further reduction in numbers may see loss of most or all female plants in such situations. Self-sterility has been demonstrated in numerous species, and it cannot be assumed that *monoecious* plants (those with both male and female flowers on one plant) are self-compatible. Certainly it should not be assumed that isolated monoecious plants will set viable seed. Although some pollinators are generalized in their behavior, others are highly specific, only visiting a small selection of species (or even a single species). Plants in very small populations may have difficulty successfully competing for pollinators, resulting in low levels of reproduction and potential population failure.

Loss of pollinators and dispersers can reduce the likelihood of long-term persistence. This points to the need, where essential associate species exist, to conserve areas large enough for the target plant species and their essential associates. Rarely, consideration may have to be given to artificial pollination and dispersal, perhaps even by hand. This is time-consuming and an intensive use of resources. Before embarking on such a program, one should undertake a survey to determine if pollination and dispersal are being carried out by other, substitute animals.

Fuchsia procumbens, a New Zealand endemic, offers a particularly interesting example of the loss of reproductive ability through elimination of sexual states (Godley 1963; Wilson and Given 1989). The species is *trioecious* (separate plants male, female, and hermaphrodite) and of 13 natural populations observed in 1963, 5 were either wholly male or female, with hermaphrodites or the opposite sex absent. *Gunnera hamiltonii* is an endangered species endemic to sand dunes in southern New Zealand (Wilson and Given 1989; C. J. Webb, pers. com.). It is dioecious, and at present there are only five known populations in the wild; at each of these only one sex is suspected to be present. Fully mature fruits have yet to be described for the species.

An extreme example from New Zealand is represented by *Pennantia baylisiana (Plectomirtha baylisiana)* (Wilson and Given 1989; A. Wright, pers. com.). This tree is confined to the Three Kings Islands of the northern tip of the New Zealand mainland. Only one tree has ever been found and this is predominently female, although a small quantity of pollen may occur on some flowers. Most pollen is sterile and in most seasons only occasional fruits are initiated. Almost invariably the inflorescence is shed before these few fruits have time to develop (rare fruits have been reported).

Finally, even when pollination is successful and dispersers are present, seed predation may mean that few fertile seeds are available to establish succeeding generations. Menges et al. (1986) showed that for the rare species *Pedicularis furbishiae,* limits to population growth may be profoundly influenced by such predation. Knowledge of dispersal methods is essential for an understanding of the colonization patterns of species and the relationships between animals and plants.

Seed banks and dormancy

Seed banks—accumulations of ungerminated seed usually found in the soil—can be the unknown factor in an estimation of population size. The size of the seed bank represents a balance between the seed rain—seeds that fall or are dispersed from fruits—and seed losses through germination, predation, and death (Archibold 1989; Louda 1989b). The existence of a seed bank should lessen harmful effects of small population size and rarity. A seed bank containing a mixture of genotypes can result from the production of seed over several growing seasons. It is possible for a census of visible plants growing above ground (seedlings through adults) to underestimate greatly the total number of plants on a site by not taking into account dormant plants or a seed bank. Long-term survival of a population may be highly dependent on these dormant plants and seeds. They offer an insurance against stochastic events and, especially for short-lived plants, a reservoir for those years when conditions are optimum for growth and germination. The seed bank may be stratified, that is, contain seed resulting from several distinct years of flowering and seeding—an advantageous strategy where environmental conditions are highly variable from year to year.

Likewise, total extirpation should not be assumed when plants are not obviously visible at a site; there may still be underground propagules. If this is suspected, every effort should be made to detect, recover, and regenerate the species by taking soil samples and examining for residual seed or other propagules such as tubers. If found, these should be germinated or induced to grow either by regenerating from scored seeds in the laboratory, or by regeneration in soil samples. Furthermore, conditions at natural sites should be manipulated to induce growth of propagules.

Development of a natural seed bank and long-term dormancy allows a species the luxury of only having to grow, flower, and fruit in the years that are most favorable. If the species is relatively short lived, populations can fluctuate wildly between great abundance and very small numbers, or even absence for a time above ground. Seed banks are generally very important for plants occurring in vegetation subject to periodic disturbance such as burning or flooding. In such sites, the presence of a significant seed bank or of dormancy should be sought. The extreme is offered by species that are rarely, if ever above ground. *Rhizanthus gardneri*, an underground orchid of Western Australia, is an example of this. Location of plants historically has been accidental, although recently satellite imagery was used to detect areas of likely habitat (Dixon and Pate 1984).

Seed bank estimates are not necessarily easy. A variety of methods are available, one of the simplest being to spread soil out on trays protected from contamination and pests, keeping it moist and identifying and counting emerging seedlings. Seeds may be separated from soil physically, followed by viability and germination tests. In situ seedlings, for instance along trails, can be collected and identified through several seasons.

Although there is considerable knowledge of seed germination and seed banks for temperate regions, relatively little is known for the tropics (Silvertown 1988). It does seem that many tropical plants have short-lived seeds, but data are far from complete. One of the problems encountered generally, but perhaps very significantly in the tropics, is the uneven distribution of seeds in the soil. Where there are coevolutionary relationships between plants and large herbivores, seeds may be concentrated in dung. This has been shown for parts of the Amazon, where concentrations of seeds in cow dung can be twenty times that of the soil itself.

In Serengeti National Park, Tanzania, regeneration from seed is important in many of the vegetation types (Silvertown 1988). For the dominant grasses, fire, grazing, and soil disturbance create the conditions for seedling recruitment. *Themeda triandra* is a major grass of the savannas that is dominant in many communities. Naturally occurring seedlings only appear after burning. The seeds have a long hygroscopic awn, which drills them into cracks in the soil where they are protected from fires. The effects of fire are probably to reduce plant cover, although some experiments testing burning against clipping of vegetation suggest that the former leads to more germination.

Metapopulation structure

A species whose range is composed of more or less geographically isolated patches interconnected through patterns of gene flow, extinction, and recolonization, is said to form a *metapopulation,* or a population made up of subpopulations. The general effect of such population subdivision is to increase total genetic variation without necessarily increasing variation within subpopulations. Although probably more widespread in animals than plants, metapopulation structure is likely to be significant in plants that have frequent long-distance dispersal of pollen or seed, and in species that have experienced relatively frequent fragmentation followed by recolonization. Three major concepts are vital to the management of metapopulations (Lande and Barrowclough 1987):

1. While particular populations become extinct and new ones are formed elsewhere, the metapopulation persists as long as extinction and colonization rates remain in equilibrium. Population sizes on various patches of habitat can be manipulated to achieve this.

2. Not all habitat for a species is likely to be occupied at any particular point in time. Failure to protect vacant habitat patches can reduce metapopulation size and viability as surely as will destruction of an existing population. It is necessary to protect suitable but vacant habitat as well as habitat where the species currently occurs.

3. The job of preserving a species or a community will never be finished with the protection of a single population or patch. A comprehensive species recovery plan should address the long-term needs of species protection by incorporation of the metapopulation concept.

Over time, the location of patches of a given type of vegetation will change with disturbance. Protection of vegetation therefore has to include enough patches of essential habitat in the landscape mosaic to ensure that sites are available for the necessary recolonization that maintains metapopulation structure. A natural metapopulation structure should not be confused with human-induced fragmentation, which has the potential to disrupt many important ecological interactions in a community, the extent of disruption depending on the magnitude, duration, and type of fragmentation. Consequences include disruption of predator–prey, parasite–host, plant–pollinator, and plant–disperser relations and mutualisms.

Conservation of hybrids

Although most conservation of populations in the wild tends to be of "pure" species, conservation of hybrids can be important when these are incipient new species or components of regional hybrid swarms. There has been a tendency not to include hybrid species on threatened plant lists.

A surprising number of plant taxa have arisen by hybridization, and sometimes quite complex strategies of polyploidy, hybridization, and vegetative reproduction have been adopted. The problem is to know what is the best means of dealing with species that appear to be of recent hybrid origin. Some may be an early stage in the evolution of a new species, before reproductive patterns have become fixed.

CASE STUDY: CONSERVATION OF *AGAVE ARIZONICA*,
A RECURRING HYBRID

Soon after its discovery in 1959, *Agave arizonica*, one of the rarest and most attractive agaves in Arizona, was known from about 10 sites over an area of about 50 square kilometers in the New River Mountains. By March 1984, 10 new sites were known from the region, but only one of the original clones had persisted. All sites are within the distribution area of two other *Agave* species—*A. toumeyana* subsp. *bella* and *A. chrysantha*. Comparison showed that *A. arizonica* is intermediate between the other two species, and thus it has been concluded that *A. arizonica* is a recurring hybrid between the two.

Source: DeLamater and Hodgson 1987.

Viable Population Planning and Risk Analysis

Over time, plants change form, grow, produce flowers and fruit, become senescent, and die. Ecosystems and populations similarly undergo change and are in a constant state of flux. The time component to plant preservation and conservation is important. Populations and ecosystems are vulnerable to change in different ways and at different rates through time. Although for a particular species or habitat there may be little chance of extinction over several decades (and it may appear "safe"), over longer periods of hundreds of years survival may be increasingly unlikely.

Vulnerability (or risk) analysis considers depletion and extinction within specified time frames. The information obtained through vulnerability analysis provides a framework for planning for the maintenance of a population and identifies key parameters

and problems (Marcot and Murphy, in press):

- Fragmentation of habitat or loss of habitat quality (e.g., through edge effects) can lead to fragmentation of populations and their decline.

- Reduction in population distribution and effective size can lead to extinction.

- Increased variation in population growth rate can lead to extinction. Large fluctuations in population size with frequent peaks and crashes will put a population at increased risk.

- Inbreeding depression coupled with decreased genetic variation can lead to risk of extinction.

- In very small populations, there is an increased possibility of chance loss of genetic material through genetic drift.

• The effects of people—policies and activities—must be considered. Interest in species and habitats change.

The *risk model* is based on the premise that viability is best estimated and expressed as a gradient of likelihoods of continued existence of a population (Marcot and Murphy, in press). There are no thresholds, such as magic numbers for minimum population size, above which the population is viable and below which it is not. Risk analysis is a facet of decision theory that helps one assess and plan for viable populations (Figure 4.2). Probabilities of chance events are estimated using such probabilities to calculate expected payoffs from each management decision at any given point. Even if these likelihoods can be expressed only in qualitative terms such as very high to very low risk, analysis can be useful. The risk analysis approach does stress the time element in conservation. This in itself may be just as important as estimates of persistence time: it is important to ask how long one wishes to conserve particular species.

Very high probability for continued existence of a population allows greater latitude for catastrophic

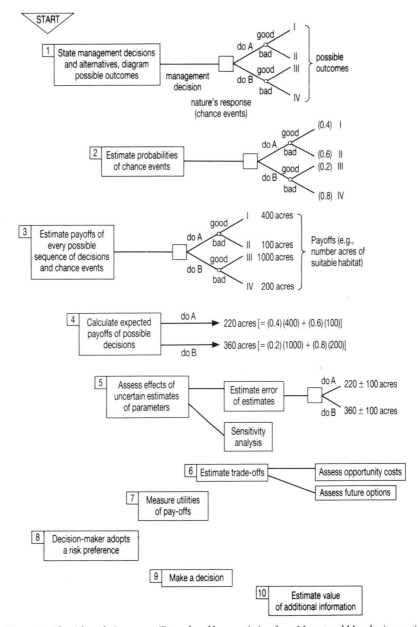

Figure 4.2. The risk analysis process. (Reproduced by permission from Marcot and Murphy, in press)

events affecting the population, for mitigating lack of flexibility in the biological requirements of species, and for demographic and genetic factors that may become significant as species experience stress. Where there is less likelihood for continued existence of a population, there is less latitude for such events. At low or very low levels of probability, catastrophic, demographic, or genetic factors will probably cause loss of populations.

Two major elements of uncertainty affect viable population planning (Marcot, in press). The first is scientific uncertainty. This arises because of the inherent variability of natural systems of populations, imperfections in the estimation of population variables (sampling problems, bias, imprecision, and inaccuracies), uncertainties over the way information is modeled and used in analysis, and uncertainty arising from asking the wrong questions (or applying a model to the wrong problem). The second factor affecting viable population planning is decision-making uncertainty. This arises from making a decision based on incomplete or imprecise information.

Both types of uncertainty probably have to be tolerated, at least in the short term. Plants are particularly affected by these uncertainties because of the wide array of reproductive options often available. This makes it extremely difficult to give accurate estimates of persistence time. A number of well-defined steps form the framework of the viable population planning process (Marcot and Murphy, in press):

Identify species for analysis. Screen the list of potential species so that attention can be focused on those for which viability is an immediate or foreseeable concern. Small numbers, limited geographic distribution, and downward population trends identify species for further consideration. There could be any number of causes for small numbers or limited distribution, including loss of habitats required for survival and sensitivity to human activities (e.g., environmental pollutants and toxicants). The causes could differ by geographic area and may change over time.

Coordinate planning. The habitats of target species may have significant alternative uses, making their conservation a matter of social, political, or economic concern. Success in planning for population viability will be more likely when these matters are taken into account. Once a range of acceptable options emerges, interest groups, management agencies, and persons with expertise in the issues can work together to find acceptable solutions to conflicts.

Develop models of species/environmental relationships. Assess the species' life history and ecological characteristics, its habitat needs, its existing and potential distribution, and its abundance. This basic information allows one to estimate trends or develop models for assessing population response to changes in the environment. No set of models, however, will be able to predict adequately and accurately the distribution and abundance of a wild population under all circumstances.

Integrate with overall planning procedures. Relevant information, models, and estimates should be brought together with other information and planning models. Habitat variables that appear to be important to target species may be defined differently in overall planning models, and there may be a need to develop criteria for consistency across land unit boundaries.

Develop a range of management options. A spectrum of management strategies provides for population viability at acceptable risk levels. The options should reflect a full range of possibilities for the species, from minimal protection and habitat enhancement to a maximum.

Evaluate viability and possible strategies. This entails estimating the likelihood of continued existence for the species in the planning area if the favored strategies were to be implemented. A coarse scale of protection levels can be used initially to screen species for more detailed analysis. The scale must reflect expected persistence for specified time periods. Many factors can be involved and combined into an ordinal scale representing probabilities of existence. A simple analysis would be an estimation of the likelihood of existence (perhaps on a five-point scale from very high to very low) assuming no change in available habitat, several different levels of human activity, and the likelihood of catastrophes such as storms and earthquakes. Very detailed study may allow greater precision and quantitative estimates of the probability of persistence over different periods of time.

Assess the best strategies. Management costs, other resource values, and legal requirements need to be evaluated for various interest groups. At this stage there should be estimates of relative costs of providing specified levels of protection. Other planning assumptions and objectives should be considered.

Choose appropriate levels. Choose levels to be set to maintain a viable population within acceptable limits, and choose the appropriate management direction. Specific objectives and actions may include monitoring, research, meeting the needs and concerns of multiple landowners, catering for recreational and other interest groups, and allowing harvesting of natural resources.

These steps and the realms in which they take place are indicated in Figure 4.3.

Most resource managers use some of the elements of viability analysis in their everyday work, although they may not recognize it as such. Nonetheless, few formal viability analyses have been carried out in resource management, especially for threatened plants. The most complete analyses have probably been those conducted for animals—for example, grizzly bears in North America. These have led to organized efforts to conserve the animal throughout its range. Viability analysis has been tested chiefly with large mammals probably because it is easier to determine demographic variables for large mammals than it is for plants and invertebrates. Nevertheless, the general principles of viability analysis can be adopted even when precise estimates of persistence time are not possible.

An endangered species is by definition at risk of extinction, and the dominant objective in the recovery process is to reduce that risk of extinction to an ac-

ceptable level. The concept of "risk" is used to define the targets for recovery, major risks to be evaluated being extinction, loss of reproductive capacity, and loss of genetic diversity. In the last several years, computer systems have been developing for analysis of the many factors that interplay to put a species at risk, and to predict future trends (Bierzychudek 1982; Menges 1990; Lacy 1992).

CASE STUDY: POPULATION VIABILITY ANALYSIS
USING VORTEX

The VORTEX computer simulation model is a Monte Carlo simulation of the effects of deterministic forces as well as demographic, environmental, and genetic stochastic events on populations. VORTEX models population dynamics as discrete, sequential events (e.g., births, mortality, catastrophes, carrying capacity truncation) that occur according to defined probabilities. The probabilities of events are modeled as constants or as random variables that follow specified distributions.

VORTEX simulated a population by stepping through a series of events that describe the typical life cycle of a sexually reproducing organism. Life events are iterated on an an-

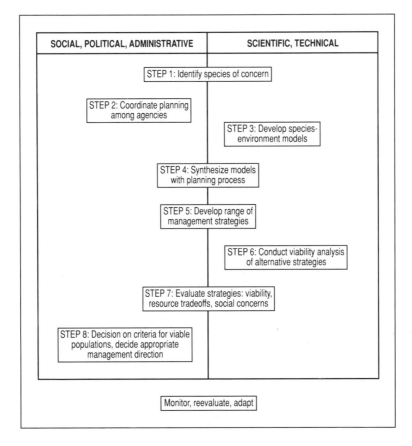

Figure 4.3. The viable population planning process. (Reproduced by permission from Marcot and Murphy, in press)

nual cycle. A pseudo-random number generator is used to determine occurrence of probabilistic events. Catastrophes are modeled as random events that occur with specified frequencies, the chances of survival and reproduction for the simulated year following each catastrophe being multiplied by a severity factor that is determined by the user.

VORTEX was originally written to model mammalian and avian populations but has now been used for a wide range of organisms including plants. It has been widely used by captive breeding programs and for determining the parameters of species recovery programs.

Source: Lacy 1992.

Maintaining Essential Habitat

Habitat loss, whether by destruction, fragmentation, or slow degradation, is a primary cause of population loss. It is often an obvious factor in depletion and may be one of the easiest to correct.

Essential habitat is determined by the interaction of biotic and abiotic factors external to the population. Essential habitat can vary through the life of a species, and the precise requirements of seedlings are unlikely to be the same as those of mature plants. The term *critical habitat* is sometimes used, but it also has a specific legal meaning, for instance, under the U.S. Endangered Species Act (1973) as,

> specific areas within the geographic area occupied by the species . . . that are . . . essential to the conservation of the species and which may require special management considerations or protection; and specific areas outside the geographic area occupied by the species . . . that . . . are essential to the conservation of the species (Bartel 1987).

An important aspect of habitats is that environmental gradients interact with general strategies of plants. Two types of gradient are especially significant. The first is stress—those things that restrict processes within the plant, including shortages of light, water, and minerals. The second is disturbance—those things that cause destruction of plant biomass, including browsing, predation, wind damage, fire, and disease. On the basis of this classification, three kinds of basic strategies can be described (Grime 1979):

1. Competitors: plants adapted to low-stress, low-disturbance habitats.

2. Ruderals: plants adapted to low stress and high disturbance.

3. Stress tolerators: plants adapted to intense stress but low disturbance.

The nature of the environment acting on a plant can differ during the lifetime of an individual. As plants germinate, grow, and mature, their size, height, crown size or spread, root volume, and geometry

change, thereby requiring a modified response to the environment. A single tree may "sample" in its lifetime many different "habitats" (Sarukhan et al. 1984).

Habitat can be looked at in terms of both quantity and quality. In "improving" habitat for target species, both aspects need to be considered. Quantity of critical habitat is not usually difficult to determine, but quality of habitat is rather more complex, partly because it tends to be a subjective concept. One should ask, Quality with respect to what? It is not sufficient to equate quality with diversity; a species-rich habitat may not suit target species. Assessment in quality also needs to take into account natural (and perhaps periodic) disturbance of habitat, for example periodic opening up of forest by winds and landslides, or natural burning of grassland and scrub.

The essential habitat of a species should be determined by field observation and not just by reference to herbarium labels and literature, or by guesswork. It should also be determined for all parts of the species' life cycle. Other species providing cover and moisture retention may be essential at seedling stages, but may inhibit maturation. On the other hand, seedlings may not germinate under mature plants until there is disturbance (e.g., by fire). One cannot assume that a target species occupies optimum sites at the present time. The plant may no longer occur in the most favorable sites. In fact, it may be growing on sites that are only marginally suitable but where threats have not led to its demise. Plants may not be able to recolonize suitable habitat because the distance between areas of suitable habitat and present populations may be greater than the dispersal range of the plant. Historic records can indicate optimum habitats occupied by species in the past. Retreat of species into suboptimal habitats is particularly likely where there is heavy predation or invasion by aggressive weeds with the capacity to displace species. In pastoral mountainous areas of New Zealand, for instance, European *Hieracium* has almost totally displaced indigenous tussock grasses on some optimum sites.

One way to test how well the essential habitat is

known is to identify areas that appear to be the right kind of habitat and then to survey these for the target species. Another test is to examine the population structure in a range of habitats: Are there flowering and fruiting adults, seeds, seedlings, and a new generation of plants developing from some of these? Natural population fluctuations and presence of a persistent but dormant seed bank need to be taken into account; decline in population size may not necessarily indicate that habitat is unsuitable, but instead may be part of natural periodic cycles of abundance. Study of related species or those with similar life histories may give a clue to the long-term nature of changes in abundance.

Preservation of the habitat required by the target species, in uncomplicated instances, may be achieved by fencing to exclude feral animals and stock, and by control of weeds and other obvious alien influences. Frequent surveys will be required—perhaps at 3- to 12-month intervals—at least for the first few years after protection starts. Habitat restoration or enhancement may have to be considered. Generally, the purpose of this is to reconstruct a presumed optimum habitat, by analogy with similar habitat types or by reference to historic accounts of sites where the target species occurred.

In extreme environments, recruitment tends to be episodic. Germination and growth to maturation correlate positively with optimum environmental conditions. In such places, it may well be that blaming reduction in numbers of species and individuals on such factors as grazing does not take account of natural processes (Williams 1981). Dormancy is a special condition of arrested growth which implies that plants temporarily opt out of the struggle for existence (Harper 1977).

Although many common species tend to be generalists and rare species are often specialists, some rare generalists exist. This can arise when a generalist species is unable to regenerate satisfactorily because of disease or intense predation, and is likely to become a more common phenomenon in the future, as fragmentation of formerly extensive vegetation types occurs. The outlook for long-term persistence of such species is dim unless they can rapidly adapt to exist as small and highly dispersed populations.

Even in regions presumed to be well explored, searches should be made of areas of habitat where the species is not known to occur at present but could be expected to grow. This becomes essential if widespread destruction of habitat is unavoidable. If resources allow, unsophisticated on-ground inspection can be supplemented by more sophisticated techniques, such as the use of a computer to process land inventories and geographical information systems to indicate likely sites. Such methods increase search cost and should be preceded by, and verified through, on-ground inspection and searching.

Field Study Techniques

Inventory, survey, and monitoring represent different levels of information gathering and use. An inventory is a geographically based assessment of a species, which often is based on literature searches and databases. Inventory leads to field survey, which determines the habitat requirements and biological relationships of the plant, population sizes and numbers, and reproductive success. Inventory and survey are usually species-based and can be followed up by monitoring—either demographic or ecophysiological studies, which concentrate on particular populations and individuals.

Levels of information gathering progress from less to more sophisticated:

1. Compilation of a list of species that may be under threat.

2. Verification of this list and assessment of various degrees of threat so that priorities can be established.

3. Establishment of a database showing locations of rare taxa from herbarium surveys, published literature, and field surveys.

4. Field verification of sites to determine current status of plants at these, and exploration to find new sites.

5. Development of a database of survey results containing a permanent record of species at the population level; this will include location, biological, and ecological information, and management and research approaches.

6. Development of a database incorporating results of monitoring—establishment of permanent plots and photo points, and collection of demographic and ecophysiological information—from selected populations.

Surveys are more time-consuming than inventories, but they provide more information at a greater level of accuracy on such factors as population structure, pollination and dispersal systems, and reproductive success. Demographic and ecophysiological studies, particularly full-scale monitoring programs, usually involve considerable time and money as they include search, data collection and marking or mapping for each plant. Many visits to a site may be needed to follow seedlings and reproduction, especially if the species has a dormant phase. Care has to be taken to ensure that sampling methods and data analysis are both practicable and statistically defensible (Palmer 1987).

Inventories can be as expensive and time-consuming as we want to make them. Even rapid inventory can give an indication of whether or not a species is threatened, but it is necessary to set priorities for inventory efforts. To make the best use of resources it is sensible to give priority to those species or communities for which information is most urgently need to promote their persistence and management. Effort should be made to find out what has already been done. Literature searches and consultation with colleagues and research and management agencies may identify past projects and techniques appropriate to situations being investigated.

Inventory will lead to selection of species for surveys, which in turn may expand into monitoring programs for selected populations. Critically threatened species should be surveyed throughout their range, and for most threatened species representative populations should be monitored on at least an annual basis if possible. Whatever techniques are adopted, the aim must be to identify critical stages in the life cycle and to predict and explain changes in the population resulting from particular types of management. Experimental manipulation of parts of a population, or of replicate populations (where population sizes allow), is one means of testing management treatments when the site or a life stage of a target species is threatened.

Results of inventory, survey, and monitoring should be readily accessible, either as reports or publications. The techniques used are likely to be of interest to those working on the conservation of similar species or sites (Palmer 1987). This does not mean that everyone has to know the precise location of study sites. Sometimes it is useful to produce a general public document in which sensitive details are omitted. More detailed information can be made available for bona fide researchers and conservation managers.

Cost is an important consideration. Therefore, more sophisticated and detailed levels of information gathering should arise from the results of less sophisticated information gathering rather than the reverse.

If survey suggests a decline in the number or health of plants or habitat, then monitoring should be considered, preferably extending over several growing seasons. Identification of problem stages in the life cycle of a species should be made a high priority effort so that monitoring and subsequent management can concentrate on this. Experiments might be designed to test ways to mitigate the problems, and these can be translated into management, which in turn is tested by further field experiments. Hence, different approaches can be flexibly alternated through time as necessary.

Planning for monitoring assumes that target populations and individuals will be available for study into the future. For endangered species there is rarely a guarantee that populations will persist for the desired length of time. A simple rule is: do not count on being able to continue the work over the long-term, even though long-term studies are the most badly needed (Ehrlich and Murphy 1987). In the short term one should concentrate on site protection and population stabilization; in the long term one should aim for self-sustained persistence.

CASE STUDY: INVENTORY, SURVEY, AND MONITORING IN GREAT SMOKY MOUNTAINS NATIONAL PARK, USA

Great Smoky Mountains National Park, in Tennessee and North Carolina, comprises over 209,000 hectares. The park is rich in endemics and in northern plants at their southern range limit, and about 10 percent of its native vascular plants are on state or national lists of rare species. The flora includes one strict endemic and four species nearly restricted to the park.

Most known data on rare species populations came from herbarium labels. Several species lists for the park, unsubstantiated by voucher collections, survive from the 1930s. Typically, such lists do not contain information on population size, and location data is often vague. Most collections can only be mapped within 100 to 10,000 meters. During the 1930s, 1500 vegetation plots each of 0.08 hectare were established. These plots were not permanently marked, and data from individual plots were never analyzed, except as they contributed to a subjective forest typing and a vegetation map. A project was initiated to analyze these data. In addition, some 300 permanent vegetation plots (50 × 20 meters, 0.1 hectare) were established; these will contribute (combined with aerial photography) to a new vegetation map for the park, but they have also been used to investigate problems of immediate concern to park managers.

Herbarium labels and field sighting forms have been designed to maximize the amount of information recorded. Photocopied sections of topographic maps, marked in the field, increase the precision of location data. Geographic position can usually be recorded within a range of 10–100 meters, and elevation within 10 meters. Labels and sighting forms also require other information on location, habitat, vegetation, and population size, details that are obvious in the field and soon lost if not recorded.

Rare plant monitoring includes three levels of permanent records: (1) populations mapped on topographic sheets and population size assessed, (2) permanent plots of 0.1 hectare for characterizing and monitoring habitats, and (3) individuals within populations marked from permanent reference points and photo points. Except for dramatic impacts, resampling at 5- to 10-year intervals is planned for rare populations and 10- to 20-year intervals for vegetation plots. Priorities for mapping of populations are established through a scale of seven weighted factors: 1–listed status; 2–geographic affinity; 3–significance of park populations to distribution as a whole; 4–number of locations; 5–population size; 6–population status; and 7–threats.

Source: White and Bratton 1981.

Survey

Field-based surveys are a logical outcome of inventory, for without surveys inventories rapidly become outdated. Surveys are particularly needed when plants grow in naturally vulnerable habitats or close to the location of proposed development projects. Sometimes survey may be required, not because of particular interest in plant species under threat but because their protection is related to other values such as wildlife protection or water quality (Nelson 1987).

Surveys cannot be done from a desk. They involve field searches, based on known or suspected ecological relations. Simple surveys may involve merely confirming the identity of a species in the field, its location, and simple descriptive statements about habitat and persistence. More sophisticated surveys use sampling methods that can be repeated to estimate community or population parameters. Many factors can be studied and measured: populations can be mapped, threats assessed, essential or critical habitat identified, land tenure investigated, plant numbers counted, and individuals scored for such factors as growth rate, size, flowering and fruiting, reproductive success, stress and competition tolerance (Palmer 1987; B. M. Pavlik, in press).

Good surveys of rare plants require preparation and forethought; a great deal of money can be wasted on poorly designed survey programs. Consideration needs to be given to the following questions (Austin 1987; Nelson 1987; Palmer 1987):

When is survey appropriate? Usually the answer is self-evident; certainly surveys are important for conservation management. Surveys are needed when information is insufficient to adequately manage a species or when a development project that may affect rare or vulnerable species is in the early stages of planning. Protection and mitigation requires factual information and not surmise. Seasonal growth patterns, land planning proceedings, and access difficulties (including the operations of adjacent landowners) may demand very precise timing of fieldwork. Rarely is it possible to survey vegetation or particular species adequately during a single visit. A calendar of flowering and fruiting times can be useful for establishing the best times to visit wild plant populations. Critical pathway planning may be required to determine timing of various aspects of the survey.

What qualifications do investigators require? Few development agencies employ full-time botanists; it is common practice to contract survey work to consultants. Skills for threatened plant survey work are not necessarily correlated with academic and professional qualifications. Qualifications that should be sought are experience as a botanical field investigator, including sampling design and methods; knowledge of the principles of taxonomy and ecology; familiarity with plants of the region; familiarity with laws, policies, and planning procedures of the region; demonstrated ability to communicate well at the level and in the manner required; and the physical capacity and enthusiasm to match the job.

What is already known? It may be that there is already a considerable amount of existing information that can be used. Field studies may have been carried out but never published. Studies of other aspects of the area may have considerable bearing on plant conservation. Agencies known to have worked in the area should be consulted even if they are not directly concerned with plant science.

What are survey requirements and objectives? A survey proposal should clearly indicate what will be achieved, a time frame for the exercise (or at least target dates for segments of it), and resource requirements. The latter may include topographic maps of the area, maps showing development proposals if they exist, records of land tenure and ownership, aerial photographs, species lists, vegetation surveys and maps, reports and notes on past botanical work in the area. If the survey requires sophisticated analysis or use of an electronic database, there may have to be computer access. Funding must be adequate to cover invisible costs such as staff salaries and wages, and report production. It is particularly important to decide what level of survey is required to answer the questions being asked. Surveys should provide the basis for attempting to answer a number of questions (Usher 1973).

- Why is the species so rare today? What is known of its history, and what trends have in species' abundance have occurred during the last 200–300 years?
- What are the environmental conditions required for optimal growth of the species? Are these conditions available at the present time? Can management establish optimal or suboptimal conditions?
- How does the species disperse? Does this species spread vegetatively, or does it set fertile seed? What are the characteristics of pollination—is it self-sterile or is it readily self-pollinated? What conditions are required for the germination of seed?

What area is required for the survey? The study area must reflect the goals of the survey. It may require expansion during the course of the project, especially if new sites are found for the target species outside the original study site. The known sites may represent only the tip of a "range extension iceberg." Often surveys are carried out in areas where little botanical investigation has occurred in the past, and field teams will not be sure what species and plant communities will be encountered. Where survey is carried out on a proposed development site it is important to survey areas likely to be affected by secondary aspects of the proposal. As an example, a hydroelectric dam affects not only the area flooded but sites required for construction of townships, campgrounds, and new hiking trails and highways. Industrial complexes may have distinct boundaries to the disturbance from construction activities, yet produce pollution that affects sites many kilometers from the construction site.

What are the most consistent and reliable methods of survey? It is worth taking the time to define objectives of the survey, and to obtain expert advice to determine the most appropriate sampling procedure. The initial number, size, and shape of plots, transects, or photopoints should be selected before getting into the field; but these also should be reviewed as the project progresses. It is very useful to ask experts in field research design and data analysis to review objectives, methods, and results of preliminary sampling, so that the techniques used are appropriate and do not give spurious results (see also Palmer 1987; Green 1979).

There is a paucity of statistically defensible survey methods for dealing with plants that occur in very low densities or populations showing high levels of contagion—both of which are characteristic of many threatened plants. Sampling and experimental design in relation to analysis of results is important and should be the result of discussion with experts in population analysis. When a survey (or monitoring exercise) is being designed, consideration should be given to the following techniques (Palmer 1987):

- Randomized sampling within each stratum in the habitat.
- Replicate experimental units in studies that compare or test management procedures.
- A design that minimizes statistical problems when the sampling is not totally randomized.
- Methods that will not give a false sense of accuracy.

What are the uses for databases? Databases are essential to research and management but there has been too great a tendency for people to assume that every project needs a computerized database, and that such a database will automatically get one out of trouble and provide all the answers. The world is full of poorly designed and incomplete databases.

There is probably no general rule of thumb to determine how often rare plant survey sites should be visited. To set a precise schedule for sampling and checking requires precise information. If flowering or fruiting (or similar seasonal features) are being measured, sites should be visited at least annually at times when these aspects can be assessed. If plants are short-lived, threats are immediate, or a site is vulnerable to catastrophic disturbance, more frequent visits are required. For instance, populations of threatened annuals should be visited several times from the commencement of germination to seed maturation. Other factors such as accessibility of a site also play a part. For extremely inaccessible sites, survey may be possible only when chance visits are made. The following list summarizes some criteria for determining both frequency and priority of survey (Given and Williams 1984, modified):

Species/habitat character	Frequency of survey	
	More often	Less often
Distribution	Few	Widespread
Population size	Small	Large
Habitat type	Successional	Climax
Life form, species	r- (annual, etc.)	K- (long-lived perennial, etc.)
Population structure	Imbalanced	Balanced (good class spread)

Species/habitat character	Frequency of survey	
	More often	Less often
Reproduction	Poor Sexual or vegetative (not both)	Good Sexual and vegetative
Breeding system	Self-incompatible Dioecious	Self-compatible Monoecious
Pollinating vector	Specialized	Unspecialized
Threats	Immediate Greater	Potential Lesser
Perturbation periodicity	Shorter	Longer
Habitat/sites protected	None or minimal	Numerous sites protected
Cultivation	Not or little	Widespread
Management	No deliberate program	Active program in operation
Taxonomic distinctiveness	Greater (endemic genus, etc.)	Less (subspecies variety, etc.)

It is important to set priorities for survey when one is faced with many tens or hundreds of species and hundreds or even thousands of populations at risk. Preliminary evaluation using broad-based questions will lead to the identification of problems deserving more detailed analysis. This is similar to the approach of a general practitioner who, on detecting a problem, may then refer the patient to an appropriate specialist for more detailed examination. If the patient is short-sighted, he or she is referred to an optometrist but is unlikely to need the attention of an ear, nose, and throat specialist or a urologist. Similarly, if broad-based questions and preliminary survey identify lack of seedling establishment as a likely reason for population decline, then specialist monitoring can concentrate on this aspect of the plant's biology. Expensive or time-consuming survey techniques should be justified by preliminary evaluation: there must be very good reason to apply them. It is not sufficient to use a technique because it looks good or gives the appearance of high technology.

An efficient survey should aim to meet the following criteria (Given 1984):

It must be easy to use. The survey may be done by people with limited biological training; questions, therefore, need to be direct and easily understood.

It must be selective. Survey should concentrate on basic questions such as, Is the species present? Is it reproducing at a rate sufficient to maintain numbers? Is the present population size dangerously low? Is the habitat suitable for the species? Is the habitat changing? What are the existing or potential threats?

It must be regular. A useful rule of thumb might be to attempt to monitor all significant sites for critically endangered or vulnerable species annually. If this is not possible for species in remote sites, a selected group of sites should be monitored to indicate trends for the species.

It must result in action. Survey is useless if observations are filed away and forgotten. If management is satisfactory, then survey may show that the status quo should be maintained. On the other hand, if there is deterioration, then decisive action is needed. This means rapid analysis of data for appropriate management authorities and research agencies who can carry out in-depth monitoring and research.

It must be cooperative. An effective survey system will require the cooperation of agencies involved in field observations, management, and research. Information needs to be disseminated to those who can make best use of it to ensure survival of the species. Ultimately, one agency should take responsibility for a monitoring system and ensure that it meets the needs of those using it.

A flow-chart to guide survey and monitoring activity is presented in Figure 4.4.

Rare plants often make up only a small percentage of the total plant cover of a site. For this reason it can be useful to conduct a complete floristic survey first, especially if an area is not well known botanically. The investigator will have to identify every plant found, which sometimes results in unexpected discoveries. Initially, floristic surveys are slow because many new species are encountered, but they speed up as they proceed. The time required for floristic surveys is greater than that required for species-targeted surveys, but it remains the best method of ensuring that all rare plants are identified during a field survey (Nelson 1987).

As mentioned earlier, many survey techniques are ill-suited to estimating numbers of plants occurring in low densities, especially species that tend to have a high level of contagion (highly "clumped" distribution) and very significant departure from a random Poisson distribution (see Figure 4.5). Even a search system as simple as random wandering and scoring plants as they are encountered can be useful and may

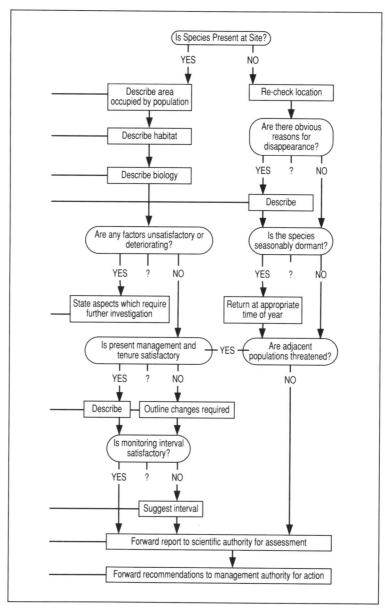

Figure 4.4. A survey and monitoring flow chart designed for use by nonexperts (D. R. Given).

be one of the few practical techniques available at present. One problem with random meanders is that some areas may be covered more than once and others not at all. In addition, there are no reliable statistical procedures that can be applied to the results. To cover all sites of interest, the study area can be partitioned so that whether random or systematic sampling is employed, the survey includes sites representative of all aspects of interest. Where precise estimation of population numbers is difficult, especially if distribution is highly contagious, it is often possible to randomly sample for density and map species in terms of density classes (DaVilla et al. 1987).

Probably more important than absolute numbers in most instances is reproductive success and the proportion of plants in various age classes (e.g., seedlings, juveniles, flowering and fruiting adults, and senescent plants). Allocation of individuals to age classes and scoring for flowering and seeding will quickly give an indication of the demographic characteristics, reproductive state, and persistence of the population and help in the design of more sophisticated monitoring studies.

Two specific survey techniques that work well with species that occur at low densities and with clumped distributions are briefly discussed below.

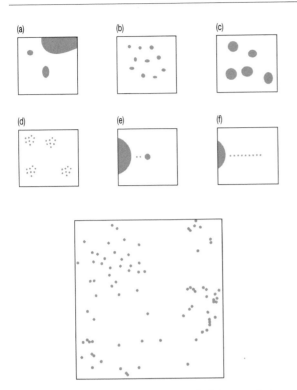

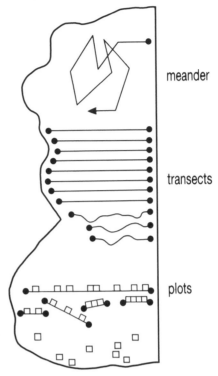

Figure 4.5. Patterns of distribution of individuals in a population: (a–f) alternative patches of two-dimensional spatial patchiness; below, patches of higher density (contagious) imposed on a general distribution of lower density, a type of distribution commonly encountered in wild populations. (Adapted by permission from Grieg-Smith 1983)

Figure 4.6. Plots, belt transects, and timed meanders are all techniques that have been used in threatened plant surveys. (Reproduced by permission from Nelson 1986)

Timed meander search procedures
for estimating population size

There has long been a need for a semiquantitative procedure that focuses on the discovery of rare, threatened, and endangered vascular plant species that often occur in very low densities, as scattered individuals, or as extremely small populations. Timed meander searches (e.g., Goff et al. 1982) are particularly suited to situations where a few target species are present at extremely low densities, or where there is extreme aggregation of plants within the study area. In such situations, transects and random plots may entirely miss the target species. For such cases, several discrete, short, random walks covering as much ground as possible are probably better than a single, longer walk; the former generally give a better indication of minor variations within different parts of the site (Figure 4.6).

Timed meander searches usually begin with the delineation of *field units*—areas of reasonably homogeneous vegetation within the search area. These units should be based on standard cover or vegetation classification as far as possible, but may also be based on

preliminary estimates of density of target species (perhaps based on a scoring system from 0 = lowest density to 5 = highest density).

Timed meander searches can be done within each field unit. A convenient point of entry is chosen and the search initiation time is recorded. Target species are recorded on a field data form as they are encountered; these include all species seen if a full vegetation analysis is being done, or it may be a single species. The transect meanders in an attempt to cover all habitat variation within the field unit. It may double back over previously covered ground, but if target plants are present in very low numbers (e.g., density is less than one percent of total cover) individuals should be recorded only once.

If all species at the site are being recorded, the search can be continued until, in the judgment of the observer, no new species are likely to be seen. If only one or a few target species are being sought, the search can last a specified time (e.g., 5 or 10 minutes), depending on the area being covered. Interruptions are considered "time out" from the process.

Maintaining equal intensity of search effort throughout the total sampling period allows comparison between different searches or even different localities. When all species are scored, a species/area curve and estimates of frequency distributions may be made.

DESCRIPTION OF VEGETATION
USING VISUAL RANKING OF SPECIES

One product of a rare plant survey should be a description of the vegetation in which a plant population occurs. Sometimes, large areas of vegetation must be covered in a limited amount of time; this can be a particular problem in areas with high species diversity. Other difficulties include the paradox of needing to describe vegetation accurately before one knows which features are most important, and the need to keep sampling broadly based yet allow for later quantification once trends are detected.

One useful technique involves listing species in order of abundance at a number of sample points within the area (Scott 1989). The sample points may be defined quadrats or plots. The means of determining abundance can vary: density of each species, percentage ground cover, or even visual estimate of aboveground dry matter. The method assumes that whatever criterion is used, visual ranking will give the same rank order as if quantitative methods were used. At least five species are ranked at each sampling point, but the number can vary. Species are ranked independently at each sampling point. The number of species ranked is generally less than the total number of species present; some species may not be ranked at every sample point.

Before the field rank data are analyzed, ranks are given to species present but not abundant; if five ranks are recognized, all other unranked species are transformed into rank 6, and those species absent are given rank 7. The data are then subjected to statistical analysis to derive summary parameters, associations between species, and significant changes of ranking. Vegetation types can be defined by rank order of constituent species. Repeated measurements allow application of the transition matrix approach to the study of vegetation trends.

The approach corresponds closely with the way people describe vegetation in conversation, by listing species in order of importance. It relies on comparison between species rather than absolute levels of species abundance. It is particularly useful for nonexpert observers, because it is simple and easily taught, and for assessing vegetation quickly over large areas; yet it is amenable to quite sophisticated statistical treatment. This makes it useful to conservation biologists and managers dealing with many, sometimes large, areas with relatively limited resources.

Monitoring

Monitoring is a quantitative assessment of the status of a population and its component individuals over time. It is commonly accomplished by marking individual plants at representative sites, and repeatedly measuring characteristics of their performance. Monitoring identifies the timing and causes of poor performance and provides specific management recommendations.

Too often, monitoring (along with survey) is regarded as third-rate science. Yet it is vital to the success of conservation of biodiversity. Plant populations are not static but vary over time. They vary in their response to competition and stress. Interactions with other species change through time and space. Monitoring allows changes to be assessed and, where necessary, enhanced or neutralized. Active management for critically threatened species must be based on good information (from survey and monitoring); likewise, its success must be determined by monitoring the results.

The design, execution, and interpretation of a monitoring program can be an awesome task, especially when resources are severely limited. Most managers of protected areas have at least a vague awareness that knowledge of life history traits, plant numbers, and genetic variability is important to plant conservation efforts. They are not always aware, however, that precise information may be necessary for effective management of species that are declining. Quite incorrect conclusions may be drawn from casual, untested observations, and a range of variables may have to be rigorously sampled to identify critical factors. As an example, study of the geysers' panicum (*Dichanthelium lanuginosum* var. *thermale*) on geothermal sites in California showed that decline in some years was not related to geothermal activity and development as some had presumed, but to levels of rainfall (Leitner and de Becker 1987).

Monitoring can be expensive and usually involves long-term commitments (at least in the order of several years). For critically threatened species there may be few plants available for study. The cost of failure can be high in terms of wasted resources and time lost. Poor design may put even more pressure on a species nearing extinction (Palmer 1987; B. M. Pavlik, in press). The two most useful monitoring approaches are essentially the same approaches applied to plant population biology as a whole. These are demographic monitoring and ecophysiological monitoring, which concentrate on genetics and resource allocation (Davy and Jefferies 1981). A large number of techniques that examine demographic, genetic, and physiological characteristics of populations are available for adaptation to monitoring programs (e.g., Wells 1967, 1981; Pavlik 1987; Pavlik and Barbour 1988; Menges 1990, 1991, 1992).

Demographic monitoring, based on numbers of individuals (or their parts), is obviously relevant to conservation of rare species. Of primary importance to a demographic monitoring program are relatively intensive studies that document population trends (stability, growth, or decline) at a specific site. Practically speaking, "intensive" may mean two to three years of following marked plants in permanent plots. These studies may have to be extended for longer to obtain meaningful data (B. M. Pavlik, pers. com.). Ideally, demographic monitoring should be a routine part of the management program for endangered plants; in practice, this is rarely achieved. If the plants being studied are extremely rare or comprise small, unstable populations, then monitoring of survivorship and propagule production is essential as a first step. Changes, for instance in seed output, will be detected by monitoring and if a variety of treatments are applied, will indicate directions for management.

The goal of demographic monitoring usually is to monitor individual plants. Frequent measuring or mapping of plants (perhaps every two to three weeks) may be necessary to achieve this resolution, so it is not surprising that these studies are rarely sustained for more than a few seasons. The physiological status and reproductive performance of each established individual becomes the primary focus of the recovery effort. Quantitative measures should be used to indicate the kinds of small-scale manipulations that would relieve unnatural stresses. If the measurements are made on manipulated plants, the effectiveness of manipulation can be evaluated; the data also may suggest other manipulations that would be appropriate. Some techniques, such as ecophysiological measurements based upon the carbon balance, can sometimes give immediate information on the effects of small-scale, experimental treatments without sacrificing individual plants. Time is an important element: for precarious populations there may be no second chance for monitoring.

Population structure needs to be considered in some instances, especially where a population is diffusely distributed over a large area in varying densities. An apparently simple population can consist of a number of smaller, genetically distinct populations (the *metapopulation* concept). This can sometimes be detected by study of pollination patterns and determination of effective neighborhood distances, both of which indicate the extent of genetic interchange between patches of individuals. At other times more sophisticated techniques such as isozyme or seed protein analysis may be necessary. Populations may be divided into subpopulations with respect to almost any aspect of their population biology, chemistry, physiology, and morphology (Davy and Jefferies 1981).

Information obtained through a monitoring program should indicate whether changes are cyclic or unidirectional. If changes are substantially cyclic, the prescription for the conservation of the rare species may be as simple as preserving a suitable area and ensuring that species and habitats survive through unfavorable phases of the cycle. Conversely, if long-term, unidirectional changes are taking place, such a strategy alone could be disastrous.

The following are general guidelines for monitoring programs (based on Davy and Jefferies 1981; Wells 1981; Palmer 1987):

- It is essential to know at the start of a monitoring program what kind of results are being sought and what the results will mean.

- Because conservation of populations requires an understanding of the dynamic aspects of the population, monitoring should examine recruitment (births), mortality (deaths), survivorship, longevity, and turnover of the population.

- It is often necessary to monitor populations several times during a twelve-month cycle. If monitoring takes place at the same time each year, only one stage in the life cycle (in annuals) or one phenological stage (in perennials) may be considered.

- Careful monitoring of populations on a regular, often annual basis, using a technique that enables the same individuals to be recorded and examined each year, will provide basic facts about the population, from which predictions can be made about future structure.

- Monitoring needs to give attention to flowering and fruiting, and to reproduction of both above- and below-ground parts of plants. Resulting information should be integrated with environmental factors and various management regimes.

- Monitoring must taken into consideration that many plants have particular biotic relationships with other organisms. For example, mycorrhizal associates of plants such as orchids and saprophytes are important but are often imperfectly understood. Special techniques must be developed before people can adequately assess the importance of such relationships.

- Implicit in intensive ecophysiological monitoring is the idea of examining responses to environmental disturbance. Disturbance may correspond with a potential management procedure such as grazing, nutrient addition, irrigation, drainage, or burning (although this should not be assumed).

- Variables such as plant size and seedling data should be examined in monitoring studies. Inferences can be based on carefully selected, random subsamples reinforced by use of controls. This may be difficult if the population is small. Under field conditions, it is not always possible to randomize or to have independent replication.

- A critical review process should assess goals, sampling methods, and experimental design of proposed projects.

If a population continues to decline despite intensive monitoring and small-scale manipulation, more drastic steps including emergency greenhouse propagation may be necessary. Even if the population becomes stable and grows, demographic monitoring should be continued, although at a less intensive level. Monitoring is important both before and after legal protection of a site. Before protection, it gives a basis for predictions and allows critical situations to be identified. After legal protection, monitoring indicates the effectiveness of protected areas in preserving and enhancing the ecosystems and species they contain. It is important not to ignore underground parts of plants, and interactions between the root systems of different plants. Although usually hidden from view, underground organs are a vital component of plant biology and ecology (St. John 1987; Stanton 1988).

Case Study: Techniques for Recording Change When Monitoring Desert Plants

Most techniques used in recording changes in populations of desert plants are variants of study of individual plants over time in permanent quadrats, fixed-point landscape photography, or surveys in which the age structure or population changes of species are estimated.

Mapping individual plants in permanent quadrats is tedious and time-consuming fieldwork, but it is the method behind most of the published studies. There are several constraints to photography: the difficulty of obtaining resolution sufficient to permit species identification, an inability to detect and identify seedlings, and the fact that small plants often are obscured by shrubs or tall grasses. Large-scale aerial photography can be used in conjunction with the charting of transects or with photo points in open desert vegetation. Fixed-point photography is usually an effective adjunct to plot studies. Even without plots, sets of photographs can be used to indicate the dynamic nature of vegetational change over time. Survey techniques rely on access to reliable age class information and the ability to determine the age of individual plants. Demographic studies are not easy to perform and they have to be maintained for many years. In Australia, population data for a number of important perennial shrubs have not yet been published because numbers on deaths and recruitment have not been obtained. Further, instead of placing exclosures and associated permanent quadrats on slightly or moderately degraded sites where some recovery of vegetation is possible, many investigators concentrated on grossly degraded and eroded sites.

In arid lands of Australia and the United States, the treatments of most interest are grazing and release from grazing for a specified number of years, experiments assessing the effect of drought, and burning and protection from burning for specified periods of time. One useful approach has been to assess vegetation response to grazing pressure within a single large paddock, taking advantage of the usual one watering point and the decreasing intensity of grazing with distance from it. Repeated sampling can give a time-specific life table, but the definition of grazing pressure presents difficulties.

Source: Williams 1981.

Population Management in the "Real" World

Are the wide range of approaches to plant population management and the many suggestions for solving the problems of endangered species practicable, given the number of regions lacking resources, the number of species in need of management, and the rapid depletion rates? Is viability analysis and detailed monitoring warranted when tens or perhaps hundreds of species are disappearing each year from some parts of the world?

Such questions should be encouraged; they raise important issues. There are reasons for urgency: there are grave problems for many plant species. Managers are frustrated trying to do too much with too few resources in too short a time. But "the only certain principle in conservation genetics is to use every available stratagem to protect variation" (Berry 1983). Population numbers are important even if they can be very hard to determine. Precise figures may not be important as long as current status and trends can be measured. Area and condition of available habitat is critical to the persistence of a species, so it is very practical to ask whether the condition, area, and configuration of available habitat is satisfactory, and whether the resources to maintain it are available.

The rarity of species may, therefore, be some function of the size and number of habitable sites, the carrying capacity of those sites, the time for which the sites remain habitable, and the probability of such sites being discovered by dispersed propagules such as seeds. This leads to a range of possibilities for decreasing the rarity of species.

The worst problems are certainly likely to come about through habitat destruction and loss; hence, a basic premise ought to be to maintain as much wild habitat as possible. Wild habitat ought not be confined to a scattering of small areas where populations are measured merely in terms of a few individuals or tens of individuals. Variability in individuals and populations must be maintained, both for the present well-being of plants and for their future maintenance and evolution.

Inventory, survey, and monitoring; assessment of population structure and genetic variability; maintenance and reconstruction of essential habitat; and control of predation must not be simply the prerogative of affluent temperate countries. Such approaches must be adopted for regions with highly distinctive floras that are at great risk, regardless of available indigenous resources. At the same time, there must be a focus on those ecosystems, habitats, and species that give the best return—for example, those whose monitoring and effective protection will in turn protect or aid in the management of many other species. This selective focus must not be based only on economic considerations—those species most likely to give an immediate dollar-based economic return—but the maintenance of the health and integrity of natural communities must be a goal as well.

It may be that, at least in the short term, the plants of some regions will receive little management beyond inventory, selective survey, and some habitat protection. This may be all that can be realistically hoped for, but it must be seen as no more than a holding operation. Conservation is not just for this year or even the next decade: it is concerned with maximizing survival rates for centuries.

CHAPTER 5

Plant Conservation in Protected Natural Areas

Preservation of plants in their natural habitat is often regarded as the mainstay of plant species conservation, but it involves more than the simple expedient of putting a fence around a few fragments of vegetation. Protected area systems have to consider a wide range of habitat types, areas, threats, social attitudes, and biogeographical variations (IUCN 1986a). Thus preservation requires a range of management options that can be tailored to the particular needs of species and ecosystems, as well as the requirements and aspirations of people living in or visiting the protected areas.

A species usually comprises far more than just one or several individuals. Most species are made up of breeding units that encompass inherent variation, which in itself is a response to, and reflection of, variations in the environment. Conservation requires preservation of species throughout their complete geographic and habitat range and a consideration of patterns of variation. Conservation of plants must also take animals into account. Plants and animals have not evolved independently but interact reciprocally with each other. Continued evolution will involve the interaction of factors both internal and external at a range of levels down to the individual and even the genome. Scholars of biogeography have raised many important questions about preservation in protected natural areas (e.g., Diamond 1975; Deshaye and Morrisset 1989). A few of these questions are listed below.

- Should all reserves be selected on the basis of strict biogeographic criteria?

- Are several small reserves better than one large one?

- Can protected areas be representative and, if so, representative of what?

- How is protection integrated with traditional use of plants and animals, and is tourism compatible with protection?

- How does one protect a mosaic of many habitat types?

- Should priority be given to protection of species richness, unique vegetation types, and high endemism?

- What approaches best protect genetic diversity within populations?

- If one protects ecosystems, are all species adequately protected along with them?

- Why not take rare species out of the wild and cultivate them in botanic gardens?

- Which is more important—the survival of all plant and animal species or people?

Most people accept the validity of these questions but justifiably argue for pragmatism. Social and economic issues are particularly sensitive ones, especially in regions of dense human habitation. Final boundary placement for reserves may have to be a compromise among financial and political factors, and existing patterns of land-ownership and use (Jensen 1987).

The purpose of a reserve is important. Many reserves have been designated with relatively little thought for their precise purpose. Is it to preserve a particular ecosystem, to maintain a successional stage, to allow an area to reach a climax, to conserve one or more target species, to preserve as many species as possible, or to maintain genetic diversity for economic reasons? Each of these purposes requires different management emphasis. Clearly, a great number of potential interrelated objectives exist for a reserve, and, in fact, there may be several conservation objectives for any particular protected area.

It is important to realize that preserving communities is not the same as preserving genes. Since communities are classified according to vegetation structure, and the dominant plant and animal species, it is quite possible to preserve a community type and still lose many species. It is also possible to preserve a species and lose genetically distinct populations. Although on-site conservation requires that biological diversity be considered as a whole, that is, in the form of intact communities, the type of conservation strategies employed and their outcome will depend on the particular focus. A protected area may focus on conserving some type of community—for example, the peat swamp forest or heath forest of Malaysia, terra firme forest in Amazonia, or *Scalesia* forest on the Galapagos Islands. Or the focus may be a particular tree species of one of those communities, such as *Gonostylus bancanus* found in the peat swamp forest or *Lippia* growing in *Scalesia* forest. A protected area also may be established to conserve genetically distinct populations of such species, rather than the whole range of variation.

Objectives interact and can be complementary. Even where conservation of unusual or threatened species may not be a primary reason for designating a particular protected area, noting the presence of such species in reserve proposals is important for several reasons (MacKinnon et al. 1986). First, it identifies areas that require urgent protection. All ecotypes deserve protection, but those whose conspicuous species are disappearing fast are obviously in need of urgent action. Second, focusing on key species gives a good indication of the effectiveness of management. If the most conspicuous rare species cannot survive, there may be something wrong with the design or management of the reserve. Third, preservation of species is something people can readily relate to and understand. Species have an appeal that wins sympathy, an important factor in raising public awareness and fund raising. Finally, species lists for proposed protected areas provide data to justify biogeographical selection of sites.

In India, the combined species and ecosystem approaches to protected areas selection have been used to advantage. Use of the tiger as the symbol of national heritage has resulted in 15 reserves totaling 24,712 square kilometers, of which 8608 are designated core areas (MacKinnon et al. 1986). The tiger has been deliberately conserved by setting aside areas of natural habitat; but many other species as well as large ecosystems are preserved along with the tiger.

It is particularly difficult to delineate objectives for a reserve without a clear idea of the length of time one wishes to conserve the target species for which that reserve was created. It is human nature to be concerned with short-term goals extending over only the immediate future, or at the most, a human lifetime. Yet design of a reserve and its management may well be dif-

ferent if the reserve is to provide a 75 percent chance that a target species will survive for 50 years, rather than a 75 percent chance of survival for 500 years. Very small populations may survive for a few generations, apparently with success, but long-term prospects for survival may be quite bleak without deliberate interventionist management. For critical species, many hundreds of years might be the most appropriate time scale for planning population persistence (Jensen 1987).

CASE STUDY: AN EXPANDED SET OF CONSERVATION OBJECTIVES FOR TROPICAL FOREST PROTECTED AREAS

Sample ecosystems: to maintain large areas as representative samples of each major biological region of the nation in its natural unaltered state to ensure the continuity of evolutionary processes, including animal migration and gene flow.

Ecological diversity: to maintain examples of the different characteristics of each type of natural community, landscape, and landform for protecting the representative as well as the unique diversity of the nation, particularly to ensure the role of natural diversity in the regulation of the environment.

Genetic diversity: to maintain all genetic material as elements of natural communities and avoid the loss of plant and animal species.

Education and research: to provide facilities and opportunities in natural areas for purposes of formal and informal education and research, and the study and monitoring of the environment.

Water and soil conservation: to maintain and manage watersheds to ensure an adequate quality and flow of fresh water; to avoid erosion and sedimentation, especially where these processes are directly related to downstream investments that depend on water for transportation, irrigation, agriculture, fisheries, and recreation; and for the protection of natural areas.

Wildlife management: to maintain and manage fishery and wildlife resources for their vital role in environmental regulation; for the production of protein; and as a base for industry, sport, and recreational activity.

Recreation and tourism: to provide opportunities for healthy and constructive outdoor recreation for local residents and foreign visitors and to serve as poles for tourism development based on the outstanding natural and cultural characteristics of the nation.

Timber: to manage and improve timber resources for their role in environmental regulation and to provide sustainable production of wood products for the construction of housing and other uses of high national priority.

Cultural heritage: to protect and make available all cultural, historic and archaeologic objects, structures, and sites for public visitation and research purposes as elements of the cultural heritage of the nation.

Scenic beauty: to protect and manage scenic resources to ensure the quality of the environment near towns and cities, highways and rivers, and surrounding recreation and tourism areas.

Options for the future: to maintain and manage vast areas of land under flexible land-use methods that conserve nat-ural processes and ensure open options for future changes in land use, incorporate new technologies, meet new human requirements, and initiate new conservation practices as research makes them available.

Integrated development: to focus and organize conservation activities to support the integrated development of rural lands, giving particular attention to the conservation and utilization of marginal areas and to the provision of stable rural employment opportunities.

Source: McNeely et al. 1987.

Considerations in Designating Protected Areas

Size and shape

Application of theory to real situations is always constrained by the practicalities of what actually can be achieved. The size and shape of a reserved area often will be determined pragmatically. Human activity is constantly cutting away at natural communities, reducing them to isolated remnants surrounded by very different urban or agricultural environments. Such remnants and fragments are becoming more like islands in a sea of highly modified vegetation, concrete, farmland, or bare ground. The principles of island biogeography reveal that this is not the ideal way to preserve natural diversity; yet there is so little suitable land left and many candidate reserves are far from ideal.

Nevertheless, some guidelines for the creation of protected areas can be summarized as follows:

- Protected areas generally should be large, and should include enough individuals of even the least abundant species to ensure the survival of those species. The type and number of species, their specific area requirements, and ecological processes necessary to maintain them all require consideration.

- The shape of these areas should be compact, and boundaries should be biologically meaningful (e.g., including whole watersheds, ecotones, and buffer zones).

- Areas should encompass year-round habitat requirements for animals associated with the target plants, especially essential pollinators and dispersers.

- As far as possible, samples of contiguous natural communities, or areas into which protected species may invade, should be included in a protected area.

- Total isolation should be avoided wherever possible; alternatively, attention should be given to habitat restoration between protected areas.

- To maintain biological diversity, a range of habitats, including successional stages, should be incorporated into a protected area network.

- Allowance should be made for manipulative management, especially where successional stages are involved or reserves are necessarily small.

Perhaps one of the most valuable contributions of island biogeographic theory is to indicate how difficult management problems may be. A reserve that conforms to the principles of island biogeography will generally be easier and less expensive to manage over the long term than one that is not (Roche and Dourojeanni 1984). Biogeographic principles will help predict the ultimate effects of habitat change and fragmentation, and the consequences for populations of plants, allowing at least an estimate of the future costs of management. Reserves, particularly small ones in urban or heavily cultivated areas, are islands in a very real sense: they have all the problems inherent to oceanic island management.

Protected reserves must take into account the patchy distribution of both species and the communities they form. Biological diversity is not evenly distributed but tends to be concentrated into areas of local endemism, the hot spots of biodiversity (Myers 1988). Areas of local endemism must be included in regional networks of protected areas even where they do not conform with the best principles of biogeographic selection of protected areas. A variety of techniques have been developed for delineation of protected area networks that achieve this. Such networks should aim to encompass both the species native to a region and the various combinations of these species that form the complex web of communities and ecosystems. It is the latter that creates the greatest problems, especially in regions that are not fully surveyed for vegetation types. A recent case study involved the Nullarbor region of Australia where four steps were combined to achieve both of the above goals (McKenzie et al. 1989):

1. Broad-scale ecological survey to acquire a database representing the geographic distributions of a wide variety of organisms.

2. Numerical classification (pattern analysis) to define species assemblages.

3. Modeling these assemblages to interpolate geographic patterns in their distribution.

4. Field sampling to test the interpolated models.

The biological reason for creating large reserves that will preserve populations above acceptable lower size limits hardly needs to be reiterated. Two other justifications for large reserves are becoming increasingly important in altered landscapes: the need for sanctuaries for wild relatives of crop plants and species that can be sustainably harvested in the wild, and the need for reserves of undisturbed ecosystems to serve as baseline areas for long-term study of ecological processes. In densely settled areas and disturbed habitats, large reserves are more and more difficult to acquire.

In recent years, a great deal of information on the evolutionary relationships of domesticated plants and their relatives has been generated. This information comes from a variety of different disciplines, including archaeology, anthropology, ethnology, plant geography, climatology, and cytogenetics. There still are, however, many gaps in our knowledge of the ancestry and relationships of some crop plants, and of their mode of domestication. Human activity has led to heavy depletion of crop relatives and the shrinkage of natural areas that constitute storehouses of useful genes and species. Representative gene pools of the major wild relatives or progenitors of cultivated plants must be established in regions rich in plant genetic resources.

Today's weeds may be tomorrow's economic plants, and today's wild relatives of cultivated plants may be tomorrow's most valuable sources of particular genes. The concept of biotype sanctuaries recognizes the need for continued evolution of wild plants within natural environments, and must always be considered a part of resource development (Maheshwari 1978).

The importance of large-scale landscape patterns has been widely recognized in planning for national parks. When properly managed, large wilderness areas provide perhaps the best opportunity to study the kinds of landscape changes that have occurred throughout geologic time—particularly processes directly affecting rare and threatened species, and the processes of speciation. Large reserves also permit a greater number of ecological processes to continue than are likely in smaller reserves.

Options for setting aside large areas of protected land are steadily becoming fewer, especially on highly fertile land that is also valued for agriculture or forestry. In such instances, the cost of outright land purchase or of compensation for land taken out of commercial production may well be greater than available conservation resources. Radical solutions may have to be sought, including reconstruction of habitat elsewhere, shifting of critically endangered species permanently to gardens and gene banks, or the creation of a highly managed mosaic of small protected areas.

Edge effects, buffer zones, and core areas

Just as an experimental plot must contain both a central measured plot and a surround, so a protected natural area should contain a central core area with stable habitat conditions and a buffer zone to absorb edge effects. A major set of effects is triggered by newly created edges and includes changes in temperature, relative humidity, and light; exposure to wind; elevated tree mortality; increased leaf fall; and the depression of populations of some animals.

As vegetation remnants become smaller, the area of both core and edge become smaller, but the ratio of edge to core increases. In very small, young, or disturbed remnants of vegetation, the entire "island" becomes an "edge." Provided the extent of edge effect is known for the particular vegetation type, it is possible to estimate the smallest viable area of habitat capable of supporting species typically found in undisturbed core sites. Care must be exercised in extrapolating such results. Although the phenomenon is universal, its qualitative expression will differ markedly from one region and vegetation type to another.

Edge effects are highly significant for species at risk (Janzen 1986c). Many inherently rare plants have very specific habitat requirements. Some will grow only in relatively undisturbed sites, although this must not be assumed. Many rare species occupy disturbed edge habitats and rely on a shifting mosaic of disturbance for their continued existence. In such instances, preservation and management of an edge has to be an integral part of the protected area concept.

A widely adopted technique for minimizing edge effects and maintaining core areas is to establish buffer zones around reserves. Buffer zones are "areas peripheral to national parks or reserves which have restrictions placed on their use to give an added layer of protection to the nature reserve itself and to compensate villagers for the loss of access to strict reserve areas" (MacKinnon et al. 1986). Various kinds of buffer zones for protected areas are illustrated in Figure 5.1.

Much more research is needed to determine appropriate widths of buffer zones in different vegeta-

tion types, particularly in the tropics. This is especially important in those countries where there is virtually no primary vegetation, and even secondary vegetation dominated by indigenous plants is becoming increasingly fragmented (Roche and Dourojeanni 1984).

Two main types of buffer zone serve rather different functions. *Extension buffering* extends habitats that are in the protected area into the buffer zone, allowing much larger breeding populations to survive than may be possible in the protected area alone. It is particularly useful for small populations of extremely

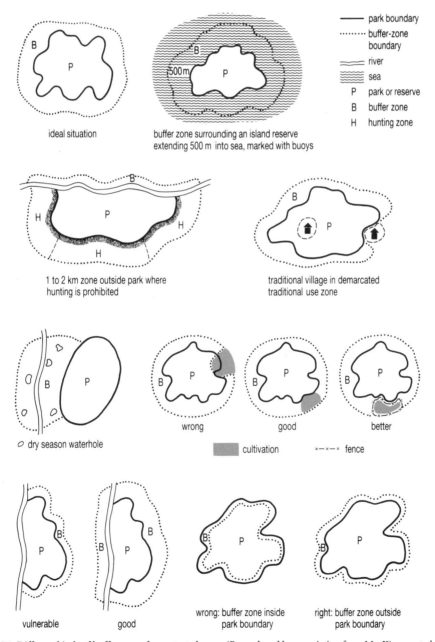

Figure 5.1. Different kinds of buffer zones for protected areas. (Reproduced by permission from MacKinnon et al. 1986)

rare species that have suffered from extreme habitat loss and shrinking geographic range. *Socio-buffering* manages a buffer zone to concentrate activities such as raising of crops or harvesting. Such use must be compatible with the objective of the core area itself. A major role of socio-buffers should be to discourage use of the core protected area by people who may traditionally use plants and animals native to the area. Where reserves are large or contain habitat traditionally used by local people, socio-buffer zones can help compensate for loss of traditional harvesting rights or privileges in core areas.

A number of factors must be taken into account when determining the extent and type of buffer zone:

- The plan for the protected area as a whole, and regional planning and development policies.

- The need to allow expansion into the buffer zone of the populations being protected or seasonal use of essential plants and animals.

- Particular regional needs for protection of soil and water and protection from fire.

- Needs of local people for land, plant and animal products, grazing and cropping, as well as traditional land use and ownership systems.

- The suitability of buffer zone crops or plantations, the general type of land use in the adjacent region, and protected area needs of managers of cultivated areas.

- The amount of land available for buffer zones.

- The jurisdiction and skill level of protected area managers (rarely have jurisdiction over land outside the legal limits of their park or reserve; may lack the training or skills to work effectively with local communities).

There is considerable scope for protected areas and buffer zones to relate to local people in a very practical way (Hanks 1984a; Infield 1988). The poverty of many tropical countries is aggravated by poor land use and the adoption of inappropriate agricultural systems. Many traditional systems of agriculture, for example multicrop and agroforestry systems, have evolved to minimize environmental impact. Their displacement can be disastrous. Protected areas are not only living laboratories for science and benchmarks against which to assess change; they also offer valuable facilities, especially in buffer zones, for education and awareness programs, and for research into low-impact systems of land use.

Lack of suitable sources of firewood is a problem in many rural tropical areas, so it may be appropriate for outer parts of a buffer zone to include plantations for village use. This can demonstrate that ecosystem protection is not antithetical to local development and economies. It is vitally important that buffer zones benefit more than just a small number of people; they must be perceived to be of value to the whole community (Oldfield 1988).

Activities allowed in buffer zones must not threaten core areas. There may have to be mandatory restrictions on the type of farming and grazing allowed, and on burning or cultivation; introduction of alien animals and plants may have to be prohibited. Ideally, the buffer zone should be incorporated into a regional conservation unit or plan in which areas for protection, multiple use, and various exploitive uses such as hunting are clearly demarcated. Care must be taken with the relative siting of such zones, and topographic boundaries should be followed wherever possible. The specific means of implementing such a system will vary from country to country, depending on the local customs and laws and nature of land-ownership and administration.

Ideally, protected area authorities have some control over land-use policies and activities within buffer zones. The situation becomes particularly complex where buffer zones lie wholly outside protected areas and come under different statutes and regulations. Integrated management then becomes a more complicated but necessary procedure. Other complications occur when the legal system under which protected areas are set up does not accord fully with traditional rights and property ownership systems. Legal protection often is not sufficient to guarantee the integrity of natural environment areas, especially where local people see their traditional rights infringed upon by establishment of a reserve. The best of laws cannot be enforced if people do not accept them, and it may be necessary to formulate new laws that provide for the needs of indigenous people while protecting core areas from use. Overall, effective dialogue is essential.

The benefits of a buffer zone for plant conservation can be divided into two broad categories as follows (modified from Oldfield 1988):

1. Biological benefits.
   A. Provides extra protection from human activities for the strictly protected core zone.
   B. Protects the core of the reserve from biological change.
   C. Provides extra protection from storm damage.
   D. Provides a large forest or other habitat unit for conservation, with less species loss through edge effects.

E. Extends habitat and thus population size for species requiring more space.

F. Allows for a more natural boundary—one relating to movements of animal species that may be essential to some plants.

G. Provides a replenishment zone for core area species including animals essential to some plants.

2. Social benefits.

A. Gives local people access to traditionally utilized species without depleting the core area.

B. Compensates people for loss of access to the strictly protected core zone.

C. Permits local people to participate in conservation of the protected area.

D. Makes more land available for education, recreation, and tourism, which in turn helps in conservation advocacy.

E. Permits conservation of plants and animals to become part of local and regional rural development planning.

F. Safeguards traditional land rights and conservation practices of local people.

G. Increases conservation-related employment.

To achieve these benefits the following basic criteria must be observed in buffer zones:

• Tree cover and integrity of all natural habitat should be maintained as far as possible.

• Vegetation of buffer zones should resemble that of the protected area, both in species composition and physiognomy.

• Buffer zones should be as biologically diverse as possible while retaining their naturalness and processes.

• The physiognomy of the vegetation should retain natural levels of heterogeneity and stratification, with locally increased heterogeneity and stratification within the buffer zone as required for utilization by people.

• The capacity of the ecosystem in the buffer zone to retain and recycle soil nutrients should be retained as far as possible. Similarly, buffer zone activities should not have negative impacts on the physical structure of the soil or on its water-regulating capacity.

• Exploitation of buffer zones should, as far as possible, make use of traditional, locally adapted lifestyles and resource management practices.

For many of the older wilderness reserves that were established decades ago, informal buffer zones made them effectively much larger than more recently established reserves. Many problems have arisen as settlement and intensive land use have increased around such protected areas and eroded these marginal areas. Land use in areas surrounding a protected area threatens the natural values of the reserve. For example, increased use of irrigation or fertilizers may destroy the soil conditions on which rare species depend. Management requirements for the protected area such as flooding and burning are seen as a threat by surrounding land-users.

The simple solution is to make the protected area larger and to incorporate buffer zones within it, but this is only possible if land is available. It may be feasible to acquire small areas of wild habitat and gradually create buffer zones in these. Another strategy is to link preexisting (and sometimes quite small) reserves by seminatural corridors to facilitate continued migration and gene flow (Wilcove and May 1986). A third strategy is to negotiate with adjacent landowners to control land use on properties bounding the protected area. This is often done in terms of fire control as a public safety measure.

It is advisable to have some legal control over land-use policies and activities for buffer zones. This in turn may depend on the precise designation of a core protected area. For instance, there may be greater legal constraints on land surrounding a national park than on land surrounding other types of protected area. The ownership of adjacent land will obviously be a major influence in determining the nature of buffer zones. The setting aside of communally owned or private freehold land for buffer zones will almost certainly involve complex negotiation including questions of compensation.

Links between natural resource conservation and rural development should be fostered as a goal in all environmental and social planning in and around protected areas. In Thailand, for example, rural "development for conservation" programs are seen as more appropriate alternatives to formal delineation of buffer zones. The aims of such a program are to improve the living standards of rural communities at the same time that protection of national parks is enhanced. Such an approach fulfills the same objectives as the buffer zone concept. A program with similar objectives is also planned for Korup National Park, Cameroon. It is important to involve local people in this way. Managers of larger protected areas such as national parks can develop a siege mentality, feeling encroachment from all sides. This attitude often heightens feelings of "them and us" and of conflict between preservationist advocates of the protected area and land-users outside the boundary. It can perpetuate a romantic vision of parks, which, in itself, may actually threaten parks by reinforcing the siege attitude.

To encourage activities causing the least impact, buffer zone activities should be graded from least harmful, through compatible, to incompatible. The rating system should take account of how buffer zones are viewed by local people. It is important that buffer zones be viewed positively and not as yet another imposition on people's rights.

Three common perceptions of buffer zones exist (IUCN 1986c). The *negative "moat" concept* suggests that the primary purpose of a buffer zone is to defend natural areas against human onslaught. More often the true objective is to promote a mosaic of compatible land uses in which the protected area fits in with and supports other zones characterized by varying degrees of exploitation. The *isolation concept* sees buffer zones encircling the protected area and isolating it from the surrounding human communities, even if some are allowed to live within the zone. Finally, *protectionist management* approaches are aimed at the protected area only in isolation from the lands and communities surrounding or in the vicinity of it. Many protected area management issues, however, can only be resolved through coordination with management of surrounding land.

No area can be viewed or managed in isolation. The extent to which activities have to be controlled depends on existing land use and on what activities that use encourages. For instance, where buffer zone rain forest is in a near natural condition and used primarily for extraction of traditional local products, it may be unnecessary and unwise to introduce new technology that leads to unsustainable exploitation. On the other hand, some new technology may actually lead to environmental stabilization and restoration, in which case it should be encouraged.

Biogeographic theory suggests that corridors of natural habitat between protected areas allow those areas to support greater numbers of species and larger populations than would be the case if the areas remained isolated. Certainly, where there is little prospect of enlarging existing protected areas, rehabilitating lost natural habitat and corridors must be considered. Such activities probably are of little direct value to plants, but they may be crucial to the long-term persistence of mobile animals such as birds and larger mammals. The fate of these, may in turn, affect the future survival of other animals and plants.

Corridors commonly are thought of as narrow connecting channels between larger areas, but there is no one pattern that must be used. They may be narrow and attenuated, for example, along riverbanks, or they may be many kilometers wide, as with a mountain range. A useful distinction can be made between transit and inhabited corridors. The former are corridors that are too narrow or do not have habitat to support permanent territories for most animals; the latter have both the width and habitat to do so. In assessing the shape required for habitat corridors, one must make allowance for edge effects. A useful rule of thumb is that an inhabited corridor should be wide enough to allow the width of an edge on either side, with the central core being at least four times this.

Vest pocket and garrison reserves

As a generalization, large protected areas have often been set aside because they include land of little agricultural or other economic value. In contrast, lands with recognized economic value for alternative uses tend to have small or few reserves. Of the 15 largest protected areas in the United States listed by IUCN, 5 are located in the arid west, 3 in Alaska, and 4 in the mountains of the far west—all agriculturally marginal regions. On more valuable lands small reserves are often the norm.

Vest pocket and garrison reserves are very small reserves (sometimes only a few hectares in extent) that are only likely to survive long term through intensive management. In some areas, small remnants of populations or natural communities may be all that remains for protection. Thus they are increasingly the last refuge of many threatened species, but small reserves cause problems for protected area managers. Nature reserves—even the smallest—have as their primary purpose to protect species of interest, preserve functioning communities, and preserve biotic diversity (Soulé and Simberloff 1986). The reserve has to have suitable habitat for target species whose habitat requirements may be exceedingly narrow. It is rarely possible to achieve a high level of diversity with long-term security.

There is also little doubt that smaller populations are at greater risk of extinction through catastrophe, or that small reserves suffer from greater impact through edge effects. For many animals, fragmentation is catastrophic, but for plants the situation is far less clear. Studies of grassland in Britain and woodland in the United States indicate that historic loss of plant species has been relatively slight. This may indicate that some plants have an ability to survive in small numbers that has not been fully appreciated (Boecklen and Bell 1987; Usher 1987). Nevertheless, it would be foolhardy to assume that all plants can survive in remnants.

Management of small reserves tends to be directed at a single purpose. Moreover, as reserves become smaller, management intensifies, so that vest pocket and garrison reserves tend to be expensive to maintain. Therefore it becomes important to manage the remnants of a region as an integrated network, and to ensure that there is reliable information on what each remnant contains (Hopkins and Saunders 1987). Ideally, small reserves should be associated with large buffer zones to minimize edge effects and the influence of adjacent land use. But this can be difficult in intensively managed regions where the price of land is high, and aggressive woody weeds are likely to be common. Even remnants often have a history of disturbance by people, and undisturbed sites simply are not available (Timmins and Williams 1987).

In extreme situations, small reserves may be the only available examples of their kind. Yet cultural, political, and economic (rather then biologic) factors often determine where reserves will be sited. In many instances, governmental or private conservation organizations either accept what is available or get nothing. Management cost may be so large that protection takes scarce resources from other conservation projects, or protection is seen as an unreasonable drain on taxpayers' money. It is very likely that garrison reserves will be biologically suboptimal, but this must not lead to the assumption that they are useless. Suboptimal habitats still have value for conservation, even aside from potential educational benefits.

The most serious problem for small reserves is that adjacent land use is likely to be very different from that in the reserve. If neighboring land right up to the boundary is intensively farmed (utilizing irrigation, high fertilizer inputs, and crops or pasture plants that can invade a reserve), long-term survival of the reserve is jeopardized. The only answer is to negotiate an adequate buffer zone around the protected area.

The problems outlined above give no reason to abandon the concept of in situ conservation in disturbed landscapes, or the value of small reserves, especially in peri-urban areas. Conservation of wild populations in natural habitats remains a fundamental principle of plant conservation. It preserves the complex ecological interactions of species and their environment. The management of small reserves is inextricably bound to management-oriented research and modeling, and a mosaic of small reserves can be advantageous in highly variable landscapes where there may be need to capture examples of environmental gradients or ecotones (Anchev, pers. com.). Linking small vegetation remnants through streamsides and road verges maintains physical continuity, which is important for animals that are intimately associated with plants (Bridgewater 1987; Russell 1987).

There are many opportunities to utilize areas of land administered by local government units (counties, municipalities, etc.), and to manage them by involving teachers, local residents, and even local politicians as well as conservation groups (Frost 1981; R. Keisling, pers. com.). Protected areas can become a source of local pride "adopted" by people living close by. Education is an important aspect of such sites. Children who visit them will be, within a few years, the adults who care for them. The efforts of one local community are likely encourage others to act.

Small protected areas do not have to be owned and managed by governmental agencies. Many people have not thought sufficiently about the effects of their own actions on biological diversity, and even the extinction of species. Concerned landowners can often do as well as the state (and sometimes even better), provided they are well advised and adequately compensated for by their efforts (Victorian Department of Conservation, Forests and Lands 1986). Devices such as covenants encourage a partnership of private and public interest to ensure that communities and wild species are conserved. Sites under covenant do not have the security of full reserves or parks, but in an era of increasing pressure to utilize land (and retain it in private or community hands), such mechanisms may be the most viable choice for conservation of key species and sites.

Representativeness

Representativeness is often given as a criterion for protected areas at local, regional, national, and international levels. The purpose of identifying representative areas is to provide a comprehensive protected natural area network protecting viable samples of the full range of global biodiversity (Specht et al. 1974; Connor et al. 1990). The concept of representativeness has been applied as a fundamental criterion for biosphere reserves. A range of "representative protected area" schemes have been proposed.

Although originally used in the sense of typical (of a biome, ecosystem, or habitat), *representative* can mean, and has come to mean, many different things, including representative of (1) species composition; (2) physical structure (forest, grassland, coral reef); (3) parameters of certain phenomena such as species diversity, percentage of endemic species; and (4) human land-use patterns and intensity (M. Soulé, pers. com.). Discrete representative areas are assumed to have similar repeating patterns of natural diversity (Margules and Usher 1984), reflect the original percentage of various habitats in natural landscapes (Connor et al. 1990), and involve comparison of the quality of representative sites (Myers et al. 1987).

Clearly, it is difficult for protected areas to be representative in all senses at once. Species composition is probably most meaningful in regions of low diversity, such as those at high latitudes. As species diversity becomes greater it becomes less meaningful, particularly where the rate of local endemism is high and species turnover occurs over very short distances.

The original intent of "representativeness" was to ensure adequate coverage—a useful aim but itself an imprecise term. It is desirable to have examples of every major type of biological community captured by a safety net of protected areas. Although this must be a major objective of a conservation strategy, current systems of ecosystem and community classification (especially at the worldwide level) are too blunt to use as a tool to preserve all local diversity and endemism. Where the concept of representativeness can be useful is in arguing that a particular site would make an excellent reserve because the landscape, soils, and microclimate are similar to that found in the surrounding region, and the site is representative in a general sense. But the use of the concept must be quite clear.

Some types of representativeness are more relevant for the tropics (especially the moist tropics), where many thousands of plant species are still undescribed and species conservation requires selection of reserves on the basis of major ecosystems. A vexing question for the moist tropics is whether there are enough protected areas and whether they are sufficiently representative of tropical forests as a whole. But the extremely high levels of species diversity and likely high geographic turnover rates of areas such as the moist neotropics means that it is very unlikely that any a priori system of classification based solely on biogeography and representativeness can capture a satisfactory level of diversity. Such systems ignore local ecosystem heterogeneity and gradients. Some communities are relatively neglected, in ecological studies as well as conservation programs, either because they are not spectacular, are regarded as impoverished, or are of very limited extent. Examples include shores of lakes, small ponds and wetlands of less than a few hectares extent, bird roosts, hot springs, and outcrops of rock (such as serpentine) that may be very different from adjacent outcrops.

Perhaps one of the more difficult situations in which to define targets for protection is when a region has an assemblage of species that are not individually threatened, but which collectively constitute a peculiar concentration of species. These have been termed *enriched communities* (Sawyer 1987). Unusual con-

centrations of species transcend broader vegetation classifications so that they tend to be overlooked in regional surveys. The occurrence of such stands emphasizes the need for finer scale surveys in areas where there are concentrations of endemics or where many distribution ranges overlap.

Ideally, a network of protected areas should include both large and small reserves, and should be designed to accommodate all endemic plants of the area and a representative sample of the range of widely distributed species. (It is easy to forget about the common or weedy species and their needs for protection.) The network should also include major genetic variants within species, especially those that may be significant as wild genetic resources for future use or for ongoing evolution of species (Roche and Dourojeanni 1984).

CASE STUDY: GUIDELINES FOR SELECTING A SYSTEM OF TROPICAL FOREST HABITATS FOR PROTECTION

Step 1: Survey
Step 2: Establish criteria
   A. Ecological criteria
     (1) Dependency
     (2) Naturalness
     (3) Uniqueness
     (4) Diversity
     (5) Integrity
     (6) Representativeness
   B. Scientific and educational criteria
     (1) Convenience
     (2) Monitoring benchmark
     (3) Research history
     (4) Demonstration
     (5) Process relationship
     (6) Awareness
   C. Social and economic benefit criteria
     (1) Economic benefit
     (2) Social acceptance
     (3) Recreation
     (4) Tourism
     (5) Landscape
     (6) Demonstration
   D. Pragmatic criteria
     (1) Urgency
     (2) Opportunism
     (3) Management feasibility
     (4) Availability
Step 3: Select areas to be included in the system
Step 4: Establish the system
Step 5: Manage the individual protected areas

Source: McNeely et al. 1987.

Local cultures and traditional economies

Few protected areas occur in totally uninhabited regions and many are in regions where people have lived for many generations. Local people have long-established patterns of living, harvesting regimes, and resource use, which can be changed drastically by the establishment of nature reserves and national parks. Even when these generate new jobs through activities such as tourism, people may resent the disruption of their traditional economy and culture. It is almost inevitable that some traditional practices will be in conflict with management objectives for protection of plants. Nevertheless, serious thought needs to be given to protection of, and respect for, traditional ways of life and economies. This is a complex and sensitive issue.

Local people may not have a profound understanding of modern conservation objectives, but there are many examples of traditional cultural practices that have themselves led to protection of ecosystems and species (MacKinnon et al. 1986). Where local practices, such as type, timing, and intensity of harvesting, are compatible with long-term conservation, management should incorporate them. Other uses of plants by local people may have to be modified, especially where there are increasing demands on grazing land, fuel plants, or food plants. Necessary changes should be introduced at a pace that allows people to adapt and understand. Common concerns provide a basis for dialogue in developing a system of management that will conserve plants and their environment yet not alienate people (Infield 1988). Hiring local people is an excellent way to integrate protected areas into the community and benefit people in the immediate vicinity. A high proportion of locally generated wealth should be shown to directly benefit communities immediately adjacent to, and perhaps otherwise disadvantaged by, a protected area.

Controlled harvesting can sometimes be incorporated into management in protected areas and may even be used to enhance habitat, for instance by creating planned disturbance patches. Any harvesting in protected areas, particularly where sensitive habitats or threatened habitats or species are present, must be adequately monitored and planned. Examples include the harvesting of wild nuts, a traditional food, in Grand Canyon National Park, United States, and cutting of reeds for thatch in English fen reserves. It is often overlooked that the "minor" forest products such as wildlife, medicinal plants, fibers, animal fodder, thatch, edible fungi, fruits, honey, and even clean water, harvested in a sustained way can often exceed the value of timber (Roche 1979; Roche and Dourojeanni 1984; Ng 1985).

Harvesting poses particular problems for plant conservation. Taking dead wood and large quantities of leaf litter may seem a harmless form of harvest, but it may remove vital nutrients as well as destroy microhabitats. Harvesting from core areas should be discouraged and only allowed if it can be unequivocally shown to have no negative effects on target species or ecosystems. Critical baseline studies to determine the extent of resources and allowable harvesting rates are an integral part of creation of protected reserves.

In some instances, some form of payment in cash or kind may be appropriate (MacKinnon et al. 1986). This is done in the Matobo National Park in Zimbabwe where grass cutters harvesting grass for thatch pay in kind by donating one bundle in ten to the park. It must not be forgotten that some forms of research also have a harvesting component that needs to be monitored. Commercial harvesting from protected areas may seem good for public relations, but it should only be allowed if it is essential, cannot be accomplished outside the area, and can be incorporated into a sustained management plan. In some instances, such as grazing or removal of feral animals, controlled utilization may serve as a management tool to maintain habitat, providing it does not lead to overstocking and habitat degradation, or to farming of feral animals to maintain their numbers at an unacceptably high level.

As in other aspects of management, care must be taken not to transplant solutions uncritically from one part of the world to another, or to create pockets of poverty that may then result in other pressures on ecosystems.

Sometimes a protected area for conservation of nature corresponds closely with the territory of an ethnic people. Such people will have an intimate association with the land and biota of the region. A body of orally transmitted knowledge of plants and their uses is likely to be part of the heritage of such people. They will usually have a particular attachment to the land, expressed as part of the culture and religion. The national conservation agency may remain the official administrator of the area, but managers must work very closely with the local, resident people. This requires good communication and a suitable model (Brownrigg 1985).

Resettlement should be avoided whenever possible. An indigenous culture will remain intact only in its home territory, where the productive capacity of the environment is intimately understood.

The protected area should be sufficiently large to accommodate its dual function—a reserve for nature with lands for indigenous people. The creation of reserves of reduced area only serves a symbolic end and begins a process of cultural devolution and ecological degradation if the indigenous people do not have access to the resources they require.

Protected area planning must accommodate population increase and cultural change. It is unrealistic to expect a group to atrophy, or worse, to return to some traditional technology long ago discarded in favor of a more modern alternative.

Park staff should be traditional residents. Threats to integrity chiefly originate from outside. This is sensible use of resources, but also helps retain necessary goodwill of the people of the area.

This model may be particularly attractive for indigenous peoples who lack formal rights to their land, who lack avenues to pursue land titles within the juridical structure of their country, and for small or rarely contacted tribal groups.

Protected Area Categories

There are many types of protected area with differing degrees of protection, permanency, and purpose. No single category will satisfy all needs, and over many decades a wide variety of protected area categories have evolved. Some have arisen to accommodate local peculiarities. Others such as national parks have universal application. The confusing range of protected areas can be broadly grouped into several different categories, such as scientific reserve/strict nature reserve, national park, natural monument/natural landmark, managed nature reserve/wildlife sanctuary, protected landscapes and seascapes, resource reserve, natural biotic area/anthropological reserve, multiple use management area/managed resource area, biosphere reserve, and world heritage site (natural) (MacKinnon et al. 1986).

Each type of protected area is particularly suited to one or several plant conservation objectives. Categories of protected area and objectives are matched in Table 5.1.

When people think of protected areas they often think first of national parks. These have wide international recognition as "jewels in the conservation crown." They enjoy a high public profile and are often of large size, preserving extensive ecosystems, but they may be too large to facilitate management of highly

Table 5.1. The most significant types of protected area for conservation of plants.[1]

Primary conservation objective	I	II	III	IV	V	VI	VII	VIII	IX	X
Maintain sample ecosystems in natural state	1	1	1	1	2	3	1	2	1	1
Conserve genetic resources	1	1	1	1	2	3	1	3	1	1
Maintain ecological diversity and environmental regulation	3	1	1	2	2	2	1	2	1	1
Provide education, research, and environmental monitoring	1	2	1	1	2	3	2	2	1	1
Produce timber, forage on a sustained basis	--	--	--	3	2	--	3	1	3	--
Conserve watershed condition	2	1	2	2	2	2	2	2	2	2
Protect sites and objects of cultural heritage	--	1	3	--	1	3	1	3	2	1
Stimulate rational, sustainable use of marginal areas and rural development	2	1	2	2	1	3	2	1	2	2

[1] Types of protected areas: I = strict nature reserve; II = national park; III = monument/landmark; IV = managed reserve; V = protected landscape; VI = resource reserve; VII = anthropological reserve; VIII = multiple use area; IX = biosphere reserve; X = world heritage site.

Ratings: 1 = primary objective for management of area and resources; 2 = not necessarily primary but always included as an important objective; 3 = included as an objective where applicable and whenever resources and other management objectives permit.

Source: MacKinnon et al. 1986, example 2.2 in part.

endangered species. They are also public areas in the sense that people traditionally have reasonably unconstrained access. On the other hand, strict nature reserves are well suited for conservation of individual species and smaller ecosystems. Yet, neither may meet the needs of relict stands of vegetation growing in highly modified, urban habitats, nor the requirements of genetic resource conservation.

Sites that are not specifically protected for nature conservation may have high conservation value and reasonable permanence. Examples include sacred sites such as churchyards and temples, lighthouse reserves, and military sites. In the United Kingdom, burial grounds and churchyards are sometimes extremely valuable for protection of wildflowers that have all but disappeared from the countryside. There is an increasing need to think "laterally" when considering sites for conservation of natural vegetation and native species. Even sports and recreation grounds and race-courses are known to provide protection for populations of threatened plants. Management may not be simple on such sites; competing uses will have to be carefully meshed with conservation needs and there are likely to be conflicts that require compromise solutions. But the reality is that there may be no other sites available or certainly no sites that can be readily given protection in the immediate future.

Some of the more significant questions to consider when selecting sites and categories of reserve for plant conservation are listed below (Roche and Dourojeanni 1984, modified).

- At the international, national, and local level, how good is the current representation of ecological and genetic diversity?

- How will representation be improved?

- Is the size of the area that will be protected sufficient for the time period envisaged?

- Is the protected area category designed to achieve the required degree and type of protection?

- Does the protected area category allow necessary manipulation and interventionist management?

- What is the acceptance of the particular protected area category by other countries (especially adjacent ones)?

- What is the legal status of the proposed category of protection and how effective is it in practice? Some categories such as national parks II, receive maxi-

mum protection in most countries, but land supposedly protected under some other categories may be little more than "paper reserves."

- What possibilities will there be for access to the protected area, including traditional harvesting, seed collection for horticulture or crop breeding, and tourism?

- What threats are posed by adjacent land use and how are these mitigated by reserve design and category?

Two kinds of protected area are likely to become increasingly important for plant conservation in the future: *nature reserves* and *biosphere reserves*. Nature reserves are those for which the primary purpose is the conservation of relatively unmodified natural communities or ecosystems. Other uses such as tourism, education, and recreation are sometimes allowed where there is no serious conflict with the primary purpose of conservation. Provisions for access vary considerably, but it is not unusual for visitor access to be restricted at least part of the year. Size can vary considerably, from less than a hectare to many thousands of hectares.

Especially where plant populations are highly vulnerable, nature reserves need to be backed up by a complementary off-site program. Transfer of plants between on-site and off-site locations can be facilitated but requires consideration of the genetic variability of the parent population, the possibility of accidental transfer of diseases and predators from one site to another, and evaluation of sites to ensure that they are ecologically equivalent.

Should people be allowed to visit reserves that contain critical species and habitats? There is no universal answer. If an area justifies nature reserve status, a management plan that controls visitor pressure and use should be implemented. But the presence of rare species or habitats in itself can attract people. Even the most careful of visitors, including legitimate researchers, cause impacts on habitat. In extreme instances, there will inevitably need to be stringent controls on entry, even by scientists. If target species are well known and of economic importance, it may even be necessary to patrol the reserve. Table 5.2 shows the protected area cover in tropical rain forest and tropical dry forest biomes. Protected area classification is under revision, a significant addition being "Protected Landscapes."

Table 5.2. Protected area cover in tropical rain forest and tropical dry forest biomes for each realm.

Realm	Tropical rain forest		Tropical dry forest and woodland	
	No. of areas	Surface area in 1000 ha	No. of areas	Surface area in 1000 ha
Afrotropical	47	10,564	204	59,920
Indomalayan	150	13,315	161	9,269
Oceanean	10	3,032	--	--
Australian	81	2,506	17	1,687
Neotropical	67	18,100	99	5,478
Total	355	47,517	481	76,365

Source: Harrison et al. 1982, in Roche and Dourojeanni 1984.

Biosphere reserves

A relatively new concept in protected areas is that of biosphere reserves, organized as part of the Man and the Biosphere (MAB) Program (Gregg 1988). This worldwide program of international scientific cooperation considers the interactions of people and their environment in a wide range of bioclimatic and geographic situations. Biosphere reserves are protected representative ecological areas linked by a coordinated international network. Biosphere reserves are designated on a regional basis to include a range of land uses from unmodified, sites through buffer zones, to compatible productive uses of land such as agriculture and sustained forestry. Areas are chosen and managed as natural or minimally disturbed representative examples of the world's ecosystems. The concept differs from that of many traditional protected areas because it combines nature conservation with scientific research, environmental monitoring, training, demonstration in resource management, environmental education, and local participation. These reserves are particularly valuable for conservation of genetic resources, especially wild crop relatives. The primary purposes of the biosphere reserves are fourfold:

1. To protect areas of representative terrestrial and coastal environments that have been internationally recognized for their value in conservation and in providing the scientific knowledge, skills, and human values to support sustainable development.

2. To form a worldwide network that facilitates sharing of information relevant to conservation and management of natural and managed ecosystems.

3. To include representative areas of minimally disturbed ecosystems, and as many as possible of the following: centers of endemism and genetic richness or unique natural features, areas for experimental manipulation, examples of harmonious landscapes resulting from traditional land use, and examples of modified or degraded ecosystems suitable for restoration.

4. To provide opportunities for ecological research, education, demonstration, and training.

An attempt is made to ensure that each reserve is large enough to be an effective conservation unit and have value as a benchmark for measurement of long-term changes in the biosphere. All biosphere reserves include buffer zones consisting of a combination of land types. Buffers may include undefined areas where activities compatible with the conservation and research objectives of the reserve are allowed. Long-term legislative, regulatory, or institutional protection is an integral part of the biosphere reserve program.

People are considered an essential component of the landscape and, as a consequence, of the biosphere reserve. Local residents are encouraged to participate in its management, which ensures strong local acceptance of conservation activities. Generally, changes in landownership or regulations are not required when a biosphere reserve is created, unless such changes are necessary to ensure strict protection of the core area or of specific research sites.

The purpose behind the biosphere reserve concept is not to create a further class of nature reserve closed to people or development, but to promote a harmonious marriage between conservation and development. Conventional reserves and national parks are unable to safeguard the whole variety of organisms under threat. Biosphere reserves are particularly useful in regions where core areas are small and there is economic, resource, or cultural pressure for intensive use of land. It is less a reserve in the traditional sense than a mosaic of representative ecosystems and landscapes in which resource use is controlled.

How this harmony is achieved is very important. A reading of biosphere reserve literature shows that there are two distinct "languages" or sets of ideas embodied in the concept: the language of resource management and the language of community. The former is concerned with the management of nature for human use, and the latter with the concept of people belonging to and sharing an ethic that stresses relationships, communication, worth, and equity—both for people and the land (Engel 1988). The language of community must receive a high level of emphasis if biosphere reserves are to be centers not only of resource management, but also for the preservation and renewal of human and natural community.

Surveys should occur early in the process of creating a biosphere reserve so that subsequent management can take due regard of the needs of target species and populations in the reserve. Involvement of local people should be sought to identify potential management conflicts. Because lifestyles evolve and change, long-term management of biosphere reserves should allow for sympathetic development in harmony with local traditions and cultures. At the same time, the important role of these reserves in plant conservation must not be forgotten (G. Sayer, pers. com.).

As wild landscapes are increasingly broken up into mosaics of developed and undeveloped areas, biosphere reserves or equivalent managed areas may become one of the few options available for plant conservation. They have potential as powerful tools of education and consciousness raising because of their emphasis on local participation and management. Every country needs to arrive at a better knowledge of its natural resources, including plants, and biosphere reserves provide a proven mechanism for promoting this (Derkatch 1987).

On-site gene banks

An on-site (in situ) gene bank is a location where wild genetic resources are conserved by maintaining gene pools of species in their natural habitat. The emphasis is on species of known or potential economic value, and a necessary function is to provide for use of the gene pool. There are two important distinctions between management for gene pool conservation and management for other types of conservation. First, the unit of management is the local gene pool rather than the species, community, or ecosystem. Second, provision must be made for collection and sustainable use by bona fide breeders and researchers, and for supply of germ plasm to off-site gene banks. The gene bank may be a formally designated protected area such as a nature reserve. It may be a zone designated within a protected area that has other objectives, such as a national park. It may be a protected area specifically set aside with genetic resource conservation as the only purpose. Where there is competition among different users of land wanted for a gene bank, there may have to be careful selection so that adequate gene pools are protected in relatively few sites. Once organized, a national system of on-site gene banks will include an array of different types of protected areas (Prescott-Allen and Prescott-Allen 1985).

The distribution of protected areas should be such that they conserve at least one viable population of each major genetic variant of the target species. Protected populations must be viable enough to be self-sustaining and so minimize loss of genes that occur in low frequency. Those sites with the highest numbers of target populations must be a priority for more detailed investigation and monitoring to ensure that plant numbers are sufficient to maintain populations over the long term, critical habitat is identified, essential associates such as pollinators and fruit dispersers are present, and other activities in the area do not jeopardize ex situ functions.

A particular value of on-site gene banks is that they demonstrate that at least some (and perhaps most) protected natural areas have value for people. Moreover, the benefits extend potentially to all humanity and not just a select few—a frequent criticism of nature tourism and the setting aside of wilderness areas.

An effective national system of on-site gene banks would maintain those wild populations that collectively contain the genetic diversity of native economic species in an array of combinations. Each protected population should be large enough to be self-regenerating and to minimize loss of low-frequency genes. The most cost-effective way of maintaining populations of climax species is by ensuring that the ecosystems of which they are part remain large and are buffered enough to be self-perpetuating. Maintenance of populations of successional species, however, will usually require more active management to avoid their replacement by components of the climax. The necessary measures will vary with the species and circumstances and include grazing or mowing to maintain a grazing subclimax; burning to maintain a fire subclimax; logging to open up the canopy; thinning and removal of competing vegetation; and control or removal of predators, parasites, or competitors. A national system of on-site gene banks should therefore combine protected areas with multiple objectives, in which particular zones can be designated for gene pool conservation, whether of climax species, successional species, or both (e.g., national parks, managed nature reserves, national forests); protected areas for which objectives do not permit artificial maintenance of seres or subclimaxes, but that instead conserve climax species through protection of ecosystems in their natural state (e.g., strict nature reserves); and protected areas for which the primary objective is gene pool conservation, where measures necessary to achieve the objective, as well as other activities compatible with the objective, are allowed (e.g., gene resource management units) (Prescott-Allen and Prescott-Allen 1985).

The distribution of these three types of protected areas should be such that they conserve at least one viable population of each major genetic variant of the native economic species identified for conservation.

Major genetic variants are genotypes that are superior, populations that are genetically unique, populations that are representative of a major genetic type, and populations that have been identified as sources of useful characteristics in the development or improvement of domesticates.

Managing Protected Areas

Research and information management

Management of protected areas benefits by close collaboration between protected area managers and research institutions, and even between agencies in different countries. Integration of management and research ensures that the needs of management are met with relevant and accurate data.

Collaboration should meet four objectives: to utilize information, to counter weaknesses in one sector by strengths in another, to understand the goals of various interest groups and minimize friction and tension between people involved, and to ensure that the primary purposes of the protected area are achieved.

Regular and meaningful feedback between research and management is a continuing collaborative process. Management can identify needs to which research can respond. In turn, the findings of a research team can alter management regimes, which then generate a new set of questions (Figure 5.2).

Basic areas of information can be identified for

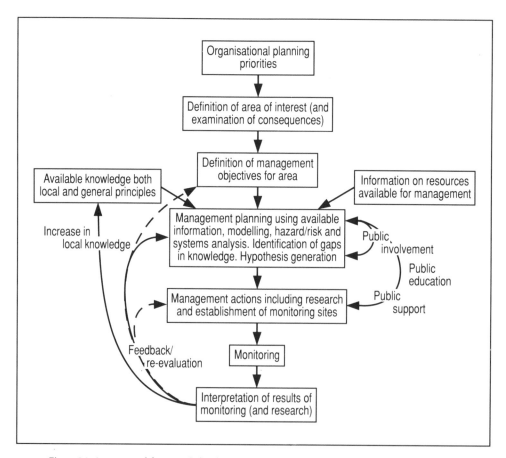

Figure 5.2. A conceptual framework for the integration of research, planning, and management.
(Reproduced by permission from Hopkins and Saunders 1987)

which the protected area manager concerned with botanical diversity should have accurate, scientifically meaningful biological data (MacKinnon et al. 1986):

Inventory. What plants, associated animals, and key natural resources are present?

Quantification. What numbers of each species are present and how are they distributed in space and time?

Ecological relationships. What eats, preys on, competes with, and depends on what? What are the primary pollinators and dispersers and what species do these in turn depend on? Although it is generally realized that breakdowns in the linkages between species may have profound effects on the reproduction, establishment, and maturation of many other organisms, essential data supporting this idea are still lacking. Even in developed countries with highly developed and sophisticated research programs there is frequently only sketchy and anecdotal information on pollinators and breeding systems.

Species needs. What are the particular habitat, food, water, and biotic requirements of plants in the reserve, especially those in need of special management?

Ecological patterns. Is the area ecologically uniform or heterogeneous, and how does this affect distribution of resources for organisms and consequent distribution of individual species?

Dynamics of change. What are the dynamics of vegetation—colonization of disturbed areas, seral succession, changes in rivers and water tables, invasion by animal and plant species, and population trends?

Predictive manipulation of ecosystems. Where the natural processes of change are contrary to objectives of management, can and should change be prevented or redirected? What are the direct and indirect, short-term and long-term effects of different management options?

Socio-economic and ethnobotanical information. The protected area manager should have information on traditional harvesting and use of plants found in the region, on effects of the reserve on the local economy, and on the interaction of core area and buffer zone usage.

Over a number of years, a surprisingly large amount of information on plant conservation may be accumulated by a protected area manager. Subject matter can cover a wide range of fields including distribution and abundance of species, flowering and fruiting times, climatic data, impact of visitor use and recreational activities, changes in abundance of spe-cies, and structural changes in vegetation. This information may be formal or anecdotal, but the value of the latter should not be underestimated. Visiting research workers will produce valuable reports and publications, and generate other information about the area. It is essential that such information be stored in a form that is accessible to management staff. Useful on-site information and resources should include the following:

Basic library. This should contain essential handbooks, textbooks, and manuals, and field guides dealing with the region and with biota found in the protected area and the immediate vicinity (including weeds and common animal pests). The library does not have to be large but access to a more comprehensive library should be sought.

Projects file. A cumulative file of research project outlines, progress reports, and results based on work carried out in the protected area is essential. Research workers are frequently tardy in providing managers with results of work in protected areas, or their reports are difficult to obtain. Managers should be firm in requiring reports and in seeking information that can be applied.

Observations file. It is useful to have a cumulative file of informal and anecdotal observations, meteorological records, and comments. Such a file requires careful indexing so that contents can be swiftly accessed when needed.

Critical sites/species database. A database of information on critical sites and species should be built. This can note such items as distribution, abundance, biology, and habitat of rare species, and location and condition of sensitive habitats. Some of the information in this database may have to be treated as confidential.

Register of plots and transects. This is a database identifying the location, significance, and recording agency for permanent transects and plots in protected areas.

Basic herbarium of plant specimens. Protected areas rarely require a comprehensive herbarium, but it is useful to have a collection that contains at least one specimen of all species found in the area including weeds. The herbarium should not duplicate larger institutional herbaria, but instead managers should develop working contacts with such collections. A management-oriented herbarium should not include important research vouchers or type specimens; these are better lodged with a more comprehensive herbarium.

Photograph library. Collections of color transparencies, photographic prints, and archival materials from known locations gain value as time passes. Where photographs or documents are unique and irreplaceable, copies should be retained and originals lodged in a secure file elsewhere.

Case history file. It is useful to maintain a file documenting management and research successes and failures both within the region and from other regions and countries with similar climate, vegetation, species, threats, and development patterns.

It is natural that managers will favor research that has an obvious application to management. Although some research proposed for protected areas may appear to be purely academic, however, it should not be discouraged unless it conflicts with management objectives, for example, by involving destructive sampling that will reduce populations below an acceptable limit. Apparently academic projects often prove to be valuable in the light of later research.

Modeling is becoming increasingly important as a means of structuring research relevant to management (e.g., Beeston 1987; Wallace and Moore 1987). Modeling also can aid communication, although any management-related model must be readily understandable by those who will use it. If the model or any other aspect of management requires use of computing time, computing requirements should be modest and designed as far as possible for desktop hardware. When modeling is desirable, it is important to have clear management objectives, a structured decision-making process, selective development of models to be tested, a clearly defined monitoring and reporting system, and recognition that all models have flaws and need both an adequate database and a good and regular system of assessment.

One of the interesting recent developments in modeling is the use of geographic information systems and statistical procedures to select sites for protection. Development of powerful personal computers and relatively inexpensive software now puts such an exercise within the reach of agencies with very modest resources. To do this requires clear and unambiguous guidelines for goals of biodiversity coverage and adequate, accurate field data.

Well-designed research by reserve staff should be encouraged. At the very least they can be alert to simple phenomena. If resources allow, an ecologist can be employed to develop programs that can be undertaken by other management staff. Local universities, schools, and research institutes are often very happy to enter into cooperative arrangements with protected areas. As an example, teachers and students can be allowed to use the area under supervision for educational purposes, in return for which they help gather data for approved projects.

Developing countries should be encouraged to carry out and develop their own research programs. This can involve the assistance of more developed countries, chiefly in the initial stages, with the goal of achieving a high degree of self-sufficiency. Such assistance might include training opportunities, financing of local researchers, free access to information, creation of specialized newsletters at regional levels, ensuring that foreign scientists use local people as assistants, progressive creation of a network of database centers, and presentation of research results at host country conferences.

CASE STUDY: RESEARCH AND MANAGEMENT ON THE GALAPAGOS ISLANDS, ECUADOR

In the 1930s, a number of islands in the Galapagos archipelago were set aside as nature reserves. Thirty years later the creation of a national park was initiated. Concomitantly, the Charles Darwin Foundation for the Galapagos Islands was set up in 1958. Between 1960 and 1964, work of the foundation was dedicated to setting up a research station with the support of UNESCO, IUCN, and the Ecuador government. The research station operates with a permanent staff as well as visiting scientists. From the beginning its mission has been threefold: scientific investigation, conservation, and education.

The 1974 management plan for the Galapagos National Park identifies research on a range of topics, several of which are key to management of botanical values:

- Monitoring of biological communities by means of censuses, particularly in critical areas such as intensive use zones, islands affected by introduced plants or animals, and areas adjacent to colonized zones.

- Research on population dynamics of certain threatened species.

- Detailed studies of the population dynamics of introduced organisms and development of programs for their eradication.

- Environmental monitoring for contaminants originating outside the archipelago.

- Synoptic study of off-shore zones (flora and fauna) within the park.

- Studies of tourism impact.

- Assessment of water resources and volcanic hazards.

Scientific research is an important function of the national park and is facilitated through the research station as part of an agreement between the government of Ecuador and the Charles Darwin Foundation. The National Park Committee considers applications from scientific institutions, and park officials supervise the activities of the research station and of researchers in the park. The research terrain for each scientific mission is determined according to protection imperatives and research needs. An important development was an international workshop in 1987 to examine and recommend future options and strategies for botanical research on the Galapagos Islands.

Sources: Black 1984; MacKinnon et al. 1986, modified.

Active management techniques

Many wildlife and threatened plant laws protect individuals or species from harvesting, but still fail to give adequate protection to the communities in which they occur. It is very important to recognize critical habitat as that which is essential to the survival and persistence of a species.

Management of critical habitat includes not only concern with the general habitat type and particular niche of a species but also regard for associated animals and plants such as pollinators and dispersers. There is also a temporal aspect to habitat management. A plant may depend on a particular stage of succession or pattern of disturbance; in fact, natural disturbance is a process on which some species depend for survival. Because there is no universal rule regarding the specific relationship of species to disturbance, management must reflect sound scientific investigation. Artificial disturbance at different scales and of different types must lead to predictable results and should not be adopted simply because they might work (Foster 1980).

For small areas of critical habitat, especially those of only a few hectares, management techniques may have to be highly manipulative; there may be no choice if declining species or habitats are involved. For plants of open habitats, this may mean removal of competing species, even though these may be indigenous plants of the region. In some shrublands, it may be necessary to prevent natural regeneration of forest, which would lead to loss of unique species.

Where manipulation of habitat has to take place, it is best that selected procedures be tested on a small scale prior to their adoption over larger areas. This may not be possible where populations or areas are particularly small or few. Ex situ research on a species should be carried out at an early stage to determine optimum microhabitat conditions.

Often, management by analogy can be adopted, where management of one reserve is based on experience gained in another. One major constraint to this is likely to be lack of knowledge of specific habitat requirements of species and lack of accuracy in predicting vegetation change under differing management regimes.

Sometimes it is necessary to restore a habitat to near-natural condition, when the original vegetation has been destroyed or grossly damaged. Natural succession depends on several factors. One of the most important is availability of parent seed: How far away are mature plants of the required species, are they producing propagules, and are dispersal vectors available? Where natural processes are slow, weedy species may regenerate rapidly and establishment of climax species may be more difficult, at least until many years have past. In such endeavors, attention should be paid to soil and hydrologic regimes. Soil erosion and degradation is a particular risk in the tropics, and greatly hinders reestablishment of forest in particular.

Managers of protected areas should be prepared to commit adequate resources for long enough to complete each task. Vegetation restoration projects of even modest size are likely to be expensive. The exact course of action will depend on the major objectives of a protected area—for example, whether it was established primarily for preservation of one or more species, a vegetation type, or an ecosystem.

Considerable controversy has been created by the use of deliberate burning and grazing as management tools to maintain particular types of vegetation and fire-dependent species (e.g., Boucher 1981; Noble and Slatyer 1981). Natural fire has had a prolonged and marked influence on the vegetation of many parts of the tropics. This is seen especially in the creation of savanna, for example, in Southeast Asia and parts of Africa. Maintenance of such sites on a large scale is likely to require periodic controlled burning; burning or harrowing may be used on smaller sites. General uses of fire include clearing scrub and grassland to reduce fire risk, not only for public safety but also to facilitate fires at times that are optimum for the species being managed; facilitating replanting with woody species, by removal of competing vegetation, especially introduced grasses; creating firebreaks to control spread of fires (e.g., spread of deliberately set agricultural fires into protected areas); encouraging the reproduction of fire-adapted species (e.g., species with woody fruits or lignotubers).

Natural disturbance regimes must be carefully distinguished from those caused by human activities, and managers have to decide whether to reestablish natural perturbations or replace them with artificial ones. Grazing with domestic stock is often regarded as incompatible with the goals of protected areas, but this is not always the case. For example, at Guanacaste National Park, Costa Rica, grazing of livestock at moderate to low densities can help encourage woody succession into pastures by reducing the amount of grass (Janzen 1986a). Such grazing must be controlled and carefully monitored, particularly to determine whether it simulates natural processes.

With any plant, it is important to remember that the species is likely to be linked in some significant way with animals. Animals may be required for pollination and dispersal, and in their absence apparently healthy populations will gradually dwindle. The long-term survival of most plants involves conservation of associated animals. This in turn may require the conservation of other plant species on which the animals themselves depend, and sometimes the conservation of distant areas or dissimilar habitats. Extreme examples involve birds that migrate thousands of kilometers between continents.

Case Study: Tropical Tree Conservation Strategies

Reserves of mature forest should be large—minimally tens of square kilometers, preferably hundreds of square kilometers.

Minimum critical population sizes are unknown for tropical trees, but low densities probably exist in some areas (e.g., Barro Colorado Island), below which obligately outcrossed trees suffer catastrophic decline.

Adequate provision must be made in tropical forest reserves to maintain the integrity of the pollinator and disperser animal communities on which many trees depend. This requires larger reserves than might seem necessary. We should err on the side of too large rather than too small in the absence of detailed information.

Large reserves also are required if forests are nonequilibrium communities. Major fluctuations in tree species abundance and spatial migrations of populations can be expected to occur, and large areas and population sizes can better accommodate and buffer these fluctuations.

If possible, reserves should encompass diverse habitats to conserve as many habitat specialists as possible. Some attention to the natural disturbance regime is desirable. For example, meandering streams that cut off oxbow lakes and cause continual long-term forest succession are an excellent complex natural disturbance regime; they are used to maintain high diversity in Manu National Park, Peru.

Many tropical trees may be local endemics. This makes it difficult to save many of these species in the face of continued loss of forest. Perhaps a more realistic goal is to design tropical forest reserves that effectively conserve populations of the many common mature forest tree species. Main centers of dispersal of rare species should be preserved. This all requires large reserves.

Reserves should have minimal perimeter-to-area ratios. This allows better buffer zone design and minimizes second-growth invasion.

Source: Hubbell and Foster 1986.

Case Study: General Principles for Implementation of New Management

If management requires active manipulation of ecosystems to preserve particular habitats or species, some general principles are appropriate. Especially where one is dealing with rare species or small areas of habitat, there is little margin for error. Blind application of management techniques without adequate trials or contingency plans can lead to disastrous loss of irreplaceable species or the need for very expensive habitat reconstruction.

- Before applying a new form of management on a wider scale, apply it to a small area first.

- Select a noncritical area for the trial. This need not be in the reserve, but it should be in a similar natural community (i.e., have similar species composition, topography, etc.) to those areas where the eventual application is planned.

- Select a control area as similar as possible in every way to the trial area to compare the effects of management.

- If the test involves introduction of species, the trial area should be isolated from similar habitat so that the introduced species can be contained and eradicated if they prove unsuitable.

- Select the most appropriate agency to do the trials; what may be of interest to scientists may be out of line with management objectives. Protected area managers must be consulted about trials and have the right to comment on or even veto the experiments.

- Keep accurate records of methods and results and test the results using the appropriate statistics before applying an apparently successful strategy elsewhere.

- If results look favorable, project the cost of the management activity in terms of labor, materials, and transport. Consider the possible risks and indirect consequences of introducing the practice. Consider what may go wrong, including inability to maintain a desirable management practice through lack of resources.

Source: MacKinnon et al. 1986, modified.

Translocations

Translocations (transfers of species of animals and plants by humans) generate strong opinions and feelings. Some conservationists and protected area managers regard translocations as unnecessary, while others see them as a routine protection mechanism fundamental to the survival of some critically threatened species. One point to consider is that translocations are not new but have been occurring for centuries. Many prehistoric translocations took place as people moved across continents and oceans and took with them such plants as the coconut and sweet potato.

Translocations for conservation purposes are essential when habitat is about to be destroyed in its entirety, and the only choice is to allow plants to be destroyed or to shift them (Falk and Holsinger 1991; Pavlik et al. 1993). Sometimes it is possible to shift plants from a site temporarily while rehabilitation is being done. In other instances the shift may have to be permanent. Translocation also may be justified where uncontrollable disease or predation threatens a population. More problematic are those instances where translocation is used on species that are unable to breed sexually (usually through loss of one sexual state). By translocating plants from two or more sites to combine elements at one location, a "new" breeding population can be established.

Precautions are necessary, particularly where key protected areas are involved. Especially where translocations involve long distances and different climates or soils, there is a risk that the target species will become weeds at the new site. Accidental disease transfer must be avoided. Careful documentation and follow-up is essential. Genetic considerations suggest that the variability of a population established at a new site should not be lower than that at a source site. Properly done, translocations are time-consuming and often expensive; they should be used only where absolutely necessary.

Managing for population fluctuations, disturbance, and stress

Sometimes it is assumed that present events and environments have existed unaltered through long periods of time. A corollary assumption is that disturbance, whether by fire, earthquake, volcanism, predation, or flood, is abnormal. In some regions disturbance is a natural, periodic, and frequent event. But there is increasing evidence to suggest that even in more stable regions, not only is disturbance normal and tolerated but it is an essential environmental factor for many species (e.g., Boucher 1981; Keddy 1985). To recognize the role of disturbance one must appreciate that rarity contains temporal as well as spatial components. Four extreme trends over time can be recognized in the behavior of plant populations (Harper 1981): (1) plants can remain common over long periods of time; (2) plants can remain rare over long periods of time; (3) plants that have been rare in the past are now more common; and (4) plants once common have since become rare.

Plant conservation is generally concerned with the last three of these trends, and particularly with second and fourth trends. The manager of threatened plants should have an ongoing interest in the third trend as well because such species may be subject to long-term fluctuations in numbers. There are many instances of previously small populations that expanded rapidly, and of abundant species that have dramatically collapsed.

Two particular points must be stressed here. The first is that both positive and negative changes in population size may not be unique events, but may be cyclic. Such fluctuations need to be identified, and if they are shown to be natural long-term events, means must be developed to maintain them. A downward trend in abundance does not necessarily mean a potential slide toward extinction. In cyclic species a trend toward rarity may be followed by a reversal back toward abundance.

A second point is that the time lapse in a monitoring program needs to take account of such fluctuations. If, for example, a species regularly goes through a 15-year cycle from rare to abundant, and a census is done each 15 years, the apparent rarity or abundance may depend on the particular stage of the cycle the species is at when sampling is done. Thus census intervals may have to be reasonably close in the initial stages of monitoring if there is any suspicion that the plants under study have large cyclic fluctuations in numbers.

When looking at the scale of natural disturbances, how does one go about determining the spatial needs of a forest fire or a flood, and how much does one attempt to manipulate such events when they occur? In remnant patches of habitat, some natural disturbances can be catastrophic, especially where there is a risk of total destruction of a species in the wild. Further, does the manager plan for an average disturbance, or for a 100- or 500-year disaster. It has been suggested that, "given the irreversible nature of most land development, it may be easiest to take a rather pessimistic view and to plan for the worst" (Wilcove and May 1986). Several strategies can help minimize the difficulties of managing for disturbance. First, protected areas must be large from the outset. Second, protected areas should allow migration and gene flow that may be important to the ecosystem as a whole. Third, use of adjacent land should be controlled, preferably by establishment of buffer zones. This means that planned disturbance can be undertaken without adversely affecting neighbors, and that major unplanned disturbances on neighboring land (e.g., uncontrolled fires) have minimal effect on the protected land.

A first step in managing plants occurring under disturbance regimes is to determine the characteristics of the system—size, frequency, intensity, and precise nature of disturbance (Boucher 1981). It is also necessary to know how target species respond to these events singly and in combination. There may be more than one disturbance agent, for example, grazing, fire, and wind throw may interact. Each will independently create different types of disturbance and create different regeneration sites. Collectively they may provide a range of necessary sites for target species.

Once the key regeneration agents, the nature and extent of disturbance, and the reactions of target species to disturbance are identified, it becomes possible to make some predictions about the general kind of disturbance that will best allow conservation of the target species. Small-scale variations in disturbance and stress should be considered. Even minor variations over a few meters in soil and microtopography can drastically alter the germination percentage of some species.

Simple manipulation of the germination regimes of seeds—of amounts of light and litter, water level, and the grazing levels of herbivores—can yield dramatic results. Longer periods of experimentation will be required to observe the effects of such factors on later stages in a plant's life cycle, but much can be inferred through study of age classes in different stands of vegetation and their distribution in relation to habitat variables.

A simple management plan for a disturbance regime might specify the following (P. Keddy, pers. com.): current abundance of target species, desired abundance of target species, major natural disturbance agents, regeneration of target species in each kind of natural disturbance, the disturbance regime to be established and methods for attaining this regime, postdisturbance manipulations (if any) to be performed, a monitoring system to assess progress toward the goal and provide further information on refinements that may be needed in the management regime. Such a series of steps can be refined to give more quantitative answers. There will always be a measure of uncertainty because of interactions between treatments and perturbations, extrapolations from the areas used in experiments, and variance in the outcome of experiments.

Like disturbance, stress is sometimes regarded as a negative factor in plant communities, perhaps because it tends to be associated with drought, floods, and storms, which cause losses of agricultural crops and stock, houses, and human lives. Both are naturally occurring events, and only in recent years has stress-tolerance in natural biological communities begun to receive the attention it should. Examples of naturally stressed communities are commonly found on extreme dry or wet sites, saline and serpentine soils, and areas that are seasonally flooded.

Three life history features are critical to the persistence of species, particularly in stress situations: life span, propagule longevity, and establishment requirements (van der Valk 1981). In combination, these lead to an array of basic life history types. In stressed environments, such as wetlands with fluctuating water levels, only a small number of life history types may persist at any one time (Keddy and Reznicek 1986). Study of the life history types present and desired can indicate the patterns of disturbance necessary to provide growing conditions for the target species.

There seems to be support for the suggestion that regular disturbance prevents competitive species from dominating and excluding weaker competitors (e.g., Keddy 1985; Reznicek 1986). It has been suggested several times that many rare plants may be weak competitors that persist only where environments prevent exclusion by more successful competitors. This concept has been recently extended with the suggestion that in some communities where competition is most intense (for instance, on highly fertile sites), not only are there fewer species but also there is morphological convergence (Keddy, in press). In contrast, a vast array of life forms and a diversity of species are found on sites where the constraints of intense competition are released. Therefore, a site's "health" for rare plants is not necessarily improved by revegetation programs if these result in the ousting through competition of the very species for which preservation is a goal.

Infertile and naturally disturbed wetlands have long been targeted for "improvement" programs under the guise of conservation (Moore et al. 1989). They are recognized as diverse and botanically interesting, with narrow endemics and other rare plants. Study of such sites indicates a predominance of stress-tolerant species. A study of wetlands in eastern Canada by Moore et al. (1989) showed that wetlands in which substrate lacked essential nutrients had higher species richness, more vegetation types, and many more rare species than did fertile wetlands. Thus disturbance and stress should not be looked on as necessarily negative.

In managing for disturbance and stress, there is need to distinguish between species density, biomass, species diversity, and morphological and genetic diversity. Increase in biomass does not necessarily correlate positively with species number; rather, the number and kinds of vegetation types and species will often increase as total biomass in the community decreases. In highly stressed situations, this may mean having to maintain many nature reserves or large areas of natural habitat in order to represent a full array of low-biomass environments.

Restoration of infertile sites to favor stress-tolerant species will not be achieved unless the role of stress is taken into account. Conventional species used for revegetation programs may be quite unsuited to high-stress situations. Recovery and recolonization rates are likely to be very slow, but it cannot be assumed that even the species normally present will respond favorably when stress is minimized; they may respond by declining.

A rather different situation arises when plants are stressed by unnatural factors. This occurs when the habitat of a species deteriorates and environmental stochasticity becomes significant. Both relatively large populations and a scattering of populations (a metapopulation structure) may be needed to ensure survival. The potential effects of environmental stochasticity are not necessarily reduced by relatively modest increases in population size; massive population numbers may be required where unnatural stresses are frequent and large. This means that in managing stressed populations there should be an indication of the relative contributions of demographic and environmental stochasticity. The primary consideration should be to maintain, or build up population numbers until obvious extinction risks can be minimized to an acceptable level. Conversely, small populations in unnatural high-stress situations may not persist for long without costly and time-consuming intervention.

Management needs of disturbance-prone ecosystems are now fairly well understood, but far less attention is given to the management and conservation of stress-prone communities and both stress-tolerant and stress-prone species (P. Keddy, pers. com.). For example, gravel or sandy areas that are seasonally flooded support many rare species. Such habitats often have peculiar nutrient levels, or are infertile—a situation that is difficult to recreate once such sites have become nutrient enriched.

Where stress and cyclic changes are part of the natural pattern for an ecosystem, conservation managers must be prepared to provide or simulate the habitat resources and natural stresses needed by the species (i.e., the right kinds, quantities, and in the right locations; Figure 5.3). Unnatural stresses must be reduced or altered to simulate closely natural patterns of stress and perturbation.

Figure 5.3. Managment techniques need to be developed for the conservation of plants in highly disturbed or stressed habitats, such as lake shores. Lake Superior, Ontario, Canada. (D. R. Given)

Control of disease, predation, and invasive weeds

Disease, predation, and competition from other plants can be limiting factors even for large populations (Drake and Mooney 1989). Well-known examples include the effects of chestnut blight and Dutch elm disease on northern temperate forests, and dieback disease caused by *Phytophthora cinnamomi,* a soil-borne fungal pathogen (von Broembsen and Kruger 1985; von Broembsen 1989). The most devastating effects tend to occur when populations are small. There is often wide variation in susceptibility of various species to disease. Dieback caused by fungi is quite common in forests but often has profoundly different effects on even quite closely related species. In Western Australia, sheoak (*Casuarina*) is only moderately susceptible to the ravages of *Phytophthora* and may persist in a diseased state for many years. In contrast, *Banksia grandis* and *Persoonia longifolia* are highly susceptible and die rapidly following infection.

Some animals are notorious for their predation on plants. Chief among these must be goats, sheep, and pigs, although the list of significant mammalian predators is very long and includes rats, various deer species, thar, Australian brush-tailed opossums, and cattle. Sometimes predation of individual species can greatly lower reproductive rates—as much as 50–80 percent destruction of seed. Intensive browsing of young leaves can lead to general weakening of plants, making them more susceptible to stresses such as drought and insect attack.

Control of predation in protected areas is rarely easy once predators are well established. Ideally, harmful predators should be eliminated while their numbers are still small and before the problem reaches epidemic proportions. This requires an early warning system that can not only detect known predators before infestation is heavy, but also predict which animals and plants may become predators once introduced to areas outside their natural areas of distribution.

Trapping, shooting, and poisoning are still probably the most widespread control methods for larger predators such as goats and pigs. Use of herbicides and fungicides is standard for many plant infestations and fungal problems. Increasing interest is being paid to biological control using organisms that themselves prey on the predators. Such an option is environmentally desirable but usually involves a long period of research, prerelease testing against possible hosts and vectors, and release trials. Trials and testing are essential. The expense of biological control methods specifically tailored to one particular pest has to be weighed against the repeated treatments needed if other control methods such as chemical sprays are considered, as well as damage to the environment caused by repeated use of chemicals.

In the case of predation by larger animals, especially herbivores, control of herbivore numbers often needs to be supplemented by exclosure fencing to keep the animals away from target plants and habitats. Fences must be appropriate to the habits of the animal; for example, fine-mesh netting is appropriate for excluding small animals such as hares and rabbits. In extreme instances, protection may have to extend to individual plants using netting cages. In a few cases, total elimination of exotic animals has been achieved, as with the removal of rabbits on Round Island, near Mauritius, and of goats on the Kermadec and Three Kings Islands of New Zealand. Such operations, to have long-term value, must be total in effect and followed up by an inspection program.

Invasive weeds can create considerable problems for the management of some species, especially endemics occurring in small numbers. Species of *Lantana, Acacia, Hieracium, Ammophila arenaria* (marram), and *Hippophae rhamnoides* (sea buckthorn) are of particularly wide occurrence as weeds. Often, the primary biological effect is to shade out competitors, but some vigorous species have a range of effects including lowering of the water table and release of growth inhibitors into soil or leaf litter. There is controversy over whether the negative effects of exotic plants are necessarily associated with general habitat disturbance—a crucial issue for protected areas with large numbers of visitors. Whatever the answer, there can be little doubt that weed control will remain a necessary strategy in protected areas if the survival in the wild of some plants is to be assured.

CASE STUDY: FOREST MANAGEMENT IN WESTERN AUSTRALIA TO COMBAT DIEBACK DISEASE

The Forests Department adopted a three-pronged attack on the dieback disease problem in state forests: the development of accurate maps of disease location, the application and continuous updating of stringent hygiene procedures, and the management of the forest ecosystem to create conditions unfavorable for the fungus.

The sequence of management began with three years of quarantine, followed by use of aerial photography, and finally the production of accurate maps of disease distribution. Operations were under strictly controlled hygiene procedures. These included confining forest activities to summer periods safe from disease, washing of vehicles, limitation of vehicle access in the forest, and specification of more appropriate equipment for some tasks. Ecosystem-oriented procedures included the following:

- Cooling and drying the surface soil by improving the density of tree crowns and promoting dense, low understory vegetation.

- Improving the proportion of certain plants in the understory such as *Acacia pulchella,* which have been shown to contain substances that actively reduce zoospore numbers and inhibit their germination.

- Improving the overall nutrient status of the site (e.g., by promoting an understory of legumes).

- Improving the ability of the most important host (jarrah) to resist infection through improvement of tree health.

- Reducing the disease inoculum potential by removal of highly susceptible species such as *Banksia grandis.*

- Avoiding any modifications to soil drainage patterns that would make soil more suitable for sporulation and zoospore survival.

- Eliminating or minimizing any disturbance that leads to the puddling of soil, which can stimulate zoospore production.

- Ensuring that water used is free of fungal inoculum.

- Ensuring that all nursery plants are free of dieback.

Source: MacKinnell 1981.

Management plans

Organisms belong to dynamic systems. Their conservation, especially in human-dominated systems, must be the result of active and deliberate management. All protected areas should have management plans (master plans) to determine priorities, guide the allocation of resources, control all development activities, and implement management actions. Management plans take into account a wide range of biological, physical, and social factors and the changing nature of ecosystems. They address the levels of genetic organization—biome, ecosystem, species, population, and individual. They promote the well-being of target species, habitats, and resources (Roche and Dourojeanni 1984). Management plans are particularly important for remnants of vegetation in highly modified landscapes. The greater the degree of intervention, the more the need for well-formulated and detailed management prescriptions (Hobbs 1987).

Recovery and management plans are essential to effective population management. They take account of the critical information needed for management and the type of program to be undertaken, consider available resources, and allow for biological and social constraints. Management plans for threatened species have particular characteristics. Some degree of urgency usually is involved, and often it is important to specify particular research requirements, numbers of individuals, and numbers of areas. Finally, an integrated approach to sampling and monitoring is required (Dawson 1987).

Core characteristics of management plans include the following (modified from MacKinnon et al. 1986):

- A statement of goals and measurable objectives, which provide a framework. Objectives can be arranged to form a priority list.

- Provision for review within a stated time period, often five years. Plans should be continuously reviewed as new information is received or new techniques become available.

- Identification of resources such as staff and funding, short- and long-term needs, and deficiencies. This requires close links and feedback between management and research, advocacy, and education.

- A highly practical presentation. Conclusions and strategies need to be expressed simply and in the language of the staff who will execute them. Technical language, lists of species, and highly scientific descriptions should be avoided; they can be appended separately to the main plan.

- Scientific and technical input. Management plans will be deficient unless there is full opportunity for input from scientific and management expert user groups and the general public.

- Presentation of the plan as a communication tool to gain understanding and support of both the general public and relevant government officials.

- Treatment of the whole planning process as an exercise in educating and training management personnel. It outlines the processes of management, and identifies priorities and points of conflict.

Prior to preparation of a comprehensive plan, which may take many months or even years to finalize, it is often necessary to prepare interim management guidelines, especially if there is a paucity of information about the region, habitat, or target species. The interim status of such guidelines should be clearly stated but should be no reason for not managing. Interim guidelines often lack statutory backing—a matter that deserves legislative attention.

One protected natural area cannot be managed in isolation from another. Clusters or networks of reserves should be managed as integrated units. This is a critical issue in regions where many small remnants of native vegetation remain. Long-term conservation may require transfer of plants from one site to another and restocking or reestablishment of vegetation and populations using adjacent sources. Two levels of management are necessary, one at the regional level and the other to deal with individual sites. Sometimes additional site plans specific to sites within protected areas may be necessary, for instance, for sensitive sites close to development areas that have high visitor use. In the case of small reserves, for instance those of about 10 hectares or less, the management plan may approximate the concept of a site plan. Site plans are particularly relevant to conservation of narrow-range endemic plants, which are likely to require management quite specific to their particular biological needs.

A necessary derivation of the management plan is the *annual operational plan*. This sets out anticipated activities for a calendar year and shows how the management plan will be put into action. Such a plan indicates objectives for the year, available resources and the budget required to achieve objectives, a time chart to show a seasonal schedule of work, factors that may prevent the achievement of objectives, further resources that may be needed, and progress in the previous year. Annual operational plans have not received wide publicity or use despite their obvious utility. They should certainly be adopted where a protected area has significant numbers of endemic species or sensitive vegetation types, or is under pressure from high use. Their use ensures that managers are aware of both long-term and sort-term objectives, and that there is at least an annual assessment of management needs and effectiveness.

Survey and monitoring must be incorporated into management plans. Sometimes it is necessary to present several monitoring options depending on the results of management. Survey and monitoring lead to ongoing feedback between research and management, each providing a check on and modifying the other. As a result, recovery and management plans are dynamic documents. They are not designed to be written then put on a shelf to gather dust. This is especially the case with plans for threatened plants. Threats, abundance, and habitat conditions may change quickly—even in a matter of weeks or days. Mechanisms must exist to amend the plan in step with this. Plans must be specific yet flexible enough to cope with rapidly changing situations.

A *recovery plan* is a form of management plan designed to mitigate factors that have led to the decline of a species. A recovery plan should summarize information on the distribution, habitat requirements, biology, threats, taxonomic status, and conservation status pertaining to the target plant, and should describe past conservation efforts directed toward that species (e.g., Schwegman 1984). Factors limiting population size and extent should be identified where possible. The plan should list objectives for management and quantified means by which these can be achieved. Needs for resources and finance should be indicated. Inventory, survey, and monitoring should be clearly differentiated in a recovery plan.

Initial management and recovery plans should be supplemented and followed up by periodic status reports outlining management activities that have been undertaken as well as recommendations for ongoing management. Such status reports are conveniently prepared on an annual basis, summarizing what has been done over the reporting period and listing priorities and a work plan for the coming period.

Where possible, single species management should be avoided, even where there is a management document concentrating on just one species. Survey and monitoring may concentrate on particular species or individuals, and clearly, certain species must be highlighted. But management plans must consider entire ecosystems. It is unfortunate that legislation as well as education programs tend to concentrate attention on single species, sometimes to the detriment of whole communities and other species (Dunn 1987).

Management of islands

Islands feature prominently in conservation strategies, but their management raises some awkward questions (Heywood 1979; Atkinson 1990). Islands are often out-of-the-way places with relatively few people living on them. Why should the conservation and future of island floras be a concern? The simple answer is that islands have many interesting plants. They are often homes to rare, narrow-range endemic species and archaic or primitive forms. Islands increasingly function as isolated sites where rare species facing extinction elsewhere can be established in the absence of competitors and feral animals. It may well be that large numbers of organisms may only survive into the twentieth century on isolated island refuges. On the other hand, islands are often highly vulnerable to change, especially to introduced predators. Also, what happens on islands is an early warning of what can happen in larger continental areas as habitats are fragmented (Given 1983).

Islands have both advantages and disadvantages

for conservation of plants. Inherent advantages as reserves are their clear boundaries, concentrations of narrow-range endemics so that many species can be conserved in the one area, and isolation from natural invasions. Disadvantages can include access, a generally narrower range of species than found in a piece of comparable habitat of similar size on the adjacent mainland, and vulnerability to both deliberate and unintentional introduction of feral animals and weeds.

Multipurpose management models often have been applied to islands. These advocate a range of uses such as grazing, forestry, and conservation on the same area of land. The uncritical adoption of such a model for management of islands that have not known intensive browsing by herbivores, where natural fires are rare events, and where human influence has been minimal may be unwise (Juvik and Juvik 1984; Meurk and Foggo 1986). On larger islands, a more appropriate approach would be a multifaceted one promoting a mosaic of developed, buffer, and natural areas; on smaller islands, a single-purpose approach is appropriate. Ecosystems of small islands are highly susceptible to disruption. This susceptibility is intensified by competition for arable land as human populations increase beyond the carrying capacity of islands. The casualties are often the unique species found on the islands. The role of islands in conservation resolves down to protection of relict species, restoration programs, and recovery programs for translocated species, but each of these has potential to create conflicts (Figure 5.4).

The following guidelines for management of small islands for nature conservation were adapted from Hall and Veldhuis (1985):

- Whenever possible, the entire island should be protected as a reserve.
- Ideally, and particularly on small islands, no residents should live in the protected area. If possible, no staff should live there either, but they should visit and patrol on a regular basis. If a base is maintained on the island (e.g., if the island is oceanic and moderately large), limits of buildings and modified areas must be clearly demarcated.
- Very strict regulations should be enforced to prevent the introduction of exotic animals or plants. If introduced species have already reached the island and are a threat to the original species, they should be eradicated.
- Where the entire population of a plant occurs on a small island, or is confined to one more or less continuous patch on a larger island, it is advisable to transfer part of the population to a second suitable site to avoid the risk of loss through natural disaster or depletion through disease.
- Efforts must be made to prevent camping by visitors to the island. Islands, especially in the tropics, are highly susceptible to fire and vegetation removal.
- If the surrounding waters have high conservation value, they should be included in the reserve, or as a buffer, so that overall use can be controlled (not necessarily discouraged).

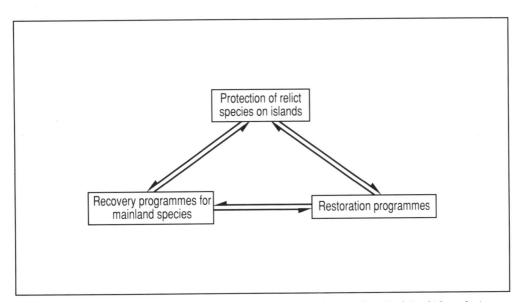

Figure 5.4. Conflicting conservation goals for islands can be expressed as a conflict triangle in which emphasis on any one goal restricts achievement of other goals. (Reproduced by permission from Atkinson 1990)

Invasive weeds and animals are a continuing threat for oceanic islands, although the example of Round Island (see below) shows that restoration is possible, at least for small islands. Where there are permanent inhabitants, things may be more complex. For instance, on the Azores, trees such as *Cryptomeria japonica* are planted close to some areas that are important for nature conservation; these trees have potential to spread. Invasive aliens such as *Gunnera* and *Hedychium* invade bare and open surfaces (Sjögren 1988). On the Galapagos Islands, *Cinchona* is a threat in the endemic cloud forest, and on Tahiti, invasive *Miconia* is rapidly spreading as a weed. Generally, sites of minor importance for agriculture are more likely to be protected than those that are accessible and have good agricultural soils.

Worldwide, many islands are given high priority for conservation, not only because of their distinctive species and the degree of damage that has already occurred to their fragile ecosystems, but also because of the lessons they teach for management of more populated and less remote regions. But the future of island floras will depend largely on political, social, and economic factors and the constraints these put on planning and protection. The role of island biologists is not just to work in the field and laboratory but to organize and communicate their knowledge so as to influence planning and protection decisions (Heywood 1979).

Case Study: Recommendations for Management of Endemic Species on Ile Aux Aigrettes, Mauritius

Ile aux Aigrettes, a small uninhabited island (ca. 25 hectares) off the southeast coast of Mauritius, was declared a nature reserve in 1965. Several of the plants found there are almost extinct on the mainland, including ebony (*Diospyros egrettarum*), bois de boeuf (*Gastonia* cf *cutispongia*), manglier (*Sideroxylon boutonianum*), and vacoas (*Pandanus vandermeerschii*). Despite legal protection, vegetation continued to deteriorate. In 1984, the island was leased to the Mauritius Wildlife Appeal Fund, and in 1985 an expedition carried out botanical and ecological surveys. Little regeneration of native trees was occurring because of competition from exotics and fruit predation. Trees had been cut for timber (especially the ebony), opening up the forest. An urgent series of recommendations were made for management:

- At least three full-time guardians should be employed to protect the island from illegal woodcutting. Accommodation should be provided for the guardians near the main jetty, and should include a good water supply.

- A boat with motor engine is essential for the guardians

along with a permanent and adequate fuel supply. Guardians should be armed for self-protection and equipped with portable radios.

- Duties of the guardians should initially include cutting and treatment of *Tabebuia*, an invasive exotic. *Casuarina equisitifolia* should also be eradicated before it spreads further.

- At least two cats were found by the expedition and should be eradicated.

The island also has several other harmful introduced animals, the worst of which is the black rat. These eat fruits and seedlings of native plants. An eradication program was started in 1986, which, it is hoped, has been successful. An eradication program is also planned to eliminate introduced Indian house shrews. A replanting program has been started using native plants. In the absence of illegal woodcutting and with intensive weeding, eradication, and propagating programs, Ile aux Aigrettes is beginning to return to its former natural state.

Sources: Wyse Jackson et al., in Strahm 1985; Strahm 1989.

Case Study: A Strategy for Island Management

1. Identify the critical conservation values associated with each island of biological significance using the following criteria:
   A. Vascular flora and presence of rare or threatened taxa.
   B. Invertebrate and vertebrate fauna and presence of rare or threatened taxa.
   C. Biotic communities present, both those representative of widespread community types and those unique to the island.
   D. Unusual geology or landforms.
   E. Human history.
2. Identify those islands where the most stringent preventative measures should be taken against the establishment of rats or mice, and other predators.
3. List all threatened species that require islands for recovery of population numbers.
4. Identify the most suitable islands for each threatened species based on their requirements for habitat and maintenance of genetic diversity.
5. Analyze the impact on each island's conservation values of those species proposed for translocation.
6. Select the appropriate protective and restorative measures for all threatened species requiring islands as refuges.
7. Integrate species-centered recovery programs with other aspects of management, including restoration

programs for biotic communities and management of the adjacent marine environment.

8. Interpret the chosen management action to the public, involving their participation whenever possible to build a broader base of public support for conservation.

Source: Atkinson 1990.

CASE STUDY: ROUND ISLAND—A SUCCESS STORY

Round Island, a 151-hectare nature reserve about 20 kilometers off the northern coast of Mauritius, is of exceptional biological importance. It supports the last remnant of a palm savanna that was once characteristic of the northern plain of Mauritius, but which is now extinct there; it is one of the few remaining rat-free tropical islands of the world; it is an important breeding site for seabirds and supports eight species of native reptiles; and it is said to support more threatened plant and animal forms than any comparable area on earth (one bird, six reptiles, nine plants).

Until the 1980s, Round Island was threatened by introduced rabbits and goats released in the nineteenth century. Much of the island's soil had been lost through erosion following the introduction of the feral animals. The goats were removed in the 1970s, but rabbits were more difficult to eradicate. By the early 1980s, the situation was critical. In 1986 three scientists were sponsored by the Jersey Wildlife Preservation Trust to spend two months on the island and poison the rabbits. The following year a follow-up for one month showed that the rabbit eradication program had been successful. Aided by an unusually wet season, vegetation recovery has been rapid. Herbs, grasses, and creepers had colonized many bare sites by mid-1987, and many palms were seeding, including over 80 rare bottle palms (*Hyophorbe amaricaulis*).

Two weeds that could cause future problems were eradicated at the time of the second visit. The sites where these grew were marked to allow future checking. Many hundreds of seeds have been collected for help in revegetation, as well as samples of long-dead wood to help gain an idea of the previous vegetation cover.

Unglamorous as it was, the removal of rabbits from Round Island is a highly significant conservation achievement that will greatly aid the survival of some of the world's most endangered species. The management plan for the next 10 years envisages three brief visits to the island each year to carry out a range of monitoring and restorative operations. Of five available options, the favored approach is to eradicate weeds, allow species recovery and reestablishment, but also to introduce carefully selected species of critically endangered animals and plants from Mauritius.

Source: Merton et al. 1989.

The special case of the tropics

The tropics present some peculiar and vexing problems for plant species management (e.g., Myers 1986c, 1988; Jacobs 1988; Collins et al. 1991). These problems largely are the result of the following:

• The large size of many tropical floras, and the lack of detailed knowledge of the species in these floras.

• The meager resources sometimes available (people, finance, expertise, and equipment).

• The perception of some governments, development agencies, and private enterprises that natural resources in the tropics provide cheap products for the developed world and allow short-term settlement of debts incurred by underdeveloped nations.

• Rapid rates of habitat deterioration and loss. This means that some tropical regions may be fortunate if inventories are completed before the areas being studied disappear. The opportunities for actual research, survey, and monitoring, and resultant management are very meager indeed.

There are two developments that affect plant species management in the tropics. The first is the focus on acquiring protected areas to cover whole ecosystems. The hope is that individual species will also receive protection. A modification of this approach is to focus on areas of known high endemism. The second major development has been a triage strategy in which species are separated into three categories—those that do not require urgent attention and will survive, at least in the short term, with no specific management; those that are beyond help (at least with present resources); and those that can be saved from extinction by appropriate management using realistically available resources. Both approaches require some hard, and at times distasteful, choices. It is difficult to see large areas of natural habitat destroyed and species allowed to drift toward extinction.

Availability of resources is an important issue. If management of large numbers of tropical species is an international concern, then the international community (and especially the developed world) must support the work. Individual countries may have to divert resources away from some of their own conservation problems toward those of the tropics. The international community must adjust trading patterns and demands for goods originating in the tropics so that they do not place further, intolerable pressures on tropical species and habitats.

Managing with limited resources

Where management resources are limited, priorities become very important. Preference has to be given to protection of particular species, sites, and ecosystems before others. Such preferences are never likely to satisfy everyone. Some questions that should be considered when setting priorities for conservation are listed:

- Are there species or ecosystems that are particularly vulnerable, either because of location, inherent characteristics (for example wetlands, which are readily polluted), or trends in land use?
- Which species are vital links (keystone mutualists) in energy and food chains?
- Which species are endangered throughout their whole range or are becoming increasingly depleted?
- Are there plants that are sole representatives of families or genera?
- Are there species related to domesticated crops that are traditionally harvested or that have potential for domesticating or harvesting?
- What programs have some chance of attracting sufficient funding?
- Are there species or habitats that are going to be so expensive to "rescue" that the quantity of funds they will absorb will jeopardize the conservation of other foci of biodiversity?

Clearly, in many regions, knowledge of ecosystems and individual species is not sufficient to make absolute judgments about values even if there was general agreement on criteria (Hopkins and Saunders 1987). Nevertheless, priority order must be considered. It is not possible to do everything at once and rarely will resources be sufficient to do everything that is desirable. Research should be directed toward species that will yield the maximum information for overall management of a reserve system, that is, species essential to the ecosystem and the persistence of other species.

Management of protected areas does not come free. It can be assumed that costs of management are more likely to escalate than to decrease. In too many instances, management has come to a standstill because it was assumed that necessary resources would become available. Similarly, it is tempting to keep adding new protected areas into a system, but each time this happens it is necessary to budget not only for setting up a reserve (land purchase, fences, signs, etc.) but also for continued management. Cuts in research funding too often occur in those areas that are of most value to the conservation of plants, including population biology and monitoring. These are not seen as revenue earning and monitoring in particular is criticized as being "open-ended." Funding must be sufficient to carry out the minimum necessary to maintain a viable conservation program. The following steps can be considered if funding becomes insufficient:

- Seek advocacy for adequate funding.
- Put management of plants and their habitats before the building of expensive visitor facilities.
- Look to alternative funding sources, such as formation of a trust or greater involvement of local interest groups.
- Seek greatest efficiencies in use of resources, and especially do not commit management to long-term, highly expensive programs that may be difficult to maintain when resources become scarce.
- Adopt a longer time frame for rescue and restorative programs. Sometimes high costs may be incurred because a very short time frame is adopted.

As already noted, volunteer groups can sometimes reduce running costs. Especially where rare species are concerned, volunteers are often very willing to work on maintaining a protected area, especially if they feel they are making a real and permanent contribution to conservation. Similarly, the cost of land purchase can sometimes be avoided by facilitating protection of habitat and species on private land using covenants and other contract agreements.

CHAPTER 6

Off-site Plant Conservation

Off-site conservation is the conservation of plants away from their areas of natural occurrence. The term does not include conservation by replanting in the wild—often termed *translocation*. The term *ex situ* is frequently used for what is described here as off-site. For many people, the term *off-site* immediately brings to mind plants growing in botanic gardens. These certainly constitute a major example of off-site conservation, but the concept extends as well to field gene banks, clonal collections, and germ plasm banks where propagating tissues and seeds are preserved for growing in the future. It also includes preservation of old cultivars and laboratory techniques such as tissue culture. Off-site conservation can involve a range of plant parts—the whole plant, seed, other tissues, or genetic material in culture. For botanic gardens, and for other off-site institutions, the conservation mission is a broad one (Ashton 1987).

Whole, living plants have particular value for conservation and will continue to be a major concern of off-site conservation. But conserving whole plants is not simple. To capture the range of genetic variation, such collections require large numbers of plants; these are expensive to establish and maintain. If the plants are annuals, they will require seasonal replication. Outside their natural habitat some plants may require hand pollination and special treatment of fruit and seeds to ensure germination. It is fortunate that improving technology is making storage as seeds, seedlings, rhizomes, tissues in culture, and even DNA an option for many plants.

A fundamental question is, Should botanic gardens (and other off-site institutions) help to save rare plants? Sometimes botanic gardens actually have hindered conservation when certain basic requirements were not observed. The conservation of plants (especially as a genetic resource) may require changes in some traditional attitudes. It certainly demands sufficient resources. Institutions that wish to become in-volved in off-site conservation need to ask themselves if they have the capability to work on the following priority species for conservation (Botanic Gardens Conservation Secretariat 1989):

1. Wild species
   A. Rare and endangered (at local, national, regional and global level) species
   B. Economically important species
   C. Species required for restoration or rehabilitation of ecosystems
   D. Keystone species (i.e., those that are known to be of particular significance in the maintenance and stability of ecosystems)
   E. Taxonomically isolated species whose loss would be serious from a scientific point of view
2. Cultivated species
   A. Primitive cultivars
   B. Semi-domesticated plants

Achieving these priorities is complex enough when one is dealing with plants whose biology is simple, particularly if they are small and do not take up too much space. It becomes much more complex with larger plants such as trees, and with parasites and species with complex biological relationships (Thompson 1975). It also becomes difficult when financial and human resources are extremely limited.

In the face of threats to much plant life, off-site conservation is becoming more important as a back-up, and sometimes a temporary replacement, for conservation in the wild (Heywood 1990). It is crucial to integrated conservation. Plants grown for many years simply for their general interest are suddenly found to be the only remaining individuals of their species, those in the wild having become extinct. For animals, the possible elimination of most tropical wildlife habitat, and a coming "demographic winter," means that off-site conservation is a necessity (Soulé et al. 1986).

For plants, the overall situation can scarcely be different. In an increasingly fragmented landscape it is not surprising that cultivation in botanic gardens and storage of germ plasm is seen as a growing need. In one example, the Xishuangbanna region in China, even if four nature reserves totaling 200,000 hectares were set up, there would probably still be some 1500 species (11 percent of the flora) outside those reserves (Xu Zaifu 1987). There are many examples of plants whose chances of survival have been increased through off-site conservation (Figures 6.1 and 6.2).

Figure 6.1. Off-site conservation has greatly enhanced the chances of survival for *Serruria florida* from southern Africa. (D. R. Given)

Figure 6.2. *Pennantia baylisiana* from the Three Kings Islands, New Zealand, has a greatly enhanced chance of survival thanks to off-site conservation efforts. (Courtesy of Anthony Wright)

CASE STUDY: *RAMOSMANIA HETEROPHYLLA*—A PLANT SAVED BY OFF-SITE CONSERVATION

The rediscovery of *Ramosmania heterophylla* on the small Indian Ocean island of Rodriquez in 1980 caused considerable excitement. It had not been seen since 1940. Attempts to ensure the survival of the one plant in the wild were jeopardized by browsing animals and insect pests.

In 1986, two cuttings were sent to the Royal Botanic Gardens, Kew, England. A medium-sized plant plus two smaller specimens were established by 1988. The poorer of the two cuttings sent from the island was used to provide material for micropropagation, but bacterial contamination has been difficult to eliminate. Nonetheless, if it works, micropropagation will allow the faster propagation of plants.

Unfortunately, little was known of the cultural requirements of this species, so temperature, light, and humidity requirements were estimated. Success so far is limited but indicates that there is still hope for even critically threatened species that have been reduced to a single individual.

The long-term future of this specimen of *Ramosmania heterophylla* is by no means certain. It is female sterile but produces viable pollen. About ten plants have now been propagated by conventional means, but in a sense this one clone is a metabolically active herbarium specimen and scarcely constitutes a species in the biological sense. It is, however, a valuable symbol for the endangered flora of the Mascarenes, the subject of a multidisciplinary program by the Mascarene government working in collaboration with the Mauritian Wildlife Appeal, WWF, Jersey Wildlife Trust, and the Royal Botanic Gardens, Kew, among others.

Source: M. Maunder pers. com. 1993.

CASE STUDY: THE DECLARATION OF GRAN CANARIA

For centuries, botanic gardens have been major centers for the scientific study of plant diversity, providing a mechanism for introduction and assessment of plants for agriculture, horticulture, forestry, and medicine. They attract more than 150 million visitors a year, affording havens of beauty and tranquility for an increasingly urban society, and a spiritual link with the plant world on which we all depend. They inform and educate; they are showcases for the living world, places where science and people meet.

For historical reasons, most botanic gardens are in the cooler, more industrialized countries of the world, but two-thirds of all plant species occur in the tropics and subtropics. More than 60,000 species risk extinction within our lifetime because of the destruction and degradation of the earth's vegetation, which is the basis of human survival. Recently, many of the world's botanic gardens have mobilized their resources for conservation action to avert this threat. They are conserving plants in the wild, cultivating them in gardens, and preserving them in gene banks.

Recognizing that they can only succeed in achieving these objectives if they work together, botanic gardens throughout the world are uniting to apply the World Conservation Strategy to the special predicament of plants. Basing their efforts on this global plan for sustainable development and conservation of living resources, they will produce, adopt, and implement a Botanic Gardens Conservation Strategy.

This declaration is the result of the 1985 Las Palmas Conference on Botanic Gardens and the World Conservation Strategy, involving more than 200 leading specialists from countries throughout the world. The declaration asserts these institutions' determination to work together to defend plant life for the benefit of all people now and in the future. It calls upon governments to provide the necessary support and resources, in accordance with their responsibilities.

Source: Bramwell et al. 1987, updated.

The Role of Botanic Gardens in Conservation

Botanic gardens have played a significant part in the exploration of the world's plant resources, introducing many economically important species into cultivation for the first time and disseminating them. Botanic gardens were the forerunners of today's agricultural experiment stations in that plants were evaluated for their potential contribution to agriculture. Botanic gardens are again assuming importance as repositories of valuable genetic material.

The origins of plant domestication, agriculture, and horticulture are lost in the mists of antiquity. The cultivation of garden plants must have began some thousands of years ago. Certainly, many cultures have grown plants for pleasure, utilitarian use, and for ceremonial purposes for many centuries. It was in the Middle Ages that the concept of a botanic garden took root in Europe and from there spread to other parts of the world. The first recorded botanic garden was probably one established in 1545 at the University of Padua in northern Italy, although similar institutions were known earlier in eastern Asia. Padua soon became an important center for acclimatization of plants gathered by botanists venturing outside Europe. By 1591, it contained 2000 species. The example was set for similar gardens to be established in other cities such as Pisa, Leiden, and Oxford.

There are many different kinds of botanic gardens and arboreta (Botanic Gardens Conservation Secretariat 1989):

- Traditional state-supported, with associated herbarium and laboratories; open to the public (e.g., Berlin, Kew, Bogor, Pera eniya).

- Municipal or civic, sometimes with an associated herbarium and laboratories, normally open to the public (e.g., Gothenberg, Glasgow, Nantes).

- University, with an associated herbarium and laboratories, usually open to the public (e.g., Cambridge, Berkeley, Hamburg, Montpellier).

- Private, often with some state support, with an associated herbarium and laboratories, usually open to the public (e.g., Missouri Botanical Garden).

- Private, without state support, usually without a herbarium or laboratory (e.g., Les Cedres, Maurimurta).

- Government/state arboretum with an associated herbarium and laboratories (e.g., U.S. National Arboretum), or without herbarium (e.g., Westonbirt).

- University arboretum with an associated herbarium and laboratories (e.g., Arnold Arboretum).

- Private arboretum with or without herbarium or laboratories (e.g., Hilliers, Bickelhaupt, Morton Arboretum).

- Botanical-zoological gardens or parks (e.g., Hong Kong, Wilhelma Stuttgart).

- Agro-botanical gardens (e.g., Godollo, Gatersleben, Castelar).

Alongside the traditional botanic garden are other off-site assemblages such as germ plasm collections, experimental gardens, medicinal gardens, mountain or alpine gardens, specialist plant group collections (e.g., cacti and succulent gardens, and orchid sanctuaries), and highly manipulated areas of quasi-natural vegetation intermediate between botanic gardens and indigenous vegetation reserves. Apart from this there is also a multitude of private gardens.

About 1500 botanic gardens and arboreta are known worldwide (Botanic Gardens Conservation Secretariat 1989). Perhaps several tens of new botanic gardens come into being each year. Most are found in temperate areas of Europe (400), North American (174), and the former USSR (158) (Figure 6.3 and Table 6.1). In contrast, there are far fewer in tropical Africa, tropical Asia, and South America, where the greatest numbers of wild plant species are found. The present pattern of gardens largely reflects patterns of eighteenth- and nineteenth-century colonialism.

Many of the earlier gardens arose to fulfill needs for acclimatization of plants, or to provide collections of medicinal and herbal plants. For example in the tropics, botanic gardens were used to introduce tropical

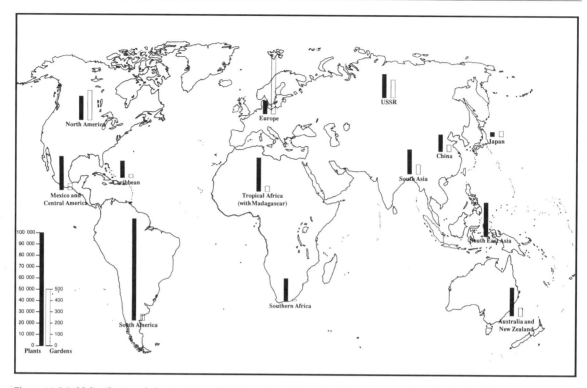

Figure 6.3. World distribution of plant species and botanic gardens. (Reproduced by permission from Botanic Gardens Conservation Secretriat 1989).

plants for economic exploitation. Consequently, many tropical gardens started with an economic rather an academic bias and thereby laid the foundations for agriculture and forestry. Botanic gardens were thus part of the exploration and introduction system from which the activities of international agricultural organizations are derived. Gardens gave rise to national botanical surveys, forestry and agriculture departments, and experiment stations.

Until recently, most botanic gardens have not regarded the conservation of plant diversity as a primary goal. Some gardens are little more than beautifully maintained public parks. It is unfortunate that the distinction between public parks and botanic gardens is not always understood by the public or by politicians. All botanic gardens, to a greater or lesser extent, maintain living collections of plants. Many carry out research; some have impressive laboratories and concern themselves with a wide range of horticultural and botanical topics. Even now, probably only a minority of gardens have a clear mandate to conserve botanical diversity (Falk 1987; Heywood 1987).

There are five main justifications for growing plants for conservation purposes: to have as many threatened plants in cultivation as practicable as insurance against their loss in the wild; to cultivate critically threatened species in sufficient numbers to ar-

Table 6.1. Geographic distribution of botanic gardens and arboreta by region.[1]

Region	No. of gardens	No. of arboreta	Population
Europe	392	64	500,899,461
Former USSR	121	34	266,674,000
Southwest Asia	14	2	134,508,085
South & Southeast Asia & Oceania	107	50	1,322,957,070
Australia & New Zealand	47	8	18,125,857
China, Japan, Mongolia, & Taiwan	66	13	1,144,269,000
North Africa	10	--	89,170,000
Tropical Africa	28	2	329,846,340
South Africa	14	1	25,590,000
North America	98	92	252,219,951
Middle America	36	--	93,133,378
South America	51	1	236,979,117
Caribbean	20	--	28,764,205

[1] Included here are only those institutions that have been identified as botanic gardens and arboreta in international surveys. Many small gardens are likely to have been omitted.

Source: Heywood 1987

rest genetic erosion; to have material available for research and assessment for economic use; to have collections of plants available for education programs and public displays; and to propagate and maintain plants suitable for reintroduction into the wild, or to reinforce wild populations.

The botanic garden can be far more than just an amusement park or a strictly research-oriented establishment. The very word *botanic* suggests a fundamental emphasis that is lacking in areas set aside purely for amenity, recreational, or horticultural use. The other word, *garden,* indicates more than just a laboratory or herbarium function. Being a garden does not mean that attempts have to be made to grow everything. Specialized gardens are just as successful and interesting to people as more generalized ones. Examples include alpine plant gardens, herbal gardens, collections of plant families or habit types such as cacti and succulents, and plants of specific habitats such as wetlands. Some gardens, such as Selby Botanical Gardens in Florida, USA, have specialized in collections of epiphytes (G. Prance, pers. com.).

The primary role played by the botanic gardens of the world is unique. No other structure can replicate their work. Botanic gardens form a worldwide network of centers with special skills in the cultivation and propagation of plants. They are visited by many tens of millions of people annually, and so influence a significant proportion of the world's population, especially in urban regions. They are an interface between the world of wild plants, botanical science, and the public.

Conservation of plant cultivars and genetic resources

To many people, *plant conservation* means preservation of wild plants. The importance of maintaining cultivars and plants with direct use for humanity is often forgotten. At their beginning, some botanic gardens served the function of evaluating crops and other economically useful plants; today, most maintain collections of specific groups of cultivated plants, especially genera and families of horticultural and medicinal value. Gardens have played a crucial role in the preservation of important species and genotypes and their subsequent introduction into agriculture and horticulture. As correctly pointed out by Williams and Creech (1987), many gardens have not been highly successful in maintaining such special purpose collections, and inflated arguments are sometimes used to justify conservation by appealing to vague possibilities of social use of plants. Nevertheless, the

role of publicly financed botanic gardens in genetic resource conservation should not be underestimated.

Some old cultivars have been discarded and will be permanently lost unless samples for future use are maintained (Brickell 1986). There may be good arguments for conserving cultivars that are now endangered. Although not usually from wild sources, they consist of unique genetic assemblages, which have potential value in a world where genetic options are narrowing. Certainly, the conservation of cultivars and of wild species should not be seen as competing, mutually exclusive exercises (Given 1987a).

Cultivar preservation requires close cooperation with a wide range of local, national, and international organizations. This may run from liaison with local horticultural groups to, at the highest level, contact with agencies such as the International Board for Plant Genetic Resources (IBPGR), international breeding stations, and agricultural gene banks. These are often in contact with databases that can assess the importance of particular garden collections. Linking with network organizations maintaining heirloom varieties of many hundreds of garden plants serves a double purpose: it ensures that botanic gardens are linking their collections with others (private and public) and it also increases public awareness and empathy.

CASE STUDY: LOSSES OF HORTICULTURAL CULTIVARS

One has only to look at lists of ornamental plants in the pre-1940 catalogs of plant growers and compare it with equivalent lists today to appreciate the decline in the range of cultivars available to the public.

What are the arguments for retaining cultivars? One could argue that 90 percent of cultivars could disappear without causing a ripple in the agricultural/horticultural calm. But among the remaining 10 percent, there may be cultivars or mutants of species containing gene complexes able to provide an irreplaceable combination of physiological or morphological characters for future breeding. Many cultivars have evolved over many centuries from species that are now extinct.

Apart from very compelling economic arguments, it is important to consider cultivars from historical, educational, and scientific viewpoints. Knowledge of cultivated plants encourages people to understand the need to conserve flora and to appreciate humanity's requirements for plants and achievements using them. Cultivars can be useful for both applied and pure research—their chemical, physical, and genetic make-up provides much useful information—especially as many can be grown more readily than wild species. The esthetic appeal of plants also should not be underestimated: they are comparable to the paintings of great artists.

Five basic questions must be asked:

1. What cultivated plants are important and what cultivars are still available?
2. Which should we maintain and why?
3. How can conserved stocks be maintained and used?
4. How are resources to be found?
5. Who is to be responsible for maintaining stocks of cultivars?

There are no simple answers to these questions. But similar issues applying to other areas of conservation have been resolved. Coordination is a key aspect of this process and needs to involve a range of organizations. In the British Isles, the setting up of the National Council for the Conservation of Plants and Gardens has been an important step toward resolving these issues.

Source: Brickell 1977.

CASE STUDY: A SET OF CRITERIA FOR BOTANIC GARDENS

Living collections give botanic gardens their name, but other criteria may be met in part or whole, including a reasonable degree of permanence; an underlying scientific basis for the collections; proper documentation of the collection, including wild origin; monitoring of the plants in the collection; adequate labeling of the plants; open to the public; communication of information to other gardens, institutions, and the public; undertaking of scientific or technical research on plants in the collections; and maintenance of research programs in plant taxonomy in associated herbaria

Source: Botanic Gardens Conservation Secretariat 1989.

CASE STUDY: THE LAS PALMAS STRATEGY

Three main objectives of living resource conservation are identified in the World Conservation Strategy: to maintain essential ecological processes and life-support systems, to preserve genetic diversity, and to ensure the sustainable utilization of species and ecosystems. Six distinct areas of activity are directed toward these objectives:

Mission. Gardens and arboreta should have a distinct mission, and should respond to changing roles and new circumstances. Each garden should have a public mission statement as well as adequate monitoring of progress.

Collections policy. The essence of a garden is its living collection. Plants grown should be of known provenance and interest to local people. They should be those that do well under local climate and soil conditions. Sometimes little use is made of plants except for display.

Documentation. The World Conservation Strategy survey showed that standards of record keeping in gardens are often poor. Recording systems should be reviewed and compatible computerized systems should be used where possible.

Conservation activity. Guidelines and case histories are useful to develop the reasons for conservation of plants in gardens. The problem of global genetic depletion needs to be appreciated. Population structure and size needs to be appreciated, as it applies to botanic gardens. There should be closer interaction between in situ and ex situ conservation. Gardens should look at ways of dealing with regions where the flora is still poorly known.

Education. About 100 million people visit botanic gardens throughout the world. Botanic gardens should function as windows into the natural world. They should, where appropriate, be involved in regional conservation issues.

Community role. Involvement of the local community in the work of gardens leads to greater appreciation of the gardens' role. A garden's mission statement should include a statement about community involvement.

Source: Botanic Gardens Conservation Secretariat 1989.

Collection of material

Sampling of plants (usually from wild sources) must be with a clear end point in mind. The purpose may be to display plants in a botanic garden for educational purposes, to exploit a population commercially for agriculture or forestry, to propagate material for translocation, to provide single genes for incorporation into domesticated plants, or to provide a last refuge against extinction (Given 1987a; Brown and Briggs 1991).

Each of these purposes may have rather different sampling requirements. The following discussion focuses on the desire to maximize genetic diversity off site, while recognizing the practical constraints of finances and personnel.

Regardless of the final destination or purpose, accurate and relevant information on incoming plant materials must be available. It is important for a garden to record and evaluate whatever information is provided. Plant material of unknown origin has limited use for ongoing conservation research and management. Such material should not necessarily be discarded, especially if the species is critically endangered. Every accession adds something to the gene pool and can help maintain genetic variability (Cullen et al. 1987), but this is no reason to be careless about documentation or seeking the appropriate sort and quantity of plant material. In the past, some botanic gardens were content with growing only one or two specimens of doubtful origin.

Many different types of plant material may arrive at a garden: seed, simple or rooted cuttings, layers, grafts, tubers, bulbs, or whole plants. Material may come from a variety of sources. It may come directly from the wild. In this case, full collecting details should be available. Second, material may come from a cultivated plant originally from a wild source. In this case, full collecting details and data on subsequent cultivation should be available. Third, material may come from a cultivated plant of unknown wild origin. This group includes plants lacking necessary documentation to confirm wild origin, as well as plants of known or unknown cultivated origin.

The type of plant material and method of collection may indicate the expected degree of genetic variability in a particular accession. Collectors should consider carefully the appropriate material for a particular purpose, although in some instances, especially with critically rare species, choices may be very limited. In general terms, incoming plant material can be classified as either seed, cuttings, bulbs (or other underground parts), or whole plants (IUCN 1985a; Brown and Briggs 1991).

Seed

Timing of collections may be critical as some seed is shed very quickly. Whether a seed sample from the wild can be regarded as a statistically meaningful sample of the genetic stock of the donor population depends on sampling techniques and the reproductive strategy of the species. For this reason, sampling details should be passed on with seed. If the seed is of cultivated origin, two possibilities must be kept in mind. First, if the seed was produced by self-pollination or controlled pollination, or the parent is known to be apomictic, the resultant material can be treated as for wild source material. If the seed came from uncontrolled open pollination, then the resultant plants cannot be assumed to be genetically pure. A great advantage of seed is that its generally small size allows storage of large numbers.

Cuttings

These can often be obtained throughout the year but have the disadvantage of fragility and very limited life while being transported to a propagation house. Use of cuttings for conservation places strict limits on size of samples, especially as each unit is only effectively sampled after it has struck and grown into a mature plant (losses with some species can be very high). Genetically, cuttings are replicates of living individual plants from the source population; they are ideal for sampling particular genetic traits such as flower color variants.

Bulbs, corms, tubers, and off-sets

This is an alternative for certain families such as Orchidaceae, Droseraceae, and Liliaceae. Advantages and disadvantages are intermediate between those of seed and cuttings. These can usually be regarded as representing the same genetic stock as the parent. Where genetic integrity is critically important, for long-lived trees and predominantly vegetatively reproducing long-lived herbs, somatic mutation may mean that there is significant genetic divergence within the plant. This may require comparison of the genetic composition of the donor and propagated plants using electrophoretic techniques. Time of collection is likely to be quite critical: it may be feasible only during periods of dormancy.

Whole plants

Collecting whole plants may be necessary if there is complete failure with propagules (seed, cuttings, etc.), or it may be the best option if a population is facing imminent destruction. Generally, taking of whole plants is inappropriate, and conservation on site should take precedence over the off-site option, although this depends on the precise circumstances. Obviously, transfer of whole individuals involves transfer of the genetic make-up of wild individuals.

Is a single specimen enough for off-site use? In the past, only single specimens often were taken; many botanic gardens and arboreta have large numbers of species represented by single-specimen accessions. A single specimen may be adequate for education or display purposes, but it is inadequate when maintenance of diversity is to be systematic (Hawkes 1987a, 1987b; Williams and Creech 1987). If the goal is to conserve biodiversity, then a fundamental objective will be to capture as much of the genetic diversity within a species as possible. Some botanic gardens have set up dedicated collections to conserve genetic diversity (Figure 6.4).

Where species are repeatedly collected from the wild, there is a tendency to take propagating material from the same sites and to collect the biggest and most vigorous plants, or those with peculiarities particularly suited to garden culture. This can lead to off-site survival of highly selective portions of the total genetic variation of a species. This becomes a matter of particular concern when a plant is critically endangered and reintroduction into the wild is contemplated (Given 1987a). The primary techniques to use

Figure 6.4. A display of *Juniperus communis* from a range of provenances demonstrates the genetic diversity of wild populations. Cambridge University Botanic Garden, England. (D. R. Given)

to achieve satisfactory representation of genetic variation are random sampling, stratified sampling (dividing the habitat into homogeneous blocks and sampling within these), systematic sampling (equally spaced grid or transect sampling), and biased sampling (based on variation in appearance). Stratified random sampling is probably the best choice, if it can be readily done (Brown and Briggs 1991). Supplementary biased samples should be handled independently from overall population samples.

A further matter involves sampling of several populations. On the one hand, differences among populations are usually not as significant as differences among species or subspecies. On the other hand, such differences are likely to be more significant than variation within a population. Sampling of several populations is a particularly important matter for inbreeding or asexual species. Clustering of populations needs to be considered: few species approach randomness in the dispersal of their populations, and clustering is reflected in patterns of genetic distribution. Clustering reflects several factors, especially patterns of original evolution and migration and habitat variation. This is likely to result in genetic differences between clusters of populations, so that different clusters may need to be regarded as distinct sampling units (as if they were different target "species"). This would allow variants such as cold-tolerant and altitude-tolerant forms to be adequately sampled.

Maintenance of genetic variability starts at the collection stage. The fact that clear guidelines for sampling, based on the reasons for collecting, are lacking has meant that (with the notable exception of wild relatives of crop plants) collectors rarely indicate how many plants were sampled, the pattern of sampling, or even when sampling was done. It is tempting to take seed or cuttings as rapidly as possible from as few plants as necessary, but a consistent and meaningful sampling strategy is important. Genetic variation is the raw material that increases the chance of a target species surviving through changed circumstances in off-site collections, and that makes the material suitable for storage, commercial use, or translocation (Brown and Briggs 1991).

Genetic variation can be expressed as *allelic richness* (the diverse array of different alleles needed to meet future environmental requirements), as *gene diversity* or *heterozygosity* (to avoid inbreeding depression), and as *genet richness* (the range of distinct genotypes in a particular population). On the basis of these three ways of looking at genetic variation, guidelines for sampling strategy can be enumerated (Brown and Briggs 1991).

First, with regards to allelic richness, the aim of sampling should be to recover in the sample at least one copy of common alleles with a guaranteed probability of about 0.90–0.95. To meet this objective a random sample of 50–100 individuals is required. Any further effort should then be spent visiting as many different and diverse sites as possible, rather than obtaining a larger sample at one site. For endangered species there may be some constraints. Large numbers of species may be involved, populations are often small, and within-population variation may be high. There may be objections to regarding some genes as more important than others, and to concentrating on common ones at the expense of those that are rare (frequency in the population of < 0.10). A counterargument to this is that in small endangered populations, frequencies are likely to be severely truncated anyway; sampling should be aimed at preserving the species as a whole. Much depends on the actual value chosen for *minimum frequency;* excessive resources will be required to collect for relatively few alleles if the value is too low. On the other hand, the prospect of climate change may mean that some low-frequency alleles governing physiological processes may become extremely important within the next few decades if some species are to survive. Overall, an appropriate minimum target for each population is probably 10 individuals, especially if this means that resources can be used to sample other populations.

Second, the assessment and measurement of gene diversity in plants is fraught with problems, especially because plants have a host of reproductive strategies available and may not be randomly mating (as is sometimes assumed). Sample size has to be very small for a real reduction in gene diversity to occur, and in terms of survival probability (the key issue in discussing gene diversity and inbreeding depression), there will be great variation among different plants. Even when off-site populations (e.g., in a botanic garden) originate from very small samples, it can be possible to achieve higher than natural levels of gene diversity through deliberate crossing of a few individuals as part of a planned propagation program.

The third way of looking at genetic variation, known as genet richness, takes no account of the nature and extent of genetic differences between each genotype or the intensity of testing for genetic differences. It is a particularly useful consideration where there is a predominance of vegetative reproduction. For outbreeding nonclonal species, the relationship between genet richness and sample size approaches linearity because each individual is unique. What is important in practice, however, is the size of sample necessary to ensure that at least one of those genets that is genetically equipped to survive off site is collected. Statistical treatment suggests that this is generally achieved by sampling at least 15 individuals per species. For dioecious species each sex should be sampled separately, with a minimum of 15 from each. Sampling and subsequent culture of propagating material should aim to maximize s/N, where s is the number of genets equipped to survive both sampling and off-site conservation, and N is the number of genets in the parent population. Where s/N is very low (e.g., < 0.1), low persistence times off site may have to be accepted.

In addition to these three ways of looking at genetic variation and sampling needs, other ways have been suggested. For instance, a goal could be to provide a 95 percent probability that all alleles with a frequency of at least 5 percent in the population are taken. As another possibility, attention could focus on rare genetic traits such as those that increase the amount of a desirable chemical in a plant.

Once plant material is collected, it is often customary to distribute small numbers of seeds or other propagating material to a relatively large number of institutions. The reason is quite logical. No institution likes to have all the material of a critical plant in one place; it is good insurance to spread it around. But this may lead to reduced genetic variability within each recipient garden or collection (similar to the bottleneck phenomenon sometimes encountered in the wild). Therefore, while some sharing should be encouraged, at least one institution, and preferably more, should hold enough material to include a fair proportion of genetic variation (Given 1987a).

Skewed genetic representation may inadvertently result from differential survival of plants under cultivated conditions. When seed is germinated away from the wild a new and unfamiliar set of selection pressures operate. As the plant passes through various stages of its life cycle it will encounter further selection pressures very different from those it would find in the wild state. Consequently, the genetic representation of individuals that survive to maturity may be very different in wild and cultivated populations (Figure 6.5). It is impractical to avoid this, but the problem should be recognized, particularly when critically important off-site collections are being rejuvenated. A solution is to make greater use of rare species in quasi-wild landscape plantings such as roadside plantations. It is important that conservation in gardens involves preservation of representative gene pools for research and practical rehabilitation and not just static museum collections (Bramwell 1979).

The collector of material for conservation is faced with many questions: What taxa? When and where to collect? What type of propagule? What type of individual? How many individuals in the sample? How many populations? Principles to keep in mind are the

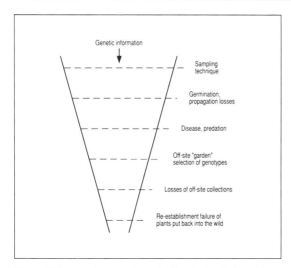

Figure 6.5. Progressive loss of genetic diversity in off-site cultivation is one consequence of selection pressure under cultivation. (D. R. Given)

purpose of collecting, constraints off site (for instance, Can a recipient garden handle the sample size and type of material?), collecting resources, and the urgency for off-site conservation. It is easy to go overboard in effort on one taxon and to fail to act on others.

Case Study: Recommended Minimum Sample Sizes From Wild Populations

Within populations. If seed is being collected for direct processing into storage, then collect sufficient seed from 10–50 individuals to give a stored sample (ideally about 1000 seed, depending on seed size). Ten is the number to strive to meet as a population minimum. Fifty represents the ideal when seed is easy to collect from such a number of plants. Maximize the diversity within the sample by collecting as many distinct fruits (to increase the number of pollination events and pollen sources), at different times, from different microhabitats. Aim to represent each source plant equally. To maintain options, it is desirable to keep the seed from individual plants separate, if this is feasible. The overall goal of 1000 seed is about a tenth of that suggested previously and is considered a more practical minimum. Samples of fewer than this will need later resampling or multiplying off site. If material (cuttings, etc.) is being collected for growing off site, sample ten individuals from varying microhabitats or randomly, but include any morphological variant to be both genetically based and of definite interest.

Between populations. Diversity usually can be increased by including more sites with fewer samples per site. A reasonable approach is to collect from all populations if there are

around five or fewer. Where there are more populations, a clustered arrangement is sensible to take account of hierarchical patterns of variation. For most threatened species the numbers would be a maximum of five clusters with one to two populations per cluster. For two to four clusters, one would sample two to three populations per cluster. The choice of five populations or five clusters per species as a maximum rests on the idea that with samples of 10 individuals per population, an overall sample of 50 is achieved.

Source: Brown and Briggs 1991.

Case Study: Variable Survival of Species Transplanted from the Wild

In Upper Teesdale, particularly on Widdybank Fell, many species rare to the British Isles are found. Over a period of ten years, attempts were made to preserve these rare plants through cultivation in the face of threats posed by dam construction. Transplants were established at Durham and Cheshire (Jodrell Bank). The primary aim of the project was to establish methods of maintaining these plants in cultivation and to judge the cost-effectiveness of such a project.

Plants were transplanted in 1970. Fifty individuals were taken from each site. They were grown in large concrete boxes using soil similar to that from the Teesdale sites. Vigorous species required dividing and replanting. Some of the Teesdale species proved to be troublesome weeds. For instance, *Thymus drucei*, once established, easily swamped other species, and *Campanula rotundifolia*, which has underground stems, was impossible to eradicate once established.

Considerable variation occurs in the long-term persistence of species in cultivation. Six of the species were highly successful in cultivation, and limited success occurred with several others. In spite of showing promise in early stages, *Gentiana verna* and *Primula farinosa* were failures. This point is important because what happens in the first season or two of cultivation may not necessarily be an indicator of long-term success.

Growing conditions in cultivation will be different from those encountered in the wild. Many of the Teesdale species are arctic-alpine plants and were exposed to unnatural conditions in the experimental plots, perhaps making them more susceptible to such factors as caterpillar attack. The growth of some species was vigorous, creating problems of division and replanting. Further, the weaker individuals in a culture could be crowded out, thus reducing the genetic variation in a sample, as, for instance, in *Saxifraga aizoides*.

Source: Cranston and Valentine 1983.

Avoiding introduction of disease and predators

Plants taken from the wild can readily acquire diseases and pathogens under cultivation. The effects of this can be devastating if plants lack natural defenses or immunity. Damage and death are not necessarily restricted to cultivated specimens, because diseases and pathogens can be transferred from garden to garden or from a garden to the wild when plants are reintroduced into their natural habitat. Attempts to reestablish plant populations in the wild through replanting can turn out to be a good intention gone wrong if diseased material is used. For critically threatened plants, quarantine procedures should be adopted even when transferring plants from one garden to another, especially where there is any possibility of reestablishment in the wild from off-site stock (Given 1987a; von Broembsen 1989).

The transfer of diseases from one country to another is an increasing problem. The risk of spreading pests, especially of crops, increases with the level of exchange of plant germ plasm. The development of rapid air transport means that there is a greater chance of viable pests being taken from one continent or island to another within a few hours. Shifting of whole plants by this means creates greater hazards than transport of seed. If propagating material requires a significant time to grow into mature plants, dormant stages in the life cycle of pests and diseases usually become apparent.

Clearly, increased surveillance and more rigid quarantine procedures are necessary (Plucknett and Smith 1989). Increasing volumes of international plant exchange strain plant quarantine services, which are frequently under pressure to reduce budgets. Fortunately, there is a trend toward use of virus-screened materials, such as callus derived from tissue culture, for transferring of important plant breeding material from one country to another. Similarly, there is increased interest in use of reconstituted DNA to transfer important genetic stock. Apart from being in a form where it can be incorporated in other genomes by laboratory techniques, such plant material can be freed from contamination by most plant diseases.

Six principles for effective quarantine of plant materials are listed (after Plucknett and Smith 1989):

1. *A wide range of scientific disciplines should be involved.* The core staff of plant quarantine services should include specialists with training in virology, bacteriology, mycology, nematology, malacology, entomology, and weed science. If such skills are not available in-house, arrangements must be made to have this expertise readily available at short notice. To reduce chances of obtaining diseased material, plant pathologists should be included in teams gathering germ plasm samples, especially when collections are extensive and involve species that may be widely disseminated.

2. *Pests and pathogens should be ranked according to the importance and chances of becoming established.* Germ plasm from centers of diversity should receive the most scrutiny, since such material is most likely to harbor the most species and races of pests and pathogens. One must keep in mind, however, that what is a pest in one region may not be in another, and sometimes quite unexpected plants and animals acquire nuisance value once they escape.

3. *Plants should be quarantined in areas isolated by ecological conditions from the respective crop or target species growing areas.* When plants need to be raised from germ plasm before release of the plant material, observation is best conducted well away from areas where the target species grows. This especially applies to important crops.

4. *Quarantine services should be reasonably flexible.* Quarantine officers should be allowed a certain amount of discretion when passing judgment on plant materials. This is especially the case when germ plasm is critically important and cannot be readily collected again.

5. *Quarantine services should be decentralized to improve efficiency.* Decentralization avoids the bottleneck that occurs when materials are brought through one processing center. It allows specialization of different parts of the quarantine network.

6. *Effective quarantine facilities should have access to good communication and transportation services.* This is vital to smooth operation of services. Delays can threaten the viability of germ plasm. Major urban centers enjoy superior transportation facilities and are also likely to have reliable supplies of electricity as well as easier access to engineers and technicians to operate laboratory equipment.

The devastation caused by *Phytopthora* root disease and Dutch elm disease is an indication of what can happen when disease spreads rapidly among plants that lack natural defense mechanisms (von Broembsen 1989). Similarly, fire blight is a long-term threat to many Rosaceous shrubs. It is essential that botanic gardens and protected area managers have access to the same range of expertise as quarantine authorities, especially if establishment of plants back into the wild from cultivated sources is contemplated.

Documentation

Good records facilitate the systematic build up and maintenance of collections, and interchange of information and plants (Cullen et al. 1987). It is useful to classify types of provenance and plant material to assess the conservation value and potential use of accessions (Figure 6.6). Documentation systems range from manual card indexes and register books with minimal information, to complex computerized systems. Garden record systems are ideal candidates for computerization. Computing systems offer many attractive features, for example, many ways to access data, flexibility of record keeping, and convenient transfer of data to other databases. Many gardens have

taken this step or are contemplating it, especially in Europe and North America. The emergence of personal computers (PCs) and proliferation of database programs specifically designed for PCs has made computer-based storage and retrieval of data an attractive proposition. The resources required to maintain a system must not be underestimated. Computer hardware, software, and systems development cost money. Record accession by machine requires ongoing expenses, which are not likely to be less than those required for equivalent manual systems.

Changes in accessions, new identifications, shifting of plants to different parts of the garden, and deaths must be faithfully recorded in the database with minimal delay. Otherwise the records system becomes misleading, of little value, and may even waste valuable time when spurious information is treated as true (Cullen et al. 1987). Problems frequently arise when multiple categories initially are created for informa-

		MATERIAL TYPE		
		Seed (Code S or O)		Vegetative Material (Code V)
P R O V E N A N C E T Y P E	Direct from the wild (Code W)	Location data, etc. from collector WS		Location data, etc. from collector WV
	From a cultivated plant of known wild origin (Code Z)	Selfed seed (including apomicts) Location data, etc. from donor ZS	Seed from open pollination No location data ZO	Location data, etc. from donor ZV
	From a cultivated plant not of known wild origin (Code G)	No location data GS	GO	No location data GV

Figure 6.6. Integrity of plant materials in relation to provenance type. (Reproduced by permission from Cullen et al. 1987)

tion that may be required some day. Often, the information is recorded for only a small percentage of plants, or it is retrieved rarely. Such an over-elaborate system can eventually "clog." At the same time, it is important to include essential information at the beginning of a project. The following list constitutes the minimal amount of documentation to strive for (Snogerup 1979; Cullen et al. 1987; Given 1987a):

Accurate identification. It is essential that specimens be accurately identified and vouchers, where possible, deposited in a herbarium. This is particularly important for plant groups such as sedges and grasses, for which flowering and fruiting specimens are often required if precise identification is to be achieved. Verification of identifications should be performed by others with duplicate plants; every effort must be made to avoid mixing or shifting of labels.

Identification of provenance. Too often information on the place of origin of plant material is imprecise. Information should be sufficient to allow another person to return to the site and replicate the original collection. If the information is altered or simplified in the database, full original details must be retained in a supplementary file.

Collection details. These include collector and date of collection, and collection number (where used).

Type of material. Type of material collected (e.g., seeds, cuttings, tubers, or whole plants) must be indicated.

Supplementary data. Other data that greatly enhance the conservation value of plants include (a) the size and condition of the parent population; (b) area covered and number of individuals; (c) the sampling method used to obtain propagating material (whether from a single individual or from many, and if the latter, then the method of choice); (d) whether material came from typical or atypical plants (Given 1987a).

Supplementary information is particularly important for critically endangered species, where most genetic variation may be restricted to off-site collections. An ongoing record of history following collection greatly enhances the conservation value of captive plants. Even quite widely cultivated plants may represent clones derived from a single introduction to horticulture. Records of propagation history give insights into the genetic variation of a captive species. On the one hand, continued vegetative propagation may perpetuate a narrow genetic base, but uncontrolled outcrossing may lead to introgression by related species growing nearby.

Full records are not always maintained to show what has been lost from cultivation and why, or to indicate where progeny has been distributed. In many instances, although botanic gardens acquire hundreds or perhaps thousands of new plants each year, their total overall number of accessions remains approximately the same. The implication is that gains are balanced by losses. Rarely is the question asked, Why has a particular species died?, but such information may give important insights into the cultivation requirements of a species or point to management problems that can be avoided.

CASE STUDY: THE INTERNATIONAL TRANSFER FORMAT (ITF) FOR BOTANIC GARDENS DATABASES

These standards deal only with international transfer of data and in no way affect transfer systems evolved regionally (although their regional use has obvious advantages) or internal use of a database by a particular garden. In fact, gardens should use ITF standards as a guideline when designing their own databases. The areas of information constituting the ITF minimum are as follows:

1. Accession data
   A. Accession number
   B. Garden code
2. Plant name data
   A. Generic, specific, and infraspecific names
   B. Cultivars and hybrids
3. Taxonomic verification data
   A. Identification qualifiers
   B. Verification
4. Source and origin data
   A. Donor
   B. Provenance and material type
   C. Geography and collecting details
5. IUCN conservation category

These items are of prime importance and are likely to be included in any form of garden records system. First priority is to produce data files in ITF to allow rapid updating of records of conservation interest by comparison with conservation database records. Building data from ITF into a garden's own system can come later. The ITF allows gardens worldwide to compare their holdings and to identify both critical species they hold and wild species that they should acquire.

Sorting out some of the categories of information is not as simple as it might seem. The naming of plants (nomenclature) is complicated by such issues as synonyms (different names for the same plant), treatment of complex hybrids, and inconsistent naming of cultivars. Common names are sometimes useful adjuncts, but they may vary widely among different countries. Assessing the significance of various types of sources may be difficult as well; there are times when origin of material is completely unknown.

Sources: Botanic Gardens Conservation Secretariat 1987; Cullen et al. 1987.

Maintenance

It is little use building up a well-documented collection to have it languish through lack of attention. This is particularly important for those gardens holding collections of critically threatened species that may be close to extinction in the wild. There may be no second chance if cultivated plants are lost through neglect.

It is of primary importance to have systematic, regular inspections of accessions. These should be done on a monthly basis, as a minimum, with more frequent inspection of critically threatened species and species that may be prone to sudden loss or disease. Regular inspection should relate to individual plants so that it does not just amount to a cursory inspection of a particular bed of plants. The following information should be noted in such an inspection: actual presence of individual plants in terms of absolute number; flowering, fruiting, or significant growth phases; significant changes in plant size and health; cultural problems such as overcrowding or soil/water problems; and damage or loss due to human influence or other biotic factors

Problems noted during an inspection should be followed up immediately. For example, if there is damage to critical specimens through trampling or visitor disturbance, increased surveillance may be necessary without delay. Flowering and fruiting should be drawn to the attention of staff who may wish to propagate the species, have drawings or photographs prepared, or study breeding.

Where plants are suffering from disease or do not appear to be growing adequately, the garden must have access to information that leads to remedial action. This requires a basic horticultural library and access to files of past case histories. Gardens should have working relationships with institutions that can diagnose pathogens and predators. Amateur growers often have a considerable store of expertise in particular plant groups; a register of local experts can provide a quick means of obtaining advice.

It is fundamental that the right kinds of habitats be maintained for the plants being grown. Some species may be amenable to cultivation in conventional plantations or garden borders, but many others have special requirements beyond those normally encoun-

tered with plants in cultivation. Where special habitats have to be constructed, it will be necessary to check periodically that such factors as soil acidity, texture, nutrition, and drainage are still satisfactory for the plants being grown (Smith 1979).

Maintenance of living collections of plants requires a wide range of professional, technical, and management skills. These skills are required not only to service gardens themselves, but also to meet the changing needs of clients. Botanic gardens should be located to provide this, but must take into account the peculiarities of wild habitats and not just the rather specialized environment of a well-manicured garden.

Are all botanic garden and gene bank staff aware of conservation issues and how they are, or should be, involved? Although many botanic gardens provide formal training and diploma courses, few adequately cover environment protection, basic principles of conservation, and the role of off-site conservation of plants. There is clearly room to develop training courses with a strong conservation orientation at various levels of expertise (Simmons and Beyer 1985). A full appreciation of the place of conservation will only be achieved by the training of new staff and by motivating experienced gardeners to seek greater understanding of the plants in their care. Such training should extend to administrators who may have little practical experience in conservation or even in horticulture (Heenan 1985; Given 1987a).

Liaison and technical training

Established gardens can assist others with fewer resources, but caution must be exercised when transferring ideas and methods from one site to another. There is no instant and universal formula for a botanic garden or for an off-site conservation program. Visits to other, established gardens can be useful, but attempts to transplant unaltered the practices of one garden to another are almost always doomed. This is particularly the case where a temperate garden is taken as the blueprint for a tropical one, or vice versa (Simmons and Beyer 1985).

Botanic gardens do those things best which cannot be done elsewhere. But they must relate to a large number of diverse institutions and interest groups (Wagner 1972). There are reasons for some gardens to support a wide range of functions; however, this must not result in pointless duplication. For example, if a well-organized independent herbarium and associated taxonomic unit is located within reasonable distance of a botanic garden, every effort should be made to ensure that the two complement each other so that there is cooperation and not competition. In this way each draws on the other's strengths while countering its own inherent deficiencies. Examples of the types of programs that benefit from cooperation and collaboration among botanic gardens and other institutions are listed here (Williams and Creech 1987):

Programs	Potential level of collaboration
Germ plasm acquisition	
Monitoring of genetic erosion	Low–high
Collecting of endangered germ plasm	Low–high
Selective collecting for diversity gaps	High
Facilitation of germ plasm distribution	Moderate
Germ plasm characterization and evaluation	
Data acquisition from accessions	Moderate
Training	
Specialized technical courses	Moderate
Genetic diversity program	
Species mapping	High
Ecogeographical studies	High
Isozyme analysis	Moderate
Wild relatives of priority crops	High

Botanic gardens are not the only places where plants are cultivated off site. Sanctuaries and parks set up for educational purposes may also play a valuable role in the cultivation of threatened plants. A significant number of rare or endangered plants are cultivated outside botanic gardens in such places as public parks, landscape plantings, school or college grounds, private gardens and collections, collections held by scientific institutions, and collections of sponsors of collecting expeditions (Botanic Gardens Conservation Secretariat 1989). Such holdings must not be ignored simply because they are not part of a formally recognized botanic garden system. The role of private gardens and collections in particular is significant and should not be overlooked. It is important that institutions and groups with related aims in conservation work with each other to ensure that effective communication channels are developed and that cooperative programs make best use of resources. Cooperation is, in fact, a key issue: it must be fostered, especially when resources for conservation are limited.

Raising plants in botanic gardens is no substitute for protecting them in their natural habitats. Botanic gardens should not merely pride themselves on holding collections of organisms that no longer exist in the wild. They should also emphasize to their visitors that preservation of habitat is of primary importance and that the role of the garden is to complement, not substitute for, preserving plants in the wild. Garden holdings, ideally, should be complemented by natural habitat reserves (Williams and Creech 1987). Gardens can conduct appropriate research on garden-grown plants, such as studies of phenology, seed physiology, and floral and dispersal biology. They can provide a source of material of known origin and cultural history for planting back into the wild. Ultimately, they act as an insurance against loss, by storing seeds and other propagating material in gene banks.

There is great potential to explore the establishment of satellite or seminatural gardens. Group or regional cooperative policies can be developed that link the programs of botanic gardens with other conservation agencies (Simmons and Beyer 1985). In some instances botanic gardens are able to maintain botanical reserves and lead programs to reestablish plants in the wild. This is especially appropriate where a facility's holdings include, or are adjacent to, areas of wild or semiwild habitat. Another, albeit costly, aspect of this is habitat reconstruction, where natural habitat is created afresh, sometimes within the garden boundaries. This requires considerable collaboration with field botanists to profile correctly the natural community being recreated.

CASE STUDY: PROPOSED FORM OF TRAINING FOR VARIOUS LEVELS OF BOTANIC GARDEN STAFF

Senior managers: study visits. Before undertaking expensive study visits, senior managers should have access to a reliable source of information on where to go and what to see.

Scientific staff: postgraduate studies. These are likely to be specific, with the participant having some knowledge of his or her particular field of study and interest.

Technical managers: summer schools. Technical managers need to know how to refine policies, within the context of development of a botanic garden, to meet specific objectives. An open-forum learning program is one way to help managers develop skills in this area. Such a setting encourages discussion of common problems among managers from different gardens, and promotes consideration of other management options. Such programs could serve a region, concentrating on problems specific to a group.

Technical staff: internships. It is necessary to offer both horticultural and management skills training to technical staff. Such training must take into account ethnic origin, level of education, and cultural/societal differences among staff.

Summary of major skills and educational background required of botanic garden staff. These include management training, horticulture, plant physiology, landscape design, media skills, conservation, biogeography, computer skills, and fund raising.

Sources: Simmons and Beyer 1985;
Botanic Gardens Conservation Secretariat 1989.

CASE STUDY: A BOTANIC GARDEN FOR CONSERVING FOREST IN CAMEROON

In January 1988, the Cameroon and British governments signed a project document for the conservation of rain forest and the refurbishment of Limbe Botanic Garden. The garden had been established in 1892 at the foot of Cameroon Mountain at the Town of Victoria, now called Limbe. The British government's Overseas Development Administration will cooperate with the Cameroon government to use the garden as a national and international base for conservation of genetic resources in the adjacent forests.

Cameroon is one of Africa's richest countries in terms of animal and plant species. A lot of primary forest still exists although it is fast disappearing. Protected areas require demarcation, legal recognition, and staff to protect them. Protection, in turn, requires funding at levels that developed countries can support. The theory behind this project is that an integral reserve can safeguard mother trees of sufficient size and variability to provide the seedlings for other plantations of timber, fruit trees, and so forth. Such an effort needs the back-up of an organization like Limbe Botanic Garden, which is ideally placed and already established, although in need of restoration.

The garden will act as a control center for several reserves. Staff will carry out training and research, be involved in education, and assemble collections. A collection of African palms will be a demonstration and resource collection of a plant family having important economic uses and further potential, as well as species still threatened with extinction. One objective is to conserve areas of degraded forest with buffer zones of agroforestry, utilizing the expertise and resources of the botanic garden. The whole scheme is an example of integrated conservation, linking the botanic garden of a developing country to a developed country, and including nature reserves of first-grade importance.

Sources: Hepper 1988; F. N. Hepper, pers. com.

Gene Banks and Germ Plasm Conservation

It is questionable whether anything approaching the full range of plant diversity can be maintained off-site using conventional techniques, especially if the gloomy prognosis for future depletions and extinctions is borne out. Numerous schemes for living gene banks have been proposed, but unless the bank is highly specialized and restrictive, the space required quickly becomes impossibly large. It is therefore essential to supplement collections of whole, live plants with collections of seeds and other propagating material to ensure a broad genetic base (Hawkes 1985).

Gene banks have three major functions (Hawkes 1985; Gomez-Campo 1987). The first function is to preserve rare or threatened plant material, thus helping to avoid possible extinctions of vulnerable or endangered species in the near future. The second function is to make plant material that would otherwise be difficult to obtain available for research or applied purposes, thus stimulating the knowledge and use of such material without damaging natural populations. The third function is to build up banks of living seeds and other tissues that represent a large proportion of the genetic diversity of wild species.

The theory behind most gene banks is quite simple. A gene bank is a collection of propagating materials that are checked for viability and then stored under conditions that retain viability for long periods (preferably in the order of tens of years at least). A gene bank can include seed, pollen, vegetative propagating material such as tubers and rhizomes, tissues grown as thallus cultures, DNA, and even whole plants grown as plantations. Storage, except as whole plants, generally involves low temperatures and sometimes low humidity, which slow down metabolic processes within the living material. Collections are regularly checked for viability and regenerated or grown to adulthood and reharvested.

About 150 botanic gardens around the world have germ plasm gene banks for wild species (Heywood 1988a). As most gene banks tend to be concerned with crop plants, wild species are highly underrepresented.

Germ plasm banks (especially for seeds) need not be difficult to set up or expensive to maintain. For seed collections, a domestic freezer can be enough to start with. Drying can be done using chemical desiccants, and once dried, samples can be kept in screw-cap containers, glass flame-sealed capsules, metal cans, or plastic-aluminum bags. The cardinal rule is that containers should be airtight. Low humidity is probably the most important factor in prolonging the life of most seeds. When used in conjunction with only modest temperature reductions, quite spectacular extensions of seed life can be obtained.

Freeze-drying generally is not used for seeds, but it has been used for pollen. A 5 percent water content is generally recommended for pollen, whereas a minimum of 8 percent water content appears to be required by most seeds to stay viable. Two factors dictate storage temperature: the cost of a suitable freezer, and the desired longevity of the seed. Extremely low temperatures may allow seed to survive for centuries, but in most instances this is ruled out by cost. Use is starting to be made of polar regions for low-temperature storage, for instance, the Nordic seed bank on Spitzbergen (Blixt 1992). Storage temperatures for most seeds are -10°C and -20°C, but range up to -5°C for some species (Plucknett et al. 1987). These temperatures are within the range of commercially available freezer cabinets, including many home deep-freeze units. With a very simple system, the money saved can be put into study of recalcitrant seeds—those which cannot be preserved by such simple means.

As with collections of whole plants, there must be adequate sampling of genetic diversity and documentation of the species and site. When sampling from a fairly uniform population, where size allows, 50 seeds should be taken from each of 50 plants to give a total of 2500 seeds in each sample. For highly variable populations, 100 plants should be sampled for the same number of seeds, giving 5000 seeds in each sample (Hawkes 1987). Such sample sizes may be difficult or even impossible to achieve for endangered species; only a few tens or hundreds of seeds may be available. Seed samples of critical species should not be rejected just because of their small size. If a small sample is all that is available, it should be stored and then regenerated and replicated at the earliest opportunity.

Efficient sampling from the wild depends on good planning—planning itineraries well in advance, multiple visits to critical sites, knowing in advance which species are to be collected, and using the appropriate collecting techniques. Sufficient time should be allocated to processing and preparing accessions, and to documenting samples; these should not be left until the end of the trip when details may be forgotten and time is lost in processing valuable samples (Gomez-Campo 1987). Once back at the laboratory, seed must be cleaned of extraneous material. Before seeds can be

stored it is necessary to ensure that they are alive; germination trials in conjunction with biochemical tests and staining techniques are useful here. Generally, 95 percent germination is satisfactory, although sometimes species have consistently low rates of germination (20–30 percent) even under ideal conditions.

Two types of seed storage should be undertaken. *Base collections* are stored under optimum conditions and are not interfered with until reduced viability, indicated by periodic germination tests, requires a new seed generation to be grown out. This latter process is called *regeneration* or *rejuvenation*. *Active collections* are those from which subsamples can be taken for experimentation, exchange, evaluation, and display. The active collection does not necessarily have to be stored under optimum conditions and can be multiplied periodically by growing up a new generation of plants and reharvesting. Every sample, no matter what size, should be divided—an important point for critically endangered species where less than desirable quantities of seed may have to be stored. Figure 6.7 outlines the series of steps and kinds of storage used in building gene bank collections of seed.

Some seeds will store well without loss of genetic integrity over relatively long periods of time. This includes many crop plants such as wheat, maize, and rice, and related wild species. Germination and storage problems are sometimes encountered; some seeds do not store well under reduced temperature and humidity. Many tropical woody plants fall into this category; however, some formerly recalcitrant seeds have now been found to be storable. Precise data on germination and storage requirements is simply not available for many wild plants. In addition, many crop plants (for which seed gene banks generally have been designed) have been intensively selected for thousands of years for such features as ease of germination.

Pollen and spore banks are less widespread but are also important. The case for spore banks for ferns and nonflowering plants is obvious, but that for pollen banks is less so. One advantage of pollen storage is that it takes up little space. Thus an immense amount of diversity can be collected and stored. Advanced techniques now allow adult plants of some species to be grown direct from pollen, and pollen can be stored and used directly in breeding and hybridizing programs. Stored pollen can be used to provide disease-free plants in instances where disease is transmitted through other types of tissue.

Biotechnology is offering an expanding range of techniques, which may well change the nature of gene banking over the next few years. One system that is widely used for crop plants is tissue culture, where cal-

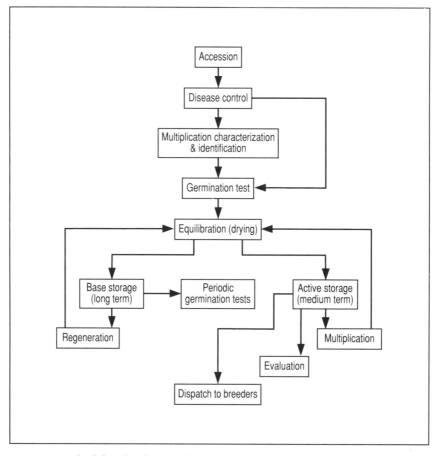

Figure 6.7. Gene bank flow chart for seed collections. (Reproduced by permission from Hawkes 1987b)

lus is stored under laboratory conditions. Another is banking of genomic DNA, which can be reconstituted and amplified for use by plant breeders (Adams 1992). Costs for a modest unit are lessening, putting them within the range of many laboratories with access to computer facilities, good water sources, a suitable centrifuge, and liquid nitrogen (if cryogenic storage is undertaken). Basic expertise is required in biochemistry and gel electrophoresis techniques. Some germ plasm storage in this form is undertaken by botanic gardens, but most is probably by organizations concerned primarily with crop and forestry breeding, or by large commercial horticultural organizations. No specific organization has a mandate to coordinate collections of laboratory germ plasm, or germ plasm of wild species in general (Heywood 1988a).

Only passing mention has been made of gene banks of whole living plants, such as plantations of trees maintained as breeding stock. These are important and may become even more so if environmental conditions, and specifically atmospheric pollution,

deteriorate in industrialized countries. Living whole plant collections are essential at least in the short term for some plant groups, such as tropical trees that produce seeds with extremely short viability times.

Where space for living collections is a problem, a solution is to screen source plants for particular genes and grow only those individuals with desired traits. Another is to limit strictly the types of plants grown. It is important to note that it will be difficult to avoid selection for plants suited to cultivation, thereby eliminating genotypes that survive in wild habitats but not in gardens or plantations. Thus living plant collections should, where possible, be supplemented by other forms of gene banks.

Gene banks in a variety of forms may be extremely important in the future if there is widespread collapse of the world's ecosystems through massive disturbance, overpopulation, and species decline. Several proposals have been made for "Noah's Ark" gene banks to be established in isolated and less polluted regions such as some oceanic islands. Arguments are made for cryogenic gene banks to be located in cold temperate or polar regions, underground, or in countries distant from possible centers of nuclear war (Blixt 1992). These banks could ensure survival of genetic material of essential species and wild and cultivated genetic resources even in the face of massive disruption and disaster.

CASE STUDY: THE COSTS OF SETTING UP A SEED BANK

Although a simple seed bank is relatively easy to set up (see Thompson 1986), an institutional seed bank that will serve as a major repository of genetic material does incur certain costs. A botanic garden wishing to set up a seed bank to handle and store up to 5000 samples will need to consider costs for three areas:

1. Capital: for building, cold storage, growth cabinets, freezer, drying facilities, laboratory equipment, and furniture.
2. Operating costs: for seed collection, seed distribution, storage materials, chemicals, office costs, index seminum/catalog, printing packets, postal costs, and utilities (e.g., electricity, water, and telephone).
3. Personnel: for a manager (graduate biologist), staff member, and assistant.

Note that in some cases access to university or research establishment facilities may be possible.

Source: Botanic Gardens Conservation Secretariat 1989.

CASE STUDY: SEED CONSERVATION GUIDELINES

Dormancy problems. A dormancy test is necessary on a small subsample before storage. Lack of germination may be the result of either lack of viability or dormancy. When judging viability after storage, this first germination figure must be considered.

Tetrazolium test. To determine which seeds are dead and which are dormant, a tetrazolium test may be used, although this does not work well with all seeds.

Prestorage treatment. Before seeds are placed in storage they should be dried and cooled. Larger seeds suffer physical damage if they are dried too quickly and to less than 8 percent water content. Seeds of wild species should not be dried to less than 5–6 percent water content, and preferably only to 7–8 percent.

Storage. Most seeds should be stored to 4°C until more is known about their reaction to lower temperatures. Oily seeds may be particularly sensitive. If tests indicate that damage is not likely to occur, then seeds should be stored at about -18°C.

Pregermination treatment. The seed coat or pericarp may have to be removed in species in which germination inhibitors are present. It is important to avoid damage to the seed when doing this.

Viability loss. After a period of time, seed viability will begin to diminish. Viability should not be allowed to fall below about 85–90 percent of what it was when first tested. If viability is allowed to drop too far, genetic changes and differential seed death will almost certainly result.

Germination tests. Samples with unknown storage qualities should be given a germination test every three years, and henceforward after longer storage periods. These tests should be carried out on base collections.

Wild seeds. Seeds from wild plants may require special conditions for dormancy breaking. This may include chemical treatment or exposure to special environmental conditions (e.g., a range of temperature conditions or temperature fluctuations).

Sequential testing. This should be carried out to avoid wasting too much seed in germination testing.

Storage containers. Store seed in metal cans (preferably aluminum), glass containers (tubes, vials, or bottles), pyrex glass ampules (heat-sealed for very long term storage), or plastic-aluminum foil bags. Minimize delays in storage.

Source: Hawkes 1985.

Experimental Gardens

Dedicated experimental gardens that primarily grow plants for research are essential for effective conservation. These are often run by research stations and universities. Such gardens facilitate research that is the basis for management of species in wild habitat, for translocation and establishment of new populations, and for rescue exercises (Timmins 1986). Experimental gardens can grow plants that are not of interest to public gardens because they lack "public interest and appeal." Such species are likely to be overlooked in the rush to conserve brightly colored and bizarre species.

A further development is an experimental propagation facility. Some threatened species are relatively easy to grow from seed, layers, or cuttings. Others, however, can be extremely difficult, and this may be the very reason why they are rare. Finding the appropriate propagation techniques may be the key not only to maintaining existing populations but to the reintroduction of species into the wild and to their continued cultivation.

Experimental gardens should have the space to grow a range of lines from different sources, and to establish temporary "populations" for replanting in bulk. They should have ready access to gene banks and to quarantine facilities, not only to prevent introduction of disease from overseas but to prevent unwitting transfer of disease and predators from cultivated plants to threatened wild plants and other gardens.

Some experimental programs are likely to be controversial, such as maintaining distinct lines from different populations, each of which may be genetically impoverished, or a breeding program to merge these and create "new" genotypes incorporating genomes from different sources (Timmins 1986).

The potential range of specialized gardens is endless. Satellite field stations and gardens can be designed specifically to demonstrate traditional uses of plants, introduce new crops, investigate fuel sources, and promote the rehabilitation of wastelands. They can also be used to demonstrate small-scale industries and to undertake pilot investigations for possible use of specific plant products in industrial processing.

An exciting development is the establishment in several countries of ethnobotanical gardens that are largely in the hands of traditional users of plants. Ethnobotanical gardens serve three major functions: to preserve traditional cultivars, to promote and teach traditional methods of cultivation and agriculture, and to promote traditional ethics and culture associated with indigenous plants. They are yet another way of making botanic gardens relevant to the basic needs of people.

Case Study: Banthra Field Station, Lucknow, India

The Banthra Research Station (a satellite of the National Botanic Garden), about 23 kilometers away from Lucknow, is a field station with about 85 hectares of alkaline land. Experiments on utilization of alkaline (*usar*) land are carried out. The approach is holistic and ecologically clean, concentrating on low-energy and minimal engineering inputs, and voluntary use of human power. The aim is to help the small-scale farmer through intensification and diversification of biomass production for food, fodder, fuel, fertilizer, small timber, aquaculture, health care, and small-scale village-based industry. Trials were conducted on various trees and shrubs known to be tolerant of alkaline conditions. Later,

less tolerant species were studied after soil conditions had improved. A Biomass Research Center (with an emphasis on firewood) was established with the assistance of the Department of Science and Technology. The whole model of ecodevelopment has five distinct components: cropland, grassland, woodland, aquaculture, and biomass-based vocations.

The transformation of barren wasteland devoid of any useful vegetation into a green area was possible through community action involving local people. This brought about environmental, social, and economic rehabilitation of the area as a whole. Today's challenge lies in converting such an example at the micro-level into a macro-level success.

Source: Khoshoo 1987.

Case Study: National Ethnobotanical Garden, New Zealand

A national ethnobotanical garden is to be established through a partnership between the Maori people and the New Zealand Department of Scientific and Industrial Research (DSIR). Other groups will be asked to participate later. The garden will assemble in one place much of the plant life that is unique to New Zealand.

The garden will provide opportunities for education about plants and their uses both before and after the arrival of Europeans in New Zealand. It will promote understanding and enjoyment of the different cultures present in New Zealand. The project seeks to establish a partnership of knowledge between the Maori and people of European origin. It will also facilitate research and will act as a national resource serving a network of regional gardens.

DSIR became involved in ethnobotany through the Commonwealth Science Council program on Biological Diversity and Genetic Resources. The department funded a study on traditional uses of indigenous plants, and this was followed by the Ethnobotany Workshop: Nga Mahi Maori O Te Wao Nui A Tane, held at the Te Rehua Marae, Christchurch, in February 1988—a workshop held according to Maori traditions.

New Zealand plants of traditional cultural and economic significance will be grown at the garden. Uses and cultural roles will be demonstrated. The garden will also give training in traditional and present day uses and science. The garden is to be established near Auckland, the location of the greatest number of people, especially of Maori and Pacific Island origin.

Sources: New Zealand Department of Scientific and Industrial Research 1989; M. Parsons, pers. com.

Other Off-site Conservation Areas

It is often difficult for conventional gardens to maintain more than a few plants of each species or to recreate natural habitat areas with a mixture of species simulating natural habitats. Amenity and landscape plantings provide an opportunity to conserve large numbers of individuals in quasi-natural surroundings, especially if plantings can be linked to the natural landscapes of the region. For example, quasi-natural areas of grassland for conservation of wild flowers and low shrubs can be maintained along motorways.

It is important to emphasize that there is a gradient of communities in which populations of threatened plants can be maintained. At one end of this spectrum are essentially natural biological communities; beyond this are natural communities in varying stages of disturbance, reconstructed communities with predominantly natural elements, reconstructed communities with increasing proportions of alien plants, plantscapes dominated by aliens, and, finally, landscapes where plants are a minor decorative element. Within this spectrum are many opportunities to use massed plantings and to reconstruct now rare communities.

Landscaping of tourist ventures (information centers, hotels, convention centers, etc.) might well include a range of plants that are characteristic of the region, notable for their uses or human associations, and critically threatened or endemic to the region. Combined with interpretive materials, the plants then become an awareness and education feature for visitors. Similarly, school arboreta and amenity plantings for shelter and shade can be promoted for education and to provide material for biology courses, but they also preserve plants of the region. Such plantings can also be used over the long term to carry out a wide range of simple experiments and observations that provide valuable information for conservation biology.

The horticultural industry and home gardens

In most developed countries, horticultural traditions run deep. Most people like to be among and grow plants, not only for obvious utilitarian value but also because they are attractive, they provide texture and color, and they are part of nature. Commercial horticulture and the nursery trade have an important role in conservation; providing there are adequate safeguards to avoid unacceptable exploitation, the nursery trade can be regarded as a potential major ally for plant conservation (Botanic Gardens Conservation Secretariat 1989).

One aspect of horticulture has particular importance for conservation. This is the growing of special, often rare, species by amateur gardeners. It is easy to underestimate the extent to which home enthusiasts are interested in threatened plants, or the expertise that has accumulated. For some groups such as alpine plants, orchids, succulents and cacti, and bulbous species (especially Liliaceae and Iridaceae), amateurs rather than professionals are often the experts on cultivation and horticultural aspects of conservation. In addition, enthusiasts tend to trade desirable plant material. It has been said that if you want to keep a plant in cultivation, give it away.

Amateur horticulture does have some problems. Although many enthusiasts are meticulous about identification and recording origin, others do not appreciate the need for good documentation and records. Some home gardeners are not aware of the degree to which open-pollinated plants can set hybrid seed. Perhaps the greatest problem is that of collection permanence. A comprehensive collection of plants from a particular region, or in a particular genus, may be quite safe during the lifetime of the enthusiast. The situation can change dramatically on the death or transfer to another locality of such individuals. Rarely do new owners have the same enthusiasm about the treasures in a private collection. Innumerable collections, painstakingly built up over decades, have been broken up, disbanded, or even dug into the soil.

One solution—perhaps a very necessary one—is to develop a system to allow people to register such collections. This means that the national (or international) value of the collection can be recognized. The collection, which may represent a lifetime of devotion and many tens of thousands of dollars investment, can be maintained according to agreed upon guidelines. The system also would provide the opportunity to establish the plants elsewhere if necessary.

Interest is growing in the creation of miniature quasi-natural habitats in domestic gardens. Instead of spending years trying to raise a wet part of a garden to drain it, or converting sandy soil to loam, some gardeners are taking the option of deliberately creating wildlike habitats where indigenous plants can thrive. Such garden habitats include a sand or desert garden; a wetland where indigenous orchids, sedges and other water-plants can thrive; or a rocky bank or slope converted into a succulent garden or shrubland. Information offering guidance to those who want to do this is often hard to come by, but the possibilities are almost without limit.

There is a need to campaign strenuously for nurseries not to sell wild-collected material (see Figure 6.8). One possibility is to issue conservation certificates guaranteeing that the material has come from nursery propagated stock or has been raised from seed and not collected directly from the wild (Botanic Gardens Conservation Secretariat 1989). Certainly, botanic gardens, commercial nurseries and garden centers, and the general public must be made aware of legal constraints on trade in endangered species (principally CITES provisions) and on collecting plants from the wild.

Figure 6.8. An endangered species, *Hebe armstrongii*, from New Zealand on sale in an English market. (D. R. Given)

CASE STUDY: THE PLACE OF HOME GARDENING AND HORTICULTURE IN THE LIVES OF AUSTRALIANS

The population of Australia is highly urbanized; almost two-thirds of the people live in the large, sprawling cities of Sydney and Melbourne. Most Australian families formerly favored detached houses set in private grounds of about 0.1 hectare. Since World War II, more and more people have been living in apartments. Australian cities therefore tend to be large, built-up areas, in the heart of which are concentrations of residents who are deprived of daily contact with nature.

A survey of recreation participation by Australians aged 14 years and over was carried out in 1985 by the Department of Sport, Recreation, and Tourism. The survey showed that 36.8 percent of people gardened for pleasure—the seventh most common activity. If participation in activities carried on outdoors is considered, gardening for pleasure had the highest participation rate, followed by walking for pleasure. Participation in gardening for pleasure and walking for pleasure increased with age for both males and females, with the highest participation rate being by those aged 55 and over.

Australia has an aging population. Based on present trends, there may be an increase in the number of people aged 55 and over—19.5 percent of the population in 1985 to 20.9 percent in 2000, 24.6 percent in 2010, and 28.2 percent in 2020. The combination of an aging population and interest in gardening provides a guide to the likely increase in community interest in botanic gardens. For residents and tourists alike, botanic gardens in mid-city locations have important recreational and educational potential.

Source: Boden and Boden 1987.

Research and Liaison Between Sites

Botanical and horticultural research is an important function of botanic gardens and gene banks even where resources allow only relatively unsophisticated studies. Before a garden embarks on a research program, needs and existing research in the region should be surveyed. The forging of links with existing organizations is preferable to setting up an in-house research structure that may duplicate others. Gardens should seek joint programs that make best use of their facilities and resources for conservation research. Examples of projects particularly suited to botanic gardens and gene banks include investigation of appropriate techniques for collecting and propagating material; trials to test appropriate methods of propagation for various plant groups, breaking of dormancy, and longevity of seed; studies on the optimization of edaphic factors in the garden, and factors involved in inducing flowering and fruiting; experimentation in predator control in cultivation and selection of resistent forms for horticulture; long-term studies on juvenility, growth forms, and phenology, including observations of flowering and fruiting times under different environmental conditions; and seed banking trials including storage at a range of temperatures.

In just one example, the Jardin Botanico Canario, Viera y Clavigo (on the Canary Islands) has undertaken a number of studies of endemic plants, including some with ornamental and agricultural potential, and some species with apparent resistance to garden pests. These include study of species of *Lotus* for forage and of *Euphorbia* species for latex production, and projects on *Tanacetum, Gonospermum, Limonium,* and *Lugoa*. Botanists and ornithologists are collaborating in studies of breeding systems and dispersal, and a group is working on marine algae as bioindicators of pollution and environmental changes (Bramwell 1987).

Many suitable projects do not require sophisticated techniques or expensive equipment. Larger gardens, or those attached to a research institution, may be able to undertake particularly sophisticated conservation biology research. It must not be assumed, however, that the more sophisticated the project, the greater its benefit to conservation.

CASE STUDY: KIRSTENBOSCH CONSERVATION LABORATORY, SOUTH AFRICA

In September 1986, a laboratory to study threatened plants was opened at the National Botanic Gardens, Kirstenbosch, South Africa. The laboratory was initially financed by a bequest, but also is supported by the South African Nature Foundation, the Botanical Society of South Africa, and the National Botanical Institute incorporating the Kirstenbosch Botanic Gardens. The laboratory eventually will include accommodation for visiting scientists and students.

The laboratory has developed methods to propagate species on the verge of extinction in the wild, and then cultivate sufficient numbers to reestablish or strengthen wild populations. Research on the economic potential of South Africa's flora also is conducted here. Sixteen staff members were involved in the program at the beginning of 1991.

Research has been broadly defined by two major goals, which are broken into the following six objectives:

1. Taxonomic studies on plant groups identified as containing a high proportion of threatened species.

2. Evaluation of the importance of threatened plants, to establish a priority list for their continued ex situ conservation.

3. Study of all aspects of threatened species, especially those aspects relating to survival.

4. Study of indigenous plants that are regarded as being important on horticultural, economic, or scientific grounds.

5. Establishment of procedures for long-term storage of viable propagating material.

6. Documentation and publication of research results.

Research activity also helps achieve goals concerned with plant utilization: identifying and developing indigenous plants with economic, horticultural, or medicinal potential; and promoting use of indigenous plant material to foster an appreciation of native plants and reduce pressure on plants in the wild.

The laboratory cooperates with other agencies involved in related projects through contracts on specific projects.

Sources: S.A.'s Major Gain for World Conservation 1986; Eloff 1988; J. N. Eloff, pers. com.

CASE STUDY: MICROPROPAGATION AT THE ROYAL BOTANIC GARDENS, KEW

The Micropropagation Unit at the Royal Botanic Gardens, Kew, England opened in 1974 to propagate rare and endangered plants and plants that are difficult or impossible to propagate using conventional methods. In addition, techniques to eliminate pathogens from infected plants are applied. Among the wide range of plants dealt with are the following:

Orchids. Most orchid germination at Kew is carried out in vitro, a technique that eliminates the need for mycorrhizal fungi. Considerable success has been achieved, and examples of success with species of high conservation interest include *Cymbidium rectum* (Sabah), *Epidendrum ilense* (Ecuador—thought to be extinct in the wild), and *Gynoglottis cymbidioides* (Sumatra). A symbiotic project is in progress, the main focus initially being on orchids native to Britain with the intention of returning these plants to their native habitats.

Ferns. Some fern propagation is carried out. The use of in vitro techniques reduces risk of contamination with spores of other species. Successes include *Angiopteris boivinii* from Mahé Island (Seychelles).

Carnivorous plants. Because most carnivorous plants show low seed viability and damping off problems, a wide range of carnivorous plants are propagated by the unit. Micropropagation has proved a useful way of increasing stocks of species that are threatened by overcollection or habitat destruction.

Succulents. Several families have been worked on. Micropropagation is used for rescuing plants that fail to establish or that develop fungal or bacterial rots. Examples of rare species successfully propagated include *Aloe patersonii* (Zaire) and *Opuntia echios* var. *gigantea* (Galapagos Islands).

Successful micropropagation often produces more plants than are needed at Kew. As a result, lists of surplus plants are produced and sent to other botanic gardens. The plants are sent out in vitro and so do not present quarantine problems. It is hoped that some material can be used for reintroduction trials. The establishment of a micropropagation newsletter will greatly help similar units to collaborate with each other.

Source: Fay 1988.

National and regional networks

The concept of coordinated networks of botanic gardens is not new, but in most regions and countries it takes considerable time to move beyond the stage of discussing the idea of a network. The three objectives of a national network should be as follows (Falk 1987; Botanic Garden Conservation Secretariat 1989). The first objective is to coordinate policies from one garden to another, encouraging exchange of plants and expertise, and discouraging duplication. Highest standards of conservation biology must be met, and collections should be a permanent resource. The second objective is to coordinate the policies of the garden network with national conservation organizations and with other relevant scientific, technical, educational, and commercial bodies and societies. The third objective is to coordinate the policies of the garden network with national groups in other countries and with international organizations such as IUCN.

Detailed activities to achieve these objectives will vary from country to country, but may include the following:

- Deciding what particular plants should be maintained in gardens and arboreta and getting agreement on what is held where. The program should be action-oriented, stressing actual conservation of plants that need it, and focusing on the most urgent.

- Organizing seed gene bank and in vitro storage for plants.

- Encouraging the establishment of nature reserves in cooperation with national conservation bodies, ensuring that garden expertise is applied where it is needed most—habitat evaluation, monitoring of rare species, and habitat gardening for endangered populations.

- Promoting and coordinating research into the cultivation, reproductive biology, and propagation of native species. The program should be scientifically valid and self-critical.

- Preparation of materials and guidelines for a botanic garden education program in conservation and plant appreciation.

- Anticipation of priorities and future needs. Conservationists should be able to look ahead rather than having always to fight rearguard actions.

National networks have a valuable public relations role, and they present a united front, which probably improves prospects of funding and resource allocation. Networks facilitate the forging of worthwhile links between organizations. Efficiently run, they should improve information flow between gardens and provide a forum for garden administrators and technical staff to talk about common problems and their solutions.

Networks must recognize the relationships between botanic gardens and local communities as unique cultural institutions. Yet they have must recognize the increasing national and international responsibility they have for conserving biodiversity. Resources for development of facilities needed at local, regional, national, and international levels are often limited. It therefore makes sense to rationalize operations to avoid undue duplication. Significant gaps are likely in coverage of species unless there is a coordinated approach to conservation in gardens.

Several types of inventory are basic to effective networking. At the broadest scale is a national inventory of plant species for which conservation is important. Also needed is an inventory of threatened plants in cultivation in network gardens (whether they are native to the country or not). Finally, the network will need an inventory of research that has been done or is being done on any of the species in the first two inventories.

Several major initiatives at the national level have taken place. The possibility of networking has been investigated in countries such as Canada and New Zealand. In addition, the American Association of Botanic Gardens and Arboreta surveyed their constituents and found that nearly half saw provision of scholarly information, conservation, and preservation as their most important functions. In 1984, eleven North American botanic gardens and arboreta joined in forming the nucleus of the Center for Plant Conservation with the intent of providing a coordinated approach to the off-site conservation of plants of the United States. Other networks include collections of national or international importance regardless of ownership (Pattison 1988). This is particularly relevant to continents with a strong tradition of horticulture, such as Europe and North America, but might also be useful in many smaller or poorer nations that cannot afford a large infrastructure.

With any sort of network it is important to set up an ongoing servicing group or secretariat committed to maintaining standards and accurate records, and capable of convincing people of the value of what the network is doing. Even a volunteer group, with basic finance from a small support group, can achieve a lot, given enthusiasm, clear goals, and resources such as a desktop computer with simple database software.

CASE STUDY: SUGGESTED MINIMUM STANDARDS FOR PARTICIPATION IN A NATIONAL NETWORK

Minimum standards for participating institutions were suggested in a report on a National Botanic Gardens System for Canada. An institution should do the following:

- Guarantee its perpetuity and the permanency of its land tenure.

- Demonstrate the ability to house and maintain living plant collections.

- Conduct appropriate research or be able to demonstrate that the institution has the staff and facilities to conduct research.

- Be accessible to the public, that is, be open to the public on a regular basis and provide public education and information.

- Maintain an accessioned plant inventory suitable for incorporation in a national inventory.

- Have the capacity to accept responsibility for collecting, maintaining, and propagating germ plasm of its region (particular emphasis should be given to endangered species, whether native or of cultivated origin).

- Have the capability to test plants to determine their adaptability to climatic zones or eco-regions.

- Be involved in formal educational programs with a recognized educational institution.

Source: Taylor 1973.

CASE STUDY: CENTER FOR PLANT CONSERVATION, USA

The Center for Plant Conservation coordinates a network of programs carried out at botanical gardens and arboreta dedicated to the conservation and study of endangered plants of the United States. Its goal is to create a systematic national program of plant conservation, research, and education within existing institutions, as a complement to the preservation of genetic diversity through habitat protection. The national office of the center coordinates and supports the activities of the participating gardens and arboreta. Institutions themselves maintain living collections of plants of their biogeographic regions.

Primary objectives of the center are as follows:

- To develop, maintain and coordinate the National Collection of Endangered Plants and its associated conservation, research, and education programs.

- To develop and maintain comprehensive and broadly accessible information systems, national networks, and databases concerning the biology, horticulture, and conservation status of all the nationally endangered native plants of the United States.

- To work with colleague organizations on collaborative integrated conservation projects combining species research, habitat management, and restoration of endangered plant populations in the wild.

- To assist botanical gardens nationally in developing public awareness of plant endangerment and conservation efforts.

The center is funded by private donations, corporate and foundation grants, federal grants and contracts, and service fees, and is developing sponsorship funds for the National Collection of Endangered Species and for international support.

The central purpose of the center is to conserve native plant species of the United States. To accomplish this, it engages in a wide variety of programs. The core programs are the National Collection of Endangered Species, setting up at least one participating institution in each major bioregion of the United States, allocating resources to priority regions, and promoting and achieving "integrated conservation, conservation research, and information and data systems." Other programs involve economic plant uses, education, and international Conservation.

Sources: Center for Plant Conservation 1985, 1991; Thibodeau and Falk 1986.

The council's primary intention is to conserve plants with horticultural merit, disease resistance, tolerance of particular soil or climatic conditions, economic or medicinal use, historical significance, or those that are rare in the wild. The large number of plant groups and collections potentially meriting recognition means that some degree of selection and evaluation is required. Priorities have been set for those plant groups that most urgently require national collection status. A small central coordinating staff based at the Royal Horticultural Society's Wisley Garden is supported by a nationwide membership of volunteers, both amateur and professional, who belong to local, usually county based, groups with national affiliation.

About 150 organizations and individuals have accepted responsibility for one or more of Britain's national collections of garden plants. These collections are, in effect, living museums, aiming to preserve a representative selection of the plants bred and grown in gardens over the centuries. The scheme now covers nearly 200 genera or groups of plants. Organizations or individual gardeners accept responsibility for collections under the scheme and must agree formally to a number of conditions of acceptance, including these:

- To keep in good health an agreed minimum number of specimens of each species or cultivar, and adding to the collection, as possible, to maintain representativeness.

- To maintain accurate records of plants and their position in the garden: identification of plants must be checked (a photographic and herbarium record system is envisaged).

- To arrange routine inspection by the NCCPG, to whom the owner is asked to submit a brief annual report (in return, owners receive help and advice to allow them to obtain specimens).

- To give sufficient notice when withdrawing to allow the NCCPG to make arrangements to house the collection.

Stocks held in national collections can act as reservoirs of material from which plants can be propagated for various purposes, including commercial sale. Holders of the collections retain the right to restrict the amount of propagating material they may wish to make available, and may charge for this. Where possible, collections are open to the public, or at least to those with an interest in the particular plant group.

Source: Stungo 1982.

International coordination

The first comprehensive attempts to involve the world's botanic gardens in conservation and threats to plants were made in 1953 at an International Colloquium of the Sub-Committee of Botanic Gardens of the International Union of Biological Sciences—the "scientific organization of botanic gardens." This colloquium looked at a wide range of matters including the definition of botanic gardens; collection, protection, and identification; seed lists; experimental gardens; finance; international relations; an index to botanic gardens; and ongoing meetings of botanic garden representatives. The most notable ongoing actions were probably the formation of the International Association of Botanic Gardens (IABG) in the following year, and the subsequent compilation of an international botanic gardens directory (Larsen et al. 1987).

In 1968, the late Ronald Melville commenced work on lists of endangered plants for an international *Red Data Book;* these included considerable information on the cultivation of species. In the same year, a paper on the international significance of botanic gardens for conservation was written by Nicholas Polunin. A symposium held in 1974 in Kuala Lumpur, Malaysia, looked at the role and goals of tropical botanic gardens. The following year, the International Association of Botanic Gardens Plenary Session, held in Moscow, recognized the important role of botanic gardens in conservation and called on botanic gardens to participate actively in the conservation of plants.

Following two conferences at the Royal Botanic Gardens, Kew, England in 1975 and 1978, IUCN has become more closely involved with botanic garden conservation. This was a natural consequence of studies to prepare regional lists of threatened plants. In the time between these two conferences, a pilot scheme was initiated to determine which threatened plants were in cultivation. After the second conference, this task was taken over by a new Botanic Gardens Conservation Coordinating Body, which by 1985 had 138 subscribing members. This body allowed gardens to keep in touch with conservation issues and was an important step forward in establishing an international network of gardens interested in plant conservation. Reports and listings of species in cultivation, on a taxonomic, regional, and individual garden basis, were issued to members. The coordinating body evolved into the Botanic Gardens Conservation Secretariat under the umbrella of IUCN, but early in 1990 became an independent organization.

Further international meetings on botanic gardens conservation have taken place. In 1984, an international symposium on botanic gardens of the tropics was held at Komter, Penang. In 1984 and 1985, conservation and international cooperation were two of the main themes of meetings of the European-Mediterranean division of the IABG. In November 1985, an international conference on botanic gardens and the world conservation strategy was held in the Canary Islands, Spain. This was followed in 1989 by the Second Botanic Gardens Conservation Congress on the Indian Ocean island of Reunion.

The three specific requirements for international cooperation are liaison, an expanded global monitoring program for ex situ conservation, and a (preferably small) coordinating body. Organizations with parallel aims, such as the various commissions of IUCN and the International Bureau for Plant Genetic Resources, interface to achieve this.

International networking can have its problems. Careful thought needs to be given to databases so that they can serve local, national, and international needs. Liaison is essential. People can quickly feel that they belong to a faceless organization, or that they are contributing to a "black box" out of which nothing relevant ever comes. Nevertheless, without global cooperation conservation quickly becomes fragmented and wasteful of resources.

Case Study: International Cooperation to Preserve the Easter Island Endemic Toromiro

The most interesting endemic of Easter Island is *Sophora toromiro*, which is the only indigenous tree to survive to the twentieth century. For some years, however, it was believed to be extinct, its history being one of decline. When discovered in 1774 it formed thickets, but by 1971 only one tree could be found. This tree was seen in 1935 at the same locality in which Thor Heyerdahl collected seeds in 1955–56.

Plants were grown from Heyerdahl's seeds at the Botanical Garden in Göteborg, Sweden. Attempts were made to reintroduce the species back to Easter Island in 1980 and 1988, but it did not survive. Other trees in cultivation are known: one in the Botanical Garden of Vina del Mar (possibly collected from Easter Island by Carlos Muñoz Pizarro in 1935), and one at the University of Bonn, Germany (of unknown origin). Plants that are reputed to be *Sophora toromiro* grow in Christchurch, New Zealand, but there is some doubt regarding their identity and provenance.

Further attempts are being made by Corporacíon Nacional Forestal (CONAF) in Chile to reintroduce the toromiro to Easter Island. International cooperators in this project include Chilean National Parks, botanic gardens, and botanists in other countries such as Sweden, England, and New Zealand.

Source: Lobin and Barthlott 1988, with additions.

Case Study: Botanic Gardens Conservation International

The Botanic Gardens Conservation Secretariat was set up by IUCN on 1 January 1987. It became an independent body as BGCI in 1990 with charitable status in the United Kingdom and its own board of trustees. It is still associated with IUCN by a memorandum of understanding. The secretariat actively recruits as many botanic gardens as possible to become members. Initial financial support has come from several foundations, but the goal is to be able to cover 70 percent of costs after three years, and to make it largely self-financing within five years. A subscription structure is based on annual operating budgets of members. Objectives of the secretariat are to promote the implementation of the Botanic Gardens Conservation Strategy; to monitor and coordinate ex-situ collections of plants worthy of conservation; to develop a program for liaison and training; to arrange a botanic gardens conservation congress every three years; and to develop an educational and training program.

Specific products will include an expanded *International Directory of Botanic Gardens* in association with the International Association of Botanic Gardens and WWF. This will be in both book and computer-readable form.

The intent is for the secretariat's monitoring of collections to develop into a program to help coordinate ex situ collections worldwide. This will reduce duplication and ensure geographic spread of collections, coverage of threatened species, and preservation of a wide range of conservation-worthy plants. Gardens contribute data on their holdings, preferably in electronic form, by predetermined standards. In return, they receive annual printouts of their collection in relation to others, general reports on the status of plants in cultivation, and answers to individual queries. A database of experience and case histories may be set up.

The secretariat should be able to act as a clearinghouse for requests for training assistance. Links at national and regional levels to encourage this will be fostered. "Twinning" arrangements between particular gardens may be appropriate, as may be multilateral agreements among several gardens.

Sources: IUCN 1987; V. Heywood, pers. com.

Constraints to Off-site Conservation

Off-site conservation often involves high collecting and maintenance costs. Long-term maintenance of collections can be problematic, especially when projects are entered into unselectively, overoptimistically, or carelessly. The objectives of a collection must be well defined. Too often projects fail to come up to expectations because the taxonomic and biological bases are inadequate, costs escalate beyond even optimistic estimates, and horticultural facilities are inadequate. It is one thing to want to save the world—it is quite another to do it.

Conservation projects must be undertaken according to a management plan that is part of the ongoing strategic function of the garden or research institution. This is a major weakness in conservation of critical species by amateurs, especially in a home garden context. Such efforts can be extremely useful, provided there is backing, support, and advice from conservation agencies and institutions. There is considerable opportunity for such organizations to liaise with and support a cadre of dedicated enthusiasts.

Acquisition of threatened species, especially through special interest groups and enthusiasts, tends to be on an ad hoc basis rather than according to a planned set of priorities. Thus collections often contain a very uneven array of species. Searches for specific genera often show that there is overduplication of some species, while other (sometimes quite critical) species are absent. This is not solely the fault of curators. Often they have not been given the facilities or the opportunity to plan systematically for conservation of target plants.

Replication of critical collections is of vital importance. Even with the carefully managed and planned garden, the unexpected can happen. Record flooding on 20 November 1990 at Waimea Arboretum resulted in collections loss and garden closure for six months; fortunately many of the critical collections were replicated elsewhere in the gardens or at other sites (Orr 1990).

Lack of full documentation is a major problem (Peeters and Williams 1984; Ashton 1987). It has been estimated that of the 2 million accessions of plant germ plasm worldwide, 65 percent lack basic data on provenance; 80 percent lack data on useful characteristics, including methods of propagation; 95 percent lack any evaluation data such as responses to germination tests; leaving only 1 percent with extensive data. Too many critically threatened plants in cultivation, or in gene banks, are similarly lacking in relevant data, or are incorrectly identified.

Because of the need to work with small samples, much off-site conservation irreversibly leads to domestication. Perhaps it would be useful to concentrate more on the preservation of gene complexes than the species themselves. Nevertheless, off-site conservation may be the only long-term choice for the components of some ecosystems. What is necessary is to decide why one is conserving a particular sample and how it may best be done. Inevitably, there will be trade-offs, but these should not jeopardize long-term plans to preserve biodiversity. On-site conservation should be a major objective as far as possible.

The long-term reliability of off-site conservation may be improved by avoiding total dependence on cultivation, and by making the fullest possible use of alternative techniques (Elias 1987a). Important among these is germ plasm storage (usually as seed), which is now being applied in a number of centers in different parts of the world. It is also important to minimize losses though careful husbandry, frequent checking of collections, and by minimizing pilfering. Sometimes an individual goes to great length to acquire or collect propagating material, only to have it lost because a propagator lacks knowledge of appropriate techniques. Gardeners and maintenance staff must be aware of the importance of endangered plants under their control.

Although the prospects for off-site conservation in botanic gardens may be very good in some instances, it is inappropriate to apply off-site techniques in a blanket fashion to all endangered species. There is a real danger that success in a few particular cases may create a misplaced confidence in the minds of those responsible for allocating support to conservation (Thompson 1975). Off-site conservation is only one of an interrelated array of techniques. A fully integrated approach to conservation must be developed that considers and applies the best of a full range of options including in situ and ex situ approaches, various types of germ plasm banks, and biological and social research (D. Falk 1991; V. Heywood pers. com.)

Too often, a simplistic view of off-site conservation is taken. The notion that one can preserve the genetic diversity of a million hectares of tropical rain forest in a botanic garden, while at the same time enjoying the financial benefits of clear cutting, is attractive. The assumed economic benefits of exploitation in the form of forestry or agriculture may persuade many that we can "have our cake and eat it too." Before any further action is taken to encourage such thoughts, conservationists would do well to ensure that their share of the cake amounts to more than a few crumbs in the form of small, poorly designed nature reserves and residual off-site collections.

It is easy to be overwhelmed by the magnitude of the challenges, responsibilities, and costs of off-site conservation and little impressed with the dividends. Those who are involved have to ask themselves the rhetorical question, Who will speak for the flowers— and if not now, when? If research institutions, botanic gardens, and arboreta do not undertake off-site conservation, it simply will not be done at all. The inevitable result will be to jeopardize the future of an enormous amount of biodiversity.

Conservation activities clearly cost money—staff, time, space, maintenance, equipment, running costs, and overhead (Botanic Gardens Conservation Secretariat 1989). Some facilities such as germ plasm banks, and experimental techniques such as micropropagation, may be relatively expensive to set up, and there must be clear commitment to long-term financial and staff support. Many other costs can be readily ab-

sorbed into the existing budget of an institution through careful planning. It is important that some botanic gardens and allied institutions make a major financial commitment to conservation (some commit 30 percent or more of their budget to conservation), but even a modest commitment will help.

If economics are a factor, there are potential dividends. These include development of sustainable agricultural and agroforestry systems, better sources and use of plant fuels, cultivation of plants with known or potential economic importance, and development of educational and awareness aids such as books on plants and educational guides. These can go some way toward making conservation a paying proposition. Over and above this, however, dividends must come in the form of a more aware and educated public—people better able to respond to calls for conservation-oriented lifestyles. This requires increasing involvement of local communities in the work of botanic gardens (Botanic Gardens Conservation Secretariat 1989). Playing a role in the local community is more than just an act of good citizenship; it encourages people from all walks of life to appreciate plant life and the need to conserve it.

CHAPTER 7

Plant Conservation in Modified Landscapes

The twentieth century has been dubbed the century of technology, but it could equally be called the century of change. Change that transforms lifestyles and landscapes in a single lifetime is something a large proportion of the world's people have come to accept as a part of the natural order. But people are rarely neutral about change: they either fear it or love it. At one time changes in most parts of the world were so slow as to be imperceptible over many generations. Now, change is often dramatic, not only within a human lifetime but even within a few years. Landscapes, ecosystems, and plant habitats are not immune to these trends.

A feature of contemporary change is that profound effects may be felt at sites far removed from the point where causal factors operate. In May 1986, the nuclear disaster at Chernobyl in the former Soviet Union made people aware of how far afield pollutants can have effect. Other global pollutants contribute to acid rain many hundreds of kilometers from emission points. In just one example, more than half of the 12 million metric tons of acid deposited on eastern Canada each year originates in the heavily industrialized parts of the eastern United States, many hundreds of kilometers to the south (Lovelock 1979). Late twentieth-century changes may be among the most profound to occur in geologic history. The greenhouse effect alone could, according to some scenarios, result in a steady warming of the planet—a projected rise of 2–4°C worldwide within the next 50 years. The effect of this temperature rise on biodiversity and extinction rates could be catastrophic.

Change can be, and often is, for the good. Few would deny the need to make better use of agricultural lands, or even the need selectively to open up and develop new areas for food and fuel production, housing, or recreation. Those activities that improve the quality of living ought to be viewed with sympathy. Change, however, does not occur in isolation and is necessary to ensure that one group of people is not advantaged at the expense of another and that changes are not at the needless expense of the natural environment—soil, water, animals, and plants.

For plant species, one of the most immediate impacts of change is the loss of wild habitats. Through modification of habitat, indigenous species disappear and are replaced by exotic animals and weeds. Remaining areas of wild habitat become fragmented, so that natural migration of species and gene exchange are restricted. Another aspect of change is the apparent contradiction that landscape patterns become fixed. Throughout geologic time, as landscapes have evolved and climates fluctuated, habitats have been created and destroyed. Superimposed on this has been local disturbance by catastrophe—flood, earthquake, fire, and storm. Much effort now goes into minimizing both short- and long-term disturbances. Landscapes are increasingly locked into a pattern of immutable land uses in which it is assumed that each land parcel is to be used now and in the future for the same particular purpose. In a sense, the land, its ecosystems, and its biota are frozen at a particular point in time with minimum opportunity for future evolution. It is paradoxical that most land-use policies deliberately minimize disturbance, with the purpose of protecting agricultural and urban lands and ensuring public safety. But this can be at the expense of species that have evolved to occupy temporary, shifting habitats.

Diversity changes as people disturb the landscape. Often in the early stages of human-induced disturbance there is a rise in species diversity. Maximum diversity probably occurs with a combination of old natural communities and new secondary assemblages. Nonetheless, as human influence increases, diversity often decreases. Secondary communities with relatively few species prevail at the expense of more diverse ones. This has been documented for several periods in the history of central Europe (Kornas

1982). An important aspect of the present period of disturbance is that probably for the first time, losses outweigh gains.

These circumstances are like those imposed by catastrophes of past geologic times. Human population growth, advancing industrial technology, and social affluence (for some) put pressure on the world's plant resources, resulting in three human-generated forces that are currently driving evolutionary change (Heslop-Harrison 1973). These forces include the absorption of living space, which reduces population size; new selective pressures imposed by the direct and indirect impact of human activities; and changing patterns of gene flow between different regions.

In former times, changing patterns of habitat were mitigated by natural means. Increasingly, pressure is such that rehabilitation will have to be by deliberate choice and will involve intensive hands-on management. For many parts of the world, preservation of remnant habitats and relict populations may be the only way to conserve a significant proportion of biodiversity. Remnants have to serve the purpose that was previously fulfilled by the whole landscape (Saunders et al. 1987).

For nature conservation to be effective in the face of rapid and continued landscape change, there must be a commitment at the grass roots level. In the absence of such a commitment, national parks and other protected areas will not be sufficient to protect the necessary array of wild species (Dasmann 1984). In the postindustrial age, governments and individuals need to be aware of options to rationalize economic viability and protection of biodiversity (McNeely 1989b).

CASE STUDY: THE GREENHOUSE EFFECT

Gases such as carbon dioxide, methane, and probably carbon monoxide play key roles in determining the earth's climate. Carbon dioxide, for instance, lets through virtually all the incoming short-wave solar energy, but traps and retains much of the long-wave energy that the earth radiates out toward space. The net effect is to keep the temperature of the earth's surface higher than it would be if these gases were not present in the atmosphere. This is popularly known as the greenhouse effect.

Since 1850, atmospheric carbon dioxide has increased by almost 30 percent, in part because of the burning of fossil fuels. In the late twentieth century, we were burning close to 5 billion metric tons of fossil fuels each year, releasing several times as much carbon dioxide by weight into the atmosphere. If fossil fuel consumption continues to rise (including the burning of forests in the tropics), by the year 2060, carbon dioxide levels could reach 600 parts per million (over twice the level in 1850).

Although exact global impacts are not certain, most experts agree that this will mean a global temperature increase of about $3°C$, with perhaps as much as a $7°C$ rise at the poles. Rainfall patterns would change, with consequences for food production and political balance. For instance, the North American grain belt could suffer, while countries of the arid Middle East could be better off. Worldwide flooding of lowlands could be expected as sea levels rise. This could have catastrophic results for the two-fifths of the world's human population that live in coastal areas.

Source: Intergovernmental Panel on Climate Change 1990.

Types of Modified Landscapes

One of the current appeals of the Antarctic for many people is that it constitutes the last great wilderness. This perception reflects the global influence of humanity. With the exception of some high mountains and parts of the Antarctic, virtually every terrestrial part of our planet has felt the direct influence of people. Even wilderness and *barrens* are not immune to modification. Long-distance pollution of water and air has its own modifying effects, sometimes thousands of kilometers from the pollution source. At the end of the twentieth century, widespread atmospheric pollution through the greenhouse effect and breakdown of ozone probably now affects every biological habitat on the globe.

Modified landscapes lie toward the far end of a

spectrum ranging from natural communities to totally artificial landscapes. Obviously, some landscapes are intermediate in nature—cultivated yet containing some elements of natural communities (Figure 7.1).

For the purposes of conservation, four categories of ecosystems can be identified (Botkin et al. 1982): those threatened by reduction in occurrence or size, those that are intrinsically sensitive, those in which there is disruption, and those that are partial.

ECOSYSTEMS THREATENED BY REDUCTION IN
OCCURRENCE OR SIZE

Certain ecosystem types are few in total number and some are small in size. These are inherently in danger of disappearing. In North America, alpine tundra is

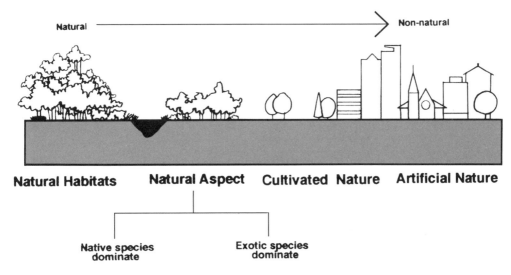

Natural ⟶ Non-natural

Natural Habitats   Natural Aspect   Cultivated Nature   Artificial Nature

Native species dominate   Exotic species dominate

Figure 7.1. The transition from fully natural to artificial urban landscapes. (Courtesy of Boffa Miskell Partners, A. Rackham and J. Roper-Lindsay)

an example of this kind of threatened ecosystem. In South Africa, the ephemeral pans of the high veld, the remaining natural forests, and estuaries and coastal wetlands all fall into this category.

Intrinsically sensitive ecosystems

Some ecosystems are sensitive to disturbance and have very long recovery times (e.g., mature rain forests and tundra). Still others depend upon periodic (but natural) perturbations for the maintenance of a steady state (e.g., barrier islands subject to overwash). Particularly sensitive ecosystems include those on geologically unstable substrata (e.g., sand dunes and steep slopes subject to landslides) or those dependent on external inputs (e.g., estuaries and mountain streams).

Ecosystems in which there is disruption

In the Northern Hemisphere, many areas are subjected to the influences of acid rain produced by industry located sometimes hundreds or thousands of kilometers away. A second example of disruption comes from Africa, where the loss of nutrients in most savannas through increased fire frequency and overgrazing has already reached serious proportions.

Partial ecosystems that are incomplete in terms of processes, the removal of species, loss of area, or introduction of barriers

Some ecosystems are unlikely to survive long term, or if they do, will only survive in highly modified form. Many remnants of forest, especially in the tropics, are included here.

Such ecosystems, or remnants of them, can be preserved in the following types of modified landscapes.

Urban areas

Toward the end of the twentieth century, about half the world's population lived in cities; this was expected to rise by the year 2000 to 75 percent, with over 20 percent living in cities with more than one million people. Predicted were nearly 60 mega-cities with over 5 million people, 42 of them in the third world. What makes these figures so disturbing is the lack of planning, overcrowding, and paucity of natural environment already characteristic of many urban areas. To quote one wildlife scientist,

> There should be no need to try to convince anyone of the ugliness and poor planning of our cities. Those with senses and sensibility will be aware of their shortcomings, and disquieted, too; because with all our insight and technical skill we continue to add to their tastelessness and inefficiency through motives that reflect little credit on the developers—public or private. . . . Until now, most urban areas have been developed without recourse to ecological advice. (I prefer not to use the word "planned," which, for me, implies more care than—obviously—has been taken). Apparently, developers and local government have had as much need for ecologists as Coffinhal had for scientists on the occasion of Lavoisier's condemnation (Williams 1971: 13).

It is not surprising that many wild plants have disappeared from urban areas. Loss of habitat has been a major factor as remnants of intact vegetation have been used for building sites and roads, or turned into parklands and gardens, in the belief that the indigenous vegetation is wasteland.

Many opportunities exist to promote and practice conservation in an urban environment (Spellerberg 1992). Peri-urban regions often have a scattering of habitat fragments where wild plants survive. Even within large cities, surveys indicate a surprising number of remnant sites with only partly modified natural habitats. A survey in the early 1970s of the closely settled Canterbury Plains, adjacent to Christchurch, New Zealand showed that several key remnants of the original, pre-European vegetation still existed (Molloy 1971). One remnant is a swampland of about 4 hectares well inside the urban perimeter, once a locality for a now nationally threatened species. In situations like this there is little point in reintroducing such plants until the habitat is in a condition that will allow for long-term survival.

General arguments can be advanced for creating green areas in urban settings regardless of their species composition (e.g., Cashdan et al. 1982). Approximately 40 square meters of greenery produce the oxygen supply for a single person, so that green areas have a very important function in maintaining clean air. Many municipalities look to vacant land for generation of revenue through development (generally buildings), despite the economic value of open spaces at both primary (benefits enjoyed by facility users) and secondary levels (economic benefits accruing more broadly). Practical projects show that in at least some urban areas, people are willing to pay, either directly or by voluntary aid, for green areas and open spaces.

The key to nature conservation in urban areas lies in effective and informed planning, and partnerships between local government and people living in the region. In many countries local authorities prepare statutory plans that include policies and maps of proposals and allowable uses. Local authorities control development and have responsibility to prepare guidelines. Local governments often have the power to protect sites for historical, cultural, or nature-preservation reasons. As part of the planning process, local authorities usually have a monitoring function.

Local bodies sometimes plead poverty when it comes to designating, procuring, and managing open land or sites for nature conservation. One solution is to acquire land and to manage it through community trusts and nongovernment organizations, and to allow local communities to develop areas appropriate to their needs. Although such open spaces are created for recreation or beautification, they also offer very good opportunities to establish small botanic gardens and reconstructed "natural" habitats, and to introduce a selection of plants that are rare or of local interest. Thus open spaces can serve an amenity function, protect species, and heighten awareness of biodiversity.

Some of the following steps that have been taken by trusts and communities in the United States at the local level are adaptable to other situations (USDA in Cashdan et al. 1982, adapted).

1. *Get organized for action.* Recruit people who are interested, if necessary going door to door to win support and generate interest in open spaces.

2. *Identify the target areas.* Find vacant and abandoned lots with potential that are available for purchase or lease.

3. *Acquire the land.* This may involve making use of tax benefits or discounting of rating payments (where they exist) to encourage owners to part with or lease land at affordable prices. It is important that the seller realize that the land will be put to good community use and will be well maintained.

4. *Organize and incorporate the organization.* There are often considerable financial and legal advantages in proper incorporation or registration of the core organizational group. For instance, in the United States such a group can incorporate as a nonprofit, tax-exempt land trust.

5. *Plan and design the site together.* Everyone in the neighborhood should be involved. Active participation by local residents ensures acceptance, use, and maintenance of open spaces.

6. *Prepare and develop the site.* Many resources are required; this calls for organization, planning, and perseverance.

7. *Maintain the site.* The trust or equivalent assumes responsibility for this. What is required is an ongoing group to take overall management responsibility, including planning and physical maintenance.

When areas are being developed for housing, industry, transport, or other purposes, legislation may require mitigation; but a better job is likely to be done if developers are involved and can see some benefit accruing. Inevitably, people are attracted to the idea of planning for obvious amenity value—for passive recreation or for landscape value. In accommodating such needs, it is important that botanical features are not subjugated to the extent that they become value-less, or are reduced in the interests of ease of maintenance. Often-encountered examples include mowing weeds along trail margins using wide gang-mowers, replacing natural lake edge vegetation with "tidy" exotic shrubs, or straightening of meandering streams. Developers and politicians have a public image to maintain and will want to be seen in a favorable light by the public and local authorities. Ultimately, the degree to which nature conservation ideals are incorporated into urban development will depend on the value put on these ideals by the constituent public.

Massed planting for landscaping along motorways and rivers and on hillsides gives considerable scope for use of plants of local and national significance, including rare species. As part of its contribution to an International Conference on Botanic Gardens and the Conservation Strategy, held in 1985, the host city of Las Palmas, Canary Islands, undertook to feature palms of the world in its municipal landscaping, thus fulfilling its name as the City of Palms. This is an example of large-scale planting to achieve both landscaping and conservation objectives.

A critical factor in such urban work is the identification of existing key sites of biological significance. These may be abandoned lots, stream and canal sides, railway and road margins, ravines, or wastelands—potentially, almost any site where indigenous plants can persist. Threatened species and fragments of natural habitat sometimes occur in the most unlikely places, such as refuse dumps, on the perimeter of sports grounds, and in parking lots (Figure 7.2). Only a systematic recording and survey system will record such occurrences.

One of the few comprehensive urban surveys of this type was used to find and describe wildlife habitats in Greater London, England (Game 1986). The survey looked at the extent, quality, and distribution of wildlife habitat in an area of 1580 square kilometers, documenting 2000 distinct sites. Surveys of this type require considerable resources and coordination, but can be very cost-effective and are likely to reveal many overlooked areas of wild habitat.

It is not enough to argue the value of a nature conservation site as if it existed in a vacuum; rather, it must be placed in a context that defines its value to the people who may enjoy it. To do this one must have data that meet the criteria of completeness, consistency, and precision (Spellerberg 1992).

Completeness. All possible sites that could be of nature conservation value within a relevant geographic

Figure 7.2. Vacant city lots have potential for preservation of local wildflowers. Aarhus, Denmark. (D. R. Given)

range should have been considered, and those of an equivalent or higher value must be surveyed. It is not enough to collect data on a sample of sites, as this leaves open the possibility that an alternative site, not included in the survey, would prove better than the one currently judged worthy of recognition. If it is not practical to survey all potential sites, this should be clearly stated in a report on the data. It is important to ensure that the plants and animals surveyed and the searching effort are sufficient to show the values to be conserved.

Consistency. It is not sufficient to exhaustively survey one potential site, as the harder one looks the more one finds. All sites to be compared must be surveyed in the same way and to the same level of scrutiny, so that comparisons can be made without bias.

Precision. Data must be clearly related to a defined land area, so that one can be sure of the relevant facts. Also, data should be recent enough that no changes remain undocumented.

Even the most detailed surveys involve compromises: the extent of geographic coverage versus detailed documentation on each site, use of professionals and amateurs, and preserving high standards of detailed data gathering while ensuring that "surveying is fun" (D. Dawson and M. Game, pers. com.).

CASE STUDY: SPECIES EXTIRPATED FROM URBAN SITES

Thismia americana

Status: Extinct. Known from one locality where it was last seen in 1913. The area is now occupied by heavy industry. The species has been searched for repeatedly in the original area and in similar sites, but without success. It is not in cultivation.

Distribution: USA. The locality was along the margin of a grass meadow in Cook County, Chicago, Illinois. The site has been identified as the bottom prairie swale on the east side of Calumet Lake.

Habitat and ecology: Occurred in low, wet prairie grassland in a stream bed. Typically, the *Thismia* grew in spots where the soil was not closely covered by liverworts, *Selaginella*, and moss. The habitat is in striking contrast to that of most of the other species of *Thismia*, which grow on decaying wood or leaves in primary tropical forests, in regions of high rainfall.

Astragalus physocalyx

Status: Rare or Endangered. Until recently it was believed extinct, since it had disappeared from its first known locality in 1902 and its second after 1961. Both were in Bulgaria. It has recently been discovered from a single locality in Yugoslavia. Cultivated plants from the first Bulgarian locality have been reintroduced into the original site, which is now a public park surrounded by the town of Plovdiv.

Distribution: Bulgaria, Yugoslavia. The locality within Plovdiv is the hill of D'zendemtepe. The second Bulgarian locality (extinct) was near the village of Kulata in the valley of the River Struma in the southwest of the country. The Yugoslav locality is in Macedonia.

Habitat and ecology: At D'zendemtepe, it grows on a rocky slope with other rare Balkan species.

Conservation measures taken: The species is legally protected in Bulgaria. Plants of wild origin are grown successfully in the Botanical Garden of the Bulgarian Academy of Sciences, Sofia; some of these were recently planted in the original locality.

Source: Lucas and Synge 1978.

CASE STUDY: THE GREATER LONDON SURVEY OF WILDLIFE HABITATS

In March 1985, a survey of sites of wildlife interest was completed for the Greater London Council in Britain. A team of eight carried out the survey on the extent, quality, and distribution of wildlife habitat throughout the 1580 square kilometers that make up Greater London. Information gathered included location and the following data on each major habitat type present: extent, stage of development, dominant plants, species richness, presence of rare or unusual species, interest for groups other than plants, other factors such as pollution. All sites larger than 0.5 hectare in inner boroughs, or 1 hectare in outer boroughs were surveyed, except for formal parks and similar areas. In all, 2000 sites were documented.

The need for information was urgent and some detail had to be sacrificed to get the survey completed. Areas lacking vegetation that were not bodies of water were not included. A minimum size guideline was adopted. A minimum quality guideline was also introduced so that intensively managed sites that seemed of relatively low value for wildlife were excluded.

The database containing the survey data is stored on computer and is now widely used. Many requests for the information are for local planning purposes. The database can be used for problems associated with specific sites, reducing the time having to be spent on inspection. Some uses have arisen out of the need for London-wide information, for example, information on the extent and quality of woodlands. A wide range of users access the database, including officers of local governments, Nature Conservancy Council, voluntary groups, students and teachers, consultants, and members of the public. An important consideration is that the database is run as part of a governmental ecology unit, and not as a separate entity. This facilitates interpretation of the data.

Source: Game 1986.

Rural areas

The shift of people to urban areas and resultant expansion of cities will not see the end of rural landscapes. What is changing is the nature of that rural landscape. Three divergent philosophies on the use and nature of rural landscapes are emerging. The first philosophy claims that the rural landscape is there to be used and developed. It ought to be tidy and controlled. Nature can be planned for as a secondary, perhaps ornamental aspect of that landscape. The second philosophy claims that nature has a part in the rural landscape, which is not necessarily subordinate to that of humanity. The rural landscape ought to be a mosaic in which activities such as farming, tree-cropping, fishing, and ranching are controlled and in balance with preservation of nature. The third philosophy claims that present needs to provide food, fuel, and shelter are paramount and nature may have to take its chances within an increasingly used and manipulated system.

Which of these philosophies predominates varies from region to region. The second viewpoint is probably most in sympathy with traditional agricultural systems, but it has been largely supplanted by the first in many developed countries, and is being replaced by the third in some less developed regions of the tropics. The view that dominates fundamentally determines the type of rural landscape and the place of wild species in it.

Rural landscape conservation is rapidly becoming a matter of protecting and managing narrow strips and fragments of wild habitat: the edges of roads and streams, strips between arable land, or pockets of habitat for which conversion to productive land is not economically viable (Kaule and Krebs 1989). Such areas have the familiar problems of need for buffer zones, edge effects, small populations, and stressed and disturbed systems.

In many instances agriculture occupies the best soil, and less-managed portions of farms are either on higher, stony ground or poorly drained wetlands. As techniques for development of marginal lands improve, agriculture encroaches on formerly unused land. What is often not realized is that many apparently "useless" sites serve functions that actually augment more obviously "economic" land use (Lowrance et al. 1984). As an example, natural wetlands serve a valuable function as nutrient filters and buffers against flooding, and also harbor valuable genetic resources.

The broad principles behind rural conservation should be to create reserves and zones that are large enough and of such a nature that a mosaic of activities can survive, to have compatible activities throughout a region (especially on adjacent land), and to educate landowners and occupiers to appreciate wild elements in the landscape and the desirability of conserving plants in wild habitats. Kaule and Krebs (1989) suggest that a priority order for conservation should be (1) protecting existing habitats, (2) creating habitats through natural succession, (3) transplanting ecosystems, and (4) planting and sowing local genetic varieties of plants.

Roadsides and riparian strips must be emphasized. In the battle for biodiversity they are increasingly important as refuges for plants and provide vital corridors for nature conservation in modified landscapes. The value of such strips tends to be neglected in planning for conservation. It has been estimated that even in a small country like New Zealand (area ca. 256,000 square kilometers), the legally defined road verges provide a potential area of about 80,000 hectares. They traverse a wide range of latitudes, climate, and altitude zones. The identification of biologically valuable vegetation remnants along roads and rivers; their preservation and protection from indiscriminate grazing, mowing poisoning, and burning, followed by restoration and repair where necessary, is urgently required in many countries (Meurk 1987).

Seminatural communities are also characteristic of many rural landscapes. These can have surprisingly high levels of diversity and some consist mostly of species native to the region, even when vegetation structure is greatly modified by human activities. Some seminatural communities are maintained by activities such as burning, grazing, and cutting. As long as disturbance occurs with reasonably natural periodicity and magnitude, is of a quasi-natural type, and the community is complex (for example, high species diversity) without being complicated (high level of obligatory interaction), biological stability is a possibility. But even small changes, such as loss of an important pollinator, alter the community to a new equilibrium.

Conservation in intensively utilized rural areas requires planning and sympathetic liaison with people in the region. Managers and investigators must be cooperative in activities such as maintenance of woodlands, riparian strips, wetlands, remnant grasslands, and connecting corridors. It may mean the imposition of quotas on harvesting, or a phasing out of exploitive utilization, such as cutting lumber from remnants of indigenous forest. It may also mean persuading farmers to leave wider hedgerows between paddocks, and use of land covenants or private land protection agreements to protect key sites on privately owned land (e.g., Lozier 1987).

Whatever the outcome, management of rural land for conservation is likely to be intensive, and to involve more and more small reserves. These will need intensive management because of structural alteration, loss of area, extreme edge effects, and increased vulnerability to invasion by weeds and exotic animals. Local farmers may see such reserves as refuges for livestock during periods of drought when grazing lands are depleted. Management under such situations will involve trade-offs and many hard decisions.

This trend will be made more acute if there is appreciable climate change over the next few decades (McGlone 1988). Complex changes in vegetation structure, seral invasions, and disruption can be expected as ecosystems adjust and move toward new equilibria. Some indigenous plants may adjust easily to new conditions and associations of species. Others will be trapped in increasingly deteriorating habitats because of inability to disperse. Invasive exotic species will probably be at an advantage, and may threaten both natural environment reserves and agricultural production lands. Survival—and especially enhancement—of biodiversity in tomorrow's rural landscapes is a challenge for the coming decades.

CASE STUDY: SEMINATURAL PLANT COMMUNITIES IN EASTERN EUROPE

For many years Polish botanists have been especially concerned with the *steppe grasslands* existing in small patches on relatively warm and dry sites in the southern and northwestern parts of the country. The most interesting stands of these xerothermic grasslands have been set aside as nature reserves. Now, after 20–50 years of strict protection, the progress of plant succession is evident, with the sole exception of the communities growing under the most extreme habitat conditions—on very shallow soils, on gypsum rocks, and so forth. In all probability, the majority of the steppe reserves are in places that were deforested by people hundreds of thousands of years ago. This is certainly the case in the Jaksiee Reserve near Miechow on the Malopolska Upland, which was established in 1923 to conserve particular grassland associations. In the absence of grazing, forest shrubs and trees from surrounding communities have extended their areas so much that the light-demanding steppe species have become locally extinct or drastically reduced. Particularly rapid succession has been observed in mesic hay meadows under protection, for example, in the mountain meadows of the forest zones in the Pieniny National Park and the Tatra National Park in southern Poland.

Successional changes do not only affect small nature reserves in heavily populated countries; data are now available for the plant communities in such larger areas as the zonal steppes of the USSR. In such communities, when human interference is much reduced, there is an excessive accumulation of dead organic matter. Consequently, xerophilous grasses are forced out by more mesophilous grasses and the steppe grassland changes its character.

Source: Medwecka-Kornas 1977.

THE SIGNIFICANCE OF WILDLIFE SANCTUARIES TO RURAL PEOPLE

How can wildlife sanctuaries, in particular national parks, be of relevance to people who live in an increasingly degraded rural environment? So much depends on the management objectives of the individual park. In simple terms, the primary objective of most national parks is to preserve in perpetuity representative examples of the plant and animal communities of that country or region. The secondary objective is usually to allow the use of the area by current and future generations for inspiration, education, and research, provided such use is consistent with the first objective. More obvious direct gain for people living in surrounding areas is usually restricted to income from tourism. Less obvious, of course, are the direct and indirect benefits from the life-supporting systems that have already been described.

The tourism and money-earning argument for nature conservation can become very counterproductive if there is no legislative, political, and administrative insurance that the income derived from tourism will be channelled back into the region in such a way that the people living there will be able to comprehend and realize this benefit in one way or another.

The ideal form of development is to have a national park surrounded by a buffer zone, where various degrees of hunting and gathering are totally accepted. Such buffer zones should also contain the major installations, such as lodges and campsites, which would not only directly benefit local people, but would also relieve the pressure on the park itself.

To gain the full support of local people, proponents of a park must demonstrate that it can provide more benefits than would accrue from shifting agriculture and forest product harvesting. A good example of this comes from Amboseli National Park, Kenya, where the total park net return amounts to U.S. $40 per hectare compared to 80 cents per hectare under the most optimistic agricultural return.

Unfortunately, many conservation plans have failed because they have been done for the people rather than with the people. Furthermore, all too often, conservation policies have been introduced in developing countries that mimic those of the developed world, and these are usually ill-suited to local conditions and social needs.

Source: Hanks 1984b.

Stressed and disturbed habitats

Natural patterns of stress and disturbance are widespread and essential to the persistence of many plants and animals. Indeed many rare species depend on regular disturbance for their maintenance. It is perhaps ironic that often the effect of creating protected areas may be to unwittingly eliminate disturbance essential to the long-term survival of a community and to persistence of particular species.

The nature, magnitude, and periodicity of disturbance and stress is important. Identification of such factors allows management for sensitive parts of ecosystems and maintenance of feedback loops. This is particularly important in systems such as oceanic islands where floras may not have coevolved with grazing mammals or where other animals such as birds have been the browsers and grazers. If the birds become extirpated, as has happened in New Zealand with the moa, simple replacement by cattle or sheep is unlikely to be successful because feeding patterns are not identical and will not have the same effect.

In continental regions, especially those with a long history of human influence, plants might be expected to be resilient to further human pressure. The effects of pollution (especially in recent decades) in Europe show that this is not always the case. Nevertheless, many so-called natural biological communities require human intervention for maintenance. For example, steppe grasslands of southern and northwestern Poland that have been protected as nature reserves (described in the case study above) have started to change back to shrubland and forest. Similar observations have been made of chalk grasslands of England. In a similar manner, shoreline communities along the edge of the Baltic sea are maintained by constant grazing or mowing. At Kolobrzeg, a nature reserve was enclosed in 1965, but after a few years it was invaded by weeds such as *Agropyron repens, Deschampsia caespitosa,* and *Phragmites communis.* This resulted in the loss of several characteristic salt-tolerant plants, which, however, survive in those sites outside the reserve that are accessible to cattle.

A sometimes unexpected source of stress following disturbance is provided by the interaction of species and predators, parasites, or disease that are new to plants of a region. Disturbance of particular species and of communities by disease and predators is of wide occurrence in natural communities. Less widely recognized is the potential for wild plants to be drastically affected by exotic diseases and predators for which they have inadequate defenses (Dobson and Hudson 1986).

Tropical moist forests may tolerate some human-induced disturbance, but often artificial disturbance even of small magnitude is risky. This emphasizes how little is really known about the function of and interactions within such vegetation. Seral vegetation, in adapting for life in landslides; forest gaps; or fire-prone, drought-prone, or flood-prone habitats is, in a sense, preadapted to live with people, invade fields, and compete with crops. Many tropical rain forest species are apparently devoid of such preadaption and everything they do might be conceived of as "wrong": lack of colonizing ability, poor synchronization of reproduction, inability of seed to remain viable, and narrow tolerance of environmental change (Ng 1983). In some tropical reserves, it is already obvious that weedy species are increasing at the expense of primary forest species. Remedial action includes the rapid restoration of canopy (to trap humidity, to recreate the proper understory environment), restoration of a multitiered structure, prevention of hunting and cutting, and careful reintroduction of animals and plants previously known to exist there.

Remnant Habitats and Relict Populations

Many natural habitats are small remnants of what were once much larger ecosystems. They range from the sides of ravines too steep for plowing, through patches of disturbed prairie and small pockets of rain forest on mountainsides, to islands of second-growth woodland surrounded by intensively cultivated farmland. Worldwide, even in many parts of the tropics, indigenous species are becoming confined to remnants of habitat (Ehrlich and Murphy 1987). In New Zealand, in the 150 years since European settlement, over 20 million hectares, or 75 percent of the land area, has been biologically modified or transformed (Meurk 1987).

True relict species whose distributions are markedly reduced by human influences are not the same as local (*narrow-range*) endemics (Ogle 1987). Local endemics, sometimes with extremely restricted distributions, are found in many parts of the world. They have evolved naturally as small populations on local "islands" that often are sharply differentiated from surrounding habitats. In contrast, human-induced relict species (*anthropo-endemics*) have had a much wider distribution in the past, their geographic ranges having only recently contracted as available habitat was destroyed. Such species may be biologically unfit for continued survival in small numbers. Many require specific management and techniques such as translocation and intervention to expand population size and number.

Fragmentation that leads to relictual distribution is rarely a random process (Usher 1987). In most parts of the world, the primary threat to natural and seminatural ecosystems has been intense, but not necessarily sustained, agricultural production. Those sites that are lost first tend to be on richest soils. This means that species that tend to aggregate on poorer sites will be well represented in fragments, whereas those that prefer more fertile sites will be under-represented in the vegetation fragments (Usher 1987).

Narrow-range endemics frequently occur on poorer, more highly stressed sites. Thus one cannot assume that remnants of vegetation will include representative overall samples of the local flora. Some species formerly confined to more fertile sites may only survive in the remaining remnants when stress can be reduced below acceptable levels.

Experimental evidence suggests that local extinc-

tions are more important influences on species richness than immigration into a site (Usher 1987). A net result of such local extinctions is likely to be a process of continued species and diversity loss. Concern should be not just with total numbers of species in habitat remnants, but also the quality of those species (Usher 1987). This does not mean that some plants cannot persist for long periods in very small relictual sites. Since retreat of the Wisconsin Ice Sheet from southern Canada and adjacent parts of the United States, approximately 8000–11,000 years ago, a surprising number of arctic-alpine species have survived in microsites where arctic climate is simulated on a miniature scale (e.g., Given and Soper 1981; Figure 7.3). Nevertheless, the monitoring of relicts and their

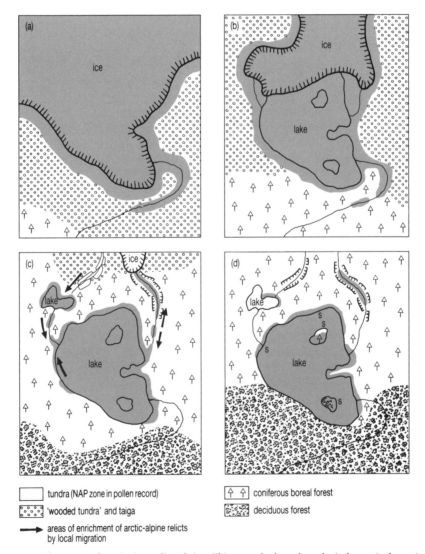

Figure 7.3. The retreat of species into relictual sites. This example shows hypothetical steps in formation of relict sites with arctic-alpine species: (a) full-glacial, (b) early post-glacial, (c) late post-glacial, (d) present day. (Reproduced by permission of the Canadian Museum of Nature, Ottawa; from Given and Soper 1981)

management is likely to use an increasingly large portion of resources in the coming decades.

Case Study: Maintenance of *Lythrum hyssopifolia* in Agricultural Landscapes in Britain

Lythrum hyssopifolia is a widespread annual species, but in Britain it is sufficiently rare to be included in the British *Red Data Book*. Like many species found in pioneer vegetation on exposed mud, it has diminished in frequency. In recent years it has been confined to only one site in Cambridgeshire and in Jersey, Channel Islands, where it occurs locally in shallow depressions in arable fields. It is dependent on both winter flooding and regular plowing of these sites for its survival.

Lythrum hyssopifolia is able to persist because the combination of local topography and agricultural practice favors an annual plant of low long-term competitive ability. Annuals predominate in this highly disturbed habitat. They germinate mostly in spring, most are self-pollinating, and most have potential dormancy of seeds (an advantage as sites may not be flooded or disturbed every year). *Lythrum hyssopifolia* was absent from one site for three years because winter flooding did not occur. The habitat is highly specialized and its survival along with the species found there depends on the peculiar combination of flooding and disturbance.

Source: Preston and Whitehouse 1986.

Figure 7.4. Plantations of *Pinus nigra* in New Zealand provide habitats for indigenous vegetation including several threatened species. (Courtesy of M. J. Parsons)

Nonindigenous Plant Communities

The potential for communities dominated by exotic species to be valuable for conservation of particular species has been generally ignored. There is, however, growing evidence that some such communities can provide valuable habitat for some plants that are quite rare. In Chile, some plantations of exotic species are known to provide a new habitat for indigenous plants such as *Lapageria rosea* (M. Arroyo, pers. com.). In New Zealand, mature forests of exotic conifers often have an understory of indigenous species including large numbers of ferns (also tree ferns) and shrubs (Figure 7.4). In one outstanding example, a large plantation of *Pinus nigra* has over 25 percent of New Zealand's native orchids, including two species at risk (Gibbs 1989a).

In some instances partial logging and conversion of previously undisturbed forest may not result in complete impoverishment of plants and animals formerly present in undisturbed sites (Roche and Dourojeanni 1984). A survey of logging effects on wildlife in primary forest at Sungai Tekam in Malaysia showed that many animals survived, and, more important, some survived better in logged than in unlogged areas. On the other hand, surveys of logged and unlogged forests elsewhere (e.g., in New Zealand) show sharp decline in numbers of indigenous birds, some of which may be crucial to long-term survival of forest ecosystems. This suggests that it is important to learn more about which animals and plants require large, undisturbed habitats; which will survive in disturbed situations; which will accommodate to the presence of exotic plants (and animals); and what are the expected persistence times in each case.

There is no doubt that exotic plants and animals, once established, are likely to remain permanent features of ecosystems. Only where they are economically important pests or threaten large numbers of indigenous species are they likely to be eradicated. It is also important to realize that if protected areas of natural vegetation are to be connected by corridors, exotic plants are likely to become significant components of these, particularly where corridors are narrow. The continued association of exotic and indigenous plants is something that people worldwide will have to learn to accept, live with, and plan for.

Case Study: Conserving Orchids in an Exotic Plantation

In 1987, a block of mature *Pinus nigra* plantation was set aside by Timberlands Bay of Plenty, a commercial lumber firm, as a reserve for New Zealand native orchids. The site is notable in having at least 27 species of indigenous ground orchids growing under a tall canopy of the exotic pine (planted in 1933). The area has a colony of rare *Chiloglottis gunnii* and has a large colony of another rare orchid, *Calochilus robertsonii*.

Some of these orchids occur outside the reserved block; attempts are being made to transplant orchids from sites on which timber will be milled into the reserve. Problems may be encountered because the reserve lacks a buffer zone and may become vulnerable once surrounding plantations are harvested. Stands of *Pinus nigra* seem to have the richest orchid floras; this may result from lack of competition under the trees. It has also been suggested that the tall *P. nigra* act as traps for windblown seed.

Only part of the *Chiloglottis gunnii* colony has been transplanted into the reserve. It seems that this species is extremely site-specific. It occurs in Australia and, of the three known New Zealand sites, two are in exotic plantations. It is hoped that one effect of retaining the *Pinus nigra* plantation as a protected area is that this will act as a source for recolonization of newly planted areas of *P. radiata*.

A grant of NZ $1000 from the Ministry of the Environment will assist with native orchid survey, recovery of orchids, and a public awareness program centered on pine forests.

Sources: Gibbs 1989a, 1989b.

Habitat Restoration

Land disturbance varies from the relatively localized disturbance caused by a small-scale farm to massive disturbance as a consequence of mining and profound land development. Factors that need to be considered when disturbed areas are to be restored are the scale and type of disturbance, the desired type of rehabilitation, problems such as chemical pollution and toxic wastes, the state of the soil, and the desired end point of restoration. A common view of restoration is that it is an attempt to reinstate biotic communities in their original prehuman (or at least premodern) state.

This is an idealistic model that has much to commend it but is seldom achievable; often we are unsure what this state actually is.

To restore in an ecological sense means no more than to put back what was there at some earlier time (Atkinson 1990). What that time is depends on the biotic community that is the desired end point. The biotic community of interest can include exotic plants, but for conservation purposes it will generally focus on indigenous plants and communities (Figure 7.5). The choice of end point community involves value

Figure 7.5. An example of prairie restoration in Michigan, USA. (D. R. Given)

judgments and not just scientific analysis (Diamond 1987).

Criteria selected to characterize ecosystem restoration must not only be scientifically sound but must encompass a broad range of attributes related to public expectations and uses (Cairns 1986). Public acceptance of the particular actions used will be influenced by the economies involved, the reliability of extrapolations from one system to another, the characteristics to be used to determine restoration success (and the precision with which they can be determined), a satisfactory methodology for determining degrees of restoration, and sensitivity of selected end points so that results can be reliably interpreted.

What are the components of a restoration program that will ensure success? Six components have been identified for island restoration but have general applicability (Atkinson 1990, modified):

Comprehensive information. This needs to cover the physical, biological, archaeological, and cultural aspects of the target region so that appropriate sites for restoration can be identified. Species inventory alone is not a sufficient description of an ecosystem.

A functional classification of sites. Restoration is only one kind of management; different areas, such as different islands, perform differing conservation functions and therefore require different kinds of management. The different management regimes are part of a spectrum of uses.

Defining restoration goals. Many different kinds of action come under the general concept of restoration. If recovery of threatened species is a primary goal, this can vary from very minor manipulation to restoration of several biotic communities to provide habitat for target species. Replacement of extinct organisms by related extant ones allows restoration of a more complete community structure. Restoration of communities themselves can range from repair work to complete restoration and reestablishment of many species. A further step is to engineer a completely new kind of community for a specific conservation purpose.

An understanding of the restorative process. Scientific understanding of natural restorative processes is necessary if the identified goal is to be achieved. It is important to be aware of plant succession on the type of site. An appreciation of nutritional needs will often be necessary to ensure that the restored community will be self-perpetuating after human intervention is withdrawn. Restoration may have to be very site-specific within the target area; for instance, unstable fertile soils on steep slopes may require different combinations of species than would a stable infertile soil on a plateau. Trials should be used to identify the most ecologically effective and therefore cost-effective method of restoring a particular community. The restoration program should be replicated and documented so that errors in methods can be identified.

Relevant practical skills. A theoretical understanding is of limited value if certain practical skills are not available. These include propagation, survey and estimation of numbers, and acute observational powers to apprehend and understand why some species are failing.

Commitment by individuals and organizations. A major restoration program extends over a long period of time. Goals cannot be achieved by a flurry of activity one year and no activity the next. A long-term commitment is essential once restoration is begun.

Where the scale of disturbance is small or its effects are relatively slight, natural regeneration may be sufficient so that minimum assistance is required. Help may only amount to periodic monitoring. Obviously, reestablishing plants with minimal interference can be very cost-effective, although natural processes are sometimes slow.

Natural succession depends on several factors. One of the most important is availability of seed of the original vegetation components. How far away are mature plants of the required species? Are they producing propagules? And are dispersal vectors available? Regeneration of weedy seral or successional species may not be difficult, but establishment of climax species may be more difficult, at least until many years have past. It is likely that soil may have become eroded, leached, or significantly degraded. This is especially true in the tropics, where reestablishment of forest frequently is hindered by the degraded condition of soils. Nutrient and moisture status of soil may have changed markedly; this also needs to be checked and remedied. Other severe constraints on natural regeneration can include grazing, factors causing accelerated erosion, lack of mature individuals in the community, and presence of weeds.

Various methods are available to establish vegetation cover artificially. For instance, to establish forest in open grassland techniques ranging from aerial seeding to planting of coppice stakes can be applied. It is essential that trees and shrubs grow quickly to shade out and overcome competition with grass and low herbs. Preferable colonizer species should be fast-growing, fire- and grazing-resistant, with capacity to fix nitrogen (unless low fertility is desired). Species forming dense, monotypic stands should not be used, as this will prevent the succession of other species and eventually a climax forest. The food and shelter plants of birds, bats, insects, and other dispersal and pollinating agents must be considered as well. Immigration of these organisms from surrounding forests will itself introduce other fruits and seeds of other plants via defecation.

For more interventionist restoration, it is necessary to perform an analytic survey to identify former biological communities and assess the impacts that led to the loss of communities and modification of others. The end product of restoration must be clearly identified. Particularly pertinent aspects of overall survey and planning for major restoration projects (Liegel 1981 in Hall 1987) include *site analysis* to obtain an understanding of the biotic and physical requirements of the desired natural community; *site preparation* to eliminate existing unwanted species or the formulation of a strategy to suppress them, and creation of an environment favorable to the desired species; *species placement* that takes into account distribution patterns and associations; and *short- and long-term management,* and provisions for review and evaluation.

On extreme sites such as those left by open-cast mining and stripping of timber, complete reconstruction of vegetation may be the only option. Sometimes it may be feasible only to restore a habitat to near-natural condition when the original vegetation has been destroyed or so grossly damaged as to be almost unrecognizable. In extreme instances, there may be no known areas of the particular vegetation type left.

In the United Kingdom alone, about 340,000 hectares of land is derelict through mining. What often results from mining, especially open-cast mining, is not only destroyed vegetation but also a complete absence of soil. Key nutrients may be deficient and the ground may be extremely acid and compacted. In such a case the first step is to restore physical factors to a level where they allow growth of plants that will colonize or can be planted at the site. If there are soil fertility or toxicity problems, these need particular treatment. Nutrient balance often can be changed through application of substantial amounts of fertilizer and establishment of nitrogen-fixing plants. It may be necessary, however, to reduce or carefully control nutrient status if the natural community is nutrient deficient. On mining wastes, phosphorus may be chemically bound. Extreme acidity due to breakdown of natural sulfides is common and is often overcome by heavy applications of lime. Mitigating the effects of heavy metals is more difficult, especially if they are present in high concentrations. Metal-tolerant species can be established, sometimes at quite low cost, or an inert covering may be placed over the ground (this will not prevent deep-rooted plants from reaching the contaminated wastes).

Sometimes quite drastic measures must be taken to restore vegetation where changed fertility is the problem (Marrs 1985; Riem and Diemont 1985). Studies of heathland show that increases in nutrient supply promote a change from heathland to grassland. Removing the upper soil horizons and stripping off the grass sod, followed by recolonization and replanting, may be necessary to restore the heathland. Other techniques that have been used to reduce fertility are planting the site with cereal crops, burning of stubble, and specific fertilizer inputs to increase the yield of temporary crops and accelerate the removal of other nutrients.

If the aim is to reestablish indigenous vegetation, exotic species should be used only as a temporary expedient when they are superior for soil rehabilitation, erosion control, or as temporary nursery plants to shelter permanent plantings, and when the intent is to eventually eliminate them. A valuable role for mixed exotic and indigenous plantings can also be played in buffer zones between agricultural land and wild habitat.

In nature reserves and other protected areas of high conservation value when natural vegetation is the desired end point, it is usually undesirable to use introduced species for reseeding, especially as there may be uncertainty of how long they may persist (Reid and Walsh 1987). One of the problems with use of exotic species is that they must be vigorous enough to establish on bare sites yet capable of being readily eliminated once their purpose has been accomplished. It is preferable to develop methods of seeding with indigenous species of flowering plants and perhaps even bryophytes. There is much room for investigation of species and techniques that will eliminate the need for use of exotic nursery crops in rehabilitation projects.

The importance of reserving or enhancing microtopography in restoration has been underestimated. In the restoration of salt marsh at Humbolt Bay, California, restoration and enhancement programs were designed to accommodate the particular habitat requirements of three rare species by providing higher elevation sites within the restored system (Newton 1987).

High-priority sites for restoration are often those

that are accessible to the public; yet pressure of use, such as high pedestrian traffic, can sometimes quite effectively negate an otherwise well-planned restoration program. At critical stages of restoration, people have to be discouraged from using sites—for instance, by the simple expedient of making adjacent ground or vegetation relatively hard to travel across by creating barriers with boulders, piles of brushwood, and ditches. Different textures of vegetation can be achieved by establishing mosaics of grasses, swards, shrubs, and trees; these may also help direct traffic. Access paths through or adjacent to sites under reconstruction should be carefully sited and so well-constructed that there is little inducement for people to stray from them.

Grazing animals may eat new vegetation as fast as it establishes at a restoration site. Mitigation of this problem involves very close liaison with local people whose livelihood may depend on the animals and who see the restoration site as "free" grazing land during times of the year when pasturage is scarce. Adjacent land-users need to realize why a degraded site is being restored. Many degraded habitats ought not to have been disturbed in the first place, but these are the sites likely to continue to be utilized as a result of pressure for food production.

Valuable opportunities exist for addressing both the problem of exponential increase in threatened species and that of damaged ecosystems, by restoring ecosystems in such a way as to enhance the chances of survival for one or more threatened species (Cairns 1986). Through computer listings of regional species that are at risk along with their habitats, and damaged ecosystem sites where rehabilitation is contemplated, needs can be matched with available sites.

Typically, either seed or container-grown plants are used for restoration programs. The use of both, however, especially with herbaceous perennials and semiwoody plants, has some clear advantages. The following considerations in a restoration program highlight some of these advantages (Evans 1988, modified):

Placement. The planner may want to place stands of a certain species in given locations as well as allow for random seed germination and establishment.

Sex ratio. Random dispersement of sexes will occur if seed germinates and plants grow on site. Container plants of known sex can be installed in ideal ratios and arrangements.

Age class. Variation and spread in actual age and maturity can be achieved by planting both seed and container-grown plants.

Ecotype. One can obtain plants from a particular region using either seed or container-grown sources, but local or superior strains can be deliberately included using container plants.

Soil biology. The use of microbial inoculants is of increasing interest. Where necessary, rootballs on container-grown plants can be inoculated before planting. Site-germinated seedlings will be infected subsequently.

Nurse crop. On many sites container-grown plants can provide protection for seedlings, or for slower growing plants.

Habitat. To obtain fast cover in shelterbelts or establish plants early to provide animal food, cover, or nest sites, seed should be used for overall cover, but container-grown plants should also be used to provide islands of habitat while seedlings become established.

Competition. Early competition with weeds can sometimes be minimized through the use of container plants.

Microenvironment. The immediate surroundings of a plant often provide microhabitat for germination and seedling growth. Thus container plants can assist germination of seeds planted at the same time or shortly after.

Success. In many species, overall survival percentages are low because of high seed mortality. Container-grown plants can act as insurance for the seed crop.

Reserves and resilience. In short drought periods, container plants will have more reserves than will seedlings.

Timing. The simultaneous seed and container plant technique allows plants to be installed at the same time or in sequence, allowing greater flexibility in timing.

Cost. The total cost for planting both seed and container plants of the same species will normally be lower than the exclusive use of container plants and slightly higher than the exclusive use of seed.

Showiness. Critical public concerns can sometimes be mitigated easily by having a few larger plants scattered through a revegetation site.

Case Study: Example of Wetlands Habitat Creation

Potentially, one of the least expensive and easiest ways to establish wetland vegetation in an area where it has not existed previously is to use donor soil from an existing wetland. This technique presupposes that viable seeds of desirable species are present in the donor soil. By spreading a layer of donor soil over a basin that is to be turned into a wetland, and then maintaining proper moisture levels, vegetation resembling that in natural wetlands can be established quickly.

There are many important questions to be answered before applying this technique: How long would it take for natural dispersal to establish wetland vegetation? Is there already a significant seed rain of wetland species? What is the species composition of the donor seed bank? What can be done to prevent the establishment of unwanted species? How long can donor soil be stockpiled before there is a significant loss in seed viability? How deep a layer of donor soil is needed?

In Florida, different thicknesses of peat from a forested wetland were deposited uniformly or in strips in experimental plots on a phosphate mine site. Many more herbaceous species did become established on the donor soils than on the control areas, but no woody species established. By August, the mean biomass of wetland species was significantly higher on sites with donor soils than on control sites. Topographic variation in the layer of donor soil was an important factor. This method of wetland creation was economically competitive with the more traditional method of establishing new wetlands by transplantation.

The absence of seeds of some desirable species in the donor soil will require the sowing or transplantation of these species. By selecting donor soils from suitable wetlands, it is possible to establish a wetland community dominated by desirable species quickly and efficiently, before natural dispersal of established unwanted, wind-dispersed species such as *Typha* or *Salix*.

The potential use of donor soils to establish vegetation in a series of wetlands being created as part of the Des Plaines River wetland demonstration project has been investigated. Altogether 120 species were found in the seed bank samples, and about 50 percent of these are considered desirable species. Two practical recommendations came from this study. First, soils should be collected at the beginning of the growing season, when they tend to have a higher diversity of desirable species. Second, soils should be collected to a depth of only 25 centimeters.

Source: Valk and Peterson, 1989.

Case Study: Example of Prairie Reconstruction and Rehabilitation

In the last 100 years the grasslands, parklands, and wetlands of the prairies have been so radically transformed by human activity as to become highly endangered in many regions. Today, in the whole of Canada, little native prairie remains in its natural state. Tallgrass prairie in Manitoba has been reduced by 99 percent; only 10 percent of the original fescue prairie remains; and 75 percent of mixed prairie and aspen parkland has disappeared. Of prairie wetland in Manitoba, 40 percent has been drained. A similar story can be told for many other parts of North America formerly covered by prairie communities.

In 1986, WWF–Canada launched a cooperative prairie program under the name Wild West. The program's primary aim is to stem habitat destruction and thereby ensure conservation of remaining prairie diversity. A range of agencies are represented on the steering committee, and there is a corresponding diversity of funding sources. More than 90 projects had been launched by early 1989, ranging from identification of critical habitat sites for prairie animals and plants, to reintroduction (translocation) programs, sustained use of private grazing lands, reservation, and restoration.

In Illinois, regrowth of prairie along roadsides and railroads is being encouraged. These strips are cut or burned in the fall, and in some instances are enriched with whole plants or seed of characteristic prairie plants. Prairie remnants are encouraged at roadside stopping points and picnic areas. Several botanic gardens are undertaking prairie recreation. One of the most ambitious programs is that of the Chicago Botanic Garden, which is gradually re-creating all of the primary prairie types within the garden area situated in the northern Chicago metropolitan area. This is requiring planting of over 100 species on a grid system at intervals of one foot, and is a slow, labor-intensive operation. A similar scheme is underway at Fernwood Botanical Garden and Nature Center in Michigan, where several acres of prairie have now been planted over a period of about 10 years. Paths and an elevated observation point allow visitors to get views from both ground level and above of tallgrass prairie.

Sources: Given, pers. obs. 1988; Dover 1989.

Translocation and Reestablishment

Translocation involves the removal of an organism from one site followed by resituating it somewhere else. For plants, this usually means propagating under controlled conditions using material obtained from a site, and then transferring young plants back into natural sites. Translocation is not a new idea, and species introductions have been attempted many times in many places (e.g., Sainz-Ollero and Hernandez-Bermejo 1979; Brooks 1981). Four types of translocation and reestablishment can be distinguished (Boitani 1976; Green 1979; IUCN 1987). *Introduction* is the deliberate or accidental release of an animal or plant of a species or race into an area in which it has not occurred in historic times; or a species or race so released. *Reintroduction* is the deliberate or accidental release of a species or race into an area to which it was indigenous in historic times; or a species or race so released. *Restocking* is the deliberate or accidental release of a species or race into an area in which it is already present. *Naturalization* is the establishment of self-regenerating populations of an introduced species or race in a free-living state in the wild.

Translocations for conservation are generally considered in these main circumstances: (1) where a habitat is likely to be destroyed and there is need to establish a population at a new location; (2) where a population is reduced in size and there is concern about its long-term persistence; (3) when it is desirable to divide a population so that risks of losing all individuals through disease or catastrophe are minimized; and (4) where there are biological problems that jeopardize persistence (e.g., a marked imbalance in the proportion of males and females).

Translocation strategies have to be carefully planned and involve both ex situ and in situ techniques (Figure 7.6). Several major problems can arise

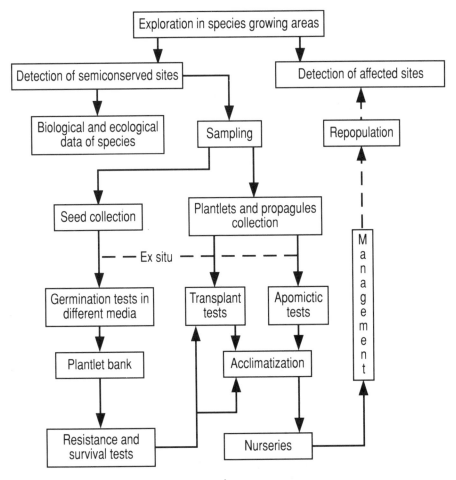

Figure 7.6. Flow diagram for study of threatened species using ex situ and in situ approaches on the Yucatan Peninsula, Mexico. (Reproduced by permission from Orellana et al. 1988)

when plants are deliberately or accidently translocated. These include transmission of pests and diseases acquired away from wild sites (Thomson 1981), hybridism with species already existing on the target site (Pritchard 1972; Green 1981), and lack of successful establishment because of inadequate research into habitat requirements. Translocations must consider the effects of predation on newly shifted plants, especially because stressed plants often are more vulnerable to the impacts of predation than are those that are less stressed (Louda 1988). Translocations are often expensive and time-consuming and should not be left to chance. They should be preceded by research into the species' habitat requirements and establishment requirements. Monitoring is essential, not only immediately following translocation, but also until plants are established and naturally reproducing.

Documentation is especially important in translocation projects and should include reasons for translocation and site selection; sources of material, methods of propagation, and precise numbers of plants handled; precise information on sites and dates of planting, and records of ongoing inventory, survey, and monitoring; and assessment of success and failure, including reasons for mortality.

In collecting material for propagation, due regard must be given to maximizing genetic variation. It is preferable that propagating material be taken from between 50 and 100 individuals. A useful technique for obtaining seed is to collect from concentric circles, initially as close as possible to plants possessing the particular characteristics being sought, and then moving outward in concentric bands as closest sources become exhausted (Ferreira and Hillyard 1987). If collections are made from fewer than 30 individuals, lines of descendants should be separated and equal numbers of progeny should be obtained from each line. It is preferable to propagate vegetatively, starting with up to 10 plants from each original (founder) specimen. Protocols are being developed for both vegetative and sexual propagation, especially when the number of founders is small (e.g., Center for Plant Conservation 1986).

Tissue culture can be considered when the number of founders is very small and there is need to build up numbers rapidly. Micropropagation techniques also have potential to store plant material as callus and release plants for translocation at predetermined times.

When young plants are released into the wild, attention must be given to pests and predators. Diseases may have been acquired off site, so plants to be used for translocation should be propagated and grown under quarantine. If plants have been grown off site for long periods of time, there may be significant alteration of the genome. Some plants should be held back and not planted out initially, in case site conditions are unsuitable or the first translocation does not succeed because of unfavorable and unanticipated events such as storms. The role of quick-growing nurse plants must be considered. These provide shelter, buffering from climatic extremes, and reduce trampling and predation.

Occasionally there may be justification for establishing a new population from a variety of sources. This may be necessary where plants are self-incompatible, natural populations consist of only one sex, or populations are so reduced in size that lack of genetic fitness is a possibility.

How many plants should be introduced into the wild and at what rate? Three guidelines are suggested for perennials. First, plant 50–75 percent of the required plants in the first three years. This allows monitoring and assessment of site suitability. Second, plant smaller amounts in subsequent years with the objectives of replacing plants that die and allowing an increase in numbers to give the desired total by the time the first plants are flowering and producing new young plants. Third, continue to translocate plants as necessary to maintain the population at a predetermined level.

An increasing range of techniques will become available to assist translocation strategies. This includes importation of genes for disease resistance and incorporation in the genomes of lines being translocated. Such techniques may be costly but should be considered for critically endangered species (Williams and Creech 1987).

Generally, translocations should be undertaken as planned exercises by organizations with long-term responsibility for conservation, although the role of observant amateurs must not be underestimated. Several attempts were made to translocate *Schoenus ferrugineus* from Loch Tummel in Scotland where it was threatened by hydroelectric development. These failed, with the exception of two transfers. One was to Cambridge from where plants eventually found their way back to Loch Tummel. The other was a transplant by an amateur on his own initiative to a different vice-county, an action for which he was, ironically, roundly criticized (Brooks 1981).

Although many translocation experiments from botanic gardens in the past have been spectacularly unsuccessful, such strategies, sometimes called species repatriation, are gaining momentum. Among recent examples are repatriation of *Gasteria baylissiana* to South Africa, *Cosmos atrosanguineus* to Mexico, and *Alsinodendron trinerve* to Hawaii (M. Maunder, pers. com. 1993).

Case Study: Creating a New Population of *Amsinckia Grandiflora*

Amsinckia grandiflora is an endangered annual plant of the winter-wet summer-dry grasslands of northern California. It is now known from only three natural populations. It is heterostylous with cryptic self-incompatibility. Habitat is deteriorating and there is high potential for anthropogenic disturbance.

Field and laboratory study indicated five potential microsites for reintroduction, the choice being finally narrowed to one by critical analysis of soils, flora, and standing crop. An experimental framework with demographic monitoring was used to follow the fate of propagules from a wild and a cultivated source with different genetic and germination characteristics. Grass cover at the site was reduced because it had significant negative effects on survivorship. The initial 3460 propagules produced 1774 germinules from which 1101 plants reproduced, resulting in a crop of about 35,800 new propagules.

Source: Pavlick, Nickrent, and Howard 1993.

CHAPTER 8

Awareness and Education

Many people are starting to acknowledge that there may be a serious environmental crisis, that it is possible we have mismanaged our planet, and that attitudes toward natural resources and nature may have to change (Myers 1984a; Raven 1986a, 1986b; Wilson 1988, 1989). The continuing dialogue between more developed (Western) nations and those that are less developed (the so-called North-South dialogue) is not only on economic and social issues: it has conservation overtones as well. Tinbergen (1986) suggests that we urgently need quantitative information in order to design an optimal policy for conservation in the world at large. To this end, a number of policy instruments can, and must, be used to warrant a safer future of humankind, thus supplying an important new dimension to the North-South dialogue.

Hundreds of millions of people do not yet grasp the arguments for a different approach to nature and its resources. Others have heard the arguments but remain unconvinced. A lot of lip service is paid to conservation but there is still far too little understanding of what it means in practical terms or active support.

The general goals of the broad field of environmental education are quite simple: to foster clear awareness of, and concern about, economic, social, political, and ecological interdependence in urban and rural areas; to provide every person with opportunities to acquire the knowledge, values, attitudes, commitment, and skills needed to protect and improve the environment; and to create new patterns of behavior of individuals, groups, and society as a whole toward the environment (International Environmental Education Program 1985).

Within this broad-brush approach to environmental education, conservation must be related to people's lives as well as to nature's needs. It is one thing to convince people that by changing their way of life they can ensure supplies of unpolluted water or increase their crop yields. It is much harder to raise awareness about soil conservation, pollution control, and forest maintenance. Often popular support for conservation of species is relatively high because of their attractiveness or oddity. But it is harder to convince people of the importance of more abstract entities such as genetic resources, or to convince people in a temperate region that their future well-being relates to the continued existence of tropical rain forests.

Several years ago a questionnaire was prepared for a natural history magazine. To the question Which of the following do you consider to be our most critical environmental problem?, six possible answers were provided (Gerlach et al. 1980): (1) water pollution; (2) air pollution; (3) nuclear and other hazardous waste build-up and storage; (4) increased societal costs of pollution control; (5) inadequate or unenforced regulatory legislation; and (6) loss of land to highways, development, and urbanization. There was no specific mention of habitat destruction, extinction of species, or loss of genetic diversity. Unfortunately, campaigns to save spectacular species such as tigers, elephants, rhinoceroses, apes, and whales probably contribute to an identification in many people's minds of conservation with preservationism.

The process of education must be one of discovery (MacFie 1987). In many instances, part of the process will be discovery of cultural roots. This can happen in a workshop that brings together people who continue to use plants in traditional ways, others who study plants from a more scientific standpoint, and people who are ignorant of both. It can happen on a field trip into the wild to rediscover the dependency of all animals (including humans) on plants. Education can be part of a project to restore roadside vegetation to its wild state. Each of these, and many other approaches, will encourage people who have never thought much about plants and their conservation to ask questions and enter on a voyage of discovery concerning the place of plants in this world.

Environmental Awareness Programs

An awareness program is an essential precursor to formal learning (Osborne and Freyberg 1985). It is important to know people's basic perceptions before educating them. The teacher needs to understand his or her own views on a topic, the views of authorities and scientists, and the views and opinions of students. A second precondition to formal education is exploration of the subject, preferably with everyday, real situations. The gaining of knowledge is largely initiated by natural curiosity or by the desire to create something that people value. A third precondition is to ensure that students clarify their own views, so they do not feel threatened by hazy or strange ideas.

The village dweller, the city person, the business person, and the technologically advanced farmer will each have a different relationship with plants. In those countries where traditional cultures still dominate, at least locally, most people probably have a greater awareness of plants than their western counterparts. A survey of environmental perceptions in the former West Germany and the Philippines indicated that children in the former were more concerned with negative factors such as pollution, technological problems, and social disruption. Children from the Philippines thought of positive aspects of the environment.

Relating conservation of plants to people's needs and aspirations may not be a matter of persuading people to accept something new so much as making them aware of what they have always felt but not recognized. Few people live without at least some plants close at hand. It can be pointed out that plants provide shade, shelter, soft surfaces to walk on, color and texture, food, medicines, clothing, and fuel. Once such an awareness is attained, it becomes possible to build on the empathy created by the initial awakening of interest (e.g., Bandyopadhyay and Shiva 1987).

The views of specialists can be introduced during an awareness program, but unless the audience is highly sophisticated it is important that matters not be too abstract. Discussion should revolve around practical and simple examples, such as determining the primary source of commonly used necessities.

Rare plants sometimes provide a starting point for creating interest in conservation of plants in general (e.g., Given 1981; Koopowitz and Kaye 1983; Huxley 1984). One thing that can be harnessed is the interest many people have in things that are rare. Despite apathy and ignorance regarding biological conservation, mention of rare plants and animals will often generate interest. For some there is genuine interest in finding out about or seeing something scarce. For collectors there is "the thrill of the hunt." One cactus hunter described the excitement of finding a new species in Mexico:

> The cactus heads were so small that it would take four to fill a thimble. To get at them, we had to scratch away pebbles of sharp volcanic tuff. We were so intent and determined that we didn't notice for an hour our fingers were dripping with blood (Goswell 1976: 83).

Hunting for rare plants can lead to depletion, but if actual collecting of plants is not the goal, such interest can support conservation. It provides information about sites, population sizes, effect of threats, and efficacy of protective measures. Worldwide, much field data comes from weekend botanists and horticulturalists. It is often easier to persuade people to look for rare species and record their flowering and fruiting times than to ask them to do the same for common plants. People may travel long distances to catch a glimpse of a rare species. On the one hand, this makes it necessary to give adequate protection to populations of well-publicized species. On the other hand, such species can act as focal points, drawing attention to the need to conserve plants generally.

Such focal species are sometimes termed *flag species*. Notable examples among animals are giant pandas, tigers, and primates. The Save a Tiger campaign in India has resulted in heightened awareness and protection of many species other than tigers. Similarly, the giant panda of southwest China is now the internationally recognized symbol of the World Wide Fund For Nature.

Species that appeal to people are obviously useful (wild relatives of crops), behave like humans (primates), are majestic (tigers), have an element of mystery (pandas), are ancient (bristlecone pines), or are bizarre (penguins). In the West, organisms are ranked according to human-related appeal: pandas and primates are favored over wolves and snakes, and animals are favored over plants. Within the plant kingdom, orchids and cycads are given greater attention than mosses, stinging plants, or spiny lianas. In the case of tidal shore beggar's ticks (*Bidens bidentioides*), it was suggested that, "as far as humans are concerned, its extinction might be good riddance" (Rolston 1985).

Flag species need to fulfill several criteria. They need to be widely known by the target audience; or if they are not well known initially, they need to be the subject of a publicity campaign. They need to have features that offer some appeal to people. They need to be genuinely under threat, and they should be *umbrella species* on which numerous other species depend.

The type of plant features that can be promoted include attractive appearance, unusual features, extreme threat (e.g., only one wild plant known, spectacular decline rate), widely known traditional use, cultural use, economic value (e.g., as a valuable wild relative of a crop plant), and horticultural potential. Size and habitat are significant: it is unlikely that a small and obscure water plant or an epiphyte found only in the tops of trees will make suitable flag species, even if they are critically endangered. Nonetheless, candidate flag species may be found in the same localities or habitats.

Sometimes awareness, particularly in a whole community, arises as a result of an environmental crisis—the construction of a hydro-dam that floods agricultural land, felling of a forest for lumber, or the draining and filling of large areas of wetland for housing. In the course of reacting to events, people will have an opportunity to increase their awareness and understanding of fundamental issues such as loss of biological diversity.

Nongovernmental organizations play a particularly important part in creating awareness (Nijhoff 1984). Enthusiastic local organizations, especially ones backed up by a national network, can gain the ear of people at all levels. Environmental groups tend to attract young people, and there can be problems through lack of political clout, technical knowledge, time, and funds. On the other hand, they often have the advantage of grass-roots support and youthful enthusiasm—something often lacking in many government agencies.

Decision-makers must not be immune to learning processes. The format and means of dispersal of information is critically important. Roughly photocopied news sheets may be quite suitable within a local interest group, but to penetrate the world of politics and commerce, one needs not only well-reasoned arguments but also a presentation appropriate to the target audience. This may mean executive summaries, glossy and well-illustrated program documents, and publicity releases designed to give a high degree of public exposure.

The success of protected area management depends very much on the degree of support and respect awarded to the protected area by neighboring communities. Where protected areas are seen as a burden, local people can make protection impossible. When the protected area is seen as a positive benefit, the local people will themselves become allied with the manager in protecting the area from threatening developments (MacKinnon et al. 1986). There is no better way for a conservation agency (especially a government one) to create antagonism than to close an area off or restrict the freedom of citizens (especially their traditional rights) without consultation. The globe is littered with examples of actions, taken in the name of conservation, that have created suspicion and resentment.

Sometimes the question is asked, "How much can local people be trusted with sensitive information on biological values?" The answer in many instances should probably be, "Far more than in the past!" There have been sad instances of key sites being revealed and then either plundered for their rare species or deliberately destroyed so that they no longer have conservation value. Nevertheless, extreme secrecy could result in more damage overall. After all, if local authorities, developers, and landowners do not know that a site or a species and its habitat are special, they cannot be blamed for the unwitting destruction of it. It is important to remember that aware and sympathetic local people make good guardians of special areas, especially where there is a shortage of guards or rangers.

A particular vegetation site or a rare species can be made a focal point for a local community. This is particularly relevant where a site or species has traditional value or cultural significance, even if it is currently overlooked or known only by a few community members.

Often, when a new site is found for a rare plant, it will not have formal protection. In such a case, conservation authorities should work cooperatively with local conservation organizations and landowners to obtain protected status for the site (Rye and Hopper 1981). Local support is often the key to success in this respect. Even where there is antagonism, sensitive personal contact with an owner or tenant can succeed where official letters fail. Where official correspondence is entered into regarding preservation, letters should be followed up with a personal visit to explain the situation openly. Cooperation and understanding cannot be expected where there is suspicion of a hidden agenda. If a key site is identified in a regional survey, it is imperative that affected landowners be contacted at an early date and made aware of the importance of the site. Only when a landowner is known to be intransigent should this approach be varied, and even then every effort should be made to approach the person in a way that will not be perceived as threatening. Often, opposition to conservation arises out of ignorance, or from fear that government will take away land and lock it up. The best guardian of a species is often a sympathetic landowner or tenant.

People who have lived close to nature for a long time develop particular feelings and relationships with the land that can be precious. Sometimes the long-term consequences of actions may not be appreciated by local people; but rather than condemning the people and actions outright, it is wise to build on existing traditions and the empathy with nature that exists. Once local values and focal points for preservation and conservation (perhaps developed over many centuries) are identified, they can be reinforced by the techniques of Western scientific investigation to the good of everyone concerned, including the plants.

CASE STUDY: KUNA INDIANS—INITIATIVES FROM A LOCAL COMMUNITY

Spontaneous colonization by non-Indians, and the construction of a new road through the previously isolated Kuna Yala Reserve in Panama, prompted indigenous residents to devise a land management plan that would protect their outstanding natural and cultural resources. With the assistance of several international agencies, the Kuna began exploring the possibility of establishing a protected conservation unit on tribal lands in the late 1970s, and by 1980 they had established their PEMASKY effort (Project for the Study of the Management of Kuna Yala Wildlands).

A team of 20 Kuna Yala (several of whom had attended wildlife management training courses) have identified and marked the reserve boundaries and are completing and implementing a management plan. The area will be administered much like a biosphere reserve, with both protection and sustainable development integrated into one management scheme. While the Kuna are still receiving some outside assistance in the planning and operation of the project, ongoing training will assure technical self-sufficiency in the near future. A scientific tourism component will also help to finance the operation of the unit.

The project is unique in its utilization of both modern wild land conservation techniques and indigenous natural resource knowledge. In addition, the Kuna have demonstrated that cultural and natural resource conservation can be achieved through appropriate park and reserve protection programs.

Source: Wright et al. 1985.

Environmental Education Programs

Awareness programs must be built upon and, where possible, consolidated by formal education. Formal education in conservation faces particular problems. Conservation biology is a relatively new science and concepts are changing from year to year. Reform of curricula tends to lag behind these developments so that basic thinking on plant conservation and its practice have yet to be generally reflected in curricula. Furthermore, because conservation biology is a holistic discipline and involves a range of aspects such as science, ethics, and social geography, it does not fit easily into the traditional teaching disciplines.

The division of education into elementary, secondary, and tertiary segments and into discrete subjects does not always fit well with the requirements of teaching about conservation (Pitt 1987a). The solution may be to recognize levels of complexity in education rather than formal, age-related grades. This will allow teachers to introduce aspects of plant conservation at appropriate levels of complexity (e.g., MacFie 1987).

There is an enormous variation in background and fundamental perceptions of students, both within and between cultures. This suggests the need for a *template approach* to education on plant conservation, in which different relevant examples are inserted into a basic text for wider use. The template approach allows the preparation of textbooks and supplementary resources with wide general application. Specific examples and emphasis can be inserted for particular regions or levels of education. This allows people to relate to those things—animals, plants, forests, environmental problems, household objects—with which they are familiar. Conservation then becomes a hands-on matter that can be related to everyday living.

Clearly, the future of our planet rests with youth. If conservation is accepted as important, it is imperative that school students be exposed to an ecologically balanced view of nature and an understanding of and concern for ecosystem function (which must include an appreciation of both common and rare species and the basics of genetic conservation). Such programs have to be realistic about some aspects of nature that may have emotive overtones, such as animal suffering.

The important objective of conservation education should be to transform patterns of thinking—to introduce new ways of looking at the range of subjects already being taught (Khoshoo 1986). Environmental concerns must be brought to all subject areas so that an environmental awareness permeates all facets of life. Environmental and conservation studies are interdisciplinary; even education in rare species should interact not only with biology, but also with economics, social studies, and mathematics.

The various interrelated components of environmental education—such as awareness, real-life situations, and conservation and sustainable development—must be matched with needs and abilities of different age and literacy levels. Balance between classroom-based and outdoor (or real-life) teaching is essential. Plant conservation studies, for instance, must include examination of plants in their natural habitats, visits to a botanic garden, and visits to industries utilizing plant materials. At the tertiary level, environmental studies have tended to be oriented strongly toward the study of biology only; but there is increasing realization that a broader scope is needed. The development of environmental impact assessment procedures has opened up new careers in environmental education, ethics, conservation economics, environmental law, conservation in relation to agriculture and forestry, and soil and water protection. One of the fundamental characteristics of conservation biology and management is that it is an activity drawing on a host of disciplines, ranging from legislation and land-use planning to reproductive biology and ethics.

Protected area managers and botanic garden staff have potential roles to play in formal conservation education. Ideally, groups of protected areas (except those of very small size or reserves for which public access is restricted) should have an education officer. This is frequently not possible, and the minimum should be an education officer or warden for each national park, for those other protected areas with high public use, and for each regional assemblage of reserves. This allows for well-planned visits by school groups and the avoidance of periods of congestion or peak management work. This is particularly important if groups are staying for several days, using full accommodation facilities on site.

As a follow-up to conservation education programs, information on conservation groups, support organizations, and natural history societies that students may wish to join should be available. This is especially important for children who are sometimes overlooked in the activities of such organizations, but who represent an invaluable investment for the future (A. C. Jermy, pers. com.). Many such organizations now have special sections that cater to junior members, for example the Watch Organization of the Wildlife Trusts in Britain, which is set up for 8- to 13-year-old children.

Programs to increase conservation knowledge of-ten tend to be aimed at those already interested in conservation. It is important to maintain awareness and wisdom among such groups, but informal education must also be directed toward the skeptical or uninformed. Because informal and continuing education projects do not have a captive audience (as in schools), it is necessary to attract interest in matters relevant to the needs of people. People must feel that what they are learning is worth the trouble. What they learn should encourage them to want to learn more. Innovative presentation is important, especially in those countries with low literacy levels. Even in technologically advanced countries, literacy levels can be surprisingly low. Considerable scope exists for nonverbal communication or for the use of theater and audiovisual techniques in teaching.

Mobile units increasingly are being used for extension work, especially where considerable distances must be covered. The simplest involve nothing more than posters and elementary display materials. In a more sophisticated form, this can extend to a vehicle with portable generator and slide, film, and video projection equipment.

Most countries have museums that could play an important role in informal and continuing education in conservation—a role unfortunately not always accepted by some museums. At such facilities, the public can be challenged to think about current issues, such as the greenhouse effect, depletion of tropical forests, and loss of genetic resources, and gain a greater appreciation for the wealth of diversity in the biological world. Another role can be to interface between research and the public. What would help is an international charter for museums along the lines of that designed for botanic gardens at an international conference at Las Palmas in 1985 (see Bramwell et al. 1987).

In urban, and especially more sophisticated, regions, a useful approach can be the formation of clubs and societies to promote conservation, especially among youth. Such clubs will usually fulfill other functions, such as acting as a social group where people can develop an identity and empathy with others. Some recently formed conservation clubs, such as Laureles in the Dominican Republic, have developed very fast, indicating that there is a demand for this type of organization (Briceno and Drake 1986). In many countries (especially of the developed world), conservation organizations and nature trusts are increasingly active in education through meetings, magazines, and campaigns on specific issues. These are a valuable component of continuing education, although such organizations may not penetrate far into the ranks of the skeptical.

There is room for considerable innovation. A recent survey of on-going conservation education in California showed that use is being made of a wide variety of approaches (Mayola 1987): touring one-person shows, spring wildflower shows, slide-tape programs (sometimes available for hire), demonstration gardens, newspaper articles, video programs, tours of rare plant sites, and even an Endangered Species Fair cosponsored with the local county. One group has begun a newsletter in which part of a page can be cut out and added to a rare plant notebook; eventually, the notebook will include information about all of the local county's rare and endangered plants.

With the world becoming increasingly urbanized there is almost unlimited potential for botanic gardens to engage in extension education. For many people, botanic gardens are (along with zoos) the window through which the world of nature is most readily seen. Because of their accessibility and ease of terrain (most gardens have at least a basic high-quality path system), they are particularly suited to use by both very young and older age groups. The general location of gardens close to areas of high population density means that education centers and permanent display buildings can often be justified. It is important that botanic gardens staff liaise closely with special interest groups such as horticultural societies, specialist plant groups, and local conservation organizations.

Continuing education is especially important for those who are living close to a protected area (e.g., Hanks 1984a, Infield 1988). It should not be assumed that people close to a protected area are aware of its function and operation. Such people can make a manager's task difficult or easy, depending on how they view the reserve or park and how well they understand and accept its objectives. In this case, education can involve a range of activities from relatively informal talks, slide shows, and open-house days, to more elaborate courses on site, and apprentice-based, hands-on research. Programs do not always have to have an obvious conservation thrust but can be incorporated into other types of extension education dealing with more general social, agricultural, and cultural issues.

The goal of conservation education must be to enhance society through increased awareness and understanding of nature and natural history, not just to preserve forests and spectacular orchids so that more people can have jobs, for example, in tourism. The latter may well be an aim, but not such that day-to-day cash return is the prime criterion for use of wild plants.

As in all areas of communication, even the simplest

of presentations must be well done. In the pursuit of the ideals of conservation, high standards of presentation have not always been regarded as necessary. But setting high standards does not necessarily mean great expense in, say, the design of posters, display materials, signs, and audiovisuals. Very simple and plain presentations can be extremely effective. Money can be saved through the use of durable materials that can be used many times over. What is most important is to carefully plan the message, assess the audience being targeted, and determine how that message can be most effectively presented to the audience. It is also important to elicit feedback to determine what information has been absorbed by people. Very often the scientific storyboard is developed well but graphic and art ability is lacking, or the presentation does not incorporate local idiom so it is not clearly understood (A. C. Jermy, pers. com. in part). This is particularly a problem where the audience is grappling with reading and writing skills. But it is worth persisting: newly literate people, especially in smaller communities, will go a long way to spread the environmental message at the grass-roots level.

Lack of properly trained personnel can hamper conservation education efforts. It puts constraints on the development of sound programs and can result in the spread of erroneous information. This not only misleads people but also can discredit the conservation movement.

In botanic gardens and nature reserves, staff involved in awareness and education programs must be familiar with the basic principles of biological conservation. All staff should appreciate the conservation role of reserves and gardens. Botanic gardens typically must grapple with such basic problems as simulating habitats and providing pollinators. These problems need to be appreciated by staff looking after the plants and can be used as starting points in conversations with visitors. The most important point is to explain to both staff and public the rarity of certain species, the need to conserve them, and the corrective measures that are available.

When specialists visit gardens they should be given the opportunity to talk with members of staff who need to appreciate the conservation problems faced by plants (Beyer 1979). A similar situation is faced by protected area managers. Emphasis can be placed on the mechanics of management, such as track and hut maintenance, at the expense of imparting basic principles of conservation to staff.

Conservation biology is a very rapidly evolving field and information only four or five years old can be hopelessly out of date. One means of keeping up-to-date is to invite specialists to visit gardens and protected areas to undertake research projects and interact with staff. Such arrangements can result in the informal sharing of much information. Seminars and workshops can also be conducted, allowing researchers and managers to interact in a more formal environment. Particular problems can be focal points of such seminars. Regular, perhaps formalized, links with research organizations in the region can further help staff to increase their knowledge.

For school teachers, such ongoing education may be more difficult. Schools operate on busy schedules and teachers rarely can be taken out of circulation for more than a few days. Nevertheless, it is essential that teachers be aware of developments in conservation biology, the philosophy of conservation, and appropriate techniques for teaching conservation. Teachers need to be encouraged to utilize resources, such as research institutions, that are well outside the usual range of school resources. Most people recognize the urgent need for environmental education, but only a few individuals have clear ideas about what needs to be done. Still fewer have either the actual experience or knowledge to teach the courses that are needed.

The Education Function of Protected Areas

As in other areas of conservation, education is an important component of on-site conservation. Even in apparently academic aspects of research such as taxonomy, attitudes and education interact. As just one example, plant taxonomy is a top research priority worldwide. In Peru, a center of plant diversity, there are only about ten botanists qualified to identify and describe plant species, and of those only half work on Amazonian species (Toledo 1986). This greatly limits ability to produce identification guides and to answer basic biological questions both for managers and the public. It means too that protected area staff may be denied the information that allows them to manage efficiently.

In many respects a protected park or reserve is only as good as the staff who administer it, including those involved in planning and policy, and even the politicians who control the purse-strings. Training courses are a vitally important aspect of plant diversity management, whatever the level. The science of conservation biology is changing at a rapid pace and concepts suggested five years ago may be quite outmoded now. Updating management staff through involvement with research scientists from a variety of disciplines should become routine. Allowing management staff to assist in research—or at least to have routine contact with researchers—pays dividends.

It is easy to see training courses, seminars, and study tours only in terms of their technical and educational value; these are prime objectives. But just as important are the opportunities they give for exchange of ideas and to appreciate points of view expressed by users of parks and reserves (Roche and Dourojeanni 1984; MacKinnon et al. 1986). Consequently, seminars, workshops, field trips, and conferences in or about protected areas and biodiversity should devote a significant amount of time to free discussion.

Valuable feedback can be fostered when protected area managers contact interest groups such as botanical and conservation organizations; such groups may be able to assist in carrying out some aspects of management such as weeding, planting, and clearing vegetation. Provided responsible and informed supervision is available, lay people can play a considerable role in interpretation services, sometimes on a volunteer basis. There are both benefits and dangers in this. Full-time staff benefit through increased contact with informed protected area users whom they might not otherwise meet. Volunteers can be vociferous advocates for the conservation of plant diversity and for funding of particular reserves. On the other hand, supervision of volunteer groups can be time-consuming and lead to an increased administrative load.

Considerable benefits result from an administrative structure that allows advisory participation by representatives of the public and interest groups. Such a system should not be seen by staff as a threat to their independence, but rather as an opportunity to interact with those who have an interest in conservation. It has immense value in promoting conservation and creating a further channel for the conservation message to reach a wider audience.

Children are increasingly recognized as an important group of protected area users who were overlooked in the past. Interest in conservation of biological diversity will remain largely undeveloped unless people are exposed to conservation education and interpretation at an early age and are shown the value and significance of these endeavors (MacFie 1987; Mayola 1987; Edwards and Paul 1988).

Favorable perception by the public is crucial to the well-being of protected areas. In the short term it may be enough for local people to know why an area is set aside. But in the long term, this needs to be communicated to the whole community, government members, and the business community. Urban people are often rather indifferent to wildlife conservation. Since most decision-makers and professionals emerge from this group, lack of concern cripples the support needed for rational conservation of plant diversity. In contrast, rural people, whose attitudes are determined by the degree of their dependence upon natural products, may have a greater appreciation of natural resources. This may not necessarily engender conservation-oriented attitudes, but it does give a valuable starting point for discussion. Initial antagonism to conservation—perhaps because people are threatened by restrictions on resource use—are best countered by a program of awareness and education, including involvement in conservation programs in protected areas.

Although the primary role of protected areas is often seen as protection of species and ecosystems, their role in education must not be devalued. Awareness and education can be at several levels: use for formal education, education of recreational users and casual visitors, and targeting of special interest groups.

Surveys of British nature reserves have indicated that information is one of the facilities in greatest demand by recreational users of the countryside. This is often given in the form of nature trails or displays and audiovisual programs in visitor centers (Usher 1973). The most direct way for people to learn about a protected area is for them to see it for themselves. Interpretation on site awakens public awareness of conservation purposes and policies and helps develop a concern for protection. Visitors can be encouraged to appreciate the value of protected areas and species to the region and the nation. Interpretation should fill the visitor with a greater sense of wonder and curiosity about the natural surroundings and make his or her visit to the area more rewarding. There is considerable scope for visitor centers to provide conservation-oriented information, entertainment, stimulation, and education in a pleasant and fascinating setting in order to win visitor support for the type of management being applied. Education service is thus a management tool, influencing behavior, soliciting support, and making the manager's job easier.

As the number of natural areas diminishes, there can be an understandable reluctance, on the part of protected area managers, to encourage visitors to reserves for fear of damage. Nevertheless, many protected areas are the most appropriate sites for the public to become aware of the diversity of the plant world. Obviously, there must be constraints that reduce visitor impact to acceptable levels, and as a general prin-

ciple, intensity of management and supervision is likely to increase in proportion to visitor pressure.

Education in protected areas will not succeed if the most appropriate areas remain best kept secrets. People need to know how to get to the area, seasonal or climatic restrictions on visitation, and services available (accommodation, meals, service stations, etc.). Visitors should be shown how they can become more involved in the protected area and in conservation organizations. A book and periodical list is useful and is enhanced by the publications being available and on sale at an on-site or regional visitor center.

Many techniques and services for nature interpretation are possible. These include brochures and leaflets; self-guided trails; wilderness trails where visitors explore and discover for themselves; guided tours; visitor information centers; education centers, which may have facilities for lectures and classes; and arboreta and gardens, which will often specialize in the plants of the region adjacent to the protected area. Some of these facilities require considerable capital or ongoing staff input, but others such as self-guide trails and basic leaflets are relatively simple and may not require a great financial outlay.

School classes are an asset to protected areas. Throughout much of the world, field teaching or conservation-related outdoor education in natural environment areas is a relatively minor component of the school curriculum. A survey of school field studies in the 1960s in Britain showed that in primary education, 6–8 hours per year were spent in out-of-doors study, while in secondary education the figure was only 2–2.5 hours per year. Nevertheless, this is not just because schools do not want to provide such education; surveys indicate that the supply of field centers for education has not kept pace with demand from schools. If more facilities were available, more schools might carry out field studies. Nature centers in many parts of the world find that, providing they liaise closely with schools and are well-organized and promoted, there is no shortage of school classes to use their facilities.

A series of guidelines can be defined for use of protected areas for education, especially for intensive use by school children (Usher 1973). Such sites should meet the following critera:

- Contain the diversity required for demonstration of a wide range of habitats, communities and species, and the operative ecological factors.

- Not be liable to destruction or irreparable damage by controlled but heavy use (e.g., certain soft bogs are easily damaged by excessive trampling and are unsuitable for large groups).

- Not contain rare features or species that ought to be permanently conserved for research and similar activities, in the national interest.

- Be reasonably accessible to users (educational reserves near to cities and towns will serve a larger number of schools than those in remote areas).

- Have paths and other access routes for safe and rapid movement of groups within the area.

- Contain a field museum or similar center.

- Have qualified staff.

The above are ideal requirements and may not always be attainable, especially where resources are extremely limited. This is where liaison with local natural history, conservation, or cultural groups can be useful; they may be able to assist with volunteer guides or setting up facilities for education. Where a site contains threatened species, a choice needs to be made between publicizing the species and risking their loss, or keeping their presence secret and not gaining support for their protection. It is probably desirable to expose people, and especially children, to some rare plants to dramatically emphasize the plight of many species. A number of sensible precautions that can be taken include boardwalks and protective barriers, view points that provide a close encounter while maintaining a reasonable protective distance, leading people to some populations but not others, or establishment of a quasi-natural population.

One means of creating an environment where awareness is fostered is the restoration of habitats in protected areas that may have low scientific standing but high educational and amenity potential. Thus an interesting, sometimes rare, species of the region could be introduced to a site to attract people to the site and remind them of the diversity of plants; at the same time, the survival of these plants is enhanced. It need not be the plants that are the initial attraction. Sites that are already well-known viewpoints or recreation areas can be selected for restoration. One of the attractive features about this approach is that it offers the opportunity to make people aware that habitats and populations are not static. As restoration proceeds, they will see processes occurring and will come to realize that nature is highly dynamic.

Reserve or park staff should act as primary guides, instructors, and interpreters, although it is also important that school teachers and local people be involved in education programs as well. Where it is difficult to provide qualified staff (perhaps because of funding problems), trained volunteers can often be used to accompany educative groups and classes to the site. In the future, teachers will need to have more knowledge and experience of field teaching techniques, the characteristics and processes operating at field sites, and of the principles and practice of biological conservation generally. Programs should ensure that those being taught interact with the ecosystem, perhaps even assisting in simple management exercises. Topics and examples must relate closely to the experience and aspirations of the audience.

A teaching tool that has proved useful in some countries is a teacher's sourcebook. This can be used both prior to and following visits to a park or reserve and during field excursions. It is important to provide follow-up material, making use of the heightened awareness and interest generated by a visit to the protected area or garden. Follow-up exercises allow the teacher to assess the type and degree of knowledge gained.

Nature trails are an important way in which protected natural areas are used to educate people about plant species and genetic resources. One of the simplest interpretive devices is to have short (5- to 10-minute) self-guided walks located at strategic stopping points and park areas. Formal trails provide a rigidly guided tour from location to location, with each stopping point demonstrating a particular feature. The more formal the system, the greater the certainty of seeing particular plants. Semiformal trails are similar to the first type, but the emphasis is placed on habitat that occupies the space between locations. Informal trails do not provide a guided tour but provide information that allows users to walk where they wish within the area, seeking out those features that are of greatest interest. On informal trails, some familiarity with the range of habitats and species is usually necessary.

Primary considerations when designing trail guides must be the type of nature trail, the amount of use, the type of user (whether school classes or casual tourists), and finances available. Where rare species are involved, it will be necessary to achieve a balance between the risk of vandalism when indicating precise locations, and the risk of habitat damage and trampling as people search for plants.

Participation in management can provide a very effective means of educating. This can range from help with revegetation and removing weeds, to participating in censuses, measurement of plots and transects, and assisting with experiments to determine suitability of habitat or degree of species persistence. Such work needs to be supervised, but a hands-on experience can be memorable for the people involved and can lead to a long-lasting interest in natural history and conservation.

For sites that receive numerous visitors, a visitor center should be considered. The form and sophistication of a visitor center is largely dependent on available resources; but at least initially, it need not be complex. Some of the educative needs of plant conservation can be met by construction of a seminatural garden where particular plants of interest can be displayed. A flag species should be considered as a theme plant for the visitor center. It is useful for visitor centers not only to feature the particular site, but to put these in a regional and even international context, so that visitors are encouraged to go on to other protected areas.

Care must be taken to ensure that management protects the features of a protected area that people go to see. Manipulative processes should be explained as part of education. As an example, Wicken Fen is one of Britain's oldest nature reserve and a very important site for conservation of wetland species and habitats. Nonetheless, at least two species have disappeared because the importance of peat digging in order to maintain open habitat was not appreciated. Such problems and conflicts should be explained in the educative program. It helps visitors appreciate the realities and expense of conservation management.

Case Study: Use of Bishop Wood for Field Teaching by Schools in Great Britain

An example of a habitat that has been used by schools for day excursions is Bishop Wood near Selby in Yorkshire. The wood, approximately 340 hectares, was largely felled during the First World War and has been managed by the Forestry Commission since 1921. The commission replanted much of it with both conifers and deciduous trees, but some of the wood has been allowed to regenerate naturally. Such areas now have a mixture of tree species with a scrub layer and a very diverse ground flora.

Although the Forestry Commission's primary object of management is to produce timber economically, it is also policy to provide rural facilities. The educational effort in Bishop Wood is a part of this policy, and the organization is jointly carried out by the Forestry Commission and the West Riding of Yorkshire County Education Department.

A survey of schools using Bishop Wood was carried out in 1969. The distribution of the schools shows that most of them are situated on the eastern fringe of the industrial zone of Yorkshire. Of the 24 schools that provided data, 20 had used the wood in summer, and 15 had used it in winter. It is known that a total of 32 schools were using or had used the wood at the time that the survey was carried out. An average visit was approximately 30 children spending half a day in the wood. The educational pressure on the wood in 1968 was approximately 1040 child days, and this was expected to increase.

In the curricular subjects covered by the school visitors, environmental studies are strongly represented, though field classes do, particularly in primary education, have a wider appeal in subject matter. The fact that seven of the schools were concerned with social questions and the preservation of the habitat indicates that some basic ideas about conservation are forming a part of the field education, though this aspect could obviously be expanded.

Sources: Taylor 1969; Usher 1973.

Case Study: Trail and Trail Guide, Barro Colorado Island, Panama

Barro Colorado Island has been a biological reserve since 1923, not long after the area was isolated from the mainland by the creation of Gatun Lake, part of the Panama Canal system. Since then it has been a major focus of biological exploration and research.

The nature trail was designed to extend the awareness and knowledge of both lay people and scientists. A printed manual is divided into two parts. The first brings together, in general terms, the diverse factors that interact in tropical forests. The second part is a self-guided tour of the nature trail with 54 stopping points. Key species are dealt with by text and sketches. The trail guide includes descriptions of ecological processes and simple experiments set up at particular stations to deal with topics such as different growth forms, leaf litter, the role of ants, and the importance of light gaps in the forest.

The following is a sample entry:

18. CUIPO
Cavanillesia platanifolia (Bombacaceae)
Los Santos, Panama, Darien
Nicaragua to Peru
Leaves lost–replaced: December–June
Flowers: March–April
Fruits: April–May
    Knock on the trunk of this tree. What do you hear? Knock on the trunk of another species nearby. What do you hear? The high water content in the trunk is responsible for the unexpected sounds you heard from Cuipo. One jungle survival manual suggests cutting a length of aboveground root from Cuipo to obtain potable water. The wood itself weighs only about 6 pounds per cubic foot and has no

commercial use, although it has been tried as a substitute for balsa. Cuipo is reported to be the most abundant tree species in upland Darien. It is also one of the easiest trees to learn in Panama. You will see why at Station 20.

Source: Wong and Ventocilla 1986.

Tourist and recreation sites

International travel is one of the fastest growing industries worldwide (Boo 1990). Tourism revenues in 1988 ranked third among all export industries, with spending on domestic and international tourism contributing to approximately 10–12 percent of the world gross product. Western affluence, allowing more resources for spending on consumer goods, is reflected in phenomenal growth in tourism. Much of this tourism is directed toward natural areas, especially national parks, as tourists throng to take their recreation in natural surroundings and experience nature firsthand. Such trends are likely to increase rather than diminish in the immediate future at least. They are fueled by decreasing opportunity to experience unspoiled nature and wilderness close to the world's large and expanding cities (Figure 8.1).

Although animal life tends to dominate as a large-scale tourist attraction, plants are important drawing cards in their own right for tourists. In western North America, the Californian redwood (*Sequoia sempervirens*) forests attract tens of thousands of tourists annually. People will travel many hundreds of kilometers to see good examples of orchids and cacti. In the Cape region of South Africa, and in parts of Australia, spectacular wildflowers are a major attraction both in their wild habitat and in regional horticultural flower shows.

Reliable sighting is very important. Tourists who travel long distances want to have a reasonable guarantee that they will see what they are interested in. This is especially the case with those sites that have been widely documented by television and the film industry (MacKinnon et al. 1986).

Plants also are increasingly appreciated for their therapeutic and transformative value. They soften landscapes, provide shade and shelter, and their patterns of color and texture evoke a range of moods and feelings. People everywhere grow plants; it can be an exciting experience to see plants that are well-known in the garden in their wild habitat. Finally, tourists may want to see what the relatives of cultivated plants look like in the wild.

Often tourism is interpreted as yet another threat to biodiversity, especially to rare and endangered spe-

Figure 8.1. Nature tourism is a growing industry worldwide. Galapagos Islands. (D. R. Given)

cies. Yet tourism has the potential to make a substantial contribution to regional development by attracting people to rural areas. It promotes construction and maintenance of facilities for protected areas, which otherwise would not be justified. Tourism provides arguments for staffing of parks and reserves at levels that otherwise would not be possible. Studies of the economic impact of major protected areas on local and national economies indicate that the benefits can be substantial. In the West Indies, the Virgin Island National Park gives an estimated tenfold return in benefits over investments for the St. Thomas–St. John economy (MacKinnon et al. 1986). As a result of nature tourism, the Gross National Product of the Galapagos Islands province of Ecuador is the highest in the country (Boo 1990).

On the other hand, uncontrolled promotion of tourism in protected areas does have its pitfalls. Even in well-regulated protected areas such as the Galapagos Islands National Park, some tourists cannot resist feeding animals or leaving trash (Boo 1990). There can be a temptation to overuse those parts of a reserve or park that are particularly attractive, or to enhance them by introducing exotic and spectacular species. Moreover, if key decision-makers are led to believe that protected areas exist mainly for economic gain and especially for vast numbers of visitors, they may begin to select and designate reserves, or manage existing ones, primarily for economic gain rather than for the conservation of biodiversity. In extreme instances, some of the species of interest even start to be regarded as nuisances that should be shifted to allow development of tourist facilities!

Some types of tourism are more compatible with the objectives of protected natural areas than others. Unless carefully controlled and within a site's carrying capacity, high visitor volumes may destroy the very things that tourists come to see and experience. Low-impact natural history tourism involving small groups under the supervision of trained guides is one example of sensitive meshing of public desire to experience nature and the conservation needs of wild species. A primary aim of such tourism is to enhance the participant's understanding of conservation. Many need no convincing, particularly those from natural history societies, but for others it will be a new experience. The emphasis is on closely supervised, low levels of human impact. Visitors learn that the impact of only a few pairs of feet on untracked sites in high rainfall forests can be dramatic. Visitor pressure on particularly fragile sites must be rigidly controlled. This can include setting an upper limit for number and size of

parties, charging higher prices, and restricting access to carefully defined entry points and routes (Boo 1990; M. Hanger, pers. com.).

Problems can be encountered with visitors who are primarily interested in acquiring plants, such as endangered palms, orchids, or ferns, for their own use. Some may see visits to reserves as opportunities to obtain seeds, cuttings, and whole plants for their gardens. In this instance, it may be advisable to make suitable propagating material available through the agency administering a protected area or through nearby commercial nurseries or botanic gardens. Similarly, photographing plants at wild sites may damage habitat or draw attention to the location of scarce species. This can be mitigated by taking people to a selected site with a viewing/photographing area, and also by having good quality photographs for sale. Some nature tourists may be interested only in seeing a rare species and ticking it off on their list—sometimes known as *twitching*. Every effort should be made to convert twitching to a sustained and genuine interest in the biological and cultural aspects of plants and their communities as well as their conservation.

Where significant numbers of visits occur, the management plan should identify specific visitor zones for different intensities of use. This allows visitors to be concentrated in parts of a protected area and in buffer zones where facilities can be appropriately developed to a high standard (MacKinnon et al. 1986). A goal may be to channel visitor activity making visitors feel they are being restricted. For example, reducing the standard of a trail surface, width, or grade may be a more acceptable means of restricting access than erecting a notice. For endangered plant species, it may be possible to translocate several plants to an accessible site and ensure that no public trails lead to the original sites.

Local communities need to benefit from tourism. Employing local people and enterprises to staff guiding services and concessions keeps a proportion of the income generated by a protected area within adjacent communities. It also helps create awareness and empathy in the local community. Selection of concessionaires is an important responsibility and may require training or additional education. Operators must possess not only adequate financial and management skills but also must demonstrate their sympathy for primary values of protected areas and for the need to conserve biodiversity.

For sites of conservation value, there should be an emphasis on *ecotourism*, which is defined as, "travelling to relatively undisturbed or uncontaminated natural areas with the specific objective of studying, admiring, and enjoying the scenery and its wild plants and animals, as well as any existing cultural manifestations (both past and present) found in these areas . . ." (Ceballos-Lascurain 1987 in Boo 1990). Even ecotourists will visit sites for a wide variety of reasons, and it is difficult to come up with universal prescriptions for dealing with tourists in natural areas (Boo 1990). Nevertheless, education and awareness of conservation values inherent in both animals and plants should be built into ecotourism, as natural areas become increasingly important in the itinerary of tourists generally.

CASE STUDY: TOURIST TREKKING IN THAILAND

The northwest section of Khao Yai National Park, Thailand, is an attractive area for wilderness trekking. It has mountain vistas, scenic rivers, waterfalls, and forests with good wildlife populations. All of this attracts both national and international visitors. Tourist trekking is seen as a way to generate income for local villagers in a manner compatible with conservation objectives. Without sufficient income, local people have, in the past, exploited park resources out of economic necessity.

Treks are taken into Khao Yai from the village of Ban Sap Tai. The first day and night are spent in the village, allowing trekkers to experience life in a rural Thai community. The visitors are welcomed by local school teachers who introduce them to the village and briefly explain the trekking program's objectives. The remaining days are spent hiking and camping in the park.

Promotion of the trekking program emphasizes the adventure of exploring tropical moist forest in a scenic and virtually unchanged area of Thailand. The wildlife interest is not promoted strongly because wildlife sightings are relatively infrequent (the nature of the forest and secretive habits of the animals keep them concealed). The treks have attracted a wide variety of participants, most of whom have been expatriate residents of Thailand.

The villagers have benefitted financially from the program; most money comes from guide and porter services and transportation. Villagers are, as a result, becoming more sympathetic to conservation, as they appreciate that the national park can provide them with tangible benefits. The trekking program has considerable potential for expansion, but it is limited by the lack of bilingual trek leaders and inadequate administration. Solutions to these problems are being sought as part of the overall management program for the park.

Source: Dobias 1985 in Oldfield 1988.

Botanic gardens

It has been estimated that 100 million people each year visit the world's botanic gardens. As widely visited institutions, they are in a powerful position to interface between botanical research, horticulture, and in-situ and ex-situ conservation. They should, in effect, be linking institutions.

Botanic gardens have the opportunity to be rich treasure houses of economic plants, displaying timbers and resins, fruits and seeds, fibers and textiles (Walters and Birks 1984). They can relate the stories of economic plants such as rubber and beverages such as tea, coffee, or cocoa, and can describe the origins of cultivation and of cultivated plants that have developed over thousands of years from wild reservoirs of genetic diversity (e.g., Edwards and Paul 1988). Displays of fascinating plants, such as orchids and carnivorous plants, offer explanations of evolution and biological mechanisms (Figure 8.2).

Botanic gardens also can be leaders in the raising of awareness about the environmental crisis, of which

Figure 8.2. An educational display on carnivorous plants, indicative of the potential for education through gardens. Missouri Botanical Garden, USA. (D. R. Given)

loss of genetic diversity is a part. Gardens can demonstrate solutions to some of the problems through their use of innovative, energy-saving greenhouses and alternative heating sources; by recycling wastes and nutrients; and by demonstrating to the community how to achieve more efficient use of resources (thus taking some pressure off natural plant resources). Without such practical steps, the educative message of botanical gardens can become somewhat theoretical.

Education is generally regarded as an overwhelmingly important function of botanic gardens. A survey in 1975 of the relative functions of botanic gardens and arboreta in the United States showed that the perceived four most important functions were education (87 percent), display (85 percent), public service (81 percent), and research (64 percent). The precise details of education programs differ from garden to garden. Each must develop its own program and promote its own species depending on needs and resources, and this is where the link between botanic gardens and many other agencies is essential. By linking into conservation departments, gardens can be used to direct people's attention to national parks. Many conservation societies have considerable experience in promotion of conservation and development of educational and interpretive materials. These same materials can be used and promoted in the gardens.

Educational materials need not be highly sophisticated. Even simple handouts and quiz sheets have proved to be very popular, especially with school children. The garden, in turn, can provide a venue for events sponsored by outside organizations.

One technique for raising awareness that can be readily initiated by a botanic garden is to promote, within the local community, the use of plants of conservation interest for amenity planting. Plant borders and beds are established worldwide in cities and towns. Some rare and endangered plants will readily grow in suburban parks, street plots, or traffic islands. In one instance in New Zealand, a county council at Heathcote, Canterbury, has planted rare species in front of their administration building. In nearby Timaru, rare plants have been used in a garden bed at an indoor swimming pool (Paterson 1987).

A botanic garden can go even further and offer, at modest prices, sets of plants of particular interest to schools, universities, and civic and youth organizations for planting around their grounds and buildings. Educational institutions require plants for experimental and class use. This, indeed, has been put forward as the justification for several university bo-

tanic gardens to grow rare plants. They have to supply plants for experimental use, so why not propagate threatened species for this purpose and thus ensure that these plants are well-established in cultivation? Botanic gardens can develop awareness and teaching packages to accompany plants distributed for amenity, classroom, or laboratory use. An outstanding example of such a project has been developed at Hanover, Germany (Winkel 1979). This is an extensive service but it could be scaled down for smaller centers. An ultimate goal should be transfer of the classroom to the gardens (Pitt 1987b). This requires an adequate education and information center with lecturing and display facilities. These same facilities can be used for short courses and for training people through continuing education. A research infrastructure and a library are useful adjuncts to an ongoing education service.

A first step toward developing education facilities might be to promote gardens as centers for outdoor instruction using nature trails and study guides. A second step would be to involve garden staff in reviewing local textbooks and curriculum organization, and producing inexpensive study guides to supplement existing textbooks. Informal educational materials can be very diversified and extend to audiovisual programs, video tapes, and educative posters focusing on particular aspects of plant conservation or use. There is sometimes resistance to use of audiovisuals and videos for education in plant conservation on the basis that plants are "not that interesting compared with animals." Educators should be challenged to change that perception!

If botanic gardens are used for formal teaching, teachers need help designing new approaches to the garden. Such help should take the form of more than just training in botany; other subjects such as mathematics, art, and literature can be applied. There is considerable potential to tailor courses for particular groups or educational levels, for instance, for mentally or physically handicapped children.

Appreciation for the role of education in botanic gardens has brought traditional approaches to plant labeling and interpretive signs under scrutiny. Traditional signs tended to be detailed, and plant labels concentrated on name and geographic origin. An improvement on this is to provide simple leaflets about the plantings in the gardens (Figure 8.3). Another is to provide simple and short interpretive signs in plain language. Even these assume some prior knowledge by the visitor and certainly some degree of self-motivation (Boden and Boden 1987). More recent innova-

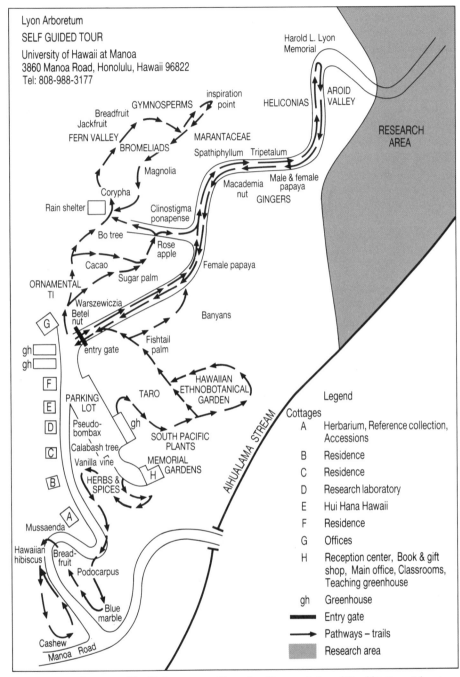

Figure 8.3. An arboretum self-guided tour route. (Reproduced by permission of Harold L. Lyon Arboretum, University of Hawaii at Manoa)

tions in this area include interpretive signs on processes or more abstract topics such as photosynthesis and pH, thematic leaflets designed to take people through a particular part of a garden or selected range of plants, and thematic trails. At the Australian National Botanic Gardens, Canberra, visitors can walk an Aboriginal Trail. This is a popular ethnobotanical resource for social studies at the primary school level (to 12 years of age), and for courses in Australian history, heritage studies, and human biology (at secondary level: 12 to 18 years of age). At other gardens such as Waimea Arboretum, Hawaii, threatened species are identified by red signs and matching interpretive text while blue is used for plants of ethnobotanical interest.

There are many possibilities for innovation in educational programs at botanic gardens (Boden and Boden 1987; Eloff 1987; Hernandez Bermejo 1987). Some groups may be responsive to education through traditional craft materials. The Australian National Botanic Garden makes use of the need for migrants to learn English; they can visit the gardens to achieve vocabulary enrichment, practice the English language, and become familiar with the plant heritage of their adopted country. Each garden must determine what is relevant to the community around it. Above all, innovation and relevance must not obscure the basic issue: it is the plants themselves that are of most interest and importance.

CASE STUDY: THE HANOVER SCHOOL BIOLOGY CENTER, GERMANY

The Hanover School Biology Center was founded in 1883, at the suggestion of teachers, to supply schools in Hanover with equipment for botany. It includes two School Botany Gardens and a Zoo School, with about 1000 square meters of greenhouse space, classrooms, and educational material. Staff total is 31, including 5 teachers and 19 gardeners. The center serves 130 schools and is under school administration; the city pays salaries and wages. The following services are performed by the center:

Supply service. In January, schools receive schedules of what can be supplied at elementary and secondary levels. Each schedule covers 15 themes. The list of materials accompanying each subject gives an evaluation of their instructional value. Teachers may order a complete package for a particular theme or make up their own. Pamphlets of 10–25 pages are received by the teacher in advance of the materials themselves. Sets of equipment remain in the schools.

Loan service. Schools may borrow specific items from a list 25 pages long. Key factors are precise planning and delivery, effective advertising at the beginning, and a dedicated team.

School gardens. Schools receive a catalog of plants for use for general cultivation, genetics, cut flowers, and so forth. Material comes as seed or as small plants free of charge to 45–50 school gardens each year. The gardener in charge shows the teachers cultivated plants, advises on their cultivation, and produces a planting scheme for each school.

Pupil and student course. Short tours and courses are held. The requests for places greatly exceed the limited capacity. For each course, the class teacher, the biology teacher, and the center teacher must first meet and discuss the course. Instruction itself is done by center teachers and is object-orientated. This gives many teachers new ideas, and young teachers appreciate watching someone else instructing their class.

Guided walks. A Sunday morning program is offered for parents to walk through the garden with their children. For educational reasons, parents must accompany their children. Six to ten teachers are available to guide walks on particular themes.

Teacher training. Every teacher in the center is in charge of young teachers. About 70 teachers are connected to the center. There is one course each year for training school assistants.

Source: Winkel 1979.

The Contribution of Professionals

There is a tendency to overlook the professional botanist as a resource for awareness and education efforts. Many botanists are engaged in education at the tertiary level. But many people believe that professionals do not have a great deal to communicate to the common person, and that even if they did, they probably would not be understood.

In reality, many professional botanists are excellent and experienced communicators and educators. Communication is an essential part of science. They also have (or should have) an essential ingredient called enthusiasm. It is increasingly important that scientists speak and explain to encourage, and sometimes to warn, the wider community. Professor Paul Erhlich has suggested that conservation scientists should be prepared to spend 10 percent of their time communicating to the general public (P. R. Erhlich, pers. com.). Professional conservationists need to be challenged to become actively involved in communicating their findings and concerns, and solutions to problems.

There are many ways in which the professional can contribute to the general conservation awareness and education effort. The most obvious is to give lectures or write articles for magazines and specialist journals. In doing so, however, it is important that the specialist not just preach to the converted. New ground can be broken by speaking to or writing for groups who may have little awareness of conservation, such as business clubs, industrial development groups, and community service organizations. The high standing of a well-known scientist in the community may allow access to such groups, which often is denied to others involved in conservation.

Perhaps the greatest problem in utilizing botanists is that the majority of professional botanists are still relatively uninterested in conservation. Bringing the plight of the world's ecosystems and the depletion of biodiversity to the world has been the task of a small group of scientists and communicators. This is well illustrated in the objectives of most botanical societies: conservation often lies well down the list. Even where individuals and groups are interested in the distribution and abundance of species, recording and mapping are often regarded as having greater priority than protection. It may be that it is not the mainstream of professional botany that will conserve the plants of the world (A. C. Jermy, pers. com., 1988).

Environmental Education Resources

Some countries cannot afford to launch and maintain their own programs for conservation education. In others, expertise is lacking or there are socioeconomic barriers to awareness of conservation issues. Such countries urgently need the help of international environmental agencies in conservation education.

It is essential that educational aid not be seen as scientific or conservationist neo-colonialism. Courses and study materials must involve and relate to local people. Workshops to train people in conservation awareness and education must equip trainees to train and educate others. Most important, educative materials must be in a form and language that the people can understand! A blackboard and chalk may be more effective than sophisticated video presentations (although the reverse may be true in other situations). The goal is to aid countries in their efforts to incorporate the environmental dimension into their educational systems. This has led, in most cases, to environmental education legislation and initiatives to integrate environmental studies into education systems.

An important role for assisting agencies is to organize specialist courses on topics such as reserve management, sustainable utilization of tropical forests, and herbarium management. The formal content of such courses is not the only benefit they provide; they also facilitate exchange of ideas and experience between participants from varied backgrounds, and the establishment of contact between technicians, scientists, park rangers, teachers, administrators, and others who would not usually meet.

Provision of educational resources will continue to be a major role of conservation organizations, many of which have become focal points in the international community for expertise. Commonly offered resources include audiovisual programs, filmstrips, posters, wall charts, booklets and leaflets, and low-cost books. The same concept can be applied within a region or a particular country: regional and national organizations (both government and nongovernment) need to assess their role in this respect.

The International Environmental Education Program (IEEP) is a cooperative response at the international level to the pressing concern of nations about their threatened or already damaged environments. In 1975, UNESCO and the United Nations Environment Program (UNEP) jointly founded the program. From the beginning, its accent has been on service to, and participation of, UNESCO's member states. Actions of IEEP have centered upon (in chronological order) development of a general awareness of the need for environmental education; development of concepts and methodological approaches in this important field of education; and efforts toward incorporating an environmental dimension into the educational system of member states.

Among the program's accomplishments from 1975 to 1985 are the following (International Environmental Education Program 1985):

- A series of international and regional meetings, culminating in the Tbilisi Conference.

- A policy of regular communication of information, notably through the IEEP's international newsletter Connect, distributed freely in five languages to 13,000 individuals and institutions throughout the world. IEEP has a computerized information system with information on 900 environmental education (EE) institutions and 300 EE projects, which is published in regularly updated directories.

- The undertaking of pilot, experimental, and research projects to aid member states in incorporating EE into their national educational programs.

- The direct involvement of over 130 countries in IEEP's activities—more than 260,000 pupils and about 10,000 teachers, educators, and administrators.

Case Study: Promoting Education Through the IUCN Tropical Forest Program

A major objective of the IUCN Tropical Forest Program is to improve training and education by strengthening existing training institutes and promoting networking among tropical forest training and research centers located in the major tropical regions. The following are important initiatives:

Anglophone Africa: Mweka Wildlife College, Tanzania. Funding is being provided to promote the conservation of a forest study area for the college students. The area is located in the moist forest zones on Mount Kilimanjaro, an area with several endemic tree species. It will give greater exposure to tropical forest conservation problems to students from 17 anglophone African countries who regularly attend the school.

Francophone Africa: College of Wildlife at Garoua, Cameroon. This initiative will promote field activities by students from the college in the Dja Forest in southern Cameroon. Though it is one of the more important moist forest areas in Cameroon, Dja Forest only has reserve status. Promotion of college field exercises in the area will give students from all francophone countries exposure to tropical forest conservation problems. It will also enhance the conservation status of the Dja Forest itself and will ultimately lead to it being upgraded to national park status.

West Africa. A proposal for a regional research and management center in the Ivory Coast is being developed in collaboration with UNEP and FAO. The center is to be a focal point of a network involving Sierra Leone, Liberia, Ivory Coast, Ghana, Togo, and Benin.

Thailand: Huai Kha Khaeng. A research and management institute, initially for Thai students and researchers, will be developed in the important Huai Kha Khaeng reserve in western Thailand. The focus will be on moist forest research, and on management techniques to upgrade national technical capacity to conserve moist forest areas and focus national attention on Huai Kha Khaeng, one of the most valuable forest areas in Thailand.

India: Peechi Forest Research Institute, Kerala State. The institute is adjacent to the Silent Valley forest, one of mainland Asia's most valuable moist forest ecosystems. International scientists will be encouraged to use the facility, bringing intellectual strength to the institute and focusing greater attention on the conservation problems of the area. Satellite activities in the Andaman Islands and Meghalaya State are anticipated.

Source: IUCN 1986b.

Case Study: The International Center for Conservation Education, England

The International Center for Conservation Education (ICCE), based in England, provides a global focus for practical conservation education activities in developing countries. Much of the work of the center emphasizes production of simple, low-cost educational materials using the wide range of staff skills and technical facilities available on the premises. Activities include filmstrip and audiovisual production, slide duplication, computer typesetting, graphic design, and offset lithography. In addition, there is a well-equipped photographic darkroom and an extensive conservation photograph library.

ICCE provides advisory and consulting services on all matters relating to the establishment and management of national conservation education programs. The center is able to assist government departments and conservation organizations with the planning and implementation of conservation education programs, public awareness campaigns, and training requirements. ICCE has also been closely involved with a number of youth activities.

ICCE provides regular training courses especially designed for nationals of developing countries. Emphasis on practical instruction, using a wide range of technical equipment, encourages the acquisition and improvement of skills for "communicating conservation" more effectively.

The center produces a lot of audiovisual (AV) programs based on the theory that AV materials are economical to produce, easily updated, and readily adapted to suit different situations and audiences. Video cassettes, posters, wall charts, leaflets, booklets, and other educational materials are also produced. Mobile conservation units are used to reach communities beyond the main centers of population. The center also is able to supply specialized equipment to field projects, conservation groups, and government departments.

Source: International Center for Conservation Education 1987.

The Media

The world is inundated with books, journals, newsletters, and bulletins. Each year millions of new books are published and daily newspapers consume prodigious quantities of paper. Much of this written information is absorbed by, and restricted to, the developed nations, which control over 80 percent of the world communications system. It is ironic that whereas the Western world is suffering from a glut of information, in many lesser developed countries there is a chronic shortage of written information. This situation is partly related to level of economy. Books and periodicals are often expensive, even by Western standards, and simply out of the reach of individuals and institutions in developing countries. In some countries the lack of written material is related to low levels of literacy and a perception that books are not needed.

Although there are many excellent presentations of animal natural history, especially on television, relatively few presentations deal with plants. Many people have the impression that "animals do things, plants do not." This perception is ironic, given the fundamental importance of plants as primary producers. This imbalance is being redressed in some respects by television programs such as David Bellamy's "Botanic Man," which has helped popularize plant science and conservation. The program, produced by Thames Television, involved back-up books, home-learning, and extra-mural courses.

Television is probably not the best of educative systems, unless it is deliberately integrated into a learning system as the "Botanic Man" series was. But there can be no doubt that newspapers, radio, and television have played a major role in raising awareness and encouraging people to learn more about conservation (Bellamy 1979).

Bad news makes good headlines, and the doomsday predictions of environmentalists about habitat loss and species destruction readily take their place alongside rape, murder, and political coups. The problem is that such messages may encourage those who can afford it to travel to "experience" rare plants and vanishing forests before they disappear, but hordes of visitors to a nature reserve, all wanting to see a rare orchid, can wreak havoc in a very short time. An additional problem with the bad news approach is the danger that overexposure to negative messages can dull the senses, so that people actually become less responsive to environmental degradation and disaster (Soulé 1988; Given 1990a).

Educative materials are of little use if they do not get to the people who need them. Even among developed countries, there is surprisingly little exchange and free availability of educative materials. A book published in Britain will probably be available there, in parts of Europe, and in North America, but it is likely to be unknown in Australia or New Zealand. A New Zealand book may be unknown elsewhere. Language poses even greater barriers so that completely separate lines of literature have arisen in major language-group areas. Thus, because much of the Latin American conservation literature is written in Spanish or Portuguese, it tends to be little known in English-speaking parts of the world. This has serious impacts on education, because unless extensive translation is done, a significant amount of the world's literature on botanical conservation remains inaccessible to much of the world. Although literature may be listed in catalogs, some libraries may be unable to purchase what is available because of cost, or may not want to because of lack of an appropriate language edition. It is not surprising that information frequently does not get to people who most need it.

The major advantage of the written word is that it provides a permanent and generally accessible form of communication. But the written word is of little direct use to people who cannot read. Illiteracy is a major impediment to the social and economic development of some countries, especially where a major part of the population lives in villages. Adults who become literate help themselves in their own particular vocations and improve the quality of their lives; quality of life also improves for their families. In India, although literacy has risen from 16.6 percent of the population in 1951 to 36.2 percent in 1981, the actual number of illiterate people has risen because of the overall increase in population (Khoshoo 1986). Thus the major use of the written word in some countries may still be to educate the educators and administrators. They, in turn, will educate by nonwritten means, using spoken local language, drama, simple audiovisuals and exhibitions, posters, and demonstrations.

CASE STUDY: *PIED CROW*—AN ENVIRONMENTAL MAGAZINE

In 1982, Dr. James Connor, professor of science education at New York University, was considering writing a secondary school textbook on environmental issues when a single fact brought him up short: 90 percent of all students in Kenya drop out before secondary school.

Changing tack and tactics, Connor fashioned instead a

product with primary schools in mind—an environment and health magazine that has come to be known as *Pied Crow.* Unlike the bird itself (*Corvus albus*), which can be found throughout Africa, the material this magazine makes available on subjects such as forests, soils, population, water, and hygiene, is extremely hard to come by. Its 16 pages of brightly colored cartoons, stories, and games printed on cheap paper are distributed free six times a year to all primary schools in Kenya and Uganda—some 50,000 copies in all—at a cost of just one U.S. cent per child.

Pied Crow proved to be the prototype for a worldwide information network for children 8–14 years old called "Outreach." Supported by WWF–UK, IUCN, the Television Trust for the Environment, UNEP, and the New York Zoological Society, "Outreach" works with cabinet-level ministries in a number of developing countries to provide twice-monthly information packs through its headquarters in Nairobi.

The copyright-free material, compiled by a research support unit in New York, comes from a wide range of sources.

Local "Outreach" contacts adopt, adapt, and add to the material and send samples back to Nairobi, making for a two-way flow of information. "Outreach" packs are also being used in Zimbabwe to prepare a magazine for distribution to upper primary and lower secondary schools in Zimbabwe, Zambia, and Botswana; in Swaziland to develop a new curriculum for environmental education; by the Arab Youth Office for Youth and Environment as resource materials for its quarterly bulletin and monthly newsletter distributed to all Arab-speaking countries; and in Indonesia to produce a children's magazine in Bahasa, the official language. The packs also are often edited for use by broadcast and print media. In addition, Television Trust for the Environment has worked through "Outreach" to provide, among other services, six programs on environment and development themes for use by the Voice of Kenya, with video copies retained at the Nairobi office for use by nongovernmental organizations.

Source: Briceno and Drake 1986.

Social Ethics

Ultimately, one goal of conservation must be the formulation of strategies for conservation at global, national, and local levels. Another must be to provide appropriate techniques with which to conserve. A third must be the integration of development with conservation. The degree to which these are achieved will depend heavily upon success in convincing all peoples of the earth that conservation is indispensable for their well-being and, indeed, their survival. This, in turn, will require a fourth accomplishment: to create awareness and educate so that we all think in terms of global conservation and stewardship. But this also means that conservation must be relevant to people at particular times and places. Within the global ethic there must be room to develop individual cultural awareness and preserve that which is distinctive. This, harnessed with social justice, will lead to the development of an adequate social ethic of the environment.

Developing societal awareness, then, demands responses from many people worldwide. The problem of tropical forests is not just a matter for the people who live there. Injustices (including destruction of forest) can result from actions within a country. But they are often external in origin, because some inhabitants of planet earth do not meet the entire costs of their expensive lifestyle. They inflict pressures on others by their demands. The development of an environmental awareness and a social ethic in a third world

country is therefore going to require reciprocal developments in the Western world.

Conservation is for people. It is also of and about people and must not be separated from the social, economic, and political contexts in which it is pursued (Porritt 1984). Conservation must deal with those things with which people are in daily contact. There is a great risk of it becoming remote—for instance, in being concerned with oceanic islands and animals that most people will never see, or global phenomena that few can comprehend. In the first place, conservation has to relate to people through common, everyday experience. Second, however powerful, ingenious, rich, or just a society might be, it will fail if it is not based on an adequate conservation ethic. The converse is also true. Every society, no matter how small, must meet the economic, social, and political needs of its people.

Conservation will have less chance of succeeding where human rights are inadequate, where there is a gulf between rich and poor, or where there is little confidence in government and its objectives. Conservation relies on social and political support, on cooperation and lack of selfishness. Where these qualities are absent, through ignorance or desperation, or because a community feels deprived of resources by others, the future of habitat and species conservation is surely bleak.

Professor Albert Baez (1986: 120) has expressed why he had been attracted to conservation and what it meant to him:

> An environmental ethic develops in a person out of respect and affection for living things. If you are a scientist this feeling is more apt to arise if you are a biologist than if you are a chemist or a physicist. My professional career was in physics and I was intrigued by phenomena which were far removed from contact with living things. I spent many hours investigating the optical properties of X-rays and worked away for hours in laboratories that didn't even have windows to let you look out at living things like birds and trees.
>
> But human beings are living things and I had a feeling of affection for people which I inherited from my parents, so I was drawn to people through contact with my students in the classroom. Eventually I switched from physics research to education and worked with UNESCO to find better ways to teach the basic sciences, principally in the developing countries. This forced me to think philosophically about the aims of education that would improve the quality of life. I hit upon the 4 Cs "CURIOSITY, CREATIVITY, COMPETENCE and COMPASSION" as the fundamental ingredients of education in general, and of science education in particular, which would help people to live better.
>
> I now believe that the development of a sense of compassion is the most important of the 4 Cs if we are going to avoid the extinction of life on earth, either through a nuclear holocaust or through the destruction of the earth's life support systems—the "fast bang" or the "slow bang." The ethical roots of a fifth C—CONSERVATION—lie, I believe, in compassion. It must be a compassion which goes beyond concern for human beings alone. It must extend as well to all living things. There are reasons for considering the earth itself as a living organism, as proposed in the Gaia hypothesis, and hence also worthy of compassion and affection.

Having come to these conclusions independently, I was heartened to read the following quotation from Albert Einstein:

> A human being is a part of the whole called by us, "universe," a part limited in time and space. We experience ourselves, our thoughts and feelings as something separated from the rest, a kind of optical delusion of our consciousness. This delusion is a kind of prison for us, restricting us to our personal desires and to affection for a few persons nearest to us. Our task must be to free ourselves from this prison by widening our circle of compassion to embrace all living creatures and the whole of nature in its beauty.

Codes of conduct

There is an educative aspect to laws and regulations. Laws to protect threatened species cannot by themselves save plants. Awareness, goodwill, and concern for plants among all people is vital to the effective functioning of laws. This means that people have to understand why laws and regulations are needed.

Yet it is a tragic fact that some of most flagrant breaches of the laws come from plant enthusiasts and collectors. For decades, plant species that are rare, attractive, and unusual have been sought. Plant groups especially favored include palms, orchids, bromeliads, cycads, ferns, cacti, and succulents. In comparison with the threats stemming from habitat destruction, the threat posed today by hobbyists and collectors often seems relatively small. It is still significant, however, because it is often focused on accessible sites rich in narrow-range endemics or in particular species.

Collectors sometimes argue that the taking of a single wild plant is insignificant alongside the taking of many hundreds or thousands by a commercial horticultural firm. Ultimately, however, there is no difference between one person or company taking 60,000 plants, and 60,000 individuals taking one plant each (Huxley 1974). In Turkey where this has been a particular problem, under GEF funding the government of Turkey is establishing courses and a series of protected areas specifically designed and managed for crop genetic resources.

One of the most successful means of diminishing the effect of collectors on wild plants and initiating understanding of legal restrictions, is to encourage the use of voluntary codes of conduct. These can be promoted by special interest groups such as horticultural societies, environmental organizations, and botanical groups. Codes of conduct can also be directed at nurseries, botanic gardens, and scientific institutions to ensure that plant populations are not depleted.

Some plant dealers get their plants from villagers who want to pick up an income from the gathering of wild species. Although this is probably only a supplementary income for people in developed countries, it may amount to a substantial income for people in poorer regions. Unfortunately, unless it is done according to strict guidelines, such collecting can be an exploitive local industry that results in extirpation of desirable plants (Bensen 1975; Gosnell 1976). Exploitation of wild plants ranges from taking a few small seedlings to uprooting orchids and total strip-collection of desert cacti by the hectare. To balance this, many commercial plant dealers are careful and very aware of the need for care and good conservation practices.

One positive way in which both collectors and commercial firms can promote conservation is by the salvage of plants from recently disturbed or imminently threatened areas, such as new road lines, building sites, forest clearance projects, and wetlands scheduled for drainage. Such plants can then be made available for establishment of new populations, and for botanical and horticultural collections. Salvaged plants can also be made available to collectors and hobbyists through special interest groups and normal retail channels, provided both salvage and subsequent sale of plants are subject to a code of conduct that protects the plant and also educates the supplier and buyer.

Codes of conduct are useful and need to address a wide range of people and situations (e.g., Hagsater and Stewart 1985; Plant Conservation Round Table 1986). Codes should apply not only to people who may want to grow a plant, but also to casual visitors and photographers who may unwittingly disturb a habitat. When people photograph a plant, disturbance often results from "tidying" the site (removing extraneous branches and other plants) or from compaction of the ground. The latter can be a problem where plants are small and the photographer must lie on the ground.

Codes of conduct are voluntary. Therein lie both their disadvantages and advantages. People cannot be forced to adhere to a code; however, once they are supported by the public there can be considerable pressure from others to encourage adherence.

Active consumerism, especially in the consumption-oriented societies of developed countries, also must aid conservation. For plants this is especially important in the nursery and florist trade (Koopowitz and Kaye 1983). Private growing of plants is an enormously profitable trade in affluent countries, and on too few occasions do consumers ask about the origin of suspicious plants. If there is enough disapproval from consumers, the horticultural trade will become sensitive to the issue, and eventually, the fact will trickle back to the plant collectors that unwarranted trade in wild-source plants and from illegitimate sources is not acceptable.

Overall, there must be an awareness of the governing function of morality in culture and society. The ethics of a culture, along with political, social, and economic factors, play a crucial role in how well people adapt to the natural environment (Engel and Engel 1990). Too often, the evangelists of modern, Western, developed world cultures are obsessed with the contribution they have to offer to poorer nations, and with such issues as raising standards of living and promulgating consumerism. In contrast to this scenario, the World Conference on Environment and Development concluded that wherever traditional cultures with positive environmental attitudes exist, they should be strengthened, whereas most modern cultures, which do not support sustainable development, require moral change. As in so many aspects of life, there must be both a meeting with dialogue and a balance—all concerned listening and caring for both humanity and the wild and cultivated plants with which humanity shares this planet.

CASE STUDY: CODE OF CONDUCT FOR ORCHID GROWERS AND COLLECTORS

To the collector of orchid species from the wild

Before collecting anything: DO acquaint yourself with national and state controls, and find out which species are protected; **DO** contact people or agencies in your own country who have the expertise to advise you; **DO** obtain all necessary permits, both for collecting and for export and import to other countries; **DO** contact interested local organizations about your intentions and respect their advice; **DO** try to discover disturbed or threatened sites from which doomed plants can be rescued.

Then: DO strictly observe restrictions on what may be collected (which species, how many specimens, what kind of material); where possible, collect seeds, offsets (pseudobulbs, keikeis), or cuttings, not the whole plant; **DO** leave large specimens for seed production; they are needed to perpetuate the wild population; **DO** set a good local example; honor local customs of land/plant ownership; **DON'T** encourage overcollection; in particular avoid encouraging random or unsupervised collection, especially that motivated by the hope of financial reward; **DO** make careful field notes, including precise locality, altitude, habitat, date of collection, and your own field number; **DO** collect plants from fallen trees, in construction sites, and where forest clearance is already in progress; **DO** take photographs and preserve representative herbarium material; submit this material, with a copy of your notes, to an appropriate institution or organization; **DON'T** underrate the value of your field observations: carefully recorded they will be a useful contribution to science and to conservation; **DON'T** take plants that you will not be able to grow under the greenhouse conditions that you can provide for them; **DON'T** take more than a few plants of each species and only take them from areas where the species appears to be common;

DON'T make a larger collection than you can care for, either during the field trip or when you reach home.

IF you plan to collect in commercial quantities: DON'T. IF you plan to sell any of the plants you collect to defray the cost of your trip: DON'T.

IF you plan to collect for research or study, obtain the agreement and (preferably the collaboration) of competent scientific authorities, such as a government agency or university department, in the host country.

To the importer, private or commercial

DON'T import wild-collected plants, even if that is legally permitted, except as a nucleus for propagation and seed-production, unless they come from authorized rescue operations.

And then: DO check the credentials of suppliers offering wild plants and satisfy yourself they are "legal"; DO observe international and national export/import regulations and phytosanitary requirements; DO ship clean plants to avoid loss in fumigation and transportation.

To the nursery operator

DO sell nursery raised or propagated material and advertise it in your catalogs as such; DO try to propagate all rare and desirable species, preferably by cross pollination; DO keep more than one clone of rare species, even self-fertile ones, for propagation; DO keep careful records of the origin of all stock, especially any with collectors' numbers or locality data, and pass on the information to interested purchasers.

To the grower/collector at home

DO make successful cultivation a prime objective of your hobby; DO enjoy the satisfaction of raising from seed. Some of the rare or "difficult" species will test your skill and patience, but reward your success accordingly; DO record when and from whom you obtained your plant/seeds, and ask your source for any data—collectors' numbers, locality, and so on—all just as vital, to the serious enthusiast, as the name on the label; DO keep your plants properly labeled; DO try to propagate rare and documented material and distribute it to other enthusiasts (remember the old proverb: To keep a plant, give it away!); DO keep rare and scientifically valuable plants marked in some way and ensure that you have made arrangements for their survival when you are no longer able to care for them or after your lifetime.

To the orchid society or club

DO endorse the precepts of this Code of Conduct, as a guide for responsible and conscientious behavior; DO discourage the advertisement of wild-collected plants for sale in your publications, either openly or by hints; DO publicize national and international regulations on the export, import, and sale of wild plants; DO sponsor or support national or international measures to protect the habitats of rare and threatened species; DO encourage local conservation groups to set up orchid gardens or reserves; these could be developed for the rehabilitation of plants rescued from areas of forest destruction nearby and for the reintroduction of plants of endangered species grown from seed in cultivation; DO help your members to make arrangements for the continued survival of their plants when they are no longer interested in them.

To the show committees and judges

DO include in the schedule some classes for orchid species raised from seed by the exhibitor; DO include in the schedule some recognition for rare or undescribed species; DO make a policy of including good cultivation in your judging criteria; DO restrict competition to plants that have been grown in cultivation for at least a year.

Source: Hagsater and Stewart 1985.

The individual response

The real dynamic of conservation, as with other movements, is in visionary and dedicated individuals. At the heart of any conservation organization, campaign, strategy, or education program will be one or a few people who are the dynamo from which enthusiasm, interest, and energy comes. Worldwide conservation depends on a small corpus of such people who are involved because they believe in it.

What can the individual do for plant conservation? The answer is: a surprising amount! It is easy to be overwhelmed by the world's environmental problems, or by the apparent powerlessness of the individual person. It is easy to be overwhelmed by the jargon of many management systems: outputs, rationalization, and corporate structure, but ultimately, individuals and teams actually make things happen.

For those to whom conservation and biodiversity are important, it is necessary to keep asking about and stressing the need to do something about plants. Compared with some animals—for instance, birds and larger mammals—most plants do not figure high in people's consciousness except as a backdrop. For other people, plants are merely a convenience to be used without regard for the future. For still other people, plants are the difference between death and starvation. For hundreds of millions of years plants have evolved alongside animals, and lately humans, to occupy an essential place in the economy of our planet. Inaction is, in the long view, as threatening as forest logging or wetland draining. Rather, it is action that will maintain the earth's essential diversity—not just single large actions, but a multitude of individual actions reinforcing each other.

CHAPTER 9

Conservation Legislation

by Cyrille de Klemm

The Basis for Legislation

Primitive humanity, emerging into organized society from a hunter–gatherer lifestyle, lived close to the land. The land and its natural products were essential to survival. So primitive tribal groups developed—perhaps often unconsciously—sustainable systems that became part of everyday life. Sustainable systems became part of traditional codes binding the daily life of individuals, villages, and tribal groups. Such codes still exist, embodied in the rural traditions of developing countries and in the writings and practices of religions around the world. Remnants persist in highly developed cultures long since wedded to urban environments and sophisticated technology.

As society evolved, however, so did the legislative basis that gradually became essential to govern relationships between human beings. In parallel with civil law, which dealt with private matters such as the family, property, contracts, torts, and successions, other branches of law developed to regulate relations between individuals and society or the state. As human activities diversified, specialized bodies of rules had to be enacted to deal with specific and complex subjects such as commerce, agriculture, forestry, taxes, and, much more recently, planning and land use, to mention but a few.

Environmental law, as a distinct branch of law, only emerged a few decades ago. Its objective is to regulate activities and behaviors that may affect any or all of the basic components of the environment, namely, air, water, soils, flora, and fauna. Where its purpose is to preserve wild species and natural ecosystems, environmental law is often more appropriately termed conservation law.

Conservation law

Conservation law has a number of specific characteristics that make it very different from the other branches of law.

Instead of governing relationships between persons, or between persons and society, its only object is to conserve wild species and ecosystems, which have generally no monetary value and the destruction of which will affect no human interest protected by law. This completely novel approach barely falls short of a legal revolution and has understandably been challenged as being illegitimate on the grounds that human interests should always come first. As a result, implementation and enforcement problems are often well nigh insurmountable.

Conservation law started as a specialized subbranch of forestry or agricultural law dealing specifically with the regulation of the exploitation of wild species and the establishment of protected areas. It has gradually evolved in a cross-sectoral way and is now increasingly integrated into other branches of law, particularly planning and land-use legislation.

From a regulatory and punitive form of legislation based on the exercise of the police powers of the state, conservation law is now increasingly developing to provide a framework for the creation of institutions and procedures designed to facilitate and encourage conservation and management programs, to organize conservation as a public service, and to promote better public awareness of conservation requirements.

International conservation law

International law governs relations between states. It is dominated by the principle of national sovereignty. As a consequence, states cannot generally be bound without their consent. This consent is usually expressed through the conclusion of a treaty, signed by plenipotentiaries duly empowered for that purpose and subsequently ratified by an Act of Parliament or equivalent measure of national legislation.

Treaties have formed the backbone of international law since early history. First, they were like contracts providing for reciprocal benefits. If one of the parties, therefore, did not comply with its treaty commitments, the other could retaliate by refusing to discharge its own obligations. Relatively recent developments in international law have, however, resulted in the emergence of a new type of treaty laying down general rules that contracting parties commit themselves to observe. Examples are conventions dealing with such matters as human rights and conditions or the protection of the environment. These "law-making treaties," as they are sometimes called, contain no reciprocal obligations, and retaliation would generally not only be useless but also self-defeating. As a result, these treaties, although binding upon the parties, are usually difficult to enforce (de Klemm 1982). This inherent weakness may, however, be remedied to a certain extent by the establishment of appropriate institutions, such as *conferences of the parties* and *secretariats,* which would continually review the implementation of the conventions concerned, promote cooperation between the parties, and provide a forum where cases of noncompliance could be discussed. The obligation for contracting parties to provide periodic reports on the manner in which they implement a convention, the powers of the "conference" to adopt specific recommendations (which, although nonbinding in law, are generally considered as giving rise to strong moral obligations), and the admission of nongovernment organizations as observers at meetings of the "conference," may also contribute substantially to ensuring compliance (Lyster 1985).

Treaties dealing with the conservation of wildlife provide for the protection of individual species, which are listed in one or several appendices, and for the preservation of natural habitats, usually by means of the establishment of protected areas. Parties to these treaties have, therefore, the obligation to protect listed species and to set up and maintain parks and reserves.

The only worldwide conservation treaty that is applicable to plants is the Convention on International Trade in Endangered Species of Wild Fauna and Flora (CITES), which was signed in Washington, D.C., USA in 1973. It is, however, restricted to control of trade. There are also a number of regional treaties that specifically list plant species that must be protected by contracting parties:

Treaty	Date	Place
Convention on Nature Protection and Wildlife Preservation in the Western Hemisphere	1940	Washington
African Convention on the Conservation of Nature and Natural Resources	1968	Algiers
Convention on the Conservation of European Wildlife and Natural Habitats	1979	Berne
ASEAN Agreement on the Conservation of Nature and Natural Resources	1985	Kuala Lumpur
Protocol concerning Protected Areas and Wild Fauna and Flora in the Eastern African Region	1985	Nairobi
Protocol concerning Specially Protected Areas and Wildlife in the Wider Caribbean Region	1990	Kingston

In addition, two worldwide treaties provide for the conservation of important ecosystems. These are the Convention on Wetlands of International Importance, especially as Waterfowl Habitat (the Ramsar Convention, from its place of signature in Iran, in 1971), and the Convention for the Protection of the World Cultural and Natural Heritage (signed in Paris in 1972, under the auspices of UNESCO).

The Ramsar Convention requires its parties to promote the wise use of wetlands situated in their territory and to designate certain wetlands for inclusion on a List of Wetlands of International Importance. Parties have the obligation to maintain the ecological character of listed sites. Among the criteria that have been developed by the Conference of the Parties for the listing of sites, the presence of rare, vulnerable, endangered, or endemic plants is of particular relevance.

The World Heritage Convention provides for the protection of natural and cultural areas of outstanding universal value to be included in a World Heritage List. Biological formations and the habitat of threatened animal and plant species may qualify for inclusion on that list (Lyster 1985).

More recently, the worldwide Convention on Biological Diversity was concluded on 5 June 1992 at the United Nations Conference on Environment and Development (UNCED) in Rio de Janeiro, but has yet to come into force (IUCN/ELC 1994). Contracting parties undertake *inter alia* to establish a system of protected areas to conserve biological diversity, to restore degraded ecosystems, and to promote the recovery of threatened species through plans and other management strategies (article 8). Unlike CITES and Ramsar, however, this treaty does not provide for an official list of such protected areas or species.

At the regional level, the European Community has now adopted a Directive on the Conservation of Natural Habitats and of Wild Fauna and Flora (Council Directive 92/43/EEC dated 21 May 1992). This directive aims to protect biodiversity by requiring member states to conserve endangered plant and animal species and natural habitats throughout the territory of the European Community. Detailed annexes set out *inter alia* some 420 plant species (including 160 *priority species*), in respect of which member states should designate *special areas of conservation*. Other *plant species of Community interest* are classified as meriting strict protection (Annex IV[b]) or as subject to restrictions on their taking (Annex V).

The legal status of plants

The legal status of plants is very different from the legal status of wild animals and is considerably more ambiguous. Wild animals are usually characterized by law as *res nullius*. This concept, inherited from Roman law, means that animals are things that cannot be subject to ownership even by the owner of the land on which they occur, unless they have been legally taken or otherwise obtained. A few recently enacted laws, however, have now replaced this characterization by that of public property. Whether this new status will result in more effective conservation remains to be seen.

In contrast, plants, being generally attached to the soil on which they grow, are considered to be the property of the landowner, whether public or private, who as a consequence is free to exploit them or destroy them at his or her will.

Private ownership of wild plants is not, however, generally sufficient to prevent collection or destruction by third parties; with the exception of trees and a few other species that have a recognized economic importance, plants continue to be considered by the pubic as a gift of nature that may be freely collected by anyone, even on private land. In certain countries, such as Norway, Switzerland, and the German state of Bavaria, this customary freedom has been embodied in legislation, or even in a constitution. For all practical purposes, therefore, property rights on wild plants must be considered as purely nominal and, in any event, extremely difficult to enforce, both on public or private land unless, of course, the land is adequately enclosed.

Renewable resources such as game, fish, wild plants, and pastures may also be the common property of a group of persons, usually a village group (Bromley 1986). This form of ownership traditionally is based on custom, not on written law. It implies a combination of rights and duties vested in each member of the group, joint decision making, and the exclusion of outsiders (Oakeson 1986). In Western Europe and Japan, surprisingly large areas of common land are still managed according to long-standing traditional rights. Examples include wet meadows in the British Isles and certain Swiss grazing lands in the mountains (Runge 1986). In many developing countries, common property regimes remain widespread.

The value of common property rights is generally limited to the conservation and sustainable utilization of the particular resources for which they have been instituted, as they are not concerned with the preservation of nontarget species, which may, therefore, be incidentally destroyed with impunity. Nonetheless, where the common resource is constituted by land reserved for certain uses, such as grazing, the maintenance of such practices will also maintain a certain form of landscape and the particular species of plants it contains.

In summary, wild plants have the worst of two worlds. As private property, they can be destroyed by their owners. As an open access resource, they may, except when they have a recognized economic value for the state or a collective of private owners, be collected or even destroyed by anyone almost anywhere. Plant conservation legislation should always be viewed against this background: any restriction on collection or destruction will always be viewed as a limitation of vested rights or property rights.

Species-centered Legislation

Species-centered legislation is concerned directly with the conservation of target species or groups of species. It should not, however, be viewed as a substitute to the establishment of protected areas and land-use controls, but rather as an often essential complement. Indeed, protected areas usually are established for purposes other than the conservation of particular threatened plants; and many species, especially when their habitat is very localized, are, therefore, likely to remain unprotected by a protected area system. In addition, even when target species are included in protected areas, specific legislation may be necessary to control their possession, transport, and trade (MacKinnon et al. 1986).

Ideally, species-centered legislation should be aimed at controlling all the factors that may adversely affect a particular species, including habitat destruction or alteration, pollution, the introduction of alien species, and threats to the survival of its pollinators or seed dispensers. In practice, with very few exceptions—the most notable being that of the Endangered Species Act of the United States—legislation is generally limited to the control of collection, destruction, and trade.

Furthermore, only a relatively small number of countries, so far, are protecting individual species of plants. These include almost all European countries, Canada, the United States, South Africa, and Australia. Almost everywhere else legislation protecting plants either does not exist at all or is very rudimentary.

An essential prerequisite to the control of activities harmful to particular species of plants is to draw up a list of protected species. The list is usually contained in a statutory instrument made under an Act of Parliament, or equivalent piece of legislation, which specifies prohibitions or restrictions and penalties for noncompliance.

Typically, criteria for the inclusion of species on the list are not specified in such legislation. Opinions vary as to the necessity of criteria. Some believe that only endangered species should be protected and that there is no justification to impose restrictions on the collection of species that are still relatively common. Others feel that species that could become threatened by overcollection should be listed and that there is no need to protect endangered species for which there is no demand.

In practice, as an analysis of plant conservation legislation in 29 European countries demonstrates, lists of protected species generally contain both endangered taxa and spectacular species such as lilies, daffodils, iris, anemones, primroses, gentians, and orchids. Many endangered species are usually omitted. On the other hand, whole genera, and sometimes whole families, as for example orchids, often appear on the lists. This constitutes a convenient means to resolve the problem of look-alikes and to facilitate identification (de Klemm 1990).

The Swiss canton of Vaud has adopted an innovative approach: a short list of attractive species is widely publicized and a long list of protected endangered species is deposited with the Botanical Museum of Lausanne where it is available to the public. Botanists, planners, and other interested persons are expected to consult it as necessary (de Klemm 1990).

By and large, lists of protected species have been relatively manageable: the number of taxa they contain, on average, seldom exceeds 100. There is, however, a growing tendency to list a far larger number of species. As an example, the Greek list comprises more than 650 taxa, including many species with a very localized distribution and which only few specialists would be able to identify (de Klemm 1990).

Lists often suffer from taxonomic uncertainties, such as the use of synonyms instead of the present accepted names; the listing of hybrids, varieties, or variants as full species; and the use of generic names that have now been split, such as *Gentiana* and *Sempervivum*. This may give rise to serious doubts as to the species actually protected and, at the very least, provide loopholes that will make the legislation less effective. Possible solutions include referring in the legislation to the particular flora (published listing of the plants of a region) on which the list is based, or using standard reference list of names such as *Flora Europea* for Europe (de Klemm 1990). When the species to be protected is new to science and has not yet been described and given a scientific name, it should be listed under its genus, or at least its family, with an indication that it is a new species (sp. nova) and when possible a descriptive colloquial name.

Lists should be revised periodically, to keep up with nomenclatural changes and to add new species in need of protection. A reasonable interval seems to be five years, as is the case under the Wildlife and Countryside Act in the United Kingdom.

Where different statutes cover the same geographic area, as in the United States where there are federal and state lists of protected endangered species, care must be taken to ensure that the lists are compatible. Where listing criteria are different, this should be clearly explained to avoid confusion (York 1987).

The listing and delisting of protected species is generally carried out in a completely discretionary way by the competent authority, usually after consultation with botanists and other interested persons. In the United States, however, the federal Endangered Species Act provides for a heavy and protracted procedure involving a preliminary listing, an enquiry, and (when requested) public hearings. The procedure may be initiated by any person by means of a petition.

This may, of course, go a long way toward securing acceptance by the public of the resulting conservation measures. On the other hand, it has resulted in a long list of candidate species that are waiting their turn for the procedures to be started. In the interim, each one remains unprotected (McMahan 1987).

Collection Controls

There are many reasons for collecting or harvesting wild plants: scientific research by professional or amateur botanists, commercial trade, traditional subsistence uses, or merely personal enjoyment or consumption of wildflowers or other plants (e.g., mushrooms).

Clearly, uncontrolled mass collection of wild plants, especially of slow-growing or of rare species, can be an important contributory factor to the extinction or depletion of species in the wild. The extinction of *Trilepidea adamsii,* an endemic mistletoe of New Zealand, and of *Tecophilaea cyanocrocus,* an endemic lily of Central Chile (Chilean Forest Service 1989), are documented cases of the effects of overcollection.

With the development of trade (particularly international trade) in many species of wild plants for the extraction of drugs or for ornamental purposes, there is an increasing risk that many more species will soon become extinct if no effective collection and trade controls are instituted. Examples of such plants at risk are the medicinal species of *Dioscorea* and *Rauvolfia,* and many ornamentals such as cacti, orchids, *Cyclamen* species, and several species of Liliaceae and Amaryllidaceae (Figure 9.1). Thus, millions of wild-collected bulbs are exported annually from countries such as Portugal and Turkey (Read 1989) or sold on the domestic market in countries like Chile (Chilean Forest Service 1989).

Types of collection controls

Protection of wild plants from collection may be total or partial.

Total protection consists of an absolute prohibition to collect whole plants, or parts of plants, belonging to listed fully protected species. Exceptions may generally be made for the purpose of scientific research, subject to the granting of a special permit.

For partially protected plants, legislation usually prohibits the uprooting or digging up of subterranean parts and restricts the collection of aerial parts to a small number of specimens, which may vary according to species and countries but seldom exceeds twenty. In certain cases, the law, instead of setting a collection limit, merely provides that the daily maximum quantity allowed is that which may be held in the hand. This "small bunch" rule considerably facilitates enforcement.

These restrictions usually apply only to listed, partially protected species. In a few cases, however, they have been made to apply to all wild plants (sometimes with some exceptions), on the theory that there is no reason to allow unrestricted collection of any species. This global restriction may be limited to uprooting, as in the United Kingdom, or also may be applicable to the picking of aerial parts, as in several Italian regions, Swiss cantons, and Austrian Länder. In these cases, there is usually a daily collection limit to allow for the picking of a small number or, again, a small bunch of flowers or twigs.

In many countries all these restrictions apply to all land, whether publicly or privately owned, and to all persons, including, therefore, landowners on their

Figure 9.1. Cacti constitute a plant group particularly requiring trade controls because of their great horticultural appeal. Waimea Arboretum, Hawaii, USA. (D. R. Given)

own land. There are, however, a few cases—in particular in Anglo-Saxon countries with a common-law tradition—where it is held that such restrictions would impose unwarranted limitations on property rights. In these countries, collection prohibitions do not apply to the owners or occupiers of land provided the specimens are not traded. Collection by third parties on private land is, however, controlled because legislation usually requires third parties to obtain the written consent of the landowner and also, sometimes, a permit from the competent administrative authority (de Klemm 1990).

Types of activities controlled

RESEARCH

Collection for scientific purposes is often regarded as a minor form of exploitation. It has, however, the potential seriously to deplete endangered species, especially where collectors visit the same sites continually. Yet scientific collection is necessary to improve our knowledge of wild plants or to obtain germ plasm for use in breeding and crop improvement.

To prevent overexploitation, legislation now usually requires special permits to be issued for collecting protected plants for scientific purposes, or for collecting any plant for such purposes from protected areas. In addition, in an increasing number of countries, scientific collection of any species on any land now requires prior permission from the appropriate state conservation agency, particularly when the collector comes from abroad. Conditions attached to the permit may specify that collecting be done in the presence of a scientist or warden of the host country and that duplicate collections be deposited with an institution of that country.

Such regulations may seem an unnecessary imposition on collectors and scientists, but they do minimize irresponsible collecting, help monitor both rare and common species, and serve to augment the scientific inventory of collections of the host nation, which may not be able to afford to send its own scientists into the field. They also promote contact and understanding between scientists, collectors, wardens, and administrators of the countries involved.

COMMERCIAL COLLECTION

The collection for commercial purposes of protected plants is generally prohibited. In addition, legislation usually also forbids the possession, for any purpose, of these plants. The main goal of this type of provision is to facilitate the enforcement of prohibitions and to re-

move potential incentives to unlawful collection.

In addition, certain countries now control the collection for commercial purposes of otherwise unprotected plants. This is achieved by requiring collectors to apply for commercial collection permits. These controls may apply to certain listed species only, or to the collection of all wild plants. As an example, Australia now has stringent state laws governing the harvesting of commercially valuable wildflowers. In particular, the state of Western Australia requires permits for the commercial collection of all species of vascular plants, even when the collection is carried out by landowners on their own land. In Switzerland, a permit is necessary for the collection of most species of wild plants. Similar rules exist in other European jurisdictions and in South Africa. In a few countries, for instance, Belgium, the commercial collection of certain species is completely prohibited, even under a permit. Collection for private use remains, however, authorized.

Article 14 of the Directive on the Conservation of Natural Habitats and of Wild Fauna and Flora provides for a permit system and other flexible restrictions to be applied to plant species of Community (European Community) interest listed in Annex V, whose taking in the wild and exploitation may be subject to management measures. This contrasts with the absolute prohibition on the keeping, transport, and sale or exchange of 480 plant species covered by Annex IV(b), which are strictly protected (article 13).

When permits have been issued, conditions generally are attached specifying the quantities that may be collected, the dates and places of collection, and sometimes the collection methods that must be used. Enforcement of these conditions is generally easy, as the possession of quantities exceeding those authorized by the permit will generally be sufficient to prove noncompliance. In cases of violations, an extremely effective penalty, which generally is imposed by a simple administrative decision, consists of withdrawing the permit and prohibiting any application for a new permit within a specified period of time. In the event of repeated offenses, the permit may be revoked permanently.

The advantage of a commercial permit system for any species of wild plant is that it allows for considerable flexibility, at the discretion of the issuing authority, as to the manner in which individual collectors must proceed. There is, therefore, no need to provide for general rules governing the exploitation of each particular species. To close an area to collection, either permanently or on a rotational basis, it is sufficient not to issue permits allowing collection in that area.

The quantities that may be collected also may be varied from one permit to another according to areas or seasons.

The total number of permits and, therefore, the total quantity that can be collected also may be limited at the discretion of the competent authority. Resultant collection pressures can be adjusted to the optimum sustainable yield of the species concerned and to its relative abundance in any given region. In addition, conditions attached to the permit also may impose the use of collection methods that are least likely to cause unnecessary damage to the plants concerned or to their habitat.

For all these reasons, the permit system appears to be an irreplaceable tool to achieve the sustainable exploitation of wild plants of commercial importance, provided scientifically sound management plans, based on species surveys and statistical returns from permit holders, are developed and adhered to. Clearly, competent staff are needed to operate such a system satisfactorily, and this costs money. Financial resources may, however, be obtained through the collection of license fees or royalties from permit holders.

Finally, an extremely important aspect of the commercial permit system is that it acts as a powerful instrument to prevent any sudden influx of commercial demand for plants that previously were not in the trade and, as a result, the devastating effects of overcollection before conservation measures can be taken.

TRADITIONAL AND SUBSISTENCE COLLECTION

In traditional closed systems, the collection of wild plants for the personal use of the collector and his or her family, for barter, or for limited trade on local markets have seldom constituted a serious threat to the survival or the sustainable use of the species concerned. The quantities collected were probably relatively small, and these customary systems were generally sufficiently well self-regulated to prevent overcollection. In addition, outsiders were generally excluded or at least unwelcome. But with economic development, many of these systems have evolved toward a market economy. Plant products that were used only locally began to be sold on distant markets, often abroad. Destructive tools, such as rakes, were used to facilitate mass collection. Outsiders came from far away attracted by high potential profits, and local inhabitants had no legal means to oppose their presence. In other words, subsistence collection has, in many cases, become commercial.

The solution to this problem has usually consisted of controlling or even prohibiting commercial collection without penalizing traditional collectors when they gather wild plants for their own use. Thus, in several Italian regions, the collection of wild berries, mosses, and lichens is limited to small daily quantities. For instance, in the region of Val d'Aosta, where the collection of medicinal plants requires a permit, landowners are exempted from this obligation for small specified quantities taken for their personal use. In many European countries, the collection of wild mushrooms is now strictly regulated, in particular, with the imposition of low daily collection limits. In several European countries, the cutting of holly, mistletoe, or Christmas trees is now severely restricted.

There may be cases, however, where the commercial collection of certain species constitutes a long-standing tradition. In depressed rural areas, people may feel that their livelihood is at stake if harvesting is prohibited or severely restricted. A possible solution may consist of granting exemptions to a limited number of persons where they can prove that they are likely to suffer from an appreciable loss of income as a consequence of the new regulations. This has been done in several Italian regions for the gathering of mushrooms. It may also be possible to provide for a transitional period during which harvesting rates will be gradually reduced to an acceptable level. This will give time for educational measures to bear fruit and for local economies to adjust. The development of alternative resources, such as substitute species, may also be considered, as well as financial or technical assistance to establish plantations and nurseries when this is possible.

COLLECTION BY THE GENERAL PUBLIC FOR
NONCOMMERCIAL PURPOSES

Most of the restrictions mentioned in the preceding paragraph are applicable not only to traditional uses but also to the public at large; the collection of many wild plants for personal consumption or use, in particular berries and mushrooms, has become increasingly popular with city dwellers. To these should be added restrictions on the picking of wildflowers, as indiscriminate mass collection of certain spectacular and popular species by thousands of weekenders may often have devastating effects. The "small bunch" rule may, in such cases, be particularly appropriate.

Finally, the Directive on the Conservation of Natural Habitats and of Wild Fauna and Flora requires member states to take appropriate measures to prohibit the deliberate picking, collecting, cutting, uprooting, or destruction of the 480 strictly protected plant species covered by Annex IV(b) (article 13[a]).

Trade Controls

Trade in fully or partially protected plant species is generally prohibited. On the other hand, trade in unprotected species is generally unrestricted. Where the commercial collection of a species is controlled, however, trade in that species must naturally also be regulated. Indeed, if a commercial collection permit is to be effective, it must be supplemented by controls applied to all the other links in the trade chain. These links include the licensing of traders, nurseries, and plant processing industries, and the obligation for licensees to keep records of their transactions and use a system of tags accompanying traded specimens as far as their final destination. Finally, there is often a prohibition against buying or selling plants obtained from persons other than licensed sellers or growers.

Examples of these elaborate trade controls can be found in several Australian states such as New South Wales and Western Australia, as well as in the Cape Province of South Africa. They were instituted because of the large volume of trade in wild cut flowers in these areas. The tagging system has been established in certain states of the United States such as California and Texas, mainly to control trade in desert plants.

Controls also are needed when commercial growers deal with the plants that are subject to collection restrictions. The objectives of such controls are to ensure that nurseries do not obtain their propagation material from unlawfully collected wild specimens, and that they do not sell wild plants under the pretense that they were artificially propagated. In certain jurisdictions, such as the Cape Province in South Africa, not only do plant growers have to be licensed, but they also must keep records of all their transactions. In France, a tagging system for artificially propagated plants was instituted in 1988. The absence of tags constitutes a presumption that the plants have been unlawfully collected from the wild.

The enforcement of all these rules requires specialized personnel to carry out inspections on the premises of traders and growers. These sophisticated controls are undoubtedly expensive and may, in addition, lead to bureaucratic heavy-handedness, especially where licenses are withdrawn or other sanctions are imposed at the discretion of a government agency. Such controls, therefore, are justified only where trade in wild plants is large and the risk of unlawful transactions high.

Interprovincial or inter-regional trade in wild plants within federal states may give rise to difficult problems where trade of a particular species is pro-hibited or restricted in one or more of the territorial entities concerned but not in the others. In such an event, specimens that have been unlawfully obtained in one state or province often may be freely sold in the others. Ideally, legislation should be enacted at a national level to ensure that uniform rules are applied throughout the country. Such legislation exists in the United States: it is called the Lacey Act. Enactment of such legislation, however, may be impossible for constitutional reasons, as in Australia. The only solution in such a case is for all the federated entities to adopt the same lists of plants subject to trade controls. This may not be easy to achieve (Good and Leigh 1986).

Where domestic trade in wild plants is controlled, prohibitions or restrictions usually extend to the import and export of specimens of protected species. Import controls are necessary to ensure that specimens that have been unlawfully collected in the importing country itself have not been exported and subsequently imported as if they were of foreign origin. Import controls also can assist exporting countries in the control of their exports.

Export controls are necessary to prevent the export of unlawfully obtained specimens, which, under such a system, would require the delivery of export permits. These should only be granted to exporters who are able to prove that the specimens they propose to export have been lawfully obtained.

The necessity of controlling international trade in endangered species was recognized as early as 1911, and provisions to that effect were incorporated into several international conventions on the conservation of wildlife, in particular, the African Convention of 1968. Because no machinery was provided to implement them, however, their effectiveness remained very low (Lyster 1985).

The Convention on International Trade in Endangered Species of Wild Fauna and Flora (CITES) was signed in Washington, D.C., in 1973. This extremely important instrument, to which 120 states were parties on 1 October 1992, constitutes the basic legal text governing international trade in wildlife throughout the world.

CASE STUDY: CONVENTION ON INTERNATIONAL TRADE IN ENDANGERED SPECIES OF WILD FAUNA AND FLORA (CITES)

The main purpose of CITES is to establish cooperative links between importing and exporting countries to ensure that unlawfully obtained specimens of species listed in the convention appendices cannot be freely traded at international level. Appendix I lists species that are threatened with extinction; commercial trade in these species is totally prohibited. Noncommercial transactions, for instance for scientific purposes, are subject to the issuing of import and export permits. Scientific authorities in both countries concerned must, before permits can be issued, certify that the transaction will not be detrimental to the survival of the species. These rules only apply, however, to wild specimens. Appendix I plants that have been artificially propagated for commercial purposes are treated as if they were listed on Appendix II.

Appendix II includes species that may become threatened with extinction unless their trade is strictly regulated. The export of specimens of these species requires an export permit, which may only be issued if the scientific authority of the state concerned has advised that it will not be detrimental to the survival of the species. Imports are allowed only under presentation of export permits.

Appendix III covers species listed by individual parties when they need the cooperation of the other parties to control the lawfulness of their exports. The export of a specimen of a species on Appendix III from the state that has listed it requires an export permit. The import of such a specimen from such a state requires the presentation of that permit. The import of Appendix III specimens from any other state requires the presentation of a certificate of origin as a proof that it does not originate from the country that has listed the species concerned.

After the seventh meeting of the Conference of the Par-

ties to the Convention, held in Lausanne in 1989, there were 99 plant taxa listed on Appendix I (most were individual species) and 48 on Appendix II, which included several families, in particular the Cactaceae, Cyatheaceae, Cycadaceae, and Orchidaceae, amounting to perhaps as much as 50,000 species in all. The only plant species so far that have been included in Appendix III are five species of trees listed by Nepal.

All the provisions of CITES apply not only to whole live or dead specimens of listed species but also to readily recognizable parts and derivatives, with a small number of exceptions. The Convention establishes a Conference of the Parties, which meets every two years, and a permanent secretariat, provided by the United Nations Environment Program and based in Switzerland.

There have been, as could be expected, many problems in the implementation of CITES. Some of these have now been resolved through increased cooperation between parties, recommendations made by the conference, and effective action by the secretariat. Others still remain. A remaining task is to obtain better enforcement of the Convention with regard to trade in listed plant species; parties have tended, as usual, to give higher priority to animals. In particular, there is a pressing need for an identification manual for CITES plant species and for a strengthening of import and export controls of plant specimens. The recent appointment of a plants officer to the secretariat will no doubt help improve the present situation.

Habitat Protection

Collection prohibitions or restrictions, important as they may be, must be supplemented by habitat protection measures if endangered plant species are to survive. Legislation protecting wild plants usually prohibits the destruction of listed species. This should be interpreted as a prohibition not only of deliberate vandalism, but also of any operation or activity, and in particular of land clearing, that may result in the destruction of protected plants.

Because it could lead to serious land-use restrictions and, therefore, to considerable political and practical difficulties, legislation is almost always deliberately ambiguous as to the extent of the prohibition on destruction. As a result, such restrictions remain largely ineffective. In many cases, moreover, a number of activities are specifically exempted from the prohibition, in particular agriculture, forestry, and, sometimes, construction, including the building of roads. In the United Kingdom, the Wildlife and Countryside

Act allows the destruction of a protected plant when it is the incidental result of a lawful operation and could not reasonably be avoided. The California Fish and Game Code exempts from the destruction prohibition not only the clearing of land for agriculture and fire control purposes, but also a host of other activities, including public works.

A relatively small number of laws, however, have gone further than merely prohibiting the destruction of protected plants and specifically provide for the protection of the habitat of listed species. As an example, the Irish Nature Conservation Act prohibits willful damage, destruction, or interference with the habitat of a protected species of plant. The Swiss canton of Zurich requires a permit to destroy or to alter the habitat of all rare and endangered species. Finland intends to apply special land-use restrictions to the habitat of species in need of special care. None of these rules establish absolute prohibitions to the destruction of endangered species habitats, but they usually set forth procedures allowing for negotiation between conservation authorities and landowners with a view to reaching a mutually acceptable solution.

In the United States, the federal Endangered Species Act of 1973 requires consultation between the Fish and Wildlife Service and any other federal agency proposing any action likely to jeopardize the existence of a federally listed endangered or threatened species. If jeopardy is found, reasonable and prudent alternatives must be sought and are binding on the federal agency concerned (Bartel 1987). Similar provisions appear in the legislation of California, with respect to state-listed species. Unfortunately, in this latter case, all that is required by the law, by way of reasonable and prudent alternative, is the removal and transplantation of the plants before the start of construction, a rather unsatisfactory solution to say the least (Cochrane 1987).

The California Environmental Quality Act of 1970, and the regulations made under that act, provide that state agencies must prepare an environmental impact report when a project has the potential to eliminate a plant or animal community or to reduce the numbers or restrict the range of a rare or endangered plant. Although it remains possible to approve a project having such an impact when specific economic, social, or other considerations make impracticable the mitigation measures and project alternatives identified in the environmental impact report, the very fact that such a report is required, with all the delays and expenses involved, will often facilitate negotiations and the adoption of less damaging alternatives (Cummings 1987).

In a few cases, legislation provides for the possibility of designating and preserving habitats that are essential to the survival of listed protected species. In the United States, under the Endangered Species Act, these habitats, called *critical habitats,* must in principle be designated for each listed species, and maps of these habitats must be published in the Federal Register. Exceptions may be made when the disclosure of critical habitat could expose the species to collection, vandalism, or other threats, or where sufficient information is lacking to make the designation. Federal agencies must ensure that any action authorized, funded, or carried out by them is not likely to jeopardize the continued existence of listed species or result in the destruction or adverse modification of their critical habitat. The official designation of these habitats gives advance notice of the areas in which federal activities will require close scrutiny to determine whether they meet the requirements of the jeopardy

prohibition (Bean 1983).

In the Australian state of Victoria, critical habitats may be designated by interim conservation orders. These orders may prohibit or regulate any activity or process likely to affect adversely the habitat concerned. They are only made, however, for a period of two years. During this period the minister must take all reasonable steps, including the conclusion of management agreements, to ensure the long-term conservation of the area.

In France, under the Nature Protection Act of 1976, the prefects (i.e., the local representatives of the central government) are empowered to make specific regulations for the conservation of the habitat of listed protected species. These orders may prohibit any activity, including farming and construction, which may be detrimental to the conservation of these habitats (de Klemm 1990).

Mention should finally be made of the few international instruments that provide for the conservation of the habitats of the species they purport to protect. In particular, the Convention on the Conservation of European Wildlife, signed in Berne in 1979, requires its contracting parties to take appropriate and necessary measures to ensure the conservation of the habitats of the species listed in the appendixes.

CASE STUDY: CONVENTION ON THE CONSERVATION OF EUROPEAN WILDLIFE

The Directive on the Conservation of Natural Habitats and of Wild Fauna and Flora now provides for the creation of a "coherent European ecological network of special areas of conservation" (article 3). Known as Natura 2000, this network will be composed of sites hosting the natural habitat types listed in Annex I and habitats containing the animal and plant species listed in Annex II. Member states are required to designate sites on their territory that correspond to scientific criteria. Pressure can be exerted upon member states to participate fully in the creation of this network: article 5 established a bilateral consultation procedure for cases where a member state omits from its national list a site that the Commission considers essential for the maintenance of a *priority habitat type* or the survival of a *priority species.* If no agreement can be reached, the final decision on whether or not to list a site is taken by the Council, acting unanimously.

From these national lists and with the agreement of member states, the Commission selects sites of Community importance based on the number of such priority habitat types or species found on the sites in question. This list must be finalized within six years of the notification of the directive. Member states must thereafter take measures to avoid the deterioration of the protected habitats or disturbance to the protected species, and must make provision for environmental impact assessments of any project liable to affect a site (article 6[3]). Subject to very limited exceptions, the competent national authorities should only authorize such a project if it will not adversely affect the conservation objectives of the site. Where such a project is carried out, the member state is obliged to undertake compensatory measures to protect the "overall coherence of Natura 2000," and the Commission must be informed of these steps.

Member states have a further six years formally to designate their sites as special areas of conservation. They are required to enact conservation measures, such as management plans, and appropriate statutory, administrative, or contractual measures that correspond to the ecological requirements of the site (article 6[1]). Land-use planning and development policies are required to be modified where necessary to encourage the management of landscape features (linear features, such as rivers and their banks, as well as stepping-stone features, like small woods and ponds) that are of major importance for wild flora and fauna (article 10).

A further innovation is that the directive provides financial incentives for member states to participate fully in the creation of a pan-European network of protected habitats. Member states may apply for Community cofinancing when they notify the Commission of their national list of sites. The Commission assesses the financial requirements of the proposed conservation measures, in relation to the concentration of priority habitats or species on a member state's territory and the relative financial burden imposed on the member state in question. It then draws up a prioritized action framework, granting cofinancing to certain projects. The action framework incorporates a review every two years, and member states that have not received funding for conservation projects may postpone such measures pending the review, provided that they refrain in the meantime from any actions likely to result in deterioration of those areas.

Financial provision will be made from the new Community Environmental Fund (LIFE), which was established by Regulation 1973/92 of 21 May 1992. Article 2(2) specifically provides for cofinancing of measures for the maintenance in or restoration to a favorable state of conservation of priority habitats and species.

It must be emphasized that these instruments, as well as national plant conservation legislation, when they deal with the protection of habitats, merely lay down general obligations, the purpose of which is to arrive at a certain result, namely the protection of the habitats of listed species. But the means that may be used to achieve this may vary considerably according to the availability of appropriate legal instruments in the country concerned and to the circumstances of each individual case.

On public land, the conservation of rare plants is usually best achieved by the establishment of nature reserves. In certain cases, botanical reserves may be sufficient provided that the collection of plants and the disturbance of natural vegetation are prohibited, even if other activities are permitted. For important plant areas situated on private land, lasting protection may require acquisition and, sometimes, expropriation by the state. This may not, however, always be possible or desirable, and other forms of protection such as the imposition of land-use restrictions by administrative order, a technique that is being more widely used, often provide an acceptable and cheaper substitute to state ownership. It is important to note that in such cases, landowners may be entitled to compensation. Finally, the conclusion of voluntary management agreements with landowners and the use of various types of financial and tax incentives also can contribute to the achievement of the desired result.

Dynamic Conservation

Although legislation protecting wild plants is generally limited to collection, destruction, and trade prohibitions or restrictions, the fact that lists of protected species now exist may have important indirect effects, especially on the development of dynamic conservation action.

Priority often is given to the conservation of the habitats of protected species when nature reserves are established or when land is purchased for conservation purposes. Environmental impact assessments generally have to take into consideration the presence of protected species and must evaluate the consequences of proposed alterations of their habitats. An additional indirect effect of such lists is the inclusion of the habitats of these species in the zones of municipal land-use plans that receive the highest degree of protection. Development permits are easier to deny when the proposed action is likely to destroy or alter the habitat of protected species. Last but not least, listing facilitates negotiations with landowners and public bodies and the taking of voluntary conservation measures such as management agreements.

Many of the measures that are required to carry out a dynamic conservation policy for endangered plant species do not need to be enshrined in the law, as they will vary from species to species and according to the circumstances of each case. They need, however, to be included in recovery or management plans that should be developed for each listed species, and the obligation to develop such plans should be embodied in the legislation as a duty of the conservation authorities. Only a few countries, so far, have made the development of these plans the subject of a legal obligation. Examples are the Endangered Species Act in the United States, which requires that recovery plans be drawn up for all listed species (except where such a plan does not promote the conservation of the species concerned) and Spain, which, under the new Nature Conservation Act of 1989, has made the development of recovery plans mandatory for all endangered species.

Recovery plans in the United States are drawn up and implemented by recovery teams composed of representatives of the federal Fish and Wildlife Service, the wildlife department of the state concerned, the agency administering the land on which the species occurs, if any, and appropriate scientific institutions. Recovery teams may propose any relevant measures to the authorities concerned, in particular, the conclusion of memoranda of understanding establishing contractual relationships between agencies for the conduct of research and conservation measures.

Recovery and management plans should deal with all aspects of the conservation of a species, including ex situ conservation in botanic gardens or gene banks, monitoring of wild populations, identification of threats, preferred habitat management methods, habitat restoration, and reintroduction of genetic stock into the wild.

Ecosystem-centered Legislation

Wild plant species also may be preserved by other legal instruments that are not specifically directed at the conservation of individual species, but which, nonetheless, provide a high degree of protection to natural or seminatural habitats and, as a result, to all the plants they contain.

The best known of these instruments is the protected area and it is generally the preferred one (when available), although conventional protected areas, such as national parks and nature reserves, will never be sufficient to safeguard the world's biological diversity. One of the main reasons for this is that in the countries where protected areas can only be established on public land, the cost of land acquisition is becoming a limiting factor. On the other hand, in those mainly Western European nations where protected areas may be created on privately owned land by government order, local opposition has made the adoption of such orders increasingly difficult. New and innovative instruments, therefore, have been developed for the conservation of biological diversity.

Land-use controls

Traditionally, land-use controls have been used to control development through the granting of permits for the construction of buildings and of infrastructure and other works. Agriculture and forestry are generally exempted from such controls. This traditional approach is changing with the growing realization that environmental conservation and land-use planning

are intricately connected. Adequate land-use controls are seen as a necessary condition for the conservation of natural resources (Rabie and Erasmus 1983).

Thus there is a growing tendency to apply land-use controls to the preservation of natural habitats. This may be done through special conservation orders to preserve important sites or landscape features; by the designation of sites of special scientific interest (as in the United Kingdom), to which certain particular rules apply; or by the establishment of specially protected zones in municipal or local zoning plans. For example, the Planning Act of the Swiss canton of Zurich and the regulations for its implementation provide that all types of wetlands and dry grasslands must be included in those areas of the local zoning plans where no construction is allowed. Because this may not be sufficient to ensure the conservation of these areas, the regulations also state that further regulations may be made to prohibit, in such areas, any activity likely to be detrimental to the preservation of the habitats concerned.

Land-use controls established in the interest of soil or water conservation often contribute to the conservation of plant species because they necessarily involve the maintenance of the vegetation cover. Controls may apply to steep slopes, river banks, or specific designated areas. Forests protected for that purpose are often called protection forests; the clearing of these usually is rigorously forbidden.

Another type of control that is increasingly used is the protection by law of certain habitat types, wherever they are located. In Denmark, for instance, the alteration of many kinds of habitats—water courses, lakes, marshes, heathlands, peat bogs, and certain coastal ecosystems—is prohibited without a permit from the conservation authorities. In the United States, a similar system applies to wetlands, both at the federal level and by a relatively large number of individual states. Nonetheless, the U.S. system has given rise to constitutional problems where the denial of a permit deprives the landowner of any possibility of using his or her land. The courts have accordingly judged it right to award compensation in such cases, and Congress may well come under pressure to repeal the restrictions in the future. In South Australia, all native vegetation is identified as potentially significant habitat under the Native Vegetation Act of 1991, which subjects the clearing of any indigenous vegetation to a permit requirement.

The need to preserve certain habitat types also appears in a number of international instruments. The Berne Convention on the Conservation of European Wildlife obliges contracting parties to preserve endangered habitat types. The Ramsar Convention on the Conservation of Wetlands of International Importance requires parties to promote the conservation of wetlands and their wise use. Annex I to the Directive on the Conservation of Natural Habitats and of Wild Fauna and Flora contains an extremely detailed list of natural habitat types of Community interest whose conservation requires the designation of special areas of conservation. Nine broad categories of habitat contain over 160 habitat types, of which around 40 are given priority designation.

Other types of controls are addressed at specific activities that may have adverse effects on natural areas, such as mining, quarrying, afforestation, the channelization of streams, and the use of off-road vehicles.

Management measures are often required to maintain nonclimax habitats, such as most marshes, peatlands, heathlands, and grasslands, at a certain stage of vegetation succession to avoid encroachment by woody plants and to preserve the animal and plant communities they contain. As land-use controls only prohibit certain activities and cannot impose positive management actions, other types of instruments are necessary to provide, where necessary, for essential management measures, such as controlled grazing, or mowing after certain dates. This is sometimes achieved by binding conservation orders, as in Denmark and the Netherlands, with appropriate compensation to landowners, or through management agreements.

Voluntary conservation

Conservation-minded landowners or private organizations that have acquired land for conservation can be encouraged to set up private reserves with government backing. Such reserves should be protected from damage caused by third parties and also, as far as possible, from the doings of government agencies and expropriation.

In France, the Nature Protection Act allows for the establishment of voluntary reserves; these benefit from the same degree of protection as state nature reserves. The National Trust in the United Kingdom has the right to declare any of its landholdings inalienable, which makes expropriation legally impossible unless Parliament itself decides to the contrary.

In some common law countries, landowners may commit themselves irrevocably not to do certain things on their land. This institution, which is called a *restrictive covenant,* gives rise to an obligation running with the land and binding upon successors in title. The advantage for owners is that they are assured that the land will be preserved after their death.

Management agreements are contracts between a public agency (or conservation organization) and an owner or occupier of land, whereby the latter undertakes to manage his or her land in a specified way and, in particular, agrees to do or not to do certain things, in exchange for the payment of a sum of money, usually on a periodic basis. Agreements of this type offer considerable opportunities to conserve natural habitats, yet they are used only in a small number of countries, as legislation does not usually provide for this possibility. In a few countries, management agreements provide for the establishment of perpetual servitudes and are binding upon successors in title. In the United States, landowners are entitled to sell certain interests in the land, such as the right to drain or to fell trees. This type of institution is called an easement. In practice it is rather similar to the establishment of a servitude.

Not all management agreements are necessarily as far-reaching as those just described. Many are concluded for a limited period of time, usually a few years, and do not, therefore, run with the land. As an example, a European Community regulation of 1985 allows for the payment of grants to farmers in designated environmentally sensitive areas who, by signing a management agreement, undertake to carry out an extensification of their activities.

Another type of voluntary conservation is achieved through the provision of financial or tax incentives to landowners and the removal of subsidies or tax benefits for activities leading to the destruction of natural habitats. In Switzerland, for instance, financial aid is provided to farmers who maintain certain habitats such as dry grasslands or tall grass meadows. These subsidies are paid as long as certain conditions are met; there are no management agreements. In Minnesota, USA, land taxes on wetlands and natural prairie areas have been discontinued when the areas concerned are maintained in their natural condition (de Klemm 1990). In the United Kingdom, areas of high natural value may be exempted from death duties provided the heirs of the estate comply with specified management requirements.

Incentives may not necessarily be provided only by government agencies. In certain countries, for instance in Switzerland, nongovernment conservation organizations compensate farmers who have agreed not to spray herbicides at the edges of their fields; this helps preserve weeds of cultivation, which are increasingly threatened with extinction.

Conversely, governments often subsidize nongovernment organizations to buy land for conservation or to carry out conservation measures. Tax exemptions are also sometimes granted for the acquisition of natural habitats for that purpose.

Disincentives supporting conservation include the refusal of subsidies and other benefits for activities that are harmful to the natural environment. The American Food Security Act of 1985 constitutes a good example of far-reaching disincentives: all federal agricultural subsidies are withheld from farmers who bring into cultivation highly erodible land or wetlands.

Conservation on public land

Conservation of natural habitats on public land should, in principle, be easy to achieve; the land is under state control and no private interests are likely to be affected by conservation measures. When the owner or manager of such lands is a conservation department, the situation is simple and the areas concerned are usually designated as protected areas. But when the manager is another department, it may not be easy to ensure that the managing agency will not carry out or authorize activities that will destroy natural habitats or threaten endangered species. Legislation is usually powerless to resolve this kind of conflict unless specific laws are enacted to provide solutions. And that can be difficult to achieve because of the opposition of the agencies concerned.

Certain legal instruments have been developed to protect natural habitats on public land. The most innovative is probably the wilderness area concept, which was initiated in the United States where vast areas of public land remain, particularly in Alaska and in the West. Wilderness areas are created by acts of Congress under the Wilderness Act of 1964. Wilderness areas are essentially roadless areas where no construction of roads or tracks and no access by motor vehicles of any kind are allowed. The system has developed rapidly and is intended to cover eventually 400,000 square kilometers of federal lands.

Public forests the world over have been and generally continue to be worked for the production of timber, often with little regard for other values. As a rule, forest departments have enjoyed a considerable degree of discretion in the way they conduct their operations. This situation is gradually changing, as legislation in some countries now requires that a reasonable balance be achieved between production activities and wildlife conservation. In the United States, the National Forest Management Act of 1976 limits the discretionary powers of the U.S. Forest Service and requires that management practices be compatible with the maintenance of the multiple functions of forests. In the Spanish region of Navarra, 2 percent of the total area of municipally owned forests must be left undisturbed.

Another important aspect of the conservation of wild plants on public land is the preservation of natural vegetation, often including endangered species, on rights-of-way along railway lines and public roads. Several countries, for instance South Africa, prohibit the picking of wild plants along highways (Hall and Rabie 1983). But the main threats result from the increasing use of machinery, fire, or herbicides to control vegetation. This matter is seldom dealt with in legislation and is usually best resolved by agreement between the conservation department and the agency responsible for roads or railways. Such agreements should result in the development of maintenance conditions that will spare important plant sites (Martz 1987).

Government-owned land held by an agency whose objectives and purpose are very remote from the objectives of nature conservation (for instance, lands in the hands of defense ministries or public roads administrations) may be difficult to protect for conservation purposes. Even if these agencies are willing to preserve important natural habitats, they may lack the necessary knowledge and capacity to carry out the necessary management work. Ways must be found to allow a conservation agency to manage the areas concerned or at least to provide advice and technical assistance. This is generally best achieved through informal negotiations. In certain cases, land can be leased to the conservation agency or to a private person or organization under a management agreement specifying certain management practices. The Flora and Fauna Guarantee Act of 1988 of the Australian state of Victoria empowers the conservation authorities to make conservation orders to conserve critical habitats of listed species on public land and to enter into management agreements with any public authority for that purpose.

Future Directions

Species-centered legislation has developed, mostly in industrialized countries, as a result of an increasing recognition of the importance of preserving endangered plants. Lists of protected species are necessary to prevent overcollection, to identify areas that must be put under protection, and to alert developers to exercise caution when their activities are likely to destroy endangered species. Trade in all wild species should, in principle, be controlled through the granting of permits, with appropriate conditions attached, to collectors, growers and traders. The improvement of international trade controls requires a strengthening of the capacity of CITES to deal with wild flora.

The main threat facing endangered plants will increasingly be the destruction of their habitats. Wherever possible, and especially in plant-rich areas, new protected areas and botanic reserves should be established to safeguard essential habitats. Lists of species requiring specific habitat conservation measures should be established for that purpose, as is the case with the detailed annexes to the European Directive on the Conservation of Natural Habitats and of Wild Fauna and Flora, and critical habitats should, as much as possible, be identified.

The preservation of habitats of endangered species and of all important natural and seminatural habitats should be accomplished primarily through improved land-use planning legislation. Land-use planning controls must be applied to all activities, including agriculture and forestry, that are likely to affect natural areas and wild species. New legislation along these lines has already been adopted in a limited number of jurisdictions, for instance, in the Autonomous Community in Spain. In Italy, Spain, and a few other countries, a new concept has appeared—the nature park, where more extensive and traditional activities are encouraged and where actions that may be harmful to the natural environment are prohibited or restricted according to the conservation requirements of each particular zone. The value of this new type of protected area lies in the fact that nature parks constitute autonomous planning units where the conservation of natural areas and the traditional activities of the local population are as fully integrated as possible.

In all matters relating to the protection of the habitats of wild plant species, emphasis should be placed on the prevention of conflicts rather than on procedures for their resolution once they have occurred. For that purpose, lists of species requiring habitat protection measures are essential as a means to provide advance warning to developers of possible future conflicts. Further, it is necessary to develop rules and techniques to ensure that endangered plant species are adequately taken into consideration in environmental impact assessments. It is also important to establish, by legislation, a general obligation not to destroy the habitats of endangered species and to specify that even when an environmental impact assessment is not required by law, adequate surveys must be carried out to ensure that no such habitats are likely to be destroyed by a proposed development.

In addition, where conflicts are unavoidable, appropriate mitigation criteria and procedures should be developed to reduce or compensate as much as possible for the impacts of approved projects on the habitats of endangered plant species or on natural habitats in general. Finally, recovery plans for endangered species and management plans for species which are subject to controlled exploitation should also be developed.

There remains the problem of implementing and enforcing legislation. Plant conservation legislation is notoriously difficult to enforce. Perhaps one reason for this is the fact that penalties are generally too low to constitute an effective deterrent. Moreover, penalties often are assigned in a haphazard way, for instance, the law rarely makes a difference between the picking of a few protected flowers by a passerby and the destruction of a whole population of the same species by a developer. But the main enforcement difficulties seem mostly to result from deficiencies in public information and a general unwillingness to prosecute. The solutions to these problems will result not from improvements in legislation but from better education, public information, training of enforcement personnel, and actions on the ground. Thus, improved protection of wild plants depends on the availability of adequate institutions, staff, and financial means to carry out necessary conservation measures. These are lacking almost everywhere.

The situation is completely different in developing countries, where almost none of the legal conservation instruments described in this chapter exist, where the number of endangered species is probably very large, and where important areas for the conservation of plants remain largely unknown. In these countries, lists of endangered or protected species would probably serve no useful purpose, with the exception of species that may be threatened by trade. These should, of course, be covered by CITES, and appropriate controls should be established at ports of export and import to prevent illegal trade.

With regard to the conservation of habitats, preference should be given as far as possible to the establishment of protected areas, particularly to preserve known centers of endemism. Generally this will be possible only in uninhabited areas.

Means must be found to ensure the conservation of wild flora, and of biological diversity in general, in areas that have so far been relatively little affected by development and where traditional land-use practices, in harmony with the environment, have persisted until today. This may be possible through the adaptation of the nature park concept to the specific conditions of the countries and areas concerned. An essential aspect of this adaptation process, however, is appreciation for the beliefs, traditions, organizations, systems, and modes of exploitation of the local populations, and the integration of these into a flexible conservation structure aimed at maintaining and developing sustainable, nondestructive practices as well as preserving the natural environment.

Particular attention should be paid to common property regimes where the livelihood of the local people closely depends on the sustainable utilization of natural resources. Such systems should be maintained as much as possible, and strengthened both from a legal standpoint (e.g., by prohibiting access to the resource by outsiders) and from a scientific or technical point of view (e.g., by assisting with research). Indeed, far too often the efficacy of these systems and their conservation potential have been denied or overlooked; when they are exposed to outside influences, the result has been overexploitation and the destruction of natural habitats.

It is not sufficient, however, merely to recognize the importance of traditional, sustainable systems and then endeavor to maintain them; it is also essential to enlist the participation of local leaders or representatives in the management of the new types of protected areas that need to be developed. Examples of these kinds of parks are still few, but the success of those that have already been established, such as the Mapimi and Sian Ka'an biosphere reserves in Mexico, augurs well for the future.

The conservation of biological diversity in devel-oping countries, and in particular, in tropical areas where it is the richest, will require, among other things, the development of new institutions and the recruitment and training of competent staff. Most of the countries concerned, however, do not have the means to devote a sufficient share of their budget to conservation. It will, therefore, be necessary to go beyond the development of legal obligations and also raise sufficient financial resources and channel these resources to the areas where they are most needed. This is one of the objectives of the new Convention of Biological Diversity, which was originally proposed by IUCN and submitted by UNEP to all nations of the world for consideration before being opened for signature at the UNCED in Rio de Janeiro on 5 June 1992 (IUCN/ELC 1994). It came into force in December 1993.

The Convention is based on the principle that states are responsible for conserving their biological diversity for the benefit of present and future generations and that special provision is required to meet the needs of developing countries in this field. This language falls short of the original IUCN draft, which designated states as the "guardians" of biological diversity with an obligation to contribute to the conservation of their "common heritage."

The Convention explicitly recognizes that the extent to which the developing country parties implement their commitments under the Convention will depend on the financial and technical contributions made by the developed country parties. It therefore establishes a financial mechanism through which developed country parties undertake to supply "new and additional financial resources to enable developing country parties to meet the agreed full incremental costs to them of implementing measures which fulfil the obligations of this Convention." In return for this significant commitment, developed country parties secured agreement that the Global Environmental Facility of the World Bank should be used as the interim funding mechanism for the Convention. Now that the Convention has come into force, the Conference of the Parties will determine the policy, strategy, program priorities, and eligibility criteria relating to the access to and utilization of such resources (article 20).

The financial mechanism is clearly critical to the effectiveness of the new Convention. Without considerable transfers of money from industrialized to developing countries, it is increasingly unlikely that biological diversity as it exists today will survive. Adequate funding and appropriate allocation of resources are therefore of paramount importance for the future of wild plant species.

CHAPTER 10

Economics and Plant Conservation

How is a balance achieved between use of plants and the preservation of botanical diversity? Attitudes about this dilemma are highly divergent, reflecting fundamental cultural and religious differences. The debate is made more intense by the growing realization that as nonrenewable resources are consumed, those remaining increase in importance. Such resources are a reservoir of opportunities for future generations. Many different questions can be asked about the use of biodiversity (Hanemann 1988): Is economic growth harmful to biodiversity? What aspects of growth are harmful? How can harmful effects be mitigated or avoided? What are the appropriate economic tools to assess biodiversity? How does one equate various types of values?

Economists have much to contribute to the debate, especially in the area of economic efficiency, but efficiency needs to be tempered by equity and value judgments. Resource economists have an obligation to measure, explain, and predict how individuals and institutions manage natural resource systems, value biological diversity, and make decisions affecting its preservation in a context of natural justice.

Because available natural resources (in a sense, stocks of natural capital) may place a serious constraint on future consumption and utilization, conservation is a necessary consideration for sustainable development. It is one of the foundations of continued economic growth. Conservation of natural resources increasingly is a major concern of both conservationists and developers (McNeely 1988). Development agencies are becoming concerned about the depletion of species and ecosystems as they realize that development itself depends on maintenance of natural biological systems. How to prevent overexploitation of biological systems is a major challenge to late twentieth-century society. The following crucial questions face most countries today (McNeely 1988): How can development be managed so that biological resources are best used to sustain development? Which economically attractive land uses are compatible with the conservation of biological diversity? What economic incentives promote conservation instead of overexploitation?

Even once there is commitment to conservation, the resources available to implement that policy are likely to be limited. Decisions about priority then must be made. Which species will be conserved ahead of others? Which courses of action give better value for money than others in terms of the amount of diversity preserved? Such decisions may lead to the abandonment of some species (and possibly their extinction) while others are targeted for funding. Furthermore, the costs and benefits must be assessed for various types of gene banks, botanic gardens, and nature reserves.

Yet a cost-benefit analysis is unlikely to yield a dependable answer to the dilemma. For a variety of valuation methods there is apparently a smattering of empirical applications (Randall 1988). What really impedes progress in the struggle to define the value of biological diversity is lack of political will, disagreement over the fundamental relationship of people to nature, and a predominance of self-interest. Until these problems are overcome, there is unlikely to be resolution of the conflicts between conservation and exploitative development.

Environmental problems themselves are difficult to define. The term has come into fashion only in the last few decades, especially with the rapid growth of the environmental movement in the affluent, industrialized countries since the 1960s. The obvious common dimensions to environmental problems are their dependence on many interacting social and resource factors, threatened survival for a wide range of organisms, and threatened quality of life for humans (Figure 10.1). Once the carrying capacity of an environment is exceeded, a reduction in survival rate or decreased standard of living is inevitable. Thus, high rates of population growth and higher rates for consumption of resources are two major driving forces that cause carrying capacities to be exceeded and environmental problems to result (Watt et al. 1977). All of this has been fueled by the premise that growth results in a better life for everyone, an assertion that may be true in some instances but not in others.

Many professional biologists care about the con-tinued existence of wildlife. Yet this attitude is in conflict with beliefs held by other people. Many species that are threatened with extinction are harvested or occupy habitats that are in high demand for human use—agriculture, water, timber and mineral extraction, or recreation. This greatly complicates planning for the maintenance of diversity and viable populations of wild species.

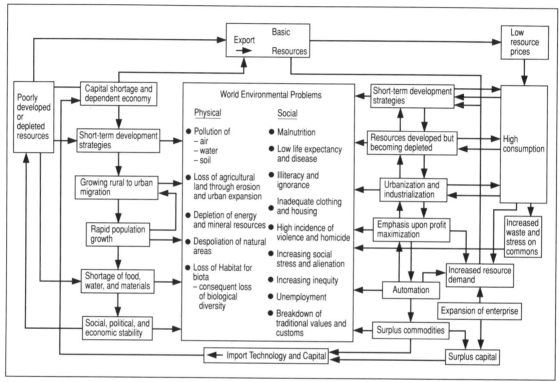

Figure 10.1. Interrelationships of world environmental problems. (Reproduced by permission from Watt et al. 1977)

Valuing Resources

In assigning value to natural resources, one must deal with preferences of both individuals and groups of people (Hanemann 1988). Preferences differ markedly from one person to another, varying according to environment and tradition as well as immediate context. A person acting in a public role may place a different weight on the welfare of future generations than he or she would when acting in a purely private role or as a developer or consumer. Furthermore, what people state in theory may not agree with what they do in practice.

Value and benefits of plant species, ecosystems, and biological diversity frequently are underesti-mated. It is important to point out that biological di-versity relates to most facets of people's lives. In fact, biological resources really are beyond value: their raw materials underpin every economic activity and many human preferences. But many people, corporations, and governments have yet to realize this (McNeely 1988). They need to have demonstrated the contribution species and ecosystems make to national economics.

Several methods have been devised to demonstrate these values. In part, these methods reflect the various ways in which people look at the world. Whether consciously or unconsciously, people classify the world of nature into what they perceive as useful and what seems useless or harmful. This tends to be a rather arbitrary process, but it does reflect a fundamental division of values into those that are essentially *anthropocentric* (human interest values) and those that do not depend on human interest. Traditional economics tends mostly to be concerned with *demand values*—those aspects of direct benefit to humanity (McNeely 1988). Values can be classified as follows as direct or indirect. Direct values include consumptive use value and productive use value—both demand values. Indirect values includes nonconsumptive use value, an intrinsic and transformative value; option value, a demand value; and existence value, an intrinsic value.

CONSUMPTIVE USE VALUE

This value applies to products that are consumed directly, without passing through a market. It can include such values as recreational experience. Consumptive use values seldom appear in national economic statements, but have considerable importance. Fuelwood is a consumptive value of high importance in rural tropical communities. A study of the use of trees by four indigenous Amazonian indians showed that the percentage of tree species used varied from 48 to 79 (Prance et al. 1987). In many countries fuelwood may provide 80–90 percent of primary energy needs, much of it gathered by users. Consumptive use value can be assigned a price in various ways. Perhaps the easiest is to estimate market value as if the goods were sold on the open market.

PRODUCTIVE USE VALUE

This value is often included in budgets and economic statements because it is more readily estimated than most others. It is the value assigned to products that are commercially harvested. Species do not have to be directly harvested as food or fuel to have direct productive use value. Plants harvested as raw products for drugs, for instance, have productive use value, this being related to the value of the end product. Productive use values can be high: counting all benefits involved, including social benefits, the value of plant-based drugs ranges from U.S. $200 billion to $1.8 trillion annually for all OECD countries (Principe 1988).

It is in developing countries that the contribution of wild plants is greatest in direct economic terms. In the humid tropics, the use of natural forests for wood export industries is usually a major source of income. Even in the United States, a detailed analysis of the contributions of wild plants and animals showed that about 4.5 percent of gross domestic product is attributable to wild species (McNeely 1988).

Direct economic values can increase rapidly as alternative sources become unavailable. As an example,

until the late 1960s, sperm oil from sperm whales was the only commercial source of liquid wax. Up to that time, 50 to 55 million tons were exported from the United States alone. Cessation of whale hunting led to the search for alternative sources. A naturally occurring liquid wax was discovered in the jojoba—a shrub of desert regions in the southwestern United States. Jojoba oil has a wide range of uses and in the early 1980s sold to Japan for U.S. $3000 per barrel (Myers 1983).

NONCONSUMPTIVE USE VALUE

Environmental resources do not have to be consumed or traded to have value. Nonconsumptive uses include a wide range of processes and functions such as photosynthetic activity, maintenance of water cycles, climate regulation, and pollutant degradation. It also includes such activities as recreational and esthetic enjoyment, education, scientific research, and inspirational benefits (the so-called transformative values) of natural environments (McNeely 1988).

At the local level, estimates of some of these benefits are not difficult to appreciate. In North America the value of coastal marshes, which provide primary productivity for fisheries, was determined in 1984 as almost U.S. $5000 per hectare per year (McNeely 1988). Tourism offers examples of nonconsumptive use benefits, although the role of plants often is not fully appreciated and probably is underestimated, especially when the dependence of animals on plants is considered. Estimates of nonconsumptive benefits on a global scale are more difficult to determine, especially regarding climate regulation and storage, and cycling of essential nutrients.

OPTION VALUE

Option value encompasses future uncertainties and the argument that society should prepare for unpredictable events. The best approach is usually assumed to be maximization of options and a safety net of diversity. This means maintaining as many gene pools as possible, particularly of potentially useful wild species (Prescott-Allen and Prescott-Allen 1986). Unfortunately, it is very difficult to know today what may be the useful plants of tomorrow, or to know precisely how much genetic diversity is going to be needed in the future. Lack of knowledge adds to this difficult situation: so few plants have been tested for useful characteristics, and knowledge of traditional uses for others is being lost.

Serendipity clearly is a significant aspect of option value, as indicated by the frequency of new discoveries from natural sources. It is likely that the rate of new discoveries will be enhanced in the future by (1) new breakthroughs in biotechnology, (2) the need for new alternatives to exploit lower-grade resources or to exploit them with less environmental damage, and (3) new needs created by novel technology.

Conservationists have emphasized the potential for species, especially those not yet discovered or investigated, to have uses as foods, genetic material, chemical sources, drug plants, and so on. Yet appeals to option value are difficult to incorporate into economic analyses; the unknown defies quantification. Still, a continuous progression of discoveries of new benefits from natural ecosystems and plant species shows that option value is significantly greater than zero (McNeely 1988).

Existence value

People can attach importance to species that they are unlikely ever to see, simply because they get satisfaction from knowing the species exist. Most people will never see Galapagos Islands iguanas and tortoises, but this does not lessen the appeal (or mystique) of these organisms. Existence values generate sympathy and concern, and are well illustrated in the use of *flag species* such as pandas, koalas, and wild primates to publicize conservation. Values of this type are very hard to quantify in monetary terms; however, the magnitude of voluntary contributions to conservation agencies does provide an indication. For WWF International, it amounts to nearly U.S. $100 million per year (McNeely 1988).

Bequest value is another aspect of existence value. It is the satisfaction derived from conserving resources now in order to benefit those living in the future. Bequest value is difficult to calculate when we do not know precise needs in the future, but it can provide a strong motivating force in people.

Both direct and indirect methods for determining people's preferences for various values have limitations (Hanemann 1988). One limitation is that every study or economic program generates winners and losers. Somehow recommendations for policy need to accommodate these limitations. It is difficult accurately to predict future demands and resources; both historical accidents and technological breakthrough play havoc with such predictions. There is, finally, the problem of attempting to establish the value people place on biodiversity, which is itself a value judgment that can be questioned.

There are other fundamental problems. Many species and ecosystems have values that do not have obvious expression in monetary terms. We do not necessarily have sufficient knowledge to convert such values accurately to monetary terms and so equate them with other values.

Consequently, in addition to the known values that economists note with respect to some small number of species, they also calculate an option value for species of unknown worth. . . . If placing a dollar figure on these option values seems a daunting task, the situation is actually far worse that it first seems. Calculations of option value can only be begun after we identify a species, guess what uses that species might have, place some dollar value on those uses, and estimate the likelihood of such discoveries occurring at any future date (so that we can discount the values across time). Once we've done all that, we can try to figure out how to translate those future, possible values into present dollars. I think that it is safe to say that despite the great theoretical interest in assigning use and option values to species, and some impressive strides in modelling these formally, it may be a long time before the total value of even one species can be stated in terms of present dollars (Norton 1988: 202).

Nevertheless, policymakers will want to put a monetary value on plant conservation. It is important that they appreciate the full range and nature of values, the sources of values, and the circumstances under which different values will dominate. Whatever figures are honestly arrived at, the actual benefits (including nonresource benefits) are always likely to be greater than estimated.

Many plants have direct economic value (Prescott-Allen and Prescott-Allen 1982; Myers 1983). Tropical rain forests in the Americas and Asia yield a number of latexes that provide income to local communities. Gutta percha from *Palaquium gutta* and closely related species, principally in Malaysia and Indonesia, is used in golf balls. Other latexes end up in the higher grades of chewing gum and bubble gum, and lower grades are used to make a range of synthetic products. Examples of these latexes are chicle from the sapote (*Manilkara zapota*), found wild throughout Central America; balata, letchi caspi, and sorva gum from *Couma rigida* and *C. macrocarpa,* trees of the Amazon basin; and jelutong or pontianale from *Dyera polyphylla,* which is restricted to peat swamp forests in Borneo.

Seaweeds are an important commodity, almost entirely gathered from the wild. Some such as the green sea lettuce *Ulva, Caulerpa,* and some brown seaweeds (e.g., *Sargassum* and *Turbinaria*) are important foods in some countries. Seaweeds provide valuable gums:

agar, algin, and carrageenan. Other seaweed extracts are used in a variety of products ranging from paints and dyes, building materials, and sealing compounds, to paper products, fire extinguishing foams, and cosmetics.

The biggest selling wild nut species is the Brazil nut (*Bertholletia excelsa*), which forms large natural stands in the Amazon basin. Brazil is the largest producer of this nut with an annual production of more than 50,000 tons. Pistachio is another highly valuable nut; although most commercial production comes from cultivated *Pistacia vera,* wild trees also account for a significant proportion of output (about 60,000 tons a year). Roughly one-third of the total harvest of allspice, and one-quarter in terms of value, comes from wild trees. Several substitutes for the spice cardamom are chiefly or entirely gathered from wild sources. They include bastard cardamom from Thailand and melegueta pepper from West Africa.

Different approaches to valuation are relevant at different levels (McNeely 1988). Consumptive use value is often most relevant at the village level, but at the national level productive use value expressed in foreign exchange opportunities tends to be more relevant. Wealthy individuals or nations emphasize option value, and the world community is likely to be interested in existence value and nonconsumptive values. Development assistance agencies increasingly work on rehabilitation of degraded ecosystems. For them, replacement value is highly relevant.

Whatever methodology is used, valuation is only the first step. It informs planners and local people about how important biological diversity may be to local government objectives, and may demonstrate that an area is important for the biological resources it contains. The second step is to determine how these areas can be conserved. It is here that economic incentives and disincentives can play their important role—ensuring that the benefits suggested in step 1 are, in fact, delivered to the community, and that the community, in turn, is empowered to protect the resources upon which its continued prosperity depends (McNeely 1988).

In general, it is appropriate for conservation to be supported through the marketplace, but the marketplace needs to be established through appropriate policies from central government (McNeely 1989b). There are ways and means of making funding for conservation and aid arrangements attractive, and of compensating the public for its support of nonconsumptive use of natural resources. Such funding and compensation must be innovative. It is important, also, to understand that although conservation agencies probably never have sufficient funding (the need for additional funding is infinite), even generous budgets will not lead to conservation if policies in other sectors are incompatible with conservation. Therefore, new funding and incentives need to be part of a package that includes appropriate policy changes.

The fundamental problems really are ethical rather than monetary. Is there inherent wrongness in reducing biodiversity? What dangers does loss of biodiversity pose? How are limited resources allocated so that they can be best conserved? How do we allocate values to organisms that are minute or not even discovered? Are any forms of life so useless as to deserve elimination? To base conservation on the marketplace and even to give conservation respectability by attempting to express values in monetary terms is to invite disaster.

If quality of life is to be a sustainable optimum, it follows that environmental problems will have to be kept at a minimum (Watt et al. 1977). This means satisfying basic physical and social needs for human development, and maintaining balance between ecosystems and economic systems. These are the fundamental dimensions of that illusive concept of quality of life, details of which differ from one society to the next.

Despite contemporary stress on economic analysis, market-driven economics is not a compelling final arbiter providing the ultimate rationale for resource use and, particularly, for preservation of a diversity of species and ecosystems. Market-driven economics provides a series of approaches to some aspects of the problems of assessing value, utilization, and preservation, both now and for the future. The way to get the environment onto the economic agenda is to demonstrate that the environment matters to national economies (Pearce 1988). But it is changed attitudes toward other people and biodiversity, and a new respect for both, that will provide and maintain the appropriate clothes for planet earth.

CASE STUDY: THE POTENTIAL VALUE OF *ZEA DIPLOPERENNIS*

In the late 1970s, a young Mexican botanist made an astounding discovery. He was searching for wild relatives of corn, particularly *Zea perennis,* a perennial teosinte thought to be extinct since the 1920s. He found the perennial teosinte in a remote mountain site, but nearby found a similar plant that was eventually determined as a species not previously known to exist. This new species was a diploid capable of producing fertile offspring when crossed with annual corn (maize).

Perennial habit is only one of this plant's traits that can

be bred into corn, and may not even be the most valuable. *Zea diploperennis* is immune to several important viral and mycoplasmal diseases, and in several instances represents the only known source of such germ plasm for corn. Testing has revealed resistent genes for foliar and root pathogens as well as insect pests such as corn earworms, stalk borers, and rootworms. It may provide genes for greater stalk and root strength, multiple ears (fruits), and tolerance to poorly drained soil. All of these are traits with considerable economic potential for the future of one of the world's most widely grown crops, which is worth U.S. $50 billion.

Source: Iltis 1988.

Genetic information and species value

It is tempting to argue that most, if not all, conservation of endangered species is of economic value for the genetic information that will be preserved now and in the future. The information carried on the genetic code (as distinguished from the code itself) is a resource that can be assigned value. The full content and resource of the genetic code can only be estimated in quite crude terms. Nevertheless, any human activity that leads to a marked reduction in numbers of individuals of organisms, or that eliminates certain individuals with particular characteristics, can be assumed to reduce the total stock of genetic information. The result: a risk for everything that derives from the stock of genetic information.

There are several reasons why it is important to consider genetic information a resource. The total plant genetic resource is fundamental to the well-being of all humanity because we depend on the carriers of genetic information for our food, clothing, and shelter. It represents the stock of information from which people obtain a flow of benefits. If equity is considered (the fair sharing of resources among all people), then a case can be made for conserving all genetic information. Nevertheless, equity involves consideration of both present and future needs, and,

> Where there is potential loss of information, a balance must be sought between the costs of manipulation on future generations, and the costs of preservation on the present generation . . . and . . . in deciding on an equable distribution of property rights all possible users of the genetic resource must be given consideration. It is not enough just to consider those with an economic interest in the resource (Blackford et al. 1986: 34).

Another aspect of genetic information and species

values is efficiency (in the sense of welfare economics). Allocative efficiency occurs when the utility of one member of society cannot be improved without a corresponding or greater loss of utility by another member. In economic terms, an ideal output situation is attained when the price (marginal benefit) of all goods is simultaneously equal to the (social) marginal costs (Mishan 1982 in Blackford et al. 1986). Efficiency cannot be applied to genetic information by itself, but only to the information and the package (species) within which it occurs.

This question of efficiency is of particular concern in the management of threatened species, when conservationists attempt to trade off present costs against future benefits. Use value (the realistic, expected value of future benefits), existence value (mere existence of genetic diversity), and bequest value (value from knowingly providing an inheritance for future generation) are each components of the total value society places on genetic diversity and willingness to pay for preservation of a gene pool. Because a greater range of uses are likely to be found for species in the future, it can be assumed that future generations will assign greater value to genetic diversity than is done at present.

To use efficiency as a criterion for determining how much genetic variation should be conserved (in practical terms likely to be measured as number of individuals to be retained in a population), one can compare the *marginal social costs* (MSC) of preserving diversity now with the *marginal social benefits* (MSB) of preserving it now and in the future (Figure 10.2). Modeling indicates that if a particular population is large enough to be sustainable, then the MSC becomes progressively steeper as more individuals are preserved; this represents the cost of acquiring or protecting increasing areas of habitat. This cost might be extremely high where agricultural land is in short supply and there are extreme food shortages. In contrast, if the target plant population is below the critical size required to sustain it, then the MSC of preserving the first few individuals is very high but progressively decreases as more individuals are preserved. When MSB are considered, values increase from low levels for few individuals to a maximum, but then decline sharply as more and more individuals are included without adding further significant genetic information; these extra individuals essentially replicate those already present. The intersection of MSC and MSB, in a viable and sustainable population, indicates the optimum size of population (number of individuals) that should be preserved.

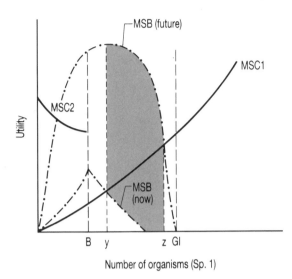

Figure 10.2. The marginal social cost (MSC) of preserving a species or population and marginal social benefit (present and future) from genetic information. MSC1 represents the marginal social cost of preserving individuals where the starting population is large and naturally sustainable; MSC2 represents the same where the population is too small for this; MSB (now) is the sum of all present benefits of the species; MSB (future) is the sum of all future benefits that genetic diversity might provide for the species in the future. (Reproduced by permission from Blackford et al. 1986)

This approach leads to the following conclusions on the basis of economics, but not necessarily on moral grounds (Blackford et al. 1986). First, in terms of their genetic information, all organisms do not need to be preserved. Second, preservation of remaining individuals of a population below a theoretical lower limit of long-term sustainability will involve high costs and potentially low benefits in terms of information because of the continuing high risk of extinction. Third, the precise point at which socially optimal preservation and manipulation will occur is dependent on the moral stance adopted by the present generation toward future generations, and is reflected by the equity criterion.

It is important to note that highly endangered species that have been reduced to extremely low numbers are likely to have lost a significant amount of genetic information. Even when numbers are increased, for instance by a propagation and translocation program, the total genetic information will remain at a reduced level. Consideration of the genetic information view is therefore an argument for conserving maximum biodiversity by not allowing particular species and populations to decline to low levels. Off-site conservation will conserve existing levels of genetic information but not increase it. It does also increase the chances that the remaining information will be passed onto the next generation.

Perhaps one of the most painful conclusions that can be made from analyses based on value of genetic information is that there may be little value in preserving some species, because their genetic information content is small and not diverse and their contribution to the total genetic information of the living world is negligible. Many endangered species would not confer high enough benefits to warrant expending the effort to save them from extinction. This is not the same as saying that they should not be conserved: there are other valid reasons for conserving, such as consideration of transformative and intrinsic values. What the genetic information approach indicates is that there are limits beyond which it is unsafe to push arguments for conservation based on demand values and utility.

This approach also indicates that consideration should be given to the relative merits and costs of conserving species that are highly distinctive in terms of genetic information value and others that are not. Thus one might put greater priority on conserving a threatened monotypic genus or a more common but highly distinctive and genetically isolated species, rather than all members of an assemblage of closely related species. There may be arguments for conserving all of the latter (for instance, lost opportunities to study recent evolution), but those arguments will have a different and noneconomic basis.

The Costs of Development

Technology now allows exploitation of natural resources at rates inconceivable to previous generations. A greater part of the resource can be taken at one bite, whether the method be mining, forestry, conversion of land for agriculture, or use of land for roads and housing. Rapid and unsustainable exploitation is likely when undifferentiated economic growth predominates—sometimes described as growthmania. Such undifferentiated growth tends to display certain features (Watt et al. 1977). It assumes that all societies must follow the same path to development, that traditional values are backward, and that promised economic take-off never happens. It ignores or does not anticipate the detrimental ecological consequences of growth, and finally, gaps between the standard of living in developed and underdeveloped countries increase.

Each of these features put pressure on the environment, and collectively they result in few resources being available to counter ecosystem degradation and loss. This does not mean that growth and development should be rejected. What is important is to avoid the assumption that the conventional pattern of undifferentiated growth of industrialized societies is the only appropriate development strategy. Each society has its own peculiarities, needs, priorities, and carrying capacity that needs to be carefully considered.

It is important to investigate the costs of exploitation when planning for long-term conservation of plants. A frequently taken attitude is that there are only two choices with respect to a resource—utilization or preservation—and that these are mutually incompatible. With care, systems of management can ensure that biological resources not only survive but that some will prosper under use. Unfortunately, many current development programs deplete biological resources at rates that render them essentially nonrenewable. Fundamentally, what drives rampant exploitation of natural resources is self-interest and emphasis on short-term benefits from exploitation. Six major factors leading to overexploitation of biological resources are discussed here (McNeely 1988).

BIOLOGICAL RESOURCES OFTEN ARE NOT GIVEN APPROPRIATE PRICES IN THE MARKETPLACE

Resources may have associated values that are not reflected in prices. Biological diversity is "public good," and individuals and industries can often gain its benefits without paying for them (the free-rider problem). The often intangible and widespread costs of depleting biological diversity usually provide ineffectual justification for conservation when balanced against projected monetary benefits of exploitation (which typically accrue to relatively few individuals).

THE BENEFITS OF PROTECTING NATURAL AREAS AND THEIR COMPONENT SPECIES ARE SELDOM FULLY REPRESENTED IN ECONOMIC ANALYSES

Some benefits of conserving biological resources (for example social benefits) are often intangible, widely spread, and not fully reflected in market prices. In contrast, the benefits of exploiting the resources supported by natural areas are often easily measured. Economic analyses usually underestimate the net benefits of conservation or overestimate the net benefits of exploitative alternatives. In short, today's land-use patterns are determined primarily by the rent-producing capacity of the area in question, irrespective of its value to society in a more natural state.

SOCIAL AND ECONOMIC COSTS OF EXPLOITATION ARE UNFAIRLY APPORTIONED

Those who benefit from exploiting seldom pay the full social and economic costs of their actions. Instead, these costs are transferred to society as a whole, or to individuals and institutions who had gained little benefit from the original exploitations. Such external costs are often accidental side effects of development projects, so the loss is not recognized in either private or social economic analyses. Timber concessionaires, for example, do not usually need to concern themselves with the downstream siltation they are causing, or the species they are depleting, because they do not pay the full cost of these effects. Once they leave, the downstream farmer generally pays for the siltation damage and the nation at large pays for flood protection as well as the reduction in biological diversity. It may well be that the greatest cause of the reduction in global biological diversity is inadvertence, an external cost of the more direct financial justification for harvesting certain biological resources.

OWNERSHIP RIGHTS MAY BE DIFFICULT TO ENFORCE

The species, ecosystems, and ecosystem services that are most overexploited tend to be the ones with the weakest ownership. Many of these are open access resources, sometimes held as common property, for which the traditional control mechanisms have failed or been overruled in the face of growing demands by centralized government, national development, international trade, and population growth. Publicly owned resources tend to be treated as free commodities for exploitation by concessionaires. When ownership rights are weakly enforced (either by the government or by a private owner), exploitation is allocated not to those who value the resource most, but rather to those who can pay the most for the exploitation rights. Where there is high consumer demand, the costs of protecting species and ecosystems from exploitation are often prohibitive for owners who often lack resources and local knowledge of management skills to control overexploitation. Common property rights are a major issue in developing countries (Bromley 1986). Many natural resources are held in collective ownership; their exploitation can result in tensions as individual and social preferences clash. Conservation may be the optimal strategy for the collective owners, but not necessarily for each individual owner.

INAPPROPRIATE DISCOUNT RATES MAY BE USED

Economic analysis usually discounts future benefits and costs because people tend to value benefits sooner rather than later. Future costs are of less significance than today's costs. Capital value is assigned in terms of its present opportunity cost. The higher the discount rate, the greater the likelihood that a biological resource will be exploited. When discount rates are high and biological growth rates are low (as in whales or tropical forests), the economically efficient use of a resource may be to deplete it, even to extinction.

CONVENTIONAL MEASURES OF NATIONAL INCOME
DO NOT ACCURATELY MEASURE THE EFFECTS
OF RESOURCE DEPLETION

Conventional measures of national income (such as per capita GNP) "do not recognize the drawing down of the stock of natural capital, and instead consider the depletion of resources, that is, the loss of wealth, as net income" (Warford 1987). Many of the national economies of the tropics are based on biological resources, especially forests, which are being depleted at a rate faster than the net formation of capital. As a result, the total assets of the economy are declining even if per capita GNP is growing. Even in countries where this problem is not obvious, there may be more subtle depletion, for example, loss of essential soil elements and water quality as a result of intensive agriculture. Warford (1987) estimates that the economic costs of unsustainable forest depletion in major tropical hardwood exporting countries ranges between 4 and 6 percent of GNP, offsetting any economic growth that may otherwise have been achieved. Growth built on resource depletion is clearly very different from that obtained from productive efforts.

The ultimate aim of good stewardship should be to eliminate or negate the effects of these factors. As a preliminary step, people must be made aware of the true costs involved in exploitation and the inadequacy of conventional economic analyses and economic growth indices with respect to environmental depletion. Stewardship is not even possible unless two commonly held views are banished: (1) the assumption that vegetation will quickly recover from exploitation, and (2) that the main purpose of vegetation is simply to clothe the landscape and give a neutral cover to soil (i.e., the species composition does not matter so long as some sort of plants are present—preferably exploitable ones).

Good stewardship involves awareness of the problems along with a commitment to manage land well. Whatever is done—develop or preserve—must be by deliberate choice and not default. Use of natural resources should be sustainable (or involve very low rates of depletion) and should be based on a consideration of all values and benefits, human and other. True costs, including both direct and indirect social costs, should be reflected, costs should be correctly apportioned, and adequate biological diversity should be preserved at all levels—genetic, species, and ecosystem.

The Costs of Conservation

Many developers see denials or restrictions on rate of use of a resource as a lost opportunity. But there is no free lunch, even for conservation. Conservation and preservation involve costs and sacrifices as do development and utilization of a resource. The question is, Who ultimately pays for conservation?

In the past, land allocated for conservation often was land that was not wanted for any other purpose—apparently valueless land. Increasingly, conflicts arise between those who want to preserve land for conservation and those who recognize the land's value for other purposes, especially mining, agriculture, and housing. Exploitation is often an attractive short-term proposition. If an indebted nation gives up short-term benefits for long-term advantages, or gives up utilization of a natural resource in the interests of preservation, it will want to know, Will those who advocate this compensate for lost financial income or assist in setting up alternative industries?

The countries with the highest levels of biodiversity are often those least able to pay for conservation. It is not surprising that such biologically rich but economically impoverished nations are criticized when they seek to use natural resources. What they often deserve is constructive assistance, not condemnation. This is a particular challenge for the 1990s; it is a problem that will not go away and that will become more acute. It is easy to speak out about what should be done with someone else's property and someone else's resources, but it is not helpful to exhort a course of action while standing back and not even demonstrating how it may be accomplished. Worse, it is hypocritical to criticize lack of conservation action while indirectly contributing to the problem. Such hypocrisy comes in the form of condemnation of forest destruction in the tropics, while allowing companies to exploit these same forests. It also includes the importation and use of products by a developed country not prepared to pay a realistic price to a developing nation.

The concept of *marginal opportunity cost* (MOC) is useful in conservation and preservation efforts. MOC is the true cost borne by society for an action or policy that depletes a biological resource. The "opportunity cost" refers to a value corresponding to the best alternative use to which a resource could be put, if it were not being used for the purpose being costed (McNeely 1988).

To demonstrate the use of MOC, a tract of land may be set aside as a nature reserve but may include stands of timber desirable for lumber. If setting the site aside as a reserve is the highest valued alternative use, then the opportunity cost of logging is the value of the nature reserve. Logging costs need to include this cost as well as the opportunity costs of labor and equipment needed to extract the trees. MOC may not always help in deciding whether to preserve or exploit such an area, but it may at least indicate the level of compensation that should be paid to developers. MOC involves three distinct elements (McNeely 1988): the direct and indirect cost to the user of depleting a biological resource, the benefits foregone by those who might have used the resource in the future (the option value), and the costs imposed on others (external costs).

The following difficulties are sometimes encountered in the application of MOC: different viewpoints over what constitutes reasonable expectations for costs, setting of profits, and choices of discount rates; exaggerated claims about development potential; and insufficient funding for compensation. Despite these, MOC probably constitutes a useful framework for assessing values of biological resources and applying these values to decision making. It focuses attention on the relationship between contemporary acts of resource depletion and their effects elsewhere in the economy and in the future, and emphasizes the role of renewable natural resources in resource use. Through MOC, development and environmental preservation are seen as interconnected (Pearce 1987).

Devices such as MOC remind people that conservation carries costs that rapidly escalate as competing claims for land use increase. As population levels rise and areas of natural habitat decrease, conservation agencies and developers alike will be under increasing pressure to assess the value of natural resources and to justify their actions.

International Trade and Foreign Aid

Civilization, at least since the Middle Ages, has been founded on trade, and in today's world, international trade is essential to the survival of nations. Nevertheless, trade and the development of a global economy sit alongside increasing human population levels and the effects of industrial and agricultural pollutants as one of three major factors that strains global ecosystems.

International trade has enabled the entire world to draw on the globe's collection of ecosystems, feeding the growing population of the world but sometimes at the expense of overexploited local resources. It requires foreign exchange, which most tropical countries earn from the exploitation of natural resources. Inevitably, this can lead to increased consumption of biological resources at unsustainable rates (McNeely 1988).

The "economic way of thinking sustains the global exchange economy" (Norgaard 1988, 209). It requires specialization of people, tools, and land in those economic activities where they have an advantage, leaving each producer with a surplus of products available for trade. In farming, for instance, diverse crops have been replaced by monocultures. A byproduct of this is a large reduction in the number of supporting species such as wild plants, soil fungi, pest predators, and pollinators. Participation in the global exchange economy transforms agricultural systems because it forces farmers to maintain a competitive edge while maintaining a commonality in use of fertilizers, pesticides, and high-yielding cultivars. This, in turn, reduces overall biodiversity (Ehrlich and Ehrlich 1981; Norgaard 1988).

Problems are magnified by fundamental differences between developed (mainly temperate) countries and the less-developed countries of the tropics. The countries of the developed world, where the average per capita income amounts to more than U.S. $9500, have less than a quarter of the people in the world but control about 80 percent of the global economy. The less-developed world, with an average per capita income of about U.S. $870, controls the rest. The developed countries consume about 80 percent of the total world supply of energy, and two-thirds of the food. Another index of the disproportionate distribution of wealth among the peoples of the world is the consumption of strategic metals. The consumption of iron, copper, and aluminum by developed countries ranges from 86 to 92 percent, and that of the less-developed countries, in this case even including China, from 8 to 14 percent (Raven 1986b).

On the basis of these figures, one might conclude that the less-developed countries of the tropics and subtropics are insignificant in the global economy and can be safely ignored. The stability of both developed and developing countries, however, is critical to economic and political stability worldwide. Despite their economic poverty, many tropical countries are rich in natural resources and have large populations of potential consumers. Countries like Japan are highly dependent on stable overseas markets to sell exports. But they are also very dependent on stable sources of supply for raw products (often obtained from less-developed countries).

In the case of Japan, about 87 percent of raw energy; 69 percent of its wood, lumber, and zinc; over 90 percent of its iron ore, tin, and copper; and all of its aluminum and nickel is imported. The continued ability to obtain these imported goods, and to maintain the precarious balance whereby Japan continues to produce about 70 percent of its food, depends on maintenance of an ecologically and economically healthy order throughout the world (Raven 1986b). If anything, the less-developed countries are more dependent than developed areas on trade with industrialized countries.

To state these relationships in a different way, a quarter of the people in the world, with a proportion rapidly dropping in size, are controlling more than four-fifths of the world's goods, and a majority of the people in the world, which is rapidly increasing in size, has access to no more than a sixth of any commodity involved in the world's productivity (Raven 1986b). It is therefore ironic that the less-developed countries of the tropics and subtropics hold so much biodiversity. To conserve this asset at the global level requires significant change in the trade and international relations policies of industrialized nations. Progress is already in evidence as aid agencies in industrialized countries are beginning to channel support into sustainable development activities and conservation of biological resources. But the potential of this often remains limited by the trade and foreign policies of these same industrialized countries.

Overpopulation places pressure on natural resources through both direct impact and the need to clear land for agriculture. But many of the crops grown are for export, to gain urgently needed foreign exchange. The example of northern Africa is instructive. In 1984, Sahelian countries harvested almost seven times as much cotton as in 1961 and imported almost nine times as much cereal grain. The cash crop trade is supported by virtually all Sahelian governments on the grounds that it earns foreign exchange to buy manufactured goods from the industrial countries, attracts support from development aid programs, and brings commercial investment from Europe. The expansion of cotton and peanut production has driven many subsistence farmers onto marginal lands too dry for farming, turning semiarid land to desert with often disastrous results for both humans and the biological resources that support them (McNeely 1988).

Government needs for foreign exchange have often led to a range of incentives, which, in turn, have resulted in overexploitation of biological resources and reduction of the economic viability of sustainable forms of development. Investments in conservation projects by aid agencies and nongovernmental organizations are welcomed by governments throughout Africa (McNeely 1988), but most of them are doomed to be overwhelmed by the more powerful trade imperatives.

What are the main problems inherent in emphasizing cash crops for export? Crops are no longer supporting the local people, but instead feed the demands of distant markets. They often require imported energy in the form of agricultural chemicals. Because they are not responding to local conditions of supply and demand, no real limit is placed on the impact that such crops can have on delicately balanced agricultural systems that have developed over long periods of time. What are needed are efforts to ensure that staple crops for local use are also produced and that there is equable sharing of export earnings.

The earnings from trade can be both positive and negative. They build up capital, which can be used to better people's way of life and to introduce appropriate technology. Yet protectionism in some developed countries works against this by restricting the ability of these countries to trade fairly. In conjunction with unrealistic commodity prices, this can set a formula for disaster. Trade itself has an unpredictable nature. Restrictions can often undermine new investments, and it is clear that developing countries must navigate a treacherous course in seeking to build sustainable economies through international trade in biological resources (McNeely 1988).

To alleviate serious problems faced by developing countries, a range of types of assistance must be provided by industrial nations to less-developed countries on a greatly increased scale. In such programs, special attention must be paid to the problems of the poorest of the poor if the long-range aim is to promote regional stability. Such goals are served well, for example, by Japan's Green Corps program in Africa, which strives to restore and maintain the ecological balance of regions that have been devastated by unwise exploitation (Raven 1986b).

Sometimes internal economic policies related to trade, rather than trade itself, may promote technocentric attitudes. Sometimes governments institute perverse incentives for social reasons, disregarding the effects of these on the environment. In the tropics, some subsidies and price controls, while instituted for apparently good social and economic reasons, actually stress the environment and biodiversity, especially through pollution, needless land clearing, and resource depletion. Considerable problems have occurred in adapting new technologies to developing country needs; often these benefit the powerful, leaving the poor even more disadvantaged.

One solution would appear to be more diversified systems of farming. More integrated agro-ecosystems will require greater investment in research, marketing infrastructure, and extension. Nevertheless, they could be at least partly financed by a reallocation of funds through the removal of some subsidies, an effective system of water charges (e.g., increased taxes on irrigated lands), and the removal of credit subsidies for some cash crops. There are sometimes hidden or unintentional disincentives in the most well-meaning of aid programs. They may divert money from other, perhaps more essential projects, and are certainly likely to divert funds from primary conservation activities.

Another solution is in the realm of intermediate technology, whereby partnerships are formed between local entrepreneurs and nongovernmental organizations. Though transfer technology is one part of such arrangements, it does not necessarily involve transfer of the highly sophisticated technology of the developed countries. Intermediate technology make use of local, and sometimes abundant, materials. Fuels provide an example: in many tropical countries there is no shortage of harvest residues that are inedible for humans but which can be eaten by animals or used as fuel. Pakistan's discarded biofuels add up to the equivalent of 54 million barrels of oil a year. Simple technology can take such fuel sources and, for instance, by making briquettes, convert these to efficient fuels.

What can be done to minimize the negative impacts of economic incentives from international sources, and to turn them into positive incentives that have lasting value? The following basic principles apply (McNeely 1988):

- Develop local capacity to manage biological resources; strive for self-reliance rather than dependence. This includes helping to design sustainable sources of income for supporting personnel, equipment, and maintenance.

- Contribute to ensuring the long-term economic viability of protected areas, which includes designing systems of sustainable utilization of biological resources.

- Contribute to projects that are designed specifically to meet the needs of the management agency, not to mold that agency into a temperate-zone model.

- Enable conservation agencies to participate fully in regional and global conservation efforts, including the various conventions and treaties relevant to biological resource management.

- Treat both the symptoms and the causes of depletion of biological resources, recalling that the causes may be very far removed from the resource management agency.

- Promote the integration of biological resource conservation (based on the principles of sustainable development) into the larger development issues of the country.

The global adoption of Western knowledge and technologies has set disparate cultures on convergent paths. Worldwide the distinctive features of local environments are disappearing as people grow the same crops, introduce the same plants for gardening and landscaping, and cope with the same weeds. With an emphasis on global markets, global values, global social organizations, and global technologies, a global uniformity has resulted. And yet, possibly half of the projects of one major agency involving technology transfer in Africa have failed. The initial losers in such situations have been the ecosystems and plant and animal species (Norgaard 1988). The ultimate losers will be humanity.

International trade in tropical timber is of great concern to those working in conservation. Many tropical countries with large forest resources have provoked wasteful export-oriented timber booms by assigning harvesting rights to concessionaires for royalty, rent, and tax payments that are only a small fraction of the net commercial value of the log harvest.

Short-term leases compound the damage caused by these incentives; they encourage concessionaires to begin harvesting at once and to adopt royalty systems that encourage loggers to harvest only the best trees while doing enormous damage to the forest land. In response, logging entrepreneurs in several countries have leased virtually the entire productive forest area within a few years and have overexploited the resource as well as unwittingly opened it for clearing by slash-and-burn cultivators. The result has been wasteful exploitation of tropical forests, the sacrifice of most of their timber and nontimber values, enormous losses of potential revenue to the government, and at the same time the destruction of rich biological resources. Reform of forest revenue systems and concession terms could raise billions of dollars of revenues; promote more efficient, sustainable forest resource use; and curtail deforestation.

Deforestation also is driven by the promotion of tropical timber imports into certain developed countries, through low tariffs and favorable trade incentives, combined with weak domestic forest policies in the tropical countries and high costs and disincentives to harvesting in the industrial countries. The industrial countries typically import unprocessed logs from tropical countries, either duty-free or at minimal tariff rates, while imposing much higher tariffs and import restrictions on processed wood products. This encourages developed-country industries to use logs from tropical forests rather than their own, a pattern that is reinforced by domestic restrictions on the amounts that can be cut in domestic forests. The situation has been relieved somewhat by the establishment in 1986 of the International Tropical Timber Organization (ITTO), based in Yokohama, Japan, which seeks to rationalize trade flows. It is the first commodity agreement that incorporates a specific conservation component (Blockhus et al. 1992).

There is wide recognition of the fact that although it is important to monitor the international trade in tropical timber, current practices are inadequate. In particular, there is urgent need for more accurate information on trade in timber species. Agreements established by ITTO aim, among other things, to improve monitoring of the tropical timber trade, by both promoting the collection and dissemination of data and improving international standards and compatibility.

Incentives and disincentives

Incentives smooth the uneven distribution of the costs and benefits of conserving biological resources (McNeely 1988). They help prevent or mitigate anticipated negative impacts on local resources, and compensate people for any extraordinary losses through such controls. They also reward local people who assume burdens in order to benefit the rest of humanity. Finally, they can open up the decision-making process to the people who are most directly affected by conservation of biological resources.

In the economic climate of the 1980s and 1990s it was difficult to protect all the natural environments that conservation agencies and individuals wanted to preserve. New mechanisms and programs of incentives and disincentives to facilitate protection and conservation must be sought. A variety of incentives are available to moderate exploitation and to apply conservation policies (McNeely 1988). Among them are institutional mechanisms, especially government regulatory agencies, but including traditional means of decision making; research programs that determine limits, appropriate rates of utilization, and points of vulnerability; legislation, and its enactment and enforcement; and development of economic devices to encourage particular courses of action and to discourage others.

Whatever incentives are used, they should achieve two objectives: stimulation of conservation-oriented activities at a lower cost than the cost of economic benefits received, and cost–benefit ratios higher than those for more exploitive proposals also competing for development capital. Incentives can be direct or indirect. Direct fiscal incentives include cash subsidies, which can be expressed as fees, royalties, loans, or payment (in part or full) of wages. Direct incentives in kind include provision of material goods, concessions and licenses, work schemes, and donations of equipment and land. Indirect fiscal measures are concerned with channeling of funds toward conservation activities. Traditionally, these include tax exemptions, price supports, tariffs, insurance provisions, and guarantees of income.

Novel fiscal measures include debt swaps, which currently are being negotiated with several Latin American countries (McNeely et al. 1990). Provision of essential services and job retraining is an appropriate recompense for communities most affected by restraints on resource use. These incentives can be associated with accelerated development of sustainable industries, or redirection into nonexploitive industries. Social incentives concentrate on enhancing quality of life and discovering ways of relating to the environment through education.

Disincentives to promote good conservation also exist. Subsidies of exploited resources are one of the more insidious forms of conservation disincentive. In smaller countries, important decisions on development projects are frequently made by small, politically influential groups with vested interests in commercial logging, ranching, plantation cropping, and large-scale irrigated farming operations. Investment incentives, tax provisions, credit and land concessions, and agricultural pricing policies are likely to favor those with power, causing losses for the economy as a whole.

Discount rates can be an incentive or disincentive. They involve estimating use of a resource in the future as against its use now. The problem of setting appropriate discount rates is compounded by the uncertainties that lie ahead. Frequent natural disasters, such as floods and storms, may be an incentive for a developer to recover investment within a few years. Even without such considerations, people are often uncertain about the future. Time horizons of individuals and private enterprises are usually rather limited, causing the discount rate to be further adapted in favor of the present (Myers 1984c). Even fear of competition may encourage increased rate of exploitation before a competitor preempts the market. There may even be a disincentive for long-term investment on the basis that technology will ensure posterity is always better off.

The selection of appropriate discount and tax rates, tax breaks, and subsidies involves ethical decisions—questions of social equity and presumed needs of future generations. The selection and level of incentives and disincentives requires great care and knowledge of local needs, institutions, and attitudes (McNeely 1988). Discount rates can be a two-edged sword: a low rate may conserve for the future, but this may be offset by greater consumption of other resources, which leads to loss of biodiversity.

What are the best ways to fund incentives? Many options are available, but the best choice will vary from region to region, depending on traditions, social systems, and the physical environment. Government funding through taxation, special local taxes, charging of entry fees to national parks and other protected areas, and charges for resource use are commonly adopted measures. Returning profits from exploitation of biological resources to the people of the region has value not only as an incentive but also creates awareness. Donations from multinational corporations investing in resource-based activities are another form of viable financing. Perhaps the key issue is that incentives should directly involve all users and owners of the resource being conserved.

Well-designed systems of economic incentives can ensure that the local communities that are most directly affected by both conservation and overexploitation can earn appropriate benefits from behavior that is in the national interest. Ideally, such a system should consist of the following elements (McNeely 1988):

1. Determine which biological resources need enhanced management.

2. Estimate the economic values of these resources.

3. Establish conservation objectives for the package of incentives and disincentives.

4. Determine reverse incentives—the national social and economic policies that have encouraged the community to overexploit biological resources.

5. Collect information about the local community, including what biological resources the community is currently using, how the resources are being managed by the community, the degree of awareness in the community about controlling regulation, and possible alternative sources of income.

6. Design specific packages of incentives to meet the highest priority needs of the villagers, and ensure that the incentives package is linked with other development activities.

7. Establish a structure of responsibility for the biological resources in the area, often through the use of village-level institutions.

8. Incorporate packages of disincentives, through legislation, regulation, taxation, peer pressure, and appropriate levels of penalties.

9. Provide appropriate information and public education on both incentives and disincentives to the target audience.

10. Establish a means of monitoring and feedback, so that necessary changes can be instituted as the incentives system adapts to changes.

When an entrepreneur wishes to exploit a natural resource, a number of decisions must be made. One of the most important is whether to exploit the resource as quickly as possible, or to spread its use out over a longer period. Usually this is resolved by calculating the amount of income that can be derived over different periods in the future and then translating this into current values by applying a discount rate—one dollar in hand is worth more than one promised next year and far more than one that may be available in 10 or 100 years time. The greater the preference for a financial return now, the higher will be the discount rate. Usual discount rates give financial incentive for the entrepreneur to limit investment to a time frame of no more than 30 years, and preferably 10 to 20 years. This means that there may be little incentive to invest for the next generation of people, or to carry out mitigating procedures (such as tree-planting) if they take more than 30 years to start providing a significant financial return.

Two possibilities have been suggested for providing disincentives for future development (Myers 1984c). The first is to set variable rates of discount, especially for high-value natural resources. Instead of rates that are based on the marketplace and preferences of the developer, it may be appropriate to devise discount rates that promote the conservation of wild habitats and biodiversity and maximize options for future generations. The rate set in each instance would reflect social, genetic, and intrinsic resource values, as well as the value of exploitation. It would, "represent a deliberate move on the part of society now to safeguard certain tracts of forest for the future, in order to keep options open for succeeding generations" (Myers 1984c). It is quite possible that such discount rates might be a sufficient disincentive in some situations to discourage any exploitation of some sites.

A second possibility is to tax nonrenewable resources. In the case of the timber industry, an international tax would raise the price of timber offered to manufacturers in developed countries and would reduce demand while providing finance for investment in conservation. It would make consumers more accountable for their actions at the workface, responding to the question sometimes asked of tropical forestry operations: Whose hand is really on the chain saw?

CASE STUDY: DEBT SWAP FOR CONSERVATION IN ECUADOR

As with many Latin American countries, Ecuador is suffering from significant external debt: its 1977 debt balance of U.S. $1.3 billion had increased to U.S. $9.4 billion by 1987, with 60 percent of the amount owed to private international lenders. Lending banks have recognized the repayment difficulties by reducing the price of Ecuador's debt. The crisis has generated austerity measures but these hamper development, including sustainable use management of biological resources.

After examining the situation, a small group of Ecuadorian professionals, including leading bankers, organized a private foundation, Fundacion Natura, to use the debt crisis as an opportunity to attract financial resources to be invested in conservation of biological diversity. The foundation is in charge of obtaining funds abroad through donations in hard currency. With these funds, a fraction of the Ecuadorean external debt is purchased at discount value on the secondary financial market. Donations are also sought directly from private lending banks. Debt notes obtained in this way are exchanged by the foundation for stabilization bonds, through an agreement between it and the government of Ecuador. The bond's interest is invested in conservation projects assessed according to a system of priorities.

The proposal was approved in October 1987 by the Monetary Board of Ecuador's Central Bank, with an initial limit being set at $10 millions. Donations are made to North American nongovernmental organizations primarily on the basis of existence value, in the hope that donations will provide incentives to developing countries to help them conserve their biological resources. The first one million dollars from WWF purchased debt at 35 percent of the face value; each $100 donation purchased $281 of debt. With interest on the bonds floating but based on the average rate paid by the five largest Ecuadorian banks on 180-day deposits, a yield of 35 percent (current in 1988) gives $98.35 on $100 per year.

Similar debt swaps are being put into operation or negotiated elsewhere in developing regions (e.g., Costa Rica, Bolivia, and the Philippines), often with support from nongovernmental organizations of developed countries. The mechanism could be adapted to debt contracted by third world governments with multilateral financial institutions. Debt swaps enable the lender to write off debts if the debtor agrees to invest the same amount of funds in projects aimed at conserving biological resources.

Sources: Sevilla 1988 in McNeely 1988; McNeely 1989b.

CASE STUDY: FUNDING CONSERVATION INCENTIVES

Many suggestions have been made as to how to fund conservation projects and incentives. A partial list of funding sources includes the following:

- Allocating a portion of the national budget.

- Establishing special budgets for the initial contribution to national funds or regional revolving funds.

- Collecting entry fees to national parks and other protected areas.

- Returning profits from exploitation of biological resources to the people of the region.

- Returning profits from investments made by those administering a protected area to the region.

- Establishing community enterprises based on sustainable use of resources.

- Levying special taxes (e.g., on timber extraction, wildlife product trade, and concession rights).

- Charging for water use from irrigation and hydro-electric installations in a protected area.

- Levying an environmental maintenance tax as part of major development projects supported with external funding, including endowment funds for continued management.

- Linking with larger development projects, including the concept of obligatory investment of part of total development costs into environmental protection.

- Swapping debt for nature.

- Making conditional agreements as part of exploitative (extractive) concessions—long-term support to various incentive programs.

- Using profits from nonextractive concessions that may not deplete natural resources.

- Encouraging voluntary support from the private sector.

- Obtaining direct support from development assistance agencies.

- Obtaining direct support from international conservation agencies.

- Deriving local currency counterpart funds from public-sector international assistance operations.

- Using donations from multinational corporations investing in resource-based activities.

- Enlisting foundations associated with specific protected areas, as a stimulus to generation of funding.

- Granting conservation concessions parallel to those provided for mining and forestry, especially for areas of outstanding conservation value.

- Issuing property rights for threatened species or important protected areas to conservation organizations or relevant United Nations agencies.

Source: McNeely 1988.

The World Heritage Convention encouraged the federal government of Australia to provide subsidies to states having world heritage properties, to compensate for loss of income through cessation of resource extraction. In the case of tropical forests in Queensland, the offer includes the following:

- Public Works: Up to $A13.5 million for enhancing regional and tourist infrastructure, creating up to 600 permanent jobs through tourism expansion.

- Reafforestation: Up to $A9.9 million for private and public schemes, providing up to 270 jobs.

- World Heritage Area Management: Up to $A17 million for management, maintenance, and presentation of the areas in the provision of tourist and visitor facilities, and the permanent employment of field staff. This will provide 300 jobs.

- Private Initiatives: Up to $A3.7 million for private initiatives creating employment for displaced workers,

enhancing attractiveness, and promoting appropriate development. This is expected to create up to 140 job opportunities.

- Community Initiatives: Up to $A300,000 provided for establishment of community committees to identify regional growth and employment opportunities and develop these to the feasibility stage.

- Adjustment Assistance: Up to $A6.5 million for a labor adjustment package including dislocation allowances, redundancy payments, wage subsidies, training allowances, and relocation assistance.

- Business Compensation: Up to $A24.4 million for businesses directly and substantially affected by the cessation of logging within the world heritage area.

Source: McNeely 1988.

Rural development

Rural regions continue to be a major refuge for biodiversity. Rural development is a frequently stated purpose of aid programs, the overall goals being to ameliorate poverty, unemployment, poor health, and inequality. A further component of rural development is maintenance and rehabilitation of ecosystems. Important links exist between environmental deterioration and economic decline, which, in turn, leads to social disintegration. Rural problems are exacerbated by inevitable rural-to-urban migration, which saps the viability and strength of rural areas (Hanks 1984b).

Something that is often forgotten in the enthusiasm of promoting regional, and especially rural, development is that traditionally effective farmers have a multidisciplinary, holistic approach to their work (Conway 1985), which preserves genetic diversity. There are significant, fundamental differences between tribal/village agricultural systems and those of technological societies (Figure 10.3). Too often in the past, agricultural problems have been approached without due regard for their impact on other parts of the biological system. Technologies have been developed in the context of wealthy societies that can afford high levels of fertilizer and water inputs, and in regions with the best-endowed climates. Short- and long-term problems with this approach include increased incidence of predation, water pollution from run-off of nutrients, and pesticide persistence. Each of these problems usually is solved, in turn, on an individual, problem-oriented basis.

Many problems of agricultural and development projects are systematic in nature; they are linked to-

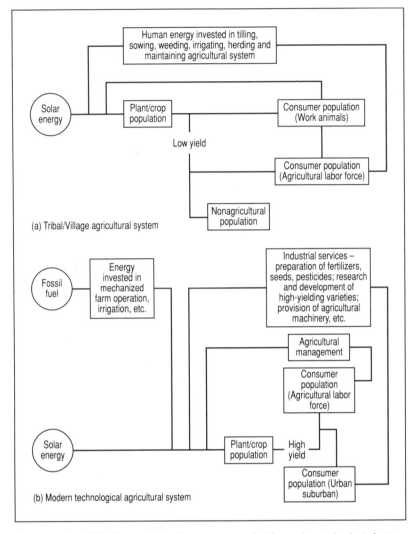

Figure 10.3. The tribal/village agricultural system contrasted with a modern, technological system. (Reproduced by permission from Watt et al. 1977)

gether and to the performance of the system as a whole (Conway 1985). So-called side effects that may not threaten agriculture in countries with access to continued advanced technology can become major problems that rapidly threaten viability of farming in poorer rural situations. To deal with such problems, it is important to understand the behavior of agroecosystems, which can be broken down into four components (Conway 1987). *Productivity* is the yield or net income per unit of resource. *Stability* is the degree to which productivity is constant in the face of small disturbances caused by normal fluctuations of climate and other environmental variables. *Sustainability* is the ability of a system to maintain productivity in spite of a major disturbance. *Equitability* refers to how evenly the products of an agroecosystem are distributed among people—perhaps a household or a village.

One does not have to know everything about an agroecosystem to be able to analyze it. What is essential is to understand key functional relationships. Improvements (and approaches toward compatibility with natural ecosystems) often require changes in only a small number of key management decisions. On the other hand, identification and understanding of the key relationships does require the formulation and then answering of appropriate questions (Conway 1985; see case study "Procedures for Analyzing Agroecosystems" below). Objectives of such an exercise should be to identify priorities for research that will improve stability of income and social structure within an agroecosystem, and to determine guidelines for improving agricultural productivity of poorer farmers in the region (leading to raising of the income of those in poverty).

Achievement of these two objectives will generally lead to accomplishment of a third, which is to relieve pressure on the environment and conserve natural biodiversity.

Part of the basis of every rural plan for conservation is to encourage farming practices that are compatible with good management of the natural environment, and which take pressure off use of scarce or vulnerable natural resources. Communication is important, not only between experts in a wide range of disciplines, but also to determine the fundamental needs and resources of a region. An obvious step particularly appropriate for many depressed rural areas is the planting of fodder trees to provide much needed animal feed and firewood. To achieve environmental compatibility while maintaining economic viability, a considerable number of models are being developed for farming strategies. In contrast to the past when many schemes transplanted temperate, high-input systems into the tropics, schemes are now being designed specifically for such critical areas as moist tropical forests and arid regions; these often are based on agroforestry techniques.

Agreement has not been reached on the suggestion that the only possible way to save significant portions of tropical forests, such as those of Amazonia, is to learn to use them as a sustainable-yield resource. Pragmatic considerations still draw heavily on sociopolitical considerations rather than ecological ones. There are instances where classical monocultural agriculture seems to be reasonably successful in places—for example, the Amazonian lowlands. In one instance, successful high-yielding oil palm plantations have been developed in the Tocache Nuevo area of Peru, the Santo Domingo area of Ecuador, and the Tumaco area of Colombia. Most of the successful plantations are on unusually fertile soils derived from the recently volcanic Andes. Successful agriculture on such patches of rich soil does not necessarily indicate a similar potential for agriculture on other soil types, at least in the absence of high inputs of nutrients. It is no accident that most of the tropical tree species that produce commercial fruits of high value—for example, bananas, cacao, coffee, and citrus—occur naturally on relatively fertile sites (Gentry 1986).

In the neotropics, the most valuable timber trees are rich-soil specialists. This observation provides part of the reason for lack of success in growing valuable timber trees on sites that vary greatly in fertility (Gentry 1986). Areas like the Amazon may appear superficially homogeneous but actually consist of a mosaic of very different habitats; this needs to be considered when assessing the success of particular projects.

The distribution of natural biodiversity in relation to fertility is very informative in this regard. While many very localized endemic species occur on high-stress, infertile sites, there is little doubt that the fertile soils that are required for agriculture are also those that often support rich and luxuriant natural vegetation.

The basis of modern agroforestry is the growing of crops for food, in conjunction with the growing of trees for fruits, fertilizers, and fuel. To these ends, a system can mobilize a wide variety of multitiered and multiuse crops (Myers 1986b). Some fully developed systems feature as many as 100 species in a single hectare. This adds up to a polycultural system of agriculture that, by virtue of its diversity, goes some way toward mimicking the ecological complexity and stability of natural forest.

Movement toward such farming systems amounts to a return to something approximating many traditional farming methods, though these are combined with the most appropriate of modern technology. In any one year, yields may not be as high as those possible from high-technology, high-input systems in developed countries. On the other hand, the system tends to be more resilient to catastrophe and change, and can be designed to give moderate and economically acceptable yields even when inputs of fertilizer and water are limited.

One of the particular compromises between preservation needs and needs for agriculture and forestry is establishment and use of buffer zones. Clearance of land for agriculture adjacent to major reserves is a continuing problem, especially in the tropics (Ramakrishnan 1983). Buffer zones can be a means of easing the pressure, especially if they are coordinated with a program to promote methods of farming that are compatible with conservation (Sayer 1987). Where population levels are still low, modification of traditional shifting agriculture may be quite sufficient—a fine-tuning of traditional practice. Where population levels are high and shifting techniques cannot be sustained, however, agroforestry offers a broad range of farming practices. Environmental benefits include retention of trees and additional tree planting for maintenance of soil and water quality, and diversity of agricultural and forestry products that promote social, economic, and ecological stability (Sayer 1987).

CASE STUDY: FODDER TREE PLANTING IN NEPAL

The Baudha-Bahunipati Project (BBP) covers 44 panchayats (village districts) of the Sindhupalchowk District northwest of Kathmandu. Total population approaches

160,000. Some 60 percent of the population live below the poverty level, and most farmers have an income of less than $40 a year. Pressure on the land is extreme, with over 11 people occupying each hectare of cultivated land—one of the highest densities in the world. Fewer than one family in six can grow enough food for the whole year. This, combined with a lack of sanitation, poor housing, and polluted water, causes many health problems. Only 15 percent of the population are literate, and few children go on to secondary school.

Many of the area's environmental problems stem from destruction of trees through fodder collecting for animals during the dry season. In the lifetime of present farmers, the nearby forest has almost disappeared, and soil and land quality has deteriorated. In 1977, discussions were held with the farmers in one community to introduce the Ipil-ipil (Leucaena), a widely used species in the Philippines. The farmers were ready to modify traditional fodder collecting practices if it did not mean replacing food crops with fodder trees. The Ipil-ipil tree offered a number of advantages over local fodder trees. It is fast-growing: it grows about three meters in the first year, and is out of reach of animals by six months after planting. It is vertical rooting, and so does not compete with nearby food crops, and plants can be grown close together on otherwise unused terrace faces. But the greatest attraction of Ipil-ipil is its coppicing characteristic, which enables it to be cut low, avoiding shading of food crops and providing fodder year-round.

A new grass variety also has been introduced to complement the Ipil-ipil and help in soil conservation. In one village studied for a recent report (Majhi village near Bahunipati) in 1986, nine years after the first Ipil tree demonstrations, 88 percent of 102 families had planted Ipil fodder trees, one-third had more than 400 trees, and about the same proportion are now self-sufficient in fodder and fuelwood. There has been reduced pressure on the nearby forest for fodder and fuelwood. Terraces have been stabilized by extensive planting of Ipil and grass, and soil erosion has been reduced. Community workers have a wide range of tasks: they also keep records and help organize the village committees, which make requests for help, raise funds, allocate benefits, and ensure the continuity of the project. This last need will be crucial in the future, and the key to this will be to build up and enable community organizations to carry on the project.

Source: Hamand 1987.

Case Study: Sustainable Farming in Moist Forests of Western Amazonia

Multitiered and multiuse agroecosystems can incorporate agriculture and aquaculture, cropping of wild and domesticated species, and harvesting of forest products on a sustainable basis. Forest utilization based on multitiered and multiuse concepts in western Amazonia seek to make self-sustaining use of such parts of the forest as are cleared, while drawing widely on renewable resources of the natural forest. In the topmost layer are palms, together with leguminous trees used for fertilizer, as well as fuel and building wood. At middle levels are cacao and coffee bushes, together with leguminous vines and beans for food and nitrogen. Also at this level are cash crops such as lemongrass, cassia, ipecac, and zingiberaceous spices. At the lower levels are short-stemmed cereals such as rice, plus root and tuber crops such as taro, yam, and sweet potato, and also vegetables and weed-type crops for green manure.

The Siona and Seocya Indians of eastern Ecuador utilize an extraordinary total of 224 plant species, spanning 166 genera and 69 families, most of them for foods, though others constitute materials for tools, construction and crafts, and medicines. The Chacobo Indians of northern Bolivia grow 40 species of food crops in their garden farms, ranging from rice and corn to papayas, watermelons, and cashews. Some of these tribes are already adept at cash-cropping of forest products. The Gavioes Indians of western Brazil are so capable in producing, transporting, and marketing of forest goods that in some areas with dense stands of Brazil nut trees, the produce generates more revenue than an equivalent area of pasture devoted to cattle ranching.

In a small locality near Iquitos in Peru, exploitation of several dozen plants—notably the fig known as oje (*Ficus antihelminthicus*), barbasco (*Lonchcarpus* species), palm heart, and several fruits (but not wild meat)—yield a household income ranging from U.S. $500 to $5000 per year, with a rough mean around $1200. A somewhat broader-ranging analysis has been developed by the Ministry of Agriculture in Ecuador. As much as 85 percent of animal protein consumed by local people is obtained from wild creatures. There is scope for sustainable cropping of forests and rivers to yield sufficient meat to provide several thousand dollars income per household each year. This means that one square kilometer of forest could produce a sustainable annual income of well over $20,000.

Source: Myers 1986b.

Case Study: Procedures for Analyzing Agroecosystems at the Local Level

Experience has shown that the procedure is best followed in a seminar or workshop environment in which meetings of the whole team are interspersed with intensive work sessions involving small groups of individuals. A suitable timetable may involve seven days with a combination of briefings, case studies, definition of the system being analyzed, small group study of particular aspects, field visits, and plenary discussion. Ultimately, a draft report and recommendations should result (Figure 10.4).

Communication is important, especially in terms of specialists presenting data so that other participants can grasp their significance. Visual aids are useful, especially when presenting pattern analysis dealing with spacial patterns, use of areas over time, flow patterns including energy use and money, and decision making. Key questions will arise throughout the exercise and reflect the particular socioeconomic/climatic peculiarities of the region. In a study of system properties in northeast Thailand some of the questions raised included the following:

- What are the most appropriate meteorological parameters for characterizing the agricultural seasons in the Chiang Mai Valley?

- Can new rice varieties be bred to produce more stable yields on the upper elevation, poorly watered paddy fields?

- Alternatively, what is the optimal application of fertilizers to traditional rice varieties under highly variable rain-fed conditions?

- How is the form and productivity of cropping systems in the Chiang Mai Valley affected by government policy on the price of rice?

- To what extent are the gains in productivity and stability from land consolidation in the Chiang Mai Valley likely to be offset by a decline in sustainability and equitability?

These key questions can be turned into testable hypotheses so that by the end of the workshop there is a list of questions, each accompanied by a hypothesis, a discussion of the issues involved, and some indication of the investigations now required. This can lead to conventional research, with testing of hypotheses by field trials, surveys, laboratory, and field experiments.

Source: Conway 1985.

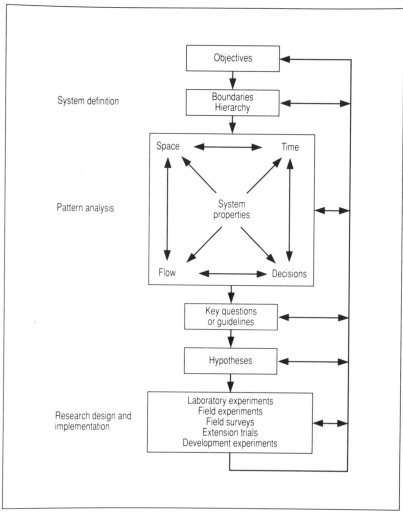

Figure 10.4. Basic steps for agroecosystem analysis. (Reproduced by permission from Conway 1985)

Allocating Resources for Conservation

Even when preservation is the most likely option, assessment of values and economic analysis should be considered. There are unlikely to be resources sufficient to permit undertaking all desired actions. Even if finance is not a critical problem, other limiting resources such as labor and equipment require the setting of priorities. The relative risks faced by key species and sites have to be clearly identified to assess which require immediate protection or mitigation and which can wait a little longer. The question always needs to be asked: For how long is one protecting or preserving: 10 years, 50 years, or 500 years?

Risk models of viability can be useful aids in such an assessment. A risk model recognizes that for a given population size, the longer the duration of time over which one wants to sustain the species, the lower the likelihood of continued existence and the greater the cost of maintaining the population. All else being equal, the likelihood of sustaining a large population for a particular span of time is likely to be greater than that for a small population.

There are no universal numbers for predicting viability; it will differ among species and between geographic locations because species differ biologically and factors causing depletion and extinction vary in their effects. There is probably no general threshold or minimum population size above which a population

is viable and below which it is not. Figures for animals are not readily translated into figures appropriate for plants. As with economic investments there are points of diminishing returns and economies of scale. For example, the last 10 percent of protection for a population may entail 90 percent of the total cost. Costs may include foregone opportunities for other uses of money. When resources for conservation are extremely limited, long-term preservation may not be a viable option.

Resources must be used with wisdom, and those species and ecosystems that need to be protected must get sufficient and appropriate attention. There is often pressure to pour time and money into the protection of a few species or areas to the detriment of others. A major problem is that much effort and finance goes toward conservation of a relatively small percentage of glamour biota, while other less glamorous (but no less deserving) species are deprived of funds.

In reality, it probably costs relatively little in many countries to conserve the majority of indigenous species at an acceptable level. Often, this may require no more than relief from pressures such as grazing and cutting for fuel. In contrast, a relatively small number of critically endangered species are likely to require large investments of money and time (Figure 10.5). They may require high technology solutions to prob-

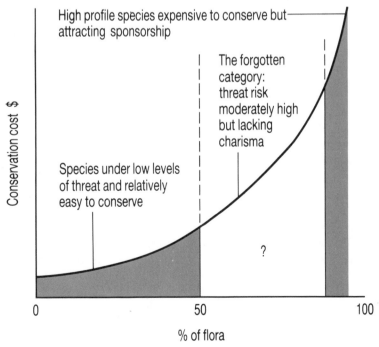

Figure 10.5. Inequalities in the allocation of resources to species conservation. (D. R. Given)

lems, or the combined efforts of many agencies including botanic gardens, scientific laboratories, and protected area staff. One should not detract from the needs of such species, but resources should not be denied to the next level of species—those that are not yet critically endangered but may well become so. Resources spent on a few highly endangered plants might be better allocated to ensuring that a far larger number of plants do not become critically endangered.

Since the world could lose many tens of thousands of plant species during the next few decades, we need to know very soon which ones would certainly leave major ecosystems at risk of collapse if they disappeared, which ones should be saved for cultural reasons, and which ones should be preserved virtually at any cost for social or scientific reasons (Spellerberg 1992). While conservation efforts need to be greatly expanded, the harsh reality is that they need also to become more selective. Many people find such choices abhorrent because it represents biological tri-

age in which cases are assigned to one of three categories: (1) those that can wait for treatment; (2) those for which treatment may be of doubtful long-term benefit; and (3) those that are likely to respond positively to immediate treatment.

It is a tragedy that such a situation (largely human-caused) has arisen. The harsh reality is that too many species and ecosystems are being depleted and destroyed. Immediate remedial action for all is not possible, given the level of conservation funding in most countries.

The most satisfactory answer to the dilemma of limited resources is greater resources for conservation and preservation, along with changed attitudes. Until this occurs, at least some species and sites may have to be abandoned or else preserved only in the short term. A particular challenge lies in the sustainable harvest of wild biota, the assigning of meaningful values to them and their habitats, and assessing positive aspects of trade for conservation.

Economic and Environmental Stability

"Regardless of the particular cultural belief system a society may follow, the one inescapable requisite for all human societies is the maintenance of ecosystem balance" (Watt et al. 1977: 44). Many factors are related to maintenance of ecosystem balance, but one of the most crucial is economic balance. Both ecosystem and economic balance exist when right and stable relationships exist between humanity and the social, economic, and environmental fabric within which people live. This means that human survival is protected and conserved; the delicate and interdependent equilibrium of the rest of the ecosystem is protected and conserved; and any departures from conditions of equilibrium are kept within manageable limits so that amplitudes in fluctuations with respect to the physical-biological environment, resource availability, food supply, prices and wages, unemployment rates, and others, can be quickly reduced or, at worst, contained in a constant condition (Watt et al. 1977).

Several factors can lead to instability of a system. Limited diversity allows the system to become vulnerable to failure of a component. This happens, for instance, where a country relies on the sales of one product for its income. Failure of the market (lower prices or demand) can result in rapid disaster for the country concerned. A second major cause of instability is increased *complexity;* this refers to size and interconnection between parts of the system. In a complex sys-

tem a shock to one part travels along the interconnected pathways and eventually affects many parts of it. A third cause of instability in complex systems is violent disturbance or catastrophe actually resulting from, or exacerbated by, the system itself. An example is conversion of primary forest to farmland, which reduces water-holding capacity of catchments and results in rapid run-off which, in turn, erodes and floods the farmland.

Some effects are readily appreciated. Pollution is a worldwide problem, especially global atmospheric pollution. The harmful effects of pollutants are often irreversible. The time lag between the addition of pollution to a system and its effects being noticed makes effective monitoring difficult. In the complex world of the industrialized countries, the effects of pollution can be particularly far-reaching, causing shocks to parts of the system that at first seem to be far removed from the point where the problems occur.

Other effects are less readily appreciated. The continued destruction of natural ecosystems and the wealth of species they contain is perceived by many people as unfortunate but hardly a crisis. The crisis aspect is only appreciated when our dependence on natural species is enumerated. History is full of examples of the collapse of civilizations that overexploited life-support systems; the ruins of hundreds of cities worldwide bear witness to the dire consequences of exhausting natural resources. Wherever people live, they will create impacts on ecosystems. They must consider not only their direct impact on the system, but also to what extent they can avoid altering the system and making it more prone to instability. Modern technologically oriented agriculture and forestry is ecologically unstable because it is analogous to an immature natural ecosystem, especially in the tropics where species diversity correlates with ecosystem resilience. In a sense, highly technological cropping based on monoculture, high nutrient inputs, and rapid turnover is

> man's attempt to reverse nature's successional sequence by artificially maintaining a highly producing, early-successional ecosystem, be it grain crops of corn, wheat or rice, herbage such as ryegrasses and clover, or plantation forests of pines (Watt et al. 1977: 55).

The four most serious impacts of highly technological cropping based on monoculture are increased erosion, reliance on cultural energy (through humanity's animals and fuels), the impact of fertilizers, and the impact of pesticides.

Further instability is likely in the future. Doubts have been expressed about the effectiveness of price mechanisms in maintaining stability. Uncontrolled population increase, changes in age distribution, and changes in geographic distribution within regions will mean that carrying capacity will be exceeded, at least in the short to medium term, for many parts of the world.

As long as species diversity drops, resilience and future options will be affected. The effect of energy and fuel shortages is another factor. Even if such novel technologies as nuclear fusion become a reality, fuel shortages are likely to continue for some decades in underdeveloped countries. Many societies are unlikely to be in a position to acquire most new energy technologies without radical changes in economic and social priorities. The exceptions are energy from solar sources, wind, and large-scale forestry plantations, but these are not likely to affect short-term shortages.

To counteract economic instability now and in the future, and its effect on species and natural ecosystems, societies must guard against reduction in diversity; ensure that there are adequate control and monitoring mechanisms; and take steps to anticipate, minimize, and contain disturbances to ecosystems. The optimistic view is that technology will provide the necessary answers. Perhaps a more realistic view is that unless human nature changes, technology's benefits will accrue to relatively few and the gulf between "haves" and "have nots" will continue to widen.

CHAPTER 11

Putting It Together: Integrated Conservation

Conservation—A Crisis Discipline

"Conservation biology differs from most other biological sciences in one important way: it is often a crisis discipline" (Soulé 1985: 227). As a scientific discipline it evolved in the late 1970s and early 1980s. It has been defined as a field "to develop scientific principles and then apply those principles to developing technologies for the maintenance of biological diversity" (U.S. Congress Office of Technology Assessment 1987, in Tangley 1988). Conservation biology overlaps considerably with other, long-established disciplines such as biology, forestry, wildlife management, ecology, and biosystematics. It relates closely to all of these and other fields but is distinguished by its broader focus on conserving the earth's biota rather than individual species that have economic or other utilitarian value (Soulé qtd. in Tangley 1988).

As with other crisis disciplines, action in conservation must often be taken before all the facts can be assembled. Because of its concern with what is rare, under threat, or disappearing, conservation of biodiversity is under severe time constraints. Nevertheless, because it is a new discipline and it deals with incomplete data, there is often a tendency to regard it with suspicion. In times of limited funding for science in general, it is sometimes looked upon as a strident upstart wanting large amounts of funding for work that it cannot justify by conventional scientific argument.

Conservation biology has other particular characteristics. For instance, it is holistic in two senses. First, a reductionist approach in which systems are examined through their various small components does not provide adequate explanation for ecological and evolutionary processes, particularly at the global level. Second, it is generally assumed that multidisciplinary approaches will ultimately be the most fruitful in conservation. Consequently, conservation biology has embraced a wide range of disciplines and theories including evolution, genetic theory, island biogeography, and hazard evaluation (Soulé 1985).

Time scales are critical in conservation biology and management. Conservation is concerned with long-term viability of systems—that is, time scales ranging far beyond individual life spans. This poses difficulties for people who are not generally used to making commitments far into the future. It is no wonder that vigorous debate occurs over such issues as, "What do we owe to the unborn?"

The above statements about conservation biology can also be made for conservation law, conservation economics, and conservation sociology. As an example, the quite sudden public appreciation of the possibility of rapid climate change through the greenhouse and ozone hole phenomena has hastened demands for reform of pollution laws. This is reflected at the political level with development of green (environmental) consciousness in many political parties, particularly in the developed world. The volume of conservation newsletters, leaflets, and journals is growing monthly, as illustrated by the growth rates of conservation bibliographies and the extremely recent publication dates of many of the items on those lists. "Humans are a brink species. They don't do much until a situation approaches a disaster. At that point they throw lots of money at a problem. I think we're beginning to see this in conservation." (Soulé qtd. in Tangley 1988).

CASE STUDY: POSTULATES OF CONSERVATION BIOLOGY

Functional postulates are working propositions based partly on evidence, partly on theory, and partly on intuition. In essence they are a set of axioms derived from ecology, biogeography, and population genetics about the maintenance of both form and function of natural biological systems. These postulates suggest rules for action. A necessary goal of conservation biology is the elaboration and refinement of such principles:

1. Many of the species that constitute natural communities are the products of coevolutionary processes. Corollaries include the following: many species are highly specialized, extinctions of keystone species can have long-range consequences, and introductions of generalists may reduce diversity.

2. Many, if not all, ecological processes have thresholds below and above which they become discontinuous or chaotic.

3. Genetic and demographic processes have thresholds below which nonadaptive, random forces begin to prevail

over adaptive, deterministic forces within populations.

4. Nature reserves are inherently in disequilibrium for large, rare organisms.

Normative postulates are value statements that make up the basis of an ethic of appropriate attitudes toward other forms of life—an ecosophy. They provide standards by which our actions can be measured. They are shared by most conservationists and many biologists, although ideological purity is not the reason for proposing them:

1. Diversity of organisms is good.

2. Ecological complexity is good.

3. Evolution is good.

4. Biotic diversity has intrinsic value.

Source: Soulé 1985.

Cross-sectoral Conservation—Integrated Approaches

In common with other crisis disciplines, conservation biology is multidisciplinary, synthetic, and eclectic. It is a science not only of uncertainty but, like other crisis disciplines such as cancer research, it necessarily draws on a wide range of information sources and both basic and applied disciplines, not all of which are biological (Figure 11.1).

The cross-sectoral nature of conservation demands that corporate and funding structures facilitate interaction between a wide range agencies, minimizing delays and ensuring that the right kinds of information are meshed with each other. Cooperation, sharing of resources, integrated research, and an atmosphere of trust are all fundamental to the success of conservation efforts. Synthetic, crisis-oriented disciplines such as conservation biology do not thrive in a free-market climate that pits one institution against another in a scramble for the crumbs falling off treasury benches.

Some of the reason for current difficulties in achieving conservation goals may be that the right institutions are not yet involved (McNeely et al. 1990). The conservation movement has been led by naturalists, who have been unable to address fully many of the basic problems of conservation, which are political, economic, social, and ethical as well as biological. Conservation action, therefore, must call on the best information from a wide range of sources. Solutions are rarely, if ever, simple, and they are dynamic in the sense that they change over time as ecological, social, and technological factors change.

Effective conservation also depends on a fusion of academic and pragmatic approaches to conservation problems, so that solutions are both innovative and realistic. Solutions must reflect sound theory yet deal with the real world. What is needed is to match theory with practice, and to adopt the best methods and philosophy for the particular situation.

> Strategically speaking, the best method is the one most closely matched to the particular conservation need, other things being equal. . . . It is a truism in conservation that needs far exceed resources, and this is most emphatically true in the tropics. Integrated conservation, by stressing the precise matching of targets and tactics, refines the discussion of priorities in ways that yield more precise cost-effect analyses. Such an approach does not necessarily make the job of choosing among options easier, but it does fine-tune the decision process (Falk 1990a).

The future effectiveness of conservation will depend not only on good techniques and changed attitudes, but on cost-effective programs that integrate a range of approaches as well. No single approach is the right approach in every instance. Protection of habitat is important but must be meshed with, and sometimes may be subservient to, off-site conservation. For one species, translocation may be a primary strategy, but for another it may be quite inappropriate.

To achieve integration requires communication—effective communication, where the emphasis is on listening and not just telling. It requires realistic as-

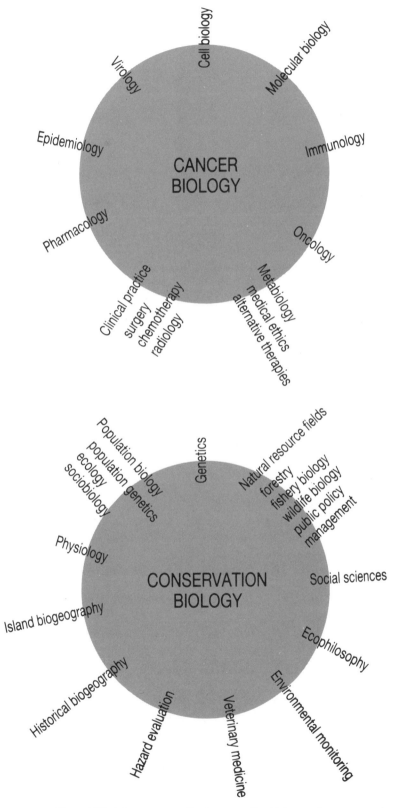

Figure 11.1. The multidisciplinary nature of both conservation biology and cancer research. (Reproduced by permission from Soulé 1985)

sessment of all resources, not just one's own but those of other people and agencies. Finally, integration demands that those involved in conservation be prepared to commit themselves to a learning curve so that each experiment and experience becomes a stepping stone to doing better in the future.

CASE STUDY: A MULTIPLE APPROACH TO CONSERVATION ON ST. HELENA

St. Helena in the Atlantic Ocean has suffered greatly from human influence since its discovery in 1502. Much of the vegetation was cut or otherwise altered by the late seventeenth century. Feral animals including goats, pigs, and cattle were introduced as people settled on the island, and many invasive weeds were brought to the island. The covering of "fine trees" and "big timber" recorded by the early Portuguese visitors had, as early as 1589, become discrete woodlands and are now almost totally gone. The island is one of the most spectacularly eroded of oceanic islands. Seven of the 60 or so endemic flowering plants have become extinct.

Conservation of St. Helena island must be by a variety of means, including protection of existing populations by fencing and clearing of exotics; propagation and widespread planting of critically endangered endemics (natural regeneration is unlikely); and restoration of soil and vegetation to halt erosion.

Since the 1970s, initiatives by local people, the island's agriculture and forestry department, and several botanic gardens (notably the Royal Botanic Gardens at Kew, England) have laid a foundation for conserving and restoring the island's flora. This has involved support from the Fauna and Flora Preservation Society; WWF–U.K.; the U.K. Ministry for Overseas Development; and several other agencies.

A cross-disciplinary team has spent seven weeks on the island undertaking social, economic, and biological surveys, interviews with island people, and public meetings. A workshop has reviewed the complete island biota using PHVA procedures. A proposed strategy addresses concerns regard-

ing food security, income, and employment alongside biological problems. The strategy presents options rather than a single solution.

Publicity through journals, books, and other media has also been an important aspect of conservation on St. Helena.

Sources: Goodenough 1985; Cronk 1989;
M. Maunder pers. com. 1993.

CASE STUDY: INTEGRATED CONSERVATION—A COST-EFFECTIVE STRATEGY FOR CONSERVING TROPICAL DIVERSITY

Traditional approaches to conservation have generally relied on the acquisition of land and establishment of legal protective measures. This is supplemented by ex-situ conservation—horticulture, germ plasm banks, and off-site preservation. Unfortunately, there has been perhaps too much attention to biodiversity at the level of species and neglect of the conservation of ecosystems and habitats.

An overemphasis on species-level conservation risks missing biologically significant diversity at higher and lower levels of organization. Conservation efforts must also be conceived in response to particular threats or impacts to the biological entity of concern. Finally, the full spectrum of conservation resources must be employed in a coordinated manner, without exclusive reliance on any single approach.

The use of a wide range of conservation methods is compelled largely by the diversity in objects of conservation and threats they encounter. It removes the obsolete dichotomy between in-situ and ex-situ conservation: neither exists in a pure form. Integrated conservation substitutes a spectrum of compatible, mutually reinforcing methods.

By integrating information, needs, and resources in the three areas mentioned, a higher degree of protection is attainable for plant diversity than is possible by any single strategy. It is this inherently multidisciplinary approach that characterizes integrated conservation strategies.

Sources: Falk 1990a, 1990b.

International Organizations

The 1980s was a period of growing awareness of the fact that environmental problems are not confined by political boundaries. Species distributions do not always coincide neatly with state boundaries, and what one country does with its pollutants and waste may profoundly affect another. This fact has been well demonstrated by the effects of acid rain: industrial pollution in one country may result in increased water and soil acidity many thousands of kilometers away.

Global telecommunications and a revolution in transport technology has shortened distances between people. For the first time in history, we are living in a truly international world where solutions increasingly must be international in scope.

Many organizations that engage in conservation work, large and small, are international in scope. Some such as FAO and UNEP fall under the umbrella of the United Nations and were not originally set up as specific conservation organizations. Other international organizations have a more specific conservation mandate. Perhaps the best two examples of the latter are IUCN (International Union for Conservation of Nature and Natural Resources) and WWF (formerly World Wildlife Fund, now World Wide Fund for Nature). IUCN was formed shortly after World War II. It is a unique organization, including in its membership sovereign states, government agencies, nongovernment organizations, foundations, and individuals. It works through a network of six commissions that harness the energies of many thousands of (usually voluntary) experts worldwide. WWF has developed alongside IUCN; originally set up as a funding and publicity organization, WWF now operates its own extensive program of research and investigation, particularly in the tropics.

Large international organizations have both strengths and weaknesses. They generally have the authority to speak to governments and multinational organizations, and can take and develop global views, using access to considerable resources. A wide range of expertise can be called on to deal with problems that may require input from various interest groups. Such organizations, however, also tend to acquire bureaucratic structures that reduce flexibility. When many contributors are involved, it can become virtually impossible to satisfy the expectations of particular donors. There is probably no easy solution to this problem, except a spirit of willingness and courage to terminate activities that have outlived their usefulness, and to avoid a top-heavy administration.

An important function of some particular international agencies is to promote and administer conventions and treaties. There are several important conservation conventions that affect plants, for instance Ramsar and CITES (Convention on International Trade in Endangered Species of Fauna and Flora). For efficient administration, most conventions have established a secretariat, which is often set up within the framework of a sponsoring international organization. This highlights a basic requirement of any international or large regional organization—the need to have a discrete, identifiable administering office answerable to the organization as a whole.

The global role of international conservation organizations is impressive. Recent examples have included the international Wetlands Program, the Plants Conservation Program, and the Tropical Forest Program. The structure of such programs is complex, requiring input beyond that of any single agency. In the case of the Tropical Forest Program, coordination has been required among IUCN, WWF, FAO, and the World Resources Institute, as well as regional and national organizations. This has meant heavy reliance on the resources of the World Conservation Monitoring Center, the Action Plan of the IUCN Commission on National Parks and Protected Areas, the IUCN Species Survival Commission, and regional expertise associated with such bodies as The Nature Conservancy based in Washington, D.C., USA. Priority goals of the Tropical Forest Program include the following (A Union Programme 1986b):

- To improve protected area systems to shield more tropical forest sites more systematically.

- To encourage conservation-conscious land use in areas adjacent to parks and reserves.

- To promote sustainable utilization of natural forests that is compatible with conservation of biological diversity and genetic resources.

- To urge reestablishment of natural vegetation in degraded areas, where feasible and desirable.

- To construct regional networks of tropical forest research and management institutes.

- To apply databases to urgent tropical forest problems.

International organizations have the capability to collaborate with governments in coordinated projects and regional campaigns. They are often in a better position than individual institutions to formulate plans for such cooperative work, although it may be more appropriate for specific institutions or individuals to undertake or provide advise for specific projects. Collaboration with governments cannot be overstressed. It is not enough for an agency to come into an area and do the "right thing," even where the agency obviously has the capacity and the expertise to do so. An organization must liaise and have the backing of both the people of the region and their operative administration and government.

Perhaps the single most important global involvement has been the development and promotion of a World Conservation Strategy (WCS) sponsored by IUCN, UNEP, WWF, FAO, and UNESCO, and its successor, Caring for the World: A Strategy for Sustainability, launched by IUCN, UNEP, and WWF in November 1990. Such strategies unify conservation and development, based on three objectives: to maintain life-support systems and essential ecological processes, to preserve genetic diversity, and to ensure that any utilization of species and ecosystems is sustainable.

The philosophy of the WCS has been recognized and accepted in principle by many governments, development agencies, and conservation organizations. It has led to the adoption of National Conservation Strategies by many countries. The WCS provides a desperately needed model into which can be linked developmental and conservation needs and constraints. It promotes the development of an overview and means by which many of a country's strengths and weaknesses can be identified.

To meet worldwide threats to plant life, IUCN and WWF launched the Plants Conservation Program in March 1984 to promote plant conservation more effectively around the world. Though the program addressed plant conservation from several directions, the emphasis was on achieving conservation of plant diversity, plant genetic resources, and plants of actual or potential economic value. The program was designed to link two traditionally distant groups: scientists, protected area managers, and conservationists on the one hand, and foresters and agronomists on the other.

The overall objective of the Plants Conservation Program was to promote, support, and formulate efforts to conserve plants, particularly in developing countries in the tropics. On a more specific level, the program consisted of a set of projects and activities to meet the following objectives (Hamann 1987):

Spreading the message. To build public awareness to help stimulate action by pressure on governments and industries, by citizen action, and by encouraging donations.

Building the capacity to conserve. To enable IUCN and WWF to promote plant conservation more effectively among their members, the world's conservation organizations, and governments.

Conserving plant genetic resources. To conserve sufficient diversity within species to ensure that all their potential is available for future use.

Conserving wild plants of economic value. To emphasize the conservation of wild plants of importance, particularly for rural people in developing countries.

Botanic gardens—a vital link. To strengthen the role of botanic gardens in conservation.

Promoting plant conservation in selected countries. To identify, develop, and implement on-the-ground model projects in priority countries.

The three partners who developed the World Conservation Strategy (IUCN, UNEP, and WWF) also set up the World Conservation Monitoring Center (WCMC) to support conservation and sustainable development through the provision of information on the world's biological diversity. The WCMC, located in Cambridge, England, collects, manages, and disseminates information relevant to nature conservation, and promotes networks to facilitate information flow. It has developed a special interest in national parks and protected areas, biosphere reserves, world heritage and Ramsar sites, and endangered species. The Protected Areas Data Unit of WCMC engages in the following activities:

- Maintains and reviews the lists of the world's protected areas, and maintains a database on these.

- Holds definitive, standardized format information documents summarizing the protected area systems of individual countries.

- Obtains maps of all protected area systems, and develops a digitized set of such maps.

- Holds definitive, standardized format information documents on major individual protected areas (particularly in developing countries).

- Collects current and historical literature on protected areas.

- Provides support to international activities, programs, and conventions relating to protected area issues.

The WCMC recently developed geographic information system (GIS) to facilitate assessment of the status and threats to the world's biodiversity and ecosystems. A series of comprehensive publications is planned for the 1990s. Through these and its databases, WCMC will provide a powerful resource for creating awareness and promoting conservation education.

Multinational and Development Agencies

One of the problems faced by many governments is that immediate economic gains hold greater political appeal than long-term gains, especially if the latter are hard to quantify in monetary terms. Where nations are poor and suffering from high levels of debt, the temptation to select development projects that provide short-term economic gains regardless of future ecological costs is often irresistible. Entrepreneurs who can produce immediate dollars are favored by governments desperate to pay off international debts and acquire foreign exchange. Questions about land degradation and loss of biological diversity are easily pushed to the background (Eckholm 1978).

The governments of many poorer countries can hardly be blamed for their skeptical view of conservation as an indulgence of the wealthy and well-educated developed countries. They are constantly told by organizations in these developed countries that they must conserve their resources. At the same time, they readily perceive that the demand for their own resources by the same countries is one of the roots of their problems.

Many development agencies and multinational corporations are very responsible and, particularly in the last decade, have developed a great degree of sensitivity to conservation and social needs, especially in the tropics. Others have been less responsible—some out of ignorance, and some out of undisguised entrepreneurial greed. Good development and responsible use of international funding increases incomes, provides jobs, and raises standards of living. Nevertheless, studies of development projects in the tropics have shown that an alarming number of projects do not achieve this and instead entail major environmental destruction and human costs. Despite the fact that many development agency projects were initiated in the third world over the last 40 years, disparity in income levels between countries remains, and poverty itself has grown (Swartzman 1986). Problems such as transmigration, degradation of natural habitats, or loss of species are easily overlooked in the chase for economic viability. International finance hastens the process, so that irreparable damage can occur before protective measures are in place.

Rural areas are often particularly affected by development programs. Unless rural development programs can be designed and implemented to meet the needs and aspirations of the people who live in the rural areas, rural-to-urban migration will accelerate. The effect of this migration will be to sap the rural areas of their vitality and strength, leaving them leached and inhabited by higher proportions of women, the old, the sick, and the very young (Hanks 1984b). Rural development, one of the most difficult problems facing any developing country, is thus in the hands of those who are least capable of dealing with it. The longer the rural areas are neglected, the more environmental degradation will increase, with ecological and economic consequences extending far beyond the present rural areas themselves.

Foreign assistance programs often lack a high public profile in donor countries. When times get hard, financial assistance for foreign countries is often one of the first items to be cut, and protective measures can be the first casualties of such cuts. Nongovernmental organizations have an important role to play in ensuring that environmental assessments and development procedures are adequate, thorough, and sensitive. "I contend that conservationists cannot allow this to continue. Our hopes for saving a significant proportion of the earth's plant (and animal) species are tied too closely to developing countries' struggles" (Campbell 1987).

The following steps must be taken to ensure that overseas development projects are environmentally acceptable (Swartzman 1986).

Consideration of a range of new ideas and alternatives. It is important that different kinds of projects be financed. Development need not destroy or damage the natural resource base, especially if it can be limited in scope. "Small is beautiful" is still a valid principle, and soft options (e.g., agroforestry in place of farming based on Western pastoral or agricultural techniques) are appropriate.

Strict environmental assessment procedures. Western donor countries often have strict environmental assessment procedures for projects within their own boundaries. There is merit in the argument that money for third world development ought to be conditional on the adoption of similar procedures.

Attention to social consequences of projects. As noted above, good social impacts go hand in hand with good conservation. One way to achieve this is by adopting a national conservation strategy based on the World Conservation Strategy. This could include guidelines for integration of social and environmental safeguards into development projects.

Establishment of environmental advisory and monitoring offices by development agencies. Such offices could ensure not only that a strong environmental component was built into all projects, but also that people in recipient countries were trained to participate in projects and monitor these along with development schemes.

Adequate involvement of nationals. Local people—landowners, administrators, scientists, members of nongovernmental organizations—should be aware of what a development project entails and should have a voice in planning it.

Can national conservation strategies to coordinate development programs actually improve environmental conditions in the nations involved? Properly carried out they should, although matching intent (as expressed in a national conservation strategy) with what finally happens on the ground may be distressingly difficult. A very significant benefit is likely to be the educational and awareness effect of preparing the strategy—possibly as important as the document itself. Further improvement can be gained by the use of environmental profiles prepared cooperatively by donor and recipient countries. Such profiles help identify conservation and development priorities, but the preparation of the document cannot of itself greatly improve the capabilities of poor nations to address environmental and resource allocation problems (Stoel 1985).

Many of the environmental problems associated with development programs in third world countries need to be laid at the feet of organizations financing the programs. There is growing public sentiment that all governments should exert stronger pressure on multilateral development banks to ensure that the environmental impacts of programs they finance are reduced (Swartzman 1986). What is needed are sensitive means to ensure that development results in not only short-term benefits but in long-term enhancement of biological diversity as well. Such benefits not only will accrue to wild habitats, species, and local people, but will trickle down to the donors and development agencies as well, who will be assured of sustainable utilization of resources and greater appreciation and support for their concepts.

Volunteers

One of the strengths of conservation should be its voluntary organizations. Worldwide, such groups number in the thousands. Almost every country has at least one national, nongovernment environmental organization; many have several that are nationwide in scope. In addition, there are a myriad of local organizations, societies, and trusts that have narrower interest areas. On top of this, groups are formed to promote (or react to) particular issues as they arise, ceasing to exist when the need is no longer there. Voluntary conservation organizations can be divided into several main categories.

National or regional organizations that have a wide mandate. These act as an umbrella, sometimes with many local branches or chapters. Examples include the Royal Society for Nature Conservation (Britain), the Royal New Zealand Forest and Bird Society, and the Sierra Club.

National or regional organizations with specialist interests. These are often formed initially as a result of a particular need or conservation issue. They do not pretend to cover the whole spectrum of conservation issues, and conservation may be only one of several objectives. Examples include specialist botanical societies.

Conservation groups set up as a subsidiary of another group. Conservation groups are sometimes established as semiautonomous groups within organizations with broader interests.

Organizations with local geographic or community interests. Many autonomous organizations have been established within just one urban area, community, or small region. They may be loosely linked with groups espousing similar aims elsewhere. Examples include local botanical trusts, friends of particular botanic gardens or reserves, and antipollution committees.

Ad-hoc groups formed to take an interest in a particular problem, species, or conservation area. Often these are not formally constituted or incorporated but are formed of a few people under the direction of an institution or formally constituted organization. Most have a limited life.

Despite the large number of voluntary organizations and public interest groups worldwide, and despite their high public profile, their role still is not always understood in the community or by governments (Bruik 1980). Sometimes the fault lies with the organization. Even if the primary goal is to press for change, its views must be defensible, authoritative, and well-presented to the appropriate audience. In this way groups can gain the respect they need to present ideas and conclusions as pointers for government policy, or as directives for attitudes in the community. Many groups have shown that it is feasible for governments and nongovernment organizations to work in partnership and not in opposition. The effectiveness of dialogue is affected by the political climate and the degree to which governments will tolerate critical viewpoints. Voluntary organizations ought to be prepared to give praise where it is due and not just look for points to criticize.

The size of some conservation organizations is surprising. New Zealand has a population of 3.2 million people; its major nongovernmental conservation organization, the Royal Forest and Bird Protection Society, has a membership of over 50,000. In the United Kingdom, the Royal Society for Nature Conservation and affiliated conservation trusts had more than 161,000 members in 1985, and Greenpeace International has a supporter group of around 4 million. Although size is sometimes regarded as important (most organizations wish to increase their membership) it is not necessarily a limiting factor. Some small organizations have influence well beyond their size. But for a small organization to achieve influence demands a clear-cut series of objectives, responsive management, and specific setting of goals and target audiences. It is better for smaller organizations to set few goals and achieve them than to set many diffuse goals and reach none. In some countries, for example, in the tropics where many people cannot afford the time and money to join an organization, extremely effective national groups may have only several hundred members.

Some very effective voluntary groups have arisen more as movements than as formerly instituted societies. Such movements usually result from grass roots pressure among local people who respond to a threat or pressure. They may be born out of frustration and feelings of powerlessness, either because of the prevailing political situation or because existing organizations do not deal adequately with the issues of concern. Such movements may remain informal or may consolidate and form structured semipermanent organizations. They may also become highly politicized, expressing themselves through the ballot box.

Voluntary service groups are extremely useful where governmental professional and technical resources are stretched. Such groups can play a major role in botanic garden education, reserve management, and survey and inventory of threatened species. There are several necessary constraints. Groups must work according to a predetermined management plan or framework of action. Their members must have sufficient competence to carry out the tasks assigned them; conversely the tasks need to be designed with the volunteers' skills in mind.

There also needs to be "something in it" for the volunteers; often this may amount to no more than knowing that they are doing a worthwhile task and are part of a long-term conservation project. Expenses, such as transport to and from sites and accommodation as necessary, should be met. Progress reports and inspection procedures are important to ensure that the results are those that were intended.

The Bureau of Land Management in the United States makes use of volunteers, who assist in conservation of rare plants. Organizations as well as individuals are encouraged to offer their assistance. The bureau has also entered into cooperative management agreements with The Nature Conservancy, whereby that organization takes over much of the responsibility for management of certain significant areas of land.

A modification of the voluntary service group idea is the setting up of organizations that are paid basic subsistence rates to work for periods of up to several months on conservation projects. It can be argued that such a system circumvents the employment of full-time labor and is a cheap way of getting a job done. Such groups must not be seen as substitutes for full-time staff. Instead they should be regarded as a means of involving the community in conservation management and research. Such groups also play a valuable role in education, especially among young people.

The use of volunteers and the concept of *conservation corps* go a long way toward breaking down barriers that sometimes arise between professionals and amateurs. Far too often research and management has been part of a mysterious "conservation priesthood" where only the qualified and professional have entry. Amateur naturalists have a great deal of expertise that should be harnessed. Their involvement breaks down suspicion, especially where land occupiers are suspicious of government-run conservation activities. Responsible volunteers, can, in fact be among the best ambassadors for conservation in a community.

CASE STUDY: VOLUNTEER ASSISTANCE AT POINT REYES NATIONAL SEASHORE, CALIFORNIA, USA

The Point Reyes National Seashore in California includes 17 cattle and dairy ranches, so potential damage to rare plants from grazing and ranch management requires U.S. National Park Service intervention. Twenty-seven plant species recorded from Point Reyes are listed as rare by the California Native Plant Society; four of these are endemic to the area. A rare plant management program developed since 1983 involved review of historical data and field surveys. A total of 143 populations for 21 species have been inventoried.

Each year a priority list is compiled indicating those species of plants needing survey. Species of interest are selected by volunteers, who are mostly members of the California Native Plant Society. The volunteers carry out monitoring programs on these species. This results in somewhat uneven coverage, but more work is accomplished than would otherwise be possible.

Most years the work of the volunteers is augmented by additional surveys conducted by seasonal employees of the National Park Service. With this combination, it has been possible to carry out a relatively successful monitoring program for rare plants at Point Reyes.

Sources: Clark and Fellers 1987; G. M. Fellowes, pers. com.

CASE STUDY: VOLUNTEER CONSERVATION OF THE MONKEY ORCHID IN ENGLAND

The monkey orchid (*Orchis simia*) had been recorded periodically in Kent from 1777 till 1923. After 1923, a period of 32 years elapsed during which no plants were recorded in the county. In May 1955, one plant was discovered growing in open grassland. During the summer of 1955, this first plant was eaten, probably by a slug, before the seed capsules matured. The following year the same plant flowered again, and four other plants on the same grassland appeared and flowered. The spring of that year was unusually dry, however, and all the flowering plants withered before setting any seed.

In 1957, a total of 35 plants were found, of which 7 flowered (including the 5 plants that flowered in 1956). Of the 7 plants that flowered in 1957, 3 were eaten or accidentally destroyed, and the remainder set seed. However, since the plants withered early in the summer, it is not known if the seed was viable. A further 28 plants, 3 of which flowered, were discovered in a nearby wood.

The first three years of observations (between 1955 and 1957) had shown the need to protect the orchid from three threats. First, many of the flowering spikes had been eaten by herbivores, the most important of which were the rabbit and the slug. Second, there was a threat from domestic animals. Third, there was the problem of the fertilization of the orchid flowers themselves. The evidence of the previous years suggested that little seed was being set, and hence the amateurs from the Kent Trust for Nature Conservation set about artificial pollination. A finely pointed pencil proved to be too clumsy, and a needle damaged the flowers. Finally, broken stems of the brome grass (*Zerna erecta*), which grew on the site, were used, and 25 percent successful fertilization was achieved. When mature, the flowering stems were cut into bags and dried, and the seeds were rubbed into the downland soil where the parent orchids were growing.

Protection from herbivores and from adverse human influence yielded good results, as did the fertilization campaign. Seed sown in 1958 produced plants with flowering spikes in 1965, a developmental period of seven years from seed to flowering.

The conservation of the monkey orchid in England resulted from the combined efforts of professional and amateur botanists. Without a dedicated effort to overcome these problems, it is unlikely the monkey orchid would be so abundant, or even present, in Kent in the 1970s.

Source: Usher 1973.

Research Priorities for Conservation

"The most intellectually challenging issue in conservation biology is to stop intellectualizing conservation biology to death and get out and do something about it" (Janzen qtd. in Tangley 1988: 445).

Conservation research can be categorized on the basis of focus. Most research uses one of three focuses: single species, communities and ecosystems, and the natural world and humanity. The first includes research on both behavior and physiology of individual organisms, and structure, dynamics, genetics, and ecology of populations. This research provides the scientific basis for protecting, managing, propagating, and reintroducing endangered species. Particular research is needed on *keystone species* (those whose presence or absence affects the functioning of entire ecosystems), *indicator species* (those used to measure the health of ecosystems), rare species, exotic or introduced species (especially invasive weeds and feral animals), and species of ecological significance (including microorganisms). A vitally important objective of

single-species research is to come to an understanding of the processes of extinction and persistence, population viability, and the genetic structure and variation within and between populations.

Research on communities and ecosystems generally focuses on four questions: What is the spatial organization of diversity? How do communities and ecosystems work? How are systems disturbed by human activity? How can human-induced degradation be stopped and damage repaired?

It is important to learn precisely where centers of diversity are located and what is happening to them, and to summarize this information. The effects of fragmentation and stress are particularly important: the future will see many more landscapes in which indigenous habitats will be islands in human-dominated habitats. Much more knowledge of how communities and ecosystems function will be needed to deal with such fragmentation.

With the third research focus—nature and humanity—conservation biology is in need of large-scale field experiments in land management, restoration techniques, reintroductions (translocations), selective removal and addition of species, and minimum size of viable protected areas. This means looking at ecosystems as laboratories. Social science research needs to be increased in scope to assess the relationship between people at all levels of sophistication and their natural environment.

These three research focuses lead to a wish list of conservation research. But what are the priorities when it comes to executing such research? The overall goals are to learn to conserve and wisely use biodiversity, and to preserve it intact. Yet there are literally hundreds of potential research projects. Norman Myers created a useful indicative list that constitutes a research agenda (Myers 1986a). He admitted that it is far from comprehensive, and that a good systematized agenda is lacking, but it does include those items that are probably the most urgent for many parts of the world, and especially the crucial hot spots of diversity. The following list is derived from Myers (1986a; 1988):

Differentiated fallout rates. Which categories of species, and what other taxonomic levels, are being most affected by broad-scale environmental degradation and destruction? Are we likely to lose most of the tropical forest biome, for instance, before we lose most of any other biome?

Linked extinctions. What prospect is there that a mass-extinction process will feed on itself through mechanisms that, by virtue of the integrative workings of ecosystems, can trigger a domino effect or cascade of extinctions?

Diversity and integrity of nature. In the light of the possible threat of linked extinctions in large numbers, should we consider switching the emphasis from safeguarding the diversity of nature to preserving its integrity? Can one be sure that an optimum number of species is necessarily a maximum number?

Mass extinctions and survivorship. What can the past tell us about the survivors of mass-extinction events, and can we gain a clearer insight into the probable make-up of biotas that appear best suited to survive the present extinction episode?

Recovery period. What does the past reveal about the potential bounce-back time required in the wake of extinctions, and what does this imply about our conservation strategies?

Conservation in practice. What scope is there for or-der-of-the-day manipulation of gene pools to maintain population viability? What other innovative techniques deserve investigation or are little known?

The greenhouse effect. What responses should be considered to the greenhouse effect and other climatic dislocations? What are the critical responses for protected area strategies?

A triage strategy. How can triage be applied in an informed and methodical manner? What are the criteria and what parameters should we seek to quantify, getting the best return for resources available?

The economics of threatened species. What are species worth to us now and in the future? How much are we prepared to pay to preserve species? How much will it cost to put a safety net under threatened species in question and is the cost socially acceptable?

Research in each of these nine issues can result in solutions applicable to a wide range of other cases. Some solutions must be found that can be applied in the immediate future. Examples of some critical, immediate research priorities are listed (Wildt and Seal 1988):

- Solutions contributing to population recovery.

- Identification and characterization of ecologically key species whose status affects or reflects the welfare of the communities in which they live.

- Conservation strategies for species that are highly distinct genetically and critically threatened.

- Conservation strategies that will work in less-developed countries, where the need for scientific expertise is greatest.

- Research in areas where a scientific presence may have extra conservation value.

- Dynamics of small populations (e.g., natural island populations).

Important research priorities may emerge if climate change becomes an overriding issue. Conservation of biodiversity in this instance must involve a great deal of research into fragmentation, the effects of stress on species, and the effects and roles of diseases and pathogens. Climate change research will bring into focus one of the more surprising gaps in conservation biology, particularly as it relates to plants—the precise mechanics of extinction.

RESEARCH PRIORITIES IN THE TROPICS

Not surprisingly, the tropics are an overwhelming problem area for conservation; they must become a primary target for research. For example, collecting and cataloging the flora of the Amazonian rain forest must be a priority. Examination of research priorities for the tropics has identified a number of particular needs (National Academy of Sciences 1980). First, scientific knowledge about tropical ecosystems is extremely incomplete. Moreover there are few data pertaining to the functioning of tropical aquatic and terrestrial ecosystems. Without the necessary knowledge, it is not possible to construct ecologically sound systems to support the numbers of people living in the tropics.

Sustainable agricultural systems still have not been achieved for the tropics. Although the conversion of tropical forest often results in immediate economic gain, and some tropical lands have been converted to timber plantations that are productive on a long-term basis, systems that lead to the sustained productivity of most tropical soils have not been achieved with existing technology.

Biological inventory of tropical ecosystems needs to be accelerated. There must be more regional studies alongside global ones, more taxonomists, greater conservation of genetic diversity on- and off-site, emphasis on selective evolutionary and biosystematic studies, more use of unusual or innovative methods of collecting specimens, and priority for known areas of high diversity.

Tropical ecosystems should be studied in depth at selected sites, and such studies should involve a wide range of disciplines. Relationships between soils, animals, and plants need to be stressed, as does study of nutrient movement and comparisons of primary and secondary vegetation systems. Tropical plant physiology requires greater attention as well.

Finally, specific tropical ecosystems and activities need to be targeted, including aquatic systems and monitoring of forest conversion.

Research at all levels must accomplish two rather different aims: satisfy short-term needs, especially where plant diversity is most threatened, and satisfy longer term needs measured in hundreds of years. It is a particular challenge to science and management to facilitate both these requirements. Concentration of research on only one of the very many issues is at best inefficient, and at worst may hasten extinction. Biosystematic research is necessary particularly in those hot spots of diversity that have been poorly studied by systematists. Case-study ecology is just as challenging and as necessary because sound conservation science must be founded on autecological studies of individual systems (Simberloff 1988).

The Funding Crisis

Conservation, whether as research, application, management, or advocacy, is grossly underfunded. In part this is because a number of damaging images of conservation persist in the eyes of its critics. Academics often regard it as a "lightweight" activity. Major funding agencies often regard conservation as too applied, although the opposite criticism—that it is too theoretical—is often made by management agencies. Conservation biology sits uncomfortably astride the divide between theoretical and applied science. It has been suggested that what conservation biology needs in the United States alone is an investment,

> comparable to what the United States spends on health and disease research.... If we find a cure for cancer, that may add one or two years to the life expectancy of Americans...but if we don't stop the loss of organic diversity, we'll be deducting 20 or more years (Ehrlich qtd. in Tangley 1988: 448).

One solution to this funding crisis may well be to increase the level of funding from the private sector. Several major U.S. foundations have now created the Consultative Group on Biological Diversity. The group's objective is to draw attention to and improve the quality of funding for the conservation of biological diversity in developing countries in the tropics. There can be no doubt that a greater amount of funding will have to come from the private sector than in the past. People are starting to realize that conservation does not come free. Simply setting aside an area of land as wilderness can involve considerable costs in the form of lost opportunities for alternative uses. A development associated with the Biodiversity Convention is the Global Environment Facility (GEF), designed to facilitate transfer of funds from richer to poorer nations to ensure the preservation and wise use of biodiversity.

It is paradoxical that although the biodiversity hot spots are mostly within underdeveloped nations, approximately 82 percent of science and technology expenditure is in the developed nations (where 20 percent of the people of the world live). Regions with greatest need of expertise may have least access to it. Colombia, with an estimated 45,000 vascular plant species, had only 47 resident botanists in 1985, in contrast to the British Isles, which support 1500 amateur and professional botanists and a flora of less than 2500 species (Toledo 1986). If GNP and flora size is compared, at one end of the scale are countries like Madagascar and Papua New Guinea, each with an index figure of 0.2, and at the other end are the United States with 225 and Japan with a staggering 481.

A 1980 study of research priorities in tropical biology recommended at least a doubling of the funds that were at that time devoted to biological inventory in the tropics and an increase by 50 percent of the professional systematists engaged in study of tropical organisms (National Academy of Sciences 1980). The study recommended establishment of centers for re-

search and major studies of critical ecosystems. Needs have grown even greater since that study, yet the increases in both funding and human effort have been only moderate, and certainly below these targets. Tragically, as time goes on, the needs are likely to accelerate and so will the urgency and consequent costs both in real money and social losses.

Biological apartheid is alive and well when it comes to conservation. One can be dazzled by the splendor of the glamour animals, the forests, and the sensational stories of impending extinction, not realizing that the mundane and less spectacular also need a share of resources.

The Information Crisis

The need for more conservation research should never be used as an excuse to delay conservation action (Tangley 1988). Everyone would like to have more information than they have already, especially when major decisions have to be made. Risk is a fact of life: every decision involves a certain number of unknowns. The nature of conservation science and management demands that decisions be taken with the minimum of information, or at least with far less than desirable.

Every conservation exercise adds to the general corpus of knowledge. It allows what has been learned, no matter how minor, to be used for subsequent decision making. Even failures have their purpose in directing attention to better alternatives. One of the critical questions that conservation biology seeks to answer is, How much, or how many, will be needed to preserve sufficient genetic diversity? Until recently, there have been too few investigations leading to formulation of general principles on this issue. Recent indications, however, are that the life form of plants is significant in this respect: annuals have appreciably more (at least four times) genetic variation among populations than woody perennials; selfing species have the greatest variation among populations and outcrossed species the least; plants have on average twice the genetic variation of animals (Mlot 1989). This allows the formulation of generalizations, which,

in time and with testing, should lead to rules for management.

An urgent and continuing need is for global monitoring and accurate global and regional databases. As Aldo Leopold (1949) once said, "The first rule of intelligent tinkering is to save all the pieces." One cannot come near to this without having the pieces in hand— knowing where species occur, where they are disappearing from, and where the concentrations of biodiversity are. This requires continued support of survey and monitoring, from remote sensing down to local ground survey. Furthermore, refinement of many techniques is needed, especially those most applicable to rapid ground survey. Long-term observations are vital:

> Long-term data series are not fashionable; they appear to funding agencies as an open-ended commitment. We must defend them because they are our only way of actually determining what is going on in the real world round us (Berry 1989).

It is important to note that observations by themselves are not sufficient. Observation and experiment are complementary and not alternatives: good observations must be the foundation for good and scientifically sound experiment that demonstrates what the observations really mean (Berry 1989).

Focal Points

There must be some doubt as to whether present and future achievements will stem the loss of biodiversity. As we move toward the twenty-first century, several focal points for efforts emerge. These needs include a

more rigorously biological approach to preservation of biodiversity, based on greater and more precise understanding of the processes of persistence and extinction; development of management strategies appropriate to ecosystems and populations subject to unnatural perturbation; acknowledgment of fundamental differences between plants and animals; a fusion of academic and pragmatic approaches to conservation problems, so that solutions are both innovative and realistic; adequate resources to get on with the job at hand; and development of a renewed conservation ethic.

More than 85 percent of biological diversity occurs in the tropics, so it is only natural that this is where conservation attention at a global level is often focused. This is where many of the present difficulties arise because the very regions with the greatest biological diversity are often also those that are least able to pay for conservation. Ironically, much of the pressure to use the resources of these regions comes from the most affluent nations.

Both within and outside the tropics, much more effort has to be concentrated in degraded and fragmented ecosystems. Although largely ignored by funding sources now, such ecosystems will be where much of the world's biological diversity will be preserved for the future.

Islands provide a further focal point for conservation effort. There is no doubt that they are particularly vulnerable to outside influences such as feral animals and invasive weeds. Many islands are also centers of endemism or harbor relics. But islands are also remote places whose future seemingly affects few people directly.

> Why are we concerned with the future of island floras? This is relatively easy to answer—because, as we have seen, they contain many interesting endemic plants. But who is interested? Which species are threatened? Does it matter and if so to whom? Why are we so concerned when apparently we do not appear capable of even identifying all of them? Are they of economic importance? . . . While it would be easy to convince our audience of botanists, they do not make the decisions. It is the general public, the voter, the taxpayer, the politician, the administrator who has to be persuaded, cajoled, convinced (Heywood 1979: 439-440).

The future of island floras will depend largely on political-sociological-economic planning decisions. The same will be true of most if not all areas where biodiversity needs to be fostered and protected. Decisions involve the input of many people: biologists, economists, social scientists, and the general public.

Myers (1988) identified 10 focal points of biological diversity. A more recent analysis (Myers 1990a) extends the number to 18, of which 14 are in tropical forests and 4 are in Mediterranean-type regions. Taking all 18 hot-spots together, they support 20 percent of known plant species and constitute 0.5 percent of the earth's land surface.

In considering focal points, it is important to remember not to be so focused that the wider view of things is lost. The late twentieth century is an age of specialization. It is also a time when, more than ever, the broader picture must be appreciated and professionals should be able, at least at certain times, to be generalists. Conservation cuts across every other aspect of life: it is a synthesis at a grand scale. Pantin (1968) warns that conservationists must be prepared to follow the analysis of their problems into every other kind of science. Without this they will not be able to accomplish major advances in their science.

Conservation biologists, managers, administrators, advocates—people involved in any aspect of conservation—have a unique opportunity and a globally significant responsibility to present this broader picture to a world that has become too introverted and specialized for its own good. The current fashion for reductionism and intellectual isolation is not the only way to solve the world's problems. In particular instances, such as protecting a particular species, it is necessary to focus; but that must not prevent the outward focus into an array of other disciplines (which each have their contribution) and toward a wider view of the universe.

The Last Frontier

The concept of the *frontier* has deep roots in most civilizations. The first frontiers were those represented by a distant range of mountains, rivers, and the simplest of technologies; later, oceans and mechanization became important frontiers. More recently, the deepest, highest, and coldest parts of the globe have been the focus of exploration and high technology, leading all the way to exploration of the solar system and universe.

But achievements in these fields divert attention from the real last frontier, which is the need to come to terms with the life-providing functions of the earth. The real challenges are to live in harmony with other species of life, to use resources sustainably, and to re-examine our cultures and institutions to achieve this. Knowledge, technologies, and institutions—traditional as well as modern—that can facilitate this effort need to be encouraged (Dahlberg 1986).

Twentieth-century civilization of the developed countries still reflects the short-sightedness evident in the pragmatism of Cotton Mather, the seventeenth-century witch hunter who proclaimed, "What is not useful is vicious" (Iltis 1988). This poses the questions, What is useful? Who is to determine usefulness? What of the species that are unstudied yet disappearing: do we know that they are any more or less useful than a hundred known "useful" animals and plants? This is the problem of serendipity—of the unknown: what we learn about the unknown may benefit future generations in ways that we can only begin to imagine (Ehrenfeld 1988).

Sometimes benefits have accrued from most unlikely beginnings. The apparently insignificant laboratory molds of Alexander Fleming were an important step in the modern development of antibiotics. The tiny, slimy seeds of an apparently useless, ugly, and weedy wild tomato have the potential to markedly increase soluble solids (chiefly sugars) in tomato fruits (Iltis 1988). Such discoveries prompted Hugh Iltis (1988: 102–103) to state,

> I have no patience with the phony requests of developers, economists, and humanitarians who want us biologists to "prove" with hard evidence, right here and now, the "value" of biodiversity and the "harm" of tropical deforestation. Rather it should be for them, the sponsors of reckless destruction, to prove to the world that a plant or animal species, or an exotic ecosystem, is not useful and not ecologically significant before being permitted by society to destroy it. And such proof, of course, neither they nor anybody else can offer!

The three components of conservation management urgently need addressing: determining the characteristics of the system of interest, selecting the goals of management, and developing the techniques for attaining these goals (Keddy et al. 1989). Each of these will require flexibility and innovation. Advances in biotechnology have already introduced techniques undreamed of a few years ago, including molecular biology, gene transfer, early flower and fruit induction, and tissue culture. There is no doubt that a host of further techniques will emerge in the future. These must be taken and applied to help conserve, preserve, and wisely use and nurture biodiversity. Yet new technology alone is not enough; it must be harnessed with wisdom and nonexploitive ethics to achieve its full potential for conservation.

Without conservation-directed ethics, biodiversity faces a bleak future. The world abounds with examples of what is *meant* to be and what actually *is*. Too often the official decrees establishing national parks fail clearly to define boundaries, or too little money is allocated to protect effectively the park values. In one instance, the official version of conservation spoke of a national park, new legislation, and the education of people. But the unofficial version—what was really happening—was dramatically different, as described by an anonymous observer:

> Nothing has changed. I think that sums up the situation here. The spiral aloe in which trade is forbidden continues to be sold by the roadside, in spite of the law; the one "National Park" (never gazetted) continues to deteriorate; there is no sign of a museum and no sign of a botanic garden other than the one at the University (for teaching). A plant survey of the highest mountain area which was conducted last February shows quite clearly what is happening. The highest mountains are, quite naturally, the most recently occupied. Yet we found people and herds virtually everywhere. The mountain bogs are being compacted by animals and will soon be useless. Such laws as do exist are openly defied. We found one shepherd with a herd of 600 animals in an area legally closed to grazing. I see very little hope for conservation.

Despite growing environmental awareness and the environmental machinery established in most countries, deterioration of environmental conditions and erosion of biodiversity continue in many parts of the world. There is no doubt that we are facing a very different world from that of fifty years ago, and the world fifty years hence is likely to be just as different, if not more so. It is likely to be a world dominated by semi-natural and cultivated landscapes where emphasis must be given to restoration and rehabilitation to conserve natural biodiversity. With such a trend, natural values become increasingly precious—too precious to be lost through mistaken management (Norton 1989). A sound scientific understanding of issues such as fragmentation, habitat modification, invasions, and population dynamics will be essential, alongside greater appreciation of social mores and interactions.

Determined and innovative action is urgently needed at national, regional, and global levels. Such innovation must be at the level of not just scientists, administrators, and government agencies; all people have responsibility—governments, public enterprises and institutions, private enterprises, citizen groups, nongovernmental organizations, educational and research institutions, as well as individuals in their personal capacities (United Nations Environment Program 1986). All have to help the world move toward a sustainable situation, which must include a stable world population; such harvesting of natural resources as would leave the earth's capital stock intact for posterity; the efficient meeting of energy needs without aggravating risks to, and harmful impacts on, health and economy; sustainable economic growth with a broad-based sharing of its benefits; and world peace and international security based on the understanding of the complementarity between the quality of life objectives of the developed and developing countries.

Innovation and flexibility must be exercised in the methods used to protect target areas, including tenure and ownership. It should not be assumed that biological reserves have to be managed by state or conservation agencies. In Paraguay, private reserves run by Itaipu Binacional are probably among the best in the country. They have guards, their flora and fauna has been inventoried, and museums have been set up for research and education. Itaipu Binacional is a semiautonomous commission that manages a large hydroelectric plant on the Rio Parana; one percent of the annual revenue of the plant goes to activities related to conservation (S. Keel, pers. com.).

CASE STUDY: INNOVATION—A TROPICAL CHRISTMAS CATALOG

Western Mesoamerica had an area of tropical dry forest equivalent to the size of France, but today less than 2 percent remains. Only 0.09 percent of this forest has conservation status. The dry forest in Guanacaste National Park (GNP) in northwestern Costa Rica wants to buy itself, replant itself, and regrow itself. This restoration of 700 square kilometers of dry forest and rainforest refugia will double the amount of Mesoamerican conserved dry forest.

How to restore it? Give it back the land it once occupied and protect it from ranching, fires, and hunting. The organisms come from the 255 square kilometers of national park restoration already within GNP, and from population fragments in the damaged habitats. Invasion by native organisms will be natural or assisted, depending on the zone. The restoration is also cultural. Its user-friendly performance as a living classroom and research laboratory will be conducted and attended largely by Costa Ricans, with an international audience as well. GNP has raised U.S. $1 million and requires $5 million more by May 1987 to purchase GNP's 160 square kilometer core. This purchase will secure the entire project.

The Christmas shopping menu—$300 buys (forever):

1 hectare or 2.47 acres
0.000029 volcano
0.001 jaguar
0.0071 bird species
0.1 adult guanacaste tree
0.04 anteater
0.01 muscovy duck
200 sphinx moth caterpillars
0.0029 herp species
0.1 agouti
25 spiny pocket mice
0.05 curassow
0.429 insect species
0.000016 of join between 330 square kilometers of dry forest and 210 square kilometers of rain forest
1,000,000 ants
0.01 white-lipped peccary
10,000 mushrooms
20 toads
400 dung beetles
0.25 tinamou
125,000 acorns
0.4 adult guapinol tree
0.023 mammal species
0.5 parrot
100 vines
5 m riverbank
5,000 bruchid beetles
0.005 tapir
1 rattlesnake
100 scorpions
200 orchids
0.000028571 peripatus species
3 million unlisted organisms
0.03 spider monkey

Your tax-deductible Christmas purchase order of any amount should be mailed to Nature Conservancy–Guanacaste Fund, 1785 Massachusetts Avenue, N.W., Washington, D.C. 20036. All purchases will be held for your on-site inspection by the Costa Rica National Park Service.

Source: Janzen 1986a.

Finally, and perhaps most fundamental, is the need for a renewed conservation ethic (McNeely 1989a; Engel and Engel 1990; Given 1990a). Conservation involves more than just knee-jerk reactions to the problems of distant oceanic islands and global issues. It means changing personal perspectives and ways of life, striving toward sustainable use of natural resources and social justice, and acknowledgment of a full range of values and cultural equity. Many people are cynical about the "green revolution" in politics. With good reason, they question whether an ethic of stewardship, sustainable development, and protection of biodiversity can be achieved under existing structures. Both capitalism and socialism have failed to deliver the environmental ethic that can safely carry the world into the twenty-first century and beyond. What is needed is the development of

> an awareness of and compassion for all life, and an appreciation of the fact that we are part of a living world. . . . we should not allow ourselves to respond only when the crises that we have caused are so extensive that they threaten our lives. To do so is to be thoroughly immoral in the fullest meaning of the word (Raven 1986a: 13).

Conservation offers a positive message for the world about plant diversity; it is not all negative. As David Ehrenfeld asserted, even scientists need to "recapture the love of diversity for its own sake" (Ehrenfeld 1986). Perhaps scientists have been too often persuaded by the expectations of others, especially politicians and technologists, to believe that theirs is a purely objective and emotionless discipline. Of ecology and ecologists, the natural science disciplines to which conservation closely relates, it was recently suggested that "the ecologist who cannot—or does not—stand back from his or her study in order to wonder, is a deprived person and possibly a poorer scientist" (Berry 1989).

Even when the overall message of conservation seems negative, there are ways to create awareness, educate, and persuade, because there is something very positive for people to believe in. This itself requires innovation and originality. Global concepts and quantities must be reduced to concepts and sizes that people can relate to. Talk of 25 million hectares of lost rain forest and associated species is relatively meaningless for many people; when translated into some number of hectares per minute, or smaller units of species, people may begin to grasp the problem.

Conservation of biodiversity is an issue of global importance for the 1990s. Biological conservation is a major plank in green politics, but its adoption as a political policy does not mean that its implications are appreciated or mechanisms understood, even by researchers, science administrators, or protected area and species managers. Indeed, as John Cobb asserted, "in the pursuit of economic gain most people do not want to be bothered by questions of biodiversity" (Cobb 1988: 481). Yet, it has also been pointed out that people want to be seen to be doing the right thing, and in an increasing number of instances, that thing is conservation-related.

Times of crisis are at hand for the conservation of plants and plant diversity. There are two aspects to this crisis: danger and opportunity. It is easy to be discouraged by the scale of the problems and the risks involved in setting out to change the world (including the risk of failure). But the opportunities are there.

> These are momentous times. They are times for great scientific investigations during a period when we shall witness the greatest upheaval ever to overtake our biological world in such a short space of time. They are times too for our scientific endeavours to make a critical contribution to the great biotic challenge of our era: that millions of species are threatened, and millions of species can be saved (Myers 1986a).

People and Plants

The conservation of plants and the needs of people converge in the increasingly important science of ethnobotany, the study of the utilization of plants by peoples, particularly, some would argue, long-standing traditional uses of plants. A multidisciplinary science that incorporates plant science, anthropology, and sometimes a variety of other disciplines such as medicine and agriculture, ethnobotany examines both the flora of a region and the culture of the people living there (Partap and Kapoor 1990). For centuries, knowledge of useful properties has accumulated for tens of thousands of plants. Forest people in many parts of the tropics frequently can distinguish the majority of plants growing in their region and have specific uses for many of them (Plotkin 1986).

Ethnobotanists can contribute towards conservation in many ways. They can determine which social groups use which plants and in what quantities; they can investigate attitudes towards the plant world and existing management practices; they can help identify areas where plant collection is not sustainable, in the sense that rates of harvesting are greater than those of natural replacement; they can assist in the development of new management practices, if desirable; and they can help to search for alternatives to wild harvesting, such as cultivation. Ethnobotanists do not necessarily deal only with perceptions and uses of "wild" plants (wild being often a matter of cultural opinion), but they also deal with cultivated plants. Ethnobotany is but one aspect of the wider subject of ethnoecology, which involves the perceptions and uses of nature by small groups in general, including relating to landscape, soils, animals and so on.

Ethnobotanists stand in a special relationship between local and scientific cultures. As such, they can help in the interchange of ideas. They can, for example, introduce appropriate new techniques and convey scientific knowledge about plant uses to local communities. Although knowledge of plant uses by local people can be profound, in some areas this knowledge is disappearing rapidly in the face of modern pressures. Loss of this knowledge represents a loss to all humanity. Ethnobotanists are in a position to record this knowledge for posterity, and in some cases they may be able to help revive fading traditions. Local knowledge about plant uses has long been devalued, which is one of the reasons why many local cultures, and also related seminatural ecosystems, have been in decline. Ethnobotanists are in a special position of responsibility to ensure that this does not continue to happen. If new commercial products from medicines to new varieties of crops are developed on the basis of local knowledge, then part of the benefits resulting from these new products should be returned to the source of the knowledge. Ethnobotanists can play a central role in ensuring that this happens.

One example of plant use by local people is as medicines. This use has contributed historically to the development of formalized systems of medicine such as the Chinese, Ayurvedic, and modern Western systems. It has been estimated that 35,000–70,000 species of plants have been used as medicines by one culture or another, while Chinese medicine employs about 5000 species. Modern pharmaceutical medicine based on single active chemical ingredients owes a major debt to ethnobotany, although chemicals that owe their original discovery to ethnobotanical research may now be synthesized, sometimes in chemically altered forms. Pilocarpine, derived from *Pilocarpus* and used to treat glaucoma, is an example of a modern medicine with its origin in local usage. *Catharanthus roseus,* the Madagascar or rosy periwinkle, yields the drugs vinblastine and vincristine, used to treat leukemia. The use of this pantropical ornamental in the treatment of leukemia was discovered fortuitously when the plant was screened following its employment in the Caribbean as a herbal remedy for diabetes.

An important area of ethnobotany concerns food plants. Our basic foods originated in several well-defined geographic areas—the Vavilov centers, named after the Russian geneticist who first identified them. The remarkable resources of the Vavilov centers are fast disappearing as clearing of forest, wetland drainage, modern agriculture, and land development take their toll. It is crucially important that the remaining traditional landraces and wild crop relatives of these regions be conserved for future generations. It cannot be assumed that the Vavilov centers have been fully explored. As an example, *Zea diploperennis,* which has been described as the "botanical find of the century," was discovered as recently as 1977.

A remarkable collection of local crops occurs in the mountains of South America, where many people still grow crops that remain outside the mainstream of agriculture. Ironically, this is the region that gave the world such major crops as the potato. When the Spanish arrived in Peru in 1591, they began introducing some new crops to Europe, but they also initiated events that led other crops into obscurity as the Inca empire collapsed. More than 20 root crops, legumes, grains, and fruits are "lost crops of the Incas," including amaranth, which is one of the most protein-rich grains known (Vietmeyer 1985).

The palms represent an outstanding plant group of vital importance to many people of the tropics. Just one group of palms, the rattans or climbing palms, is used by local people to make baskets, cordage, bridge hawsers, rafts, hammocks, sleeping mats and toothbrushes (Dransfield 1981, Myers 1984a). This group is also used in the manufacture of a range of industrial products such as dyes, varnishes, and medicines. The main commercial use of these climbing palms is, however, for furniture, for which there is an insatiable demand worldwide. Rattans have extraordinary strength yet retain malleability. Although many of the rattans are collected in the wild, their conservation was neglected until recently, though demand generally outstrips supply. There is an urgent need to find methods of managing wild rattans for sustained yields, of placing more species in cultivation to take the pressure off wild populations, and of taking active measures to conserve the germplasm of the species.

Conservation problems for rattans are well demonstrated by a critically threatened species, *Ceratolobus glaucescens,* which is known only from a few clumps confined to one nature reserve in West Java. Being situated in a reserve has not guaranteed the survival of this species; the only hope for it may be in botanic gardens. Widespread clearing of forest lowlands that are rich in rattans is likely to lead to the extinction of other species.

CASE STUDY: OIL CONTENT OF *FEVILLEA* SEEDS

Seeds of the liana *Fevillea* contain an emetic seed oil and are used by the Campa Indians of Amazonian Peru as candles. The plants have more oil per seed and fruit than any other dicotyledon. Calculations show that if the naturally occurring lianas of an otherwise intact forest were replaced by *Fevillea* vines producing fruits at their normal rates, the oil yield per hectare would be as great as that produced by any extant oil crop. *Fevillea* has extractable oil amounting to 55 percent of the seed body's weight. Genetic improvement might be expected to raise yields to about 800 kilograms of oil per hectare without felling any trees.

Sources: Myers 1984a; Gentry 1986.

Ethnobotany leads to sustained utilization of plants, including the science of plant breeding, which is as old as agriculture itself. From early beginnings has evolved a highly complex industry worth billions of dollars worldwide. Plant breeding is essential to the survival of humanity, but it also has engendered many social problems, some of which have generated bitter controversy in recent years. Much of this controversy revolves around questions regarding who ultimately owns plant genetic resources, and the role of multinational companies in developing new cultivars. There is also the issue of equity between the developed and developing world. Solutions are not likely to be simple, and consensus is not likely to be reached with ease.

Two of the most contentious matters in genetic resource conservation are plant variety rights (also known as breeders' rights) and plant patenting (Plucknett et al. 1987). Many people would accept restrictions of access to advanced breeding lines and finished varieties, and would agree that charging a royalty for the use of these is desirable. Ultimately, someone has to pay for such breeding work, whether it be the customer, governments, or international foundations. On the other side of the equation is the principle of farmers' rights, especially the recognition that the local landraces which have been evolved for particular local environments worldwide are the results of plant breeding and the intellectual efforts of local people over many hundreds of years. These varieties are often well adapted to local environments, and

their genes have often been used in breeding programs for "modern" high-yielding cultivars without any recognition or compensation. Why should the intellectual effort and energy which has produced local landraces also not be rewarded?

The other major area of controversy in plant breeding, after plant patenting and variety rights, concerns biotechnology. This has been defined as "the use of living organisms or their components in industrial processes" (NASULGC 1983 in Plucknett et al. 1987) or as "the use of a biological system to produce a product, the use of a biological system as a product, or the use of the techniques of biotechnology to indirectly provide a product, process, or service" (Hardy 1983 in Plucknett et al. 1987).

What equitable steps can be taken to harness traditional knowledge of plant uses, ethnobotanical skills, and conservation techniques? It is important that this process includes full consultation, and that people of other cultures be respected as custodians of knowledge about life-support species (Partap and Kapoor 1990). Educative aspects and full respect for traditional value systems and people-land relationships are also fundamental (Park 1990). Systematic approaches to ethnobotanical projects have been outlined (e.g., Given 1990b, Plotkin et al. 1986, Given and Harris 1994, Martin 1994), but need to be pursued in a spirit of respect, cooperation, and sharing of benefits to all who have an interest in the plants under study and evaluation.

People who have long lived closely with nature have often developed sustainable methods of using natural resources, such as forests, without destroying them. Consequently, their knowledge is vital to both development and conservation of resources. Failure to acknowledge the importance of this knowledge represents a tremendous cultural, economic, and scientific loss, particularly when the high degree of current local use is considered. As just one example, over 1000 plants in Xishuangbanna, of the Yunnan tropics, have been used by local people (Xu Zaifu 1987). Inextricably, the history of humanity and development of civilization is largely the story of people's relationships with the diversity of plant life around them. The conservation of that diversity and its wise use on a sustainable basis is one of the most important tasks entrusted to this and future generations.

Conversion Formulas

°F	$= (9/5 \times °C) + 32$

1 millimeter	= 0.04 inch
1 centimeter	= 0.4 inch
1 meter	= 3.3 feet
1 kilometer	= 0.6 mile

1 square meter	= 11 square feet
1 square kilometer	= 0.4 square mile
1 hectare	= 2.5 acres

1 cubic meter	= 1.3 cubic yards

Bibliography

Abawickrama, B. A. 1983. Threatened or endangered plants of Sri Lanka and the status of their conservation measures. In *Conservation of Tropical Plant Resources*. Eds. S. K. Jain and K. L. Mehra. Howrah: Botanical Survey of India. 13–18.

Adams, M. W., A. H. Ellingboe, and E. C. Rossman. 1971. Biological uniformity and disease epidemics. *BioScience* 21(21): 1067–1070.

Adams, R. P. 1992. DNA Bank-net to use DNA technology to save endangered germplasm. *Diversity* 8: 23.

Adisewojo, S. S., S. Tjokronegoro, and R. T. Tjokronegoro. 1984. Natural biological compounds traditionally used as pesticides and medicines. In *Traditional Lifestyles, Conservation and Rural Development*. Ed. J. Hanks. Gland, Switzerland: IUCN/Ecology Commission, Paper 7. 11–14.

Allen, R. 1974. Does diversity grow on cabbages? *New Scientist* 63: 528–529.

Altieri, M. A., M. K. Anderson, and L. C. Merrick. 1987. Peasant agriculture and the conservation of crop and wild plant resources. *Conservation Biology* 1: 49–58.

Anderson, A. B., and D. A. Posey. 1985. Manejo de cerrado pelos indios Kayapo. *Boletim do Museo Paraense Emilio Goeldi Botanica* 2(1): 77–98.

Antonovics, J. 1984. Genetic variation within populations. In *Perspectives in Plant Population Biology*. Eds. R. Dirzo and J. Sarukhan. Sunderland, MA: Sinauer.

Archibold, O. W. 1989. Seed banks and vegetation processes in coniferous forests. In *Ecology of Soil Seed Banks*. Eds. M. A. Leck, V. T. Thomas, and R. L. Simpson. London: Academic Press.

Ashton, J., and D. S. Mitchell. 1989. Aquatic plants: patterns and modes of invasion, attributes of invading species and assessment of control programmes. In *Biological Invasions: A Global Perspective*. Eds. J. A. Drake and H. A. Mooney. Chichester, England: Wiley. 111–154.

Ashton, P. S. 1976. Factors affecting the development and conservation of tree genetic resources in South-east Asia. In *Tropical Trees: Variation, Breeding and Conservation*. Eds. J. Burley and B. T. Styles. Linnean Society Symposium, Series 2. London: Academic Press. 189–198.

———. 1981. Techniques for identification and conservation of threatened species in tropical forests. In *The Biological Aspects of Rare Plant Conservation*. Eds. H. Synge. Chichester, England: Wiley. 219–232.

———. 1987. Biological considerations in in situ vs ex situ plant conservation. In *Botanic Gardens and the World Conservation Strategy*. Eds. D. Bramwell, O. Hamann, V. Heywood, and H. Synge. London: Academic Press. 117–130.

———. 1992. Species richness in plant communities. In *Conservation Biology*. Eds. P. L. Fiedler and S. K. Jain. New York: Chapman and Hall. 3–22.

Atkinson, I. A. E. 1990. Ecological restoration of islands: prerequisites for success. In *Ecological Restoration of New Zealand Islands*. Eds. D. R. Towns, C. H. Dougherty, and I. A. E. Atkinson. Conservation Sciences Publication No. 2, Department of Conservation, Wellington, New Zealand. 73–90.

Austin, M. 1987. The uses of surveys and data bases for conservation. In *Nature Conservation: the Role of Remnants of Vegetation*. Eds. D. A. Saunders, G. W. Arnold, A. A. Burbidge, and A. J. M. Hopkins. Chipping Norton, Australia: Surrey Beatty. 367–368.

Baez, A. V. 1986. Back to basics: "The 4 Cs". *IUCN Bulletin* 17: 120.

Baker, H. G. 1965. Characteristics and modes of origin of weeds. In *The Genetics of Colonizing Species*. Eds. H. G. Baker and C. L. Stebbins. New York: Academic Press. 147–169.

Bandyopadhyay, J., and V. Shiva. 1987. Chipko: rekindling India's forest culture. *The Ecologist* 17: 26–34.

Barney, G. O. 1980. *The Global 2000 Report to the President of the U.S.*, vol. 1, The Summary Report. Oxford: Pergamon.

Bartel, J. A. 1987. The federal listing of rare and endangered plants: what is involved and what does it mean. In *Conservation and Management of Rare and Endangered Plants*. Eds. T. S. Elias. Sacramento: California Native Plant Society. 15–22.

Bawa, K. S., and C. J. Webb. 1984. Flower, fruit and seed abortion in tropical forest trees: implications for the evolution of paternal and maternal reproductive patterns. *American Journal of Botany* 71: 736–751.

Bean, M. J. 1983. *The Evolution of National Wildlife Law*. New York: Praeger.

———. 1987. Legal experience and implications. In *The Road to Extinction*. Eds. R. Fitter and M. Fitter. Gland, Switzerland: IUCN. 39–43.

Beardsley, K., and D. Stoms. 1993. Compiling a digital map of areas managed for biodiversity in California. *Natural Areas Journal* 13: 177–190.

Beeston, G. 1987. Modelling: its role in understanding the position of the remnants in their ecosystems and the development of management strategies. In *Nature Conservation: the Role of Remnants of Native Vegetation*. Eds. D. A. Saunders, G. W. Arnold, A. A. Burbidge, and A. J. M. Hopkins. Chipping Norton, Australia: Surrey Beatty. 355–356.

Bell, A. D. 1985. On the astogeny of six-cornered clones: aspects of modular construction. In *Studies of Plant Demography: a Festschrift for John L. Harper*. Ed. J. White. London: Academic Press. 188–208.

Bellamy, D. 1979. The role of the media in conservation. In *Survival or Extinction*. Eds. H. Synge and H. Townsend. Kew, England: Royal Botanic Gardens. 165–170.

Benedetti, S. H. de. 1987. Management of feral pigs at Pinnacles National Monument. In *Conservation and Management of Rare and Endangered Plants*. Ed. T. S. Elias. Sacramento: California Native Plant Society. 193–198.

Bennett, P. S., R. R. Johnson, and M. R. Kunzmann. 1987. Cactus collection factors of interest to resource management. In *Conservation and Management of Rare and Endangered Plants*. Ed. T. S. Elias. Sacramento: California Native Plant Society. 215–224.

Bensen, 1975. Cacti. Bizarre, beautiful, but in danger. *The Environment Journal* (July): 85–89.

Berry, R. J. 1983. Genetics and conservation. In *Conservation in Perspective*. Eds. A. F. Warren and F. B. Goldsmith. Chichester, England: Wiley. 141–156.

———. 1989. Ecology: where genes and geography meet. *Journal of Animal Ecology* 58: 733–759.

Beven, S., E. F. Conner, and K. Beven. 1984. Avian biogeography in the Amazon basin and the biological model of diversification. *Journal of Biogeography* 11: 383–399.

Beyer, R. I. 1979. The appreciation of the conservation role by staff of botanic gardens. In *Survival or Extinction*. Eds. H. Synge and H. Townsend. Kew, England: Royal Botanic Gardens. 171–175.

———. 1988. Propagating *Ramosmania heterophylla* (Rubiaceae) at Kew, one of the world's rarest plants. *Botanic Gardens Conservation News* 1(3): 40–41.

Bierzychudek, P. 1982. The demography of jack-in-the-pulpit, a forest perennial that changes sex. *Ecological Monographs* 52: 335–351.

Black, M. J. 1984. The path of conservation. Part 1. In *Key Environments. Galapagos*. Ed. R. Perry. Oxford: Pergamon. 265–268.

Blackford, C., B. de Ronde, N. Gibbs, M. Jebson, J. Keenan, T. McClurg, R. Pemberton, D. Shearer, A. Sheppard, G. Smitheram, C. Turbott, and P. Wallace. 1986. *An Approach to the Management of Genetic Resources.* Case Study 603. Christchurch: Centre for Resource Management, University of Canterbury and Lincoln University.

Blixt, S. 1992. Gene banks for plant conservation. In *Conservation of Biodiversity for Sustainable Development.* Scandinavian University Press. 204–213.

Blockhuis, J., M. Dillenbeck, J. A. Sayer, and P. Wegge, eds. 1992. *Conserving Biological Diversity in Managed Tropical Forests.* Gland: IUCN; Yokohama: ITTO.

Boden, R. W., and E. A. Boden. 1987. Botanic gardens and community education in Australia. In *Botanic Gardens and the World Conservation Strategy.* Eds. D. Bramwell, V. Hamann, and H. Synge. London: Academic Press. 67–74.

Boecklen, W. J., and G. W. Bell. 1987. Consequences of faunal collapse and genetic drift to the design of nature reserves. In *Nature Conservation: the Role of Remnants of Native Vegetation.* Eds. D. A. Saunders, G. W. Arnold, A. A. Burbidge, and A. J. M. Hopkins. Chipping Norton, Australia: Surrey Beatty. 141–149.

Boitani, L. 1976. *Proceedings, Reintroductions: Techniques and Ethics.* Morges, Switzerland: WWF International.

Bond, W., and P. Slingsby. 1984. Collapse of an ant–plant mutualism: the Argentine ant (*Iridomyrmex humilis*) and myrmecochorous Proteaceae. *Ecology* 65: 1031–1037.

Boo, E. 1990. *Ecotourism: The Potentials and Pitfalls.* 2 vols. Washington, D.C.: WWF–U.S.

Botanic Gardens Conservation Secretariat. 1987. *The International Transfer Format (ITF) for Botanic Garden Plant Records, Version 01.00.* Kew, England: IUCN.

———. 1989. *The Botanic Gardens Conservation Strategy.* Kew, England: WWF, IUCN, Botanic Gardens Conservation Secretariat.

Botkin, D. B., B. R. Davies, D. Edwards, P. H. G. Frost, G. L. Lucas, G. Newman, A. Rabinovitch-Vin, G. C. Ray, R. L. Specht, R. Van Der Elst, and B. H. Walker. 1982. Ecological characteristics of ecosystems. In *Conservation of Ecosystems: Theory and Practice.* Eds. W. R. Siegfried and B. R. Davies. South African National Scientific Programmes Report No. 61, Council for Scientific and Industrial Research, Pretoria. 17–27.

Boucher, C. 1981. Autecological and population studies of Orothamnus zeyheri in the Cape of South Africa. In *The Biological Aspects of Rare Plant Conservation.* Ed. H. Synge. Chichester, England: Wiley. 343–355.

Boyd, J. M. 1984. The role of religion in conservation. *The Environmentalist* 4: 40–44.

Bradshaw, M. E. 1981. Monitoring grassland plants in Upper Teesdale, England. In *The Biological Aspects of Rare Plant Conservation.* Ed. H. Synge. Chichester, England: Wiley. 241–252.

Bramwell, D. 1979. A local botanic garden: its role in plant conservation. In *Survival or Extinction.* Eds. H. Synge and H. Townsend. Kew: Royal Botanic Gardens. 47–52.

———. 1987. The role of the Jardin Botanico Canario, "Viera y Clavijo" in the conservation of endangered Canarian endemics. In *Botanic Gardens and the World Conservation Strategy.* Eds. D. Bramwell, O. Hamann, V. Heywood, and H. Synge. London: Academic Press.

———. 1990. Conserving biodiversity in the Canary Islands. *Annals of the Missouri Botanical Garden* 77: 28–37.

Bramwell, D., O. Hamann, V. Heywood, and H. Synge, eds. 1987. *Botanic Gardens and the World Conservation Strategy.* London: Academic Press.

Briceno, S., and S. Drake, comps. 1986. Special report: education for a viable future. *IUCN Bulletin* 17(10–12): 111–127.

Brickell, C. 1976. *The Vanishing Garden: A Conservation Guide to Garden Plants.* London: Royal Horticultural Society / John Murray.

———. 1977. Conserving cultivated plants. *The Garden* 102(5): 197–201.

Bridgewater, P. B. 1987. Connectivity: an Australian perspective. In *Nature Conservation: the Role of Remnants of Native Vegetation.* Eds. D. A. Saunders, G. W. Arnold, A. A. Burbidge, and A. J. M. Hopkins. Chipping Norton, Australia: Surrey Beatty. 195–200.

Briggs, J. D., and J. H. Leigh. 1989. *Rare or Threatened Australian Plants.* Special Publication No. 14, Australian National Parks and Wildlife Service, Canberra.

Broady, P., D. Given, L. Greenfield, and K. Thompson. 1987. The biota and environment of fumeroles on Mount Melbourne, Northern Victoria Land. *Polar Biology* 7: 97–113.

Bromley, D. W. 1986: The common property challenge. In *Proceedings, Conference on Common Property Resource Management.* Washington, D.C.: National Academy of Sciences. 1–5.

Brooks, B. S. 1981. The discovery, extermination, translocation, and eventual survival of *Schoenus ferrugineus* in Britain. In *The Biological Aspects of Rare Plant Conservation.* Ed. H. Synge. Chichester, England: Wiley. 421–430.

Brown, A. H. D., and J. D. Briggs. 1991. Sampling strategies for genetic variation in ex-situ collections of endangered plant species. In *Genetics and Conservation of Rare Plants.* Eds. D. A. Falk and K. E. Holsinger. New York: Oxford University Press. 99–122.

Brown, A. H. D., and D. R. Marshall. 1986. Wild species as genetic resources for plant breeding. In *Plant Breeding Symposium DSIR 1986.* Eds. T. A. Williams and G. S. Wratt. Wellington: New Zealand Department of Scientific and Industrial Research. 9–15.

Brownrigg, L. A. 1985. Native cultures and protected areas: management options. In *Culture and Conservation: the Human Dimension in Environmental Planning.* Eds. J. A. McNeely and D. Pitt. Beckenham, England: Croom Helm. 33–44.

Bruce, J. P. 1990. Myths and realities of global climate change. *Ecodecision* 1: 89–92.

Bruik, V. C. 1980. The role of non-government organizations whose interests bear on the subject of threatened species and threatened habitats in British Columbia and the Yukon. In *Threatened and Endangered Species and Habitats in British Columbia and the Yukon.* Eds. R. Stace-Smith, L. Johns, and P. Joslin. Victoria, Canada: British Columbia Ministry of Environment. 282–284.

Bunnell, F. L., and R. G. Williams. 1980. Threatened species and habitats—why bother? In *Threatened and Endangered Species and Habitats in British Columbia and the Yukon.* Eds. R. Stace-Smith, L. Johns, and P. Joslin. Victoria, Canada: British Columbia Ministry of Environment. 260–281.

Burrough, P. A. 1986. *Principles of Geographic Information Systems for Land Resources Assessments.* Monographs on Soil and Resources Survey No. 12. Clarendon, Oxford: Oxford Science Publications.

Cairns, J., Jr. 1986. Restoration, reclamation, and regeneration of degraded or destroyed ecosystems. In *Conservation Biology.* Ed. M. J. Soulé. Sunderland, MA: Sinauer. 465–484.

Campbell, D. G., and H. D. Hammond. 1989. *Floristic Inventory of Tropical Countries.* New York: New York Botanical Garden.

Campbell, F. 1987. The potential for permanent plant protection. In *Conservation and Management of Rare and Endangered Plants.* Ed. T. S. Elias. Sacramento: California Native Plant Society. 7–14.

Cashdan, L., P. R. Stein, and D. Wright. 1982. Roses from rubble: new uses for vacant urban land. *New York Affairs Local Initiatives* 7: 89–96.

Ceballos-Lascurain, H. 1987. *Estudio de Prefactibilidad Socioeconomica del Turismo Ecologico y Anteproyecto Arquitectonico y Urbanistico del Centro de Turismo Ecologico de Sian Ka'an, Quintana Roo.* Study, SEDUE, Mexico.

Center for Plant Conservation. 1985. *Development Plan. Center for Plant Conservation, Jamaica Plain.* Jamaica Plain, MA: Center for Plant Conservation.

―――. 1986. *Recommendations for Collection and Ex Situ Management of Germplasm Resources from Rare Wild Plants.* Jamaica Plain, MA: Center for Plant Conservation.

―――. 1991. Program summary. Center for Plant Conservation, St. Louis, MO.

Chilean Forest Service. 1989. *Red List of Chilean Terrestrial Flora.* Santiago: Chilean Forest Service (CONAF).

City of Cape Town. 1982. Table Mountain Nature Reserve: Western Table master plan. City of Cape Town City Engineers' Department, South Africa.

Clark, R. A., and G. M. Fellers. 1987. *Rare Plants at Point Reyes National Reserve.* Cooperative National Parks Resources Study Unit, Technical Report No. 22, University of California, Davis.

Cobb, J. B., Jr. 1988. A Christian view of biodiversity. In *Biodiversity.* Ed. E. O. Wilson. Washington, D.C.: National Academy of Sciences. 481–485.

Cochrane, S. A. 1987. Endangered plants and Californian state laws. In *Conservation and Management of Rare and Endangered Plants.* Ed. T. S. Elias. Sacramento: California Native Plant Society. 33–38.

Cohn, J. P. 1989. Gauging the biological impacts of the greenhouse effect. *BioScience* 39(3): 1442–1445.

Colinvaux, P. A. 1984. The Galapagos climate: present and past. In *Key Environments: Galapagos.* Ed. R. Perry. Oxford: Pergamon. 55–69.

Collins, N. M., J. A. Sayer, and T. C. Whitmore, ed. 1991. *The Conservation Atlas of Tropical Forests (Asia and the Pacific).* Cambridge, England: IUCN.

Commonwealth Science Council. 1987. *Executive Summary: Genetic Resource Conservation in SADCC Region: Regional Training Workshop on Conservation Biology, 16–22 May 1987, Lusaka, Zambia.* London: Commonwealth Science Council.

Connor, K. F., F. B. Overmars, and M. M. Ralston. 1990. *Land Evaluation for Nature Conservation.* Conservation Sciences Publication No. 3, New Zealand Department of Conservation, Wellington.

Conway, G. R. 1985. Agroecosystem analysis. *Agricultural Administration* 20: 31–55.

———. 1987. The properties of agroecosystems. *Agricultural Systems* 24: 95–118.

Cranston, D. M., and D. H. Valentine. 1983. Transplant experiments on rare plant species from Upper Teesdale. *Biological Conservation* 26: 175–191.

Crawley, M. J. 1989. Chance and timing in biological invasions. In *Biological Invasions: a Global Perspective.* Eds. J. A. Drake and H. A. Mooney. Chichester, England: Wiley. 407–423.

Crist, R. E. 1971. Migration and population change in the Irish Republic. *American Journal of Economics and Sociology* 30: 253–258.

Cronk, Q. C. B. 1986. The decline of the St. Helena ebony *Trochetiopsis melanoxylon. Biological Conservation* 35:159–172.

———, comp. 1988. *Biodiversity. The Key Role of Plants.* Kew, England: IUCN/WWF.

———. 1989. St. Helena and Ascension Island. Unpublished report.

Csuti, B. A. 1984. Applying conservation biology to the preservation of natural diversity in natural areas. Report, Center for Conservation Biology, Stanford, CA.

Cullen, J., M. Lear, D. C. Mackinder, and H. Synge. 1987. Principles and standards for the computerisation of garden records schemes, as applied to conservation, with proposals for an International Transfer Format. In *Botanic Gardens and the World Conservation Strategy.* Eds. D. Bramwell, O. Hamann, V. Heywood, and H. Synge. London: Academic Press. 301–340.

Cummings, E. W. 1987. Using the Californian Endangered Species Act consultative provisions for plant conservation. In *Conservation and Management of Rare and Endangered Plants.* Eds. T. S. Elias. Sacramento: California Native Plant Society. 43–50.

Curran, J. 1985. *Principles of Remote Sensing.* London: Longman Group.

Curtis, J. T. 1956. In *Man's Role on Changing the Face of the Earth.* Ed. W. L. Thomas, Jr. Chicago: University of Chicago Press.

Dahlberg, K. A. 1986. The Earth, not space, is our last frontier. *Bulletin of Science, Technology and Society* 6(4): 337–338.

Daldjoeni, N. 1984. Pranatamangsa, the Javanese agricultural calendar—its bioclimatological and sociological function in developing rural life. In *Traditional Lifestyles, Conservation and Rural Development.* Ed. J. Hanks. Ecology Commission Paper 7. Gland, Switzerland: IUCN. 15–18.

Dasmann, R. 1984. The role of governments and international agencies in conservation and rural development. *The Environmentalist* 4: 8–11.

Davilla, W. B., D. W. Taylor, R. D. Stone, and J. W. Willoughby. 1987. Determining population sizes of narrowly endemic but locally common plants in the Red Hills, California. In *Conservation and Management of Rare and Endangered Plants.* Ed. T. S. Elias. Sacramento: California Native Plant Society. 167–172.

Davis, S. D. 1983. *WWF Plants Campaign: the World's Crop Plants.* Plantpac 2. Gland, Switzerland: WWF.

Davis, S. D., S. J. M. Droop, P. Gregerson, L. Henson, C. J. Leon, J. Lamlein Villa-Lobos, H. Sunge, and J. Zantovska. 1986. *Plants in Danger. What do we know?* Gland, Switzerland: IUCN.

Davy, A. J., and R. L. Jefferies. 1981. Approaches to the monitoring of rare plant populations. In *The Biological Aspects of Rare Plant Conservation.* Ed. H. Synge. Chichester, England: Wiley. 219–232.

Dawson, B. E. 1987. Development of management plans for sensitive plant species. *Conservation and Management of Rare and Endangered Plants.* Ed. T. S. Elias. Sacramento: California Native Plant Society. 455–460.

De Becker, S. M. C. 1984. Geysers panicum monitoring study: 1983 annual report. Department of Engineering Research Report No. 417-84.19, Pacific Gas and Electricity Company, San Francisco, CA.

———. 1985. Geysers panicum monitoring study: 1984 annual report. Department of Engineering Research Report No. 417-85.11, Pacific Gas and Electricity Company, San Francisco, CA.

De Klemm, C. 1982. Conservation of species: the need for a new approach. *Environmental Policy and Law* 9: 117–128.

———. 1990. *Wild Plant Conservation and the Law.* Gland, Switzerland: IUCN.

Delamater, R., and W. Hodgson. 1987. *Agave arizonica,* an endangered species, a hybrid or does it matter. In *Conservation and Management of Rare and Endangered Plants.* Ed. T. S. Elias. Sacramento: California Native Plant Society. 305–310.

Derkatch, M. 1987. UNESCO programme on biosphere reserves as centres for conservation of gene pools of life support species. Workshop on Life Support Species, New Delhi, India.

Deshaye, J., and P. Morisset. 1989. Species–area relationships and the SLOSS effect in a subarctic archipelago. *Biological Conservation* 48: 265–276.

Deshmukh, I. 1986. *Ecology and Tropical Biology.* Palo Alto, CA: Blackwell Scientific.

Di Castri, F. 1989. History of biological invasions with special emphasis on the old world. In *Biological Invasions: a Global Perspective.* Eds. J. A. Drake and H. A. Mooney. Chichester, England: Wiley. 1–30.

Diamond, J. M. 1975. The island dilemma: lessons of modern biogeographic studies for the design of nature reserves. *Biological Conservation* 7: 129–146.

Diamond, J. 1986. The design of a nature reserve system for Indonesian New Guinea. In *Conservation Biology.* Eds. M. J. Soulé. Sunderland, MA: Sinauer. 485–503.

———. 1987. Reflections on goals and on the relationship between theory and practice. In *Restoration Ecology—a Synthetic Approach to Ecological Research.* Eds. W. R. Jordan, III, M. E. Gilpin, and J. D. Aber. Cambridge: Cambridge University Press. 329–336.

Dixon, K. W., and J. S. Pate. 1984. Biology and distributional status of *Rhizanthella gardneri* Rogers, the Western Australian underground orchid. Kings Park Research Note 9, Kings Park, Perth, Australia.

Dobias, R. J. 1985. Elephant conservation and protected area management. Final report, WWF International/IUCN Project 3001.

Dobson, A. P., and P. J. Hudson. 1986. Parasites, disease and the structure of ecological communities. *Tree* 1: 11–14.

Dover, P. 1989. Saving wildlife on Canada's prairies. *WWF News* (April/May): 3–6.

Drake, J. A., and H. A. Mooney, eds. 1989. *Biological Invasions: a Global Perspective.* Chichester, England: Wiley.

Dransfield, J. 1981. The biology of Asiatic rattans in relation to the rattan trade and conservation. In *The Biological Aspects of Rare Plant Conservation.* Ed. H. Synge. Chichester, England: Wiley. 179–186.

———. 1987. *The Palms of the New World: a Conservation Census.* IUCN/WWF Plants Programme, Publication 2. Kew, England: IUCN/WWF Plants Programme.

Drury, W. H., and I. C. T. Nisbet. 1973. Succession. *Arnold Arboretum Journal* 54(3): 331–368.

Dunn, P. V. 1987. Endangered species management in southern California coastal salt marshes: a conflict or opportunity. In *Conservation and Management of Rare and Endangered Plants.* Ed. T. S. Elias. Sacramento: California Native Plant Society. 441–446.

Eckholm, E. 1978. *Disappearing Species: the Social Challenge.* Worldwatch Institute Paper 22. Washington, D.C.: Worldwatch Institute.

Edwards, I., and H. Paul. 1988. A rain forest child. *Botanic Gardens Conservation News* 1(3): 25–29.

Ehrenfeld, D. 1986. Thirty million cheers for diversity. *New Scientist* 110: 38–43.

———. 1988. Why put a value on biodiversity? In *Biodiversity.* Ed. E. O. Wilson. Washington, D.C.: National Academy of Sciences. 212–216.

Ehrlich, P. R. 1986. Extinction: what is happening now and what needs to be done. In *Dynamics of Extinction.* Ed. D. K. Elliott. New York: Wiley-Interscience. 157–164.

———. 1988. The loss of diversity. In *Biodiversity.* Ed. E. O. Wilson. Washington, D.C.: National Academy of Sciences. 21–27.

Ehrlich, P. R., and A. H. Ehrlich. 1981. *Extinction: The Causes and Consequences of the Disappearance of Species.* New York: Random House.

Ehrlich, P. R., and D. D. Murphy. 1987. Monitoring populations on remnants of native vegetation. In *Nature Conservation: the Role of Remnants of Vegetation.* Eds. D. A. Saunders, G. W. Arnold, A. A. Burbidge, and A. J. M. Hopkins. Chipping Norton, Australia: Surrey Beatty. 201–210.

Elias, T. S. 1987a. Can threatened and endangered species be maintained in botanic gardens? In *Conservation and Management of Rare and Endangered Plants.* Ed. T. S. Elias. Sacramento: California Native Plant Society. 563–566.

———, ed. 1987b. *Conservation and Management of Rare and Endangered Plants.* Sacramento: California Native Plant Society.

Elliott, S., and J. Brimacombe. 1985. *The Medicinal Plants of Gulung Leuser National Park, Indonesia.* Report to WWF International.

Eloff, J. N. 1987. Botanic gardens and education in South Africa. In *Botanic Gardens and the World Conservation Strategy.* Eds. D. Bramwell, O. Hamann, V. Heywood, and H. Synge. London: Academic Press. 85–102.

———. 1988. The threatened plant laboratory: a significant step in the research of the NBG. *Veld and Flora* (June): 59–61.

Elton, C. S. 1958. *The Ecology of Invasions by Animals and Plants.* Methuen.

Engel, J. R. 1988. The symbolic and ethical dimensions of the biosphere reserve concept. In *Fourth World Wilderness Congress Worldwide Conservation. Proceedings, Symposium on Biosphere Reserves.* Washington, D.C.: U.S. Department of the Interior. 21–32.

———. 1990. Introduction: the ethics of sustainable development. In *Ethics of Environment and Development.* Eds. J. R. Engel and J. G. Engel. London: Belhaven. 1–23.

Engel, J. R., and J. G. Engel, eds. 1990. *Ethics of Environment and Development.* London: Belhaven.

Evans, J. M. 1988. Direct seeding and container plant installation techniques: justification for simultaneous use in revegetation. Paper presented at Second Native Plant Revegetation Symposium, San Diego, CA.

Everett, S. 1988. Rare vascular plant survey of southern England. Contract Survey 50/DA01/F2C/420, Nature Conservancy Council, Peterborough, England.

Falk, D. A. 1987. Endangered species in botanic gardens. In *Conservation and Management of Rare and Endangered Plants.* Ed. T. S. Elias. Sacramento: California Native Plant Society. 553–562.

———. 1990a. Integrated strategies for conserving plant genetic diversity. *Annals of the Missouri Botanical Garden* 77: 38–47.

———. 1990b. Endangered forest resources in the United States: integrated strategies for conservation of rare species and genetic diversity. *Forest Ecology and Management* 35: 91–117.

————. 1991. Joining biological and economic models for conserving plant genetic diversity. In *Genetics and Conservation of Rare Plants*. Eds. D. A. Falk and K. E. Holsinger. New York: Oxford University Press. 209–224.

Falk, D. A., and K. E. Holsinger, eds. 1991. *Genetics and Conservation of Rare Plants*. New York: Oxford University Press.

Farnsworth, N. R. 1984. How can the well be dry when it is filled with water? *Economic Botany* 38: 4–13.

————. 1988. Screening plants for new medicines. In *Biodiversity*. Ed. E. O. Wilson. Washington, D.C.: National Academy of Sciences. 212–216.

Farnsworth, N. R., and R. W. Morris. 1976. Higher plants—the sleeping giant of drug development. *American Journal of Pharmacy* 148:46–52.

Farnsworth, N. R., and D. D. Soejarto. 1985. Potential consequence of plant extinction in the United States on the current and future availability of prescription drugs. *Economic Botany* 39: 231–240.

Fay, M. F. 1988. Micropropagation at the Royal Botanic Gardens, Kew. *Botanic Gardens Conservation News* 1(3): 42–45.

Fearnside, P. M. 1989. The charcoal of Carajas: a threat to the forests of Brazil's eastern Amazon region. *Ambio* 18: 141–143.

Ferreira, J., and D. Hillyard. 1987. Genetic conservation issues in land restoration: an open discussion. In *Conservation and Management of Rare and Endangered Plants*. Ed. T. S. Elias. Sacramento: California Native Plant Society. 523–524.

Fiedler, P. L. 1986. Concepts of rarity in vascular plant species, with special reference to the genus *Calochortus* Pursh (Liliaceae). *Taxon* 35: 502–518.

————. 1987. Life history and population dynamics of rare and common mariposa lilies (*Calochortus* Pursh, Liliaceae). *Journal of Ecology* 75: 977–996.

Fiedler, P. L., and S. K. Jain. 1992. *Conservation Biology*. New York: Chapman and Hall.

Fitter, R. 1986. *Wildlife for Man: How and Why We Should Conserve our Species*. London: Collins.

Fitter, R., and M. Fitter, eds. 1987. *The Road to Extinction*. Gland, Switzerland: IUCN/UNEP.

Food and Agriculture Organization of the United Nations. 1989. Interpretation of the international undertaking on plant genetic resources. Report to FAO, Rome, Italy.

Foose, T. J. 1986. Riders of the last ark: the role of captive breeding in conservation strategies. In *The Last Extinction*. Eds. L. Kaufman and K. Mallory. Cambridge, MA: MIT Press. 141–165.

Foster, R. B. 1980. Heterogeneity and habitat disturbance in tropical vegetation. In *Conservation Biology*. Eds. M. J. Soulé and B. A. Wilcox. Sunderland, MA: Sinauer. 75–92.

Frankel, O. H., and E. Bennett. 1970. *Genetic Resources in Plants: Their Exploitation and Conservation*. IBP Handbook 11. London: Blackwell.

Frankel, O. H., and M. J. Soulé. 1981. *Conservation and Evolution*. Cambridge: Cambridge University Press.

Frost, L. C. 1981. The study of *Ranunculus ophioglossifolius* and its successful conservation at the Badgeworth Nature Reserve, Gloucestershire. In *The Biological Aspects of Rare Plant Conservation*. Ed. H. Synge. Chichester, England: Wiley. 481–490.

Fuller, W. A. 1987. Synthesis and recommendations. In *The Road to Extinction*. Eds. R. Fitter and M. Fitter. Gland, Switzerland: IUCN/UNEP.

Furtado, J. I. 1987. Some problems. In *The Road to Extinction*. Eds. R. Fitter and M. Fitter. Gland, Switzerland: IUCN/UNEP. 62–63.

Futuyma, D. J., and G. Moreno. 1988. The evolution of ecological specialisation. *Annual Review of Ecology and Systematics* 19: 207–233.

Gadgil, M., and O. T. Solbrig. 1972. The concept of r- and K-selection: evidence from wild flowers and some theoretical considerations. *American Naturalist* 106: 14–33.

Galloway, J. N. 1989. Atmospheric acidification: projections for the future. *Ambio* 18: 161–166.

Game, M. 1986. The use and impact of the Greater London Ecology Database. Manuscript notes, Greater London Ecology Unit.

Gee, H. 1989. Desperate fight for life in the Last Chance Mountains. *The Times* (March 7).

Gentry, A. H. 1979. Extinction and conservation of plant species in tropical America: a phytogeographic perspective. In *Systematic Botany, Plant Utilization and Biosphere Conservation.* Ed. I. Hedberg. Stockholm: Almquist and Wiksell. 110–126.

———. 1982. Neotropical floristic diversity: phytogeographical connections between Central and South America: Pleistocene climatic fluctuations, or an accident of the Andean orogeny. *Annals of the Missouri Botanical Garden* 69: 557–593.

———. 1986. An overview of neotropical phytogeographic patterns with an emphasis on Amazonia. In *Anais, lo Simposia do Tropico Umido. Volume II. Flora e Floresta.* Brasilia, DF, Brazil: Departmento de ifusao de Tecnologia. 19–35.

Gerlach, L. P., V. Hine, and E. Radcliffe. 1980. You and the ecology movement. *Natural History* 89(7): 6–8.

Gibbs, M. 1989a. Report on the native orchids at Iwitahi. *Orchids in New Zealand* 15: 38–41.

———. 1989b. Iwitahi grant. *Orchids in New Zealand* 15: 69.

Gilbert, W. 1980. Food web organization and conservation of neotropical diversity. In *Conservation Biology.* Eds. M. J. Soulé and B. A. Wilcox. Sunderland, MA: Sinauer. 11–34.

Gilpin, M. E. 1987. Spatial structure and population vulnerability. In *Viable Populations for Conservation.* Ed. M. J. Soulé. Cambridge: Cambridge University Press. 125–140.

Gilpin, M. E., and M. J. Soulé. 1986. Minimum viable populations: processes of species extinctions. In *Conservation Biology.* Ed. M. J. Soulé. Sunderland, MA: Sinaeur. 19–34.

Gilpin, P. 1983. *Quantitative Plant Ecology.* 3rd ed. Oxford: Blackwell.

Given, D. R. 1981. *Rare and Endangered Plants of New Zealand.* Wellington, New Zealand: Reed.

———. 1983. Conservation of island floras. In *Conservation of Tropical Plant Resources.* Eds. S. K. Jain and K. L. Mehra. Howrah: Botanical Survey of India. 82–100.

———. 1984. Monitoring and science—the next stage in threatened plant conservation in New Zealand. In *Conservation of Plant Species and Habitats.* Ed. D. R. Given. Wellington, New Zealand: Nature Conservation Council. 83–102.

———. 1987a. What the conservationist requires of ex situ collections. In *Botanic Gardens and the World Conservation Strategy.* Eds. D. Bramwell, O. Hamann, V. Heywood, and H. Synge. London: Academic Press. 103–117.

———. 1987b. Plant conservation in the Antarctic. *Species* (March): 15 [reprinted in *IUCN Bulletin* 18 (10–12): 11].

———. 1987c. Plant variety rights: some implications for conservation. *Tuatara* 29: 13–18.

———. 1990a. Conserving botanical diversity on a global scale. *Annals of the Missouri Botanical Garden* 77: 48–62.

———. 1990b. A framework for conservation of plant genetic resources. In *Nga Mahi Maori o Te Wao Nui a Tane: Contributions to an International Workshop on Ethnobotany.* Eds. W. Harris and P. Kapoor. Christchurch, New Zealand: Department of Scientific and Industrial Research, Botany Division. 119–126.

Given, D. R., and W. Harris. 1994. *Techniques and Methods of Ethnobotany as an Aid to the Study, Evaluation, Conservation and Sustainable Use of Biodiversity—A Training Manual.* London: Commonwealth Science Council.

Given, D. R., and D. A. Norton. 1993. A multivariate approach to assessing threat and for priority setting in threatened species conservation. *Biological Conservation* 64: 57–66.

Given, D. R., and J. H. Soper. 1981. The Arctic-alpine element of the vascular flora at Lake Superior. Publications in Botany no. 10, National Museum of Canada, Ottawa.

Given, D. R., and P. A. Williams. 1984. *Conservation of Chatham Island Flora and Vegetation.* Christchurch, New Zealand: Department of Scientific and Industrial Research.

Gleason, H. A., and A. Cronquist. 1964. *The Natural Geography of Plants.* New York: Columbia University Press.

Gleick, P. H. 1989. Climate change and international politics: problems facing developing countries. *Ambio* 18: 333–339.

Godley, E. J. 1963. Breeding systems in New Zealand plants. 2. Genetics of the sex forms in *Fuschia procumbens. New Zealand Journal of Botany* 1: 48–52.

———. 1979. Flower biology in New Zealand. *New Zealand Journal of Botany* 23: 687–706.

Goff, F. G., G. A. Dawson, and J. J. Rochow. 1982. Site examination for threatened and endangered plant species. *Environmental Management* 6: 307–316.

Gomez-Campo, C. 1987. A strategy for seed gene banking in botanic gardens: some policy considerations. In *Botanic Gardens and the World Conservaion Strategy.* Eds. D. Bramwell, O. Hamann, V. Heywood, and H. Synge. London: Academic Press. 151–160.

Good, R. 1974. *The Geography of Flowering Plants.* London: Longman.

Good, R. B., and J. H. Leigh. 1986. Guidelines for the formulation of uniform flora legislation in all states. Report to Australian CONCOM Ad Hoc Working Group on Endangered Flora.

Goodenough, S. 1985. St. Helena—a conservation success. Report. Manuscript notes, Royal Botanic Gardens, Kew, England.

Goodman, D. 1987. The demography of chance extinction. In *Viable Populations for Conservation.* Ed. M. J. Soulé. Cambridge: Cambridge University Press. 11–34.

Goodman, P. J., E. M. Braybrooks, and J. M. Lambert. 1959. Investigations into 'die-back' in *Spartina townsendii* agg. I. The present status of *Spartina townsendii* in Britain. *Journal of Ecology* 47: 651–677.

Gorham, E. 1989. Scientific understanding of ecosystem acidification: a historical review. *Ambio* 18: 150–154.

Goswell, M. 1976. Please don't pick the butterworts. *National Wildlife* (April/May): 33–37.

Green, B. H., ed. 1979. *Wildlife Introductions to Great Britain.* London: Nature Conservancy Council.

———. 1981. A policy on introductions to Britain. In *The Biological Aspects of Rare Plant Conservation.* Ed. H. Synge. Chichester, England: Wiley.

Greenslade, P. J. M. 1983. Adversity selection and the habitat template. *American Naturalist* 122: 352–365.

Gregg, W. P., Jr. 1988. On wilderness, national parks, and biosphere reserves. In *Fourth World Wilderness Congress on Worldwide Conservation. Proceedings of the Symposium on Biosphere Reserves.* Washington, D.C.: U.S. Department of the Interior.

Grenell, P. G. 1987. Innovative programmatic approaches to resource conservation. In *Conservation and Management of Rare and Endangered Plants.* Ed. T. S. Elias. Sacramento: California Native Plant Society.

Grieg-Smith, P. 1983. *Quantitative Plant Ecology.* 3rd ed. Studies in Ecology Vol. 9. Oxford: Blackwell Scientific.

Grime, J. P. 1977. Evidence for the existence of three primary strategies in plants and its relevance to ecological and evolutionary theory. *The American Naturalist* 111: 1169–1191.

———. 1979. *Plant Strategies and Vegetation Processes.* Chichester, England: Wiley.

Grubb, P. J. 1977. The maintenance of species richness in plant communities. The importance of the regeneration niche. *Biological Review* 52: 107–145.

Grumbine, E. 1990. Protecting biological diversity through the greater ecosystem concept. *Natural Areas Journal* 10: 114–120.

Gunatilleke, C. V. S., I. A. U. N. Gunatillake, and B. Sumithraarachchi. 1987. Woody endemic species of the wet lowlands of Sri Lanka and their conservation in botanic gardens. In *Botanic Gardens and the World Conservation Strategy.* Eds. D. Bramwell, O. Hamann, V. Heywood, and H. Synge. London: Academic Press.

Gunn, A., and A. Edmonds. 1986. Why preserve species? In *Environment and Ethics: A New Zealand Contribution.* Ed. J. Howell. Wellington: New Zealand Environment Council. 23–60.

Gupta, R., and K. L. Sethi. 1983. Conservation of medicinal plants in the Himalayan region. In *Conservation of Tropical Plant Resources.* Eds. S. K. Jain and K. L. Mehra. Howrah: Botanical Survey of India.

Gwynne, M. 1985. GRID: jewel in GEMS. *IUCN Bulletin* 16(10–12): 125–126.

Haga, R. 1989. Logging. *Whispering Aru* (unpaged).

Hagsater, E., and J. Stewart. 1985. *Code of Conduct for Orchid Growers and Collectors.* Gland, Switzerland: IUCN/ SSC Orchid Specialist Group.

Hall, A. V. 1974. Museum specimen record data storage and retrieval. *Taxon* 23: 23–38.

———. 1978. Endangered species in a rising tide of human population growth. *Transactions of the Royal Society of South Africa* 43: 37–49.

———, ed. 1984. Rare plants gazette no. 4. Bolus Herbarium, University of Cape Town.

Hall, A. V., and M. A. Rabie. 1983. Indigenous plants. In *Environmental Concerns in South Africa.* Eds. R. F. Fuggle and M. A. Rabie. Capetown, South Africa: Juta. 164–189.

Hall, A. V., and H. A. Veldhuis. 1985. *South Africa Red Data Book: Plants—Fynbos and Karoo Biomes.* South African National Scientific Programmes Report no. 117, Council for Scientific and Industrial Research, Pretoria.

Hall, A. V., M. De Winter, B. De Winter, and S. A. M. Van Oosterhout. 1990. *Threatened Plants of Southern Africa.* South African National Scientific Programmes Report no. 45, Council for Scientific and Industrial Research, Pretoria.

Hall, L. A. 1987. Transplantation of sensitive plants as mitigation for environmental projects. In *Conservation and Management of Rare and Endangered Plants.* Ed. T. S. Elias. Sacramento: California Native Plant Society. 413–420.

Halloy, S. 1986. The highest bryophyte taxoccnes on earth? *Bryological Times* 367: 6–7.

Hamand, J. 1987. Fodder trees and family planning in Nepal. *Earthwatch* 28: 4–5.

Hamann, O. 1987. The IUCN/WWF Plants Conservation Programme in action. In *Botanic Gardens and the World Conservation Strategy.* Eds. D. Bramwell, O. Hamann, V. Heywood, and H. Synge. London: Academic Press. 31–46.

Hanemann, W. M. 1988. Economics and the preservation of biodiversity. In *Biodiversity.* Ed. E. O. Wilson. Washington, D.C.: National Academy of Sciences. 193–199.

Hanks, J., ed. 1984a. *Traditional Life-styles, Conservation and Rural Development.* Commission on Ecology Paper no. 7. Gland, Switzerland: IUCN.

———. 1984b. Conservation and rural development: towards an integrated approach. *The Environmentalist* 4: 60–67.

Hardy. 1983. Chemical, biological, genetic and agronomic approaches to improved or alternative technologies to provide fixed nitrogen. In *Chemistry and World Food Supplies: The New Frontiers.* II. Ed. L. W. Shemilt. Oxford: Pergamon. 585–599.

Harper, J. L. 1977. *Population Biology of Plants.* London: Academic Press.

———. 1981. The meanings of rarity. In *The Biological Aspects of Rare Plant Conservation.* Ed. H. Synge. Chichester, England: Wiley.

———. 1984. Forward. In *Perspectives in Plant Population Biology.* Ed. R. Dirzo and J. Sarukhan. Sunderland, MA: Sinauer. xv–xviii.

Harris, W., and P. Kapoor, eds. 1990. *Nga Mahi Maori o Te Wao Nui a Tane: Contributions to an International Workshop on Ethnobotany.* Christchurch, New Zealand: Department of Scientific and Industrial Research, Botany Division.

Harrison, J., K. R. Miller, and J. McNeely. 1982. The world coverage of protected areas: development goals and environmental needs. In *World National Park Congress.* Bali. 7–28.

Hartmann, H. E. K. 1981. Ecology, distribution and taxonomy in Mesembryanthemaceae as a basis for conservation decisions. In *The Biological Aspects of Rare Plant Conservation.* Ed. H. Synge. Chichester, England: Wiley. 297–303.

Hastey, E. L. 1987. Conservation of rare plants on public lands in California. In *Conservation and Management of Rare and Endangered Plants.* Sacramento: California Native Plant Society. 51–60.

Hawkes, J. G. 1985. A strategy for seed banking in botanic gardens. Unpublished report to International Conference on The World Conservation Strategy and Botanic Gardens, Las Palmas, Canary Islands.

———. 1987a. A feasibility study for the preparation of a list of economic plants for conservation and development. Report to IUCN/WWF.

———. 1987b. A strategy for seed gene banking in botanic gardens. In *Botanic Gardens and the World Conservation Strategy.* Eds. D. Bramwell, O. Hamann, V. Heywood, and H. Synge. London: Academic Press. 131–150.

Heenan, P. B. 1985. Rare plant conservation in parks departments. *Royal New Zealand Institute of Horticulture Annual Journal* 13: 13 -21.

Henifen, M. S., L. E. Morse, J. L. Reveal, B. MacBryde, and J. I. Lawyer. 1981. Guidelines for preparation of status reports on rare and endangered plant species. In *Rare Plant Conservation: Geographical Data Organization.* Eds. L. E. Morse and M. S. Henifin. New York: New York Botanical Garden. 261–282.

Hepper, F. N. 1988. A botanical garden for conserving the forest in Cameroon. *Botanical Gardens Conservation News* 1(2): 38–39.

Hernandez Bermejo, J. E. 1987. The Cordoba Botanic Garden in the local community. In *Botanic Gardens and the World Conservation Strategy.* Eds. D. Bramwell, O. Hamann, V. Heywood, and H. Synge. London: Academic Press. 75–84.

Heslop-Harrison, J. 1973. The plant kingdom, an inexhaustible resource? *Transactions of the Botanical Society of Edinburgh* 42: 1–15.

Heywood, V. H. 1979. The future of island floras. In *Plants and Islands.* Ed. D. Bramwell. London: Academic. 431–442.

———. 1987. The changing role of botanic gardens. In *Botanic Gardens and the World Conservation Strategy.* Eds. D. Bramwell, O. Hamann, V. Heywood, and H. Synge. London: Academic Press. 3–18.

———. 1988a. Botanic gardens and germplasm conservation. *Botanic Gardens Conservation News* 1(3): 15–16.

———. 1988b. Rarity: a privilege and a threat. In *Proceedings of the 16th International Botanical Congress.* Ed. W. Greuter and B. Zimmer. 277–290.

———. 1990. Botanic gardens and the conservation of plant resources. *Impact of Science on Society* 158: 121–132.

Hobbs, R. J. 1987. Disturbance regimes in remnants of natural vegetation. In *Nature Conservation: The Role of Remnants of Vegetation.* Eds. D. A. Saunders, G. W. Arnold, A. A. Burbidge, and A. J. M. Hopkins. Chipping Norton, Australia: Surrey Beatty. 233–240.

Holland, R. F. 1987. Is *Quercus lobata* a rare plant? Approaches to conservation of rare plant communities that lack rare species. In *Conservation and Management of Rare and Endangered Plants.* Ed. T. S. Elias. Sacramento: California Native Plant Society. 129–132.

Holt, S. J. 1987. Categorization of threats to and status of wild populations. In *Road to Extinction.* Eds. R. Fitter and M. Fitter. Gland, Switzerland: IUCN/UNEP. 19–30.

Hopkins, A. J. M., and D. A. Saunders. 1987. Ecological studies as the basis for management. In *Nature Conservation: The Role of Remnants of Vegetation.* Eds. D. A. Saunders, G. W. Arnold, A. A. Burbidge, and A. J. M. Hopkins. Chipping Norton, Australia: Surrey Beatty. 15–28.

Hopper, S. D. 1977. Biogeographical aspects of speciation in the Southwestern Australian flora. *Annual Review of Ecology and Systematics* 10: 399–422.

Hoyt, E. 1988. *Conserving the Wild Relatives of Crops.* Rome: IBPGR/IUCN/WWF.

Hubbell, S. P., and R. B. Foster. 1986. Commonness and rarity in a neotropical forest: implications for tropical tree conservation. In *Conservation Biology.* Ed. M. J. Soulé. Sunderland, MA: Sinauer. 205–232.

Huenneke, L. F., and K. Holsinger. Plant population biology and viable plant populations. In *Managing for Viable Populations.* Eds. B. G. Marcot and D. D. Murphy. In press.

Huffaker, C. B., D. L. Dahlsten, D. H. Janzen, and G. G. Kennedy. 1984. Insect influences in the regulation of plant populations and communities. In *Ecological Entomology*. Eds. C. B. Huffaker and R. L. Rabb. Chichester, England: Wiley. 659–690.

Hunt, D. 1986. Responsibility to future people. In *Environment and Ethics: A New Zealand Contribution*. Ed. J. Howell. Wellington: New Zealand Environmental Council. 61–76.

Huxley, A. 1974. The ethics of plant collecting. *Journal of the Royal Horticultural Society* 99: 242–249.

———. 1984. *Green Inheritance*. London: Collins/Harvill.

Iltis, H. H. 1983a. From teosinte to maize: the catastrophic sexual transmutation. *Science* 222: 886–894.

———. 1983b. What will be their fate? Tropical forests. *Environment* 25: 55–60.

———. 1987. Maize evolution and agricultural origins. In *Grass Systematics and Evolution*. Eds. T. R. Soderstrom, K. W. Hilu, C. S. Campbell, and M. E. Barkworth. Washington, D.C.: The Smithsonian Institution. 195–213.

———. 1988. Serendipity in the exploration of biodiversity. What good are weedy tomatoes? In *Biodiversity*. Ed. E. O. Wilson. Washington, D.C.: National Academy of Sciences. 98–105.

Infield, M. 1988. Attitudes of a rural community towards conservation and a local conservation area in Natal, South Africa. *Biological Conservation* 45: 21–46.

Intergovernmental Panel on Climate Change. 1990. Policymakers summary of the scientific assessment of climate change. Report prepared for IPCC by Working Group 1. WMO/UNEP.

International Centre for Conservation Education. 1987. *ICCE: Communicating Conservation*. Annual Report. Cheltenham, England: International Centre for Conservation Education.

International Environmental Education Programme. 1985. The *International Environmental Education Programme*. Paris: UNESCO.

IUCN. 1980. *World Conservation Strategy*. Gland, Switzerland: IUCN.

———. 1985a. *Botanic Gardens and the World Conservation Strategy. An International Conference*. Gland, Switzerland: IUCN.

———. 1985b. *Implementing the World Conservation Strategy*. IUCN Programme Series 1/1985. Gland, Switzerland: IUCN.

———. 1986a. *The Nahuel Huapi Action Plan for Protected Areas of the Neotropics*. Gland, Switzerland: IUCN.

———. 1986b. *Tropical Forest Conservation Programme*. Gland, Switzerland: IUCN.

———. 1986c. *Tropical Forest Advisory Group Meeting. Proceedings*. Gland, Switzerland: IUCN.

———. 1987. *Translocation of Living Organisms*. IUCN Position Statement. Gland, Switzerland: IUCN.

———. 1989. A union programme. *IUCN Bulletin* 17: 15.

IUCN Plant Conservation Office. 1990. *Centres of Plant Diversity*. Kew, England: IUCN.

IUCN/UNEP/WWF. 1990. *Caring for the World. A Strategy for Sustainability*. Second draft. Gland, Switzerland: IUCN/UNEP/WWF.

Jablonski, D. 1986. Causes and consequences of mass extinctions: a comparative approach. In *The Last Extinction*. Eds. L Kaufman and K. Mallory. Cambridge, MA: MIT Press.

Jacobs, M. 1984. The study of non-timber products. In *Traditional Lifestyles, Conservation and Rural Development*. Ed. J. Hanks. Ecology Commission Paper 7. Gland, Switzerland: IUCN. 77–79.

———. 1987. *The Tropical Rain Forest: A First Encounter*. Berlin: Springer-Verlag.

Janzen, D. H. 1984. Dispersal of small seeds by big herbivores: foliage is the fruit. *American Naturalist* 123(3): 338–351.

———. 1985. On ecological fitting. *Oikos* 45: 308–310.

———. 1986a: *Guanacaste National Park: Tropical Ecological and Cultural Restoration*. Costa Rica: EUNED-FPN-PEA.

———. 1986b. Lost plants. *Oikos* 46: 129–131.

———. 1986c. The eternal external threat. In *Conservation Biology.* Ed. M. J. Soulé. Sunderland, MA: Sinauer. 286–303.

———. 1986d. *A Tropical Christmas Catalogue.* Pamphlet.

Jeffries, R. L. 1984. The phenotype: its development, physiological constraints and environmental signals. In *Perspectives in Plant Population Biology.* Eds. R. Dirzo and J. Sarukhan. Sunderland, MA: Sinauer. 347–358.

Jensen, D. B. 1987. Concepts of preserve design: what we have learned. In *Conservation and Management of Rare and Endangered Plants.* Ed. T. S. Elias. Sacramento: California Native Plant Society. 595–604.

Johannes, R. E., and B. G. Thatcher. 1986. Shallow tropical marine environments. In *Conservation Biology.* Ed. M. J. Soulé. Sunderland, MA: Sinauer. 371–382.

Johnson, A. E. 1989. The "Selva Misionera," its present survival, threats and its conservation. Report to Fundacion Vida Silvestre, Argentina.

Johnson, D. V., R. W. Read, and M. J. Ballick. 1986. Economic botany and threatened species of the palm family in Latin America and the Caribbean. Part 1. Economic botany of the palm family in Latin America and the Caribbean. Final report to WWF International Project 3322.

Juma, C. 1989. *The Gene Hunters, Biotechnology and the Scramble to Seeds.* African Center for Technology Studies Research Series No. 1. Princeton, NJ: Princeton University Press.

Juvik, J. O., and S. P. Juvik. 1984. Mauna Kea and the myth of multiple use. Endangered species and mountain management in Hawaii. *Mountain Research and Development* 4(3): 191–202.

Kaneshiro, K. 1989. Uniqueness of Hawai'i's biota. In *Conservation Biology in Hawai'i.* Eds. C. P. Stone and D. B. Stone. Honolulu: University of Hawaii Press. 7–10.

Kapoor, P. 1988. Biological diversity and genetic resources. Status report. Technical Series 258, Commonwealth Science Council, London.

Kaufman, L. 1986. Why the ark is sinking. In *The Last Extinction.* Eds. L. Kaufman and K. Mallory. Cambridge, MA: MIT Press. 1–42.

Kaufman, L., and K. Mallory, eds. 1986. *The Last Extinction.* Cambridge, MA: MIT Press.

Kaul, V. 1983. Conservation of plant resources in aquatic ecosystems with reference to some aquatic habitats of Kashmir. In *Conservation of Tropical Plant Resources.* Eds. S. K. Jain and K. L. Mehra. Howrah: Botanical Survey of India. 118–131.

Kaule, G., and S. Krebs. 1989. Creating new habitats in intensively used farmland. In *Biological Habitat Reconstruction.* Eds. G. B. Buckley. London: Belhaven. 161–170.

Keddy, P. A. 1985. Wave disturbance on lakeshores and the within-lake distribution of Ontario's coastal plain flora. *Canadian Journal of Botany* 63: 656–660.

———. 1990. Competitive hierarchies and radial organization in plant communities. In *Perspectives on Plant Competition.* Eds. J. Grace and D. Tilman. San Diego, CA: Academic Press.

Keddy, P. A., and A. A. Reznicek. 1986. Great lakes vegetation dynamics: the role of fluctuating waterlevels and buried seeds. *Journal Great Lakes Research* 12: 25–36.

Keddy, P. A., I. Wisheu, B. Shipley, and C. Gaudet. 1989. Seed banks and vegetation management for conservation: towards predictive community ecology. In *Ecology of Soil Seed Banks.* Eds. M. A. Leck, V. T. Thomas, and R. L. Simpson. London: Academic Press. 347–363.

Keel, S. 1987. The ephemeral lomas of Peru. *The Nature Conservancy Magazine* (November/December): 17–20.

Kennedy, P. 1989. Monitoring the vegetation of Tunisian grazing lands using the normalized difference vegetation index. *Ambio* 18: 119–123.

Khadka, R. B. 1983. Mountain flora and their conservation in Nepal. In *Conservation of Tropical Plant Resources.* Eds. S. K. Jain and K. L. Mehra. Howrah: Botanical Survey of India. 132–141.

Khoshoo, T. N. 1986. Environmental priorities in India and sustainable development. Presidential address, 73rd session of Indian Science Congress Association, New Delhi.

———. 1987. A botanic garden in the Indian context: a case study. In *Botanic Gardens and the World Conservation Strategy.* Eds. D. Bramwell, O. Hamann, V. Heywood, H. Synge. London: Academic Press. 197–216.

King, F. W. 1987. Thirteen milestones on the road to extinction. In *The Road to Extinction.* Eds. R. Fitter and M. Fitter. Gland, Switzerland: IUCN/UNEP. 7–18.

Koopowitz, H., and H. Kaye. 1983. *Plant Extinction: a Global Crisis.* Washington, D.C.: Stonewall.

Kornas, J. 1982. Man's impact upon the flora: processes and effects. *Memorabilia Zoologica* 37: 11–30.

Krebs, C. J. 1978. *Ecology, the Experimental Analysis of Distribution and Abundance,* 2nd ed. New York: Harper and Row.

Kruckeberg, A. R. 1986. An essay: The stimulus of unusual geologies for plant speciation. *Systematic Botany* 11: 455–463.

———. 1987. Serpentine endemism and rarity. In *Conservation and Management of Rare and Endangered Plants.* Ed. T. S. Elias. Sacramento: California Native Plant Society. 121–128.

Lacy, R. C. 1992. VORTEX: a computer simulation model for population viability analysis. In *Population and Habitat Viability Analysis (PHVA). Briefing Book Core Materials.* Apple Valley, MN: CBSG–IUCN.

Lammers, T. G., T. F. Steussy, and M. Silva. 1986. Systematic relationships of the Lactoridaceae, an endemic family of the Juan Fernandez Islands, Chile. *Plant Systematics and Evolution* 152: 243–266.

Lande, R., and G. F. Barrowclough. 1987. Effective population size, genetic variation, and their use in population management. In *Viable Populations for Conservation.* Ed. M. J. Soulé. Cambridge: Cambridge University Press. 87–124.

Lanley, J. P., and J. Clement. 1979. Present and future forest and plantation areas in the tropics. *Unasylva* 123: 12–20.

Laptev, I. 1990. Raising the biosphere to the noosphere. In *Ethics of Environment and Development.* Eds. J. R. Engel and J. G. Engel. London: Belhaven. 117–126.

Larsen, K., B. Morley, and H. Ern. 1987. The role of the International Association of Botanic Gardens (IABG) in conservation world-wide. In *Botanic Gardens and the World Conservation Strategy.* Eds. D. Bramwell, O. Hamann, V. Heywood, and H. Synge. London: Academic Press. 277–284.

Lavieren, L. P. van. 1983. *Wildlife Management in the Tropics with Special Emphasis on Southeast Asia: a Guidebook for the Warden.* 3 vols. Prepared for Ciawi School of Environmental Conservation Management, Bogor, Indonesia.

Lawesson, J. 1987. Exotic plants in the Galapagos Islands, a summary. White paper to Workshop on Botanical Research and Management in Galapagos Islands, April 1987.

Ledig, F. T. 1986. Heterozygosity, heterosis and fitness in outbreeding plants. In *Conservation Biology.* Ed. M. J. Soulé. Sunderland, MA: Sinauer. 77–104.

Ledig, F. T., and M. T. Conkle. 1983. Gene diversity and genetic structure in a narrow endemic, Torrey pine (*Pinus torreyana* Parry ex Carr.). *Evolution* 37: 79–85.

Le Houérou, H. N., and H. Gillet. 1986. Desertization in African arid lands. In *Conservation Biology.* Ed. M. J. Soulé. Sunderland, MA: Sinauer. 444–462.

Leigh, J., R. Boden, and J. Briggs. 1984. *Extinct and Endangered Plants of Australia.* South Melbourne: MacMillan Australia.

Leigh, J., and J. D. Briggs, eds. 1992. *Threatened Australian Plants: Overview and Case Studies.* Canberra: Australian National Parks and Wildlife Service.

Leigh, J., J. Briggs, and W. Hartley. 1981. *Rare or threatened Australian plants.* Special Publication No. 7, Canberra: Australian National Parks and Wildlife Service.

Leitner, B. M., and S. L. de Becker. 1987. Monitoring the Geyser's panicum (*Dichanthelium lanuginosum* var. *thermale*) at the Little Geysers, Sonoma County. In *Conservation and Management of Rare and Endangered Plants.* Ed. T. S. Elias. Sacramento: California Native Plant Society. 391–396.

Leopold, A. 1949. *A Sand County Almanac.* (Rpt.) New York: Ballantine Books, 1970.

Lesica, P., and F. W. Allendorf. 1992. Are small populations of plants worth preserving? *Conservation Biology* 6: 135–139.

Lesouef, J. Y. 1988. The rescue of *Ruizia cordata* and the possible extinction of *Astiria rosea. Botanic Gardens Conservation News* 1(2): 36–39.

Levin, D. A. 1984. Immigration in plants: an exercise in the subjunctive. In *Perspectives in Plant Population Biology.* Eds. R. Dirzo and J. Sarukhan. Sunderland, MA: Sinauer. 242–260.

Lewin, R. 1982. Never ending race for genetic variants. *Science* 218: 877.

Lewis, W. H. 1972. University and graduate education at botanical gardens. In *Proceedings, A National Botanical Garden System for Canada.* Hamilton, Canada: Royal Botanical Gardens. 34–40.

Liegel. 1981. Restoring American prairie. *Oryx* 16: 171–177.

Ling, K. A., and M. R. Ashmore 1987. Acid rain and trees. Nature Conservancy Council Report 19, Nature Conservancy Council, Peterborough, England.

Lobin, W., and W. Barthlott. 1988. *Sophora toromiro* (Leguminosae) and the lost tree of Easter Island. *Botanic Gardens Conservation News* 1(3): 38–39.

Loope, L. L., and D. Mueller-Dombois. 1989. Characteristics of invaded islands, with special reference to Hawaii. In *Biological Invasions: a Global Perspective.* Eds. J. A. Drake and H. A. Mooney. Chichester, England: Wiley. 257–274.

Lord, J. M., and D. A. Norton. 1990. Scale and the spatial concept of fragmentation. *Conservation Biology* 4: 197–202.

Louda, S. M. 1988. Insect pests and plant stress as considerations for revegetation of disturbed ecosystems. In *Rehabilitating Damaged Ecosystems,* vol. 2. Ed. J. Cairns, Jr. Boca Raton, FL: CRC Press. 51–67.

———. 1989a. Differential predation pressure: a general mechanism for structuring plant communities along complex environmental gradients. *Trends in Ecology and Evolution* 4: 158–159.

———. 1989b. Predation in the dynamics of seed regeneration. In *Ecology of Soil Seed Banks.* Eds. M. A. Leck, V. T. Thomas, and R. L. Simpson. London: Academic Press. 25–51.

Lovejoy, T. E., R. O. Bierregaard, Jr., A. B. Rylands, J. R. Malcolm, C. E. Quintela, L. H. Harper, K. S. Brown, Jr., A. H. Powell, G. V. N. Powell, H. O. R. Schubart, and M. B. Hays. 1986. Edge and other effects of isolation on Amazon forest fragments. In *Conservation Biology.* Ed. M. J. Soulé. Sunderland, MA: Sinauer. 257–285.

Lovelock, J. E. 1979. *Gaia: A New look at life on earth.* Oxford: Oxford University Press.

———. 1988. The Earth as a living organism. In *Biodiversity.* Ed. E. O. Wilson. Washington, D.C.: National Academy of Sciences. 486–489.

Lowrance, R., R. Todd, J. Fail, Jr., O. Hendrickson, Jr., R. Leonard, and L. Asmussen. 1984. Riparian forests as nutrient filters in agricultural watersheds. *BioScience* 34: 374–377.

Lozier, L. L. 1987. Californian Nature Conservancy landowner contact and registry programme and voluntary protection for rare plant sites. In *Conservation and Management of Rare and Endangered Plants.* Ed. T. S. Elias. Sacramento: California Native Plant Society. 567–573.

Lucas, G. L., and H. Synge. 1978. *The IUCN Plant Red Data Book.* Morges, Switzerland: IUCN.

Lyster, S. 1985. *International Wildlife Law.* Cambridge: Grotius.

Maarel, E. van der. 1984. Dynamics of plant populations from a synecological viewpoint. In *Perspectives in Plant Population Biology.* Eds. R. Dirzo and J. Sarukhan. Sunderland, MA: Sinauer. 66–82.

MacDonald, I. A. W., L. L. Loope, M. B. Usher, and O. Hamann. 1989. Wildlife conservation and the invasion of nature reserves by introduced species: a global perspective. In *Biological Invasions: a Global Perspective.* Eds. J. A. Drake and H. A. Mooney. Chichester, England: Wiley. 215–245.

Mace, G. M., and R. Lande. 1991. Assessing extinction threats: towards a reevaluation of IUCN threatened species categories. *Conservation Biology* 5: 148-157.

MacFie, C. 1987. *In Touch: Nature Awareness Activities for Teachers, Leaders, and Parents.* Auckland, New Zealand: Longman Paul.

Mack, R. N. 1981. Inavasion of *Bromus tectorum* L. into western North America: an ecological chronicle. *Agroecosystems* 7: 145–165.

———. 1989. Temperate grasslands vulnerable to plant invasions: characteristics and consequences. In *Biological Invasions: a Global Perspective*. Eds. J. A. Drake and H. A. Mooney. Chichester, England: Wiley. 155–180.

MacKinnon, J., K. MacKinnon, G. Child, and J. Thorsell. 1986. *Managing Protected Areas in the Tropics*. Gland, Switzerland: IUCN/UNEP.

Madulid, D. A. 1985. The botanist's role in Philippines conservation. *Enviroscope* 5(1): 2.

Maheshwari, J. K. 1978. Biotype sanctuaries as an aid to the development of Himalayan resources. In *National Seminar on Resources, Development and Environment in the Himalayan Region*. New Delhi: NCEPC. 146–152.

Maltby, E. 1986. *Waterlogged Wealth*. London: International Institute for Environment and Development.

Marangio, M. S., and R. Morgan. 1987. The endangered sandhills plant communities of Santa Cruz County. In *Conservation and Management of Rare and Endangered Plants*. Ed. T. S. Elias. Sacramento: California Native Plant Society. 267–274.

Marcot, B. G. Concepts of risk analysis as applied to viable population assessment and planning. In *Managing for Viable Populations*. Eds. B. G. Marcot and D. D. Murphy. In press.

Marcot, B. G., R. S. Holthausen, and H. Salwasser. An assessment framework for planning for viable populations. In *Managing for Viable Populations*. Eds. B. G. Marcot and D. D. Murphy. In press.

Marcot, B. G., and D. D. Murphy, eds. *Managing for Viable Populations*. In press.

Marcot, B. G., and H. Salwasser. Viable population planning. In *Managing for Viable Populations*. Eds. B. G. Marcot and D. D. Murphy. In press.

Margules, C. R., and M. B. Usher. 1984. Conservation evaluation in practice. I. Sites of different habitats in north-east Yorkshire, Great Britain. *Journal of Environmental Management* 18: 153–168.

Marrs, R. H. 1985. Techniques for reducing soil fertility for nature conservation purposes: a review in relation to research at Roper's Heath, Suffolk, England. *Biological Conservation* 34: 307–332.

Marshall, N. T. 1993. *The Gardener's Guide to Plant Conservation*. Washington: WWF.

Martin, G. 1994. *Ethnobotany and Plant Conservation*. London: Chapman and Hall.

Martz, C. 1987. Endangered plants along California's highways: consideration for right-of-way management. In *Conservation and Management of Rare and Endangered Plants*. Ed. T. S. Elias. Sacramento: California Native Plant Society. 79–84.

May, P. H., A. B. Anderson, M. J. Balick, and J. M. F. Frazao. 1985. Subsistence benefits from the babassu palm (*Orbignya martiana*). *Economic Botany* 39: 113–129.

Mayola, K. A. de. 1987. Opportunities for involvment in endangered plant education. In *Conservation and Management of Rare and Endangered Plants*. Ed. T. S. Elias. Sacramento: California Native Plant Society. 619–622.

McClintock, E. 1987. The displacement of native plants by exotics. In *Conservation and Management of Rare and Endangered Plants*. Ed. T. S. Elias. Sacramento: California Native Plant Society. 185–188.

McGlone, M. 1988. Climatic change: the New Zealand response—impact on ecosystems. New Zealand Ministry of Environment Seminar, Wellington.

McKenzie, N. L., L. Belbin, C. R. Margules, and G. J. Keighery. 1989. Selecting representative reserve systems in remote areas: a case study in the Nullarbor region, Australia. *Biological Conservation* 50: 239–261.

McKinnell, F. H. 1981. Review of the dieback disease situation. Technical Paper No. 2, Forestry Department of Western Australia, Perth.

McMahan, L. R. 1987. Plant conservation laws: how effective are they? Ecology Forum no. 65. *Nature Conservancy* (November/December): 21–23.

McNaughton, S. J. 1983. Grassland-herbivore dynamics. In *Serengeti*. Eds. A. R. E. Sinclair and M. Norton-Griffiths. Chicago: University of Chicago Press. 46–81.

McNeely, J. A. 1988. *Economics and Biological Diversity: Developing and Using Economic Incentives to Conserve Biological Resources.* Gland, Switzerland: IUCN.

―――. 1989a. Protected areas and human ecology: How national parks can contribute to sustaining societies of the twenty-first century. In *Conservation for the Twenty-first Century.* Eds. D. Western and M. C. Pearl. New York: Oxford University Press. 150–157.

―――. 1989b. How to pay for conserving biological diversity. *Ambio* 18: 308–313.

McNeely, J. A., K. R. Miller, W. V. Reid, R. A. Mittermeier, and T. B. Werner. 1990. *Conserving the World's Biological Diversity.* Gland, Switzerland: IUCN/World Resources Institute/Conservation International/ WWF–U.S. / World Bank.

McNeely, J. A., K. R. Miller, and J. W. Thorsell. 1987. Objectives, selection, and management of protected areas in tropical forest habitats. In *Primate Conservation in the Tropical Rain Forest.* Eds. C. Marsh and R. A. Mittermeier. New York: Liss. 181–204.

Medwecka-Kornas, A. 1977. Ecological problems in the conservation of plant communities with special reference to Central Europe. *Environmental Conservation* 4: 27–34.

Melville, R. 1973. Relict plants in the Australian flora and their conservation. In *Nature Conservation in the South Pacific.* Eds. A. B. Costin and R. H. Groves. Canberra: Australian National University. 83–90.

Menges, E. S. 1986. Predicting the future of rare plant populations: demographic monitoring and modeling. *Natural Areas Journal* 6(3): 13–25.

―――. 1990. Population viability analysis for an endangered plant. *Conservation Biology* 4: 41–62.

―――. 1991. The application of minimum viable population theory to plants. In *Genetics and Conservation of Rare Plants.* Eds. D. A. Falk and K. E. Holsinger. New York: Oxford University Press. 45–61.

―――. 1992. Stochastic modeling of extinction in plant populations. In *Conservation Biology.* Eds. P. L. Fiedler and S. K. Jain. New York: Chapman and Hall. 253–276.

Menges, E. S., D. M. Waller, and S. C. Gawler. 1986. Seed set and seed predation in *Pedicularis furbishiae,* a rare endemic of the St John River, Maine. *American Journal of Botany* 73(8): 1168–1177.

Merton, D. V., I. A. E. Atkinson, W. Strahm, C. Jones, R. A. Empson, Y. Mungroo, E. Dulloo, and R. Lewis. 1987. A management plan for the restoration of Round Island, Mauritius. Jersey Wildlife Preservation Trust/ Ministry of Agriculture, Fisheries and Natural Resources, Mauritius.

Messick, T. C. 1987. Research needs for rare plant conservation in California. In *Conservation and Management of Rare and Endangered Plants.* Ed. T. S. Elias. Sacramento: California Native Plant Society. 99–108.

Meurk, C. D. 1987. Conservation objectives in pastoralism. *Proceedings of the New Zealand Grasslands Association* 48:71–74.

Meurk, C. D., and M. N. Foggo. 1986. Vegetation response to nutrients, climate and animals in New Zealand's "Subantarctic" islands, and management implications. Manuscript, Land Care Research, Ltd., Christchurch, New Zealand.

Millar, C. L. 1987. The California Forest Germplasm Conservation Project: a case for genetic conservation of temperate tree species. *Conservation Biology* 1: 191–193.

Mishan. 1982. *Introduction to Political Economy.* London: Hutchinson.

Mlot, C. 1989. Blueprint for conserving plant diversity. *BioScience* 29: 364–368.

Molloy, B. P. J. 1971. Problems and possibilities for nature conservation in a closely settled area. *Proceedings of the New Zealand Ecological Society* 18: 25–27.

Mooney, H. A., and J. A. Drake. 1989. Biological invasions: a SCOPE program overview. In *Biological Invasions: A Global Perspective.* Eds. J. A. Drake and H. A. Mooney. Chichester, England: Wiley. 491–506.

Mooney, P. R. 1982. Switching off the gene machine. *New Internationalist* 108: 12–13.

Moore, D. R. J., P. A. Keddy, C. L. Gaudet, and I. C. Wishau. 1989. Conservation of wetlands: do infertile wetlands deserve a higher priority? *Biological Conservation* 47: 203–217.

Moran, G. F., and S. D. Hopper. 1987. Geographic population structure of eucalypts and the conservation of their genetic resources. In *Nature Conservation: the Role of Remnants of Vegetation.* Eds. D. A. Saunders, G. W. Arnold, A. A. Burbidge, and A. J. M. Hopkins. Chipping Norton, Australia: Surrey Beatty. 151–162.

Morse, L. E. 1982. Refugia: places from the past. *The Nature Conservancy News* (November/December): 5–11.

Morse, L. E., M. S. Henifin, J. C. Ballman, and J. I. Lawyer. 1981. Geographical data organization in botany and plant conservation: a survey of alternative strategies. In *Rare Plant Conservation: Geographical Data Organization.* Eds. L. E. Morse and M. S. Henifin. New York: New York Botanical Garden. 9–32.

Moyseenko, H. P. 1981. Limiting factors and pitfalls in environmental data management. In *Rare Plant Conservation: Geographical Data Organization.* Eds. L. E. Morse and M. S. Henifin. New York: New York Botanical Garden. 237–254.

Munton, P. 1987. Concepts of threat to the survival of species used in Red Data Books and similar compilations. In *Road to Extinction.* Eds. R. Fitter and M. Fitter. Gland, Switzerland: IUCN/UNEP. 71–112.

Myatt, M. M. 1987. Predicting the habitat geography of sensitive plants and community types. In *Conservation and Management of Rare and Endangered Plants.* Eds. T. S. Elias. Sacramento: California Native Plant Society. 173–179.

Myers, N. 1979. *The Sinking Ark.* Oxford: Pergamon.

———. 1980. *Conversion of Moist Tropical Forests.* Washington, D.C.: National Academy of Sciences.

———. 1983. *A Wealth of Wild Species: Storehouse for Human Welfare.* Boulder, CO: Westview.

———. 1984a. Problems and opportunities in habitat conservation. In *Conservation of Threatened Natural Habitats.* Ed. A. V. Hall. South African National Scientific Programmes Report No. 92, Council for Scientific and Industrial Research, Pretoria. 1–15.

———. 1984b. *The Primary Source: Tropical Forests and our Future.* New York: Norton.

———. 1984c. Tropical moist forests: over-exploited and under-utilised. Consultant's report 3233 to WWF International/IUCN.

———. 1985a. The plant kingdom—a natural underpinning of our daily lives—is grossly threatened. *Journal Royal Society Arts* (December): 38–47.

———, ed. 1985b. *The Gaia Atlas of Planet Management.* London: Pan.

———. 1986a. Nature conservation at the global level: the scientific issues. Inaugural lecture for the new Chair and Visiting Professorship, University of Utrecht, Netherlands.

———. 1986b. Forestland farming in Western Amazonia: stable and sustainable. *Forest Ecology and Management* 15: 81–93.

———. 1986c. Tropical deforestation and a mega-extinction spasm. In *Conservation Biology.* Ed. M. J. Soulé. Sunderland, MA: Sinauer. 394–409.

———. 1988. Threatened biotas: "hot spots" in tropical forests. *The Environmentalist* 8(3): 1–20.

———. 1990a. The biodiversity challenge: expanded hot-spots analysis. *The Environmentalist* 10: 243–156.

———. 1990b. Mass extinctions: what can the past tell us about the present and the future? *Palaeogeography, Palaeoclimatology, Palaeoecology* (Global and Planetary Change Section) 82: 175–185.

Myers, S. C., G. N. Park, and F. B. Overmars. 1987. *A Guidebook for the Rapid Ecological Survey of Natural Areas.* Biological Resources Centre Publication No. 6, Department of Conservation, Wellington, New Zealand.

Nabham, G. P. 1987. Nurse plant ecology of threatened desert plants. In *Conservation and Management of Rare and Endangered Plants.* Ed. T. S. Elias. Sacramento: California Native Plant Society. 377–384.

National Academy of Sciences. 1980. *Research Priorities in Tropical Biology: A Report of the Committee on Research Priorities in Tropical Biology.* Washington, D.C.: National Academy of Sciences.

———. 1990. *Firewood Crops: Shrub and Tree Species for Energy Production.* Washington, D.C.: National Academy of Sciences.

National Association of State Universities and Land-Grant Colleges. 1983. *Emerging Biotechnologies in Agriculture: Issues and Policies.* Washington, D.C.: Division of Agriculture, Committee on Biotechnology, National Association of State Universities and Land-Grant Colleges.

National Research Council. 1989. *Lost Crops of the Incas: Little Known Plants of the Andes with Promise for Worldwide Cultivation.* Washington, D.C.: National Academy of Sciences.

National Research Council, Panel on Common Property Management, eds. 1986. *Proceedings, Conference on Common Property Resource Management.* Washington, D.C.: National Academy of Sciences.

Navarro Valdivielso, B. 1987. The botanic garden as a vehicle for environmental education. In *Botanic Gardens and the World Conservation Strategy.* Eds. D. Bramwell, O. Hamann, V. Heywood, and H. Synge. London: Academic Press. 59–66.

Nelson, J. R. 1986. Rare plant surveys: techniques for impact assessment. *Natural Areas Journal* 5(3): 18–30.

———. 1987. Rare plant surveys: techniques for impact assessment. In *Conservation and Management of Rare and Endangered Plants.* Ed. T. S. Elias. Sacramento: California Native Plant Society. 159–166.

Newton, G. A. 1987. The ecology and management of three rare salt marsh species of Humboldt Bay. In *Conservation and Management of Rare and Endangered Plants.* Ed. T. S. Elias. Sacramento: California Native Plant Society. 263–266.

New Zealand Department of Scientific and Industrial Research. 1989. National Ethnobotanical Garden. Project proposal.

Ng, F. S. P. 1983. Ecological principles of tropical lowland rain forest conservation. In *Tropical Rain Forest: Ecology and Management.* Eds. S. L. Sutton, T. C. Whitmore, and A. C. Chadwick. British Ecological Society Special Publication No. 2. Oxford: Blackwell. 359–375.

Nichols, G. R. 1986. Silverglen Nature Reserve medicinal plant project. City of Durban Parks, Recreation and Beaches Department, South Africa. Unpublished Notes.

Nichols, G. R., and K. H. Pegel. 1989. Is there an answer to the mass extinction of Africa's medicinal flora? *Newsletter of Medicinal and Aromatic Plants* 2: 45–48.

Nijhoff, P. 1984. Environmental conservation in Indonesia project. Unpublished report, Utrecht.

Noble, I. R. 1989. Attributes of invaders and the invading process: terrestrial and vascular plants. In *Biological Invasions: a Global Perspective.* Eds. J. A. Drake and H. A. Mooney. Chichester, England: Wiley. 301–313.

Noble, I. R., and R. O. Slatyer. 1981. Concepts and models of succession in vascular plant communities subject to recurrent fire. In *Fire and the Australian Biota.* Eds. A. M. Gill, R. H. Groves, and I. R. Noble. Canberra: Australian Academy of Science. 311–335.

Norgaard, R. B. 1988. The rise of global exchange economy and the loss of biodiversity. In *Biodiversity.* Ed. E. O. Wilson. Washington, D.C.: National Academy of Sciences. 206–211.

Norton, B. G. 1987. *Why Preserve Natural Variety?* Princeton, NJ: Princeton University Press.

———. 1988. Commodity, amenity, and morality: the limits of quantification in valuing biodiversity. In *Biodiversity.* Ed. E. O. Wilson. Washington, D.C.: National Academy of Sciences. 200–205.

———. 1989. Scientific basis for the conservation management of New Zealand plant communities. Unpublished manuscript, University of Canterbury, School of Forestry, New Zealand.

Norton, D. A. Scientific basis for the conservation management of New Zealand plant communities. Unpublished manuscript.

———. 1992. Disruption of natural ecosystems by biological invasion. In *Science and the Management of Protected Areas.* Eds. J. H. M. Willison, S. Bondrup-Nielson, C. Drysdale, T. B. Herman, N. W. P. Munro, and T. L. Pollock. Amsterdam: Elsevier.

Oakeson, R. J. 1986. A model for the analysis of common property problems. In *Proceedings, the Conference on Common Property Resource Management.* Washington, D.C.: National Academy of Sciences. 13–30.

O'Connor, K. F. 1984. Stability and instability of ecological systems in New Zealand mountains. *Mountain Research and Development* 4: 15–29.

Odum, S. 1978. *Dormant Seeds in Danish Ruderal Soils.* Royal Veterinary and Agricultural University, Horsholm, Denmark.

Ogden, J. 1985. An introduction to plant demography with special reference to New Zealand trees. *New Zealand Journal of Botany* 23: 751–772.

Ogle, C. C. 1987. The incidence and conservation of animal and plant species in remnants of native vegetation within New Zealand. In *Nature Conservation: the Role of Remnants of Native Vegetation*. Eds. D. A. Saunders, G. W. Arnold, A. A. Burbidge, and A. J. M. Hopkins. Chipping Norton, Australia: Surrey Beatty. 79–87.

Oldfield, S. 1988. *Buffer Zone Management in Tropical Moist Forests: Case Studies and Guidelines*. Gland, Switzerland: IUCN.

Olwell, P., A. Cully, P. Knight, and S. Brack. 1987. *Pediocactus knowletonii* recovery efforts. In *Conservation and Management of Rare and Endangered Plants*. Ed. T. S. Elias. Sacramento: California Native Plant Society. 519–522.

Opler, P. O. 1980. A parade of passing species. *Oregon Wildlife* 35: 8–9.

Orellana, R., N. Ayora, and C. Lopez. 1988. Ex situ studies on five threatened species in the Yucatan Peninsula, Mexico. *Botanic Gardens Conservation News* 1(2): 38–39.

Orr, D. 1990. Flood report. *Notes from Waimea Arboretum and Botanical Garden* 17(2): 12–14.

Osborne, R., and P. Freyberg. 1985. *Learning in Science*. Auckland, New Zealand: Heinemann.

Outerbridge, T. 1987. The disappearing Chinampas of Xochimilco. *The Ecologist* 17: 76–83.

Palmer, M. 1987. A critical look at viable population monitoring in the United States. *Biological Conservation* 39: 1–15.

Pantin, C. F. A. 1968. *Relations Between the Sciences*. Cambridge: Cambridge University Press.

Park, G. 1990. Traditional plants in the natural landscape—the values to conserve. In *Nga Mahi Maori o Te Wao Nui a Tane: Contributions to an International Workshop on Ethnobotany*. Eds. W. Harris and P. Kapoor. Christchurch, New Zealand: Department of Scientific and Industrial Research, Botany Division. 114–118.

Parsons, P. A. 1989. Environmental stresses and conservation of natural populations. *Annual Review of Ecology and Systematics* 20: 29–49.

Partap, T., and P. Kapoor. 1990. Ethnobotanical research and life support species. In *Nga Mahi Maori o Te Wao Nui a Tane: Contributions to an International Workshop on Ethnobotany*. Eds. W. Harris and P. Kapoor. Christchurch, New Zealand: Department of Scientific and Industrial Research, Botany Division. 103–113.

Paterson, G. 1987. The role of parks departments—what can members do? *Proceedings: New Zealand Institute of Park and Recreation Administration Conference, Invercargill*. 166–170.

Pattison, G. A. 1988. The National Council for the Conservation of Plants and Gardens (NCCPG) in the U.K. *Botanic Gardens Conservation News* 1(3): 38–39.

Pavlik, B. M. 1987. Autecological monitoring of endangered plants. In *Conservation and Management of Rare and Endangered Plants*. Ed. T. S. Elias. Sacramento: California Native Plant Society. 385–390.

Pavlik, B. M., and M. G. Barbour. 1988. Demographic monitoring of endemic sand dune plants, Eureka Valley, California. *Biological Conservation* 46: 217–242.

Pavlik, B. M., D. L. Nickrent, and A. M. Howard. 1993. The recovery of an endangered plant. I. Creating a new population of *Amsinckia grandiflora*. *Conservation Biology* 7: 510–526.

Pearce, D. W. 1987. Marginal Opportunity Cost as a planning concept in natural resource management. *University College London Discussion Papers in Economics* 87(6): 1–21.

———. 1988. Economists befriend the Earth. *New Scientist* (19 November): 34–39

Peeters, J. P., and J. T. Williams. 1984. Towards a better use of genebanks with special reference to information. *Plant Genetic Resources Newsletter* (FAO) 60: 22–32.

Perring, F. H., and L. Farrell. 1983. *Vascular Plants. British Red Data Books: 1*. 2nd ed. Nettleham, England: Royal Society for Nature Conservation.

Peters, C. M., A. H. Gentry, and R. O. Mendelsohn. 1989. Valuation of an Amazonian rainforest. *Nature* 339: 655–656.

Peters, R. L., II. 1988. The effect of global climate change on natural communities. In *Biodiversity*. Ed. E. O. Wilson. Washington, D.C.: National Academy of Sciences. 450–464.

Pickett, S. T. A., and J. N. Thompson. 1978. Patch dynamics and the design of nature reserves. *Biological Conservation* 13: 27–37.

Piggott, C. D. 1981. The status, ecology and conservation of *Tilia platyphyllos* in Britain. In *The Biological Aspects of Rare Plant Conservation.* Ed. H. Synge. Chichester, England: Wiley. 305–318.

Pimm, S. L. 1986. Community stability and structure. In *Conservation Biology.* Ed. M. J. Soulé. Sunderland, MA: Sinauer. 309–329.

Pitt, D. 1987a. A feasibility analysis for a template textbook on botany and conservation. Unpublished report to IUCN, Gland, Switzerland.

———. 1987b. Outline for a book on education and botanic Gardens. Unpublished report to IUCN, Gland, Switzerland.

Plant Conservation Roundtable. 1986. Conservation Guidelines. *Natural Areas Journal* 6(3): 31–32.

Plotkin, M. 1986. Conservation and ethnobotany in South America. Report to WWF–U.S.

Plotkin, M., V. Randrinasolo, L. Sussman, and N. Marshall. 1986. Ethnobotany in Madagascar. Report to IUCN/WWF International.

Plucknett, D. L., and N. J. H. Smith. 1989. Quarantine and the exchange of crop genetic resources. *Bioscience* 39(1): 16–23.

Plucknett, D. L., N. J. H. Smith, J. T. Williams, and N. M. Anishetty. 1987. *Gene Banks and the World's Food.* Princeton, NJ: Princeton University Press.

Porritt, J. 1984. *Seeing Green.* Oxford: Blackwell.

Prance, G. T. 1974. Phytogeographic support for the theory of Pleistocene forest refuges in the Amazon basin. *Acta Amazonica* 3(3): 3–28.

———. 1977. The phytogeographic subdivisions of Amazonia and their influence on the selection of biological reserves. In *Extinction is Forever.* Eds. G. T. Prance and T. S. Elias. New York: New York Botanical Garden. 195–213.

———. 1981. *Biological Diversification in the Tropics.* New York: Columbia University Press.

———. 1986. The conservation and utilization of the Amazon rain forest. *Revista de la Academia Columbiana de Ciencias Exactus, Fisicus y Natureles* 16(61): 77–128.

Prance, G. T., W. Balee, and B. M. Boom. 1987. Quantitative ethnobotany and the case for conservation in Amazonia. *Conservation Biology* 1(4): 296–310.

Prescott-Allen, R. 1984. Threatened habitats: the challenges for humanity. In *Conservation of Threatened Natural Habitats.* Ed. A. V. Hall. South African National Scientific Programmes Report No. 92, Council for Scientific and Industrial Research, Pretoria. 16–45.

Prescott-Allen, R., and C. Prescott-Allen. 1982. *What's Wildlife Worth? Economic Contributions of Wild Plants and Animals to Developing Countries.* Earthscan Paperback.

———. 1984. In situ conservation of wild genetic resources. Report to IUCN/FAO.

———. 1985. In situ gene banks for maintenance of wild genetic resources in tropical forest countries. A pilot project for northwest South America. Report to WWF/IUCN/TRF 3224.

———. 1986. *The First Resource: Wild Species in the North American Economy.* New Haven: Yale University Press.

———. 1991. How many plants feed the world? *Conservation Biology* 4: 365–374.

Preston, C. D., and H. L. K. Whitehouse. 1986. The habitat of *Lythrum hyssopifolia* L. in Cambridgeshire, its only surviving British locality. *Biological Conservation* 35: 41–62.

Principe, P. P. 1988. *The Economic Value of Biological Diversity Among Medicinal Plants.* Paris: Environment Directorate, Organisation for Economic Cooperation and Development.

Pritchard, N. M. 1972. Where have all the Gentians gone? *Transactions of the Botanical Society of Edinburgh* 41: 279–291.

Pritchett, D. A., and W. R. Ferren, Jr. 1988. *Vernal Pools of the Del Sol Reserve, Santa Barbara County, Santa Barbara.* Unpublished manuscript for the California State Coastal Conservancy.

Pusat Luar Lembah Danum. (n.d.) Yayasan Sabah, Malaysia: Danum Valley Field Centre, Public Affairs Department.

Rabie, M. A., and M. G. Erasmus. 1983. Environmental law. In *Environmental Concerns in South Africa.* Eds. R. F. Fuggle and M. A. Rabie. Capetown: Juta. 30–81.

Rabinowitz, D. 1981. Seven forms of rarity. In *The Biological Aspects of Rare Plant Conservation.* Ed. H. Synge. Chichester, England: Wiley. 205–218.

Rabinowitz, D., S. Cairns, and T. Dillon. 1986. Seven forms of rarity and their frequency in the flora of the British Isles. In *Conservation Biology.* Ed. M. J. Soulé. Sunderland, MA: Sinauer. 182–204.

Ralls, K., P. H. Harvey, and A. M. Lyles. 1986. Inbreeding in natural populations of birds and mammals. In *Conservation Biology.* Ed. M. J. Soulé. Sunderland, MA: Sinauer. 35–56.

Ramakrishnan, P. S. 1983. Problems and prospects of conservation of plant resources in the north-eastern hill region of India. In *Conservation of Tropical Plant Resources.* Eds. S. K. Jain and K. L. Mehra. Howrah: Botanical Survey of India. 172–180.

Randall, A. 1988. What mainstream economists have to say about the value of biodiversity. In *Biodiversity.* Ed. E. O. Wilson. Washington, D.C.: National Academy of Sciences. 217–223.

Ranney, J. W., M. C. Bruner, and J. B. Levenson. 1981. The importance of edge in the structure and dynamics of forest islands. In *Forest Island Dynamics in Man-dominated Landscapes.* Eds. R. L. Burgess and D. M. Sharpe. Berlin: Springer-Verlag. 67–95.

Ranwell, D. S. 1981. Introduced coastal plants and rare species in Britain. In *The Biological Aspects of Rare Plant Conservation.* Ed. H. Synge. Chichester, England: Wiley. 413–420.

Rao, A. N., H. Keng, and Y. C. Yee. 1983. Problems in conservation of plant resources in South East Asia. In *Conservation of Tropical Plant Resources.* Eds. S. K. Jain and K. L. Mehra. Howrah: Botanical Survey of India. 181--204.

Raup, D. M., and J. J. Sepkowski, Jr. 1982. Mass extinctions in the marine fossil record. *Science* 215: 1501–1503.

Raven, P. H. 1986a. We're killing our world. Keynote address to American Association for the Advancement of Science, 14 February 1986, Chicago.

———. 1986b. Biological resources and global stability. Address at award of International Prize for Biology, 22 November 1986, Kyoto, Japan.

Raven, P. H., R. E. Evert, and S. E. Eichorn. 1986. *The Biology of Plants.* 4th ed. New York: Worth.

Ray, G. C. 1984. Conservation of marine habitats and their biota. In *Conservation of Threatened Natural Habitats.* Ed. A. V. Hall. South African National Scientific Programmes Report No. 92, Council for Scientific and Industrial Research, Pretoria. 109–134.

Read, M. 1989. The bulb trade: a threat to wild plant populations. *Oryx* 23: 127–134.

Reid, T. S., and R. C. Walsh. 1987. Habitat reclamation for endangered species on San Bruno Mountain. In *Conservation and Management of Rare and Endangered Plants.* Ed. T. S. Elias. Sacramento: California Native Plant Society. 493–500.

Reid, W. V., and K. R. Miller. 1989. *Keeping Options Alive: the Scientific Basis for Conserving Biodiversity.* Washington, D.C.: World Resources Institute.

Reveal, J. L. 1981. The concepts of rarity and population threats in plant communities. In *Rare Plant Conservation: Geographical Data Organization.* Eds. L. E. Morse and M. S. Henifin. New York: New York Botanical Garden. 41–48.

Ricklefs, R. E. 1987. Community diversity: relative roles of local and regional processes. *Science* 235: 167–171.

Riem, F., and W. H. Diemont. 1985. Pflege und restauration von heideflachen. *Vegetationstechnik* 8: 19–22.

Roche, L. 1979. Forestry and the conservation of plants and animals in the tropics. *Forest Ecology and Management* 2: 103–122.

Roche, L., and M. J. Dourojeanni. 1984. A guide to in situ conservation of genetic resources of tropical woody species. Forest Resources Division Report No. FORGEN/MISC/84/2, Food and Agriculture Organization of the United Nations.

Rodhe, H. 1989. Acidification in a global perspective. *Ambio* 18: 155–160.

Rolston, H., III. 1985. Duties to endangered species. *BioScience* 35(11): 718–726.

Runge, C. F. 1986. Common property and collective action in economic development. In *Proceedings, the Conference on Common Property Resource Management.* Washington, D.C.: National Academy of Sciences. 31–60.

Russell, E. 1987. Workshop report: ecotones, patchiness and reserve size. In *Nature Conservation: the Role of Remnants of Native Vegetation.* Eds. D. A. Saunders, G. W. Arnold, A. A. Burbidge, and A. J. M. Hopkins. Chipping Norton, Australia: Surrey Beatty. 363–364.

Rye, B. L., and S. D. Hopper. 1981. A guide to the gazetted rare flora of Western Australia. Department of Fisheries and Wildlife, Western Australia, Report 42.

St. John, T. V. 1987. Mineral acquisition in native plants. In *Conservation and Management of Rare and Endangered Plants.* Ed. T. S. Elias. Sacramento: California Native Plant Society. 529–536.

S.A.'s "major gain for world conservation." 1986. *Our Living World* (September 7): 2.

Sainz-Ollero, H., and J. E. Hernandez-Bermego. 1979. Experimental reintroductions of endangered plant species in their natural habitats in Spain. *Biological Conservation* 16: 195–206.

Salim, E. 1981. *Conservation and Development.* Second World Conservation Lecture. London: WWF.

Sarukhan, J., M. Martinez-Ramos, and D. Piñero. 1984. The analysis of demographic variability at the individual level and its populational consequences. In *Perspectives in Plant Population Biology.* Eds. R. Dirzo and J. Sarukhan. Sunderland, MA: Sinauer. 83–106.

Sastrapradja, S. 1983. Activities on plant genetic resources in Indonesia. In *Conservation of Tropical Plant Resources.* Eds. S. K. Jain and K. L. Mehra. Howrah: Botanical Survey of India. 205–210.

Saunders, D. A., G. W. Arnold, A. A. Burbidge, and A. J. M. Hopkins. 1987. The role of remnants of native vegetation in nature conservation: future directions. In *Nature Conservation: the Role of Remnants of Native Vegetation.* Eds. D. A. Saunders, G. W. Arnold, A. A. Burbidge, and A. J. M. Hopkins. Chipping Norton, Australia: Surrey Beatty. 387–392.

Sawyer, J. O. 1987. The problem of the Salmon Mountain. In *Conservation and Management of Rare and Endangered Plants.* Ed. T. S. Elias. Sacramento: California Native Plant Society. 155–158.

Sayer, J. 1987. Buffer zone management in tropical rain forest protected areas. Unpublished manuscript, IUCN, Gland, Switzerland.

Sayer, J. A., and T. C. Whitmore. 1991. Tropical moist forest: destruction and species extinction. *Biological Conservation* 55: 199–213.

Schwegman, J. E. 1984. State of Illinois recovery plan for *Iliamna remota* Greene. Unpublished report of the Botany Program, Illinois Department of Conservation.

———. 1986. Procedures for demographic monitoring, census and compiling life history information on special plants. Unpublished report for the Botany Program, Illinois Department of Conservation.

Scott, D. 1979. Use and conservation of New Zealand native grasslands in 2079. *New Zealand Journal of Ecology* 2: 71–75.

———. 1989. Description of vegetation using visual ranking of species. *New Zealand Journal of Ecology* 12: 77–88.

Seed Savers Exchange. 1987. Historic apple orchard: a project of Heritage Farm. Grant proposal.

Sevilla, R. L. 1988. Debt swap for conservation: the Ecuadorean case. Paper presented at IUCN Workshop on Economics, 4–5 February 1988, San Jose, Costa Rica.

Shaffer, M. 1987. Minimum viable populations: coping with uncertainty. In *Viable Populations for Conservation.* Ed. M. J. Soulé. Cambridge: Cambridge University Press. 69–86.

Sheean-Stone, O. 1989. Mexico's wonder weed. *WWF Reports* (August/September): 9–16.

Shetler, S. G. 1974. Demythologising biological data banking. *Taxon* 23: 71–100.

Shevock, J., and D. W. Taylor. 1987. Plant exploration in California, the frontier is still here. In *Conservation and Management of Rare and Endangered Plants*. Ed. T. S. Elias. Sacramento: California Native Plant Society. 91–98.

Shmida, A., and S. Ritman. 1985. The Israel Plant Data-base: a unified approach to ecology, phytosociology, floristics, teaching, and conservation. In *The Role of Data in Scientific Progress*. Ed. P. S. Glaeser. Amsterdam: Elsevier. 91–95.

Silvertown, J. 1988. Seeds in natural populations and their significance for plant conservation in the tropics. In *Conservation Biology Training Manual for Africa*. London: Commonwealth Science Council.

Simberloff, D. 1986. Are we on the verge of a mass extinction in tropical rain forests? In *Dynamics of Extinction*. Ed. D. K. Elliott. New York: Wiley-Interscience. 165–182.

———. 1988. The contribution of population and community biology to conservation science. *Annual Review of Ecology and Systematics* 19: 473–511.

Simmons, J. B. E., and R. I. Beyer. 1985. Cooperation in training and technical liaison between botanic gardens. Paper presented at International Conference on Botanic Gardens and the World Conservation Strategy, November 1985, Las Palmas, Spain.

Sioli, H. 1986. Tropical continental aquatic habitats. In *Conservation Biology*. Ed. M. J. Soulé. Sunderland, MA: Sinauer. 383–393.

Sjögren, E. 1988. The protection of Azorean plant communities—suggested areas and methods. *Las Journadas Atlanticas de Proteccao do Meio Ambiente in Angra do Heroismo (Acores)* 1 January–1 February 1988.

Skolimowski, H. 1990. Reverence for life. In *Ethics of Environment and Development*. Eds. J. R. Engel and J. G. Engel. London: Belhaven. 97–103.

The slow march of technology. 1990. *The Economist* (January 13): 99–101.

Smith, J. P., Jr. 1987. California's endangered plants and the CNP's rare plant program. In *Conservation and Management of Rare and Endangered Plants*. Ed. T. S. Elias. Sacramento: California Native Plant Society. 1–6.

Smith, M. 1979. Creating specialised habitats in a garden. In *Survival or Extinction*. Eds. H. Synge and H. Townsend. Kew: Royal Botanic Gardens. 219–222.

Snogerup, S. 1979. Cultivation and continued holding of Aegean endemics in an artificial environment. In *Survival or Extinction*. Eds. H. Synge and H. Townsend. Kew: Royal Botanic Gardens. 85–90.

Soulé, M. J. 1984. Conservation in the real world: real-conserve or conservation-as-usual? In *Conservation of Threatened Habitats*. Ed. A. V. Hall. South African National Scientific Programmes Report No. 92, CSIR, Pretoria. 46–65.

———. 1985. What is conservation biology? *BioScience* 35: 727–734.

———. 1986. Patterns of diversity and rarity: their implications for conservation. In *Conservation Biology*. Ed. M. J. Soulé. Sunderland, MA: Sinauer. 117–121.

———. 1987. Where do we go from here? In *Viable Populations for Conservation*. Ed. M. J. Soulé. Cambridge: Cambridge University Press. 175–184.

———. 1988. Mind in the biosphere; mind of the biosphere. In *Biodiversity*. Ed. E. O. Wilson. Wasington, D.C.: National Academy of Sciences. 465–469.

———. 1990: The real work of systematics. *Annals of the Missouri Botanical Garden* 77: 4–13.

Soulé, M., J. Gilpin, W. Conway, and T. Foose. 1986. The millenium ark: how long a voyage, how many staterooms, how many passengers? *Zoo Biology* 5: 101–113.

Soulé, M. J., and D. Simberloff. 1986. What do genetics and ecology tell us about the design of nature reserves? *Biological Conservation* 35: 19–40.

Sousa, W. P. 1984. The role of disturbance in natural communities. *Annual Review of Ecology and Systematics* 15: 353–391.

Southwood, T. R. E. 1977. Habitat, the templet for ecological strategies. *Journal of Animal Ecology* 46: 337–365.

Specht, R. L., E. M. Roe, and V. H. Broughton. 1974. Conservation of major plant communities in Australia and Papua New Guinea. *Australian Journal of Botany* (Supplement Series No. 7): 1–667.

Spellerberg, I. F. 1992. *Evaluation and Assessment for Conservation.* London: Chapman and Hall.

Stafford, R. 1989. Botanists find cactus better neighborhood. *The Center for Plant Conservation* 4(1): 3.

Stanton, N. L. 1988. The underground in grasslands. *Annual Review of Ecology and Systematics* 19: 573–589.

Stebbins, G. L. 1980. Rarity of plant species: a synthetic viewpoint. *Rhodora* 82: 77–86.

Stoel, T. B., Jr. 1985. Pulling out the plug. *IUCN Bulletin* 16: 114.

Strahm, W. 1985. Mauritius and Rodrigues: conservation of endemic plants. Report on project 3149 to WWF International/ IUCN.

———. 1989. Mauritius—a paradise being lost. *WWF Reports* (February/March): 2–11.

Stungo, R. 1982. National reference collections. *The Garden* 107: 472–474.

Swartzman, S., ed. 1986. *Bankrolling Disasters.* San Francisco, CA: Sierra Club.

Synge, H., and V. Heywood. 1987. *IUCN Plant Information Programme.* Kew, England: IUCN Threatened Plants Unit.

Tangley, L. 1988. Research priorities for conservation. *BioScience* 38: 444–448.

Taylor, A. E. 1969. *The Role of Bishop's Wood and Strensall Common as Natural Resources with Special Reference to Education.* B.A. Thesis, University of York, England.

Taylor, P. W. 1986. *Respect for Nature: a Theory of Environmental Ethics.* Princeton, NJ: Princeton University Press.

Taylor, R. L., comp. 1973. A national botanical garden system for Canada. Report of the Organizing Committee for National Botanic Gardens System for Canada, Hamilton, Ontario.

Temple, S. A. 1977. Plant-animal mutualism: coevolution with dodo leads to near extinction of plant. *Science* 197: 885–886.

Templeton, A. R. 1986. Coadaptation and outbreeding depression. In *Conservation Biology.* Ed. M. J. Soulé. Sunderland, MA: Sinauer. 105–116.

Terborgh, J. 1986. Keystone plant resources in the tropical forest. In *Conservation Biology.* Ed. M. J. Soulé. Sunderland, MA: Sinauer. 330–344.

Thibodeau, F., and D. Falk. 1986. The Center for Plant Conservation: a new response to endangerment. *The Public Garden* (January): 14–19.

Thompson, P. 1975. Should botanic gardens save rare plants? *New Scientist* 11 (December): 636–638.

Thompson, P. 1986. Long life seeds. *Newsletter of the National Council for the Conservation of Plants and Gardens* 8: 9–10.

Thomson, A. D. 1981. New plant disease record in New Zealand: cucumber mosaic virus in *Myosotidium hortensia* (Decne) Baill. *New Zealand Journal of Agricultural Research* 24: 401–402.

Timmins, S. M. 1986. The role of experimental gardens in the conservation of threatened plants. Paper presented at Botany Division, New Zealand Department of Scientific and Industrial Research Symposium, June 1986, Christchurch.

Timmins, S. M., and P. A. Williams. 1987. Characteristics of problem weeds in New Zealand's protected natural areas. In *Nature Conservation: The Role of Remnants of Native Vegetation.* Eds. D. A. Saunders, G. W. Arnold, A. A. Burbidge, and A. J. M. Hopkins. Chipping Norton, Australia: Surrey Beatty. 241–247.

Tinbergen, J. 1976. *Reshaping the International Order.* New York: E. P. Dutton.

Tokalau, F. 1990. Kava drinking in Namosi village, Fiji: its significance and rituals. In *Nga Mahi Maori o Te Wao Nui a Tane: Contributions to an International Workshop on Ethnobotany.* Eds. W. Harris and P. Kapoor. Christchurch: New Zealand Department of Scientific and Industrial Research, Botany Division. 27–36.

Toledo, V. M. 1986. The floristic richness of Latin America and the Caribbean as indicated by the botanical inventories. Unpublished report to The Nature Conservancy, Arlington, VA.

Tryon, R. 1986. The biogeography of species, with special reference to ferns. *The Botanical Review* 52(2): 117–156.

Turkington, R., and L. W. Aarssen. 1984. Local-scale differentiation as a result of competitive interactions. In *Perspectives in Plant Population Biology.* Eds. R. Dirzo and J. Sarukhan. Sunderland, MA: Sinauer. 107–127.

UNEP 1986. *Environmental Perspective: Second draft.* Report, Intergovernmental Intersessional Preparatory Committee on the Environmental Perspective to the Year 2000 and Beyond. United Nations Environment Programme, Nairobi.

Usher, M. B. 1973. *Biological Management and Conservation.* London: Chapman and Hall.

———. 1987. Effects of fragmentation on communities and populations: actions, reactions and applications to wildlife conservation. In *Nature Conservation: the Role of Remnants of Native Vegetation.* Eds. D. A. Saunders, G. W. Arnold, A. A. Burbidge, and A. J. M. Hopkins. Chipping Norton, Australia: Surrey Beatty. 103–121.

Valk, A. G. van der. 1981. Succession in wetlands: a Gleasonian approach. *Ecology* 62: 688–696.

Valk, A. G. van der, and R. L. Peterson. 1989. Seed banks and the management and restoration of natural vegetation. In *Ecology of Soil Seed Banks.* Eds. M. A. Leck, V. T. Thomas, and R. L. Simpson. New York: Academic Press. 329–346.

Vietmeyer, N. D. 1985. Lesser known plants of potential use in agriculture and industry. *Science* 232: 1379–1384.

von Broembsen, S. L. 1989. Invasions of natural ecosystems by plant pathogens. In *Biological Invasions: a Global Perspective.* Eds. J. A. Drake and H. A. Mooney. Chichester, England: Wiley. 77–84.

von Broembsen, S. L., and F. J. Kruger. 1985. *Phytophthora cinnamomi* associated with mortality of native vegetation in South Africa. *Plant Disease* 69: 715–717.

Vovides, A. P. 1979. Practical conservation problems of a new botanic garden. In *Survival or Extinction.* Eds. H. Synge and H. Townsend. Kew, England: Royal Botanic Gardens. 165–170.

Wagner, W. H., Jr. 1972. Botanical research at botanical gardens. In *Proceedings, A National Botanical Garden System for Canada.* Ed. P. F. Rice. Hamilton, Ontario: Royal Botanical Gardens. 28–53.

Wallace, K. J., and S. A. Moore. 1987. Management of remnant bushland for nature conservation in agricultural areas of southwestern Australia—operational and planning perspectives. In *Nature Conservation: the Role of Remnants of Native Vegetation.* Eds. D. A. Saunders, G. W. Arnold, A. A. Burbidge, and A. J. M. Hopkins. Chipping Norton, Australia: Surrey Beatty. 259–268.

Walls, G. 1986. Cook Islands visit. Report on a visit as part of the Commonwealth Science Council Biological Diversity of Perennial Plants Programme. Report to New Zealand Department of Scientific and Industrial Research, Botany Division.

Walters, S. M., and H. Birks. 1984. *Plantpac V. WWF Plants Campaign: Botanic Gardens and Conservation.* Gland, Switzerland: WWF.

Wang, S., and J. B. Huffmann. 1981. Botanochemicals: supplements to petrochemicals. *Economic Botany* 35: 369–382.

Warford. 1987. Environment, growth and development. Economic Development Committee, World Bank, Washington, D.C.

Watkinson, A. R. 1981. The population ecology of winter annuals. In *The Biological Aspects of Rare Plant Conservation.* Ed. H. Synge. Chichester, England: Wiley. 253–264.

———. 1985. Plant responses to crowding. In *Studies of Plant Demography: a Festschrift for John L. Harper.* Ed. J. White. London: Academic Press. 275–290.

Watt, K. E. F., L. F. Molloy, C. K. Varshney, D. Weeks, and S. Wirosardjono. 1977. *The Unsteady State.* Honolulu: University of Hawaii Press.

Weil, O. S. 1986. Beyond the WCS: integrating development and environment in Latin America and the Caribbean. *IUCN Bulletin* 17(4-6): 64.

Weins, D., C. L. Calvin, C. A. Wilson, C. I. Davern, D. Frank, and S. R. Seavey. 1984. Reproductive success, spontaneous embryo abortion and genetic load in flowering plants. *Oecologia* 71: 501–509.

Weins, D., C. I. Davern, and C. L. Calvin. 1988. Exceptionally low seed set in *Dedeckera eurekensis*: is there a genetic component of extinction? In *Plant Biology of Eastern California*. Eds. C. A. Hall and V. Doyle-Jones. 19–29.

Wells, T. C. E. 1967. Changes in a population of *Spiranthes spiralis* (L.) Chevall. at Knocking Hoe National Nature Reserve, Bedfordshire, 1962–65. *Journal of Ecology* 55: 83–99.

———. 1981. Population ecology of terrestrial orchids. *The Biological Aspects of Rare Plant Conservation*. Ed. H. Synge. Chichester, England: Wiley. 281–296.

White, P. S., and S. P. Bratton. 1981. Monitoring vegetation and rare plant populations in U.S. national parks and reserves. *The Biological Aspects of Rare Plant Conservation*. Ed. H. Synge. Chichester, England: Wiley. 265–280.

Whitmore, T. C. 1980. The conservation of tropical rain forest. *Conservation Biology*. Eds. M. J. Soulé and M. Wilcox. Sunderland, MA: Sinauer. 303–318.

Whitson, P. D., and J. R. Massey. 1981. Information systems for use in studying the population status of threatened and endangered plants. In *Rare Plant Conservation: Geographical Data Organization*. Eds. L. E. Morse and M. S. Henifin. New York: New York Botanical Garden. 217–236.

Wilcove, D. S., and R. M. May. 1986. National park boundaries and ecological realities. *Nature* 324: 206–207.

Wilcove, D. S., C. H. McClennan, and A. P. Dobson. 1986. Habitat fragmentation in the temperate zone. In *Conservation Biology*. Ed. M. J. Soulé. Sunderland, MA: Sinauer. 237–256.

Wilcove, D. S., and D. D. Murphy. Fragmentation and extinction: the conceptual backdrop. In *Managing for Viable Populations*. Eds. B. G. Marcot and D. D. Murphy. In press.

Wilcox, B. A. 1980. Insular ecology and conservation. In *Conservation Biology*. Eds. M. J. Soulé and B. A. Wilcox. Sunderland, MA: Sinauer. 95–118.

Wildt, D. E., and U. S. Seal, eds. 1988. Research priorities for single species conservation biology. National Science Foundation/National Zoological Park, Washington, D.C.

Williams, G. R. 1971. The city and natural communities. *Proceedings of the New Zealand Ecological Society* 18: 13–17.

Williams, J. T., and J. L. Creech. 1987. Genetic conservation and the role of botanic gardens. In *Botanic Gardens and the World Conservation Strategy*. Eds. D. Bramwell, O. Hamann, V. Heywood, and H. Synge. London: Academic Press. 161–174.

Williams, O. B. 1981. Monitoring changes in populations of desert plants. In *The Biological Aspects of Rare Plant Conservation*. Ed. H. Synge. Chichester, England: Wiley. 233–240.

Willson, M. F. 1984. Mating patterns of plants. In *Perspectives in Plant Population Biology*. Eds. R. Dirzo and J. Sarukhan. Sunderland, MA: Sinauer. 261–276.

Wilson, C. M., and D. R. Given. 1989. *Threatened Plants of New Zealand*. Wellington: New Zealand Department of Scientific and Industrial Research.

Wilson, E. O. 1988. The current state of biological diversity. In *Biodiversity*. Ed. E. O. Wilson. Washington, D.C.: National Academy of Sciences. 3–20.

———. 1989. Threats to biodiversity. *Scientific American* (September): 60–66.

Winkel, G. 1979. The work of the Hanover School Biology Centre as an example for teaching methods in botanic gardens. In *Survival or Extinction*. Eds. H. Synge and H. Townsend. Kew, England: Royal Botanic Gardens. 165–170.

Wong, M., and J. Ventocilla. 1986. *A Day on Barro Colorado Island, Panama*. Panama City: Smithsonian Tropical Research Institute.

Woodin, S. J. 1988. *Acid Rain and Nature Conservation in Britain*. Peterborough: Nature Conservancy Council.

Woolliams, K. R. 1976. The propagation of Hawaiian endangered species. In *Conservation of Threatened Plants*. Eds. J. B. Simmons, R. I. Beyer, P. E. Brandham, G. L. Lucas, and V. T. H. Perry. London: Plenum. 73–83.

World Resources Institute, The World Bank United Nations Development Programme. 1985. *Tropical Forests: A Call For Action*. 3 vols. Washington, D.C.: World Resources Institute.

World Wildlife Fund. 1986. *The Assisi Declarations.* Gland, Switzerland: WWF.

Wright, R. M., B. Hounseal, and C. de Leon. 1985. Kuna Yala: indigenous biosphere reserve in the making? *Parks* 10: 25–27.

Wyatt, R. 1983. Pollinator-plant interactions and the evolution of breeding systems. In *Pollination Biology.* Ed. L. Real. Orlando, FL: Academic Press. 51–96.

Wyse Jackson, P., J. Parnell, and Q. Cronk. 1985. Ile aux Aigrettes—some urgent recommendations. In *Mauritius and Rodrigues: conservation of endemic plants.* Ed. W. Strahm. Report on project 3149 to WWF International/IUCN.

York, R. P. 1987. A list is a list . . . or is it? In *Conservation and Management of Rare and Endangered Plants.* Ed. T. S. Elias. Sacramento: California Native Plant Society. 39–42.

Xu Zaifu. 1987. The work of Xishuangbanna Tropical Botanical Garden in conserving the threatened plants of the Yunnan tropics. In *Botanic Gardens and the World Conservation Strategy.* Eds. D. Bramwell, O. Hamann, V. Heywood, and H. Synge. London: Academic Press. 239–254.

Zedler, P. H. 1987. The ecology of southern Californian vernal pools: a community profile. National Wetlands Research Center, Fish and Wildlife Service Biological Report 85(7.11), U.S. Department of the Interior, Washington, D.C.

Index

AABGA, *see* American Association of
    Botanic Gardens and Arboreta
Aarhus (Denmark), 149
Abies alba, 31, 32
Acacia spp., 108
Acacia pulchella, 109
Acid rain, 31–32
Acts, legislative
    California Environmental Quality
        Act (USA), 198
    Endangered Species Act (USA),
        192–193, 198, 200
    Flora and Fauna Guarantee Act
        (Victoria), 203
    Food Security Act (USA), 202
    Forest Management Act (USA), 202
    Lacey Act (USA), 196
    Native Vegetation Act (South
        Australia), 201
    Nature Conservation Act (Ireland),
        197
    Nature Conservation Act (Spain),
        200
    Wilderness Act (USA), 202
    Wildlife and Countryside Act (UK),
        192
Adaptability, 19
Agave arizonica, 68
Agave chrysantha, 68
Agave toumeyana subsp. *bella*, 68
Age-classes, 64, 78
Agriculture
    modern, 151–152, 155, 215–216,
        222–224
    traditional, 95, 145–146, 212, 216,
        220–224
Agro-ecosystems, 221–224
Agro-forestry, 222–223, 227, 235
Agropyron repens, 153
Alaska (USA), 202
Aigrettes, Ile aux (Mauritius), 112
Algeria, 190

Algiers, 190
Alien plants, 14, 28, 29, 30, 31
Allelic evenness, 18
Allelic richness, 18, 122
Allozymes, 65, 129
Aloe patersonii, 138
Aloe, spiral, 243
Alpha-numeric code, 38
Alsinodendron trinerve, 163
Altamaha River (USA), 21
Amaranth spp., 246
Amaryllidaceae, 193
Amazonia, 33, 34, 36, 67, 86, 222–223,
    240
Amboseli National Park (Kenya), 152
Amenity plantings, 136, 149
American Association of Botanic
    Gardens and Arboreta
    (AABGA), 138
Ammophila arenaria, 108
Amsinckia grandiflora, 163
Analysis
    clustering, 42
    economic, 205, 208, 221, 223–225,
        230
    ranking, 40–43, 205, 208, 221,
        223–226, 230, 241–242
Andaman Islands (India), 182
Angiopteris boivinii, 137
Apocynaceae, 26
Apostasiaceae, 26
Aquatic habitats and plants, *see* Habitat
    types, wetland
Arab Youth Office, 184
Argentina, 25
Argyroxiphium macrocephalum, 29
Arizona (USA), 68
Asclepiadaceae, 26
ASEAN Agreement on the Conser-
    vation of Nature and Natural
    Resources, 190
Assisi Declaration and Initiative, 11, 12

Asteraceae, 26
Astiria rosea, 14, 15
Astragalus physocalyx, 150
Atlas Mountains (Morocco), 56
Atlas of the British Flora, 56
Auckland (New Zealand), 134
Australia, 23, 67, 82, 136, 175, 220
    endangered plants of, 25, 39, 55
    forest management in, 108–109
    plant protection in, 192, 194, 196,
        203, 220
Australian National Botanic Garden
    (Canberra), 179–180
Austria, 193
Awareness programs, 166
Azores, Islands, 112

Baeticus, Cordillera (Spain), 56
Baez, Albert, 185
Ban Sap Tai (Thailand), 177
Bangladesh, 35
Banksia grandis, 108
Banthra Field Station (India), 134
Barbasco, 223
Barro Colorado Island (Panama), 174
Bartram, John and William, 21
Beggar's ticks, 166
Belgium, 194
Bellamy, David, 183
Benin, 182
Berne (Switzerland), 190, 198
Berne Convention, *see* Conventions,
    Conservation of European
    Wildlife
Bertholletia excelsa, 209
BGCI, *see* Botanic Gardens
    Conservation International
BGCS, *see* Botanic Gardens
    Conservation Secretariat
Bidens bidentioides, 166
Biodiversity hot spots and centers, 8,
    39, 240, 242

Biomass Research Center (India), 134
Biosphere regulators, 23
Biosphere Reserves, 97–99, 204
Biotechnology, 162, 208, 243, 247
Biotype Sanctuaries and Reserves, 7, 88
Bishop Wood (UK), 174
BLM, *see* Bureau of Land Management
Bois de bouef, 112
Bolivia, 219, 223
Bonn, University of (Germany), 141
Borneo, 55
Botanic gardens
　databases, 47, 120
　management, 128–129, 139,
　　142–143, 178, 180
　networks, 136, 137–141, 177
　priorities, 115, 119–120, 128, 178,
　　180
　role, 115, 117–120, 133–134, 137,
　　177–180
　staff, 128–130, 169–170, 178
Botanic Gardens Conservation
　Congress, 141
Botanic Gardens Conservation
　Coordinating Body, 140
Botanic Gardens Conservation
　International (BGCI), 140–141
Botanic Gardens Conservation
　Secretariat (BGCS), 140–141
Botanic Gardens Conservation
　Strategy, 116–117, 141, 149
Botswana, 184
Bottle palm, 113
Brazil, 25–26, 33, 55, 190, 204, 207–208,
　223, 240
Brazil nut, 209
British Isles, *see* United Kingdom
Brome grass, 238
Bromeliads, 185
Buffer zones, 88–92, 98, 152, 176, 222
Bulgaria, 150
Bulgarian Academy of Sciences Botanic
　Garden, 150
Bureau of Land Management (USA),
　237

Cacti, 27, 135, 166, 175, 185, 186, 193,
　197
California (USA)
　conservation education, 170
　Fish and Game Code, 197
　plant conservation, 163
　plant management, 65, 80
　plant threats, 19, 29,
　R-E-V-D code, 38
　site restoration, 158
　trade controls, 196

California Environmental Quality Act
　(CEQA), 198
California Native Plant Society
　(CNPS), 237–238
Calochilus robertsonii, 155
Cambridge University Botanic Garden
　(UK), 122, 162
Cameroon, 55, 91, 130, 182
Campa Amerindians (Peru), 247
Campanula rotundifolia, 124
Canada, 107, 138, 145, 154, 192
Canary Islands (Spain), 116, 137, 141,
　149, 169
Cape Floral Kingdom (South Africa),
　19, 35, 175, 196
Caribbean Islands, 45, 190
Carnivorous plants, 27, 137
Carrying capacity, 205
Casuarina spp., 108
Casuarina equisitifolia, 112
Catastrophic shocks, 6, 36, 63–64, 72,
　92
Catharanthus roseus, 246
Caulerpa spp., 208
Cavanillesia platanifolia, 174
CBA, *see* Cost-Benefit Analysis
Center for Plant Conservation (CPC),
　48, 139
Centers of Plant Diversity Project, 55–56
Centro Internacional de Mejora-
　mienmto de Maiz y Trigo
　(CIMMYT), 54
CEQA, *see* California Environmental
　Quality Act
Ceratolobus glaucescens, 246
Channel Islands, 155
Charles Darwin Foundation, 102, 103
Chernobyl (Russia), 145
Chiang Mai Valley (Thailand), 224
Chicago (USA), 150, 160
Chicago Botanic Garden (USA), 160
Chile, 141, 155, 193
Chiloglottis gunnii, 155
China, 32, 116, 166, 215, 246–247
Christchurch (New Zealand), 134, 141
CIMMYT, *see* Centro Internacional de
　Mejoramienmto de Maiz y Trigo
Cinchona succirubra, 30, 112
CITES, *see* Convention on Inter-
　national Trade in Endangered
　Species of Fauna and Flora
Climate change, 14, 33–34, 51,
　145–146, 154, 239
CNPS, *see* California Native Plant
　Society
Cobb, John, 245
Codes of conduct, 185–187

Coevolution, 63, 85
Coffea spp., 25
Coffea arabica, 25
Collections
　clonal, 121
　commercial, 135–136, 194–196
　controls on, 99, 193–196
　DNA genetic, 125
　documentation of, 126–128, 135,
　　139–140, 142, 162
　ex situ, 115, 120–124
　gene bank, 99, 115
　herbarium, 74, 101, 128
　in situ, 74, 185–186
　maintenance, 121–122, 128
　network, 136–141
　replication, 142
　registration of, 135–136, 139–140
College of Wildlife (Cameroon), 182
Colombia, 25, 34, 43, 222, 240
Commonwealth Science Council
　(CSC), 1, 134
Community
　complexity, 5, 226
　enrichment, 94, 156–160
Community involvement, 167, 171,
　209, 235, 237, 245–247
　and economic benefits of plant
　　conservation, 176–177, 216, 218
　and plant databases, 49
　in protecting specific areas, 90–91,
　　99–110, 146, 157, 195
　in rural areas, 220–224
　in urban areas, 148–151
Competition between plants, 64, 72, 80
CONAF, *see* Corporacíon Nacional
　Forestal
Connor, James, 183–184
Conservation
　clubs, 169, 180
　incentives, 216–220
　integrated, 115, 139, 142–143, 230,
　　232, 235
　international, 149, 233
　postulates, 229–230
　strategies, 1, 184
　urban, 136, 146–150, 172
　volunteer, 185–187, 236–238
Consultative group on Biological
　Diversity, 240
Consumption, 2, 205–206, 214–215
Convention conference of parties, 190,
　197, 199
Convention on International Trade in
　Endangered Species of Fauna
　and Flora (CITES), 136, 190,
　196–197, 203–204, 233

Conventions (on)
  Biological Diversity, 190–191, 204, 240
  Conservation of European Wildlife (Berne Convention), 190, 198, 201
  Conservation of Nature and Natural Resources (Africa), 190, 196
  Nature Protection and Wildlife Protection in the Western Hemisphere, 190
  Protection of the World Cultural and National Heritage, 190, 220
  Wetlands of International Importance (RAMSAR), 190, 201, 233, 234
Cooktown orchid, 9
Corn, see *Zea mays*
Corporacıon Nacional Forestal, Chile (CONAF), 141
Corridors, 91, 92, 151, 155
Cosmos atrosanguineus, 163
Cost-Benefit Analysis (CBA), 205, 217
Costa Rica, 4, 9, 104, 219
Costs
  conservation, 74, 114, 212–214
  development, 211–213
  marginal opportunity, 214
Couma macrocarpa, 208
Couma rigida, 208
Covenants, 93, 114, 201–202
CPC, *see* Center for Plant Conservation
Critical area, minimum, 16–17
Crops
  traditional, 4, 119–120, 220, 222–223, 245–247
  wild relatives of, 53, 88
Cryptomeria japonica, 112
CSC, *see* Commonwealth Science Council
Cultivars, preservation of, 115, 119–120, 135–136
Culture
  indigenous and traditional, 95–96, 134, 195
  local, 86, 95–96, 98, 165, 184
Cyatheaceae, 197
Cyathula ceylonica, 26
Cycads, 27, 185, 197
Cyclamen spp., 27, 193
Cymbidium rectum, 137

Data
  batch processing, 59
  descriptors, 46, 126–127
  elements of, 43–46, 126–127, 149, 157

management, 44–45, 56–57
  oral, 56, 224, 247
  redundant, 45, 58
  reliability, 57, 126–127, 149
  sources, 46, 49, 58, 149, 221, 224
  transfer formats, 50–51, 127–128
Databases
  availability, 59–60, 150, 241
  back-up, 60
  bibliographic, 37, 48–49
  botanic garden, 47, 139–140
  general purpose, 37–38, 73–76, 100–101
  networks, 45, 49, 139–140
  protected area, 74–75, 101
  specialist, 40, 150
  structure, 48
  universal, 40
Date palm, 9
Debt swaps, 217, 219
Dedeckera eurekensis, 65, 66
Demography, 15, 17, 70, 74–75, 78–83, 105
Denmark, 149, 201
Deschampsia caespitosa, 153
Desertification, 23–24
Deterministic events, 15–16, 64
Development
  agencies, 235
  costs, 211–213
  disincentives, 216–220
  integrated, 87, 98, 235
  mitigation, 99, 235
Dichanthelium lanuginosum var. *thermale*, 80
Dioscorea deltoidea, 28, 193
Diospyros egrettarum, 112
Directive on the Conservation of Natural Habitats and of Wild Fauna and Flora, 191, 194–195, 198–199, 201, 203
Discount rates, 55, 213, 218–219
Disease, 97, 108–109, 125–126, 128, 162
Disturbance regimes
  and habitat restoration, 157–160
  and impact on plants, 64, 72, 152–153
  and plant management, 5–6, 82, 105–107, 109
Diversity, 37, 38
  centers of, 39, 55–56, 94, 238, 246
  maintaining, 5, 86, 121, 145, 226
Dja Forest (Cameroon), 182
Documentation, 126–128, 157, 162
Dominican Republic, 169
Dormancy, 62, 67, 73, 133
Drosera spp., 121

Durham (UK), 124
Durian, 25
Durio spp., 25
Dyera polyphylla, 208
D'zendemtepe (Bulgaria), 150

Easter Island (Chile), 141
Ebony, 112
Ebony, St. Helena, 27
Economics
  disincentives in, 113, 216–220
  efficiency of, 152, 210
  incentives in, 216–220
  patterns of, 3, 143, 146, 166, 177, 216
  traditional, 4, 95–96
  welfare, 210
Ecosystems
  conservation, 86–87, 94, 96, 98, 111, 142, 212
  degraded, 72, 132, 145–147, 153–155, 205 226–227
  function, 62–63, 68, 105–107, 145
  legislation, 197–201
  management of, 61–62, 107, 150–151
  modified, 108–109, 112, 146–147, 152, 220
  overlooked, 94
  rehabilitation of, 209
  types of, 146–147
  urban, 147–150
Ecuador, 25, 137, 219, 222, 223
Edge effects, 10, 88–90, 92
Education
  botanic garden, 119–120, 169–170, 237
  botanists in, 170–171, 180–181
  continuing, 166, 170, 247
  informal, 166, 170–171
  interpretive, 168, 170
  media-based, 170, 182
  protected area, 86, 99, 102, 110, 169–175
  restoration strategies for, 156, 160
  resources, 180–182
  template, 168
Ehrenfeld, David, 245
Ehrlich, Paul, 181
EIA, *see* Environmental Impact Assessment
Einstein, Albert, 185
Element Stewardship Abstracts, 60
Ellipanthus unifoliatus, 26
Endemism, 38, 87, 110–111, 113, 153
England, *see* United Kingdom
Environmental Impact Assessment (EIA), 199–200, 235

Environmental stochasticity, 15–16, 105–107
Epidendrum ilense, 137
Ethics, 185, 218, 226, 243–245
Ethiopia, 25
Ethnobotany, 134, 179–180, 245–247
Eucalyptus spp., 25
Eucalyptus globulus, 25
Eugenia spp., 26
Eugenia jambos, 30
Euphorbia spp., 137
European broom, 29
Exploitation
    factors in, 2–3, 22, 25, 27, 205
    economics of, 211–212, 214
Extinction
    cascade, 22, 29
    human-induced, 14, 20, 31, 206, 241
    mega-, 13, 35
    natural, 15, 20
    proneness, 39, 43
    rates, 14, 20, 145, 241
    vortices, 15–16, 21

FAO, *see* Food and Agricultural Organization of the United Nations
Fauna and Flora Preservation Society, 232
Ferns, 40, 137, 155, 176, 185
Fernwood Botanic Garden and Nature Center (USA), 160
Feral animals, 14, 28–31, 47, 112–113, 155, 157, 159, 162
Fevillea spp., 247
Ficus antihelminthicus, 223
Fish and Wildlife Service (USA), 200
Flagship species, 166, 174, 208
Fleming, Alexander, 243
Florida (USA), 119, 160
Food and Agricultural Organization of the United Nations (FAO), 25, 48–49, 232–234
Food plants, 4, 53, 134, 166, 222–223
Forest, *see also* Habitat types, forest
    conservation of, 86, 94, 98, 104, 174, 182, 220
    loss of, 23–26, 31–34, 50, 108–109, 113, 155
    management of, 108–109, 113, 177, 220, 222–223
    non-timber values, 113, 207, 223, 246–247
    temperate, 31–33, 36, 108–109
    threats to, 23, 24–26, 33–34, 36, 147, 152, 153, 155, 184
    tropical, 36, 153, 184, 208
Forest Service (USA), 202
Forestry Commission, 174

Fragmentation, 110, 116, 145–146, 151
    and biodiversity, 239, 242
    human-induced, 67, 87
France, 15, 112, 141, 190, 198, 201
Franklinia altamaha, 21
Fuelwood, 4, 27, 53, 90, 207, 223
Fundacion Natura, 219
Furcraea hexasepala, 30
Future options, 8, 87, 227

Galapagos Islands (Ecuador), 10, 30, 86, 102–103, 112, 138, 175, 208
Galapagos National Park (Ecuador), 102–103, 175–176
Garoua (Cameroon), 182
Gasteria baylissiana, 163
Gastonia cf *cutispongia*, 112
Gatun Lake (Panama), 174
GEF, *see* Global Environment Facility
GEMS, *see* Global Environment Monitoring System
Gene bank
    off-site, 115, 122–125, 130–133, 142
    on-site, 99–100
Genet richness, 122–123
Genetic
    bottlenecks, 18–19
    depression, 16, 18, 20–21, 65–66
    diversity, 122, 124
    engineering, 243, 247
    erosion, 28, 118–119, 124
    fitness, 15, 123–124
    flow, 65, 67–68
    heterozygosity, 65, 122
    information, 18, 65, 70, 122, 124, 210–211
    minimum frequency, 123–124
    mosaic, 17
    reserve, 99–100
    structure, 65
    variability, 83, 86, 94, 100, 115, 122–124, 162, 241
Genotype, 28, 122
Gentiana spp., 192
Gentiana verna, 124
Geographic Information Systems (GIS), 51–53, 102, 234
Georgia (USA), 21
Germ plasm
    bank, 53–55, 99–100, 128, 130–133, 232
    evaluation, 54–55
Germany, 31–32, 141, 166, 178, 180
Geysers' panicum, 80
Ghana, 182
Gippsland (Australia), 25
GIS, *see* Geographic Information Systems

Global Environment Facility (GEF), 204, 240
Global Environment Monitoring System (GEMS), 51
Global monitoring, 51–53, 239–240
Global Resources Information Database (GRID), 51
Gonospermum spp., 137
Gonostylus bancanus, 86
Gorse, 29
Göteborg (Sweden), 141
Gran Canaria (Spain), 116
Grand Canyon National Park (USA), 95
Grassland, *see also* Habitat types, grassland
    restoration of, 156, 157, 160, 163
    threats to, 34, 146–147, 152–155
Great Britain, *see* United Kingdom
Great Smoky Mountains National Park (USA), 74–75
Greece, 192
Green Corps, Japan, 216
Greenhouse effect, *see* Climate change, greenhouse effect
Greenpeace International, 237
GRID, *see* Global Resources Information Database
Guanacaste National Park (Costa Rica), 104
Guava, 30
Guishow (China), 32
Gunnera spp., 112
Gunnera hamiltonii, 66
Gynoglottis cymbidoides, 137

Habitat
    changes, 6, 14, 17, 68, 111–113, 137
    critical, 99, 103–104, 147, 198
    destruction, 22–23, 29, 35, 68, 151–152, 235
    diversity, 85
    essential, 22, 68, 72–73, 75, 83, 155
    infertility, 106–107
    monitoring, 81–83
    protection, 73, 197–199
    remnant, 145–147, 151, 153–155
    restoration, 156–160
    specialization, 64–66, 72, 154–155
Habitat types
    arid, 23–24, 40, 52, 65, 82, 147
    coastal, 153, 158, 207
    forest, 98, 108–109, 113, 208, 220;
        see also Forest
    grassland, 23, 28, 72
    scrub and shrubland, 72, 103
    serpentine, 94, 106
    wetland, 23–24, 31, 33, 40, 150–151, 160, 207

Haleakala silversword, 29
Hanover (Germany), 178, 180
Hanover School Biology Center, 180
Harold L. Lyon Arboretum (USA), 178–179
Harvesting systems, 27–28, 35, 95, 99, 246–247
Hawaiian Islands (USA), 29, 163, 179, 193
Hedychium, 112
Heyerdahl, Thor, 141
Hieracium spp., 72, 108
Himachal Pradesh (India), 28
Himalayan Mountains, 26–28
Hippophae rhamnoides, 108
Horticulture, 135–136, 142, 148
Huai Kha Khaeng (Thailand), 182
Human population increase, 34–35, 146–147, 205, 215
Hybrid conservation, 68, 162
Hyophorbe amaricaulis, 15, 113
Hyophorbe vaughanii, 15

IABG, *see* International Association of Botanic Gardens
IBPGR, *see* International Board for Plant Genetic Resources
ICCE, *see* International Center for Conservation Education
IEEP, *see* International Environmental Education Program
Illinois (USA), 150, 160
Iltis, Hugh, 243
India, 27–28, 86, 134, 166, 182–183
Indicator species, 6, 63, 238
Indonesia, 208, 246
Information
    crisis, 58–59, 241
    minimum requirements, 44, 62, 72–75
    point locality, 47
Intermediate technology, 216
International Association of Botanic Gardens (IABG), 140–141
International Board for Plant Genetic Resources (IBPGR), 48–49, 54, 119, 141
International Center for Conservation Education (ICCE), 182
International Conservation Union, *see* IUCN
International Environmental Education Program (IEEP), 181
International Transfer Format (ITF), 50–51, 127–128
International Tropical Timber Organization (ITTO), 217
Invasive animals, *see* Feral animals

Inventory, 73–75, 83, 138, 237
Ipilipil, 223
Iran, 190
Ireland, 197
Iridaceae, 135
Island
    biogeography, 87–92
    management, 30, 110–113, 242
    restoration, 112–113, 232
    oceanic, 9, 20, 28–29, 30, 55, 110–113, 232
Israel, 37
Itaipu Binacional, 244
Italy, 117, 193, 195
ITF, *see* International Transfer Format
ITTO, *see* International Tropical Timber Organization
IUCN (International Conservation Union), 49, 140, 184, 233
    Species Survival Commission (SSC), 233
    Threatened Plant Unit (TPU), 48
    Tropical Forest Program, 233
    Working Group on Ethics and Conservation, 3
Ivory Coast, 182

Jaksiee Reserve (Poland), 152
Jamaica, 190
Japan, 215–217
Jardin Botanico Canario Viera y Clavigo (Spain), 137
Java (Indonesia), 246
Jersey (Channel Islands), 155
Jersey Wildlife Trust, 116
Jojoba, 23, 55, 207
Juniperus communis, 122

Kalanchoe pinnata, 30
Kashmir, 28
Kent Trust for Nature Conservation (UK), 238
Kenya, 152, 190
Kerala State (India), 182
Kermadec Islands (New Zealand), 108
Kew, Royal Botanic Gardens (UK), 116, 137, 140
Keystone species, 20, 63, 86, 238
Khao Yai National Park (Thailand), 177
Kikuyu grass, 29
Kilimanjaro, Mount (Tanzania), 182
Kinabalu National Park (Borneo), 55
Kingston (Jamaica), 190
Kirstenbosch Botanic Gardens (South Africa), 137
Kolobrzeg (Poland), 153
Komter, Penang (Malaysia), 141
Korup National Park (Cameroon), 91

Kuala Lumpur (Malaysia), 140, 190
Kuku (India), 28
Kulata (Yugoslavia), 150
Kuna Indians, 168

Landowners, 89–91, 194–195, 197–201, 221–222, 224
Landraces, 53, 88
Lantana spp., 29, 108
Lantana camara, 30
Lapageria rosea, 155
Las Palmas, 117, 149, 169
Las Palmas Strategy, 117, 120
Laurales, 169
Lausanne (Switzerland), 192, 197
Legislation
    environmental, 40–41, 148, 185
    international, 190–191
    and planning, 91, 110, 203
    species-centered, 191–193
    treaties (law-making), 40, 190
Leguminosae, 40
Leibig's law of the minimum, 20
Leiden (Netherlands), 117
Leucaena leucocephala, 223
Liaison, 173, 180
Liberia, 55, 182
Lichens, 32, 43
Life-history, 104, 121, 123, 137, 161–163
    features of, 62
    and persistence of species, 106
    and plant management, 65–67, 71–74, 77–78, 81
Life support species, 226–227, 247
Lilies, 27, 121, 135, 193
Limbe Botanic Garden (Cameroon), 130
Limonium spp., 137
Lippia spp., 86
Listing and delisting, 192, 198–199, 203
Liverworts, 43
Loch Tummel, 162
Lonchocarpus spp., 223
London (UK), 149–150
Lotus spp., 137
Lucknow (India), 134
Lugoa spp., 137
Lythrum hyssopifolia, 155

MAB, *see* Man and the Biosphere Program Organization
Madagascar, 34, 241
Mahé Island (Seychelles), 137
Mahogany, 40
Maize, see *Zea Mays*
Malawi, 55
Malaysia, 25, 55, 86, 140–141, 155, 190, 208

Man and the Biosphere Program
  (MAB), 49, 51
Management
  agreements, 90–91, 99, 201
  burning-based, 103, 106, 157–158,
    257
  grazing-based, 103–104, 157–159
  guidelines, 109, 111, 172
  information, 70, 109, 172
  integrated, 100–102, 230–232
  interventionist, 68–82, 99, 100–101,
    103, 105–107, 112–113,
    156–160, 174
  land-use options, 85, 220–224
  multipurpose, 86, 99, 109, 111
  objectives, 61, 70, 83, 152, 165
  objectives for protected areas,
    100–101, 103–104, 106, 109,
    111–112, 114
  plans, 109–110, 142–143, 241–242
  rehabilitation-based, 103, 107,
    112–113, 149, 156–160, 173
  research, 102–104, 109, 194
  trials, 104
Mangifera spp., 25
Manglier, 112
Mango, 25
Manilkara zapota, 208
Manitoba (Canada), 160
Manu National Park (Peru), 104
Mapimi Biosphere Reserve (Mexico),
  204
Marginal social benefits (MSB), 210–211
Marginal social costs (MSC), 210–211
Marram grass, 29, 108
Marshall, Moses, 21
Mather, Cotton, 243
Matobo National Park (Zimbabwe), 95
Mauritian Wildlife Appeal, 116
Mauritius, 14, 112
Media, 170, 182–184
Medicinal plants, 4, 40, 53, 137
Mediterranean regions, 23
Meghalaya State (India), 182
Melville, Ronald, 140
Metapopulation, 18, 67–68, 81
Mexico, 23, 161, 163, 166, 204, 209
Michigan (USA), 160
Miconia spp., 30, 112
Milne Bay (Papua New Guinea), 25
Minimum Viable Density (MVD), *see*
  Population, minimum viable
  density
Minimum Viable Population (MVP),
  see Population, minimum viable
  size
Ministry for Overseas Development
  (UK), 232

Mojave Desert (USA), 65
Monitoring
  for data bases, 53, 57–58, 73
  demographic, 16, 22, 74–75, 80–81,
    105, 238
  design, 74, 80–82, 102, 110
  ecophysiological, 74, 80, 82
  guidelines, 73, 75, 80–83, 157–159,
    162
Monkey orchid, 238
Moraea loubseri, 19
Moscow (Russia), 140
Mosses, 32, 43
Mountfort, Guy, 9
MSB, *see* Marginal Social Benefits
Mulanje, Mount (Malawi), 55
Multinational agencies, 28, 209,
  233–236
Muñoz Pizarro, Carlos, 141
Mutualisms, 17, 63
MVD, *see* Population, minimum viable
  density
MVP, *see* Population, minimum viable
  size
Mweka Wildlife College (Tanzania),
  182
Myers, Norman, 25

Nairobi (Kenya), 184, 190
Narrow-range endemic, 110–111,
  153–154
National Collection of Endangered
  Species (USA), 139
National Conservation Strategy,
  234–236
National Council for the Conservation
  of Plants and Gardens
  (NCCPG), 140
Natura 2000, 198
Natural Heritage Inventory Program,
  46
Navarra (Spain), 202
NCCPG, *see* National Council for the
  Conservation of Plants and
  Gardens
Nepal, 26–27
Nephelium spp., 25
Net Primary Production (NPP), 6
Netherlands, 117, 201
New River Mountains (USA), 68
New South Wales (Australia), 196
New York (USA), 184
New York Zoological Society, 184
New Zealand, 29, 43, 72, 138, 153
  ethnobotanical garden, 134
  nonindigenous plants, 155
  overcollection in, 193
  and rare species, 66, 141, 178

road verges of, 151
Threatened Plants Register, 42
Nigeria, 32
Nimba, Mount (Liberia), 55
Noosphere, 11
North Carolina (USA), 74–75
Norway spruce, 32
NPP, *see* Net Primary Production

Oak, 29
Oje, 223
Opuntia echios var. *gigantea*, 138
Orchids, 9, 26, 27, 40, 121, 135, 137,
  155, 175, 176, 185, 186, 187, 193,
  197
Orchis simia, 238
Organization of African States (OAS),
  49
"Outreach" Program, 184
Oxford (UK), 117
Ozone depletion, *see* Climate change,
  ozone depletion

Pakistan, 216
Palaquium gutta, 208
Palms, 27, 179, 185, 223, 246
Panama, 168
Pandanus vandermeerschii, 112
Papua New Guinea, 25, 241
Paraguay, 244
Parana, Rio (Paraguay), 244
Paris (France), 190
Passport data, 53–54
Patch dynamics, 18, 68
PECS, *see* Plant Existence
  Categorization Scheme
Pedicularis furbishiae, 66
Peechi Forest Research Institute
  (India), 182
PEMASKY, *see* Project for the Study of
  the Management of Kuna Yala
  Wildlands
Penang (Malaysia), 141
Penicillium spp., 10
Pennantia baylisiana, 66, 116
Pennicetum purpureum, 30
Permits and licenses, 194–200
Persoonia longifolia, 108
Perturbation, 73, 221, 226, 242
Peru, 23, 25, 40, 222–223, 246–247
Pest control, 67
Philippine Islands, 35, 166, 219, 223
Phragmites communis, 153
Phytopthora cinnamomi, 108, 125
Picea abies, 32
Pied Crow magazine, 183–184
Pieniny National Park (Poland), 152
Pilocarpus spp., 246

Pinnacles National Monument (USA), 29
Pinus nigra, 155
Pinus sylvestris, 32
Pinus torreyana (Torrey pine), 19
Pisa (Italy), 117
Pistachio, 209
Pistacia vera, 209
Planning
    annual operational, 110
    management, 74, 142–143, 206
    recovery, 110–111, 200
    status reports, 110
    viable population, 107
Plant Existence Categorization Scheme (PECS), 47
Plants Conservation Program, 233–234
Plectomirtha baylisiana, 66
Plovdiv (Bulgaria), 150
Point Reyes National Park (USA), 237–238
Poland, 152–153
Pollen bank, 130–131
Pollution, 14, 31–33, 76, 137, 145, 153, 226
Polunin, Nicholas, 140
Population
    characteristics, 64–65, 68
    critical area, 16–17
    decline, 19–20, 82
    density, 79–80
    dynamics, 68, 73–74, 80–82, 123
    effective size, 20, 107
    manipulation, 74, 105–107
    minimum viable density (MVD), 18
    minimum viable size (MVP), 16–17, 20, 64
    sample sizes, 122–124
    temporal changes, 19, 20, 72, 73
Population Viability Analysis (PVA), 15, 17, 68–72, 225, 232
Portugal, 193
Predation, 17, 97, 108, 125–126, 153
Primula farinosa, 124
Priorities and ranking
    of environmental problems, 165
    factors in, 17, 40–41, 54, 76–77, 94, 114, 211
    necessity of, 43, 241
Project for the Study of the Management of Kuna Yala Wildlands, 168
Propagation
    nursery, 121, 124–125, 130, 136, 159, 162
    tissue culture and micropropagation, 116, 131, 137–138
Property regimes, 90, 191, 194, 204, 210, 212, 247

Protected area
    activity controls, 90–92, 95–97, 99, 112–113, 152, 176, 199
    buffer zones, 88–92, 104
    categories, 88–89, 92–93, 96–100
    network, 94, 99
    perimeter-area ratios, 87–89
    private, 93, 114, 199, 201–202
    staff, 96, 112, 169–171
    visitor centers, 93, 172, 174
    visitor impacts, 97, 111–112, 152, 159, 167, 173, 176
Protocols
    Protected Areas and Wild Fauna and Flora in the East African Region, 190
    Specially Protected Areas and Wildlife in the Wider Caribbean Region, 190
Psidium guajava, 30
Psophocarpus spp., 55

Quarantine, 125, 126, 134, 138, 162
Queensland (Australia), 220
Quercus lobata, 29

Rafflesia spp., 9
Rambutan, 25
Ramosmania heterophylla, 116
Ranking, *see* Priorities and ranking
Rapa Island (French Polynesia), 55
Rarity, 40–42, 83
Rattan palms, 246
Rauvolfia serpentina, 28, 193
Red Data Books, 39–42, 60, 140
Redwood, 175
Refugia, 111
Rehabilitation, 115, 123, 134, 146, 156–160, 220
Remote sensing, 43, 51–53
Representativeness, 93–94
Reproductive biology, *see also* Life-history
    demography, 63–64, 66, 81–82, 162–163
    dispersal, 66
    pollination, 66, 104, 123, 162, 238
    vegetative, 66, 121
Reserves
    design, 85, 87, 104
    garrison, 92–93, 112
    maintenance, 86
    manipulation, 99, 103–104
    network, 99
Resources
    bibliographic, 37, 46, 48–50, 101
    limitations of, 62, 103, 109, 113–114, 213

photographic, 46, 51, 102, 128
Restoration, 106, 112–113, 156–160
    and botanic gardens, 129
    and conservation, 1, 73, 151
    of islands, 111
Reunion Island (France), 15, 141
Rhizanthus gardneri, 67
Rights traditional, 90–91, 204
Rio de Janeiro (Brazil), 190, 204
Riparian strips, 151
Risk modeling, 68–72, 102, 225
Rodriques Island, 15, 116
Rosy periwinkle, 246
Round Island (Mauritius), 108, 112–113
Royal Forest and Bird Protection Society (New Zealand), 237
Royal Horticultural Society, 140
Royal Society for Nature Conservation, 237
Rubus spp., 30
Ruderals plants, 53, 72
Ruizia spp., 15
Rural conservation, 150–152, 214
    and development, 220–224, 234
    and farming systems, 216, 227
Russia, 140, 145

Sabah, 137
Sacred sites, 97
Sahel, 23, 215
St. Helena Island, (UK), 232
Sampling, 73–75, 79–80, 162
    for ex situ use, 120–124
    seeds, 121, 131, 159–160, 162
Santo Domingo (Ecuador), 222
Sapote, 208
Sargassum spp., 208
Satellite imagery, *see* Remote sensing
Save a Tiger Campaign, 166
Saxifraga aizoides, 124
Scalesia spp., 30
Schoenus ferrugineus, 162
Scots pine, 32
Sea buckthorn, 108
Seaweeds, 208
Sechuan (China), 32
Seed bank, 66–67, 73, 124, 130–131, 133, 138
Selby (UK), 174
Selby Botanical Gardens (USA), 119
Sempervivum spp., 192
Sequoia sempervirens, 175
Serendipity, 35, 55, 207–208, 211, 243
Serengeti National Park (Tanzania), 67
Serruria florida, 116
Seychelles Islands, 137
Sheoak, 108

Sian Ka'an Biosphere Reserve (Mexico), 204
Sideroxylon boutonianum, 112
Silver fir, 31, 32
Simla Hills (India), 28
Simmondsia chinensis, 23, 55
Sir Seewoosagur Ramgoolan Botanic Garden (Mauritius), 14
Sites, critical and key, 97, 163, 167
Sitka spruce, 32
Soils, 23, 62, 91, 94, 157–160
Sophora toromiro, 141
Sophora zeylanica, 26
Sorghum spp., 55
South Africa, 19, 29, 35, 175
  and conservation, 116, 163
  and conservation laws, 192, 194, 196, 202
South African National Botanical Institute, 58, 13
South African National Herbarium, Pretoria, 58
South African Nature Foundation, 137
South Australia (Australia), 201
Soybean, 55
Spain, 116, 137, 141, 169, 200, 202
Sri Lanka, 26
SSC, *see* IUCN, Species Survival Commission
Stewardship, 11, 213
Stochastic events, 15–17, 64, 67, 106–107, 207
Strategies, k- and r-, 64
Stress regimes, 64, 72, 80, 105–107, 152–153
Succession, 29, 99, 145, 152, 157–158, 201
Sungai Tekam (Malaysia), 155
Superior, Lake (Canada), 107
Survey
  field methods, 74–80
  meander searches, 78–80
  objectives, 61, 73–75, 83, 110, 112, 237
  qualifications for, 75
  records, 47–48, 57–58, 101–102, 104
Sustainable development, 186, 211–213, 215–218
  and conservation, 1, 169, 205
  education for, 181
  examples of, 168, 220, 223
  reasons for, 11
  in the tropics, 240
  and tribal groups, 189
Sweden, 141
Switzerland, 190, 192–193, 197, 200, 202
Syon Park (UK), 14
Systems failure, 66, 68

Tahiti (French Polynesia), 112
Tanacetum spp., 137
Tanzania, 67, 182
Target species, 62–63, 73, 76
Tatra National Park (Poland), 152
Tbilisi Conference, 181
Te Rehua marae (New Zealand), 134
Tecophilaea cyanocrocus, 193
Tectiphiala ferox, 15
Tennessee (USA), 74–75
Texas (USA), 196
Thailand, 91, 177, 182, 224
The Nature Conservancy (TNC), 46, 60, 233, 237
Theobroma cacao, 25
Thismia americana, 150
Threat categories, 38, 40–43, 47
Three Kings Islands, 66, 108, 116
Thymus drucei, 124
TNC, *see* The Nature Conservancy
Tocache Nuevo (Peru), 222
Togo, 182
Tourism services, 86, 99, 102, 135, 152, 175–177, 207
TPU, *see* IUCN, Threatened Plant Unit
Trade, 27, 185–186, 196–197, 215
Trails, visitor, 172–174, 179–180
Training, 128–130, 134, 170–171, 180, 182, 204
Transfer formats, *see* Data, transfer formats
Translocation, 105, 110, 115, 161–163
Triage, 226, 239
Trilepidea adamsii, 193
Trochetia melanoxylon, 27
Trophic cascade, *see* Extinction, cascade
Tropical Agronomic Center for Research and Instruction (CATIE), 49
Tropical moist forest, *see* Forest, tropical
Tumaco (Colombia), 222
Tunisia, 52
Turbinaria spp., 208
Turkey, 185, 193

Uganda, 35
Ulva spp., 208
Umbrella species, 63, 167
Undescribed taxa, 39
United Kingdom, 42, 92, 158, 240
  botanic gardens in, 117, 122, 137–138
  and conservation, 95, 97, 140–141, 155, 162, 238
  and conservation education, 169, 174
  and conservation laws, 197, 200–202

national plant collections, 48
National Trust, 201
  and plant trade, 136, 193
United Nations (UN) programs
  UNCED (UN Conference on Environment and Development), 190
  UNEP (UN Environment Program), 49, 181, 184, 204, 232–234
  UNESCO (UN Educational, Scientific and Cultural Organization), 181, 190, 233
United States of America, 35, 43, 82, 145, 150, 154, 156
  and conservation, 46, 92, 139
  and conservation laws, 192–193, 198, 200, 201, 202
  and plant trade, 27, 207
Upper Teesdale (UK), 124
Urban conservation, 136, 148–150, 175

Vacoas, 112
Values
  bequest, 208, 210
  consumptive use, 207
  cultural, 3, 99, 168
  demand, 10, 99, 150–151, 207
  economic, 3, 17, 99, 117, 119, 136, 177, 206, 208
  esthetic, 9, 17, 149
  existence, 208, 210
  intrinsic, 10, 150–151
  moral, 3, 9, 17, 165, 168
  nonconsumptive use, 207
  option, 207
  productive use, 207, 210
  scientific, 3, 8, 157, 158
  transformative, 10, 168, 175, 207
Vaud (Switzerland), 192
Vavilov Centers, *see* Diversity, centers of
Vegetation ranking, 80
Venezuela, 32, 55
Vest pocket reserves, *see* Reserves, garrison
Victoria (Australia), 198, 203
Vina del Mar, Botanic Garden (Chile), 141
Virgin Islands National Park, 176
Voice of Kenya, 184
Volunteer groups, 114, 171, 173, 236
VORTEX, 71–72

Waimea Arboretum (USA), 179, 193
Washington (USA), 190, 196
Watch Organization, 169
WCMC, *see* World Conservation Monitoring Center
WCS, *see* World Conservation Strategy

West Indies, 176
Western Australia, 67, 108, 194, 196
Weeds, 14, 47, 88, 108, 112–113, 157
Wetlands Program, 233
Wicken Fen (UK), 174
Widdybank Fell (UK), 124
Wilderness, 88, 99, 146, 175
Winged bean, 55
Wisconsin (USA), 22
Wisley, RHS Botanic Garden (UK), 140
Working Group on Ethics and
    Conservation, *see* International
    Conservation Union, Working
    Group on Ethics and
    Conservation
World Charter for Nature, 3

World Conference on Environment and
    Development, 186
World Conservation Monitoring
    Center (WCMC), 233–234
World Conservation Strategy (WCS), 1,
    3, 9, 233–234
World Conservation Union, *see* IUCN
World Heritage Convention, *see*
    Conventions (on), Protection of
    the World Cultural and National
    Heritage
World Resources Institute, 233
Worldwide Fund for Nature (WWF),
    141, 116, 160, 166, 184, 208,
    232–234
WWF, *see* Worldwide Fund for Nature

Xishuabanna (China), 116, 247

Yorkshire (UK), 174
Yucatan Peninsula (Mexico), 161
Yugoslavia, 150
Yunnan Province (China), 25, 247

Zaire, 138
Zambia, 184
Zea diploperennis, 209, 210, 246
Zea perennis, 209
Zea mays, 209
Zerna erecta, 238
Zimbabwe, 95, 184
Zurich (Switzerland), 197, 200

Permissions Acknowledgments

The author, sponsoring organizations, and publisher gratefully acknowledge permission to reproduce the following figures.

Figure 1.2   Courtesy P. H. Zedler and the U.S. Department of the Interior, Washington, D.C.

Figure 2.1   From "Causes and Consequences of Mass Extinctions: A Comparative Approach," by D. Jablonski. In *The Last Extinction*, edited by L. Kaufman and K. Mallory. Copyright © 1986 by The MIT Press, Cambridge, Massachusetts. Redrawn by permission.

Figure 2.2   From "Threatened Species and Habitats—Why Bother?" by F. L. Bunnell and R. G. Williams. In *Threatened and Endangered Species and Habitats in British Columbia and the Yukon*, edited by R. Stace-Smith, L. Johns, and P. Joslin. Copyright © 1980 by British Columbia Ministry of Environment, Victoria, Canada. Redrawn by permission.

Figure 2.3   From "Riders of the Last Ark: The Role of Captive Breeding in Conservation Strategies," by T. J. Foose. In *The Last Extinction*, edited by L. Kaufman and K. Mallory. Copyright © 1986 by The MIT Press, Cambridge, Massachusetts. Redrawn by permission.

Figure 2.4   From "Thirteen Milestones on the Road to Extinction," by F. W. King. In *The Road to Extinction: A Symposium Held by the Species Survival Commission, Madrid, 7 and 9 November 1984*, edited by R. Fitter and M. Fitter. Copyright © 1987 by IUCN/UNEP, Gland, Switzerland, and Cambridge, England.

Figure 2.5   From "Minimum Viable Populations: Processes of Species Extinction," by M. E. Gilpin and M. E. Soulé. In *Conservation Biology: The Science of Scarcity and Diversity*, edited by M. E. Soulé. Copyright © 1986 by Sinauer Associates, Inc., Sunderland, Massachusetts.

Figure 2.6   From *Man's Role on Changing the Face of the Earth*, edited by W. L. Thomas, Jr. Copyright © 1956 by The University of Chicago Press, Chicago, Illinois.

Figure 3.1   From *Threatened Australian Plants: Overview and Case Studies*, edited by J. H. Leigh and J. D. Briggs. Copyright © 1992 by Australian National Parks and Wildlife Service, Canberra, Australia.

Figure 3.2   From "Some Problems," by J. I. Furtado. In *The Road to Extinction: A Symposium Held by the Species Survival Commission, Madrid, 7 and 9 November 1984*, edited by R. Fitter and M. Fitter. Copyright © 1987 by IUCN/UNEP, Gland, Switzerland, and Cambridge, England.

Figure 3.4   From *IUCN Plant Information Programme*, by H. Synge and V. Heywood. Copyright © 1987 by IUCN Threatened Plants Unit, Kew, England.

Figure 3.5   From "Predicting the Habitat Geography of Sensitive Plants and Community Types," by M. M. Myatt. In *Conservation and Management of Rare and Endangered Plants*, edited by T. S. Elias. Copyright © 1987 by the California Native Plant Society, Sacramento.

Figure 4.1   From "The Meanings of Rarity," by J. L. Harper. In *The Biological Aspects of Rare Plant Conservation*, edited by H. Synge. Copyright © 1981 by John Wiley & Sons, Ltd., Chichester, England. Reprinted by permission of John Wiley & Sons.

Figure 4.2   From *Managing for Viable Populations*, edited by B. G. Marcot and D. D. Murphy. In press.

Figure 4.3   From *Managing for Viable Populations*, edited by B. G. Marcot and D. D. Murphy. In press.

Figure 4.5   From *Quantitative Plant Ecology*, by P. Grieg-Smith. 3rd edition, Studies in Ecology, Volume 9. Copyright © 1983 by Blackwell Scientific Publications Ltd., Oxford, England. Adapted by permission.